HARLAXTON MEDIEVAL STUDIES

VOLUME SEVEN

ARMIES, CHIVALRY AND WARFARE
IN MEDIEVAL BRITAIN AND FRANCE

HARLAXTON MEDIEVAL STUDIES

NEW SERIES

1. ORMROD, W. M. (ed.), *England in the Thirteenth Century*, Proceedings of the 1989 Harlaxton Symposium (1991).
2. HICKS, Carola (ed.), *England in the Eleventh Century*, Proceedings of the 1990 Harlaxton Symposium (1992).
3. ROGERS, Nicholas (ed.), *England in the Fourteenth Century*, Proceedings of the 1991 Harlaxton Symposium (1993).
4. ROGERS, Nicholas (ed.), *England in the Fifteenth Century*, Proceedings of the 1992 Harlaxton Symposium (1994).
5. THOMPSON, Benjamin (ed.), *The Reign of Henry VII*, Proceedings of the 1993 Harlaxton Symposium (1995).
6. THOMPSON, Benjamin (ed.), *Monasteries in Medieval Britain*, Proceedings of the 1994 Harlaxton Symposium (1998).
7. STRICKLAND, Matthew (ed.), *Armies, Chivalry and Warfare in Medieval Britain and France*, Proceedings of the 1995 Harlaxton Symposium (1998).

OLD SERIES

1. ORMROD, W. M. (ed.), *England in the Thirteenth Century*, Proceedings of the 1984 Harlaxton Symposium (Harlaxton, 1985).
   (1b. Sheets of the above paperback reissued with a new title-page in hardback by Boydell & Brewer, Woodbridge, 1986).
2. ORMROD, W. M. (ed.), *England in the Fourteenth Century*, Proceedings of the 1985 Harlaxton Symposium (Woodbridge, 1986).
3. WILLIAMS, Daniel (ed.), *England in the Fifteenth Century*, Proceedings of the 1986 Harlaxton Symposium (Woodbridge, 1987).
4. WILLIAMS, Daniel (ed.), *Early Tudor England*, Proceedings of the 1987 Harlaxton Symposium (Woodbridge, 1989).
5. WILLIAMS, Daniel (ed.), *England in the Twelfth Century*, Proceedings of the 1988 Harlaxton Symposium (Woodbridge, 1990).

HARLAXTON MEDIEVAL STUDIES, VII

ARMIES, CHIVALRY
AND WARFARE
IN MEDIEVAL BRITAIN
AND FRANCE

Proceedings of the 1995
Harlaxton Symposium

Edited by
Matthew Strickland

PAUL WATKINS
STAMFORD
1998

.

Published in 1998 by
Paul Watkins
18, Adelaide Street,
Stamford,
Lincolnshire, PE9 2EN

ISBN
1 871615 89 5

Typeset from the discs and essays of the authors
by Paul Watkins (Publishing)

Printed on long-life paper

Printed and bound by Woolnoughs of Irthlingborough

CONTENTS

ARMIES AND ORGANISATION

RAVAGING AND LOGISTICS

THE PRACTICE OF WARFARE

LIST OF CONTRIBUTORS

Christopher Allmand	University of Liverpool
Andrew Ayton	University of Hull
Matthew Bennett	Royal Military Academy, Sandhurst
Jim Bradbury	Selsey, West Sussex
Sonya Cameron	University of Glasgow
Charles Coulson	University of Kent
Anne Curry	University of Reading
Kelly DeVries	Loyola College, Baltimore
Carol Edington	University of St Andrews
Anthony Goodman	University of Edinburgh
Jennie Hooper	University of Leeds
Maurice Keen	Balliol College, Oxford
Kay Lacey	London School of Economics
Frédérique Lachaud	Université de Paris-Sorbonne
Richard Morris	University of Warwick
John Palmer	University of Hull
Pam Porter	Department of Manuscripts, British Library
Michael Prestwich	University of Durham
Toby Purser	St Alfred's College, Winchester
Matthew Strickland	University of Glasgow

LIST OF ILLUSTRATIONS

18 (Morris) Kenilworth Castle, great hall, view from the keep (History of Art Photo Library, University of Warwick: R. K. Morris).

19 (Morris) La Ferté Milon, entrace façade (History of Art Photo Library, University of Warwick: R. K. Morris).

20 (Hooper) The Aberlemno Stone, Angus (c.8th century) detail (Historic Scotland).

21 (Hooper) Sculptured frieze (c.11th century) from Winchester (Conway Library, Courtauld Institute of Art).

22 (Hooper) The Bayeux Tapestry, birds and beasts in the margin above the final battle scenes (drawn by Jennie Hooper).

23 (Hooper) British Library, Cotton MS Claudius. B. IV, f. 15r (Aelfric's *Hexateuch*, Canterbury, early 11th century), detail of Noah's Ark (drawn by Jennie Hooper).

24 (Hooper) British Library, Cotton MS Claudius. B. IV, f. 24v (Aelfric's *Hexateuch*), the battle of the Kings and the capture of Lot (Conway Library, Courtauld Institute of Art).

25 (Porter) British Library, Additional MS 44985, f. 4v. (Italian, late 14th century), the use of the grappling hook (reproduced by permission of the British Library Board).

26 (Porter) British Library, Royal MS 20. B. xi, f. 3 (French, early 14th century), exercises for recruits (reproduced by permission of the British Library Board).

27 (Porter) British Library, Royal MS 15. E. I, f. 209 (Flemish, late 15th century), cannon and accoutrements (reproduced by permission of the British Library Board).

28 (Porter) British Library, Cotton MS Nero C.iv, f. 14 (English, c.1150), the massacre of the Innocents (reproduced by permission of the British Library Board).

29 (Porter) British Library, Additional MS 23145, f. 37v (French, late 14th century), St Maurice (reproduced by permission of the British Library Board).

30 (Porter) British Library, Egerton MS 859, f. 27 (German, 15th century) St Maurice (reproduced by permission of the British Library Board).

31 (Porter) British Library, Royal MS 12F. xiii, f. 11v (English, early 13th century), mail armour (reproduced by permission of the British Library Board).

32 (Porter) British Library, Royal MS 10. E. IV, f. 65v (Italian with English illustrations, early 14th century),m single combat (reproduced by permission of the British Library Board).

33 (Porter) British Library, Arundel MS 66, f. 45 (English, c.1490), the constellation of Argo (reproduced by permission of the British Library Board).

34 (Porter) British Library, Yates Thompson MS 12, f. 40v (French, c.1250–60), the siege of Jerusalem (reproduced by permission of the British Library Board).

35 (Porter) British Library, Yates Thompson MS 33, f. 155v (French, late 15th century), the battle of Hastings (reproduced by permission of the British Library Board).

36 (Porter) British Library, Royal MS 19 D.I, f. 111 (French, mid 14th century), the siege of Saianfu (reproduced by permission of the British Library Board).

37 (Porter) British Library, Stowe MS 17, f. 243v (Maastricht, c.1300), a siege engine (reproduced by permission of the British Library Board).

38 (Porter) British Library, Royal MS 16 G.VI, f. 388 (French, 1325–50), two trebuchets in action (reproduced by permission of the British Library Board).

39 (Porter) British Library, Cotton MS Nero D.ix, f. 77v (French, c.1470), a battle scene (reproduced by permission of the British Library Board).

40 (Porter) British Library, Burney MS 169, f. 21v (Flemish, 1468–75), the destruction of Thebes (reproduced by permission of the British Library Board).

41 (Porter) British Library, Cotton MS Nero E.ii, pt. 1, f. 124 (French, early 15th century), Roland fights Feragaut (reproduced by permission of the British Library Board).

42 (Porter) British Library, Royal MS 16. G. ix, f. 76v (Flemish, c.1470–80), an army advancing in formation (reproduced by permission of the British Library Board).

43 (Porter) British Library, Harley MS 326, f. 90 (English, c.1480), an army on the move (reproduced by permission of the British Library Board).

44 (Porter) British Library, Egerton MS 3028, f. 8 (English, 1325–50), the beginnings of plate armour (reproduced by permission of the British Library Board).

45 (Porter) British Library, Additional MS 47680, f. 44v (English, 1326–27), a primitive cannon (reproduced by permission of the British Library Board).

46 (Strickland) Corpus Christi College, Cambridge MS 26, p. 160 (Matthew Paris' *Chronica Majora*, c.1240–58), the legendary duel between Edmund Ironside and Cnut (Corpus Christi College, Cambridge; The Conway Library, Courtauld Institute of Art).

47 (Strickland) Two lead-glazed tiles from Chertsey Abbey, Surrey, c.1250, showing Richard Coeur de Lion's joust with Saladin (The British Museum).

48 (Strickland) British Library, Additional MS 42130, f. 82 (Luttrell Psalter, c.1325–35), Richard I unhorsing Saladin (reproduced by permission of the British Library Board).

49 (Lachaud) Trinity College, Cambridge, MS 0.0.34, f. 20 (Thomas of Kent's *Roman de toute chevalerie*, c.1240–50), horses with mail barding (by kind permission of the Master and Fellow of Trinity College, Cambridge).

50 (Lachaud) Bodleian Library, MS Douce 366, f. 55v (Ormseby Psalter c.1310), a knight with chapel de fer, ailettes, poleyns and couters (The Bodleian Library, Oxford).

51 (Lachaud) Bodleian Library, MS Auct. DIV.17, f. 7v (Apocalypse, 13th century), two knights, one wearing a chapel de fer and surcoat, the other with gamboised cuisses with poleyns (The Bodleian Library, Oxford).

52 (Lachaud) Metz, Médiathèque de Pontiffroy, MS 1.184, f. 5 (Metz Apocalypse, c.1250–55), knight with reinforced armorial surcoat and poleyns (by kind permission of the Conservateur du fonds ancien et précieux).

53 (Lachaud) Dublin, Trinity College MS 177, f. 55v (Matthew Paris' *Vie de Seint Auban*, c.1245–52), King Offa setting out on an expedition (by kind permission of the Board of Trinity College, Dublin).

54 (Lachaud) Bodleian Library, Bodley Roll, row 3 (*Genealogy of the Kings of England*, late 13th century), battle scene (The Bodleian Library, Oxford).

PREFACE

Few subjects could be more admirably suited to the interdisciplinary approach to medieval studies fostered by the Harlaxton Symposium than that of 'War and Chivalry', adopted as the theme of the 1995 Symposium. For chivalric culture itself was a rich and inseparable amalgam of military, political and social influences which profoundly affected, and equally were profoundly affected by, literature and art. The complexity of this interface is reflected throughout this volume, and directly addressed by studies of chivalric literature, of the influence of Arthurian romance on secular aristocratic architecture, of the development of the tournament in Scotland, and of the powerful and ubiquitous motif of single combat.

Equally, few elements of medieval society escaped the reverberations of war, whether through direct experience of warfare or the demands of supply and recruitment. Here a series of complimentary studies examines aspects of recruitment and organisation of English armies from the fourteenth to the early sixteenth century, revealing the extensive militarisation of all levels of the aristocracy under Edward III, the complexities and sophistication of army structure in Lancastrian Normandy, and the tensions inherent in the crown's continued reliance on, yet growing mistrust of, noble retinues in the early Tudor period. The same theme of 'privatised' defence, only occasionally bolstered by an impecunious government in times of emergency, pervades a study of the border defences of northern England in the later middle ages. Yet if the English crown might relinquish ownership of key border castles, a parallel study of Valois fortress policy reveals the French kings ruthlessly manipulating their regalian rights of rendability to enhance Valois power under the thinnest pretexts of military necessity.

The continued influence of the classical past on military thinking is revealed by an analysis of late medieval redactions of Vegetius' *De Re Militari*, a text which both inspired a body of technical illustrations and challenged its translators to achieve contemporary relevance by the paraphrasing of Latin vocabulary and the addition of new weaponry such as the cannon. One of the first recorded uses of such weapons in open battle rather than in siege, at Bevershoutsveld in 1382, also forms a case study, while the effectiveness of the more traditional arm of knightly cavalry is critically reassessed. To qualify the mounted role of knights, however, is not to advocate their military redundancy, but rather to stress their tactical versatility and ability to fight equally effectively on foot. Much of their continued military significance rested on the quality of the knights' defensive equipment, and here the crucial period of transition from mail to plate during the thirteenth and early fourteenth centuries is explored through the evidence of both record material and contemporary illustration. The challenges and pitfalls of employing the latter form of evidence for the study of medieval warfare form the subject of a separate enquiry, while the depiction of the slain in the manuscript illumination and poetry of Anglo-Saxon England explores a central but hitherto largely neglected facet of combat.

Yet if such images of war are disturbing, they pale by comparison with the picture of appalling brutality and localised genocide revealed by the formulaic and emotionally disengaged entries for 'waste' recorded in Domesday Book, here re-analysed in a forceful reassertion of the cataclysmic nature of William the Conqueror's 'Harrying of the North' in 1069–70. Though William and his boyhood companions such as William fitzOsbern, whose career receives a separate study, were raised in a developing chivalric milieu, this campaign was exceptional in its ferocity even by the standards of the great chevauchées of the first part of the Hundred Years War. These large-scale mounted raids, where armies lived off the enemy's land, marked a departure from an elaborate, but as a case study of the logistics of Edward II's Scottish expedition of 1322 reveals, not always successful logistical system developed by Edward I and his son for their operations against Scotland.

Contemporary writers, confronted by the brutality, suffering and profiteering engendered by war, struggled to reconcile these realities with equally forceful and pervasive notions of chivalry. Some, such as Chaucer and his Scottish contemporary John Barbour, succeeded to a considerable degree in so doing. Their very different handling of the tensions between ideal and reality examined here furnish a highly instructive comparison.

Taken together, the following papers reflect both the great diversity of themes and approaches current in the study of medieval warfare and its cultural context, and the continued potential of so central a subject. My thanks are due to many people; to all the contributors for their efforts and their patience; to members of the Harlaxton Committee and in particular to Sean O'Harrow for his invaluable and unstinting support in the organisation of the 1995 Symposium: and especially to Shaun Tyas of Paul Watkins Publishing for his quiet forebearance and expert advice during the preparation of this volume. Also, his assistant Marion Cutforth carefully set the original text and processed the corrections at proof stage.

The 1995 Conference itself was overshadowed by the tragic death of Andrew Martindale, with whom I had the pleasure of working for all too short a time. The 1996 Symposium Proceedings will form a special memorial volume, but it is fitting to acknowledge here the important role he played in the early stages of the formulation of the 1995 War and Chivalry Conference, at which his presence was sorely missed.

Matthew Strickland

Chaucer and Chivalry Re-visited

MAURICE KEEN

Since Terry Jones's remarkable book, *Chaucer's Knight,* appeared in 1980, there has been a good deal of discussion of Chaucer's attitude toward chivalry, to which many of us, myself included, have contributed.[1] Two new contributions to the debate tempt me to return to it. One is Terry Jones's own introduction to the revised version of his book that appeared in 1994: the other is the extremely interesting article by Anthony Luttrell, 'Chaucer's Knight and the Mediterranean', which appeared – also in 1994 – in the first volume of *The Library of Mediterranean History.*[2] Though they have very different things to say, both seem to me to say things that are illuminating in the context of Chaucer and chivalry.

I should make it clear at the start that, although I admire Terry Jones's book and have found his comments on the *Knight's Tale* useful and perceptive, I remain quite unable to accept his thesis that the portrait of the knight in the *General Prologue* is a satiric send-up of a free-booting mercenary soldier. What Jones and Luttrell in their different ways have reminded me of sharply, however, is the need to nuance very carefully the attitude of Chaucer, or rather perhaps of Chaucer's age and circle, whose reactions his

---

[1] The present paper is not based on new research, but on the reconsideration, in the light of the work of others, of what I wrote in 1983 ('Chaucer's Knight, the English Aristocracy and the Crusade' in V. Scattergood and J. Sherborne, eds., *English Court Culture in the Later Middle Ages* (London, 1983), pp. 45–61). Beside the work of Terry Jones and of A. Luttrell, cited below, the writings that have most influenced me are J. Barnie's chapter on 'Conservatives and Intellectuals; the Debate on War', pp. 117–38 of his *War in Medieval Society* (London, 1974): A. Blamires, 'Chaucer's Re-evaluation of Chivalric Honour', *Medievalia,* 5 (1979), pp. 245–67: J. Catto, 'Sir William Beauchamp between Lollardy and Chivalry', *The Ideals and Practice of Medieval Knighthood,* III, ed. C. Harper-Bill and R. Harvey (Woodbridge, 1990): A. Hudson's chapter on 'The Context of Vernacular Wycliffitism', in her *The Premature Reformation: Wycliffite Texts and Lollard History* (Oxford, 1988), pp. 390–445: and P. Mrockzkowski, 'Chaucer's Knight and Some of His Fellow Fighters', *Genres, Themes and Images in English Literature,* ed. P. Boitani and A. Torti (Tübingen, 1988).

[2] T. Jones, *Chaucer's Knight* (revised edn, London, 1994): A. Luttrell, 'Chaucer's Knight and the Mediterranean', *Library of Mediterranean History,* I (1994), pp. 127–60.

1

writing inevitably reflects, to knightly and martial issues. 'Chaucer's flair for verisimilitude in detail', writes Luttrell, 'was accompanied by a deliberate ambiguity and reticence which enable him to present his Knight as a standard or ideal representation of a class, as a figure against which he could level implicit and perhaps ironic social criticism.'[3] 'To suppose', Terry Jones writes with typical forcefulness, 'that they [Chaucer's contemporaries] all subscribed to the idea of crusading and all unquestionably thought warfare was a good thing is like supposing that twentieth century England is made up entirely of readers of *The Sun* and *The Daily Telegraph*. Let us celebrate the differences of opinion that existed in Chaucer's day as well as our own'.[4] This emphasis on ambiguities, on reticences and differences of opinion, is what I wish here to follow up.

I will start by saying that, as it seems to me, there *were* people in Chaucer's day – not everyone but a great many people – who did think rather in the way of Jones's *Telegraph* readers of the fourteenth century. There were a great many who readily subscribed to the view so pithily put by Jean de Bueil in a later chivalrous generation, that poor soldiers 'may earn their salvation by arms just as well as one may by living in contemplation on a diet of roots'.[5] Similarly widely held was the view of Geoffrey de Charny, that there was more honour to be won at the tournament (because it was more perilous) than in jousting, more through war service than through the tournament, and that the greatest honour of all was to be won fighting in strange lands far afield – above all for the faith.[6] These are conventional chivalric views, open to all sorts of qualifications: among the English, it would seem, there were those ready to go a bit further. In England, says Froissart, on account of their great and high victories in the time of Edward III and the Prince of Wales, and on account of their great conquests and the riches won in them, 'the whole community of the land is always more inclined to war than peace'.[7] He eloquently re-evokes this same theme in the speech that he puts into the mouth of Thomas Duke of Gloucester inveighing against the pacific policies of Richard II: 'the people of this land desire war, for they cannot live without it ... but we have a king who is too heavy in the arse, who wishes for nothing but to eat and drink and sleep: that is no way of life for men at arms who desire to win honour

---

[3]   Luttrell, 'Chaucer's Knight and the Mediterranean', p. 158.

[4]   Jones, *Chaucer's Knight*, p. xxi.

[5]   J. de Bueil, *Le Jouvencel*, ed. C. Favre and L. Lecestre (Paris, 1887–9), II, p. 21.

[6]   G. de Charny, *Livre de Chevalerie*, in *Oeuvres de Froissart*, ed. K. de Lettenhove, 25 vols (Brussels, 1870–77), I, pt. iii, pp. 464–72.

[7]   *Oeuvres de Froissart*, ed. K. de Lettenhove, XIV, p. 384.

in arms'.[8] The speech of course is imaginary, but Froissart was not ill informed about English politics in the 1390s, and it tallies well with what we otherwise know of Duke Thomas's opinions. Its message, moreover, chimes rather neatly with the words that Langland gives to Lady Meed, upbraiding Conscience for his advocacy of peace: 'Conscience should never be my Constable if I were king ... I wager that if I had been Marshal of his (the king's) men in France, he should have been lord of that land in its length and breadth, and would have made the least brat of his brood a baron's peer there'.[9]

Chaucer would clearly have known and understood the sort of attitude that Langland satirised, and that Froissart attributed to Thomas Duke of Gloucester. He knew the contemporary martial, chivalrous world from the inside. When he gave testimony to the commissioners for the Court of Chivalry in the great armorial dispute between Richard Lord Scrope of Bolton and Sir Robert Grosvenor, in 1387, he was able to say that he had been armed for 27 years. The Court's clerk identified him as an esquire, a martial degree, and he was a man of coat armour.[10] Many of the military men who gave witness with him in that case would have been known to him: some were his friends. The overall flavour of their testimony is powerfully resonant of the glory and bellicosity of chivalry that Froissart's *Chronicles* reflect so vividly. A series of witnesses spoke of the prowess that the Scropes of an earlier generation had shown in the tourneying field.[11] The ageing veteran, Nicholas Sabraham, spoke of how he had seen members of the Scrope clan, clad in their arms *azure a bend or*, 'in many a place, where many a deed of chivalry was done' – in Scotland, at Crécy and Poitiers, and 'beyond the great sea'.[12] He told also of how he had seen Stephen Scrope, 'armed in the said arms', kneeling to receive knighthood from King Peter of Cyprus before the assault on Alexandria in 1365.[13] John

---

8   *Oeuvres de Froissart*, XVI, pp. 3–4.

9   William Langland, *Piers Plowman*, C. Text, Passus IV, ll. 256–63:

> For sholde nevere Conscience be my Constable,
> Were ich a kyng ycoroned, by Marye, quath Mede,
> Ne be mareschal of my men there ich moste fyghte.
> Ac hadde ich, Mede, be hus mareschal over hus men in Fraunce,
> Ich dorst have leid my lyve and no lasse wedde,
> He had be lord of that londe in lengthe and in brede.
> And al-so kyng of that cuth hus kyn to have holpen,
> The leste brol of hus blod a barones pere.

10 *The Scrope and Grosvenor Controversy*, ed. N. H. Nicolas (London, 1832), I, pp. 178–9. Chaucer's arms appear to have been *per pale argent and gules, a bend counterchanged (ibid.*, II, p. 412).

11 *Ibid.*, I, pp. 133, 142, 155.

12 *Ibid.*, I, p. 125.

13 *Ibid.*, I, p. 124.

Rither esquire spoke of how Geoffrey Le Scrope the Younger had fallen fighting the pagan Lithuanians on a *reise* with the Teutonic knights.[14] The glamour of tournaments, of great campaigns, of crusading adventure, all these are reiterated themes with the witnesses among whom Chaucer stood up to give his evidence in the Court of Chivalry in the case of Scrope v. Grosvenor.

It is no wonder, then, that Chaucer's writing should show how well he understood the spirit of chivalry that their testimony breathes. The knight of his *Prologue* had seen service in Prussia, at Alexandria and beyond the 'grete see'.[15] The tournament of his *Knight's Tale* shows him an acute observer of chivalry's colour and pageantry, with its panoply of gold hewn helms, coat armours, its foaming steeds, gnawing at the bridle, its chief herald on his scaffold, making 'an Ho!'[16] His picture of the pomp of Arcite's funeral *cortege* seems likewise to be drawn from the life, and can be usefully compared with the directions for their funerals of such as the Black Prince and Sir Brian Stapleton.[17] Chaucer clearly understood well the purpose of such a *cortège*, with its white horses with trappers of Arcite's arms and mourning men bearing his spear and shield, which was to do fitting honour to a dead knight of renown:

> In as muche as the service sholde be
> The more noble and riche in his degree[18]

To understand, however, is not necessarily the same thing as to approve. 'Let us celebrate the differences of opinion that existed in Chaucer's day as well as in our own', Terry Jones reminds us. Evidence is clear enough that, in the very years when the case of Scrope v. Grosvenor was being heard, war-weariness was beginning, at the political level at least, to take some of the gloss off English chivalrous bellicosity. These were the years of the complex diplomatic processes in quest of *détente* between France and England, born of exhaustion and disappointment with military effort that seemed to be leading nowhere, and culminating in the twenty-eight year truce of 1396. That diplomatic policy, and that truce, were what the Duke of Gloucester and others like him who thought that 'war was a good thing' – for England anyway – so deplored. But there were

14 *Ibid.*, I, p. 146.
15 *Canterbury Tales*, General Prologue, ll. 42–59.
16 *The Knight's Tale*, ll. 1625–78.
17 For the Prince's instructions, see J. Nichols, *A Collection of all the Wills ... of the Kings and Queens of England* (London, 1780), p. 68. For Stapleton's instructions see M. Vale, *Piety, Charity and Literacy among the Yorkshire Gentry, 1370–1480* (St Anthony's Hall Papers, York, 1976), p. 12; and for further discussion of chivalric funerals see his *War & Chivalry* (London, 1981), pp. 88 ff.
18 *The Knight's Tale*, ll. 2029–30.

others, clearly, who thought rather differently, in the light of experience. Hoccleve put their view neatly, a little later; 'This werre waxeth al to hor and old.'[19]

There is also some evidence that hints at English reactions to the late fourteenth-century military experience that seem to go a little further than mere war-weariness at the political level, that had a more profound, ideological dimension, stirring serious questions about the current ethos of chivalry. The significance of that evidence, and its purport, is the major issue that the comments of Terry Jones and Anthony Luttrell, which I quoted at the beginning of this paper, seem to me to raise.

It is their clear suggestion, though there is a difference in their emphasis, that Chaucer was among those touched by just such reactions. Luttrell in particular, with a sure insight in my view, suggests that in this context we need to look carefully at the attitudes of the so-called Lollard Knights, several of whom were Chaucer's friends and three of whom, by coincidence, were fellow witnesses with him in the Scrope v. Grosvenor dispute. Their attitudes and Chaucer's may be compared with those of other thinking and literate contemporaries who seem to have been interested in raising questions about contemporary chivalric values, like Gower and Langland, and the great French crusade propagandist, Philippe de Mézières.

Three perceived stains on the character of contemporary chivalry seem particularly to have struck home to the fourteenth-century satirists, intellectuals and soldiers who raised questions about its values: cruelty, avarice and vainglory. Criticism of knighthood on these grounds was not then new, but what was said by them, by men of Chaucer's circle and by others, sounds to me as if it was born of experience, or at the very least crystallised into an attitude as a result of experience, direct or indirect. The cruelty and the bloodthirsty waste of war is what Chaucer himself, I think, evokes most vividly. At the very beginning of his *Knight's Tale*, his picture of the pillagers in their unpleasant occupation of ransacking the dead, and stumbling on the bodies of the wounded cousins Palamon and Arcite, shows his vivid awareness of the darker side of the martial trade.[20] His description of Mars's mansion and his temple rises to a more powerful rhetorical level. What does war, the business of chivalrous men and of Mars, God of War, mean? It means

---

19 T. Hoccleve, *The Regement of Princes*, ed. F. J. Furnivall (E.E.T.S., Extra Series 72, 1897), l. 5341.
20 *The Knight's Tale*, ll. 146 ff. On 'pilours' and their professional role in hosts of this period see N. A. R. Wright, '"Pillagers" and "Brigands" in the Hundred Years War', *Journal of Medieval History*, 9 (1983), pp. 15–23.

The careyne in the bush with throat y-corve:
A thousand slayn, and nat of qualm y-storve;
The tyrant, with the prey by force y-raft;
The tourn destroyed: there was nothing laft.[21]

"There is ful many a man that cryeth "werre! werre!"" says the wise man in the *Tale of Melibeus* 'that woot ful little what werre amounteth'.[22] Chaucer saw very clearly to what 'open werre, with woundes al bi-bledde' amounted, in terms of blood and cruelty.

Some of the imagery that Chaucer uses in his description of Mars's mansion is very similar to that of Philippe de Mézières, in his near contemporary *Letter to Richard II*, describing Nimrod's 'Garden of War'. Chaucer's painted forest of 'knotty, knarry, barren trees old', 'where dwelleth neither man ne beste' recalls the land in Nimrod's garden, stripped bare by gigantic locusts so that no blade could sprout and no fruit ripen.[23] Just as in Mars's mansion wall paintings recalled the murder of Caesar and the death of Antony, so in the old roofless palace in Nimrod's garden were figured the wars of the giants 'who shed human blood without measure', the slaughter at Cannae, and the death of Antony.[24] Philippe was equally sharply aware with Chaucer of war's potential – and the potential of chivalrous bellicosity – through evil to spawn further evil. In his *Songe du Vieil Pélérin* he charged the English – specifically – with turning all Christendom upside down in their intoxication with knighthood, 'drunk as you are with your stories of Lancelot and Gawain and of worldly valour'.[25] Yet Philippe, like Chaucer, was one who knew his chivalry from the inside. He had enjoyed a distinguished martial career and his life's ambition was to found a new order of chivalry of the Passion, in which the ideal of crusading would be revived. One such as Chaucer's Knight, who had fought for the faith at Algeciras and Alexandria and in Prussia, would have been a man after his own heart. Chaucer's Knight loved chivalry and truth and honour, as would have de Mézières' ideal knights of the Passion Order. There is no outright condemnation of chivalry by either, rather the reverse: but of the bloodthirstiness of contemporary knighthood there is, and it is emphatic.

---

21 *The Knight's Tale*, ll. 1115–8.
22 *The Tale of Melibeus*, E 12, l. 2228.
23 *The Knight's Tale*, ll. 1117 ff: P. de Mézières, *Letter to King Richard II*, ed. G. W. Coopland (Liverpool, 1975), pp. 58, 132.
24 *The Knight's Tale*, l. 1174 ff: *Letter to King Richard II*, pp. 57, 131.
25 P. de Mézières, *Le Songe du Vieil Pélérin*, ed. G. W. Coopland (Cambridge, 1975), I, p. 197.

The streams in Philippe's garden of war were full of bloodsucking leeches, bloated with feed: these leeches, he wrote 'represent the captains and their men at arms, who suck the blood of the poor, that is their livelihood, by ransoms, pillage, taxes and oppressions without measure'.[26] The covetousness of freebooting soldiery, here allegorised, is a theme powerfully echoed by English writers of the same age, among whom covetousness is singled out again and again as one of the darkest smirches on contemporary chivalry. Gower was much concerned with it:

> Mais certes je ne say
> De cez gens d'armes quoy diray,
> Q'ensy disant les ay oiz:
> 'Es guerres je travailleray,
> Je serray riche ou je morray
> Ains que revoie mon païs
> Ne mes parens ne mes amys?
> Ains sont de convoitise epris.'[27]

Langland saw things the same way. It is no accident that in *Piers Plowman* it is Lady Meed, mistress of bribery and corruption, who rallied King Edward's troops in France:

> There I lafte with my lorde his lyf for to save,
> And made his men meri, and mornyng to lette.
> I batered hem on the bakk, and boldede here hertis,
> And dede hem hoppe for hope to have me at wille.[28]

– that is to say, to have riches at their will.

The shaft here goes home surely. The hope of 'good and great spoils', said the Duke of Gloucester in his speech in Froissart, is what makes it so sure that 'if we had a good king, who was desirous of war, ... he would find 100,000 archers and 6,000 men at arms who would willingly cross the sea in his service'.[29] Avarice was the reason why, thought Hoccleve, the Anglo-French war went on and on;

> To wynne worldly tresour and richesse
> Is of your stryf the long continuance.[30]

The 'cursednesse of covetyse', Chaucer declared, was what first brought in strife, when after the Golden Age tyranny entered and Nimrod began to build his high towers

> Thise tyrants put him gladly not in pres,

---

[26] *Letter to King Richard II*, pp. 58, 132.
[27] J. Gower, *Mirour de l'Omme*, ll. 24048–56.
[28] *Piers Plowman*, B Text, Passus III, ll. 196–9.
[29] *Oeuvres de Froissart*, XVI, p. 3.
[30] Hoccleve, *The Regement of Princes*, ll. 5342–3.

No wildnesse, ne no busshes for to winne ...
But ther as bagges been and fat vitaille,
Ther wol they gon, and spare for no sinne
With al hir ost the cite for t'assaille.[31]

Sir John Clanvowe, in one of his most powerful passages in his
homiletic *The Two Ways*, manages to combine together in a single
denunciation all the three great vices of chivalry: cruelty, the lust for blood;
covetousness, the greed of riches; and vainglory, the thirst for worldly
honour:

> For the world holt hem worsshipful that been greet werreyours and
> fighters and that distroyern and wynnen manye loondis, and waasten and
> geven muche good to hem that han ynough: and that dispenden
> oult-rageously in mete, in drynke, in cloothing, in buyldying ... And also
> the world worsshipeth hem muche that woln bee venged proudly and
> dispitously of every wrong that is said or doon to hem. And of swyche
> folke men maken bookes and soonges and reden and syngen of hem for
> to hoolde the mynde of here deedes the lengere heere upon eerth, ffor
> that is a thing that worldely men desiren greetly that here naame myghte
> laste loonge after hem heere upon eerth.[32]

One could find hundreds of echoes, in contemporary writing, for what
Clanvowe says here; in Chaucer's jibe at the lovers of chivalry who
thronged to the tournament at Athens in hope to earn 'a passant name';[33] in
Melibeus' warning against warlike vengeance that only engenders further
causes for vengeance;[34] in Gower's question, where be they now that made
strong wars for 'ven honour or for the worldes good?'[35] But I am not sure
that I can think of anyone who went as straight for the jugular as Clanvowe
did with his 'of swyche folke men maken bookes and soonges ... to hoolde
the mynde of here deedes the lenger heere upon eerth'. Froissart avowed in
the preface to his chronicles that his purpose in writing was 'so that the
great deeds of arms done in the wars of France and England shall be
notably enregistered and held in perpetual memory'.[36] Clanvowe's
denunciation calls into question as mere vainglory the whole aim and
conception of the arch-chronicler of chivalry, whose work had such an
impact and who held out explicitly to his knightly informants the reward of
having their name set down in his book.[37]

---

[31] *The Former Age*, ll. 33–40.
[32] Sir J. Clanvowe, *The Two Ways*, in *The Works of Sir John Clanvowe*, ed. V. J. Scattergood (Cambridge, 1965), p. 69.
[33] *The Knight's Tale*, l. 1249.
[34] *The Tale of Melibeus*, 36 (ll. 2579–82).
[35] Gower, *To King Henry IV, in Praise of Peace*, ll. 99–101.
[36] *Oeuvres de Froissart*, II, pp. 1, 7, 11.
[37] E.g. *ibid.*, XI, p. 108.

Sir John Clanvowe is a very interesting figure.[38] As is well known, he was a considerable soldier, a poet, a friend of Chaucer, and one of the group of those identified by the chroniclers Walsingham and Knighton as 'Lollard Knights'. He served with distinction in the French wars, and also further afield: in 1390 he joined the Barbary Crusade led by the Duke of Bourbon, and then travelled further east. He died of sickness in Constantinople. Three days later, his friend and fellow 'Lollard Knight', William Neville, who had accompanied him, died. Over their tomb was laid a marble slab which commemorated their chivalrous bonding by displaying the arms of Neville impaling the arms of Clanvowe. It seems almost certain that they were sworn brothers in arms[39] – as were Palamon and Arcite in the *Knight's Tale*.

There is a tension, clearly, between this memorial, with its evocative heraldic symbolism commemorating a partnership in chivalry, and what Clanvowe wrote about the desire to be remembered on earth. The easiest resolution is that here we have a memorial to true chivalry (as opposed to false, vainglorious chivalry), to two knights faithful unto death in their dedication to a crusading enterprise that was different from the wars of France and England, and more worthy of honour and respect.[40] That there was such a difference was clearly contemporarily understood. The distinction between salvific fighting for the faith and the bloodthirsty wars of the English and French was the underlying theme of all de Mézières, writing; the object of his Order of the Passion was to draw men out of worldly service into salvific chivalrous service. Chaucer, as Luttrell points out, says nothing of his Knight's service in wars between Christians: crusading is the clear theme of the litany of his battle honours in the *General Prologue*. If Luttrell is right, he was thereby quite deliberately seeking to make the same point as de Mézières.[41]

---

[38] The fullest account of Clanvowe's career is that given by K. B. McFarlane in his *Lancastrian Kings and Lollard Knights* (Oxford, 1972); see especially chapters 2 and 3, pp. 151–85.

[39] See S. Düll, A. Luttrell and M. Keen, 'Faithful unto Death: The Tomb Slab of Sir William Neville and Sir John Clanvowe, 1391', *Antiquaries Journal*, 71 (1991), pp. 174–90.

[40] Vale, *Piety, Charity and Literacy*, pp. 11–12 suggests, in general terms, a different resolution of the tension between 'contemptuous language towards the body' and 'elaborate armorial display', when they are found together: 'The knight may die but his arms live on: the mortal body may be described as caitiff but the arms are immortal''.There is much in this, but it hardly fits this particular case, where the unusual marshalling of the arms seems clearly to be a memorial to a particular relationship between two individual knights, and so lacks the armorial 'immortality' he refers to.

[41] Luttrell, 'Chaucer's Knight and the Mediterranean', pp. 155, 157.

Among the 'Lollard Knights' there were others besides Clanvowe and Neville who showed an interest in crusading. Sir John Montagu fought alongside the Teutonic Knights against the heathen in Prussia.[42] Sir Lewis Clifford, who was a close friend of Chaucer's, was enrolled in the Order of the Passion, as well as being a Knight of the Garter.[43] These biographical details fit well with the very interesting conclusion to which they help to lead Anthony Luttrell in his consideration of Chaucer's perception and purpose in his description of the Knight and in the *Knight's Tale*. He notes Chaucer's connections with the Lollard Knights, and the strong Lollard condemnation of the crusades against Christians launched by the schismatic popes in the 1380s. With the Lollard Knights, as he sees it, 'the ideas of Wyclif formed one element in the awareness of a group of knights who gave conventional military and diplomatic service to the crown, while engaging, with certain incoherences, in literary activity and theological speculation'.[44] The martial career of their friend Chaucer's Knight fits well, he goes on to suggest, with the slightly ambiguous framework of their approach, reflecting 'a war weary rejection of the Anglo-French conflict conceived in the spirit of de Mézières' crusade vision and of Lollard protests against crusades against Christians'.[45]

It seems to me that Luttrell's suggestions here are both perceptive and sure; and that his delicately nuanced interpretation of Chaucer's Knight and his Tale in the context of chivalry is more convincing than Terry Jones's reading of his portrait as a satiric 'send up' of mercenary freebooters and their ways. As Luttrell emphasises, Chaucer's depiction of his Knight has a 'genuine reality', based on contemporary 'English presence in infidel parts of the Mediterranean', which had nothing much to do with freebooting.[46] Those who chose to travel east were much more likely to encounter problems with meeting their expenses than to return home rich with the spoils of war.

There remains one point on which this leaves me not quite comfortable, though and to which I am alerted to some of Terry Jones's remarks on fourteenth-century crusades.. The critics of chivalrous vainglory clearly recognised it as the most insidious of the temptations leading knighthood astray, the one which 'lied like the truth'. When it came to crusading, they gave no more shrift to those who sought worldly honour by riding to fight in Prussia or beyond the great sea than they did to those who sought a 'passant name' nearer home. Chaucer placed it high among

---

[42] McFarlane, *Lancastrian Kings and Lollard Knights*, p. 178.

[43] *Ibid.*, pp. 178–9.

[44] Luttrell, 'Chaucer's Knight and the Mediterranean', p. 159.

[45] *Ibid.'*, p. 157.

[46] *Ibid.'*, p. 160.

Duchess Blanche's virtues in the *Boke of the Duchesse* that she had not bidden her admirers to seek worship by running 'hoodless' to Prussia or to Alexandria or into Tartary.[47] Gower was equally explicitly suspicious of those who went to Prussia or crossed the great sea to win reputation and *los* – praise – to gain esteem from their lady loves.[48] Clearly, one did not need to be a full blooded Wycliffite to look askance at knights 'who runnen to hethenesse to get themselves a name for sleying men'.[49]

Sir John Clanvowe, the Lollard Knight who denounced the desire of worldly men, that their name might last long after them here on earth, was buried in the East, under a marble slab finely carved with heraldic blazon. His friend Lewis Clifford was more consistent with puritan principles in his funerary directions:

> I, most unworthy and God's traitor, recommend my wretched and sinful soul wholly to the grace and to the mercy of the blissful Trinity, and my wretched carrion to be buried in the furthest corner of the churchyard ... And I pray and urge my executors, as they will answer before God ... that on my stinking carrion be neither laid cloth of gold nor of silk, but a black cloth, and a taper at my head, and another at my feet, and no stone nor other thing whereby any man my know where may stinking carrion lieth.[50]

In a lower key, Chaucer I think was trying to make a point against vainglory similar to that which Clanvowe made in his homily and Clifford in his will, when he dressed his knight in a doublet of simple fustian, travel stained by his hauberk. Each of these three in his own way struck out at the flamboyance that was the outward symptom of chivalry's vainglory.

That brings me to my paradoxical conclusion. In Clanvowe's homily, in Clifford's will, in Chaucer's pictures both of the Knight and of the Parson in the *General Prologue* and in his *Persone's Tale*, as also in many passages in Langland and Gower, there is a streak of puritanism that was clearly characteristic of intelligent moral speculation in their time; a streak that is not specifically Wycliffite but that is sensitive and receptive to many views that Wyclif and his followers espoused. At the same time, Clanvowe and Clifford in their martial careers and Chaucer in his poetry made apparent their appreciation of what they saw as best in knighthood and its ethos. In doing so, however, they explicitly distanced themselves, in their different ways, from the vainglory of the chivalrous world that they saw round about them. Their ideal for the knight was not that of Froissart or of the

---

[47] *Book of the Duchesse*, ll. 1024–32.
[48] *Mirour de l'Omme*, ll. 23893–916.
[49] *Selections from English Wycliffite Writings*, ed. A. Hudson (Cambridge, 1978), 28 (no. 10 of the 'Twelve Conclusions of the Lollards').
[50] *Testamenta Vetusta*, ed. N. H. Nicolas (London, 1826), I, p. 164.

Arthurian romances, coming much closer to Jean de Bueil's later encapsulation of his office, to be ready to take up arms but only in causes manifestly just, 'in the fear of God and in great humility'. Humility is the antithesis of vainglory: Chaucer deliberately described his Knight as being 'of his port as meke as is a mayde'.[51]

Unfortunately, as Jeremy Catto has pointed out, chivalry and Lollardy make uncomfortable bedfellows.[52] Chivalrous culture was dependent on the visual, on the symbolism of heraldry and pageantry, to a degree that could not in the long run find accommodation with the denunciation of books (or tapestries or paintings) that hold in the mind men's high deeds or with the quest for a final resting place with no stone or other thing whereby men might know whose bones were underground. I do not suppose that Chaucer and his thoughtful contemporaries were fully aware of or had fully worked out the implicit contradictions in their questioning outlook on chivalry. It is a common human capacity to be able to sustain and uphold at one and the same time views which are in tension with one another. The implicit tensions, and in particular those relating to the vainglory of chivalry, do help though to explain why it is so difficult to pin down what they really did think about knighthood, its culture and *mores*, and, in particular, to decide just precisely how we should interpret Chaucer's portrait of the Knight and his *Knight's Tale*.

---

51   *Le Jouvencel*, I, p. 121: *General Prologue*, l. 69.
52   Catto, 'Sir William Beauchamp between Chivalry and Lollardy', p. 39.

Chivalry and Warfare in Barbour's Bruce

SONJA CAMERON

The Scottish romance *The Bruce* was written *c*.1375 by John Barbour, archdeacon of Aberdeen. It narrates the events (or what Barbour claimed were the events) of the Scottish War of Independence against England, 1306–29. The main heroes of the romance are King Robert I (or Robert Bruce), who fought to regain the Scottish throne, and James, lord of Douglas, his closest friend and most successful captain in war. There are also two important lesser heroes, Edward Bruce, earl of Carrick (the king's brother), and Thomas Randolph, earl of Moray (the king's nephew). Although all are historical figures, there is often little or no evidence to confirm the actions or opinions attributed to them by Barbour. Like any romance writer, Barbour insists on his own *suthfastness*,[1] and indeed he has clearly taken some care to research his subject. Nonetheless, it is evident to anyone with a knowledge of the historical background that when it suits him the poet is perfectly ready to omit facts which he dislikes,[2] and to invent or modify episodes in order to make particular points. In the composition of his romance, then, he was not constrained by historical fact. For what follows, it is important to bear in mind that the incidents we find in Barbour's *Bruce* are described because the author *chose* to describe them, and, in fact, to a large extent invented them. *The Bruce* is a romance, not a chronicle.

And indeed, we have Barbour's own word for this. In a much-quoted couplet at the beginning of his narrative, he addresses his audience: 'Lordingis quha likis for till her, / Ye romanys now begynnys her'.[3] The use of the term 'romanys' would have raised certain expectations with his

---

[1]   I.7.13.36. All references are to John Barbour, *The Bruce*, ed. M. P. McDiarmid and J. A. Stevenson (Scottish Text Society, 4th series, 12, 13, 15, Edinburgh, 1980–5). A new paperback edition, *John Barbour, The Bruce*, ed. A. A. M. Duncan (Edinburgh, 1997), has recently been published, at last making Barbour's work accessible to a wider audience. Book and line references are virtually identical to the McDiarmid edition.

[2]   His hero's doubtful and ever-changing allegiances before 1306 are a conspicuous example.

[3]   I.445–6.

audience, who were, after all, used to the genre. Romances dealt with knights and their adventures, with courts and with noble deeds – in a word, with chivalry.

The main heroes of this particular romance are the king, two earls, and a baron whose nobility is constantly referred to and who, indeed, ends up being accorded the epithet 'good' – James Douglas, or the 'good Sir James'.[4] The elevated cast might lead an audience to expect elevated deeds. The king is on a quest to win his inheritance, a popular romance activity[5] which tends to involve the fighting of heathens, the marrying of princesses, the washing of dishes[6] and anonymous participation in tournaments, in varying combinations and not necessarily in this order. However, to anyone introduced to the concept of chivalry on a diet of *Horn Childe*, *Havelok the Dane*, *Guy of Warwick* or *Sir Gawain and the Green Knight* (the latter contemporary with Barbour's *Bruce*), the heroes' pursuits as portrayed in Barbour's work may appear rather peculiar. They fail to engage in the popular chivalric pursuits of winning ladies, fighting in tournaments, and sleeping with their lord's wife. Instead, they sneak around in the woods at night, they ambush their enemies, and they do all they can to avoid what Barbour calls 'playne fechting'.[7] While this may have been a perfectly normal course of action in the real-life chivalric warfare of the middle ages, such fighting methods are less commonly found in romances, which were after all the escapist fiction of the time.

As the title of this paper suggests, it deals with Barbour's treatment of chivalry in just one of its aspects: that of knightly conduct in waging war. The intention is primarily to concentrate on passages that stand out because in them, Barbour's heroes are not merely shown engaging in particular activities, but are found commenting on their reasons for choosing a specific course of action. The aim is to trace how, throughout *The Bruce*, a

---

[4]   This, of course, only in a Scottish context. The English called him 'black' – 'ye blak Douglas' (XV.562).

[5]   Winning back an inheritance, though not necessarily a throne, was a very common concern of romance heroes: examples include the King Horn romances – *Horn et Riemenhild* (Anglo-Norman, 1170–80), *King Horn* (English, c.1225), *Horn Childe* (c.1320) – *Havelok the Dane* (c.1280), and to some extent *Bevis of Hamptoun* and *William of Palerne*.

[6]   Thus Havelok the Dane, in his throne-seekers' job-specification: 'Fir and water Y wile you fete, / [th]e fir blowe an ful wel maken, / Sticks kan Ich breken and kraken, / and kindlen ful wel a fyr, / And maken it to brennen shir. / Ful wel kan Ich cleuen shides, / Eles to-turuen of here hides; / Ful wel kan Ich dishes swilen, / And don al [th]at ye euere wilen.' (*Havelok*, ed. G. V. Smithers, ll. 913–21).

[7]   IX.750.

dialogue takes place about what constitutes acceptable fighting methods for a king or a noble knight.

King Robert's first successful action in his fight to gain his throne[8] is a massacre of sleeping enemies at Turnberry.[9] With his men he enters the town noiselessly at night, breaks into the houses and kills everybody in their beds, regardless of rank. Amongst candidates for thrones in the romance tradition, such behaviour is exceptional; but the most interesting point about this exercise is that Bruce not merely indulges in it but talks about it and justifies his action to his followers. This would be unnecessary if his behaviour was conventional, or even readily acceptable, and therefore the mere fact that a defence of his action is required indicates that according to the norms of the society portrayed in *The Bruce*, it is neither of these things. Bruce argues as follows:

And yocht we slepand slew yaim all
Repruff yar-off na man sall,
For werrayour na fors suld ma
Quheyer he mycht ourcum his fa
Throw strenth or throw sutelte
Bot yat gud faith haldyn be. (V.83–8)

The rationale that anything was compatible with a chivalric code of honour as long as promises and covenants were kept is not unique; it is found in medieval chronicles (the *Histoire de Guillaume le Maréchal* probably being the outstanding example) and is occasionally applied to the definition of chivalry even today. By that token, 'chivalry' in war is reduced to 'keeping faith', and very little besides. It certainly makes it easier to deal with a concept for which no clear guidelines can be found, and which at times appears full of contradictions. In real life, this reduction to keeping faith may well have applied. However, it is by no stretch of the imagination a prominent feature of romances. As can be seen, although the rationale may be adopted and acted upon by King Robert, he (or the author) recognises the need to defend his actions. Bruce's defensiveness implies some tension between the conventions recognised by his followers, and the king's own favoured tactics.

That there is indeed tension within the narrative between the accepted conventions of warfare and guerrilla tactics in which Bruce engages soon becomes obvious and explicit. For Bruce's nephew, Thomas Randolph earl of Moray, disagrees with Bruce's policy of reducing knightly behaviour merely to 'keeping faith'. He disagrees so much that he deserts his uncle and joins Bruce's enemies, at a crucial time in Bruce's career. He is finally

---

[8]   Apart from killing his rival in church, a point which will be raised again later.
[9]   V.89–116.

15

captured by Douglas, who is conducting a guerrilla war in Selkirk Forest,[10] and brought before the king to answer for himself. Bruce reproaches him for changing sides and asks him to be reconciled. Moray retorts angrily:

> ...Ye chasty me, bot ye
> Aucht bettre chastyt for to be,
> For sene ye werrayit the king
> Off Ingland, in playne fechting
> Ye suld pres to derenyhe rycht
> And nocht with cowardy na with slycht. (IX.747–52)

In his opinion, Bruce ought to be ashamed of himself, and if he was going to wage war, he ought to do it 'right', properly, and not sneak about like a coward. The words used are 'cowardy' and 'slycht', with 'slycht' best translated as 'slyness' or 'cunning', but in a sense that is clearly related to treacherous behaviour. These are serious accusations, and it is obvious that Bruce's methods are not part of the knightly code of conduct as Moray knows it; they are not even remotely acceptable. Moray upholds the chivalric code of conventional romances. 'Right' knightly warfare, he implies, is out in the open, and therefore courageous and brave. This conjures up the more accustomed world of romance warfare: pitched battles, challenges, perhaps trial by combat – a type of warfare worlds removed from King Robert's methods.

If Moray considers Bruce's methods cowardly and unacceptable, he is not the only one. Somebody who obviously feels the same way but is perhaps too closely connected to the king to desert him is Bruce's brother Edward, earl of Carrick. Throughout the romance, Carrick behaves like a knight who has just emerged from the court of King Arthur – from a courtly, chivalric romance. Despite his fidelity to Bruce, Carrick never relinquishes his conventional approach to warfare. While Douglas, and after a while even Moray, recover the Scottish castles one by one through cunning, backstabbing, and with the help of common peasants, Carrick, who has been charged with recovering Stirling castle, persists in carrying out a conventional, fruitless siege.[11] Later he enters into a typical chivalric agreement with the commander of the castle: an English army is to come and relieve Stirling Castle by midsummer, but if they do not arrive in time, it is to be yielded.

---

[10]   IX.696–724.

[11]   The contrast between the successes of Douglas and Moray with their lowly born associates and the ineffectiveness of Edward Bruce's orthodox approach to siege warfare has been noted earlier: cf. B. W. Kliman, 'The Significance of Barbour's Naming of Commoners', *Studies in Scottish Literature*, 11 (1973), pp. 108–13, at p. 109.

This agreement elicits a variety of reactions. The English are delighted, which, by the lights of this particular romance, is already a bad sign. The poet himself calls it 'outrageous',[12] or 'excessive'; and the more restrained King Robert remarks that it was 'unwisely done'.[13] Clearly, Barbour is at pains to affirm that the chivalrous deal was not one of Edward Bruce's more popular contributions to the war effort. By implication, the 'good lord' Douglas's exploit of disguising himself as a cow, letting a peasant lead the way up and over the walls of Roxburgh castle, surprising the garrison at their Fastern Eve's celebrations and killing them all 'but pite',[14] is much to be preferred. However, Carrick refuses to learn his lesson. Throughout the romance, he is never shown involved in guerrilla warfare, he never tries to limit the odds, and clearly never grasps the concept of functional fighting.

The circumstances of his death are symptomatic. The situation: he faces a large host with a considerably smaller one, but his companions point out that help is on its way and should arrive within a day. The following dialogue ensues:

In hy schyr Eduuard ansuerd yen
And said yat he suld fecht yat day
Youcht tribill and quatribill wan yai
Schyr Ihone Stewart said, 'Sekyrly
I reid nocht yhe fecht on sic hy,
Men sayis my broyer is cummand
With fyften thowsand men ner-hand,
And war yai knyt with yhow yhe mycht
Ye traystlyer abid to fycht.'

Yan with gret ire 'Allace,' said he,
'I wend neuer till her yat of ye.
Now help quha will for sekyrly
Yis day but mar baid fecht will I,
Sall na man say quhill I may drey
Yat strenth of men sall ger me fley.
God scheld yat ony suld ws blam
Gif we defend our noble nam.'

...yar mycht na consaill awaile,
he wald algat have bataile. (XVIII.28–36; 49–56; 69–70)

Carrick wants to fight on the spot. When his companions try to persuade him to wait until the reinforcements arrive, he displays anger and amazement; his comment along the lines of 'I never thought to hear you say something like that!' suggests that he finds the mere thought ignoble

---

[12]   XI.32.
[13]   XI.38.
[14]   X.373–459.

beyond belief. His Irish allies are the next group to try and dissuade him, without success. Carrick insists on fighting and obligingly, he lets the audience know why: 'No man shall say that I will flee from a stronger enemy; and nobody can blame us for defending our noble name'.[15] Predictably, he falls in the ensuing battle with most of his men, committing various deeds of heroism in the process. This, one may presume, is Moray's 'right' type of warfare. But the poet's comment is exceptionally harsh:

> On yis wis war yai noble men
> For wilfulnes all lesyt yen,
> And yat wes syne and gret pite
> For had yar owtrageous bounte
> Bene led with wyt and with mesur
> Bot gif ye mar mysawentur
> Be fallyn yaim, it suld rycht hard thing
> Be to lede yaim till owtraying,
> Bot gret owtrageous surquedry
> Gert yaim all deir yar worschip by.[16]

The references to 'wilfulness' and 'surquedry'[17] as well as lack of 'wit' and 'mesur' may tempt critics to dismiss Carrick's attitude as simply hot-headed and slightly stupid. The significant point, however, is that the instinct he follows is obviously deeply rooted. Furthermore, it is clearly founded upon a social convention – Carrick acts as he does because he is worried about what others might say of him. The implication is that the society of his time is more likely to approve of a heroic and moreover unnecessary last stand than of a judicious retreat to fight some other time. Like Bruce himself at the beginning, Carrick worries about public opinion; but unlike Bruce, who departs from convention and tries to justify it, Carrick decides on the 'safer' course of action – the one which he considers socially acceptable.

Clearly, the convention which is the backdrop to the action of Barbour's narrative is one with values different from those of which the poet himself approves. Carrick is criticised for lack of 'mesure', of moderation. 'Mesure' is an important chivalric virtue, but to some extent it lives in a state of tension with other chivalric virtues, most notably courage,

---

15. An interesting detail to note here is that everybody else usually speaks in terms of defending their country or their freedom rather than their reputation: e.g. Bruce at Methven (II.343–4); Bruce at Bannockburn (XII.247–8; 2381–3); Bishop Sinclair when faced with an English invasion (XVI.607). That is not to say that honour is never mentioned; Bruce refers to it both at Methven (II.340–1) and Bannockburn (XII.315), but in neither case is it rated as the prime motivation for engaging in battle.

16. XVII.175–84.

17. Translated as 'excessive arrogance', and perhaps reminiscent of the much-debated 'ofermod' of the Battle of Maldon.

and finding a working compromise is not an easy achievement. Carrick is particularly concerned that nobody should be able to say that he ran away, that he is a coward. We have seen that Moray also accuses the king of cowardice. Barbour obliges with a discourse on the importance of finding a mean between cowardice and foolhardiness, but he is of no help regarding the practical application of his wisdom.[18] It is a question of where the boundaries lie between cowardice, courage, and foolhardiness; and the comments of Moray and Carrick make clear that the poet is redrawing them according to his own agenda. Actions that the two earls, attached to a conventional code of conduct, consider cowardly are suddenly simply prudent, while actions which those two consider reasonable (and indeed unavoidable) affirmations of courage are by Barbour criticised as foolhardy, and, if carried out, are shown to have dire results.

Here it is instructive to consider Moray again; for if Carrick is unwilling to compromise his courage, Moray, in fact, 'sees the light', and embarks upon a career of employing 'sum slycht',[19] sneaking about 'in a myrk nycht',[20] and killing priests.[21] Despite his conversion, however, Moray floats uneasily between the two codes of conduct and suffers a significant and extended relapse into chivalric mode towards the end of the romance. In the passage in question, Moray and Douglas with a small raiding party are intercepted by an entire English army. The situation produces an interesting exchange between Douglas and Moray. Douglas has been sent to reconnoitre, and:

> Quhen he [Douglas] yat folk [the English] behaldyn had
> Towart his ost agayn he rad.
> Ye erle speryt gift he had sene
> Yat ost. 'Yha schyr', he said, 'but wene'.
> 'Quhat folk ar yai.' 'Schyr mony men.'
> Ye erle his ayth has suorn yen.
> 'We sall fecht with yaim yocht yai war
> Yhet ma eftsonys yan yai ar.'
> 'Schir lowyt be God,' he said agayn,
> 'Yat we haiff sic a capitayn
> Yat swa gret thing dar wndreta,
> Bot be saynct Bryd it beis nocht swa
> Giff my onsaill may trowyt be,
> For fecht on na maner sall we
> Bot it be at our awantage,
> For me think it war na owtrage

---

[18] VI.338–54.
[19] X.520; also 524.
[20] X.593.
[21] XVII.537–88.

To fewar folk aganys ma
Awantage quhen yai ma to ta.'
(XIX.291–308)

As we see, Moray's response to Douglas's report that they are wildly outnumbered is worthy of the earl of Carrick: 'We shall fight them, even if they were still more than they are'. Douglas's reply is carefully constructed and illuminating: he actually begins by complimenting Moray on his courage, almost as though to reassure him on this crucial point. Only then does he argue against fighting, and he does so in a rather apologetic fashion. He reminds Moray that it should not be considered 'an outrage', or wrong, to try and secure an advantage. His insistence on 'advantage' echoes Bruce's attitude at the beginning of the narrative. This, of course, is the strategy of which Douglas and the king have become masters, and which Moray, to some extent, has also pursued with great success. But Moray, despite his intermittent career as a guerrilla, still instinctively favours 'praiseworthy' combat. Like Carrick, he appears to subscribe to a different social convention. By resurrecting this conflict at so late a stage, Barbour ensures that the tension between convention and expediency, between the different ways of fighting and different attitudes towards what is to be considered acceptable knightly conduct, is sustained throughout the romance.

Moray gives in to Douglas the first time round, but a few days later, he reiterates his suggestion:

Ye erle said, 'Sen yat it swa is
Yat we may nocht with iupertys
Our feloune fayis fors assaill
We sall do it in plane battail.' (XIX.635–8)

Again Douglas, this time with considerably less patience, contradicts him, mentioning the concept of 'folly' in the process (a reminder of Carrick's 'foolhardiness'):

Ye lord Dowglas said, 'Be saynct Brid
It war gret foly at yis tid
Till ws with swilk ane ost to fycht
Yat growys ilk day off mycht
And has wittaill yar-with plente,
And in yar countre her ar we
Quhar yar may cum ws na succourys.'
(XIX.635–45)

It it unlikely that Barbour wished to portray Moray as incorrigibly stupid. Like Carrick, Moray is one of the king's most effective lieutenants, and certainly one of the main heroes of the narrative. It is far more likely that the author simply wished to reinforce his message that normal conventions, as followed partly by Moray and consistently by Carrick, are constantly being violated, and justifiably so.

Considering the four heroes again, we find a rough division into two and two: Moray makes his first major appearance in a scene where he voices his disgust at Bruce's methods, and even though he adopts these methods later, they never become a spontaneous response. Carrick simply refuses to employ them. These two important heroes of the romance obviously subscribe to a different code from that favoured by the other two. Moreover, it is evident that this code is founded upon the conventions of their society, while that of Bruce and Douglas departs from it. If chivalry is the sum of knightly conventions, Bruce's fighting methods are therefore not chivalric within the terms of this romance. By allowing Carrick and Moray to challenge the rationale of functional fighting without success, Barbour reinforces it. The fact, however, that he does so not just once, but regularly throughout the romance, may suggest that he was conscious of arguing a case; that he knew that the style of fighting he portrayed appeared dubious, not just to some characters in his poem, but to members of his own audience. It is possible that we are dealing with another, external point of tension – between the poet's portrayal of his heroes' actions and the norms and conventions associated with 'ideal' chivalry in the 1370s.

Certainly, if the massacre of sleeping enemies had been what contemporary audiences expected to find in a romance as an act perpetrated by a noble knight, any explanation would have been superfluous and the incident would have passed without comment. By the same token, if the author needs to emphasise something repeatedly, the impression is that it is not self-evident. The objections Bruce encounters in the poem may reflect, and indeed anticipate, the objections Barbour expected from his audience. In this context, we may consider Moray, with his arguments both early and towards the end of the romance, the mouthpiece of Barbour's audience – of conventional expectations and reservations. Barbour's methods of making his point are skilful and varied. Characters within the story are made to uphold the conventional code of conduct either verbally or in actions. Verbal challenges are deflected by other characters (usually Douglas) who argue the case for Barbour's 'alternative warfare', or are simply proven misguided by events (Moray's accusation of Bruce). Conventional actions are shown to be either fruitless (Carrick before Stirling) or disastrous (Carrick in Ireland), while the schemes based on the alternative concept are always shown to succeed. Occasionally, the poet himself will interfere and criticise acts of conventional chivalry which he considers particularly unfortunate.

So far, it has been possible to identify a dialogue which deals with tension between a pre-existing convention of knightly conduct, upheld by some characters in the romance, and a more expedient, albeit less clean, method of warfare favoured by the king and James Douglas. Since this method involves the avoidance of battle and the killing of defenceless enemies, a second area of tension is created involving the concepts of cowardice, courage, and foolhardiness, and the question of where to locate the middle ground. The poet himself favours the unconventional, expedient method of waging war, and uses various episodes in the romance to demonstrate, explain, and justify his preference. The frequent reiteration implies that he feels it necessary to justify the mode of warfare he portrays not only within the romance itself, but to his audience, so that we may assume a third area of tension between the conduct which an audience would have expected of the knightly protagonists of a romance, and what Barbour is aiming to present as acceptable behaviour for his romance heroes.

Throughout the romance, the attitude towards fighting itself is simply functional. The aim is less personal distinction than killing the enemy. Single combat occurs only when the heroes are forced to it, as for instance by Henry de Bohun descending on them on a well-nourished charger.[22] They never initiate challenges and usually try to avoid fighting against the odds (although to keep the story interesting they rarely succeed).[23] Barbour's attitude towards fighting is important because almost his entire narrative deals with it. If we give brief consideration to other features of romances which could perhaps be considered elements of a chivalric culture, we find that many of the more commonly encountered ones are either simply absent in *The Bruce*, or have been given a slight twist.

In *The Bruce*, for example, we find no court or the various rituals associated with a courtly community. The only ceremonies of knighting are dealt with perfunctorily, along the lines of: 'Ye king maid Walter Stewart knycht / And Iames of Dowglas yat wes wycht'.[24] There are no tournaments. The only hunt is one in which the king is hunted with hounds by his enemies.[25] Service to ladies is reduced to procuring food for them in

---

[22]   XII.25–59.

[23]   Barbour is adept at placing his heroes in a multitude of hopeless 'heroic' situations while ensuring that they carry no blame for getting there in the first place. At one point, he manages to engineer a (historically undocumented) fight between Douglas with just a handful of men and a 'gret cumpany' of English soldiers in such a way that even the most pragmatic realist can hardly criticise Douglas for fighting against such odds (XV.321–417).

[24]   XII.417–18.

[25]   The hunt takes place in the deer-forest of Glentrool, as if to place special emphasis on the twist which replaces the conventional quarry with the hero of the romance himself. To make up for the lack of orthodox hunting, this variation even occurs twice: VI.32–180, 486–600.

the form of four different kinds of fish while the company is on the run;[26] love affairs happen between a soldier's son and an unspecified 'wench in town',[27] or in a sub-clause between King Robert and women who can give him information.[28] *Courteoisie* is most strikingly evident in the king's treatment of a pregnant laundress – not the most conventional 'weak party requiring protection' of chivalric romance.[29] Even acts of daring are left to simple peasants when these seem in the best position to perform them.[30]

If Barbour is twisting the conventions, this is unlikely to have happened by accident. It is even less likely to have been necessitated by historical fact – very few of the episodes mentioned are confirmed in historical record as having actually taken place, and even these Barbour could have omitted if he had wished. Of course, conventional chivalric elements do appear in *The Bruce*, but then usually in clusters, and at points where the Scots have the upper hand: for instance, after the battle of Bannockburn, in Bruce's treatment of his prisoners and his mourning of a fallen enemy;[31] or after the conclusion of peace at the end of the romance. The implication is that there is a time and place for such things, and for most of the time, the Scots have more important, less conventional matters on their minds. This corresponds again to the style of fighting, where convention is also ignored in the interests of efficiency.

Ever since literary scholars began to take notice of *The Bruce*, these peculiarities have caused learned and lengthy discussions regarding whether it should be considered a romance at all, rather than perhaps an epic or a chronicle.[32] Of neither of these, it was felt, would we have to expect the

---

[26] II.573–88. Douglas is the obliging hero; but as his only interaction with the opposite sex, his services lack a certain something with regard to the courtly tradition. Had he provided 'comfort', the case might be different; but Barbour shows Douglas as a knight of unusual priorities. While the ladies are charmed with fish, the recipient of comfort is the king: 'And ye king oft comfort wes / Throw his wyt and his besynes' (II.589–90).

[27] X.554–63.

[28] V.542–4.

[29] XVI.275–96.

[30] A farmer defeats the English garrison of the peel of Linlithgow (X.150–244) and a ropemaker is the first to scale the walls of Roxburgh Castle and kill the sentries (X.410–44).

[31] XIII.505–50.

[32] E.g. F. Brie, *Die nationale Literatur Schottlands* (Halle/Saale, 1937), p. 93; B. Goedhals, 'John Barbour's *The Bruce*, and Bannockburn', *Unisa English Studies*, 2 (1968), p. 41; A. M. Kinghorn, 'Scottish Historiography in the Fourteenth Century: A New Introduction to Barbour's Bruce', *Studies in Scottish Literature*, 6 (1960), p. 139; and finally Janet Smith, to whom goes the prize for approvingly mentioning all three main possibilities in one short sentence:

lofty ideals of a romance. However, Barbour himself called his work a romance, and it is worth entertaining the idea that he believed he could justify his departures from convention within the framework of romance tradition. Definitions of romance, like definitions of chivalry, vary. The field at its widest comprises the politeness of *William of Palerne*, the inanities of *Sir Ambrose* and the brutalities of the *Siege of Jerusalem*. Still, romance is always closely interlinked with chivalry – its heroes are knights, its subject is their adventures, the challenge and confirmation of their knightly virtues, and their interaction with other members and ranks of society – ladies, heathens, headless knights or humble peasants. Romances were addressed to a knightly audience and thus portray, like any popular fiction, an ideal version of knighthood with which this audience could identify and to which it could aspire.

Barbour had extensive knowledge of romances and refers to the heroes of several in his poem. However, one romance in particular is singled out for attention; it is the only one mentioned by name, and by its position in the text we may assume that Barbour considered it particularly relevant. This is the romance of *Firumbras*, based on the French romance *Fierabras*, of which several versions circulated in the fourteenth century. It is a romance of the Charlemagne cycle, its heroes are the *douzepers* and a heathen called Firumbras who, after single combat with Olivier, consents to be baptised and joins Charlemagne's warriors. The exact version which Barbour knew has not survived, so that a brief survey of Bruce's narrative may be in order: the *douzepers* are imprisoned by heathens, they are being given no food and the situation is desperate. Finally, they manage to escape and warn Charlemagne. The French then return to defeat the Saracens in battle, rescue several holy relics, and live happily for another few years.[33] Barbour claims that King Robert read this romance to his men while they were being ferried across Loch Lomond, to keep up their spirits. The immediate application is obvious: Bruce and his party are at the lowest ebb of their fortunes, they are soon to run out of food, and the intended message is clearly that others have been in similar difficulties but managed to triumph. But it is also significant that we are dealing with a crusading romance, and that this is what Barbour considered appropriate in the circumstances.

Romances dealing primarily with the crusade against unbelievers show a reduction of courtly and chivalric elements to a bare minimum similar to that observed in Barbour's *Bruce*: more warfare, more violence, few ladies,

---

'Barbour's great poem *The Bruce* – epic, we might call it – is half way between chronicle and romance' (*The French Background to Middle Scots Literature* (Edinburgh, 1934), p. xiv).

[33]   III.435–62.

negligible court scenes, no hunting, and few tournaments.[34] We also encounter atrocities which not only rival but easily surpass the more radical passages of *The Bruce*.[35] In the crusading romances, the emphasis is clearly on fighting to win at any cost, rather than fighting beautifully, fairly, and for fun. The reason why conventional chivalric norms are out of place and methods do not matter is that the heathens, whether Saracens, Vikings, or third-century Persians, are portrayed as intrinsically bad and barely human. Thus it is acceptable to cheat them in fighting and eat their flesh.[36] Christianity, civilisation, the known order of the world has to be protected from them at all costs. By the same token, the war against the heathens is, with very few exceptions, essentially a communal enterprise with little room for personal aggrandisement.[37]

In order to explain Barbour's approach to warfare, it would be convenient to accept *The Bruce* as a romance in the crusading mould. However, one feature of crusading romances cannot be ignored: religious matters are of some importance. 'The Faith' provides all the emotional and dramatic tension; it is the cause for the fighting, the *raison d'être* of the narrative; and it is the fight to save Christianity which justifies all manner of crude methods. And although *The Bruce* matches the crusading romances in stylistic features such as the approach to fighting and the de-emphasis of courtly elements of chivalry, its approach to the Christian faith is not only patently less fervent, but is in fact another peculiarity which requires comment.

First of all, for most of the time Barbour's heroes are of course not fighting to save Christianity – they are fighting *against* Christians. This is a very unusual occurrence in romance literature.[38] When the heathen Saracens finally surface in *The Bruce*, it is at the very end of the narrative where various other conventions also make a re-appearance, and the manner of their entry is revealing. At this point, after the Scottish kingdom has been saved from its enemies, the dying King Robert expresses the wish that his heart should be taken on a crusade against the infidel. Douglas obliges by carrying Bruce's heart into battle against the heathen Moors in Spain, where

---

[34] Despite the lack of these elements there is, of course, no doubt that the knights are noble knights. Lack of civilised amenities does not equal lack of chivalric virtue.

[35] The *Siege of Jerusalem* is probably the outstanding example.

[36] Richard Coeur de Lion acquires this habit in the romance of the same name.

[37] An exception is *Octavian*, in which the crusading constitutes only a minor part of the action and is treated more in the fashion of a tournament.

[38] It does happen in *Morte Arthure*, but there it is justified by the assumption that the ruler of Italy and Lorraine, against whom Arthur starts an expedition, is in league with the infidel.

he meets his end. This part, the one which might show most similarities to the romances dealing with crusades, is in fact disappointingly perfunctory. The Moors are not particularly evil and do not commit any particular offences – they simply happen, conveniently, to be there to be fought.[39] Compared to the description of the English host at the battle of Bannockburn,[40] Barbour's visualisation of the heathen savages is a pedestrian affair. The Moors are purely functional; not the smallest amount of emotion is wasted on them. Archdeacon Barbour is simply not interested in the heathens. Neither, truth to tell, is Douglas – he is only there to please Bruce. Not surprisingly, once the heroes are dead, angels fail to descend from heaven to uplift their souls in glory – a service they do not omit to perform elsewhere.[41]

Similarly, the upholding of, or even respect for, the Christian faith is remarkably underdeveloped in Barbour's poem. An earlier critic has noted the poet's casual attitude towards holiness.[42] The passage referred to was Barbour's dismissive comment about a sainted martyr:

> Men said syne efter yis Thomas
> Yat on yis wis maid marter was
> Was saynct and myrakillis did ...
> Bot quheyer he haly wes or nane
> At Pomfret yus was he slane. (XVII.873–5, 877–8)

In fact, this is rather harmless. More remarkable is the fact that Barbour's chivalric heroes distinguish themselves by desecrating churches. The trend is set by the king, who murders his rival at the altar of Greyfriars' church in Dumfries. Emphatically, this is not upholding the Christian faith in crusading style; it is not even acceptable knightly behaviour, and the author feels compelled to moralise about it in the best didactic fashion:

> He mysdyd yar gretly but wer
> Yat gave na gyrth to ye awter,
> Yarfor sa hard myscheiff him fell
> Yat ik herd neuer in romanys tell
> Off man sa hard frayit as wes he
> Yat efterward com to sic bounte. (II.43–8)

---

[39]   XX.402–6.

[40]   XI.83–141, 467–81.

[41]   E.g. *Otuel & Roland*, ed. M. J. O'Sullivan, *EETS* 198 (London, 1935), ll 2439–47.

[42]   B. W. Kliman, 'The Idea of Chivalry in John Barbour's *Bruce*', *Medieval Studies*, 35 (1973), pp. 477–508, at p. 487. For further comments on religiosity (or lack thereof) in *The Bruce* see also J. Schwend, 'Religion and Religiosity in *The Bruce*', in D. Strauss and H. W. Drescher (eds.), *Scottish Language and Literature, Medieval and Renaissance* (Frankfurt am Main, 1986), pp. 207–15.

Still, although the evil deed led to many hardships for Bruce, it is not said to devalue him as a hero, and Bruce is not required to embark on an active programme of penance.

No criticism at all is invoked by the second murder, indeed mass-murder, in a church, which is perpetrated by Barbour's second main hero, his particular favourite, James Douglas. Douglas objects to the English garrison in his family's castle, and cold-bloodedly plans to surprise them 'during the Palm Sunday mass when they will expect no evil' – as no reasonable person in the middle ages would:

> Yai ordanyt yat he still suld be
> In hiddillis and in prewete
> Till Palme Sonday yat wes ner-hand
> Ye thrid day efter folowand,
> For yan ye folk off yat countre
> Assemblyt at ye kyrk wald be,
> And yai yat in ye castell wer
> Wald als be yar yar palyms to ber
> As folk yat had no dreid off ill
> For yai thocht all was at yar will ...
> ... Yen suld yai full enforcely
> Rycht ymyddys ye kyrk assaill
> Ye Inglismen with hard bataill
> Swa yat nane mycht eschap yaim fra... (V.305–14, 324–7)

Douglas carries out his attack, kills everybody, again regardless of rank – and the king approves, as does the poet.

Douglas turns out to be a veritable scourge of churchmen. He later kills a cleric called Ellis (who had admittedly been asking for trouble),[43] and together with Moray he manages to kill three hundred priests during a battle at Mitton in Yorkshire.[44] The poet is unconcerned, and merely takes care to share with his audience the joke that the preserve and death of so many priests led to the designation of the battle as the 'chapter of Mitton'.[45] Scottish churchmen, when they appear (which is not very often), are treated with slightly more respect. But even about them there is something odd. A sturdy friar with armour under his habit thinks nothing of spying on the English and leading an attack on them during which he kills a man.[46] The outstanding ecclesiaste is Bishop William Sinclair, another rather unusual figure in a romance context. When the earl and the sheriff of Fife retreat before an English invasion, Bishop Sinclair gathers his own host and

---

[43]   XVI.444–60.
[44]   XVII.537–88.
[45]   XVIII.585–8.
[46]   XVIII.300–17. Cf. Kliman, 'The Idea of Chivalry in John Barbour's *Bruce*', p. 486.

shames the earl and sheriff into joining him to intercept the invaders.[47] On the whole, bishops rarely figure in romances, and fighting clerics were certainly not part of the standard repertoire of chivalry. The ones that do appear are at least conventional in that they kill (or attempt to kill) heathens. These are Charlemagne's Archbishop Turpin, who gives an unrivalled performance in the *Sege of Melayne*, and an incompetent militant pope in the *Sowdowne of Babylon*. Sinclair is unique in romance literature as a bishop who cheerfully slaughters Christians, and gets away with it.

Why should all this be acceptable? Killing heathens is acceptable because, being unbelievers, they stand against the God-given order of the world and subvert its laws. Therefore they have to be fought and destroyed. The defence of established order is a typical feature of romance and of the chivalric ethic. Heathens are one personification of the chaos outside established order, Green Knights and similar supernatural antagonists another. These chaotic forces show their evil nature by overturning human or divine law, by refusing to accept the conventions, hierarchies or faith of the virtuous Christian knights, through exhibiting unwarranted brutality and through acting in a tyrannous fashion when given a chance.

At the beginning of *The Bruce*, Barbour describes the behaviour of the English regime in Scotland:

> Y[ai] worthyt yan sa rych fellone
> And sa wykkyt and cowatous
> And swa hawtane and dispitous
> Yat Scottis-men mycht do na thing
> Yat euer mycht pleys to yar liking.
> Yar wyffis wald yai oft forly
> And yar dochtrys dispitusly
> And gyff ony of yaim yar-at war wrath
> Yai waytyt hym wele with gret scaith,
> For yai suld fynd sone enchesone
> To put him to destruccione.
> And gyff yat ony man yaim by
> Had ony thing yat wes worthy,
> As hors or hund or oyer thing
> Yat war plesand to yar liking,
> With rycht or wrang it have wald yai,
> And gyf ony wald yaim withsay

---

[47]   XVL.560–682. Sinclair is an interesting parallel to Archbishop Turpin in *The Sege of Melayne*, who threatens to excommunicate Charlemagne if he refuses to go and fight the heathens (*The Sege of Melayne*, in *Six Middle English Romances*, ed. M. Mills (London, 1973), ll. 680–709). Although Sinclair does not go as far as threatening excommunication, he uses fairly strong language by Barbour's standards (XVI.600–8).

Yai suld swa do yat yai suld tyne
Oyir land or lyff or leyff in pyne,
For yai dempt yaim efter yar will,
Takand na kep to rycht na skill.
A quhat yai dempt yaim felonly,
For guid knychtis yat war worthy
For litill enchesoune or yan nane
Yai hangyt be ye nekbane. (I.194–218)[48]

They are haughty, covetous and spiteful. They do not respect the sacrament of marriage, they oppress women, and kill men on a pretext. They hang knights. They have no respect for either property or law. One editor of *The Bruce* has called them 'ruthless subverters of native rule, law and custom'.[49]

If Barbour's heathens are a tame affair, it is because their place as the personification of evil has been usurped. As the English regime in Scotland replaces the customary heathen antagonists of crusading romances, so the fighting methods justifiably employed against the heathens are legitimate against them. They are the forces of chaos which have to be destroyed. Even the priests are English priests, and therefore legitimate targets. Like the war against the heathens, Barbour's war is a deadly serious business, a communal, urgent fight which has to be won by any means, and which leaves no room for considerations of personal honour or glorification. Carrick with his concern for his noble name is simply in the wrong book.

This is the context in which Bruce's dialogue with his two earls, and Barbour's dialogue with his audience, takes place – the context in which actions conventionally defined as cowardly become simply prudent, and actions conventionally called courageous or perhaps chivalric become foolhardy and almost criminal. From a historical perspective, this crusading spirit finds an interesting parallel in recorded events of the early fourteenth century. The bishops of Robert I's reign did indeed preach that fighting the English was as good as fighting the infidel, with all the merit and instant bliss which that entailed and that the patriotic war was a holy war. Barbour may have been aware of this. Within *The Bruce* itself, the equation is also made by the king: 'He yat deis for his cuntre / sall herbryit in-till hewyn be' (III.43–4). In his romance, Barbour thus adopts the rhetoric and ethics of the holy war as it was preached in 1306, and argues (for his constant reiteration amounts to an argument) that the fighting ethics of the crusading romances are a fitting vehicle for a patriotic war.

---

[48] Another passage reiterates: 'For off ye lordis sum yai slew / And sum yai hangyt andsum yai drew, / And sum yai put in presoune / For-owtyn caus or enchesoun' (I.277).

[49] McDiarmid (ed.), *The Bruce*, I, p. 49.

The Fifteenth-Century English Versions of Vegetius' De Re Militari

CHRISTOPHER ALLMAND

The work of Publius Flavius Vegetius Renatus, recently termed 'the most influential military manual in use during the middle ages',[1] was a medieval best-seller. Part of its importance lay in the fact that it was a work which might be read at different levels. Already widely known in the early and central middle ages, the translations added a whole dimension to the text's significance. Thus made available in Anglo-Norman,[2] French (some four times before the sixteenth century), Tuscan, Castilian, English (twice in the fifteenth century), German, and (in part) even Scots, it was to become a text which interested the student of languages and translations, as well as the student of the large corpus of classical literature which was rendered into the vernacular languages at the end of the middle ages.[3] Besides all this, the text is one which should be of interest to the historian of late medieval military culture, and to the historian of the transmission of ideas.

What had been Vegetius' aim when he compiled his *Epitome Rei Militari* most probably during the dying years of the fourth century?[4] The work is in four long books, or chapters, each divided into sections of varying length. It is quite possible that the first book was written to stand on its own, and that the remainder of the work was compiled at the request of the emperor to whom Vegetius had dedicated the first book after appreciative remarks

---

[1] G. Lester (ed.), *The Earliest English Translation of Vegetius' De Re Militari*, Middle English Texts, 21 (Heidelberg, 1988), p. 7. See also p. 12 for further, similar views.

[2] See L. Thorpe, 'Mastre Richard, a Thirteenth-Century Translator of the *De Re Militari* of Vegetius', *Scriptorium*, 6 (1952), pp. 39–50; M. D. Legge, 'The Lord Edward's Vegetius', *ibid.*, 7 (1953), pp. 262–5.

[3] Lester, *The Earliest English Translation of Vegetius*, pp. 14–16. See also C. R. Shrader, 'A Handlist of Extant Manuscripts Containing the *De Re Militari* of Flavius Vegetius Renatus', *Scriptorium*, 33 (1979), pp. 280–305; J. Monfrin, 'Humanisme et traductions au moyen âge', in A. Fourrier (ed.), *L'humanisme médiéval dans les littératures romanes du XIIe au XIVe siècle* (Paris, 1964), pp. 217–46.

[4] On the dating, see W. Goffart, 'The Date and Purpose of Vegetius *De Re Militari*', *Traditio*, 33 (1977), pp. 65–100.

had been made about it.[5] In this, Vegetius had been looking back to the past when Rome had ruled the world, something which it no longer did in his lifetime. Its failure to do so, the author implied, was the result of poor standards of recruitment and training, as well as of a decline in the organisation, strategies and effective use of equipment in the army of his day. As Vegetius told the emperor, the greatness of Rome could be revived if the army were restored to its former efficiency when few had stood against it. The reasons for successes achieved in the past were not difficult to work out: or so Vegetius thought. As we discover on reading his work, he was a great believer in the basic military doctrine that victories were won as the result of proper training and preparation, as well as through the use made of the past experiences of others. Soldiers must be taught the basics about their arms and about the strategies which won wars. They could hear about these from their leaders, but they should on no account ignore the lessons of past experience which could be learned and absorbed from the written word: 'they of Atthenes ... writen ... bookys and reweles, and commaunded the maystres of her yong chiualrie to teche and to rede thilke bookys to the yonge [werriours]'.[6] Several times Vegetius refers to the *doctrina armorum*, translated as the 'teching and lore of armes' in English, and as *l'usage et la science des armes* by Jean de Meun in the first French rendering of 1284.[7] All three translations of the phrase give the sense that fighting is something which can be taught and, therefore, learned. Thus it was the duty of those with experience to preserve it in writing for it to be passed down to succeeding generations. The *De Re Militari* falls into the category of didactic works intended to instruct.[8]

The first book is therefore packed full of principles, sound if often general in nature. It was after a favourable reception had been given it that its author decided to continue his work. His book, then, should probably not be seen as a proper *Art of War* as such, conceived as a whole,[9] but rather as an attempt, by a reformer, to bring an improvement to the army of 400 A.D. by breathing new life into an institution which, all knew, had seen

---

[5]   P. Önnerfors (ed.), *P. Flavi Vegeti Renati Epitoma Rei Militaris* (Stuttgart andLeipzig, 1995), pp. 52–3; N. P. Milner (trans.), *Vegetius: Epitome of Military Science*, Translated Texts for Historians, 16 (2nd edn, Liverpool, 1996), p. 29.

[6]   Lester, *The Earliest English Translation of Vegetius*, p. 103/12–16. (Here and in subsequent references, citation is by page followed by line number.)

[7]   Önnerfors, *Epitoma Rei Militaris*, p. 19?243–4; Lester, *The Earliest English Translation of Vegetius*, p. 56/19; U. Robert (ed.), *L'Art de Chevalerie; traduction du De Re Militari de Végèce par Jean de Meun*, Société des Anciens Textes Français (Paris, 1897), p. 14; L. Löfstedt (ed.), *Li Abregemenz noble homme Vegesce Flave René des establissemenz apartenanz a chevalerie* (Helsinki, 1977), p. 75.

[8]   M. Keen, *Chivalry* (New Haven and London, 1984), p. 111.

[9]   Milner, *Vegetius: Epitome of Military Science* (1st edn, 1993), p. xviii.

better days. Some, trying to look at Vegetius' work from the viewpoint of the middle ages, have found it strange that so little is said about cavalry. It should be remembered, however, that in the days of Rome's greatness the cavalry had not been the state's most powerful arm, nor, indeed, was that arm in need of fundamental reform at the time when Vegetius was writing. On neither count, then, did it fall within the author's self-imposed brief. However, one cannot ignore the fact that some of Vegetius' views were old-fashioned even by the standards of his own time, and that he emphasised the role of the footsoldier at the expense of cavalry and cavalry tactics.[10]

What were the author's qualifications for writing this work? Vegetius was not a military man, but a well-read and versatile functionary who may have had experience of high-level finance and, in particular, of the recruiting and provisioning of armies. Since he was no great military expert he depended, for the detail, upon the experience and wisdom of others.[11] Should this work, then, be regarded mainly as an ordered résumé of the works of others, or, rather, as an original creation of the author, however eclectic in its use of sources and ideas? Recent scholarship suggests the second of these, although at times Vegetius appears to have been following known texts quite closely, in particular the works of Cato the Elder, Cornelius Celsus and, perhaps above all, that great source of examples, the *Stratagemata* of Julius Frontinus, written in the first century A.D.[12] From these, and from others, Vegetius drew material to compile his own work, of which more than 320 manuscripts, ranging from the seventh to the seventeenth centuries, and written in both Latin and the vernacular languages, have survived.[13]

Why was Vegetius' work so popular in medieval Europe? Some will have seen it as part of the general culture, others as part of the military culture, inherited from the ancient world. But it was more than that. Here was a work which was both informative and didactic, one from which men could learn lessons useful for their own time. One wonders whether the medieval translators realised when the work was written and, in particular, what intentions had lain behind its compilation? One suspects not, so that the first task of the translator, to provide his readers with a translation which reflected the author's intentions, may not have been regarded as a

[10]   Lester, *The Earliest English Translation of Vegetius*, p. 11, n. 10.
[11]   'For I claim no authority to myself, but merely write up the dispersed material of those whom I have listed above, summarising it as if to form an orderly sequence' (Milner, *Vegetius: Epitome of Military Science* (2nd edn), p. 10).
[12]   C. E. Bennett (trans.), *Frontinus, The Stratagems and the Aqueducts of Rome*, Loeb Classical Library (London and Cambridge, Mass., 1969).
[13]   Shrader, 'A Handlist', especially pp. 286–305. See also below, pp. 104–5.

prime obligation. The translator's options were limited. Either he could try to aim for accuracy but, in so doing, produce a work which, because of its rather technical nature and, consequently, very specialised vocabulary, might not make great sense to the contemporary reader, whoever that reader might be; or alternatively, he might try to produce a version which reflected the spirit rather than an accurate rendering of the original text. Furthermore, what if the work being translated had been written almost one thousand years earlier? What might the late medieval reader expect to learn from studying Vegetius? Cited by two Benedictine monks, Bede in the early eighth century, Hraban Maur a century or so later, Vegetius was to come into his own in the twelfth and thirteenth centuries, when not only do the number of copies of his work appear to have increased, but he also came to be cited, or 'moralised', often at length, by such as John of Salisbury, Vincent of Beauvais, Giles of Rome and other compilers of the princely 'mirror' literature, as they tried to show why rulers should have armies and proper leaders to command them.[14] To such writers, the importance of Vegetius lay not so much in what he could teach them about the administration of the Roman legion, or the details of good tactics to follow either in the field or at the siege, but rather what guidance he could offer the rising national monarchies regarding successful preparations for war which had to be carried out irrespective of time, place, or circumstance. An army consisting of well selected troops (selection, Vegetius taught in Book I, was crucial) trained and drilled in the disciplines of war achieved its own sense of confidence, and was thus ready to face the enemy. For the purposes of their works, which soon came to be widely disseminated, these writers concentrated on what was, broadly speaking, the message shared with the first Boy Scout: 'Be prepared'.

Vegetius was first translated from Latin into a vernacular language in the second half of the thirteenth century. We cannot be certain which translation was the first to be completed: Domincia Legge thought that the one into Anglo-Norman dialect could have been made about 1254–55, or else in the very early years of the fourteenth century; Lewis Thorpe, on the other hand, argued that this translation was intended for Edward I, and was made in about 1271, when the future king of England was on crusade.[15] In any event, it seems likely that by the late thirteenth century the text was already regarded as important enough to justify a complete translation. In France, the first of these, in prose, was made in 1284 by Jean de Meun, who had already completed the text of the *Roman de la Rose* begun more than a generation earlier by Guillaume de Lorris, and who was already proving himself a translator of skill. The work on Vegetius, he tells us, was

14 Lester, *The Earliest English Translation of Vegetius*, pp. 14, 11.
15 See above, n. 1.

done in response to a request made to him by Jean de Brienne, count of Eu, who had only recently served on crusade with the saintly king, Louis IX.[16] A few years later (certainly before 1291), Jean Priorat of Besançon produced a verse version of Meun's translation.[17] The work is that of someone who had had at least some practical experience of war, and suggests that the original prose version was already known, certainly among military men, within a short time of completion and (although the point is more speculative) that it was achieving a measure of success.

What was to be the approach of the first English translator who, more than a century later, 'at the ordenaunce & biddynge of the worthi & worschipful lord sire Thomas of Berkeley', an active campaigner at the time engaged under Prince Henry [V] in Wales, tackled the Latin text and completed the task, as the colophon informs us, on All Souls' Eve, 31 October 1408?[18] The problem confronting the translator faced with great changes, such as those of military organisation or terminology or, at another level, with great developments such as the invention of new arms, can be considerable. How is he to react to the letter of his text? Is he to treat it as an 'archaeological' relic to be left as it was found, a text which fossilises an age and, in this case, its army?[19]

Lacking a fully developed technical vocabulary (some of it would have had to refer to officers, weapons, and practices now totally 'historical') the translator was soon forced into compromises, in spite of the fact that, living in an age which saw itself as the heir of the Roman/Latin past and which still shared a Latin culture with it, he may have wished to produce a rendering which was close to the original, both to do honour to that original and to demonstrate the relevance of the book's content to his own day. It is likely that the middle ages looked upon Vegetius' work as one and whole, a handbook whose practical teachings were more appropriate in some sections than in others: siege warfare, for example, had not changed all that much until the middle ages were very well advanced. To make the handbook more comprehensible to his own day, the translator was obliged to make some concessions; where possible, terms had to be up-dated; some passages could be omitted because their practical relevance was very

---

16   Robert, *L'Art de Chevalerie*, p. 177; Löfstedt, *Li Abregemenz noble homme vegesce*, p. 195.

17   U. Robert (ed.), *Li Abrejance de l'Ordre de Chevalerie*, Société des Anciens Textes Français (Paris, 1897).

18   Lester, *The Earliest English Translation of Vegetius*, p. 189/32–3.

19   On the translations into French, see C. Buridant, 'Jean de Meun et Jean de Vignay, traducteurs de l'*Epitoma Rei Militaris* de Végèce. Contribution à l'histoire de la traduction au Moyen Age', in *Etudes de langue et de littérature française offertes à André Lanly* (Nancy, 1980), pp. 51–69.

doubtful; others, too, were dropped because the translator could not understand them;[20] while others, by contrast, were developed and 'augmented' in respect of both vocabulary and content.[21] In practice, the translator did what he could to transform parts of the *De Re Militari* into a useful guide on how to achieve success in war. Of the eleven surviving manuscripts of this translation, five are found on their own, six are bound with other works, most frequently John Lydgate's *Book of Governance of Kings and Princes*.[22] In spite of much research and scholarly ingenuity, the name of the translator is still not known.[23] His rendering is normally fairly close to the original, but its effect, in the word of one critic, is to make it rather wooden. Nor is it always the needs of clarity or explanation which lead to the expansions of the text; the use of otiose language helps to make the translation more than twice as long as the published text of the original Latin.[24]

Just as there was a verse rendering of Vegetius into French, so fifty years after the English prose version had been completed, an English verse translation was made by a priest (or parson, as he styled himself) residing in Calais.[25] How did this translator confront the problems which faced him? The simplest answer is to say that the work is not a translation as we understand the term, but at best a paraphrase in verse. Apart from facing the problems inherent in his chosen medium, the parson is obliged to omit whole passages, radically paraphrase others, or set out the text in an order which is not that of the original. By contrast with that of Jean Priorat, which stuck closely to Meun's original, the parson's translation was his own and was completed in the relatively short space of some 3,028 lines. Although not a soldier, he says that he hopes that soldiers will read him, and it is not surprising, in view of the difficulties which he had in rendering a complicated vocabulary into an English suitable for verse, that he should ask his readers at the end to help improve his work.[26] One of the great differences between this and the earlier prose translation is that the Calais parson regards this as a book about knighthood in a rather traditional, hierarchical sense. 'Knyghthode an ordir is', the pre-eminent one, whose

[20] On omissions, see Lester, *The Earliest English Translation of Vegetius*, pp. 33–4.
[21] On the translator's expansions, see *ibid.*, pp. 30–3.
[22] *Ibid.*, pp. 17–23.
[23] R. Hanna, III, 'Sir Thomas Berkeley and his Patronage', *Speculum*, 64 (1989), pp. 878–916.
[24] Lester, *The Earliest English Translation of Vegetius*, pp. 29–31.
[25] R. Dyboski and Z. M. Arend (eds.), *Knyghthode and Bataile. A XVth Century Verse Paraphrase of Flavius Vegetius Renatus' Treatise "De Re Militari"*, Early English Texts Society [EETS], o.s., 201 (London, 1935).
[26] *Ibid.*, ll. 117–20, 3022–5.

members are born noble, are possessed of land and fee, and who will defend the country with honour to the last. The obligation to fight, and in particular to lead, stems from the traditional qualifications of land ownership.[27] The translator appears to have completely (perhaps wilfully) missed the fundamental point made by Vegetius that the best fighting men come from rural society which enjoys few of the material pleasures of life, and that men qualify for positions of responsibility not through birth, wealth or social origins, but by virtue of the skills, attributes and soldierly qualities which they show.[28]

Since it is the more important text, let us concentrate on the prose translation of 1408. The work was said to have been commissioned for 'lordes and alle worthi werrioures that ben apassed by wey of age al labour & trauaillyng, and to greet informacioun & lemynge of yonge lordes & knyghtes that ben lusty & loueth to here & see and to vse dedes of armes and chyualrie'.[29] How did the translator deal with the problems of rendering a technical work written so long ago into a rapidly developing vernacular language?

As examples, let us observe how he deals with some significant terms. The Latin word frequently used by Vegetius to describe the recruit is *tiro/tirones*. In the late thirteenth century both Jean de Meun and Jean Priorat had normally rendered this as *chevalier(s)*, Meun sometimes as *jones chevaliers* or *nouviaus chevaliers ou li aprentis*.[30] In 1408, the English translator also used a wide range of terms for the original Latin: 'knighte', 'newe chosen knightes', 'yong knighte', 'newe chosen fighteres', 'werriours' and 'yong werriours'.[31] By contrast, the 1458 translator seemed largely content with 'chivalerys'. The Latin word *miles/milites* was almost always *chevalier(s)* in French; in 1408, the most commonly used English term used was 'knight(es)', although 'fightares' was also employed, as would be 'werryourys' and 'chiualerys' in 1458.[32] The accusative singular form of *eques* (*equitem*) was a *homme àc heval* in French, or a 'horseman' in English in

---

[27]   *Ibid.*, I. 131; 'Nobiles sint milites ... ignobiles non sint milites' (*Ibid.*, ll. 271, 278). See also D. Bornstein, *Mirrors of Courtesy* (Hamden, 1975), pp. 34–6; *idem*, 'Military Manuals in Fifteenth-Century England', *Mediaeval Studies*, 37 (1975), pp. 472–3.

[28]   This is made clear in Book II.

[29]   Lester, *The Earliest English Translation of Vegetius*, p. 190/1–5.

[30]   Robert, *L'Art de Chevalerie*, pp. 7, 9–10, 105; Löfstedt, *Li Abregemenz noble homme Vegesce*, pp. 70, 73, 143.

[31]   Lester, *The Earliest English Translation of Vegetius*, pp. 94/28, 57/19, 53/9, 133/34, 104/26, 56/4.

[32]   Robert, *L'Art de Chevalerie*, p. 11; Löfstedt, *Li Abregemenz noble homme Vegesce*, p. 74; Lester, *The Earliest English Translation of Vegetius*, pp. 54/27, 133/25; Dyboski and Arend, *Knyghthode and Bataile* ll, 250, 1735.

1408 and a man 'on hors' half a century later.[33] The plural form, *equites*, was rendered as *chevaliers* in French, 'horsmen' in English.[34] The *bellator* was always a *batailleur* or *batilleur* in French, while the English translations offered 'werriour' or the higher-sounding 'men of armes'.[35] There appears to have been little attempt at consistency here. Was there ever intended to be such? Are we too 'modern' in expecting it? Probably so.

The use of a vocabulary bearing implications of rank and social order which did not exist in the fifteenth century could thus create a difficulty. Another concerned the most effective way of rendering a technical vocabulary into English. The Latin *acies* or battle line, normally *bataille* in French, became 'scheltromes or batailes' or 'ege' in English.[36] The different means of protection afforded to those approaching a wall were called by a variety of terms, 'targattes', 'pauyses', and 'scheldes',[37] the 'snayle' being the smaller version of *testudo*, the covered battering ram: 'for, right as the snayl hath his hous ouer hym, whether he walke or reste, and out of his house he scheteth his heued whan he wole & draweth him yn agen, so doth this [en]gyn, and therfore he is icleped the snayl'.[38] The not infrequent use which the translator makes of two or more English words to render one in Latin suggests that he may feel that his readers will not always be familiar with every English form which he employs to translate technical terms. His desire to help the reader understand ancient meanings is made clear by this practice, as is that of adding a phrase, or clause, sometimes even a sentence, by way of explanation or enlightenment. The 'tabil' of what must be unusual words or forms included, with references to the text, at the end of two manuscripts of the 1458 verse translation[39] is further evidence of the way that translators went out of their way to explain an unfamiliar vocabulary to their readers. In the prose version the translator, confronted with rendering the ranks and titles of the legions' leaders into comprehensible vernacular, admits to 'grete difficulte to Englisshe the

---

[33] Robert, *L'Art de Chevalerie*, p. 9; Löfstedt, *Li Abregemenz noble homme Vegesce*, p. 72; Lester, *The Earliest English Translation of Vegetius*, pp. 52/32; Dyboski and Arend, *Knyghthode and Bataile*, ll, 216.

[34] Robert, *L'Art de Chevalerie*, p. 46; Löfstedt, *Li Abregemenz noble homme Vegesce*, p. 98; Lester, *The Earliest English Translation of Vegetius*, 82/22.

[35] Robert, *L'Art de Chevalerie*, p. 111; Löfstedt, *Li Abregemenz noble homme Vegesce*, p. 147; Lester, *The Earliest English Translation of Vegetius*, pp. 51/28, 170/10.

[36] Robert, *L'Art de Chevalerie*, p. 57; Löfstedt, *Li Abregemenz noble homme Vegesce*, p. 106; Lester, *The Earliest English Translation of Vegetius*, pp. 49/19; Dyboski and Arend, *Knyghthode and Bataile*, ll, 579, 1783.

[37] Lester, *The Earliest English Translation of Vegetius*, pp. 162/28.

[38] *Ibid.*, p. 168/18–22.

[39] Dyboski and Arend, *Knyghthode and Bataile*, pp. xii–xiii.

names of officeris'.[40] Responding to this problem as a schoolboy might do, he simply omits some and fudges others in a manner which is not always satisfactory.

In the work's opening sentence, the 1408 prose translator tells his reader that his 'tretys techith holliche of knighthod and chiualrye'.[41] How are we to understand these two terms? In one sense in which he uses the word we note that 'knighthod' means no more than fulfilling the role of the soldier whose obedience is due to the emperor and, since Vegetius was almost certainly a Christian, to God, too.[42] Used as it was to be in the title of the 1458 paraphrase, in conjunction with the word 'bataile' (hence *Knyghthode and Bataile*) as the translation of *De Re Militari*, it comes to mean something like the 'Art of War'. As for the word 'chiualrye', or *la chose de chevalerie*, used in the phrase *l'art de chevalerie*, it was taken by Jean de Meun as the translation of *res militaris*,[43] in English, the Latin phrase would be rendered simply as 'chiualrye' or 'knighthode and dedes of armes'.[44] What is clear in this case is that the sense of the word 'chiualrye' which is being emphasised is the art, craft, or making of war, regarded as an almost scientific activity to which the wisdom of the past, set out in books and manuals, has much to contribute. This is underlined in another phrase containing the word 'knyghthode'; this is 'the lore and the teching of knighthoode' which the 1408 translator used to render the Latin term *disciplina militaris*,[45] the word *disciplina* being something which can be taught and instilled into the minds of soldiers who, as *eruditos* 'in dedes of armes wel vsed and lerned', will go forward to win wars.[46] It is in this roundabout way that we reach another meaning of 'chivalry'. Used as a verb in the form 'to chyualry', it meant exercising military power for the common benefit, for 'hereynne stondeth al the helthe and profight of the comynalte'.[47] Chivalry, then, was not merely an attachment, through obedience, to the legally constituted authority. It was a sense of responsibility to society as a whole exercised by those selected by the emperor for their marked military virtue, not for their birth, to prepare themselves and keep themselves ready

---

[40] Lester, *The Earliest English Translation of Vegetius*, p. 83/18–19.

[41] *Ibid.*, p. 47/3–4.

[42] *Ibid.*, pp. 81/29–82/7; Dyboski and Arend, *Knyghthode and Bataile*, ll. 684–704.

[43] Önnerfors, *Epitoma Rei Militaris*, pp. 47/646, 54/60; Robert, *L'Art de Chevalerie*, pp. 36, 40; Löfstedt *Li Abregemenz noble homme Vegesce*, pp. 91, 94.

[44] Lester, *The Earliest English Translation of Vegetius*, pp. 74/10, 77/15, 147/17–18.

[45] *Ibid.*, p. 57/4–5.

[46] *Ibid.*, p. 88/14–15. See also similar phrases on pp. 51/9–10, 53/10.

[47] *Ibid.*, p. 55/3–5.

to act *pro reipublicae salute*, 'for the helthe of [the] common profit'.[48]

Modern commentators, noting the increase in the number of surviving manuscripts of Vegetius' text, have remarked how his popularity appears to have been on the increase well into the sixteenth century, by which time his work was available in print, and was being produced with other works of a military character. Why was there this long-standing interest in a thousand-year old text? Take, first, the idea that man may help himself to work out his destiny through his own conscious efforts. The notion lay at the very heart of what Vegetius had written and of the manner in which he had presented it.[49] We have already seen how important it was, in his view, for each generation to pass on its experience and wisdom to those which followed, the only way to do this effectively being to write things down for transmission to posterity. But it is the manner of justifying this which was significant. Vegetius recalled that we have much to learn from history.[50] But how much? Therein lies the heart of the matter. History recounts what happened, but usually fails to tell us what we should be seeking to know, how it happened. To record victories is one thing; to understand the manner of their achievement is quite another. Hence his book is an attempt to answer the questions 'Hou ... hou ...'.[51] To Vegetius, who here followed a long Roman tradition, it was possible to explain rationally how wars were lost and won. The soldier, in particular the commander, must be a thinking soldier or commander. If he is so, then he has every chance of being successful. The knight, already endowed with the attributes of *sapientia* and *fortitudo*, acquires *prudentia* towards the end of the eleventh century. From that time, the intellectual approach to war is something which grows, and which helps to explain the popularity of Vegetius' text from the twelfth century onwards.[52] Thought, particularly forethought, can win wars. That is precisely what Vegetius, following authors such as Frontinus, had argued, so that it is not surprising that he should have become an author whose ideas were very much quoted, for example, in the 'mirror' literature of the age. Since wars could, to a certain extent, be planned, rulers had a duty to look to the future and have their deterrent forces ready to be called upon in necessity. It was important to fight wars with a background of knowledge and experience, what the French called *science*. It was the recognition that soldiers commonly found the Latin language difficult to understand that

---

[48] Önnerfors, *Epitoma Rei Militaris*, p. 7/75; Lester, *The Earliest English Translation of Vegetius*, p. 48/22–3.
[49] Man should not be 'in happes of fortune' (*ibid.*, p. 55/13).
[50] See Book I, ch. 8.
[51] This is what Vegetius is saying in his 'prologue' (Lester, *The Earliest English Translation of Vegetius*, pp. 47–8) as well as Book I, ch. 8, pp. 56–7.
[52] A. Murray, *Reason and Society in the Middle Ages* (Oxford, 1978), pp. 124–7, 134.

had led Jean de Vignai to translate Vegetius into French about 1325. He did so because he was among those writers *[qui] ont dit aucunes choses qui mout sont profitables a savoir a ceus qui veulent estre sages et apris darmes.* It was good to be well informed, Vignai wrote at the end of his translation, *car en toutes batailles seulent plus donner victoire sens et usage darmes que force ne multitude de gens mal endoctrinés.*[53] As the English prose translation would put it in the next century, 'he concludith and scheweth that in alle manere werres on lond or on water noght multitude and vnkunnyng, ne strengthe vntaught is cause of ouercomynge, but craft, usage, and exercise of armes getith victorie & ouercometh enemyes'.[54]

So, in the first and fundamental book of the *De Re Militari* Vegetius dealt with the basic requirements of any army, the recruitment, selection and training of young soldiers. Here he established the bases of any successful army. Recruits must be those tested and chosen, the implication being that some, perhaps many, would be rejected as unsuitable. They must be trained in the use of arms; how to act and react together; how to conquer fear. All this should be achieved through regular training and exercises with the implied responsibility owed by each recruit to the legion, to the emperor and, as indicated earlier, to the good of the wider society.

The favourable reception accorded to his first book led Vegetius to write three more which, together, make up the work. In the second book he dealt with the general matter of the army's organisation, its command structure, its duties and its equipment. Significantly, he stressed the importance of war fought at sea.[55] Significantly, too, although recognising the fact that mounted soldiers generally move more quickly than do others, Vegetius stressed that it was the foot soldier who should assume the central position in battle, the cavalry being accorded a position, although not an insignificant one, on the wings. It was the foot soldier, too, whom Vegetius recognised as being more versatile than his mounted counterpart owing to his ability to fight in a greater variety of situations in which physical factors were likely to play an important, if not dominant, role. Nor should it be forgotten that the foot soldier was cheaper than the cavalry: 'men may se and vndirstonde that footmen ben most profitable for the communalte, for thei mowe profighte in alle places bothe in londe and on water, and also more multitude of werriours wel vsed to dedes of armes may with lasse cost be norschid than of any other degre'.[56] Vegetius then returned to a point which he had made before. An army should not be drawn from

---

[53]   P. Meyer, 'Les anciens traducteurs français de Végèce, et en particulier Jean de Vignai', *Romania*, 25 (1896), pp. 412, 421–2.

[54]   Lester, *The Earliest English Translation of Vegetius*, p. 47/17–21.

[55]   *Ibid.*, p. 77/18–19, 25–7.

[56]   *Ibid.*, pp. 77/32–78/2.

anybody or everybody, but from men specially selected for their suitability. Great responsibility rested upon them. Equally important was the fact that society depended heavily upon the selectors to act with a sense of communal responsibility as they chose those who were to serve in the army, a responsibility which was seen as extending as far as the emperor himself.[57] In the same line of argument, the ordinary soldier, too, was regarded as a servant of the public good and the recipient of public money, who should fulfil no other service than that of furthering the emperor's wars. Vegetius was critical of those who left the public for the private service.[58]

This part of the work produced several ideas which could fall on fertile ground. The first was the emphasis placed upon the active role attributed to the foot soldier now, by the end of the middle ages, fully prominent again in war, as well as upon archery. The second idea was of a different kind. The translation of *tiro* as 'knyght' was not as inappropriate as it might have seemed. According to Vegetius, the *tiro* was distinguished by two important characteristics. First, he was a man accustomed to the use of arms who had acquired skills through regular training and practice. Secondly, Vegetius saw the soldier's role essentially as a public one with strong social connotations, that of protecting territory and property. He regarded the army (the 'oost') essentially as a public instrument whose existence was specifically justified by the need to defend and promote the common good. It was a notion to which Vegetius returned time and time again. It follows quite logically that every member of that army, every soldier, can be regarded as a servant of the common interest, whose skills, acquired by training, are available to defend that interest. Nor was 'knyght' simply or chiefly a word which reflected position or rank in society, a word implying privilege. On the contrary, it entailed certain obligations which were essentially 'social' in scope, that is to say that the privileges of position implied a moral compulsion upon the 'knyght' to serve the society of which he was a member. *Noblesse oblige*. When Vegetius wrote about the societal obligations of the late fourth-century soldier, what he was saying could be translated accurately in terms of what was expected of the knight in medieval Europe and what, one day, would be expected of the soldier, seen increasingly as the servant of the society whose wage he was now coming to accept.[59] In other words, the fundamental first book, in which Vegetius

---

[57]   *Ibid.*, pp. 78/14–17, 94/32–4.

[58]   *Ibid.*, p. 95/27–9.

[59]   'Antiquity's example taught that the soldier must regard his trade in the light of defined obligations' (Keen, *Chivalry*, p. 111). On this matter see C. Allmand, 'Changing Views of the Soldier in Late Medieval France', *Guerre et société en France, en Angleterre et en Bourgogne, XIVe et XVe siècle*, ed. P.

justified the need for and the position of the army in society, may have been a strong theoretical influence in creating the thinking behind the development of national armies, which were already coming into being in the fourteenth century, armies whose existence was to be justified as being required for national defence, the need which, in turn, would be used to demand taxation at a national level.[60]

In his third book Vegetius turned to the practical side of war. Here the message was 'Don't let things drift; much can be achieved if precautions are taken in anticipating events.' This view was consistent with the notion, running right through the work, that for experience to have a lasting benefit, it must be passed on through the written word. Much of this chapter is common sense. The general rules of battle, which bring it to an end, sum up its character best: adequate supply and its opposite, famine, are two decisive factors in deciding the outcome of war; the ability to seize an opportunity is often more effective than force of numbers; likewise, military virtue, by which Vegetius means obedience, discipline and proper training, putting experience to the best use, as well as the maintenance of a high level of morale in the army, is of greater avail than numbers. The outcome of war must not be left to fortune, whose unpredictable wheel was all too well known in the middle ages. Soldiers must be ready, versatile, properly trained, for only skill in arms would be regularly rewarded with victory.

Having dealt with war in the field, Vegetius turned his attention in the fourth and final book to siege warfare and to the ways of fighting at sea. In a series of short chapters he discussed different kinds of defences as well as a variety of approaches which an attacker might use. Not all the practical means of pressing a siege were out of date by 1408; his observation that a round tower rendered a ram less effective could be translated into the advice given by late medieval architects that, in the age of the cannon, it was best to avoid the full frontal wall. But in chapter 22 the translator suddenly realised that the text he was rendering into English was no longer adequate to describe the artillery pieces of his day. In the most blatant 'up-dating' in the entire work, he suddenly referred to the 'grete gunnes that schete nowadayes [stoones] of so grete peys [weight] that no wall may withstonde hem, as hath ben wel schewed bothe in the north cuntrey and eke in the werres of Wales'.[61] Writing half a century later, the verse paraphraser could not resist referring to 'the canonys, the bumbard & the gunne [which] bloweth out the voys and stonys grete',[62] as well as to

---

Contamine, C. Giry-Deloison and M. H. Keen (Lille, 1991), pp. 171–88.

[60] In France attempts to create a 'national' army under the king were made in the 1370s and 1440s.

[61] Lester, *The Earliest English Translation of Vegetius*, p. 173/4–7.

smaller pieces, the serpentine, covey, culverin, crappaud, and fowler.[63] This is one of the clearer examples of the difficulties faced by both translators who, without a blush, introduced instances of up-to-the-minute technology into the ancient text.

What do such 'augmentations' suggest? The importance of the text lies not only in the interest which the philologist may have in it (although that should on no account be forgotten) but in the historical significance of a work, already one thousand years old, being rendered into the vernacular for what it had to offer a contemporary readership, a process which the translator was helping along by referring to technical developments and their very recent use in the north of England and in Wales. In other words, the translation was not so much a rendering of a 'historical', 'archaeological' or 'fossilised' treatise as one which, by the omission of certain material, the addition of up-to-date examples, and the modernising of the vocabulary could be shown to have some practical contemporary value. We may note that Jean de Meun's translation of 1284 was, on the whole, careful to follow the original as far as this could be done; yet it would not be long before 'augmentations', some of them references to events in the history of both Greece and Rome, others to events of relatively recent times, such as the battle of Bouvines or the defeat of Conradin, or to happenings *de nostre tens et de nostre souvenance*, came to be added to the text, such illustrations being evidence of the importance of the topical status being accorded by copyists to the work in hand.[64]

Topical, too, was the emphasis on wars at sea, 'schippewerre' or 'waterwerres' as the 1408 translator called them.[65] In a series of some fifteen short chapters he rendered Vegetius' text into an English which, he hoped, his readers would understand. Trying to be helpful, he described how vessels 'that beeth galeyes in Englische'[66] were used in the past, an explanation intended to assist his readers understand what went on in a battle at sea. One wonders how many persons, reading the text of 1408, would have observed the similarities of tactics used in a naval battle fought at that time with that described by Vegetius a millennium earlier. The galley still existed, after all, even in the waters of the north now increasingly dominated by the high-sided ship. The emphasis on the kinds of weapons used in naval battles, the similarity of the need to grapple and board, and to hurl and drop missiles from a height, had not greatly changed. Yet it was important and significant that observations on war fought at sea, taken as a

---

[62] Dyboski and Arend, *Knyghthode and Bataile*, ll. 2854–5.
[63] *Ibid.*, ll. 1849–52.
[64] See Löfstedt, *Li Abregemenz noble homme Vegesce*, pp. 11–13.
[65] Lester, *The Earliest English Translation of Vegetius*, p. 178/19, 23.
[66] *Ibid.*, p. 179/33.

more general view of warfare, should have been made at this time. The message will have been understood by those with recent experience of war against France, Genoa, and Castile. The consistent message of the *De Re Militari*, to be prepared for all forms of war and to be ready to learn from written experience, will have applied to naval war as much as it did to war on land.

What is the significance of these translations? England was rather late in rendering Vegetius into the vernacular; there were already four French versions in existence by about the year 1380, although the German translation was not made until 1475, just in time for it to be put directly into print in that year. When we seek the owners of such translations, we find that one was owned by a king, Richard III;[67] one by John Smert, first Garter King of Arms; another by a succession of later Kings of Arms; another by Sir John Astley, K.G.; and another still by Sir John Paston. When Thomas Hoccleve warned Sir John Oldcastle of the dangers of reading books on theology, he suggested instead a diet of works to include, 'Vegece, *Of the aart of chiualrie*'.[68] We do not know whether Henry V read him, but granted the date of the first translation and the fact that Henry, as both prince and king, encouraged translations from Latin, it is not unlikely that he had done so, particularly as John Lydgate referred to Henry training and exercising his body in the manner Vegetius had taught. Certainly the *Brut* chronicle records the king acting at the siege of Rouen in ways which resembled recommendations made by Vegetius to those besieging a fortified position. We may also note that the anonymous member of Henry's clerical household who wrote the *Gesta Henrici Quinti* was familiar with Giles of Rome's *De Regimine Principum*, for he cites passages from that work which reflect a knowledge of Vegetius.[69]

Vegetius was to make an indirect impact upon England through a number of fifteenth-century works written in English. It has been argued convincingly that Thomas Malory liked Vegetius' realism and, far from regarding a knight as a romantic figure, preferred him as a proper soldier influenced by *prudentia* rather than by considerations of romance. Examples of his work show how he had accepted Vegetius' realistic and unromantic message on the need to fight when circumstances and conditions were favourable, and that espionage should be used if it could procure an advantage.[70]

---

[67] A. F. Sutton and L. Visser-Fuchs, 'Richard III's Books: IV. Vegetius, *De Re Militari*', *The Ricardian*, 7 (1987), pp. 541–52. For much of what follows, see Lester, *The Earliest English Translation of Vegetius*, pp. 16–17.

[68] M. C. Seymour (ed.), *Selections from Hoccleve* (Oxford, 1981), p. 66.

[69] J. Taylor and J. S. Roskell (eds), *Gesta Henrici Quinti. The Deeds of Henry the Fifth* (Oxford, 1975), pp. 28 n. 4, 40 n. 1, 42 n. 2.

The influence of Vegetius also came to England through translations of the works of Christine de Pisan, especially her *Faits d'Armes et de Chevalerie*, written about 1410, which was translated and printed as *The Book of Fayttes of Armes and of Chyualrye* by William Caxton in 1489.[71] Most of that work's first book relies heavily upon the teachings of Vegetius, and it is of interest to note which passages from the *De Re Militari* Christine chose to cite or emphasise; they included his ideas on the choice of leaders in war; his insistence that, in choosing which man to promote to command, experience is more important than is 'the gretenes of his lignage & hye blood of his persone' (although it is admitted that respect due to a man as the result of his lineage will help the person appointed); his insistence on practice and training; and the importance of securing adequate and regular supplies. The book ends with what was doubtless intended to be a useful 'short recapytulacyon', 'inmanere of prouerbys' (or maxims) of what Vegetius had taught.[72]

Using several means of access to his thought, men were anxious to cite Vegetius as the leading authority on military thinking in fifteenth-century England. Through his own work in Latin (copies of which were still being made at this period) or in French (Humfrey, duke of Gloucester, owned one such), through two English versions of his treatise, and through the translation of French works in which he was cited, Vegetius was being given the opportunity to set out not only the old, timeless advice, but also his more philosophical ideas about war which had been the source of his reputation for centuries, and which would ensure the survival of his influence until at least the seventeenth century, and later.

---

[70] D. Bornstein, 'Military Strategy in Malory and Vegetius' *De Re Militari*', *Comparative Literature Studies* (Univ. of Illinois), 9 (1972), pp. 123–9. Jean de Boucicaut, a lover of the romantic aspects of chivalry, also developed a 'passion for physical training, which has strong echoes of Vegetius' (Keen, *Chivalry*, pp. 111–12).

[71] A. T. P. Byles (ed.), *The Book of Fayttes of Armes and of Chyualrye*, EETS, o.s. 189 (London, 1932).

[72] *Ibid.*, pp. 20, 28–32, 43–4, 98.

The Tournament in Medieval Scotland

CAROL EDINGTON

Following the footsteps of the knight-adventurers they study, scholars of the tournament have found themselves tracking this particular aspect of chivalry throughout medieval Europe.[1] Hitherto, however, the Scottish experience has been largely neglected. There are good – or at least understandable – reasons for this, not least the scant, often fragmentary, nature of the evidence. But this occupational hazard of medieval Scottish history should not blind us to the fact that Scots, like their European counterparts, were deeply committed to the chivalric ideals which informed secular life and, like them, were enthusiastic devotees of the various pursuits through which an attachment to the knightly ethic received tangible expression. This paper, therefore, offers a preliminary survey of that most striking chivalric exercise, the tournament; tracing its development from the encounters of the thirteenth century – great *mêlées* virtually indistinguishable from actual battle – to the elaborate *pas d'armes* of the sixteenth – individual jousts more akin to celebratory pageants than military training exercises. As this suggests, the evolution of the tournament in Scotland followed a broadly similar pattern to that found elsewhere. This is hardly surprising: after all, as has already been intimated, Scottish knights were part of a cosmopolitan chivalric community with members the length and breadth of Christendom. Indeed, if we are to obtain a complete picture, we must consider not just those encounters staged in Scotland but also Scottish tourneying activity elsewhere in Europe.

---

[1]   For an overview, see R. Barber and J. Barker, *Tournaments: Jousts, Chivalry and Pageants in the Middle Ages* (Woodbridge, 1989); see also J. Barker, *The Tournament in England, 1100–1400* (Woodbridge, 1986); J. Larner, 'Chivalric Culture in the Age of Dante', *Renaissance Studies*, 2 (1988), pp. 117–30, esp. pp. 122–4; T. Knighton, 'Northern Influence on Culture in the Iberian Peninsula during the Fifteenth Century', *Renaissance Studies*, 1 (1987), pp. 221–37, esp. pp. 224, 227; W. H. Jackson, 'The Tournament and Chivalry in German Tournament Books of the Sixteenth Century and in the Literary Works of Emperor Maximilian I', *The Ideals and Practice of Medieval Knighthood: Papers from the First and Second Strawberry Hill Conferences*, ed. C. Harper-Bill and R. Harvey (Woodbridge, 1986), pp. 49–73.

It is, in fact, continental combat which provides the earliest extant evidence for Scottish participation in tourneys. The Scottish king, William I, is recorded as fighting in France in 1166 and again nine years later in 1175.[2] Such exploits are testimony not only to personal interest but also to William's concern to take his place amongst the chivalric rulers of northern Europe. Indeed, such activity may even have represented a deliberate attempt to rehabilitate his knightly reputation following the humiliation of the Treaty of Falaise.[3] That tourneying should prove attractive to Scots during this period is only to be expected. The well-charted Anglo-Norman and Flemish immigration of the twelfth and thirteenth centuries had brought with it the chivalric ideology of a new military and political élite. Although geographically limited to the more feudalised society of lowland Scotland, this enormously important cultural shift stimulated Scottish participation in activities as diverse as tourneying, crusading, and the commissioning of romance literature. Indeed, by the second half of the thirteenth century, the Scottish reputation for knightly excellence, and for combat in particular, was such that an encounter with the Scottish champion was used as the dramatic climax of the French romance, *Le Sone de Nansay*.[4]

When it comes to tournaments fought on Scottish soil, the early evidence is much less satisfactory. Given William the Lion's evident enthusiasm, it is not unreasonable to suppose that he initiated similar competitions at home: indeed, it has been claimed that his reign saw tournaments take place at Roxburgh, Stirling and at Edinburgh.[5] Unfortunately, surviving sources fail to support this intriguing assertion which seems simply – and more accurately – to reflect William's long-lived reputation for chivalric prowess.[6] Nevertheless, by the middle of the

---

[2] F. J. Amours (ed.), *The Original Chronicle of Andrew of Wyntoun*, 6 vols, Scottish Text Society (hereafter STS) (Edinburgh, 1903–14), V, p. 3 (hereafter *Chron. Wyntoun*). As Wyntoun was writing some considerable time later, the 1166 reference may not be that reliable, though William certainly was in France at that time. For 1175, see P. Meyer (ed.), *L'Histoire de Guillaume le Maréchal*, Société de l'Histoire de France (hereafter SHF), 3 vols (Paris, 1891–1901), I, pp. 48–9.

[3] I am grateful to Dr Matthew Strickland for this suggestion.

[4] Michel Parisse, 'Le tournoi en France, des origines à la fin du XIIIe siècle', *Das Ritterliche Turnier in Mittelalter*, ed. J. Fleckenstein (Göttingen, 1986), pp. 175–211, p. 189.

[5] A. Nisbet, *A System of Heraldry: Speculative and Practical with the True Art of Blazon According to the Most Approved Heralds in Europe*, 2 vols (Edinburgh, 1816), I, p. 7.

[6] Noted by the chroniclers John of Fordun and Andrew Wyntoun. See W. F. Skene (ed.), *Johannis de Fordun, Chronica Gentis Scotorum*, 2 vols (Edinburgh,

thirteenth century, there is at least some evidence for tournaments being held in Scotland. Andrew of Wyntoun, admittedly writing in the 1420s, describes what he terms a 'gret iustinge' held at Haddington in 1242.[7] The brutal murder of Patrick, earl of Atholl, associated with this occasion rendered it something of a *cause célèbre* and it seems likely that other – less sensational – tournaments were also being staged unremarked upon by the chroniclers. This is certainly the impression given by Matthew Paris, who implies that the 1242 encounter was but one of several unfortunate contests held in the border region at this time.[8]

As the events at Haddington suggest, tournaments could provide the focus for serious unrest. Large numbers of knights gathered together in one place represented a potentially dangerous threat to peace and, even if no violence ensued, the nature of the fighting itself was often enough to devastate the surrounding countryside. It was largely in response to such problems that the English king, Richard I, issued the well-known writ of 1194 laying down specific conditions under which tournaments could be held by royal licence. Crown regulation of this type appears to have been unique to England and there is nothing to suggest that similar measures were introduced by Richard's Scottish counterparts. This may, of course, reflect nothing more than a failure of the evidence, but it is more likely that tournaments were simply less common north of the border, for it is surely significant that the surviving sources all refer either to Scottish exploits overseas or to fights staged south of the Forth.

The continental *mêlées* in which William the Lion acquired his reputation brought together knights from all over northern Europe. Offering what has been termed a form of 'chivalrous apprenticeship', they served to disseminate chivalric ideas and foster a sense of knightly solidarity capable of cutting across national boundaries.[9] At the same time, however, the practice of pitting teams of knights drawn from different regions against one another must have sharpened local loyalties. The internationalism of chivalry which the Scots were undoubtedly keen to be part of has often been commented upon, but it is equally important to

---

1871–2), II, p. 256 (hereafter *Chron. Fordun*); and *Chron. Wyntoun*, V, p. 4.

[7] *Chron. Wyntoun*, V, p. 99. The earl of Atholl and several of his men were killed when his lodgings were set alight as they slept. The episode, described in essentially similar terms, is also found in Bower, who was probably working from the same source; see D. E. R. Watt (ed.), *Scotichronicon by Walter Bower in Latin and English*, 9 vols (Aberdeen, 1987–), V, pp. 178, 277 (hereafter *Chron. Bower*).

[8] H. R. Luard (ed.), Matthew Paris, *Chronica Majora*, 5 vols (Rolls Series. London, 1872–83), II, p. 200.

[9] Barber and Barker, *Tournaments*, p. 10.

recognise the nationalist element which co-existed somewhat uneasily with it and which increasingly came to colour Scottish chivalric culture.

This trend is clearly discernible in the Wars of Independence, during the course of which the chivalric ethic with its stress upon military prowess and loyal service was readily and increasingly appropriated in support of the Scottish cause. The image of the ideal knight became that of the patriot-hero, with Robert Bruce himself viewed as no less than the tenth worthy of chivalric historiography.[10] This association was to prove highly significant for the future aspirations of Scottish kings as well as the nature of Scottish national identity more generally. More pertinent to this study, however, is the impact of the wars on the history of the tournament. There are, of course, obvious links between tourneying and warfare, with the former providing training for the latter. Even the individual jousts which by this time had replaced the great *mêlées* served to hone practical skills, promoting a martial ethos amongst those expected to fight, and providing participants and organisers alike with the ideal opportunity to make a political point. Both Edward I and Edward III staged tournaments whilst campaigning in Scotland and both drew attention to their military successes, celebrating victories there with jousting.[11] The Scottish crown on the other hand was in no position to encourage similar contests, as first John Balliol and then Robert Bruce fought a desperate struggle for military and political survival.

Nevertheless, Scots were not inactive tourneyers during this period. As Juliet Barker has shown, contests between English and Scottish knights or

[10] C. Edington, 'Paragons and Patriots: National Identity and the Chivalric Ideal in Late Medieval Scotland', *Image and Identity: The Making and Re-Making of Scotland through the Ages*, ed. D. Broun, R. Finlay and M. Lynch (forthcoming).

[11] In 1302 Edward I staged a tournament at Falkirk, scene of the great English victory of 1298; R. L. Loomis, 'Edward I: Arthurian Enthusiast', *Speculum*, 28 (1953), pp. 118–19. A tournament was also held while the English king was at Roxburgh in October 1305; J. Bain (ed.), *Calendar of Documents relating to Scotland*, 5 vols (Edinburgh, 1881–8), V, no. 471 (hereafter *CDS*). Following the siege of Stirling Castle, Edward also reportedly called upon the knights of his army to joust before their departure at the close of the siege; Herbert Maxwell (ed.), *Scalachronica: The Reigns of Edward I, Edward II and Edward III as recorded by Sir Thomas Gray* (Glasgow, 1917), p. 26. In 1341, his grandson spent Christmas at Melrose where he licensed jousting against the Scots; J. R. Lumby (ed.), *Henrici Knighton Chronicon*, 2 vols (Rolls Series, London, 1895), II, p. 23; E. M. Thomson (ed.), *Adae Murimuth Continuatio Chronicorum* (Rolls Series, London, 1889), p. 123. Tournaments were also organised to celebrate the end of campaigning in Scotland in 1347; Barker, *The Tournament in England*, p. 68.

between small teams frequently took place alongside regular hostilities.[12] During the Weardale campaign of 1327, for example, military stalemate was punctuated by what John Barbour termed 'iustyn of wer', while the following year, James Douglas and Thomas Randolph were involved in jousts during the Scottish siege of Alnwick castle.[13] Although at least one such Anglo-Scottish combat is recorded as having taken place near Edinburgh (in 1328), it was along the border that most of these jousts were staged.[14] And as early as 1303, the area played host to what Thomas Gray terms 'great passages of arms'.[15]

These Anglo-Scottish clashes were often associated with the conduct of sieges. During any siege the feelings of those thrown together must have run high, inflamed no doubt by the sustained proximity of the enemy, or stimulated perhaps by sheer boredom. Some contests, possibly more akin to judicial duels, were also mounted specifically to uphold a point of war. This seems to have been the case in 1403 during the siege of Cocklaws castle when a negotiated truce was allegedly broken by the Scots.[16] In order to defend Scottish honour, the captain of the castle offered himself in a duel against any Englishman 'who was his equal'. Whether all siege-related combats were fought over such a precise point of honour is unlikely; nevertheless many surely reflect a desire to uphold not just an individual's reputation, but also the national cause more broadly understood.

Several examples of this type of siege-related tourney occurred during the renewed, extremely bitter, conflict of the 1330s. Despite considerable English success in the early part of the decade, by 1338 tenacious guerrilla warfare had reduced the English presence north of the Forth to just two strongholds, Cupar and Perth, both of which were besieged by the Scots and both of which were the scene for Anglo-Scottish jousts. Alexander Ramsay of Dalhousie jousted with a squire (presumably English) at Cupar while John de Bruce, squire of William Douglas, later known as the knight of Liddesdale, fought three courses of war during the siege of Perth.[17] The fact that these episodes date to this period of Scottish revival illustrates not

---

12   Barker, *The Tournament in England*, pp. 31–40.
13   M. P. McDiarmid and J. A. C. Stevenson (eds), *Barbour's Bruce*, 3 vols, STS (Edinburgh, 1980–85), III, p. 227; *Scalachronica* (Maxwell), p. 82; also J. Stevenson (ed.), *Scalachronica by Sir Thomas Gray of Heton, Knight* (Edinburgh, 1836), p. 155. Cf. Barker, *The English Tournament*, 32, who mistakenly dates this to 1340.
14   G. Burnet (*et al.*), *The Exchequer Rolls of Scotland*, 23 vols (Edinburgh, 1878–1908), I, p. 238; (hereafter *ER*).
15   *Scalachronica* (Maxwell), p. 23; *Scalachronica* (Stevenson), p. 126.
16   *Chron. Bower* (Watt), VIII, pp. 51–3.
17   *Chron. Wyntoun*, VI, pp. 93, 125, 129. Barker also assumes the squire to have been English, *The Tournament in England*, p. 32.

only the increasing military and political confidence of the Scots, but also the way in which the secular ideologies of chivalry and nationalism were increasingly fused together in Scottish thinking. Ramsay and Douglas were key figures in this respect: closely associated with the struggle to recover Scottish independence, such exploits set the seal on their growing and long-lived reputation as the flower of Scottish chivalry. Significantly, both men were also involved in a celebrated border tourney in 1342, jousting against Henry, earl of Derby, first at Roxburgh and subsequently, after an injury to Douglas led to the contest being abandoned, at the rematch at Berwick.[18]

Just as the late 1330s and early 1340s saw a flurry of tourneying activity in the borders, so too did the 1380s, a time when a Franco-Scottish force was raiding northern England and feelings were once more running high.[19] At least five English knights received safe conducts to perform feats of arms in the Scottish marches against Scottish opponents at this time. while the Scot William Halyburton was licensed to carry harnesses and weapons to Carlisle for a tourney there in 1393.[20] The hostility generated by a century of intermittent conflict inevitably coloured these encounters. The clashes were often brutal and fatalities were not uncommon. That held at Berwick in 1342, for example, was fought – at the suggestion of the Scots – with raised visors. Unsurprisingly, two men were killed and William Ramsay was fortunate to escape with his life when a spear was driven through his helm and buried in his head. In an English context, it has been argued that these border jousts *à outrance* offered knights a comparatively rare chance of adventure, an opportunity to prove themselves in a form of tourney which was increasingly losing ground to the stylised jousts *à plaisance*.[21] Moreover, the national dimension provided additional motivation, the added frisson of fighting in some sense for one's country against its enemies. It is not surprising, therefore, that English knights were also enthusiastic in tourneys fought against the French.[22] For the Scots, however, there was only one enemy and, arguably, their antagonism was

---

[18] W. Goodall (ed.), *Johannis de Fordun Scotichronicon cum supplementis et continuatione Walteri Bower*, 2 vols (Edinburgh, 1759), II, p. 329; *Chron. Wyntoun*, VI, pp. 103–9; F. J. H. Skene (ed.), *Liber Pluscardensis*, 2 vols (Edinburgh, 1880), II, p. 218; Knighton, *Chron.*, II, p. 23; *Scalachronica* (Maxwell), p. 112. According to Gray, Derby and Douglas jousted first at Melrose in the presence of Edward III.

[19] Barker, *The Tournament in England*, p. 35.

[20] D. MacPherson (*et al.*), *Rotuli Scotiae*, 2 vols (London, 1814–19), II, pp. 87, 90, 111, 117, 119 (hereafter *Rot. Scot.*); *CDS*, IV, nos 425, 439, 452, 453.

[21] Barker, *The Tournament in England*, p. 14.

[22] *Ibid.*, pp. 36–8.

peculiarly sharp. War fought against England represented a powerful element of the Scottish chivalric ideal and border tourneys were an attainable, not to say exciting, means of realising that ideal.

Tournaments between English and Scottish knights were not only an adjunct to war. Paradoxically, they could also be viewed as a way of fostering good relations between the two kingdoms, and a shared enthusiasm for the pursuits of chivalry was an important factor in the close relationship which existed between David II and Edward III. While a captive in England, David had jousted in a tournament at Windsor (possibly also in London), and during regular visits south thereafter he would, according to Wyntoun, 'at Lundynge ... play'.[23]

It has been argued that the late 1380s/early 1390s saw Edward's successor, Richard II, deliberately invoke chivalry's supra-national appeal as part of a foreign policy designed to promote Anglo-French peace.[24] Events such as the Smithfield tournament of October 1390, the great St Inglevert joust fought earlier that year, and participation in the Prussian crusades, were all encouraged to this end. This period of temporary amity therefore saw a new phase in Anglo-Scottish tourneying and the performance of arguably the most celebrated of all Scottish exploits in the lists: the joust fought on London Bridge between Sir David Lindsay (later first earl of Crawford) and Lord Welles in the presence of Richard II, in May 1390.[25] 1390 also saw a tourney fought in London between John Dunbar, earl of Moray, and Thomas Mowbray, earl of Nottingham and earl marshal, while another Scot active in London at this time was William Dalzell who fought with the experienced English jouster, Sir Piers Courtney, son of the earl of Devon.[26] The outcome of this third encounter is not clear; Walter Bower

---

[23] For the Windsor tournament, see G. F. Beltz, *Memorials of the Order of the Garter* (London, 1841), p. 380; for London (1357), see W. J. Thoms (ed.), *A Survey of London Written in the Year 1598 by John Stow* (London, 1876), p. 142; *Chron. Wyntoun*, VI, p. 243.

[24] J. J. N. Palmer, *England, France and Christendom 1377–90* (London, 1972), pp. 181–5.

[25] *Chron. Bower* (Watt), VIII, p. 12; *Chron. Wyntoun*, VI, pp. 359–61; L. C. Hector and B. F. Harvey (eds), *Westminster Chronicle 1381–94* (Oxford, 1982), p. 434; B. D. D. Turnbull (ed.), *Extracta e Variis Cronicis Scocie* (Edinburgh, 1842), p. 204; *Rot. Scot.*, II, pp. 103–4; *CDS*, IV, nos 404, 410, 411. See also C. O. Parsons, 'A Scottish "Father of Courtesy" and Malory', *Speculum*, 20 (1945), pp. 51–64.

[26] *Westminster Chronicle*, p. 436; *CDS*, IV, nos 411, 412; 'Part of the Ynglis Cronikle', *The Asloan Manuscript*, ed. W. A. Craigie, 2 vols, STS (Edinburgh, 1923), I, pp. 197–214; *Chron. Bower* (Watt), VIII, pp. 17–19, 156; *Westminster Chronicle*, p. 437. For the dating of this encounter, see *Chron. Bower* (Watt), pp. 14, 156.

accords the honours to Dalzell while the Westminster Chronicle (probably referring to the same event) reckons the Englishman to have been the victor. Such partiality strongly suggests that even these peacetime jousts fought before the king and court were not free from the deep-seated antagonism associated with border tourneys. Indeed, all three of these combats were fought *à outrance* with unrebated lances and, in at least one case, continued on foot with battle axes, and finally with daggers, a format more commonly associated with border jousts. Even though no-one was actually killed, these were still extremely dangerous affairs and, according to the Westminster Chronicle, the strikingly vicious clash between Dalzell and Courtney led to a royal ban on any such tournaments taking place in future.[27]

Tournaments were also staged in Scotland – albeit somewhat sporadically – in the course of the fourteenth and fifteenth centuries. As suggested above, David II was keenly interested in the pursuits of chivalry, reportedly devoted to 'iustinge, dawnssynge and playinge'.[28] This chronicle tradition is borne out by entries in the Exchequer Rolls.[29] Between 1342 and 1343 at least three payments were made for jousting equipment for the king and, following his return to Scotland, tournaments were organised in 1364 and 1365. These were held in Edinburgh but David may also have used Stirling as a tournament site. In later years, Stirling would prove an extremely popular venue for royal tournaments, possibly in part owing to the belief linking Stirling castle – or Snowdon as it was known – with Arthurian legend. This tradition seems to have been rooted in the chivalric culture of David's reign, being first articulated by Jean Froissart, who himself visited Scotland in 1365 and spent three days with the king at Stirling.[30] There he was told not only that the castle had been known as Snowdon since the days of Arthur, but also that it was often frequented by the knights of the Round Table. Froissart also associates Stirling with the staging of splendid tournaments, making the connection explicit in his Arthurian romance, *Méliador*.[31] It is tempting to speculate, therefore, that David did indeed begin the tradition of holding royal tournaments at Stirling and moreover that, influenced by his experiences in England and in

27 *Westminster Chronicle*, p. 437.
28 *Chron. Wyntoun*, VI, p. 161.
29 ER, I, pp. 493, 528, 531; II, pp. 129, 177, 222.
30 R. S. Loomis, 'Scotland and the Arthurian Legend', *Proceedings of the Society of Antiquaries of Scotland*, 89 (1955–56), pp. 1–21, p. 15.
31 *Méliador, Roman Comprenant les Poésies lyriques de Wenceslas de Bohême, Duc de Luxembourg et de Brabant, publie par la première fois par A. Longnon*, 3 vols, Société des Anciens Textes Français (Paris, 1895–9), II, 14759–66.

particular by Edward III's Order of the Garter, he may have staged these encounters with deliberate reference to the tales of Arthurian chivalry.

With the accession of the Stewarts in 1371, royal interest in the tournament appears to have declined. A lone surviving reference in the Exchequer Rolls represents practically all we know relating to the reign of Robert II. There was, it is true, a tournament held on the Eden sands at St Andrews in 1382 but with the king in Inverness at the time, this could not have been a royal initiative.[32] Neither was Robert III a patron of the tournament. Although an encounter between the English challenger, Sir Robert Morley, and Sir James Douglas of Strathbok was arranged at Stirling, it never in fact took place and, when Morley subsequently fought three Scottish knights at Berwick on his way home, the combat had more in common with a traditional border tourney.[33]

Towards the end of the reign, however, tournaments were held at Perth and Stirling in 1401 and 1404 respectively.[34] Little is known about these occasions but it is reasonable to assume that they were not staged at the behest of the ailing and politically isolated monarch. We do, however, know appreciably more concerning a tournament in 1398 when Queen Annabella Drummond arranged for twelve knights to fight at the Nor Loch in Edinburgh.[35] The leading figure at this tourney was the heir to the throne, David, earl of Carrick, who became duke of Rothesay that same year and was subsequently appointed Lieutenant of the country in 1399. This tournament, also the occasion of Carrick's knighting, may well have been connected with Annabella and Rothesay's own ambitions, and the attempted revival of a more splendid court culture seems designed to parallel the prince's emergence as an assertive player on the political stage.[36]

The failure of the early Stewarts to patronise the tournament to any significant degree is easy to note yet difficult to explain. As contests held outside Scotland illustrate, Scottish knights entertained a perfectly healthy appetite for tournaments and were willing to travel considerable distances to indulge it. Moreover, the crown could not have been unaware of the tournament's capacity to enhance prestige and tighten the royal grip on the patronage of honour. Certainly Annabella and Rothesay seem to have been

---

[32] ER, III, p. 37; Scottish Record Office (SRO) GD 82, MakGill Charters, no. 6. I am grateful to Dr Stephen Boardman for this reference.

[33] ER, III, p. 436; Chron. Bower (Watt), VIII, p. 10.

[34] ER, III, pp. 526, 596.

[35] Chron. Bower (Watt), VIII, p. 10.

[36] For Rothesay's career, see S. Boardman, 'The Man who would be King: The Lieutenancy and Death of David, Duke of Rothesay, 1378–1402', People and Power in Scotland: Essays in Honour of T. C. Smout, ed. R. Mason and Norman Macdougall (Edinburgh, 1992), pp. 1–27.

attempting something along these lines in 1398. Possibly for Robert II this was a policy too closely associated with his predecessor, David II, who, together with a similarly-minded group of chivalric enthusiasts, had represented a dangerous political threat to the Steward before 1371. Robert III on the other hand was probably just too old and infirm to act as a credible chivalric leader, even had he wished to do so.

Thus, it was not until the personal reign of James I (a monarch who like David II had spent many years a prisoner in England), that the trappings of chivalry were once again associated with the person of the king. Ceremonial knighting, for example, played an important role not only in raising royal prestige, but also in defining crown-noble relations during the reign.[37] However, although Walter Bower was to describe the king as 'a knowledgeable jouster', only the evidence of a royal tournament held at Perth in 1434 supports the picture of James as tourneying enthusiast.[38]

It is not until the reign of his son, James II, that we find the first really substantial evidence relating to a Scottish tournament. This, the great Stirling tournament of 1449, is recorded in several sources both Scottish and continental. The *Auchinleck Chronicle* relates that in 'the zeir of god 1449[8] the 25th day of February, the master of Douglas callit James and twasum with him, that is to say James of Douglas, brother to the laird of Lochleven, and the laird of Haukat faucht in the barres at Stirling agains twa knichtis and ane sqwyar of Burgunze'.[39] Much fuller accounts are provided by the continental chroniclers, Mathieu d'Escouchy, Georges Chastellain, and Olivier de la Marche, who describe how the joust arose from a challenge issued in July 1448 by the Burgundian knight Jacques de Lalain, whose celebrated tourneying career took him the length and breadth of Europe, performing feats of arms in France, Navarre, Castile, and Portugal, as well as in Scotland.[40]

Clearly, the Stirling tourney was not a 'royal tournament' initiated by the crown. Although held at the royal castle of Stirling and paid for – partly at least – out of the royal purse, it was essentially an aristocratic

---

[37] M. Brown, *James I* (Edinburgh, 1994), pp. 132–3.

[38] *Chron. Bower*, VIII, p. 304; *ER*, IV, p. 561.

[39] *Auchinleck Chronicle*, printed in C. McGladdery, *James II* (Edinburgh, 1990), pp. 160–73, p. 164. See too *Chron. Extracta*, p. 238; *Chron. Bower* (Goodall), II, p. 515.

[40] J. A. Buchon (ed.), *Chronique de Jacques de Lalain par Georges Chastellain*, Collection des Chroniques Nationales Français 40 (Paris, 1825), pp. 189–207; G. du Fresne de Beaucourt (ed.), *Chronique de Mathieu d'Escouchy*, 3 vols, SHF (Paris, 1863–64), I, 148–53; H. Beaune and J. d'Arbaumont (ed.), *Mémoires d'Olivier de la Marche*, 4 vols, SHF (Paris, 1883–8), II, 104–10.

competition undertaken with royal licence and patronage.[41] Nevertheless, the king was undeniably eager to exploit the situation. Whether James was, like his father, 'a knowledgeable jouster' is not clear. Certainly, he enjoyed a considerable posthumous reputation for his interest in military affairs and, although he is best remembered for a fatal fondness for artillery, his grant of land in Edinburgh for the burgesses to joust upon and the purchase of armour and lances for his use suggest an active interest in more traditional knightly pursuits.[42]

The Stirling tournament of 1449 provided James II with an ideal opportunity to project a positive – and very public – image of royal authority at a time when he was beginning to emerge from the personal and political tutelage of the minority. Like his marriage to Mary of Gueldres, the niece of Philip of Burgundy, a few months later, the tournament represents an unambiguous statement of the young king's growing self-confidence as well as the strengthening of Scoto-Burgundian ties, an important cultural theme of the reign.[43] However, the tournament spoke as much to James's own subjects as to the Burgundian visitors he so anxiously sought to impress. For the powerful Livingston family, chief beneficiaries of the minority administration and closely associated with Stirling castle, what must have seemed an occasion of Livingston triumph swiftly gave way to despair when, a few months later, the renewed royal authority hinted at in the chivalric celebrations became a political reality and James moved against the family, successfully engineering their political downfall.[44]

It could be argued that the Douglases similarly misinterpreted the affair. Although Douglas participation in the tournament was to a certain extent foisted upon them, they – like the king – were not slow to exploit the image-building opportunity. From the days of Good Sir James onwards, sources both in Scotland and abroad had portrayed members of the Black Douglas family as the epitome of knightly valour, lauded in particular for their military service in the borders and for their loyalty to the crown. As we have seen, Douglases were particularly prominent in border tourneys,

---

[41] ER, V, p. 385.

[42] A. Constable (ed.), J. Mair, *A History of Greater Britain as well England as Scotland (1521)*, Scottish History Society (Edinburgh, 1892), p. 386; ER, V, pp. 345, 503; *Charters and Documents Relating to the City of Edinburgh 1143–1540*, Scottish Burgh Record Society VII (Edinburgh, 1871), p. 82.

[43] R. Nicholson, *Scotland: The Later Middle Ages* (Edinburgh, 1989), p. 348. The two events, tournament and marriage, were not directly connected although, in the midst of negotiations for the marriage, James would have taken pains to send the right signals to his prospective in-laws. For details of the negotiations, see J. H. Baxter, 'The Marriage of James II', *Scottish Historical Review*, 25 (1928), pp. 69–72.

[44] McGladdery, *James II*, pp. 49–50.

and their role as the military guardians of Scotland – initially dictated by their own territorial interests – became central to what might be termed the Douglas legend.[45] This was strikingly enunciated in the great Middle Scots poem, *The Buke of the Howlat*, written by Richard Holland and dedicated to Elizabeth Dunbar, countess of Moray and wife of Archibald Douglas, twin brother of James.[46] The dating of this poem has been the subject of considerable debate but the most plausible suggestion is that it was written sometime in the summer of 1448 – that is at the same time as arrangements were being made for the tournament.[47] Unsurprisingly, both tournament and poem articulate the same message. Thus, in 1449, James Douglas reportedly laid great stress on the family traditions of loyalty and service, showing the king great reverence and requesting that he gird him with the honour of knighthood.[48] This ritualised obedience undoubtedly recalled not only the Douglases' celebrated history but also more recent events. Some four months previously, a Scottish army under the Douglas earl of Ormond (James's brother), had defeated an English force in the west marches. Against this background, such a timely reminder of the family's carefully cultivated reputation as the 'wer wall' or rampart of Scotland would have been particularly pertinent.[49] This message was reinforced by an impressive show of Douglas strength. According to the chroniclers, Douglas was accompanied into Stirling by his brother the earl, various other magnates and between four and five thousand men.[50] Although the Douglases were unquestionably the most powerful family in Scotland, the idea that they posed any sort of threat to the crown is largely a creation of later writers: as they made clear to James II in 1449, the Douglases saw themselves as heirs to a unique relationship with the Bruce/Stewart line.[51]

---

[45] Between 1414 and 1415, William Douglas of Drumlanrig fought at Carlisle; *Rot. Scot.*, II, p. 212; *CDS*, V, no. 944. The tourney was licensed in December 1414, so may not actually have taken place until the following year. Douglas had also received a safe-conduct to perform feats of arms in England in August 1413 and seems to have spent a considerable part of 1413–14 in England (partly engaged in negotiations concerning the release of James I), *Rot. Scot.*, II, pp. 207, 209.

[46] 'The Buke of Howlat', *Scottish Alliterative Poems*, ed. F. J. Amours, STS (Edinburgh, 1897), pp. 47–81.

[47] F. J. Riddy, 'Dating the Buke of Howlat', *Review of English Studies* 37 (1986), pp. 1–10.

[48] Chastellain, *Chronique*, p. 199; *Chronique de Mathieu d'Escouchy*, I, p. 150.

[49] A. I. Dunlop, *Life and Times of James Kennedy, Bishop of St Andrews* (Edinburgh, 1950), p. 93.

[50] Chastellain, *Chronique*, p. 199; *Chronique de Mathieu d'Escouchy*, I, p. 50.

[51] The origins of the idea that the Douglases were over-mighty subjects who sought to challenge the crown is traced by N. Macdougall, 'Bishop James

Although unusual in a Scottish context, the Stirling tournament was but one example of the chivalric links forged between Scotland and Europe in the middle years of the fifteenth century. It was also in 1449 that Scottish knights were invited to participate in an elaborate *pas d'armes* held at St Omer by the celebrated jouster, Jean de Luxembourg. Three years previously, Jean and thirty of his men had made a pilgrimage to Scotland and it is clear that he hoped – vainly as it transpired – that some of those Scottish knights he had met on that occasion would respond to his challenge.[52]

Following the lead provided by the Burgundian court, the fifteenth century saw something of a mania for these elaborate, allegorical, *pas d'armes*, one of the most celebrated of which was the *Pas de la Fontaine de Pleurs* held at Chalon-sur-Saône between November 1449 and October 1450, and organised by that gallant knight errant, Jacques de Lalain.[53] The choice of this venue in the south-east of France was determined partly by the fact that it lay in the path of anyone travelling to Rome from France, England, Spain, or Scotland.[54] 1450 was the year of the papal jubilee and de Lalain clearly hoped to capitalise on the large number of pilgrims expected in Rome on this important occasion. Indeed the letters proclaiming the tournament specifically stated that any knight or squire on pilgrimage and lacking the necessary horses and harness would be suitably kitted out by the officer of arms stationed at the fountain.[55] Whether the anticipated knight-pilgrims would have travelled in such a commendably modest manner is, perhaps, questionable. Amongst those who certainly did not were the earl of Douglas, accompanied by that intrepid tourneying trio, his brother, Sir James, his kinsman, Douglas of Ralston, and the laird of Hawkhead; all of whom were members of the large party which left Scotland for Rome in October 1450.[56] Is it possible that the Douglas

---

Kennedy: a Reassessment of his Political Career', *Church, Politics and Society: Scotland 1408–1929*, ed. N. Macdougall (Edinburgh, 1983), pp. 1–23, esp. pp. 2–12.

[52] *CDS*, IV, no. 1184; *Chronique de Mathieu d'Escouchy*, I, p. 261 (dated 1448); *Mémoirs d'Olivier de la Marche*, I, pp. 118–35.

[53] Chastellain, *Chronique*, p. 225. Chastellain's account is, however, chronologically muddled. The text of the proclamation he gives is dated December 1448, during which month de Lalain was in Scotland, yet he is quite clear that the idea for the *pas* originated several months later. For a more detailed discussion, see A. Planche, 'Du tournoi au théâtre en Bourgogne: Le Pas de la Fontaine des Pleurs à Chalon-sur-Saône 1449–50', *Le Moyen Age*, 81 (1975), pp. 97–128.

[54] *Mémoires d'Olivier de la Marche*, II, p. 143.

[55] Chastellain, *Chronique*, p. 225.

[56] *CDS*, IV, nos 1229, 1232.

58

pilgrimage (the timing of which historians have often found difficult to explain) was motivated, in part at least, by a desire to renew the family's tourneying links with Jacques de Lalain?

Although Scottish knights were clearly part of a cosmopolitan chivalric culture, it has to be stressed that the 1449 tournament does not fit altogether snugly within the European framework. Unlike the elaborate continental *pas d'armes*, the Scottish combat was a straightforward battle of physical strength and martial skill and in many ways this fight *à outrance* with lances, daggers, and axes appears rather more similar to the border and siege-related tourneys of the thirteenth and fourteenth centuries. Nevertheless, the Stirling tourney was notably less brutal than earlier competitions (though in such circumstances accidental death was always a possibility). In some senses, therefore, Stirling marks an important stage in the development of the Scottish tourney as – influenced by Burgundian court culture – military proficiency and undisguised aggression gradually gave way to the stylised courtly jousts more readily associated with continental chivalric spectacle.

This development was to reach its apogee in the sixteenth century. Both James IV and James V were enthusiastic jousters and during their reigns tournaments were a regular feature of court life, usually staged, for instance, as part of the annual pre-Lenten festivities.[57] Even more splendid *pas d'armes* were associated with national celebrations, occasions of state, or the visits of important foreign dignitaries. As such, they represented a significant element in a carefully crafted programme of court revelry intended not only to entertain but also to communicate an important message concerning the nature of Stewart kingship.

In 1496, for example, James sponsored the marriage of the English pretender, Perkin Warbeck, to Catherine Gordon, daughter of the earl of Huntly. Attention was drawn to this deliberately provocative move by the extravagance of the celebrations, including a joust in Warbeck's honour in which the king himself took part.[58] James's own marriage to Margaret Tudor in 1503 was also marked by the staging of a grand *pas d'armes* designed both to celebrate the dynastic union and to give visual expression to James's kingship.[59] This can be clearly seen from the elaborate pageantry

---

[57]   T. Dickson and J. Balfour Paul (eds), *Accounts of the Lord High Treasurer of Scotland*, 12 vols (Edinburgh, 1877–1916), II, p. 363 (1502); II, pp. 202, 386 (1503); II, p. 476 (1505); III, p. 182 (1506) (hereafter *TA*).

[58]   *TA*, I, pp. 257, 262–3.

[59]   *Ibid.*, II, pp. 388–9; 'The Fyancells of Margaret, eldest Daughter of King Henry VIIth to James, King of Scotland: Together with her Departure from England, Journey into Scotland, her Reception and Marriage there, and the great Feasts held on that Account. Written by John Younge, Somerset Herald,

surrounding the event when, on entering Edinburgh, Margaret and her party were met by two knights, one of whom robbed the other of his paramour. Stepping in to break up the ensuing brawl, James proclaimed a 'very fair Tourney' to settle the matter, thereby making manifest his qualities as both knightly defender and wise judge; two of the central virtues of Christian knighthood and late medieval kingship alike. Clearly James intended that Margaret – or more pertinently the important dignitaries who accompanied her – should be impressed by these Scottish celebrations, celebrations designed to rival – or rather outshine – those staged at the proxy marriage ceremony in England.

Amongst the most unusual tournaments of the early sixteenth century must have been the water-borne affair at Leith in 1508 when the king was entertained by men jousting in boats.[60] However, the most celebrated tournaments of the period were undeniably those held by James IV in 1507 and 1508.[61] These can be vividly reconstructed from the Treasurers' Accounts which, as well as recording the expenditure usual on such occasions, include payment for a magnificent 'tree of Esperance' hung with eighteen dozen leaves, six dozen flowers and thirty-seven pears.[62] The jousts also involved what the records refer to as 'wild men' dressed in goat skins, wearing harts' horns, and possibly mounted on the fabulous winged beasts equipped with reins and saddles which also appear in the accounts. James himself fought in the guise of the 'wyld knycht', though whether he led or vanquished the company of wild men and beasts is not at all clear.[63]

A comprehensive interpretation of the iconographic significance of these fantastic tourneys remains elusive. Perhaps it was never intended in the first place. Although the pears of the Tree of Esperance were surely there to be won, we also know that the contests centred on a much more

---

who attended the said Princess on her Journey', *Johaniis Lelandi Antiquarii de Rebus Britannicis Collectanea*, 6 vols (London, 1774), IV, pp. 265–300, esp. pp. 288–91.

[60]   *TA*, III, pp. 141, 143.

[61]   For the 1507 tournament, see *TA*, III, pp. 393–7; for 1508, see *TA*, IV, pp. 117–25; also AE. J. G. Mackay (ed.), *The Historie and Chronicles of Scotland by Robert Lindsay of Pitscottie*, 3 vols, STS (Edinburgh, 1899–1911), I, pp. 241–4 (Pitscottie misdates the tournament 1505).

[62]   In 1508, a further twelve dozen leaves, five dozen flowers and forty-nine pears were ordered and payment made for the repair of fifty-two leaves.

[63]   James's participation is alluded to by the sixteenth-century chroniclers, Lindsay of Pitscottie and John Lesley (the former incorrectly identifying the king as 'the black knicht'); Pitscottie, *Historie*, I, pp. 242–3; E. G. Cody (ed.), *The Historie of Scotland Written first in Latin by the most Reuerand and Worthy Jhone Leslie Bishop of Rosse And Translated in Scottish by Father James Dalrymple ... 1596*, 2 vols, STS (Edinburgh, 1888–95), II, p. 128.

symbolically ambiguous prize, the favours of the 'Black Lady'. It is, however, worth noting another symbolic reading of the *pas d'armes* suggested by the sixteenth-century historian, John Lesley.[64] In this account, James determines that 'he wald be called a knycht of King Arthuris brocht vp in the wodis', a story-line which would certainly support the cast of wild men and beasts. It has been suggested that this recourse to Arthurian symbolism represented a deliberate manipulation of chivalric spectacle to make a political point, with James underlining the uncertainty of the Tudor succession and his own claims to the English crown.[65] Certainly, relations with England at this time were frosty and the barely civil reception accorded Henry VIII's ambassador provides a striking contrast to that given to Bernard Stewart, Lord d'Aubigny, a member of the embassy recently arrived from Louis XII, and guest of honour at the 1508 tournament. The overt nationalism associated with the border and siege-related tourneys of the thirteenth and fourteenth centuries had clearly given way to a more subtle form of national posturing.

Like the Stirling tournament of 1449, those of 1507 and 1508 also addressed a domestic audience. As well as proclaiming the tournament in extravagantly illuminated letters sent to France in 1507, it was also announced, according to Pitscottie, to 'the heill lordis and barronis of Scotland'.[66] And, despite the presence of French competitors, his account – focusing on Scottish exploits in the lists – probably provides a more accurate impression of the actual competition.[67] Recording the triumphs of individual knights, Pitscottie relates how they were rewarded with golden weapons to be kept 'in memorie for the kingis honour and thair gloire in tymes cuming that thair posteritie micht sie eftir quhat nummer that haue beine and how thay vsit thame sellffis to the kingis graice thair maisteris pleasour and to the adwancment of thair awin honour'.[68] As this suggests, the tournament conveyed a powerful message to the Scottish nobility stressing the king's role as the fount of patronage and honour and calling upon the loyalty that this ought properly to evoke.[69]

---

[64] Leslie, *Historie*, II, p. 128.

[65] N. Macdougall, *James IV* (Edinburgh, 1989), p. 295.

[66] *TA*, III, p. 365; Pitscottie, *Historie*, I, p. 242. Pitscottie also asserts that the articles proclaiming the tournament were sent to England and Denmark.

[67] Pitscottie, *Historie*, I, p. 243.

[68] *Ibid.*, I, p. 243.

[69] Along with activities such as the creation of chivalric orders and the ceremonial dubbing of knights, the tournament was frequently used by monarchs to tighten their grip on the patronage of honour, see M. Vale, *War and Chivalry: Warfare and Aristocratic Culture in England, France and Burgundy at the End of the Middle Ages* (London, 1981), p. 168. For a more general discussion of state control of honour, see M. James, 'English Politics and the Concept of

With the great *pas d'armes* of 1507 and 1508, it may not be going too far to say that a Renaissance cult of honour centred on service to the crown had replaced the celebration of physical strength and military skill more traditionally associated with tourneying activity. Lying on the geographical fringes of Europe, Scotland was often and perhaps inevitably tardy to respond to cultural developments elsewhere in Europe. Certainly, Scotland seems to have come late to tourneying in the first instance and the Stewarts were definitely slow starters in the tournament stakes. Nevertheless, as illustrated by this brief analysis of Scottish tourneying history, Scots were clearly determined to plug themselves into European chivalric activity. To a large extent, therefore, Scottish tournaments followed a familiar pattern. What rendered them – and Scottish chivalric culture in general – more distinctive was a markedly nationalist and anti-English character. Of course, such patriotic chauvinism was by no means unique to Scotland, but these two related – though not necessarily identical – concepts exerted a powerful influence on jousts both *à outrance* and *à plaisance* throughout the later middle ages.

Honour', *Past and Present*, Supplement no. 3 (1978).

The Architecture of Arthurian Enthusiasm: Castle Symbolism in the Reigns of Edward I and His Successors[1]

RICHARD K. MORRIS

The castles of King Edward I in North Wales have long been acknowledged as one of the crowning achievements of European military architecture.[2] They mark the culmination of almost two centuries of development, from the first crusading experience in the Near East, through the castles of the Plantagenets and Philip Augustus in France; resulting in virtually impregnable fortresses relying on such features as concentric walls and heavily fortified gatehouses. The Edwardian castles are a virtuoso demonstration of such ideas, characterised especially by their enormity of scale and their variety of type. Flint has a detached keep, Conwy is planned for consecutive defence, Harlech and Beaumaris rely on concentric defences of near perfect symmetry; Caernarfon experiments with polygonal towers, Conwy with a very early example of stone machicolation, and so on. The impression is firmly given of an elite group of men-of-war, long-standing comrades in arms of the king, indulging in an orgy of military

[1]   Versions of this paper have been given to various audiences during the past twenty years, starting as a series of undergraduate course lectures in 1974; with its major previous public airings to the British Archaeological Association in 1979 and Le Comité International d'Histoire de l'Art in 1985. Its content has benefited from the comments of many people too numerous to acknowledge individually. I thank them all, and I am particularly grateful to Professor Alan Gowans, whose teaching at the University of Victoria (Canada) introduced me to socio-architectural history: and to Professor Julian Gardner and other staff and students in the History of Art and English Departments at the University of Warwick for their continuing interest in this subject: and to the Harlaxton Symposium committee for the opportunity finally to publish it.

[2]   The standard modern account is by Arnold Taylor, 'The King's Works in Wales 1277–1330', in H. M. Colvin (ed.), *The History of the King's Works*, I, *The Middle Ages* (London, 1963), pp. 293–408; reissued with minor revisions as A. J. Taylor, *The Welsh Castles of Edward I* (London, 1986). See also the Cadw Guidebook series – *Beaumaris Castle* (1988), *Caernarfon Castle* (1993), *Conwy Castle* (1990), *Flint Castle-Ewloe Castle* (1995), *Harlech Castle* (1988), *Rhuddlan Castle* (1987). I am much indebted to Dr David Robinson (Cadw) for considerable assistance with the Welsh material in this paper.

architectural expression on an almost unlimited budget:[3] a medieval forerunner of the recent American 'star-wars' programme.

No-one doubts that the English castles in North Wales represent an overkill. One has only to compare a castle of the Welsh princes, such as Dolbadarn in Snowdonia,[4] with Harlech or Conwy to gain a visual appreciation of this phenomenon (Pls 4, 5, 6). Clearly the explanation for these excesses goes beyond basic military function, and two further motives will be examined here – artistic effect and symbolism – as exemplified particularly at Caernarfon, the viceregal centre of the English administration after 1284.

The idea that real castles might also incorporate decoration found no place in Sidney Toy's style of military history,[5] but Caernarfon displays a series of features which can be construed as consciously artistic. Decoration can be observed earlier in the fabric of some Anglo-Norman keeps like that at Castle Rising, Norfolk (c.1140), and recent research has heightened our awareness of such factors at work in the twelfth century.[6] Nevertheless, the extent of the decorative vocabulary at Caernarfon marks it out as a turning point: the progenitor of the late medieval castle as a work of art. The relevant effects include geometrical variety in plan, banded masonry in the walls, a surfeit of turrets, and battlements carved with figures; to all of which we shall return shortly. Probably the feature most symptomatic of the new spirit, however, and one which has received least attention from scholars, is the façade of the King's Gate (Pl. 3). Here the presence of an elaborate sculpted niche enclosing the seated figure of a king appears to have been inspired by the imperial precedent of Frederick II's triumphal gate at Capua,[7] which Edward or a member of his court was likely to have seen during his return from crusading. In 1272 he wintered in southern Italy, and in February 1273 he travelled north to the papal court at Orvieto. The design of the King's Gate is repeated in the gatehouse of the lordship castle at Denbigh, with the additional chequer-board pattern of coloured

---

[3] For example, Sir Otto de Grandison (Edward's closest friend), Sir William de Cicon and the engineer Master James of St George; see further Taylor, 'The King's Works in Wales', pp. 293–408. For a recent study of the potentially withering firepower from some of these castles, see Q. Hughes, 'Medieval Firepower', *Fortress*, 8 (1991), pp. 31–43.

[4] See further R. Avent, *Castles of the Princes of Gwynedd* (Cardiff, 1983); and Cadw Guidebook *Dolwyddelan Castle-Dolbadarn Castle* (Cardiff, 1994).

[5] S. Toy, *A History of Fortification from 3000 B.C. to A.D. 1700* (London, 1955).

[6] T. A. Heslop, 'Orford Castle, Nostalgia and Sophisticated Living', *Architectural History*, 34 (1991), pp. 36–58.

[7] For a reconstruction of this gate, see C. A. Willemsen, *Kaiser Friedrichs II Triumphtor zu Capua* (Wiesbaden, 1953), pl. 106.

stones above emphasising the artistic effect.[8] Caernarfon and Denbigh appear to incorporate the first surviving examples in England – perhaps even in northern Europe – of castle gatehouses adorned with carved imagery, an idea more familiar in ecclesiastical entrances of the period.[9] It thus stands at the head of a trend which became the fashion for pretentious castles in the later middle ages, such as the gatehouses at Bodiam and Herstmonceux, or Pierrefonds and La Ferté-Milon in France (Pls 7, 19).

Symbolism of a political kind has been discerned in the fabric of Caernarfon, linking it with the antiquity of the location – the Roman Segontium – and with a wider imperial imagery. The most salient points are the carved eagles of the eponymous west tower, and especially the imitation of the late fourth-century Theodosian walls of Constantinople through the combination of polygonal towers with bands of two different colours in the wall fabric (Pl. 1).[10] Affirmation of the link with Constantinople is provided by the contemporary record in the *Flores Historiarum* that the body of Magnus Maximus, the legendary father of the Emperor Constantine, was discovered when preliminary work was under way on the castle in 1283. All this information and its interpretation has been precisely recorded and analysed by Arnold Taylor.[11] However, one may venture to suggest that the intended symbolism goes beyond the merely political to a specific

---

[8]   See D. W. Dykes (ed.), *Alan Sorrell: Early Wales Re-Created* (Cardiff, 1980), p. 61, for an artist's impression. It is possible that the Denbigh gatehouse façade was actually completed before that at Caernarfon. Both presumably stem from a general design probably established in the 1280s, though not completed for several decades at Caernarfon; see further Taylor, 'The King's Works in Wales', pp. 333–4 and 388 (reference of 1320 to *ymaginem Regis* over the King's Gate); and most recently J. M. Maddison, 'Building at Lichfield Cathedral during the Episcopate of Walter Langton (1296–1321)', *Medieval Archaeology and Architecture at Lichfield*, British Archaeol. Assoc. *Conference Trans.*, XIII, ed. J. M. Maddison (Leeds, 1993), pp. 77–8.

[9]   For example, the Judgement porch of Lincoln Cathedral Angel Choir (1255–80).

[10] The Theodosian walls are stone and tile, whereas the Caernarfon walls are two types of stone (carboniferous limestone with darker bands of Carboniferous sandstone); see Royal Commission for Ancient and Historic Monuments (RCAHM) (Wales), *Caernarvonshire*, II, Central (1960), p. 130.

[11] Taylor, 'The King's Works in Wales', pp. 369–71. For the identity of 'Constantine', see J. J. Parry, 'Geoffrey of Monmouth and the Paternity of Arthur', *Speculum*, 13/3 (1938), pp. 271–7; and R. S. Loomis, 'From Segontium to Sinadon; the Legends of a "Cité Gaste"', *Speculum*, 22 (1947), pp. 520–33. For a recent archaeological account of Segontium, see P. J. Casey (*et al.*), *Excavations at Segontium (Caernarfon) Roman Fort*, Council for British Archaeology Research Report, 90 (London, 1993).

association with the fashionable contemporary world of Arthurian romance: and herein lies the main objective of this paper.

At this juncture, it is necessary to turn away temporarily from the Welsh castles to consider the historiography of Arthurian art. In 1938, when Roger Sherman Loomis and Laura Hibbard Loomis published their survey, *Arthurian Legends in Medieval Art*, they found only modest evidence in England in the decorative arts and in a few undistinguished manuscripts.[12] This was all the more surprising for, as they remarked, medieval England was 'the homeland ... of some of the finest versions of Arthurian story';[13] and subsequently R. S. Loomis was to go on to detail one aspect of the story in his 'Edward I, Arthurian Enthusiast'.[14] Recently Alison Stones has usefully updated our knowledge of 'Arthurian Art since Loomis', though keeping to literal representations of Arthurian episodes and characters mainly in manuscript illumination, as the Loomises had done.[15] There is thus still a place for an examination of the potential architectural examples of 'Arthurian enthusiasm'; even though it must be admitted at the outset that identifications will be less definitive because of the abstract language of building fabric and the need to argue through association.

Since the early versions of this paper over twenty years ago, the academic climate has become more receptive to my main hypothesis, particularly regarding changing attitudes to secular architecture. Charles Coulson has diagnosed the 'structural symbolism' of castellation, whilst Colin Platt and Michael Thompson have introduced respectively the terms 'castles of chivalry' and 'show castles' for later fourteenth- and fifteenth-century castles.[16] Thompson has also brought out the

---

12   R. S. Loomis with L. H. Loomis, *Arthurian Legends in Medieval Art* (New York, 1938), pp. 40–1 (stained glass and the Winchester round table), 44–8 (the Chertsey tiles), 68 and 79 (misericords), 138–9 (manuscripts).

13   *Ibid.*, p. 138.

14   R. S. Loomis, 'Edward I, Arthurian Enthusiast', *Speculum*, 28 (1953), pp. 114–27.

15   M. A. Stones, 'Arthurian Art since Loomis', *Arturus Rex*, eds. W. van Hoecke (*et al.*), II (Leuven, 1991), pp. 21–55, especially pp. 27–30 for Britain; 'Arthur's Hall' at Dover Castle is noted, but without any discussion of the architecture.

16   C. L. H. Coulson, 'Structural Symbolism in Medieval Castle Architecture', *Jnl of the British Archeol. Assoc.*, 132 (1979), 73–90; C. Platt, *The Medieval Castle in England and Wales* (London, 1982); M. W. Thompson, *The Decline of the Castle* (Cambridge, 1987). Recent critical reviews of changing attitudes to castle studies are D. Stocker, 'The Shadow of the General's Armchair', *Archeol. Jnl*, 149 (1992), pp. 415–20; and C. L. H. Coulson, 'Freedom to Crenellate by Licence – an Historical Revision', *Nottingham Medieval Studies*, 38 (1994), pp.

contemporary realism of the *Gawain*-poet's description of the Green Knight's Castle,[17] and the relationship of military architecture to romance literature now warrants a section in a general textbook like Tom McNeill's English Heritage book of *Castles*.[18] Away from castles, a milestone has been Paul Binski's re-assessment of the decorative scheme in the former Painted Chamber of Westminster Palace, demonstrating *inter alia* the association of its Maccabees cycle with Edward I's heroic notion of kingship and with the Arthurian climate of the late thirteenth century.[19]

In addition it is pertinent to note here three other discoveries which are strongly suggestive of the Arthurian climate in Edward's time, and which could not have been known to R. S. Loomis or were not identified by him. The first is the recent revelation through scientific dating methods that the famous Round Table hanging in the former great hall of Winchester Castle was formed from trees which are now known to have been felled *c*.1250–80.[20] Thus although the extant Arthurian painting of the surface belongs to the early Tudor period, the table was almost certainly created initially for one of the royal round table festivities of Edward's reign.[21]

As in life, so in death: for, secondly, a case can be made that Edward's tomb chest, surprisingly austere amongst the regal splendours of Westminster Abbey, is based on or related to the former tomb of Arthur at

---

86–137.

[17] M. W. Thompson, 'The Green Knight's Castle', *Studies in Medieval History Presented to R. A. Brown,* ed. C. Harper-Bill *et al.* (Woodbridge, 1989), pp. 317–25. I am grateful to Dr Christopher Norton for first drawing my attention to this reference. See also A. Putter, *"Sir Gawain and the Green Knight" and French Arthurian Romance* (Oxford, 1995), p. 38, for Gornemant's castle in the *Conte du Graal* 'fully abreast of the latest developments in castle construction'.

[18] T. E. McNeill, *Castles* (London, 1992), pp. 109–11.

[19] P. Binski, *The Painted Chamber at Westminster,* Society of Antiquaries Occasional Paper, New Series IX (London, 1986), especially ch. 3 and Conclusion; most recently see P. Binski, *Westminster Abbey and the Plantagenets: Kingship and the Representation of Power* (New Haven and London, 1995), especially pp. 104–6, 139, 197–8, for images of Edward's kingship.

[20] M. Biddle and B. Clayre, *Winchester Castle and the Great Hall* (Winchester, 1983), pp. 37 and 40; see further M. Biddle, ed., *King Arthur's Round Tables: An Archaeological Investigation* (London, forthcoming).

[21] Biddle and Clayre, *Winchester Castle,* p. 40, '[the scientific tests] place the making of the table ... in the later part of the reign of King Henry III ... or the earlier part of the reign of King Edward I ... with the latter being for various reasons – scientific, political, personal – the more likely'. Loomis, *Arthurian Legends,* pp. 40–1, noted that the table was potentially earlier than Tudor, but could not tell what date.

Glastonbury.[22] The latter had been inspected personally by Edward and Queen Eleanor in 1278, and as a result of this visit the remains of Arthur and Guinevere were reburied with ceremony before the high altar, where their tombs were displayed for the rest of the middle ages:[23] which suggests how highly Edward regarded his association with them. The salient points of comparison between the Westminster and Glastonbury tomb chests are that both were fashioned from 'marble' and were devoid of an effigy on the lid,[24] the latter a remarkable omission in the case of Edward's tomb and distinguishing it from all the other comparable monuments at Westminster. The suggestion that the use of marble may also have been intended to evoke associations with antiquity through the porphyry sarcophagi of royal burials in southern Europe[25] need not preclude the Arthurian connection, for the visual imagery of Edward's monarchy was multiple and eclectic.[26] Indeed, the only English tomb surviving to a member of the royal family actually called Arthur – the Tudor Prince Arthur (d. 1502) buried in Worcester Cathedral – quotes the same formula of a marble topped tomb

22   This association, which I first expounded publicly in a lecture to the British Archaeological Association in 1979, has also been suggested by Paul Binski and Nicola Coldstream. See respectively M. A. Stones, 'Aspects of Arthur's Death in Medieval Illumination', *The Passing of Arthur: New Essays in Arthurian Tradition*, eds. C. Baswell and W. Sharpe (New York, 1988), pp. 52–86 (n. 38 citing personal communication with Binski); and N. Coldstream, *The Decorated Style: Architecture and Ornament 1250–1350* (London, 1994), p. 127, where she also suggests a link with the tomb of Louis IX of France.

23   A. Gransden, 'The Growth of the Glastonbury Traditions and Legends in the Twelfth Century', *Jnl of Ecclesiastical History*, 27 (1976), p. 355, citing Adam of Domerham. See also E. K. Chambers, *Arthur of Britain* (London, 1927), p. 125; Loomis, 'Edward I, Arthurian Enthusiast', pp. 114–16; and J. Vale, *Edward III and Chivalry: Chivalric Society and its Context, 1270–1350* (Woodbridge, 1982), p. 19.

24   For Arthur's tomb, see Chambers, *Arthur of Britain* n. 23, pp. 125–6; and Gransden 'Glastonbury Traditions', pp. 349–57. For depictions in manuscript illumination, see Stones, 'Aspects of Arthur's Death' n. 22, pp. 61–4. For Edward I's tomb, see Royal Commission for Historical Monuments in England, *London, I, Westminster Abbey* (London; 1924), p. 29 and Pl. 48; his tomb is made of English Purbeck marble, as presumably was Arthur's at Glastonbury.

25   See J. Déer, *The Dynastic Porphyry Tombs of the Norman Period in Sicily* (Cambridge, Mass., 1959); and B. Rosenman, 'Tomb Canopies and Cloister at Santes Creus', *Studies in Cistercian Art and Architecture*, II, ed. M. P. Lillich (Kalamazoo, 1984), pp. 229–31, for the tomb of Peter III of Aragon (d. 1285).

26   See Binski, *The Painted Chamber at Westminster*, Conclusion; and Binski, *Westminster Abbey*, pp. 104–6.

chest without an effigy.[27] This observation has not been made before to my knowledge, and it tends to corroborate the Arthurian association for Edward's earlier memorial.

The employment of romance imagery owed as much to his courtiers as to the king himself, and their tombs provide an insight into the chivalric lifestyle of English noble society. Here we are concerned with the meaning of the cross-legged pose for military effigies, which constitutes the third piece of contextual evidence not considered by Loomis. Significantly the posture is almost entirely restricted to English monuments,[28] appearing during the first half of the thirteenth century in a few effigies mainly connected with the Knights Templar and becoming fashionable in a wider context at about the beginning of Edward's reign, from the 1270s to the 1340s; including notably the tomb of Edward's brother, Edmund, earl of Lancaster, in Westminster Abbey, with chivalric details in the gable tympanum and elsewhere.[29] The suggestion that the pose denoted a Crusader has long since been replaced by the more general idea of the knight as 'soldier of Christ',[30] but it may have been associated more specifically in contemporary minds with romance allusions to the knights on quest. In the case of the Grail Quest, with its potential for personal salvation, this might be highly appropriate as an image for a knight's tomb.[31] The most obvious visual parallel is the depiction on a series of early fourteenth-century ivories of Gawain on the Perilous Bed, in an agitated pose in full armour, and usually with his legs crossed; an episode probably derived from the *Conte du Graal* of Chrétien of Troyes.[32] The bed translates well into a tomb chest; or vice-versa, for it cannot be certain that the version in the portable arts preceded the monumental tombs. In manuscript illumination, sleeping cross-legged figures in full armour which also relate to this theme include 'Lancelot asleep as the Grail appears' and 'the soul of Roland carried to heaven'.[33]

---

[27]   Illustrated in N. Pevsner, *Worcestershire* (Harmondsworth, 1968), Pl. 44.

[28]   For a survey of English cross-legged effigies and reference to continental examples, see H. A. Tummers, *Early Secular Effigies in England: The Thirteenth Century* (Leiden, 1980), pp. 107–26. The continental specimens are restricted to Spain, to a small group of the later thirteenth century in northern Castile; and a link with England through Edward's Spanish marriage would be worth investigating further.

[29]   *Ibid.*, p. 112.

[30]   See Coldstream, *The Decorated Style*, pp. 111–12.

[31]   See further M. Whitaker, *Arthur's Kingdom of Adventure: The World of Malory's Morte D'Arthur* (Cambridge, 1984), ch. 4.

[32]   Cited in Loomis, *Arthurian Legends*, pp. 71–2 and Figs 136–42; but without drawing any parallel with monumental tombs.

[33]   The former illustrated in M. A. Stones, 'Sacred and Profane Art: Secular and

Perhaps the most extreme version of this pose in sepulchral monuments comes towards the end of the trend, in three well known East Anglian tombs depicting cross-legged knights lying on beds of stones; of which that to Oliver de Ingham (d. 1344) at Ingham in Norfolk (Pl. 8 is considered here. Various explanations have been proposed for this peculiar imagery, including the late Andrew Martindale's suggestion of a possible link with the Roman statue of a recumbent river-god, misinterpreted in the middle ages as depicting Mars.[34] However, in the early nineteenth century Stothard recorded painted hunting and forest scenes as the backdrop to the Ingham effigy. Taken together with Sir Oliver's restless slumber, his right hand resting (formerly) on the pommel of his sword, this suggests an allusion to the knight on quest, sleeping rough in the forest; vowing never to sleep twice in the same place until he achieved his goal.[35] This was the vow of Perceval in the *Conte du Graal*, and its continuing significance for the Edwardian period is emphasised by its use as a model for the chivalric oaths taken at the Feast of the Swans in Westminster Palace in 1306, as noted by Loomis.[36]

What the Ingham example demonstrates, together with the other tombs cited, is how the general interest in Arthurian romance in continental

Liturgical Book Illumination in the Thirteenth Century', *The Epic in Medieval Society*, ed. H. Scholler (Tübingen, 1977), Figs 5 and 6 (two depictions, dated to *c*.1285 and *c*.1315–25); the latter in M. Keen, *Chivalry* (New Haven and London, 1984), Fig. 8 (*Les Grandes Chroniques de France*). Obviously one must beware of the pose being employed as a convention for sleep, as for example in some of the sleeping knights in the carved Easter sepulchres at Heckington and Hawton; which is why the extra visual and contextual evidence is vital at Ingham.

[34] A. Martindale, 'The Knights and the Bed of Stones: a Learned Confusion of the Thirteenth Century', *Jnl of the British Archeol. Assoc.*, 142 (1989), pp. 66–74, where all three tombs at Ingham, Reepham and Burrough Green are described and illustrated; including Stothard's record of the painting on the back wall of the Ingham recess (Pl. XVIIB). Related to this group is the monument at Saleby (Lincolnshire) showing a cross-legged knight lying on a bed of flowers; I am grateful to Loveday Gee for this observation. For a suggestion that the Ingham knight's pose signifies a 'penitent spirit', see J. and M. Vale, 'Knightly Codes and Piety', *Age of Chivalry: Art and Society in Late Medieval England*, ed. N. Saul (London, 1992), pp. 26–7.

[35] For example, *Sir Gawain and the Green Knight*, ed. W. R. J. Barron (Manchester, 1974), lines 691–739, e.g. 'Almost slain by the sleet, he [Gawain] slept in his irons night after night amongst the naked rocks' (729–30). For a convenient selection of forest episodes from old French romance, see Putter, 'Sir Gawain and the Green Knight', pp. 16–20.

[36] Loomis, 'Edward I, Arthurian Enthusiast', pp. 122–3; see also A. Gransden, *Historical Writing in England c.550 to c.1307* (London, 1974), pp. 453–4.

Europe, evidenced in relatively 'mass produced' personal artefacts like ivory caskets and mirror-backs, manifests itself in England rather in monumental works of art which are more specifically personal in patronage. The conclusion to be drawn is that certain elements in the circle of Edward I had adopted Arthurian ideals as a lifestyle, more so than even Loomis had envisaged when he wrote of Edward's 'Arthurian enthusiasm'.[37] This corresponds with how his military activities in Wales and Scotland may be viewed almost as re-enactments at sites associated with Arthur by poets and chroniclers;[38] and, in artistic terms, with how the English Decorated style magnified small-scale ornament (often of foreign derivation) into monumental architectural creations.[39]

Armed with such ideas, we may return to Caernarfon to consider the full meaning of the castle's architectural sources. In 1283, the year work began, Edward received the crown of Arthur from the Welsh, and in the following year he held a round table festivity at Nefyn, south-west of Caernarfon and the Snowdonia range.[40] Moreover, 'Sinadon' (Snowdon) or Segontium had long been known to conteurs and writers of Arthurian romance as the birthplace of Perceval and a site 'where Arthur sits at the Round Table'.[41] In such circumstances it would be astonishing if contemporaries did not recognise automatically that the incontrovertible architectural links with Constantinople (as described above) also implied an association with Arthur, as grandson of Constantine, following the pedigree stemming from Geoffrey of Monmouth's *Historia Regum Britanniae*.[42] The continuing relevance of the latter is shown by Edward's use of Arthurian material from the *Historia* in a letter to the pope in 1301 to support his claim to Scotland.[43] Overall it is hard to accept Loomis's assertion that, with Edward's re-use of stones from Segontium for his new castle, 'the

[37] Loomis, 'Edward I, Arthurian Enthusiast', p. 114, '... in his cult of Arthur Edward was influenced by a vogue not exclusively English but shared by most of the aristocracies of Christendom in his day'. See also Vale, *Edward III and Chivalry*, pp. 16–24, for the international Arthurian prestige of Edward I and English knights.

[38] See Loomis, 'From Segontium to Sinadon', pp. 521–9.

[39] Especially in tracery patterns: see J. Bony, *The English Decorated Style: Gothic Architecture Transformed, 1250–1350* (Oxford, 1979), ch. 3; Coldstream, *The Decorated Style*, pp. 35–52.

[40] Loomis, 'Edward I, Arthurian Enthusiast', p. 117.

[41] Loomis, 'From Segontium to Sinadon', pp. 527–8.

[42] See Parry, 'Geoffrey of Monmouth and the Paternity of Arthur', pp. 271–7 for how Geoffrey conflated three historical Constantines, including Constantine the Great. See also Loomis, 'From Segontium to Sinadon', pp. 521–4.

[43] Gransden, *English Historical Writing*, pp. 443, 477–8.

magic departed'.[44] Rather the evidence suggests that Caernarfon is an Arthurian castle in all but name.

The potential implications of this conclusion for the design of castellated architecture will now be examined. It would be naive to imagine that every feature discussed below bears a connotation which must be specifically or exclusively Arthurian. Nor can it be certain that images are always being transferred from literature to architecture, rather than vice versa.[45] Vinaver has demonstrated that the interaction between visual art forms and the constructions of romance story-telling could be very close.[46] The later thirteenth century in England was a period of great artistic invention, known best through the development of the Decorated style. So it is to be expected that architects, like poets, would wish to entertain and dazzle their patrons, designing works of novelty and complexity as far as the constraints of the architectural process would permit. In certain instances, their creations would be derived from the content, or inspired by the climate, of Arthurian romance, as the largest body of literary chivalric material available. But it is important to stress that the general application of artistic imagination to castle architecture is potentially as relevant to the theme of this paper, even where no specific literary source can be discovered.

At Caernarfon, the turrets of the Eagle Tower and the variety of geometrical planning may be interpreted as such attributes of Arthurian enthusiasm. Both constitute decorative features well beyond the requirements of military and domestic function, evoking the wonder and excitement of the wish-fulfilling castles of romance.[47] A single turret projecting above the battlements of a tower can be justified as a look-out post and as housing a staircase; even two turrets can evolve from the latter purpose, as in the later Guy's Tower at Warwick Castle. However, the employment of three turrets in the Eagle Tower was unprecedented and, though logical explanations have been posited,[48] the telling impression which it still produces today suggests that it was designed rather (or also) for conscious effect (Pl. 1). Here, then, is an important progenitor of the

---

[44] Loomis, 'From Segontium to Sinadon', p. 531.

[45] For example, the (admittedly later) *Gawain*-poet's famous description of Sir Bertilac's castle may be based on an existing castle; see Thompson, 'The Green Knight's Castle', pp. 318–19.

[46] E. Vinaver, *The Rise of Romance* (Oxford, 1971), ch. 5.

[47] Whitaker, *Arthur's Kingdom of Adventure*, ch. 2.

[48] For example, imperial and heraldic meanings in Taylor, 'The King's Works in Wales', pp. 370–1; also Professor John White, in a personal communication, has suggested to the author that such a large tower could require three observation positions in a military contingency.

spectacular fighting decks of some later medieval towers, such as Caesar's Tower at Warwick (after 1356) and the gatehouse at Herstmonceux (c.1440, Pl. 7).[49] A similarly visual approach to the deployment of turrets is found at Conwy Castle, where single turrets crown each of the four corner towers of the inner ward and thus signify the position of the royal apartments (Pl. 5). This idea is more familiar in later palaces, notably the turreted ranges of the royal lodgings at Richmond (c.1498–1501) and the show façade to the royal lodgings at Nonsuch (1537–47),[50] both taking inspiration from the chivalric castle image. By this date continental intermediaries also deserve consideration, such as the existing rooftop architecture of the châteaux of the Loire, but behind all these streams may lie the Edwardian castles as a fundamental source.

Analysis of the plan of Caernarfon Castle reveals a designer playing with geometrical shapes for effect. The plan for the King's Gate seems to be based on three octagons linked in a triangular formation, the rear octagon intended as a vaulted reception hall presumably with side doors leading out to both wards. Strategists would argue that the 'bent entrance' is good defence, as appreciated at the better preserved example of this gatehouse design at Denbigh: but it is also dramatically chivalric, in the same spirit of display as the five sets of doors and six portcullises for which the King's Gate was provided. For the plan of the Eagle Tower, a decagon was chosen, with both hexagons and octagons employed for the smaller mural chambers.[51] The intended effect may be to impress and entertain the visitor, rather like the social circuit of variously shaped and decorated rooms in the 'social house' of the eighteenth century.[52] A similar repertoire

---

[49] There is no need to look invariably, or ultimately, to French precedent for these; see further R. K. Morris, 'The Architecture of the Earls of Warwick in the Fourteenth Century', *England in the Fourteenth Century*, ed. W. M. Ormrod (Woodbridge, 1986), pp. 172–4.

[50] See S. Thurley, *The Royal Palaces of Tudor England: Architecture and Court Life 1460–1547* (New Haven and London, 1993), pp. 27–32 (Richmond), 60–5 (Nonsuch).

[51] The only published plans which show the geometrical intricacies of the Eagle Tower satisfactorily are in RCAHM *Caernarvonshire*, II, between pp. 150–1. The best study of the geometry of the Welsh castles and its influence is J. M. Maddison, 'Decorated Architecture in the North-West Midlands: An Investigation of the Work of Provincial Masons and their Sources', unpublished Ph.D. thesis, University of Manchester (1978), especially ch. 1. It is worth noting that the decoration of the Eagle Tower, like that of the King's Gate, was not finally completed until the second decade of the fourteenth century.

[52] M. Girouard, *Life in the English Country House* (New Haven and London, 1978), ch. 7, esp. pp. 194–8.

of octagons, hexagons and triangles appears in miniature in the Eleanor Crosses of the 1290s, a suggestively chivalric series of monuments in the homage they pay to a lady (herself a known collector of romances)[53] and in their heraldic display. Elsewhere in castles of Edward's period, unusual geometry is used in the triangular plan of Caerlaverock (c.1300–10), which suggests that the castle's association with the chivalric poem the *Siege of Caerlaverock*, may be more than coincidental.[54] The visual qualities of triangular and polygonal geometry continued to hold an attraction for some later medieval castle-builders in England and on the continent, in spite of the dominant uniformity of quadrangular planning. The Château du Clain of John, Duke of Berry, shown as triangular in the month of July page of the *Très Riches Heures*, may be related to Caerlaverock; and hexagonal planning is to be seen, for example, at Old Wardour and Raglan Castles. The compact courtyard house at Wardour (1393) is an amazingly creative piece of planning, an architectural evocation of the world of romance: with a first-floor hall contrived above a fan-vaulted entrance passage, and formerly with a labyrinth of chambers more in keeping with the ingenious Elizabethan designs of Robert Smythson.[55]

Water defences and castellation are two other military features which lend themselves as well to an Arthurian interpretation in certain examples from Edward I's reign. It goes without saying that the origin of wet moats generally relates to issues of security, and that numerous castles were built adjacent to a river for strategic reasons. Nevertheless, new meanings could be added in the course of time, and it is proposed here that the romance image of the 'castle across water' is such a development, blurring the distinction between the real castle (originally the model for the literary image) and the castle in literature. In the thirteenth century *La Mort le Roi Artu*, the Castle of Douloureuse Garde is approached across a river, and King Arthur could see the arrival of the boat carrying the body of the maid

---

[53] See Loomis, 'Edward I, Arthurian Enthusiast', p. 116; Binski, *The Painted Chamber at Westminster*, p. 97.

[54] Caerlaverock was probably built by the English in the 1290s, and is described in the poem as shaped like a shield; B. H. St J. O'Neil, *Caerlaverock Castle* (Edinburgh, 1952), p. 3. For the poem and roll of arms, see Vale, *Edward III and Chivalry*, p. 23; she observes that Edward I is implicitly identified with King Arthur in the poem.

[55] For the design of Wardour (Wiltshire), see B. Morley, 'Aspects of Fourteenth-Century Castle Design', *Collectanea Historica: Essays in Memory of Stuart Rigold*, ed. A. Detsicas (Gloucester, 1981), pp. 111–12. Robert Smythson was familiar with Wardour from the conversion works he carried out there in c.1576–8; M. Girouard, *Robert Smythson and the Elizabethan Country House* (New Haven and London, 1983), pp. 78–81.

of Escalot from the hall windows of Camelot;[56] and there are many more examples throughout romance literature. A castle from Edward I's reign which would fit this identification is Leeds in Kent, well away from the active 'war zones' of the later thirteenth century.[57] It was acquired by King Edward and Queen Eleanor in 1278, and became one of their favourite residences, more of a country house in usage than a castle. For today's visitor the most striking feature is the moat which surrounds the two islands of the castle like a lake, and contributes to the picturesqueness of the whole (Pl. 10). That contemporaries thought similarly about the castle is implied by its thirteenth-century nickname, 'La Mote', and the fact that the smaller island housing the king's chamber was known as 'La Gloriette' (Pl. 11).[58] Significantly 'glorieta' is a Spanish word almost certainly introduced into England by Queen Eleanor of Castile, deriving from the Arabic term meaning a 'garden pavilion'.[59] In this respect, the Gloriette at Leeds compares to a toy castle, and the delicacy of its pedestrian bridge (originally wooden) conjures up in the romantic imagination the episode of Lancelot balancing on the sword-bridge as he crosses the water to rescue Guinevere from Meleagant's castle.[60] The visual and symbolic qualities which can thus be inferred for the moated setting at Leeds suggest that the perceived images of some other water-borne castle sites should be reconsidered. One thinks of Warwick, for example, with its association with Guy of Warwick; and Kenilworth, formerly flanked by its great mere, the setting for Roger Mortimer's round table event in 1279 and where Queen Elizabeth I was welcomed by the Lady of the Lake in 1575.[61] Indeed, at Bodiam Castle, the

---

[56]   J. Cable (ed.), *The Death of King Arthur* (Harmondsworth, 1971), pp. 71, 92.

[57]   In that there was no French threat to the south coast during the castle's main period of rebuilding, in contrast, say, to the situation a century later when Bodiam Castle was constructed. Charles Coulson's recent re-assessment has overstated the case against Bodiam's military capacity; C. H. L. Coulson, 'Bodiam Castle: Truth and Tradition', *Fortress*, 10 (1991), pp. 3–15.

[58]   *The History of the King's Works*, I, *The Middle Ages*, ed. H. M. Colvin *et al.* (London, 1963), pp. 695–6. The term 'gloriette' is also used at Corfe Castle from this period; *idem*, p. 622.

[59]   J. H. Harvey, *Medieval Gardens* (London, 1981), p. 106. See also T. Tolley, 'Eleanor of Castile and the "Spanish" Style in England', *England in the Thirteenth Century*, ed. W. M. Ormrod (Stamford, 1991), pp. 167–92.

[60]   For the popularity of toy castles at Edward I's court, see Binski, *The Painted Chamber at Westminster*, pp. 74–5. For depictions of the Lancelot episode, see Loomis, *Arthurian Legends*, pp. 70–1 and Figs 136–8.

[61]   For the Kenilworth round table, see Loomis, 'Edward I, Arthurian Enthusiast', pp. 116–17. For Elizabeth's visit, see F. J. Furnivall (ed.), *Robert Laneham's Letter: Describing a Part of the Entertainment unto Queen Elizabeth at the Castle of Kenilworth in 1575* (London, 1907), pp. 6–7.

moats have recently been reinterpreted as 'landscape features'.[62]

Evaluating the extent to which battlements might be perceived to be primarily for display is complicated by the relative lack of surviving or unrestored examples, especially from earlier periods like Edward I's reign. Indeed a full survey still needs to be published of merlons, loops and other such military fixtures. The documentary research of Charles Coulson into the socio-architectural implications of royal licences to crenellate validates the perception of such features as evoking a chivalric culture, whilst warning against classifying some smaller castles as 'merely ornamental' or 'sham', such as Acton Burnell.[63] It might be supposed that militarily functional battlements may be identified by the occasional survival of slots or sockets on the merlons to house shutters in the embrasures as, for example, on the south tower of Stokesay Castle (c.1291) and at Maxstoke Castle (c.1345). There is evidence, though, that such fixtures could be added later, thus potentially confusing the historical record.[64] Anyway, it appears that the more complete the array of military apparatus, the better it came to suit the literary romance image, as the description of Sir Bertilac's castle in *Sir Gawain and the Green Knight* suggests.[65]

On the other hand, display is clearly intended (in addition to any other function) where merlons are surmounted with carved figures, as on the Eagle Tower at Caernarfon (Pl. 1) and the contemporary residential tower of Roger Bigod at Chepstow Castle.[66] Additionally, battlements which survive without any signs of protecting the embrasures and without loops in the merlons are potentially non-military in function, especially where other circumstances are favourable. Such a case is the great hall and chapel

---

[62]   Coulson, 'Bodiam Castle', pp. 11–15, citing the RCHME survey of 1988.

[63]   See most recently C. H. L. Coulson, 'Specimens of Freedom to Crenellate by Licence', *Fortress*, 18 (1993), pp. 3–6. I am grateful to Charles Coulson for several discussions on matters concerning crenellation, and for setting me right about the 'sham' nature of Acton Burnell.

[64]   See L. F. Salzman, *Building in England Down to 1540: A Documentary History* (Oxford, 1952), p. 90: in 1313 at the Tower of London, John de Lynne was paid for 'piercing into the battlements for the insertion of hekkes [hatches]'.

[65]   Thompson, 'The Green Knight's Castle', pp. 318–22. Pierced merlons are common in micro-architecture in painting, e.g. in the Painted Chamber at Westminster, and the Peterborough Psalter (Brussels); see respectively Binski, *The Painted Chamber at Westminster*, colour Pl. III, and R. S. Loomis, 'The Allegorical Siege in the Art of the Middle Ages', *American Jnl of Archeol.*, 13 (1919), pp. 255–69, Fig. 4.

[66]   For the wider context, see Coldstream, *The Decorated Style*, pp. 45–6. The Caernarfon eagles are virtually unrecognisable today, and evidence presented by Arnold Taylor implies that they have been restored and augmented at least once; 'The King's Works in Wales', p. 371, note 1.

added to the bishop's palace at Wells by Edward's chancellor and most trusted official, Bishop Robert Burnell, in *c.*1285–90 (Pl. 14). The enormous windows beneath the crenellated parapets visually contradict any idea of defence, even though iron bars and shutters actually provided security, as also probably the enclosure of the site.[67] Moreover, the archaeology of the chapel's roof-line shows that the creasing was once higher, suggesting that the parapet may not have afforded adequate protection for men-at-arms (Pl. 9).[68]

The fabric of Burnell's other famous surviving work, Acton Burnell Castle in Shropshire (*c.*1284), provides evidence just as compelling for viewing its castellation as primarily for effect. It is a compact rectangular house with crenellated walls and four crenellated angle towers (Pl. 12), and has been compared to Anglo-Norman keeps.[69] Though much disfigured through ruin and later use as farm buildings, the original interior organisation can still be clearly read in its fabric. At the upper end of a first-floor hall was a two-storey chamber block, through which was the only purpose-built access to the wall-walk by way of a first-floor staircase in the south-west tower (Pl. 13).[70] As these were the best chambers, the design is distinctly inconvenient had its intentions been primarily military. The building's impracticality for this purpose is further revealed by the fact that it must originally have had a service range attached to the east wall, apparently timber-framed. The obvious prominence given to symbolism at Acton Burnell has been interpreted as establishing personal political authority,[71] but chivalric fashion may also be relevant to the crenellated appearance. Edward and his retinue stayed at Acton Burnell in 1283[72] and more visits may have been anticipated, which would have encouraged Bishop Burnell to build in a style suitable for court entertainment: rather like the later builders of Elizabethan prodigy houses. In which case, the

---

[67] For the palace, see R. W. Dunning, 'The Bishop's Palace', *Wells Cathedral: A History*, ed. L. S. Colchester (West Compton, 1982), ch. 10. Dunning (p. 235) asserts that the moat and outer walls are works of *c.*1340, but it seems highly probable that some form of enclosure existed before this date.

[68] This point needs checking further with measurements and a thorough investigation of the roof.

[69] J. West, 'Acton Burnell Castle, Shropshire', in *Collectanea Historiana: Essays in Memory of Stuart Rignold*, p. 91, n. 55.

[70] *Ibid.*, Fig. 14, for plans.

[71] *Ibid.*, p. 92.

[72] *Ibid.*, p. 90. Exactly when Burnell built this part of his castle – for there obviously was more – is an interesting issue, as implied in West's ultimately inconclusive text. The conventional view is that the work follows on from Edward's 1283 visit and the 1284 licence to crenellate, but it could predate them.

battlemented settings that appear in contemporary ivories and manuscript illumination, forming a backdrop to enactments of the 'Castle of Love' and other such festivities, are as pertinent an image for a courtier's residence.[73]

Architectural settings influenced by romance literature may also be detected in some churches of the period, especially those with a strong reliance on baronial patronage and in regions with a tradition for inventive stone-carving.[74] One related example is the unusual flower-patterned vault over the mausoleum of the Despenser family in the sanctuary of Tewkesbury Abbey (c.1320–40), perhaps evoking the Paradise Garden and the spiritual salvation of a knightly class.[75] Another is the east arm of St Augustine's Abbey at Bristol (now the cathedral), which was the burial place of the lords of Berkeley Castle throughout this period, a family risen to prominence in the military service of Edward I. The work, dating mainly to c.1310–40, is relatively small but enjoys an unique reputation amongst English churches for combining a hall church elevation with internal bridges across the aisles.[76] It also represents the earliest example in England of horizontal transoms consistently applied to a series of ecclesiastical windows (Pl. 16).[77] Both the bridges and the transoms are redundant in a general structural sense, in that much larger aisles and windows had been constructed successfully in preceding Gothic buildings; for example, Lincoln Cathedral, or Tintern Abbey, to name a more local and monastic comparison.

The designer's purpose may have been no more than to show off his artistic virtuosity, which in itself is relevant to our theme: but a deeper symbolism may also have been intended. A clue lies in the mimetic form of the bridges, which loosely recalls such features of contemporary timber construction as arch braces and tie-beams, and perhaps crown-posts too

---

[73] For the Castle of Love and related images, see Loomis, 'The Allegorical Siege', p. 255–69; and Binski, *The Painted Chamber at Westminster*, pp. 74–5.

[74] Here I refer particularly to early Gothic architecture in the west of England, which includes features antipathetic to the orthodoxy of French Gothic; see H. Brakspear, 'A West Country School of Masons', *Archaeologia*, 81 (1931), and most recently M. Thurlby, 'The Lady Chapel of Glastonbury Abbey', *Antiquaries Jnl*, 75 (1995), pp. 115–27.

[75] R. K. Morris, 'Tewkesbury Abbey: the Despenser Mausoleum', *Bristol and Gloucestershire Archeol. Soc. Trans.*, 93 (1974), pp. 142–55.

[76] The bridges and Bristol's numerous other idiosyncrasies have generated a considerable literature; see Bony, *The English Decorated Style*, pp. 35–6, n. 9.

[77] Earlier occurrences of the 'transom' derive from French Rayonnant ecclesiastical tracery effects, such as the group of Yorkshire churches of the late thirteenth century/early fourteenth century (e.g. York Minster nave, Bridlington Priory); from which derive 'feature' windows like Howden west window, which come closest to the Bristol form but only in single windows.

(Pl. 16).[78] The quotation, though not literal, is from the open roof of a secular great hall, and this is as likely a source for the transoms at Bristol as French rayonnant curtain tracery. Transoms had been used in an English secular context since at least the great hall of Winchester Castle (1222–36), and by the late thirteenth century they were fashionable in aristocratic great halls. Excellent examples survive in the west in the castles of Goodrich, Chepstow and Acton Burnell; and, finest of all, in Burnell's great hall at Wells (Pl. 15), which might even have influenced the Bristol design.[79] In these hall windows the transom was employed to divide a lower area with shutters and grilles from a glazed upper area, which might also have shutters, as may be seen in the background of many fifteenth-century Flemish paintings such as Jan van Eyck's *Arnolfini Wedding Portrait* (London, National Gallery). At Bristol, the transom loses any such function and has been subsumed under the fully glazed format of ecclesiastical traceried windows. It has been copied for effect, which the context here suggests is to make an association with a secular hall. It is a singular fact that the tombs of the Berkeleys line the aisles, which incorporate the transomed windows and mimetic bridges (Pl. 16); whereas the abbots are buried in the centre vessel (choir and Lady Chapel) under a more conventional Decorated lierne vault and devoid of secular architectural associations. The image from romance literature which would best explain the various references of the Bristol aisles is the Grail Hall, where the successful knight errant meets his Maker. The imaginative filigree stellar recesses which house the effigies intensify the other-worldly effect (Pl. 16, right).[80] Overall this is as appropriate an architectural setting for knightly burial as is the quest iconography of Ingham for an individual knight's monument.

A possible corollary of this interpretation is that some secular great halls were themselves viewed by contemporaries as evoking the Grail Hall or the feasting hall of one of the other romance castles.[81] The case would be stronger if the great hall is particularly magnificent, or if the site has relevant historical associations: criteria which are both satisfied at Burnell's

---

[78] See Bony, *The English Decorated Style*, p. 36. The analogy with a crown-post roof (Bony's 'king-post') is based on the way the ribs spring from a point in the centre of the bridge (equivalent of a collar beam), recalling the curved braces diverging from a crown-post.

[79] The great hall at Berkeley Castle also has transomed windows, though with simpler tracery and of slightly later date (*c*.1320–40).

[80] Bristol also has crenellated parapets like the Wells hall, and is thus one of a select group of churches at the head of a fashion which became popular in late Gothic architecture.

[81] See Thompson, 'The Green Knight's Castle', p. 324, for the importance of the great hall in *Sir Gawain and the Green Knight*.

79

great hall at Wells. The splendour of its windows and its display of crenellations has already been noted, and it was also one of the largest aristocratic halls to have been built in England in its time, at 115 feet by 59½ feet. Historically the most significant factor is the palace's situation only five miles from Arthur's resting place at Glastonbury. Burnell was building on a regal scale probably in anticipation of further royal visits, following that to Glastonbury in 1278. However, it could also be that the conception of the hall was influenced by a local Arthurian micro-climate recreated by Edward's opening of Arthur's tomb.

The image may have continued to capture men's minds in later periods, such as the rebuilding of the great halls at Westminster Palace and Kenilworth Castle in Richard II's reign. In favour of this interpretation at Kenilworth is the former approach to the castle across water and the documented Arthurian festivities there in the thirteenth and sixteenth centuries, described above. The great hall itself is one of the most sumptuously appointed large halls surviving from the later middle ages (Pl. 18). Everything about it excites wonder in the beholder[82] – the symmetry of the hall and towers seen from across the mere; its elevation to the first floor as an extension of the state apartments: the elaborately carved porch entrance and the enormous double-transomed windows: the fireplaces decorated with the latest Perpendicular tracery patterns, and with provision for tapestries to hang above. The builder of the hall and new apartments was John of Gaunt, duke of Lancaster, in whose circle of patronage it has been suggested that the *Gawain*-poet may have worked.[83] Moreover, Lancaster was commemorated in a chivalric style tomb in Old St Paul's, dressed in full armour beneath a shrine-like canopy hung with the knightly accoutrements of lance, helm and shield (Pl. 17):[84] a more orthodox

[82] Contemporary literary interest in fantastic halls, though architecturally more surreal than related to built examples, is represented in Chaucer's Hall of Fame, *c*.1379–80; see J. A. W. Bennett, *Chaucer's Book of Fame: an Exposition of "The House of Fame"* (Oxford, 1968), ch. III.

[83] R. S. Loomis, *Arthurian Literature in the Middle Ages* (Oxford, 1959), p. 529, n. 6. More recently Bennett has suggested that the poem was written to entertain the itinerant royal household; M. J. Bennett, 'The Court of Richard II and the Promotion of Literature', in B. Hanawalt (ed.), *Chaucer's England: Literature in Historical Context* (Minneapolis, 1992), pp. 3–20, esp. pp. 12–15. Goodman found no actual proof that Gaunt commissioned a literary work or rewarded an author, though he was a patron of Chaucer and one of his retainers was 'a voluminous writer of courtly verse'; A. Goodman, *John of Gaunt: the Exercise of Princely Power in Fourteenth-Century Europe* (Harlow, 1992), pp. 37–8.

[84] See Goodman, *John of Gaunt*, for Gaunt's 'lifelong delight in the finer points of jousting' (p. 37) and as 'a devotee of the combat' (p. 360). It was fairly common practice in the period for a knight's military accoutrements to be

rendition of themes from knightly tombs of the earlier fourteenth century and ultimately of Edward I's reign.

The architecture of his reign has been the main subject of this paper, which has endeavoured to show that at a particular moment in time, in particular buildings, Arthurian symbolism informed their design through the aspirations of their patrons and the imagination of their craftsmen. The Edwardian court had captured the spirit of Arthurian romance literature and, more significantly, had created a style which had given its ideals permanent monumental expression in stone. This new perception of castle architecture is as much a part of the Decorated style as the curvilinear tracery of churches, and its influence at least as great in late medieval Europe. The vocabulary of the Arthurian castle worked out in Edward's reign is the language of Warwick, Herstmonceux, Mehun-sur-Yèvre and la Ferté-Milon (Pls 7, 19); even if the phraseology becomes more clichéd and mannered as it enters the vernacular of late Gothic architecture.

---

given to the church in which he was buried; see J. and M. Vale, 'Knightly Codes and Piety', p. 27. Gaunt's tomb follows the general pattern of that of the Black Prince (d. 1376) in Canterbury Cathedral. For the latter, see C. Wilson, 'The Medieval Monuments', in P. Collinson et al. (eds), *A History of Canterbury Cathedral* (Oxford, 1995), pp. 494–8, where the practice of hanging arms on knightly graves is discussed; and Binski, *Westminster Abbey and the Plantagenets*, p. 197–8, placing the tomb firmly in a chivalric context.

The 'Rows of the Battle-Swan': The Aftermath of Battle in Anglo-Saxon Art[1]

JENNIE HOOPER

War is a bloody business. The manner of the fighting may vary from a pitched battle to a minor unplanned skirmish, but whatever the scale there are usually casualties. Written sources record the causes of war and the events of the campaigns, and at times give vivid descriptions of the field of battle. The visual impact of war is conveyed by the artist. War artists, be they medieval or modern, provide a differing interpretation of war. Unlike the written sources, artists stress either particular images or visual messages to their audiences. The artists of the First World War conveyed differing images of war, from the stark devastation of Paul Nash to the symbolism of Colin Gill, from the heroic advances of François Flameng to the horrors of death and injury depicted by Eric Kessington.[2] These artists conveyed the emotion and atmosphere of war in a way that photographs could not.

For the medieval artist the task was more complicated. The 'emotional' input of the artist was limited. It would be misleading the suggest that all medieval artists were totally restricted in their choice of illustrations by the dictates of the written sources. The medieval artist when illustrating war was expected to remain relatively faithful to the events that he was depicting and to capture the 'spirit' of the fight. The illustrations in the chronicles of Froissart, which provide seemingly accurate pictorial sources for the events and warfare of the Hundred Years War, are often cited as an example of this. In reality these illustrations are anachronistic products of the fifteenth century.[3] Images produced in the so-called 'chivalric' era are deemed by many to contain the true nature and essence of medieval warfare. However, the accuracy is debatable in some instances. There seem to be traditional artistic *topoi* which are followed. For example, one image

---

[1] In *Tøgdrápa* the ranks of the dead are described as 'the rows of the battle-swan', by Thorarin Loftunga (*English Historical Documents* [*EHD*], Vol. I, p. 340). D. Whitelock translates the 'swan' element as birds of prey which attend after a battle, or the 'ranks of slain men'.

[2] For example, Paul Nash, *Oppy Wood* (1917); Colin Gill, *Heavy Artillery* (1916); François Flameng, *American Advance at St Pierre* (1918); Eric Kessington, *Gassed and Wounded* (1918).

[3] A. Curry, *The Hundred Years War* (London, 1993), p. 15.

which has a long iconographic tradition is that of the symbolic decapitation.[4] The 'victim' kneels before his executioner, unarmed and almost sacrificial. The 'aggressor' clasps the hair of the victim and raises his sword high above his own head ready to complete the deed. Examples of this set iconography can be traced within all areas of medieval art, both secular and religious. However, not all aspects of warfare iconography were retained throughout the medieval period. Some images seem to disappear. The question arises whether certain images fell from grace. Did some images fall outside the acceptable repertoire of 'chivalric' warfare? Were artists, or their patrons, censoring the more graphic and unsavoury aspects of war? Were others excluded because they had become obsolete and deliberately omitted as a direct response to changes in military practice?

The changing nature of English warfare in the eleventh and twelfth centuries has received much detailed scholarship. The 'chivalric' era is clearly associated with the arrival of the Normans and the shift of emphasis towards French culture and military practice away from the Anglo-Danish. John Gillingham suggests that there existed within twelfth-century Anglo-Norman society a conception that 'barbarian' or 'native' warfare was, by its very nature, inferior to that practised by the more 'civilised' French.[5] In reality many of the elements traditionally associated with 'chivalric society' can be traced prior to the twelfth century, for example both in ninth-century Francia and in Anglo-Saxon England. The importance of courage, largesse, loyalty to one's lord and comrades, as well as feats of arms, were the prerequisites of most military-based societies. Gillingham argues convincingly that it was a shift in the technology of warfare that led to fundamental changes in attitudes. Prior to this there were certain aspects of war that had been universal. The taking of slaves was a traditional by-product of campaigning throughout Europe. Armies which engaged in battle suffered high casualty rates, as the majority of fighting was hand to hand combat. Advances in body armour, increased use of cavalry, the growing financial rewards of ransoming, and other factors, resulted in the older traditions of war retreating into areas where Anglo-Norman influence did not penetrate. The campaigns launched by the Anglo-Normans against the Scots, Welsh and Irish brought these two styles of warfare into direct

---

4   J. Kiff, 'Images of War: Illustrations of Warfare in Early Eleventh-Century England', *Anglo-Norman Studies*, 7 (Woodbridge, 1985), p. 180. Also D. Bernstein, *The Mystery of the Bayeux Tapestry* (London, 1986), pp. 171–4.

5   J. G. Gillingham, 'Conquering the Barbarians: War and Chivalry in Twelfth-Century Britain', *The Haskins Society Journal*, 4 (1993), pp. 57–84; see also M. J. Strickland, 'Slaughter, Slavery or Ransom? The Impact of the Conquest on Conduct in Warfare', *England in the Eleventh Century. Proceedings of the 1990 Harlaxton Symposium*, ed. C. Hicks (Stamford, 1992), pp. 41–59.

contrast in the twelfth century and for the Anglo-Norman sources advanced the concept that 'barbarian' warfare was inferior and that the enemy, by default, did not deserve the same 'courtesy' afforded in 'civilised' warfare.[6]

The general tenet of Anglo-Norman sources is that warfare prior to the Norman conquest lacked a proper sense of honour and was essentially 'barbaric'. This is clearly untrue. One has only to look at the poem of *The Battle of Maldon* to see the acts of 'honourable' men and the scorn placed upon those who lacked 'honour'. Chansons de geste and other 'chivalric' texts do not have the monopoly of heroic deeds on the battlefield. Literary sources describe battles in terms of their 'heroic' elements, including 'heroic' deaths. The brave Byrhtnoth, although wounded and his sword arm 'unstringed', was still able to exhort his men to continue the fight before being 'hewed' down along with Wulfmear and Aelfnoth; 'the two followers followed in death'.[7] The injuries inflicted in battle and the manner of death are often graphically described by the poets. In *The Battle of Maldon*, Byrhtnoth

> old in war-skills let the weapon drive
> through the man's throat, his thrust steered
> so as to reach right to the reaver's life-breath.
> And afresh he struck him, stabbed so swiftly
> that the ring-braid burst apart; breast pierced
> through the locked hauberk, in his heart stood
> the embittered ash-point.[8]

Byrhtnoth's own death, which began with an injury to his sword arm, would appear to be based upon more than mere poetic licence. In Sarah Wenham's report on Anglo-Saxon skeletons buried at Eccles in Kent, the variety of injuries incurred testify to the accuracy of some literary descriptions.[9] These skeletons are attributed to the ninth/tenth century. Skeleton II had extensive injuries to the head, lower back and arms. The blow to the right forearm would, in Wenham's opinion, have made it almost impossible for the man to have held a sword, and the injury to the left elbow would have had the same effect. It would seem that Byrhtnoth's

---

[6] *Ibid.*, p. 183; cf. M. J. Strickland, *War and Chivalry: The Conduct and Perception of War in England and Normandy, 1066–1217* (Cambridge, 1996), pp. 1–7, 19–30 and esp. pp. 291–340.

[7] *The Battle of Maldon*, in M. Alexander (trans.), *The Earliest English Poems* (London, 1977), ll. 181–4.

[8] *The Battle of Maldon*, ll. 140–6.

[9] S. J. Wenham, 'Anatomical Interpretations of Anglo-Saxon Weapons Injuries', *Weapons and Warfare in Anglo-Saxon England*, ed. S. Chadwick Hawkes (Oxford, 1989), pp. 123–41.

'unstringed' arm, which rendered him unable to defend himself and led to his being hewn down, was not a unique fate. Some of the skeletons also show evidence of injuries to the back that may have been incurred either in the battle itself, after they had fallen, or in the flight from the field.[10] Those who met a similar fate to the men at Eccles are not excluded from the literary sources. In the *Finnsburg* fragment the poet refers to them; 'good men lay around, a pale crowd of corpses'.[11] The fate of the fallen did not end with death. The carnage of the battlefield led to bodies being left *in situ*, prey to the attentions of wild animals and birds. Nearly all literary sources which relate to Anglo-Saxon battles make some reference to this consequence of war. In *The Battle of Maldon*, 'the fighting was now imminent, glory was at hand; the time was come when doomed men were to perish there. A din was upraised there; ravens wheeled about, and the eagle greedy for carrion.'[12] The *Brunanburh* poem describes the birds, ready to devour the bodies of the slain; 'the dusky-coated one, the black raven with its horned beak, [remained on the field] to share the corpses, and the dun-coated, white-tailed eagle, the greedy war-hawk, to enjoy the carrion, and that grey beast, the wolf of the forest'.[13] These descriptions were not just a feature of the Anglo-Saxon sources. In *Knútsdrápa* there are references to the wolf's jaw and the raven enjoying the aftermath of battle. In *Eríksdrápa* reference is made to warriors giving 'swollen flesh to the raven' and to the wolves which 'waded in blood, and the wolf-pack got plenty of wolves' fodder. The wolves enjoyed the grey beasts' ale.'[14] The description of the battlefield at the end of the fighting could be just as graphic as that of the combat itself. Given the intended audience for these poems it is unlikely that the poets were presenting an image that was not in essence realistic.[15]

One would expect to find the harsh realities of pre-Conquest warfare, evident in literary and archaeological sources, mirrored in the art of the period. Medieval battles can be depicted in a variety of media including wall-paintings, manuscript illuminations, sculpture and metalwork. In the

---

[10] *Ibid.* Six skeletons are discussed in the study. I, V and VI show cranial injuries to the left side indicating sword blows to the head. Skeletons II, III and IV exhibit a variety of injuries attributed to 'disorganised fighting'.

[11] *The Fight at Finnsburg*, in Alexander, *The Earliest English Poems*, p. 56, ll. 36–7.

[12] *The Battle of Maldon*, ll. 103–6.

[13] D. Whitelock (trans.), *The Anglo-Saxon Chronicle* (New Jersey, 1961), p. 70, 'C', *s.a.* 937.

[14] *EHD*, I, p. 336; *Knútsdrápa*, l. 11, p. 334, *Eríksdrápa*, ll. 13–14.

[15] D. Whitelock, 'The Audience of Beowulf', *From Bede to Alfred. Studies in Early Anglo-Saxon Literature and History* (London, 1980), pp. 1–105. *The Gododdin*, written *c.*600, refers to a warrior being 'food for the ravens', K. Jackson (ed.), *The Gododdin: The Oldest Scottish Poem* (Edinburgh, 1969).

allegedly 'barbaric' period some depictions of battle occur in stone carvings and sculpture. The Aberlemno stone (Aberlemno no. 2) has been closely associated with the events of the battle of Nechtansmere where the Northumbrians were defeated by the Picts in 685 (Pl. 20). The exact dating of this sculpture is problematic, and although an eighth-century date is generally accepted, this is largely based upon comparisons with similar stones and the dating of Pictish art is ripe for reassessment.[16] The Aberlemno stone shows three rows of warriors, each row engaged in a different aspect of the conflict. The upper row depicts a mounted Pict in pursuit of a Northumbrian horseman who appears to be fleeing the field, discarding his shield, sword and spear in the process. The central section shows three men on foot facing a mounted warrior. The final row depicts two horsemen facing each other. The exact narrative sequence of these figures can be debated, but the remaining figure has no such ambiguity. To the lower right-hand side of the scene a figure appears in the process of falling backwards. He has no visible injury or weapon and his round shield lies useless by his side. A bird pecks at the base of his intact helmet, attacking either the lower portion of his face or neck. The bird's wings are closed, implying that it is not attacking while in flight. This suggests that the figure, although depicted as almost vertical, is intended to represent a victim of the battle. Here the fate of men killed on the field of battle is not minimised but is given equal emphasis with the major events of the battle itself. This dead man forms an integral part of the composition, not an additional afterthought. The position of this figure is possibly no accident. In manuscript illumination the bodies of the dead or injured are usually shown directly under the feet of the fighting troops or under the hooves of their horses. In Carolingian manuscripts such as the Golden Psalter of St Gall and the Utrecht Psalter, contorted bodies, usually in conjunction with their shields, lie beneath advancing troops. In Anglo-Saxon manuscript illumination the same configuration appears. In sculpture too the image of a figure contorted beneath the hooves of a mounted warrior has a long pedigree. The late first-century tomb of the cavalryman Flavius at Hexham Abbey is not in essence that far removed from the cast plate on the Sutton Hoo helmet.[17] However, the artist creating the Aberlemno sculpture does

---

[16]   N. Hooper, 'The Aberlemno Stone and Cavalry in Anglo-Saxon England', *Northern History*, 29 (1993), pp. 188–96; L. Alcock, 'The Rhind Lectures 1988–89: A Synopsis. An Heroic Age: War and Society in Northern Britain, A.D. 450–850', *Proceedings of the Society of Antiquaries of Scotland*, 118 (1988), p. 331.

[17]   J. Campbell (ed.), *The Anglo-Saxons* (Oxford, 1982), pl. 66, p. 66. The tombstone of Longinus at Colchester has a similar scene. A decorative plaque on the Sutton Hoo helmet also shows a figure holding onto the bridle of the

not attempt to place the 'dead' beneath the importance of the living. Both elements have parity and importance in the total picture of the battle.

This theme continues, in part, in another carving, this time in ivory rather than stone. The Franks Casket, attributed to the first half of the eighth century, contains a scene of warfare, which probably illustrates Egil (Wayland's brother) defending his house against attack.[18] Egil uses arrows to repel his attackers. These are seen lodged in the shield of one of the front line as well as embedded in the chest of one of the fallen, who still holds his sword. Those men killed in the encounter form the central section of the composition, and their odd arrangement in part derives from the position of the central boss, which is no longer extant.[19] The fallen men in the lower part of the composition are much smaller than Egil and considerably smaller than the warriors to the left of the scene. One lies, apparently naked, upon his back holding his shield above his chest. At his feet a figure is bent over, the left hand is held to the head and the hair falls forward towards the fallen man. Whether this small figure is injured or is adopting a traditional iconographical stance implying grief and mourning is difficult to establish. Neither of these figures has any visible injuries, although their stance indicates that they are both 'victims' of the conflict. An even more intriguing figure appears at the top of the scene, directly above these latter victims. In many ways this larger figure mirrors that of the fallen man at the base of the boss. Both are reminiscent of the depictions of the fallen Goliath found in insular art.[20] While the figures balance the composition it is unclear whether the upper figure has fallen from the top of Egil's house or whether the artist is implying that the dead were lying all around.

From the ninth and tenth centuries there are fewer examples of English sculpture that contain specific battle images. Although the Lindisfarne grave marker depicts a group of warriors intent on fighting there is no visual evidence which records the aftermath of a pitched battle.[21] In

horse which tramples him.

[18] *Ibid.*, p. 94.

[19] L. Webster and J. Backhouse (eds), *The Making of England. Anglo-Saxon Art and Culture A.D. 600–900* (London, 1991), pp. 101–3. Also I. N. Wood, 'Ripon, Francia and the Franks Casket in the Early Middle Ages', *Northern History*, 26 (1990), pp. 1–19.

[20] For example at the top of the Cross of Muiredach, Monasterboise, mid-tenth century, there appears to be a hand to hand combat with spears and round shields. One of the spears seems to be piercing a bird which rests behind his opponent. Also see B.L. Cotton, MS Vitellius, F. XI, folio 1, produced in Ireland in the first half of the tenth century, and Cambridge, St John's College MS C.9(59), folio 7v, an early eleventh-century manuscript.

[21] Webster and Backhouse, (eds), *The Making of England*, p. 155.

contrast, many of the Gotland 'stelae' (memorial stones) contain images of hand to hand combat which form a part of other symbolic elements illustrating the mythology of Odin. In many of these carvings a wolf and raven are depicted in close attendance, although taking no active part in the aftermath of the fighting. In a few of these carvings the conflict is more graphically portrayed, for example the Lärbro I stone. In the upper portion of the carved stone, which is divided into horizontal sections, a battle takes place. The action moves from left to right, opening with two men within a house; the central section contains infantry which advance towards the final figure, on the right, who lies underneath his horse. Above the combatants two huge birds are flying, both with hooked beaks. A third bird sits behind a fallen man, pecking and pulling at his body.[22] In another stone from Tjägvide a bird appears to be sitting upon a fallen spear and pecking at the feet of a figure, although the figure is hard to distinguish as the stone is partially damaged.[23] The evidence is fragmentary, but the implication could be that the artists of the Gotland 'stelae' were familiar with carrion birds and considered them to be an acceptable part of the battlefield iconography.

A fragment of English sculpture, dating from the eleventh century, contains an intriguing and problematic scene which may relate to a possible depiction of a battlefield (Pl. 21). The exact date of this piece is difficult to determine.[24] The scene depicted has been interpreted by Biddle as representing the story of Sigismund and the she-wolf in the *Volsunga Saga*. He identifies the image of the wolf licking honey from the face of Sigismund, who then bites off the wolf's tongue and avoids death.[25] The choice of the *Volsunga Saga* was, Biddle suggests, in response to Cnut's commission to visually symbolise the common ancestry between the

---

[22]   G. Jones, *A History of the Vikings* (Oxford, 1975), p. 343, pl. 13.

[23]   Statens Historiska Museum, Stockholm. The stone was dedicated to Iurulf by his brother. See P. H. Sawyer, *The Age of the Vikings* (London, 1971), plate 5.

[24]   J. Backhouse, D. H. Turner and L. Webster (eds), *The Golden Age of Anglo-Saxon Art, 965–1066* (London, 1984), pp. 133–5, no. 140. Martin Biddle suggests a dating between 1016 and 1035, although George Zarnecki in *English Romanesque Art, 1066–1200* (London, 1984), pp. 150–1 disagrees and favours a later, post 1070 date. David Wilson in *The Bayeux Tapestry* (London, 1985), pp. 206–8 discusses the relative problems of both suggestions.

[25]   The wolf plays an important part in Viking mythology; for example wolves pursue the Sun and the Moon, they are associated with Odin, and the wolf Fenrir is Odin's enemy at Ragnarok. See H. R. Ellis Davidson, *Gods and Myths of Northern Europe* (London, 1964), pp. 48–69. The raven also has close associations with various Odin stories. The wolf appears too in Pictish imagery, for example the Ardross fragment at the Inverness Museum and Art Gallery.

English and Danish royal houses. In short, the sculpture formed part of a larger frieze which, by implication, was a propaganda exercise to give additional legitimacy to a conquering king. As such it could be argued that it performed a similar purpose to that of the Bayeux Tapestry.[26] However, the explanation for the figure to the left of this Sigismund scene, clad in mail and armed with a 'straight broad-bladed sword' is lacking.[27] Given the close proximity of the departing warrior and the fallen figure might this scene not simply have represented the end of a battle? The mail-clad figure is departing from the scene of conflict, his sword re-sheathed and hanging from a strap around his waist. Contemporary iconographical comparisons depict soldiers departing the battlefield in a similar manner, with their backs to the fighting. The figure nearest to a battle depicted in Ælfric's Hexateuch, an eleventh-century English manuscript, has his sword clearly placed in the scabbard and his hand firmly holding the pommel, indicating that he has ceased hostilities. His departure is emphasised by the wide step of his legs and the separation of his tunic. The mail figure on the Winchester fragment has distinct iconographical similarities. The fallen man in the Winchester sculpture, one could conjecture, has become prey to those wolves and dogs so frequently attested to by the literary sources as feasting on the bodies of the slain and mortally wounded.[28]

Biddle suggests that this frieze fragment may well fit into the tradition of the embroidered narratives of the Bayeux Tapestry and the lost Ely tapestry which recorded the battle of Maldon. Is it possible that this frieze may also record a battle, possibly a Danish victory and the conquest of England by Cnut? It could be argued that the Viking predilection for stone memorials, as opposed to embroidered records of monumental events, was more in tune with contemporary Danish attitudes.[29] This hypothesis relies upon accepting the dating of the sculpture suggested by Biddle. However, Zarnecki rejects the Biddle hypothesis as relying on too many assumptions. The similarity of the armour in the Winchester fragment to that depicted in

---

[26]   C. R. Dodwell, *Anglo-Saxon Art. A New Perspective* (Manchester, 1982), p. 138.

[27]   Backhouse, Turner and Webster (eds), *Golden Age of Anglo-Saxon Art*, p. 133.

[28]   It is difficult to reconstruct the original composition of this fragment, although Biddle suggests that it forms part of a much larger frieze. It certainly contained six other sections, which would have shown the remaining parts of the soldier and the horizontal figure. Whether this was one independent panel or part of a larger scheme is unknown. The Aberlemno stone also shows a man attacked by a bird with his back to the battle. B. L. Cotton MS. Tiberius C.VI shows the followers of Goliath leaving the battle scene in a similar manner, as do many other Anglo-Saxon manuscripts.

[29]   The recording of heroic events in narrative embroideries was more of an English tradition, although the eighth-century Oseburg hangings clearly indicate that it was not an English monopoly.

the Bayeux Tapestry, and the lack of any other Anglo-Saxon works which have stylistic comparisons to the Winchester fragment, prompt Zarnecki to suggest a date post-1070. The dating of this fragment is problematic. As an iconographical witness to military activity in the eleventh century it remains ambiguous.

In the embroidery genre there is one undisputed masterpiece of the eleventh century which has a strong military theme. The Bayeux Tapestry is the most graphic visual description of a near contemporary battle and includes many insights into the reality of the battlefield. In the lower borders, beneath the feet of those still fighting, the dead appear as the Normans advance against the English shield wall. The carnage continues with broken weapons and contorted bodies littering the ground. Some lie, almost peacefully, directly under their shields while elsewhere there are severed heads and three fallen horses. The advance of the archers in the lower border forms a visual break between the falling dead in the midst of battle and the next scene. Here a figure from the main narrative falls into the lower border in a three-scene fall. Firstly he is shown with an arrow either in his mouth or at the base of the nose-piece of his helmet. He is then shown in fall, and finally lies horizontal in the border. The archers then reappear briefly before the scene of Harold's death is shown in the main narrative. Beneath Harold's death the aftermath of the battle is depicted. The dead are dispossessed of their mail, pulled unceremoniously over their heads. A figure collects swords, bundling them under his arm as he tries to add another to his collection. Shields are being gathered up as well, although two figures seem to be disputing the prize of a green shield. At the very end of the battle, as the Normans pursue the remaining English forces, the lower border shows naked bodies lying close to each other, perhaps suggesting a pile of corpses.

The artist has made no attempt to disguise the activities of people on the battlefield as the conflict ends. The looting of the dead by the 'lesser ranks' was not considered an unsuitable topic. This degree of reality is impressive, but there initially appears to be no reference to the other fate that could await the dead besides the looting of their persons. However, in the upper border, directly above the battlefield debris in the lower border, a pattern seems to emerge. The main part of this section is inhabited by a collection of birds and dogs or wolves. It opens and closes with a tripartite depiction of a bird, one which is not found elsewhere in the Tapestry's zoomorphic repertoire (Pl. 22). The artist has gone to considerable lengths to indicate the hooked beak and the white feathers. In the first scene the bird appears to be landing, looking back towards the end of the battle. In the second scene a slightly cruder version of the white bird appears to prepare to fly away from the battlefield. The final image immediately follows; a part of a white bird's wing apparently extended for flight is visible, although the body of the bird has been lost. This common Anglo-Saxon practice of a three-scene narrative appears elsewhere in the Tapestry. It is of course open to interpretation whether the artist is attempting to convey the arrival and departure of carrion birds in the wake of the battle. Another feathered bird, possibly a raven as it has dark feathers, is placed opposite the first white bird in this sequence, which suggests that the placing of these birds in the borders was deliberate. Given the detailed depictions of the other elements associated with the aftermath of fighting, it would be surprising to find the role of the 'greedy war-eagle' overlooked. The inclusion of such a theme may imply another element in the 'Englishness' of the Tapestry.

This close association of carrion birds with the bodies of the dead is most strikingly illustrated in an early eleventh-century Canterbury manuscript, British Library MS Cotton Claudius B. IV, which is also known as Ælfric's Hexateuch (Pl. 23). The drawing appears in the Genesis story, in the context of the ark. The text, which follows the Genesis A tradition, recounts that Lamech's son released a black raven to see if land had reappeared after the flood. The raven did not find land, but it 'perched exulting upon a floating corpse; the dun-feathered bird was unwilling to return'.[30] The artist provides an alternative image to that created by the text. The raven is clearly shown sitting on a man's head, pecking at the face. However, the man is not floating in the water. He would seem to be decapitated, and the head placed upon a pole on the prow of the ark. The artist has taken some pains to be accurate, adding streams of blood to the pole, and carefully showing the beard, hairstyle and ears of the man. The eyes are missing, possibly eaten by the raven. The raven sits, with its talons extended, in a strongly naturalistic pose. Exactly why the artist chose this form is unclear. The reference to the 'dun-feathered bird', which is a feature of the heroic literature relating to warfare, may have misled the artist into incorporating a drawing more in keeping with secular realities rather than the biblical story. It is impossible to be precise as to the artist's exact motivation. The drawing of the raven is interesting in itself. There are visual parallels with the birds of the Bayeux Tapestry, especially in the details of the banding at the top of the tail, the delineation of tail feathers and other feathers. The strong curve of the beak and the open mouth are also similar. While the iconography of the raven in Ælfric's Hexateuch is not identical to those above the close of the battle in the Bayeux Tapestry, there are stylistic links.

---

[30]   G. P. Krapp (ed.), 'The Junius MS', *Anglo-Saxon Poetic Records*, I (New York, 1931), p. 45, ll. 1447–8. In Genesis 8:6–7, the raven only goes 'to and fro, until the waters were dried up from off the earth'.

The association between the bodies of the fallen and the activities of carrion was not unknown in the corpus of manuscript illumination prior to the eleventh century. One of the most important Carolingian imports of the period, the Utrecht Psalter, contained images of battles which are extremely detailed and influential. On folio 46v, there are illustrated bodies which are 'given to be meat unto the fowls of heaven, the flesh of thy saints unto the beasts of the earth'.[31] Birds fly off carrying limbs in their beaks. Lions, foxes and dogs/wolves stand on the bodies, while others eat. One body has a dog/wolf standing upon his back while it bites his head. The drawing is extremely graphic, and another similar drawing is shown on folio 86r.[32] These Carolingian pictures were copied c.1000 and the English artists faithfully reproduced many of the original compositions. Other eleventh-century English psalters contain similar images. The eleventh-century artist of the Bury Psalter included a bird flying with a hand held in its talons and a head grasped within its beak.[33] The head is held by the forehead or eyes. This bird is stylistically similar to the other birds already referred to. There is also a dog/wolf which is in the act of eating other parts of the dismembered body, possibly the legs. These two detailed and striking images appear at the very top of the drawings which surround the text and they are treated in the same manner as other more traditional religious themes on the same folio, such as the martyrdom of St Stephen.

The Anglo-Saxon manuscripts produced in the tenth and eleventh centuries followed many of the existing conventions representing warfare in a largely biblical context. However, this did not preclude the artist from incorporating some aspects of contemporary warfare within his visual repertoire. Although the text was biblical in Ælfric's Hexateuch the artist illustrates the battle of the kings and the capture of Lot in a contemporary manner (Pl. 24).[34] The main features of the narrative are shown, including Lot's capture and the departing figure of the escaping messenger who informed Abraham of the events. However, there is a visual emphasis on certain themes. In the battle scene the artist pays particular attention to the role and importance of the sword, which is enlarged in proportion to the figures. The importance of the sword to the higher military classes of Anglo-Saxon England is well attested.[35] A later artist has clearly added extra

---

[31] Psalm 79:2–3.

[32] B.L. MS Harley 603. See D. Tselos, 'English Manuscript Illumination and the Utrecht Psalter', *Art Bulletin*, 41 (1959); Kiff, 'Images of War', pp. 177–94.

[33] Biblioteca Apostolica Vaticana, MS. Reg.Lat.12, folio 87v; Psalm 78(79), Bury St Edmunds c.1025–50; E. Temple, *Anglo-Saxon Manuscripts 900–1066* no. 84, pp. 100–2.

[34] B.L. MS. Cotton Claudius B. IV, folio 24v; Genesis 14:10–13.

[35] H. R. E. Davidson, *The Sword in Anglo-Saxon England. Its Archaeology and*

emphasis to certain elements of the original drawing that he regarded as important, such as the byrnie. Despite additions the original composition is intact and the battle is visually dramatic and descriptive. The flow of the picture from left to right follows the start of the battle and the eventual flight to the mountain. The realities of war are not ignored: two figures are shown huddled behind a shield while their colleagues begin the flight from the battlefield. The kings are shown in hand-to-hand fighting, their heads being held by the crown and the beard as their bodies are attacked by swords. Beneath them lie the dead, who have suffered a bloody decapitation. The general impression given in this drawing is one of movement and a sense of reality. The centre of the battle is confused. The composition, following the text, illustrates the terrain and gives the indication that the battle takes place in a valley, which in this picture almost takes on the appearance of a pit into which the combatants have tumbled. In this respect the artist evokes not only the story but also some of the emotional tumult of war.

The battle continues on the next folio showing Abraham informed of Lot's capture, followed by a mounted retinue setting off to recover Lot, leading to the ensuing hand-to-hand combat of battle and the triumphant return on horseback.[36] Although the depictions of hand-to-hand combat are effective, they all fit into a particular convention that is applied to most of the illustrations of fighting in this manuscript.[37] The manner of death is decapitation, stylised and following models regularly used throughout ecclesiastical art. The narrative of the battle scenes moves from left to right. The enemies are shown departing the scene at the extreme right, turning their backs on the battle and smartly walking away with their swords

---

Literature (Oxford, 1952); I. Peirce, 'Arms, Armour and Warfare in the Eleventh Century', *Anglo-Norman Studies*, 10 (1987), pp. 237–58. Swords had social status attached to them in the 'lower ranks' the spear was more usually used, sometimes a knife. In the Bayeux Tapestry, the English fighting on the hill lack any armour and fight with shield and spear. One man seems to have a sword still in the scabbard, and uses both hands to wield an axe. The looting of the dead is undertaken by those also lacking armour, which seems to imply that this was an activity undertaken by the 'lesser ranks' as a means of equipping themselves.

[36] C. R. Dodwell and P. Clemoes (eds), *British Library Manuscript Cotton Claudius B. IV. Early English Manuscripts in Facsimile*, 18 (Copenhagen, 1974).

[37] B.L. MS Cotton Claudius B. IV. Some of the battle scenes are shown in a three-tiered composition, a similar concept to that used in the Aberlemno stone. On folio 127v, a woman is put to the sword (Numbers 31:6–18), but shows no physical injury although the intent is clear. On folio 152v, kings are shown hanging by their arms from trees before their bodies are placed into a cave (Joshua 10:26–7).

sheathed – an iconographical convention which has already been mentioned in this paper. Although the illustrations in Ælfric's Hexateuch follow certain iconographical *topoi*, they also reflect some aspects of contemporary warfare. On folios 24v–25v the men ride to battle, dismount to fight and return on horseback. Bodies are depicted as mutilated and dismembered. However, there is no hint of the fate of those bodies left on the battlefield. Carrion beasts, in this instance, form no part of the visual imagery. The exclusion of birds and wolves could well be a direct response to a lack of textual references. Alternatively, it could be an early reflection of changing conventions of military iconography. The same story illustrated in Ælfric's Hexateuch appears in part in a late eleventh-century wall painting at St Savin-sur-Gartempe. This representation of the story is highly stylised.[38] The text describes an attack at night by Abraham and his trained household 'servants' where the enemy are forced to flee and are pursued into Hobah. The text is clear that Abraham and his retinue 'smote' the enemy prior to their flight. In this wall painting the action portrayed is static and somewhat passive. Abraham and his forces adopt the stance of a more defensive group in close order, using spears to repulse a cavalry attack that could be offered by the enemy. The artist has represented a military tactic that was in use in contemporary society. He is clearly receptive to transferring 'common practice' to a biblical story and cannot be accused of slavish adherence to antiquated exemplars. However, there is no suggestion of any violence having taken place. There are no fallen horses or dismembered bodies. The main thrust of the narrative for this artist is of paramount importance and the reality of the carnage of military engagements is not deemed as relevant, or possibly even as appropriate, for the ecclesiastical setting.

It has been argued that in manuscript illumination the role of war and conflict is far more related to theological and moral lessons than concerned with depicting a totally accurate image of a battlefield.[39] Such texts as the *Psychomachia* of Prudentius relate specifically to the battle between good and evil, the virtues and the vices.[40] The battlefield is the soul of man. The artistic debts to late antique exemplars are well known. It is generally

---

[38] O. Demus and M. Hirmer, *Romanesque Mural Painting* (London, 1970), pls 138–9.

[39] J. J. G. Alexander, 'Ideological Representations of Military Combat in Anglo-Norman Art', *Anglo-Norman Studies*, 15 (Woodbridge, 1992), pp. 1–24. In B.L. MS. Harley 603 the illustration to Psalm VII shows a lion standing upon the naked contorted body of a man, waiting to 'tear out my soul and pull it to pieces'.

[40] H. Woodruff, 'The Illustrated Manuscripts of Prudentius', *Art Studies*, 7 (1929), pp. 3–49.

accepted that the battle between the virtues and the vices is symbolic and the outcome never in doubt. Manuscript illumination played to a particular audience in the same way that vernacular poetry was directed towards certain members of secular society. The story was important, the rights and wrongs of the conflict and the role of the main protagonists were of primary concern. Alexander illustrates how the 'moral' lessons of warfare in the illuminated manuscripts of the late eleventh and twelfth centuries were enforced and ideals of 'acceptable' combat, to reach moral goals, were promoted.[41] This sanitised battle created images which were, in general, devoid of the unpleasant realities of war. Although death was shown, illustrations followed acceptable conventions dictated by the text. Bodies are thrown from chariots, fall upon their swords, are pelted with stones or meet other fates. In a few instances additional elements were introduced, contemporary armour, mail coats and helmets, as well as swords. In a few of the twelfth-century manuscripts there are minor compositional changes. In a manuscript produced at Regensburg c.1150 the artist has included two dogs which feast upon the back of Jezebel, who represents a defeated vice.[42] This image is reminiscent of the psalter tradition, which was noted in the Utrecht Psalter and elsewhere. In this illustration there are no carrion birds and the body of Jezebel, which the animals eat, is intact. The artist appears to be following biblical iconography rather than introducing a perceptive allusion to any element of contemporary warfare. The fate of the vices was deserved, the moral victory won. In this battle the leaders were of primary concern, everything else was of secondary importance to the main narrative.

Religious texts had their own agenda where warfare was concerned. It is important to remember that the commissioning of art was not an ecclesiastical monopoly. Art created for a secular audience; had to fulfil the same criteria as literature created for a secular audience, it must depict the reality of their experiences. Ecclesiastical art was concerned with the spiritual or moral issues the depiction of battles was part of this ethos. Realism was not essential. It has been suggested that those texts which do include more contemporary elements were directly commissioned by members of the laity. The commissioning of manuscripts by lay patrons was not a new phenomenon. A manuscript produced in the early tenth century, the Leyden Maccabees, contains not only illustrations of warfare based upon I Maccabees but also the text of Vegetius.[43] This configuration

---

[41]   Alexander, 'Ideological Representations of Military Combat', p. 5.
[42]   Munich, Bayerische Staatsbibliothek, Clm. 13002, f. 3v, 4r.
[43]   J. Dunbabin, 'The Maccabees as Exemplars in the Tenth and Eleventh Centuries', *Studies in Church History*, Subsidia 4, ed. K. Walsh and D. Wood (Oxford, 1985), pp. 36–8. Religious writers used the example of military

strongly implies that the text was commissioned by a secular person with an interest in warfare and the lessons that these texts could teach. Anglo-Saxon manuscripts were also commissioned and possibly represent the more contemporary aspects of warfare as a direct response to the interests of the patron. Certainly religious texts which contained military themes and allegories were addressed to secular persons.[44] Yet the images used even in these manuscripts become increasingly symbolic rather than descriptive.

In contrast to the artistic trends of the late eleventh century, the literary sources of the Anglo-Norman 'chivalric age' are filled with graphic descriptions of war and the carnage that resulted. Guy of Amiens' description of the battle of Hastings, although considered to be later than the events recounted, creates a vivid picture. The exact manner of Harold's death is not for the squeamish; '... cleaving his breast through the shield with his point, drenching the earth with a gushing torrent of blood; the second smote off his head below the protection of his helmet and the third pierced the innards of his belly with his lance; the fourth hewed off his thigh and bore away the severed limb; the ground held the body thus destroyed'.[45] The description of the demise of the English 'rank and file' is confined to the midst of the battle where emphasis is mainly upon the quantity of the dead, especially within the English shield wall; '... bodies could not be laid down, nor did the dead give place to living soldiers, for each corpse though lifeless stood as if unharmed and held its post'.[46]

The aftermath of the battle at Hastings is only described briefly and provides an interesting insight. The Norman dead, according to Guy, are taken up by the duke, who 'buried them in the bosom of the earth'. One would assume that this implies at least some nominal form of Christian burial. In marked contrast, 'the corpses of the English, strewn upon the ground, he left to be devoured by worms and wolves, by birds and dogs'. These actions are also referred to in other sources. William of Jumièges is characteristically succinct; William returned to the battlefield during the

leaders to flatter their patrons.

[44] M. Godden, 'Apocalypse and Invasion in Late Anglo-Saxon England', *From Anglo-Saxon to Early Middle English: Studies presented to E. G. Stanley*, ed. M. Godden, D. Grey and T. Hoad (Oxford, 1994), pp. 130–62. Godden refers to Ælfric's connections with Sigeweard, Æthelwaerd and Æthelmaer, all of whom would be categorised as *bellatores* by Ælfric, *ibid.*, pp. 138–40.

[45] C. Morton and H. Munz (eds), *The Carmen de Hastingae Proelio of Guy of Amiens* (Oxford, 1972), pp. 35–7. Guy does not include an arrow in the eye in Harold's death, but generally follows the account illustrated by the Bayeux Tapestry including the injury to Harold's thigh. See Strickland, *War and Chivalry*, pp. 4–6.

[46] *The Carmen de Hastingae Proelio*, p. 37.

night and 'at first dawn, having despoiled the corpses of his enemies and buried the bodies of his dear comrades, he took the road which leads to London'.[47] William of Poitiers is typically more descriptive and reflects that William '... could not gaze without pity on the carnage, although the slain were evil men, and although it is good and glorious in a just war to kill a tyrant'. It is this source which refers to William taking Harold's body to his camp and giving it to William Malet for burial. The refusal to hand Harold's body to his mother for burial is used to present William the Conqueror in a better light and inflate his reputation. For William

> ... considered it wrong that Harold should be buried as his mother wished, since so many men lay unburied ... it would have been just if wolves and vultures had devoured the flesh of these English who had rightly incurred their doom, and if the fields had received their unburied bones. But such a fate seemed cruel to the duke, and he allowed all who wished to do so to collect the bodies for burial.[48]

The reference to 'vultures' may reveal more about Poitiers' learning and desire for classical parallels than an accurate picture of the aftermath of Hastings. William of Poitiers is more concerned with stressing the 'courtesy' of the Normans in the matter of the disposal of the dead in marked contrast to other sources.

The sources appear to agree that the Norman dead after the battle of Hastings were buried. It would seem that in general the right of burial largely applied only to the victors who 'held the field'. The burial of the enemy was a matter for the victorious commander's discretion. Other eleventh-century English sources would appear to support this. In the *Encomium Emmae Reginae* the Danish victors, led by Thorkell, 'buried such of the remains of their comrades as they could find'.[49] After the battle of Ashingdon the Danish dead were also buried and the survivors 'stripped the spoil from the limbs of their enemies, but left their bodies to the beasts and the birds'.[50] This practice seems to have continued after the Norman conquest had been completed. Richard of Hexham's account of the aftermath of the battle of the Standard (1138) records that:

> by the righteous judgement of God, those who cruelly massacred multitudes and left them unburied, giving them neither their country's nor a foreign rite of burial (leaving them prey to dogs, birds and wild beasts), were themselves either dismembered and torn to pieces or left to

---

[47] William of Jumièges, *Gesta Normannorum Ducum*, in *EHD*, II, pp. 229–30.

[48] William of Poitiers, *Gesta Willelmi ducis Normannorum et regis Anglorum*, in *EHD*, II, p. 244.

[49] A. Campbell (ed.), *Encomium Emmae Reginae*, Camden Society, Third Series, 72 (London, 1949), p. 23.

[50] *Ibid.*, p. 29.

decay and rot in the open air.[51]

Increasingly the post-conquest sources become less interested in these distasteful post-battle details. The consequences of battle for the 'rank and file' were not even worthy of description and the fate of the leading protagonists of the battle becomes the main theme. Even in these instances only succinct details are included, but rarely embellished.[52] The 'chivalric' texts do not negate the horrors of war, but the emphasis is more on the deeds of the living and the manner of death, not the fate of the corpse. In Anglo-Norman literature it would seem that the dramatic impetus moves quickly on to the rest of the campaign after the individual battle has been won or lost.

This trend seems to be reflected in the contemporary illustrations of war. Cavalry engagements increasingly take precedence over infantry encounters. Bodies are included in many of these illustrations lying underneath the hooves of horses and the feet of men. They are bloodied, often dismembered and in some instances extremely graphically portrayed. The extent of the injuries incurred is, in some instances, shown to indicate the prowess of the victors. Certain earlier elements are clearly lacking in the iconographical repertoire. Although there are some references in written sources to the wolf, raven and eagle being present in the wake of battle, there are no comparable visual scenes. The absence of these elements may reflect the gradual changing of artistic conventions in the depictions of battles, with the increasingly ecclesiastical monopoly on the production of the visual arts having a different iconographical agenda. Although the ravens, eagles and dogs survived despite artistic neglect, the disappearance of the wolf from the battlefield imagery could be linked to a rapid process of extinction, as wolves retreated to remote areas to escape hunters.[53] Their

---

[51]   *EHD*, II, p. 347. Archaeological evidence at Repton suggests that bodies were left outside *c*.875 and became disarticulated prior to later burial. The bodies show no evidence of violence upon the bones, implying that they were not the victims of a violent battle. It is tempting to conjecture that these skeletons, with their large dimensions, were either the unfortunate victims of plague or epidemic, or all met their deaths through injuries which left no trace on the bones, such as strangulation. It is difficult to assess the Repton information fully, as publication of the full archaeological report is still pending.

[52]   After the battle of Evesham (1265) Montfort's mutilated body was buried though, as the Evesham chronicler records, in 'less than honourable fashion'. The remaining troops are described as lying around the town and monastery like 'slaughtered sheep'; D. Carpenter, *The Battles of Lewes and Evesham 1264/5* (Keele, 1987), pp. 64–6.

[53]   There are references to wolves in northern England in 1070: Florence of Worcester, *Chronicon ex Chronicis*, ed. B. Thorpe, 2 vols (London, 1848–9), II,

absence could also possibly be accounted for by fewer battles, lower mortality rates in response to technical changes in the manner of fighting and a more general usage of mass burial. These changes would in turn create less carrion for wolves, dogs and birds.[54] The violent deaths on the battlefield continued. The excavation of the burial sites related to the battle of Wisby (1361) revealed the extent of the injuries as well as invaluable information about armour and weaponry.[55] Common mass graves, where the dead were interred shortly after the battle, appear to be used. The inclusion of arms and armour suggests limited looting by the victors, and the largely intact skeletons would imply that there was no major carrion activity.[56]

The fate of the dead after a battle is an aspect of war that few care to dwell upon. In this paper I have attempted to question whether the visual perceptions of the fate of the dead reflect the literary and archaeological sources or followed a separate agenda. There are inherent problems in this study. Although warfare was an important element in Anglo-Saxon history the visual sources are limited. Many are unique, often being difficult to interpret and compare. The chronology of these images is sometimes impossible to establish accurately. The illustration of war by Anglo-Saxon artists largely represented their perceptions and values, although some external influences, such as the Utrecht Psalter, were absorbed into the English repertoire. New external influences, in the wake of the Norman conquest, were also largely assimilated into English art. To the Anglo-Norman artists of the twelfth century some of the visual pre-conquest traditions did become redundant, representing part of an older era which had no place in the image of 'modern' warfare. The eagles and the wolves may well have been hungrier, with fewer battlefield bodies to feed upon, but what 'feasting' there was went unrecorded by the Anglo-Norman 'war artist'.

---

p. 4. By 1200, most wolves were confined to unpopulated areas in Wales, Westmoreland and the moors; J. Steane, *The Archaeology of Medieval England and Wales* (London, 1985), p. 167.

[54] Gillingham, 'Conquering the Barbarians', pp. 75–7.

[55] B. Thordeman, *Armour from the Battle of Wisby 1361*, 2 vols (Uppsala, 1939).

[56] Recent excavations of a burial pit near the site of the battle of Towton (1461) also revealed fully articulated skeletons, but without clothing or weapons. The extensive injuries to the heads suggest the men, possibly infantry, were poorly equipped. The majority of the bodies are buried on an east/west alignment, suggesting some form of religious observance. I am grateful to A. Boylston for this information.

The Ways of War in Medieval Manuscript Illumination: Tracing and Assessing the Evidence

PAMELA PORTER

'For before the historian can try to make valid use of a visual source, however undemanding, however simple, he has to know what he is looking at, whether it is authentic, when and for what purpose it was made ...'.[1] In relation to the practicalities of waging war in the middle ages, visual representations have a particularly important role to play as source material. Thanks both to the wear and tear of frequent use and the destructive effects of damp and corrosion, direct evidence of military artefacts from the medieval period, particularly the earlier centuries, is sparse. Consequently historians and others with a special interest in the use and development of armour and military equipment are forced to rely heavily on secondary sources unless some more ingenious way of exploring the topic can be devised.[2] Although written accounts may contain terminology and descriptions which are extremely valuable for this purpose, visual sources have, at least in theory, the advantage of being able to offer immediate concrete evidence of the type that could otherwise be gained only from the direct observation of an artefact. The extent to which the information that they offer is reliable, however, is an aspect that must be well understood if they are to have any real value as documentary sources.

Although visual images may be transmitted through a variety of objects, the pictorial representations of war that survive from the middle ages are dominated in terms of sheer numbers by the illustrations appearing in manuscripts – a state of affairs which occurs not only because books tend to have a lower casualty rate than other kinds of object, but also because individual volumes are very likely to contain multiple examples, most of them rather well preserved after leading a sheltered existence in closed volumes on shelves.[3] Such an abundance of material offers

---

[1] F. Haskell, *History and Its Images* (New Haven and London, 1993), p. 2.

[2] E.g. adopting a practical approach for considering the construction of mail. See E. M. Burgess, 'The Mail-Maker's Technique', *The Antiquaries Journal*, 33, 1, 2 (1953), pp. 48–55; *idem*, 'Further Research into the Construction of Mail Garments', *The Antiquaries Journal*, 33, 3, 4 (1953), pp. 193–202.

[3] For example, a manuscript of the *Grandes Chroniques de France ou de Saint Denis*, made in France in the second quarter of the 14th century and now in the

enormous scope to those with an interest in the ways of war, but only a very small proportion of these illustrations have ever come to light, chiefly because there is neither a quick nor a convenient way of tracing them, nor is there even any obvious way of specifying the range of volumes in which they appear. Descriptions in library catalogues frequently lack details of miniatures or list only brief captions so that a wide variety of subsidiary and incidental material remains totally unrecorded, and subject indexes which might provide assistance with the task are rare, while those that do exist frequently obscure military elements by incorporating them under wider and less specialised topic headings. In most cases the only certain way of tracing fresh material is to make a systematic search through the manuscripts themselves, an undertaking which can pose problems both of identification and difficulties of access, as well as demanding unlimited quantities of time.

The purpose of this paper is to provide some general guidance for those interested in tracking down new visual material relating to warfare in manuscripts, and to consider some of the factors that need to be taken into account when assessing the historical reliability of the information that they contain.[4] The miniatures selected as accompanying illustrations, with a couple of exceptions either English, French or Flemish, are all taken from the collections of the British Library. One or two will certainly be familiar, but for the most part they are believed to be relatively unknown as representations of military subjects.

The first important point that needs to be made about warfare images in manuscripts is that they are universal, but before examining the portrayal of war in the wider context some consideration needs to be given to illustrated military manuals, ostensibly the class of source material with the highest potential for providing accurate and reliable technical information on the topic of military operations. The practical conduct of war in the middle ages had its roots in theories inherited from Graeco-Roman Antiquity, an age when the treatment of warfare as an exact science gave rise to a vast corpus of technical literature in which successive generations of writers sought to clarify, refine and modernise the work of their predecessors. The manuals that they produced covered all aspects of the topic, and the technical and highly detailed texts that these manuals

---

British Library (B.L. Royal MS 16G VI), contains a total of 418 miniatures of which approximately half portray either military scenes or armed figures.

4   This paper has its origins in an after-dinner talk at the 1995 Harlaxton Symposium where it was illustrated with a large number of slides. As such it does not represent a piece of focused research, but is intended as a general survey covering some of the points that are not always well understood by those who are unfamiliar with manuscript illustrations.

contained were routinely supplemented by detailed explanatory drawings, included as an integral component of the work; the complex applied mechanics involved in the construction of siege machines, for example, could have been extremely difficult to master from a verbal account alone.[5]

There is a lack of direct information about the survival of manuscripts of these works in western Europe during the years immediately after the fifth century when many texts became lost or neglected, but Greek illustrated manuals are still known to us through eleventh-century copies made in the Byzantine Empire, where the study of military science in the antique tradition continued to flourish.[6] New manuals, modelled on Greek prototypes, were also produced. More of these Byzantine manuscripts remain available than have actually survived to the present day, thanks to some industrious copying in the sixteenth century when there was a revival of interest in the study of military science in western Europe. The charge that repeated copying has corrupted the visual aids and deprived them of their technical value[7] need not concern us here, as the illustrations still have sufficient content to demonstrate quite clearly that they were conceived as a tool for a more complete understanding of the text.[8] This can be seen from a treatise on poliorcetics compiled by the tenth-century theorist of uncertain origin who is generally identified as Heron of Byzantium. Although the original is no longer extant, Heron's work, an adaptation and 'modernisation' of the works of early Greek writers, survives in a near-contemporary manuscript of the eleventh century[9] of which there is also a faithful sixteenth-century copy.[10] The text is furnished with a large number of attractive coloured drawings which, not least because of the inclusion of figures, resemble book illustrations rather than technical visual aids, but which are so full of detail and linked so closely to the text that there can be little doubt that they were included to fulfil an explanatory

---

[5] Some of these texts are translated and discussed in E. W. Marsden, *Greek and Roman Artillery: Technical Treatises* (Oxford, 1971).

[6] The Byzantine theorists are detailed in A. Dain, 'Les stratégistes byzantins', *Travaux et Mémoires*, 2 (Paris, 1967) pp. 317–92.

[7] E.g. Marsden, *Greek and Roman Artillery*, p. vi.

[8] For reproductions of some of these illustrations, see e.g. R. Schneider, 'Geschütze auf handschriftlchen Bildern', *Jahrbuch der Gesellschaft für Lothringische Geschichte und Altertumskunde*, Ergänzungsheft 2, 1907; *idem*, 'Griechische Poliorketiker', *Abhandlungen der Königlichen Gesellschaft der Wissenschaften zu Göttingen*, phil.-hist. Klasse, N.F., XI (Berlin, 1908), pp. 1–109, pls I–XI; XII, 5 (Berlin, 1912), pp. 1–87, pls I–VII.

[9] Codex Vaticanus Graecus 1605.

[10] B.L. Additional MS. 15276, made in northern Italy in about 1542. Described, together with the Vatican manuscript, in A. Dain, *La tradition du texte d'Héron de Byzance* (Paris, 1933), pp. 25–33, 51–8.

WAYS OF WAR IN MEDIEVAL MANUSCRIPTS

function. There is, for example, an account of an elaborate battering ram supported on an eight-wheeled mobile penthouse, which can be moved in any direction. The accompanying drawing follows the text precisely, showing the ram suspended from the structure by strong ropes, its battering end equipped with a crossbeam bearing a net that can be used for scaling walls, while an enclosed area surmounting the structure provides a shelter for observing the defensive measures of the enemy. In proportion to the figures using it the entire structure is massive, confirming the statement in the text that it is so heavy that it requires a hundred men to move it. Another drawing shows two floating structures designed to be employed in attacking a fortified town from the sea, each consisting of a pair of small boats bridged by a platform, one carrying a ram for weakening the fortifications, the other bearing a structure with a high bridge for entry over the top of a wall. A technical note is introduced by the portrayal of massive busts, one at each end of the platforms, which in the text are identified as stabilisers to enable the structure to be more easily positioned for safe access in rough weather. The mutual dependence of narrative and illustrations, the sophisticated and sometimes extravagant nature of some of the devices described and the fact that such warfare treatises are frequently found in manuscripts in association with other technical works, often by the same authors, all suggest that these antique and Byzantine works on military science were almost certainly written as much for academic interest as for any practical needs that they may have served.

The evidence of surviving manuscripts suggests that this widespread tradition of the study of military science as a discipline for its own sake seems not to have survived into the middle ages in western Europe, although it made a reappearance during the fifteenth century with the renewal of interest in the teachings of antiquity.[11] Otherwise there is an almost total absence of what might be termed 'technical' illustrations in those works dealing with military theory that appeared in the manuscripts of western Europe from the tenth to the fifteenth century.

This is perhaps all the more surprising as the practice of war was dominated throughout the middle ages by the military thinking of antiquity. The most influential theorist was the fourth-century writer, Flavius

---

[11] For example, manuscript evidence of this is provided by B.L. Additional MS. 24945, a 15th-century Italian luxury copy of *De re militari*, a manual compiled soon after 1450 by Roberto Valturio of Rimini. There was a particularly strong atmosphere of technological creativity in Italy at this time; the personal sketch-book of a near-contemporary anonymous engineer from Siena, also in the British Library (Add. MS. 34113), contains many designs for military machines and equipment, adapted from the works of the early 15th-century engineer known as Taccola.

Vegetius Renatus, whose *De Re Militari* was widely circulated both in Latin and in vernacular translations and adaptations, a fact that can be deduced not only from the number of extant medieval book lists and library catalogues in which it is included, but also from the fact that over three hundred manuscripts of the work survive.[12] Another ancient work that was popular, although apparently to a somewhat lesser extent if the number of surviving manuscripts can be taken as evidence, was the early second-century manual of Sextus Julius Frontinus, a collection of examples of military stratagems from Greek and Roman history which would have served as a useful adjunct to a more theoretical treatise such as that produced by Vegetius. Medieval manuscripts of Frontinus are frequently decorated or illuminated, but in general they lack 'technical' illustrations. One exception to this is an unusual fragment, now in the British Library, which consists of nine leaves from a copy made in Naples in the mid to third quarter of the fourteenth century (Add. MS. 44985). Here the text is written in double columns of two to thirteen lines above large coloured drawings without borders or background, occupying about three-quarters of the page. Assuming that the text was complete and the same format was followed throughout, the entire volume must have been extremely grand and was undoubtedly produced for an important, most probably royal, patron. The drawings, dominating the pages in relation to the text, portray the individual stratagems with a precision that implies that their primary function was intended to be explanatory. Thus an illustration may simply demonstrate the use of equipment such as the grappling hook devised by C. Duellius and employed against the Carthaginians (Pl. 25) or it may include representations of different stages of a single confrontation to demonstrate a particular set of consequences, as when Hannibal is shown harassing the Roman camp with night attacks, making the Romans too exhausted to withstand a morning assault.[13] The format of the manuscript, so unusual

---

[12]   C. R. Shrader, 'A Handlist of Extant Manuscripts containing the *De Re Militari* of Flavius Vegetius Renatus', *Scriptorium*, 33 (1979), pp. 280–305, lists 243 Latin versions, seventy-eight vernacular translations and three manuscripts in more than one language. This list includes only those volumes available at the time at which it was made; Shrader also refers to four Latin versions known to be lost or destroyed and to a further 200 references which he was unable to link positively to any of the extant manuscripts, some at least of which are likely to refer to untraced copies. These figures, which exclude other lost or undiscovered examples, are likely to represent a mere fraction of the total number actually produced; see also Professor Allmand's study in this volume, above, pp. 30–45.

[13]   Sulla's defences against Archelaus (f.1v) and his success with Archelaus's battle-line in confusion (f.2) are reproduced in J. Alexander, 'Italian Manuscripts in British Collections', *La Miniatura Italiana fra Gotico e*

for its time, suggests that it may possibly have been copied from a much earlier volume, now lost, although it may of course simply reflect a conscious attempt to mimic the antique style.

This fragment is something of a curiosity, and as far as I have been able to ascertain has no counterpart in the surviving manuscripts of the *De Re Militari* of Vegetius, where the use of illustrations is in the main very restrained, whether the text occurs in an individual volume or as part of a composite collection. Individual copies, either in the original Latin or in vernacular translation, are frequently small enough to have been portable,[14] suggesting that they were designed to be carried on campaign for reference as well as – or possibly rather – than for study. The practical constraints of size militate against the inclusion of an elaborate scheme of illustration in these volumes and many are totally plain, while those that appear to have been intended as luxury copies have extensive decoration, but little if any pictorial material.[15] Occasionally miniatures are used at the start of the work or to indicate the beginnings of chapters, but any such illustrations that have a military theme are normally of a generalised nature – a siege scene or knights in combat, for example – and are clearly not intended to be didactic. Even when illustrations appear to have a direct connection with the text, their function is illustrative rather than explanatory. This is demonstrated by a miniature at the beginning of an early fourteenth-century manuscript of one of the French translations. Beside the presentation scene, the most commonly found image in this type of manuscript, the artist portrays two young men in armour practising vital military skills, the one fighting at the pile, the other mounting a horse fully armed (Pl. 26). Although these two activities are appropriate to the training of recruits as described in chapter 1, the representations appear to have no clear explanatory function. At least one other similarly-dated French manuscript of this translation of Vegetius[16] makes use of the same two figures in an opening miniature, suggesting a standard illustration which may well have been widely used.

Rinascimento' I, Atti de II Congresso di Storia della Miniatura Italiana (Cortona, 24–26 September 1982), figs. 3, 4.

[14] E.g. B.L. Add. MS. 4713, a late 15th-century copy of the English translation made in 1408 for Thomas, Lord Berkeley, measures 220 x 160mm and is 30mm deep. B.L. Royal MS. 18 A.XII, another copy of the same translation made in 1483–5 for Richard III, measures 244 x 152 x 45mm.

[15] E.g. B.L. Add. MS. 11698, made in France in the late 13th century, which has exquisite decorated initials throughout.

[16] Dresden, Oc. 57, f.1, reproduced in G. G. Vitzthum, *Die Pariser Miniaturmalerei* (Leipzig, 1907), Pl. IV.

Military manuals thus prove rather disappointing in terms of tracing specific visual source material, and so representations must be sought in a less focused context. Away from the military manuals it is true to say that warfare images are universally found, appearing either as complete miniatures where the main subject is a scene of combat, or in an incidental way where there are, for example, armed figures included in a non-military setting. The classes of manuscript in which such material is likely to occur are sometimes rather easy to specify, as with illustrated chronicles and works based on historical events. Later in the period the demands of wealthy patrons gave rise to the production of some sumptuous volumes containing historical narratives, and a small body of detailed and exceptionally well-executed fifteenth-century warfare scenes from these volumes[17] has become the stock-in-trade of picture researchers, with the result that certain images are reproduced in all sorts of appropriate, and frequently inappropriate, contexts. Because the easy availability of these well-known illustrations in published volumes can readily satisfy demand, smaller miniatures in the same manuscripts, perhaps less striking in their overall impact but often extremely valuable in portraying details of military dress and equipment, have often been overlooked. A case in point is an illustration of a siege showing cannon and accoutrements (Pl. 27), one of a number of relatively unfamiliar small miniatures in a handsome late fifteenth-century volume containing William of Tyre's *History of the Crusades* in French translation (Royal MS. 15 E.I). Made in Flanders for Edward IV, this manuscript is extremely well known for its excellent large miniatures which, despite their anachronistic content, have become very familiar by virtue of their frequent appearances in all manner of illustrated literature on the Crusades. Such grand fifteenth-century volumes might be assumed to represent the culmination of a long tradition of chronicle illustration but this tradition is in reality rather a short one, as the practice of adding illustrations to what were essentially factual records did not gain ground until comparatively late in the medieval period. Nevertheless there is still much scope for tracing relevant representations among the illustrated chronicle manuscripts produced from the late thirteenth century onwards, in particular an extensive sequence of copies of *Les Grandes Chroniques de France*. Although exceptionally well-endowed with relevant images,[18] these volumes are very under-exploited as a resource for military material.[19]

---

17 Some of the most notable examples are the large miniatures in volume III of Jean de Waurin's *Chronique d'Angleterre* (B.L. Royal MS. 14 E.IV), a luxury volume made for Edward IV in Bruges in the late 15th century.

18 See note 3.

19 Surviving manuscripts are listed in A. D. Hedemann, *The Royal Image*, California Studies in the History of Art (Berkeley and Los Angeles, 1991), pp.

Battle scenes and individual armed figures may also confidently be sought in illustrated Bibles and liturgical works with sequences of biblical illustrations. It is not difficult to identify certain subjects, like the Massacre of the Innocents, which can be expected to offer some kind of portrayal of military dress (Pl. 28), while other subjects like David and Goliath are often worth exploring. Lives of the saints or representations of saints in other works should not be overlooked. In this context the figure of St George most readily springs to mind, but other warrior saints such as St Maurice are likely to be portrayed in the guise of a medieval soldier, as is demonstrated by the mounted knight in a late fourteenth-century French Book of Hours (Pl. 29). Although the general presentation of such figures may conform to a universal stereotype, their arms and armour normally reflect the variations of contemporary or near-contemporary usage, as illustrated by the difference between the elaborate full plate-armour of St Maurice in a German prayer book of the fifteenth century (Pl. 30) as against the mail and surcoat of the earlier representation.

Although with a little imagination certain other categories of manuscript likely to be worth exploring can be identified easily enough – for example universal histories, biographies or chivalric literature – there are also many very unexpected places where representations of military dress and equipment can be found. An extensive review of these would not be appropriate here, but three examples are included to suggest something of the variety of these unusual sources. The first is an early thirteenth-century bestiary where the representation of the elephant, illustrating the brief statement in the text that Persians and Indians place wooden towers on elephants in order to fight from them, offers a recognisable representation of contemporary armour and weapons (Pl. 31). Perhaps even more surprising is the occurrence of military material in an early fourteenth-century volume containing a compilation of the Decretals issued by Pope Gregory IX. Although written in Italy, this manuscript was illuminated in England where its lower margins were filled with lively illustrations taken from a wide variety of sources including biblical tales, popular literature and the activities of everyday life in the middle ages. Among these illustrations there are numerous detailed representations of armed knights (Pl. 32), chiefly in a chivalric rather than a military context but valuable nevertheless for details of their arms and armour; also included in the volume is a rather well-known depiction of a battle at sea (Royal MS. 10 E.IV, f. 19). The last of my examples is an illustration to Ptolemy's star catalogue, which appears in a manuscript thought to have been made for Henry VII in about 1490 (Pl. 33). Although the depiction of

187–92. The work also includes a catalogue of many of the manuscripts (pp. 193–268) and reproductions of some miniatures.

Mars as a warrior in an astrological manuscript is perhaps not so surprising,[20] a portrayal of the southern constellation 'Argo' certainly does not readily suggest itself as a likely candidate for the representation of a military subject, yet in this miniature the configuration of stars in the constellation is superimposed on a realistic image of a medieval warship with cannon blazing.

The diversity of these examples goes some way towards hinting at the ubiquity of warfare representations in manuscript miniatures, indicating that those seeking to locate such material should not rely on inspiration alone but should be prepared to make thorough and diligent searches through a very wide range of illuminated material, a task which is not only time-consuming in itself but also complicated by potential difficulties of access. So do the ends justify the means? Representations of medieval warfare are certainly evocative, but how is the historian to make valid use of them after they have been found? Haskell's observations, quoted earlier, underline the need to have a thorough understanding of the nature and purpose of a visual source before trying to extract information from it. His last point, namely the need to know the purpose for which the illustration has been made, has particular relevance in the case of medieval miniatures, where it is important to be aware of the fact that these pictures are illustrations in books lacking the kind of space and freedom available to full-scale paintings, a fact which may well have repercussions for sizes and perspectives. A historiated initial showing the siege of Jerusalem in a mid thirteenth-century French manuscript of William of Tyre's *History of the Crusades* (Pl. 34) demonstrates that a skilled artist may be able to condense a highly detailed scene into a very small area,[21] while it also reveals how perspectives are likely to be altered to emphasise important figures or activities. Of course this is not necessarily true in all miniatures, and without external corroborating evidence it can be practically impossible to tell whether relative dimensions within a scene are accurate or not, or whether the artist has been constrained in certain respects by the limited space available. Consequently the drawing of any conclusions based on visual estimates of size is an exercise that must be approached with the utmost caution.

Haskell's other points concern authenticity, the identification of subject matter and date. Taken in the broadest sense there can be no question that manuscript miniatures are authentic in that they offer a view of warfare as seen through medieval eyes – but to what extent are these eyes to be regarded as truthful and objective? It is a fact almost too well known to repeat that medieval artists display little sense of historical accuracy or

---

[20]   See e.g. B.L. Add. MS. 41600, f. 54v.
[21]   The initial measures approximately 42 x 45mm.

commitment, so that specific events such as the battle of Hastings are likely to be portrayed in contemporary terms (Pl. 35). This carries the implication that artists were relying heavily on what they knew and thus were producing an accurate record of their own times, but it is important to remember that they were using this material in a creative way rather than documenting information either for their own or for future generations. In their terms it was necessary only to convey recognisable images, and in cases where no confirmatory evidence is available from surviving artefacts, written descriptions or technical illustrations in manuals, it is difficult to know whether or not details are to be trusted. For example, medieval artists used a number of different techniques for portraying mail, yet there is no material evidence to confirm that such a wide variety of patterns actually existed. Accurate portrayal of mail on such a small scale would have been a very intricate and time-consuming task, and in all probability artists merely made use of accepted artistic conventions or used their powers of imagination to convey their meaning, occasionally putting different techniques to practical use in order to make distinctions between groups of opponents or different types of armour.

Medieval artists generally had no trouble in conveying an unambiguous representation of military objects, but there is no reason at all to suppose that they must have possessed specialised technical knowledge of military equipment, and frequently it is evident that such knowledge has been completely lacking. A mid fourteenth-century manuscript of a French translation of Marco Polo's travels contains an account of the attack on the city of Saianfu, an episode in which siege engines hurling huge stones play such a prominent role that the artist is almost under an obligation to indicate their presence in the accompanying miniature (Pl. 36). Here the artist's portrayal of one of these giant engines has clear pictographic value but virtually no technical credibility, suggesting that its originator was barely familiar with such a piece of equipment. This is clearly not true of the artist responsible for an illustration in the lower margin of a Book of Hours made in Maastricht in about 1300, the subject of which is probably taken from a fable or allegorical tale (Pl. 37). Here an ass operates a very convincing trebuchet, credible in its proportions and with its construction details clearly visible, which has every appearance of complete technical accuracy. Its similarity to examples portrayed in later, and presumably earlier, military manuals[22] suggests that its artist either possessed direct knowledge about this type of siege engine through design or observation

---

[22] The technical reliability of such machines has recently been demonstrated through reconstructions and computer simulations. See P. E. Chevedden, L. Eigenbrod, V. Foley and W. Soedel, 'The Trebuchet', *Scientific American* (July, 1995), pp. 58–63.

or, more likely, that he was an extremely accurate copyist. Perhaps not surprisingly such machines are found comparatively rarely in medieval miniatures of sieges, suggesting that artists either found difficulty in trying to represent their complexities in such confined spaces, or that they simply had little idea of how such a specialised structure was to be portrayed. Even where there is evidence of some knowledge on the part of the artist representations are often schematic rather than realistic. The two giant machines portrayed in one of the siege scenes in Royal MS. 16 G.VI (Pl. 38) are typical of the kind of representations that appear; the basic structure is conveyed, but there is little evidence that any principles of applied mechanics underlie their construction.

The common practice of copying illustrations from one manuscript to another led to a multiplication of individual images, both accurate and otherwise, a circumstance which restricts the usefulness of any such representations as original factual sources. Confidence is most likely to be inspired by those illustrations which are clearly the creative work of a skilled artist. Such are the miniatures in the only known illustrated manuscript of the romance of Jehan de Saintré (Pl. 39), a luxury volume written and illuminated in France in about 1470, which offers a battle scene of convincing realism with minute attention to detail. Within the lively and tumultuous clash of two opposing armies each individual figure is given a separate identity, which differentiates him from those around him. Closer examination reveals numerous details of fighting dress and weapons, portrayed with extreme precision in terms of style and texture, their variety creating the impression that they have a factual basis. While there is no immediate way of telling whether this is indeed the case, or whether these representations are limited by conventional features, it is clear that the miniature merits closer study in the light of what is known from other sources. There may be an even stronger case for suspecting realism when precise and apparently accurate details occur in the work of a lesser artist. A late fifteenth-century Flemish manuscript containing a French translation of the life of Alexander portrays the assault on Thebes in terms of a contemporary army using cannon-fire to bombard the city (Pl. 40). The artist in this manuscript displays only average skill in handling landscape and figures, which are very stylised, but he has lavished much attention on depicting carefully crafted armour and weapons thereby, creating a distinct air of realism. In particular the clear differentiation between the two forms of cannon – the one cast, the other of hooped construction – would appear to reflect a degree of knowledge on the part of the artist and not just reliance on a merely conventional representation.

The identification of artefacts in manuscript illustrations cannot necessarily be regarded as a straightforward process, and even where information is accepted as reliable it may be limited in scope because miniatures are static and two-dimensional. This can be a distinct disadvantage in interpreting details; for example, only the external appearance of armour can be portrayed, and the most natural way for it to be seen is from the front. In manuscript illustrations it is quite rare to find any clear evidence of garments worn beneath the visible outer protective layers, while the excellent and detailed back view of the armed figure of Roland confronting Feragut in an early fifteenth-century manuscript of *Les Grandes Chroniques de France* (Pl. 41) must be viewed as a somewhat isolated example. Despite the limitations of space miniatures can sometimes convey wider information about corporate activities such as the advance of troops in battle formation as portrayed in a French version of the *Cyropaedia* of Xenophon made in Flanders in about 1470–1480 (Pl. 42), or the movement of an army with its baggage in a manuscript of the English romance *The Three Kings' Sons* produced at approximately the same date (Pl. 43). Together with general battle scenes such operations are suited to the 'snapshot' technique, but it is virtually impossible for visual representations to convey any more specific details of tactics or manoeuvres, although changes in procedures may sometimes be inferred by observing subtle differences in pictures produced at different points in time. Thus it has been suggested that the standard procedure for single combat in warfare and tournaments may have changed over the course of the years, since earlier portrayals generally depict an attack off-side to off-side with lances pointing straight forward and held to the right of the horses' heads, while later illustrations tend to show the opponents attacking near-side to near-side with lances placed diagonally across the horses' necks.[23]

It remains only to consider Haskell's other point concerning the importance of knowing the date of a visual source for the purposes of interpretation. Manuscripts pose some problems in this respect since comparatively few can be dated precisely, either directly or from internal evidence. More often than not an estimate of date has to be made on the basis of the iconographic and palaeographical features of a volume, a process not necessarily straightforward in itself, as text and illustrations may have been produced at different points in time.[24] Such judgements allow miniatures to be placed only within a certain chronological context, quite often a very broad one, but such lack of precision in dating is of small consequence for certain general purposes such as documenting the use of

---

[23]   D. J. A. Ross, 'Breaking a Lance', *Guillaume d'Orange and the Chanson de Geste. Essays Presented to Duncan McMillan in Celebration of his Seventieth Birthday by his Friends and Colleagues of the Société Rencesvals* (Reading, 1984), pp. 127–35.

[24]   An example is provided here by the manuscript of the Decretals of Pope Gregory IX (see Pl. 8).

weapons or tracing the evolution of armour, since cumulative evidence from a range of illustrations can be evaluated against an overall pattern built up from a range of secondary sources. Although within this framework specific information in miniatures should be treated with a certain amount of caution – an artist may have been following an accepted convention or copying an earlier exemplar so that his information may be out of date – the general principles established can sometimes be employed as a tool for a more general dating process. For instance an English manuscript of an abridged version of Wace's *Brut* contains an illustration of Arviragus, depicted as a figure dressed in mail armour with clearly identifiable plate reinforcements to the limbs (Pl. 44). The style of drawing is unusual but palaeographical features place the volume in the fourteenth century, and since the text contains a continuation of the chronicle to the year 1338 it is not unreasonable to suppose that the manuscript was completed at this date or shortly after. If this is so, the conclusion can be drawn that plate reinforcements to the limbs would have been a familiar feature during the second quarter of the fourteenth century. The mail-clad figures in two near-contemporary English manuscripts, the Queen Mary Psalter (Royal MS. 2 B.VII) and the Holkham Bible Picture Book (Add. MS. 47682), lack such reinforcements, a factor that has been cited as supporting evidence for a rather earlier dating for these two volumes.[25]

Although some caution is required in interpreting details within a chronological context, a specific date has the advantage of furnishing a *terminus post quem* for the existence of an identifiable artefact and so may be critical in documenting the earliest appearance of a particular item. Perhaps the most celebrated of all miniatures relating to medieval warfare is a picture of a weapon powered by gunpowder which appears in a manuscript, now in Oxford (Christ Church MS. 92, f. 70v), containing a treatise on royal duties compiled by a certain Walter de Milemete for presentation to Edward III. The manuscript can be dated 1326–1327 from the rubric at the beginning of the volume, so that the illustration is generally acknowledged as the earliest visual representation of a cannon and has been widely reproduced as such. A similar representation which appears in a companion volume containing the *Secreta Secretorum* attributed to Aristotle, another book of instruction for a king (Pl. 45), is popularly ignored in this context although the volume appears to have been presented to Edward before the Milemete treatise, a fact which implies that this might well be the earlier of the two illustrations.[26]

Both miniatures show a curious vase-shaped weapon, the Milemete gun apparently smaller than that of the *Secreta* and with the touch-hole on the

[25] W. O. Hassall (ed.), *The Holkham Bible Picture Book* (London, 1954), p. 27.
[26] Hassall, *The Holkham Bible Picture Book*, p. 28, n. 1.

side rather than at the end, suggesting that the one is not merely a copy of the other. Taken together these two miniatures illustrate the fact that all aspects of an illustration ought to be taken into account if full and valid use is to be made of its historical content. Although there can be no question that the two weapons demonstrate the use of gunpowder for the purposes of warfare, the guns themselves bear small resemblance to those types of cannon commonly portrayed in manuscripts produced in subsequent years; this makes it difficult to know whether the artist is recording fact or merely inventing a plausible representation of the very latest in weaponry, which he is anxious to include but which is known to him only by hearsay. Authenticity may perhaps be suggested by the accuracy of the other, more traditional weapons portrayed elsewhere in the two volumes, but this in itself is hardly conclusive. However, some concrete support for the rather curious appearance of the weapons has been put forward through comparison with two artefacts, the first a comparably shaped Japanese gun of the early nineteenth century which affords the representations some technical credibility,[27] the second a smaller but similar gun of likely medieval origin, excavated at Loshult in Sweden, which supports the existence of such vase-shaped weapons at a comparatively early date.[28]

The other questions of some concern in view of the Milemete miniature's reputation as the earliest extant illustration of a weapon powered by gunpowder are whether the miniatures share the 1326–27 date indicated by the opening rubric of the Milemete treatise, and whether the *Secreta* weapon may perhaps be the earlier of the two representations. In the past doubt has been cast on a contemporary date for these illustrations on the grounds that weapons of this size were not technologically viable until nearer the end of the fourteenth century, indicating that the miniatures must have been added to the volumes at a considerably later date.[29] The application of an external criterion such as this may sometimes be valid, but

---

[27] P. Post, 'Die frühste Geschützdarstellung von etwa 1330', *Zeitschrift für historische Waffen-und Kostümkunde*, Neue Folge 7, Sammelheft: Geschützwesen (1938), pp. 137–41.

[28] T. Jakobsson, 'Ein waffengeschichtlich wertvoller Geschüzfund im Armeemuseum von Stockholm', *Zeitschrift für historische Waffen-und Kostümkunde*, Neue Folge 8, Heft 5/6 (1944), pp. 124–7. Interestingly enough, this gun (now SHM 2891, Statens Historiska Museum, Stockholm) has not yet been subjected to research using modern techniques for a more accurate dating than that reported by Jakobsson (pre-17th century), and so is currently considered to have been made in about 1350 or somewhat earlier on the basis both of its primitive shape and of its similarity to the Milemete and *Secreta* illustrations. I am indebted to Hans A. Lidén, Keeper of the Medieval Department at Statens Historiska Museum, for supplying information on this.

[29] B. Rathgen, *Das Geschütz im Mittelalter* (Berlin, 1928), p. 61.

here it is highly unsatisfactory because so little is known about the military capabilities of gunpowder at this date, while skills were certainly available by the early fourteenth century to fashion the type of weapon portrayed.[30]

A further approach to dating can be made through the stylistic features of the miniatures, a specialist task which may be quite complicated as in the case of the two volumes under consideration. Here the miniatures in each manuscript are the work of more than one artist while some of the *Secreta* images are unfinished, indicating that the illustrations may not necessarily have been produced at the same time as the text or even as a unified project. In the introduction to an early facsimile of the Milemete Treatise[31] a thorough attempt was made to distinguish the work of the various artists, but without questioning the 1326–1327 date. Only recently have the problems of artist and date been studied in greater depth,[32] resulting in the conclusion that both volumes appear to have been the subject of more than one campaign of decoration, with at least some of the work on each stretching over a number of years. Within this framework stylistic features indicate that both cannon images were executed by artists working on the manuscripts in the initial stages, perhaps as early as 1325–1326 for the *Secreta* volume and contemporaneously with the text, possibly after the death of Edward II, in the case of the Milemete Treatise. This would seem to confirm that the *Secreta* image should displace its counterpart as the earliest known visual representation of a gunpowder weapon, but it is still not possible to make this claim because the artist could easily have continued to have access to the volume for quite some time.

Tracing and interpreting visual representations of war in miniatures can be both arduous and tantalising, but the potential rewards are great. Although modern knowledge of the ways of war in the middle ages cannot help but be of a fragmentary nature, the vast reserves of untapped visual sources in manuscripts may well contain crucial information that in the future will enable some of the many missing pieces of the jigsaw to be put in place.

---

[30] See Post, 'Die frühste Geschützdarstellung', n. 27 above.

[31] M. R. James, *The Treatise of Walter de Milemete*, Roxburghe Club (London, 1913).

[32] M. A. Michael, 'The Artists of the Walter of Milemete Treatise' (unpublished Ph.D. thesis, University of London, 1986).

The Civil War of Stephen's Reign: Winners and Losers

JIM BRADBURY

This is a case which is the reverse of normal. An ancient rule of war is 'To the victor the spoils', but in this instance, King Stephen seems to have won the war but lost the peace. In this paper, the war is treated in two separate phases, divided by the retreat of Matilda to Normandy in 1148.

By 1147 Stephen had emerged from the Matildine conflict better than his opponents. The deaths of Miles, earl of Hereford, in a hunting accident on Christmas Eve 1143, and of Geoffrey de Mandeville in 1144, the taking of Faringdon in 1145, the death of Robert of Gloucester in 1147, the retreat of Matilda to Normandy by March of 1148 never to return, all point in the same direction with regard to the war in England.

In 1143 Geoffrey de Mandeville II had been arrested. Stephen was prone to this ploy, attempting to enforce his rights over castles. He gained control of key castles, but he alienated a succession of magnates. Stephen's motive was a belief that he could win control of the kingdom by dealing with any magnate who threatened his authority. However, time after time, having received the castles demanded, and taken oaths over future behaviour, he released the offender who then rebelled against him. The example of Geoffrey was in some ways unfortunate, in that it succeeded. Geoffrey was arrested at St Alban's, and forced to hand over his main castles: Pleshey, Saffron Walden and the Tower. He 'unwillingly gave up his fortifications with the deepest bitterness of heart'. On release, angered by his 'unjust treatment', he fled to the Isle of Ely. Stephen built a series of castles against Geoffrey.[1] One was at Burwell in Cambridgeshire, which Geoffrey sought to destroy before it was completed. He unwisely approached without his helmet on, and a low-born bowman hit him. Geoffrey was taken off to Mildenhall, where he died a week later, 'penitent from the bottom of his heart', according at least to the chronicle of his own foundation at Walden. The *Gesta Stephani* says: 'a kind of darkness and dread filled all the king's enemies, and those who had thought that the king's efforts were greatly weakened by the revolt for which Geoffrey was

---

[1] H. Collar, 'The Book of the Foundation of Walden Abbey', trans. C. H. Emson, *Essex Review*, 45 (1936), pp. 73–85, pp. 80–2.

responsible'.[2]

Faringdon castle had been built by Robert of Gloucester for his son, Philip. It was an attempt to protect Malmesbury. Stephen took the castle and destroyed it. One reason for the perceived significance was that Robert of Gloucester's son then deserted to Stephen, perhaps because his father had failed to come to its relief. By 1145 Stephen was seen as the victor in the war, and the success of Henry a forlorn hope rather than a foregone conclusion.

On 31 October 1147 Robert of Gloucester died. He had been the mainspring of Matilda's efforts. His desertion of Stephen in 1138 had made the war possible. More than Matilda, he held the Angevin forces together and conducted the war.[3] Without him the Angevin cause seemed in tatters. Matilda had nineteen years to live, but she gave up the fight in England. It cannot be said that she stood down in favour of her son. When she retired to Normandy, Henry had only the unsuccessful 1147 expedition to England behind him. It looks rather as if she were abandoning the struggle.

There was sporadic fighting after 1145, which went largely in Stephen's favour: the episode with Ranulf of Chester in 1146; the rebellion in Kent which saw Stephen capture three castles from the earl of Hertford; the recapture of Henry of Blois' castle of Downton from Earl Patrick in 1148. But although the Matildine war was a victory for Stephen, it was not a complete one. Matilda's son Henry was growing to manhood and seemed intent on claiming his mother's rights; parts of England, which had been consistently Angevin, were still not under Stephen's authority. And in Normandy, where Stephen had lost the war against Geoffrey, the outcome seemed more final than in England. The count of Anjou had settled the issue with the taking of Rouen in 1144, and completed it with the capture of Arques in 1145. From 1144 he referred to himself as duke. From 1150 he associated his son Henry in the government of the duchy.

In the Henrician episode of the war in England, it is less clear who was the military victor. Some historians have seen Henry's final expedition in 1153 as a triumph. Politically it was, but not militarily. Henry's previous efforts in England had been largely humiliating. Before 1153 he made little impact.

He had come in 1147 in response to urgent requests for aid from the pro-Angevins in England. They wanted Geoffrey's intervention; all they got was the teenage Henry, with a few mercenaries, whom he could not even

---

[2]   *Chronicon Abbatiae Ramesiensis*, ed. W. D. Macray (Rolls Series, London, 1886), p. 332, 'quidam vilissimus sagittarius'; Walden Chronicle, p. 82; *Gesta Stephani*, ed. and trans. K. R. Potter (Oxford, 1976), pp. 166–7.

[3]   'Angevin' is used here to denote supporters of Matilda and Henry in England, and 'royalist' for supporters of King Stephen.

afford to pay. Neither his uncle, Robert of Gloucester, 'brooding like a miser over his moneybags', nor his mother was prepared to underwrite his costs.[4] Only a desperate appeal to Stephen provided cash to pay off the mercenaries and for return to Normandy.

Henry came again in 1149, a little older and wiser, but not much stronger. He reached Carlisle, and was knighted by King David on 22 May. There he made contact with Ranulf de Gernons, earl of Chester, one of the 'major troublemakers' of the reign, who gave hope to the Henrician phase of the war as Robert of Gloucester had to the Matildine phase.[5] He was a powerful magnate with lands stretching from the Welsh border, across the midlands into the north and Lincolnshire. He had obstructed all Stephen's attempts at peace since causing the Battle of Lincoln by seizing the castle in 1141, but he had not been a staunch Angevin either. Round was not far wrong in believing that 'the real springs of his policy are found in Carlisle and Lincoln'.[6] In 1146 he deserted back to Stephen. A formal agreement was made with the king, giving Lincoln to Ranulf.[7] Ranulf aided Stephen in the capture of Bedford, and accompanied him to Wallingford. The worst move Stephen ever made was to alienate this powerful if unreliable magnate. Stephen arrested Ranulf on the advice of his courtiers, chained him up, and demanded his major castles, including Lincoln. Ranulf was arrested on 'bad counsel', and released 'on worse counsel'; upon which he 'flew to arms'.[8] It is true that he failed to take Coventry or recover Lincoln, but he became a powerful aid to the failing Angevin cause, prepared even to give up Carlisle to the Scots.

Let us pursue Henry's 1149 visit. The allies at Carlisle planned an attack on York, but Stephen turned up before expected, the coalition broke up and made a run for it, each to his own base. Henry evaded ambushes laid by Stephen and his son Eustace, having to leave Dursley in the middle

---

[4]   *Gesta Stephani*, pp. 206–7.

[5]   C. W. Hollister, 'The Magnates of Stephen's Reign: Reluctant Anarchists', *Haskins Society Journal*, 5 (1993), pp. 77–86, p. 79. On Ranulf also see P. Dalton, 'In Neutro Latere: The Armed Neutrality of Ranulf II Earl of Chester in King Stephen's Reign', *Anglo-Norman Studies*, 14 (1991), pp. 39–59; and H. A. Cronne, 'Ranulf de Gernons, Earl of Chester, 1129–1153', *TRHS*, 4th ser., 20 (1937), pp. 103–34.

[6]   J. H. Round, 'King Stephen and the Earl of Chester', *EHR*, 10 (1895), pp. 87–91, p. 87.

[7]   *Regesta Regum Anglo-Normannorum, 1066–1154*, III, ed. H. A. Cronne and R. H. C. Davis (Oxford, 1968), no. 178, pp. 64–5.

[8]   *The Anglo-Saxon Chronicle*, ed. D. Whitelock, D. C. Douglas and S. I. Tucker (London, 1961), p. 201; *The Peterborough Chronicle*, ed. C. Clark (Oxford, 1970), p. 58: 'thurhc wicci raed ... thurhc waerse red'; *Gesta Stephani*, pp. 198–9: 'ad arma conuolauit'.

of the night to do so. Once back in Angevin territory he made one or two aggressive moves, including the capture of Bridport, but the 1149 visit produced little for his supporters to crow over. Most of England remained in Stephen's hands; he was 'holding the upper hand everywhere'.[9] The pro-Angevin leaders, Reginald of Cornwall and Roger of Hereford, appealed to Henry to come to England because they were 'in sore distress'.[10] It was four years before he returned, a period of difficulty for his supporters, with Stephen in the ascendant, taking Newbury in 1152, and besieging the now isolated Wallingford.

Only in comparison to his earlier efforts can the 1153 campaign be seen as a success for Henry. In practice, even in 1153, he won but a few new strongholds, and made little impact on the steadily royal regions. At best, he reopened a war that seemed dead, which was perhaps sufficient to be the kernel of his overall victory. Henry, now duke of Normandy, arrived in England on 6 January 1153, bringing a mere 140 knights, with 3,000 infantry, in 36 ships. His mercenaries proved unpopular, and he was persuaded to send them back to Normandy, many drowning during the return voyage.

The 1153 campaign is seen by Leedom as a triumph; Henry 'won impressive victories over King Stephen'.[11] But this view simply does not hold up to examination. Politically it proved a triumph, but the account of the military campaign shows no such thing. Henry failed at both Bedford and Nottingham. His successes were moderate and not on their own decisive. The armies twice confronted each other but there was no battle, and on at least one of these occasions it was Henry rather than Stephen who refused battle.

The delicacy of Henry's position is clear. He could not be absent from Normandy for long. The Normans had believed, when Louis VII invaded, that Henry would lose all his possessions. There had also been rebellion in Aquitaine, and his brother Geoffrey had caused problems in Anjou. There were some desertions from Stephen, but in truth only a few. Robert earl of Leicester was Henry's main new acquisition, perhaps to defend the family

---

[9] *Gesta Stephani*, pp. 206–7.
[10] *Gesta Stephani*, pp. 227–32; pp. 228–30: 'in summa erant tribulatione'.
[11] J. W. Leedom, 'The English Settlement of 1153', *History*, 65 (1980), pp. 347–64, p. 347. For contrary views see G. J. White, 'The End of Stephen's Reign', *History*, 75 (1990), pp. 3–22; D. Crouch, 'Earl William of Gloucester and the End of the Anarchy: New Evidence Relating to the Honor of Eudo Dapifer', *EHR*, 103 (1988), pp. 69–75, and H. G. Richardson and G. O. Sayles, *The Governance of Medieval England* (Edinburgh, 1963), especially p. 254. I should like to thank Richard Eales for reminding me of the significant contribution to this subject in this now elderly work.

position, but probably out of self interest. Other deserters to Henry were Richard de Lucy and William Mauduit, a royal chamberlain.

The recent support Henry had received from such as Ranulf and Hugh Bigod could not be greatly relied on, and was bought dear. Ranulf was promised the honour of Peverel of Nottingham, a promise which antagonised Robert de Ferrers, earl of Derby. Robert of Leicester was promised the restoration of the honour of Breteuil in Normandy for his son, and was himself made steward to Henry in England and Normandy. William Mauduit was rewarded with the castellanship of Rockingham Castle.

Henry attacked Malmesbury Castle. An appeal for help went to Stephen, who came to its relief 'as though he meant to fight a pitched battle'. The armies faced each other over the Avon, their banners glittering gold.[12] Stephen sought battle, Henry with a smaller army refused. But Stephen gained nothing because of the heavy rain, which blew 'in the faces of the king and his troops, so that they could hardly support their armour or handle their spears'; it proved impossible to cross the river, so the king tamely gave up and returned to London. 'It seemed as if the Almighty Himself were fighting for the duke.' Both leaders reluctantly agreed a truce.[13] The castellan Jordan, who was supposed to destroy the castle, surrendered it to Henry. Henry had successes in the midlands, marching through Worcestershire, Warwickshire, Northamptonshire and Bedfordshire. He took Tutbury, and Warwick was surrendered to him by the countess, though her husband was with Stephen at the time, and is said to have died of the shame. Henry improved the Angevin position in the midlands in 1153, largely because he now had the support of Ranulf of Chester and Robert of Leicester. He captured a few castles, but in truth, his gains had been from new allies; militarily he had achieved little.

Henry now approached Wallingford and besieged Stephen's counter-castle at Crowmarsh, guarding the bridge over the Thames. The armies faced each other across the river, but again 'shrank on both sides from a conflict'. Stephen was thrown from his horse three times as it reared, which may have shaken him up enough to agree what seems an unnecessarily submissive truce.[14] Although Stephen was not defeated on

---

[12] *Gesta Stephani*, pp. 232–3; Henry of Huntingdon, *Chronicle*, ed. and trans. T. Forester (London, 1853), p. 291; Henry of Huntingdon, *Historia Anglorum*, ed. T. Arnold, Rolls Series (London, 1879), p. 286: 'insignibus aureis coruscus'.

[13] *Gesta Stephani*, pp. 232–3; Henry of Huntingdon, ed. Forester, p. 291; Henry of Huntingdon, ed. Arnold, p. 286: 'ut Deus ipse videretur pro duce rem agere ... Apertes etenim cataractis coeli tantas in facies eorum misit inundationes'.

either occasion, his loss of Malmesbury and his agreement to the destruction of Crowmarsh shows that, in the negotiations, Henry was gaining the upper hand, which, given their relative strengths, is curious. The explanation lies in the unwillingness of the magnates to fight. 'The nobles, nay rather the traitors of England, arose and discussed terms of peace among themselves. They loved indeed nothing better than discord, but were unwilling to commit themselves to battle; for they desired to raise up neither one nor the other of the claimants to the throne, lest by vanquishing the one they might become entirely subject to the other.' The chronicler adds that both leaders were 'aware of the treachery of their followers, and were reluctantly compelled to make a truce'. The two conferred on an island, and 'both complained bitterly of the betrayal of their barons'.[15]

At Nottingham, Henry again suffered a military reverse, and was forced to move on. At Winchester the armies approached each other once more, but this time a more lasting peace was agreed. Henry had not won a war, but he was to do better from the peace. To clarify the picture, we must examine the settlement of 1153.[16] It was the result of several meetings and prolonged negotiations. These were pressed upon the contestants by churchmen, as was often the case. It has been argued that the terms were made earlier, and that Eustace reacted against them. Leedom claimed that Eustace's death 'came after peace had already been made'.[17] But this is not what the chronicles say. Eustace reacted against a peace negotiation between his father and Henry. He reacted angrily, which suggests he did not like what was happening, probably the tame surrender of Crowmarsh, but this does not prove what terms if any had been agreed. The *Gesta Stephani* says he raged 'because the war, in his opinion, had reached no proper conclusion'.[18] He took to arms and ravaged Cambridgeshire, but died on 17 August 1153. Before that time there had been negotiations but no settlement: the sides were still at odds; the truce lasted only five days.

We should revert to an earlier view of events, which sees the death of Eustace as vital in the process. William of Newburgh clearly states that his death 'offered a great opportunity of creating peace', a peace which had been impossible during his lifetime because of his 'youthful aggression'.[19]

14   *Gesta Stephani*, pp. 238–9; Gervase of Canterbury, *Opera Historica*, ed. W. Stubbs, 2 vols (Rolls Series, London, 1879), I, p. 154.
15   Henry of Huntingdon, in *English Historical Documents, vol. II, 1042–1189*, ed. D. C. Douglas and G. W. Greenaway, 2nd edn (London, 1981), p. 336; Henry of Huntingdon, ed. Arnold, pp. 287–8: 'proceres imo proditores'.
16   *Regesta*, pp. 97–9, no. 272.
17   Leedom, 'The English Settlement', p. 347.
18   *Gesta Stephani*, pp. 238–9: 'quod bellum, uti aestimabat, ad effectum nequaquam processerat'.

After the Wallingford meeting, there was no peace. Both leaders rejected the truce and resorted to arms, Henry taking Stamford, while Stephen captured Ipswich.

It was only at Winchester, in November, that agreement was reached, confirmed by Stephen's charter, recently reconsidered by Professor Holt.[20] Now peace was agreed, and Stephen marked it by leading the duke in procession through the streets. It is from chroniclers' descriptions of Winchester, and Stephen's Westminster charter, that we know the terms. The charter was a document for action to those who must enforce the new arrangements, not a formal treaty. There is no 'treaty' of Westminster. The charter refers to an agreement made in the past, that is to Winchester. Henry became Stephen's adopted son and heir. Stephen was recognised as king for life. At Winchester they agreed that recently built castles were to be demolished, and that holders of land disinherited since the time of Henry I should be restored. Mercenary troops were to be sent home, and according to William of Newburgh they 'slid off'.[21] The Westminster charter repeated the main terms which could be implemented without difficulty, but left the more sensitive points, on new castles and repossessions, to be tackled quietly with individuals.

The feeling of relief throughout the country was great. Of Winchester, Henry of Huntingdon exclaimed: 'What a happy day!' Osbert of Clare, prior of Westminster, wrote to Archbishop Theobald, congratulating him on his part in making the peace, late in 1153: 'you have restored order to our distracted country'. He wrote also to Henry, calling him a 'new light ... a leader given to us by God ... (who) shall found a new Jerusalem'.[22]

We need to look at the results of the peace for those who had been engaged in the war. Few barons lost lands or positions through royal action. This was partly because Henry was not vindictive. Those who submitted might be penalised, and some got less than they hoped for, but most retained their lands. Henry laid down principles: that there should be a return to the position as under Henry I, that those who had been unlawfully dispossessed should be repossessed, that the castles built since

---

[19]   William of Newburgh, *The History of English Affairs*, Book I, ed. and trans. P. G. Walsh and M. J. Kennedy (Warminster, 1988), pp. 124–7.

[20]   J. C. Holt, '1153: The Treaty of Winchester', in *The Anarchy of Stephen's Reign*, ed. E. King (Oxford, 1994), pp. 291–316.

[21]   William of Newburgh, '*Historia Rerum Anglicanum*', in *Chronicles of the Reigns of Stephen, Henry II and Richard I*, ed. R. Howlett, 4 vols (Rolls Series, London, 1884–89), I, p. 101: 'in brevi dilapsi sunt'.

[22]   Henry of Huntingdon, in *EHD*, II, p. 337; Henry of Huntingdon, ed. Arnold, p. 289: 'quam beata dies!' *The Letters of Osbert of Clare*, ed. and trans. E. W. Williamson (Oxford, 1929), pp. 122, 130.

the time of Henry I should be demolished.[23] In practice none of these things was pursued with vigour: few who had gained from Stephen were dispossessed, few castles were destroyed. Amt shows how few castles were destroyed in certain areas, for example in Gloucestershire (Angevin) or Oxfordshire (divided). Even in royalist Essex, where several new castles had been built, only a handful were demolished, and those mainly belonging to Geoffrey de Mandeville. Allowing castles to stand proved a useful form of patronage. Coulson suggests that Stephen was more successful in demolishing castles than Henry. William of Newburgh gives the game away when he says that those new castles which were 'conveniently located' were to be kept by 'himself or peaceful men for the defence of the kingdom'.[24] After revolts caused by Henry's efforts to recover castles from his own followers, Roger of Hereford (Gloucester and Hereford) and Hugh Mortimer (Bridgnorth, Wigmore, and Cleobury, the latter being actually destroyed), Henry used his discretion and let the matter drop. The truth is that almost no-one was a loser, at least in any comprehensive way.

Few of the leading royalists lost everything. Some even recovered their positions. Stephen kept his throne, and his son William of Blois was to keep the family lands, as well as his gains through marriage to the Warenne heiress. Henry treated him with caution at first, holding fire over his danegeld exemptions.[25] Henry demanded castles from him, and reneged on his generosity of 1153, but William stayed loyal. Henry knighted him in 1158, and William died returning from the Toulouse campaign with Henry. He had not expected the throne while Eustace lived, and so far as we know made no effort to gain it thereafter. He was much better off after 1153 than he had been before. Perhaps not everyone wishes to be a king.

Simon de Senlis, like many main contestants, died before the end of the reign, in 1153. He was seen as Henry's most determined enemy. Yet his son was not a total loser, since Henry split the old earldom of Huntingdon and gave him part of it with the title earl of Northampton.

---

23   C. Coulson, 'The Castles of the Anarchy', in *The Anarchy of Stephen's Reign*, ed. King, prefers not to call these castles adulterine, but William of Newburgh, eds Walsh and Kennedy, p. 130, does refer to 'munitiones adulterae'; compare William of Newburgh, ed. Howlett, p. 102: 'castella nova' for the same castles.
24   William of Newburgh, ed. Stevenson, p. 444; Coulson, 'The Castles of Anarchy', p. 69; William of Newburgh, ed. Howlett, p. 102: 'praeter pauca in locis opportunis sita, quae vel ipse retinere, vel a pacificis ad regni munimen retineri voluit'.
25   E. Amt, *The Accession of Henry II in England, Royal Government Restored, 1149–1159* (Woodbridge, 1993), p. 27.

William de Chesney was one of Stephen's new men. Gilbert Foliot, his nephew, tried to encourage him to good works, warning that his castles would be left behind, but his sins would follow him to heaven.[26] In the last year of the reign, anticipating losses from the settlement, Stephen compensated William with new grants. He did not lose his lands in the new reign, nor was his castle at Deddington demolished. He received grants from Henry and danegeld exemptions, though not for Deddington until 1157.

William of Ypres was one of the few losers by the settlement, perhaps the only serious one. He was an illegitimate descendant of the counts of Flanders, had twice sought to win the county for himself, and twice failed. He had become a mercenary captain in Stephen's employ, and his foremost lieutenant. He received rich rewards. He was the scapegoat of the peace: a mercenary, a Fleming, a dedicated opponent, and he lost his lands: some to Angevins supporters, more to the crown. But he was by 1154 a back number, not active since at least 1148 because of ill health and blindness. Henry could afford to treat him roughly, but he did not press; the demesne lands in Kent were not repossessed for two years and William retired to Loo in Flanders. There he repented his many sins, gave alms to the poor, restored churches and made pious foundations before his death in 1162.[27]

Faramus of Boulogne is a counter to the case of William of Ypres. Faramus was also a continental mercenary who had been valuable to Stephen. He was descended from an illegitimate line of the counts of Boulogne, and had been castellan of Dover. Henry took over Dover for himself, but early in his reign granted lands to Faramus in compensation. These he held till his death in about 1183, when they passed to his heir.

William of Aumale had been made earl of York by Stephen in 1138. He did not relish Henry II's policy of taking back royal castles, and rebelled. He was forced to submit and to hand over Scarborough, but only because of this revolt after the accession. Henry's policy with regard to royal castles was applied also to pro-Angevin magnates, and with similar results. Such men lost not for supporting for Stephen but for rebellion after 1154.

William Peverel of Nottingham was one of the few barons forced out of England after the change of dynasty, not because of his activities in the war but because he tried to poison Ranulf of Chester. The exile seems to have been his own choice.

---

[26]   E. King, 'The Anarchy of Stephen's Reign', *TRHS*, 34, p. 153; Amt, *The Accession of Henry II*, p. 52; *The Letters and Charters of Gilbert Foliot*, ed. A. Morey and C. N. L. Brooke (Cambridge, 1967), pp. 54–5.

[27]   *Biographie Nationale*, VIII, Brussels (1884–85), columns 436–9.

Other Stephen supporters were treated well. Hugh de Lacy, for example, had Pontefract restored to him. Alan of Penthièvre (Alan II, the Black) had been a supporter of Stephen, becoming earl of Richmond and dying in 1146. He had been made earl of Cornwall by Stephen, in opposition to the Angevin Earl Reginald. His son Conan did not get Cornwall, but was recognised by Henry as earl of Richmond. Henry's benevolence did not always pay off. When Conan took up his claims in Brittany, he caused problems for Henry there.

Henry of Essex was a significant figure in the county for Stephen, holding the castle of Rayleigh which he rebuilt, but if anything he bettered himself under Henry, becoming sheriff of Hertfordshire, and later of Buckinghamshire and Bedfordshire. Amt has shown that even in Essex, a mainly royalist county, no major landholders were disinherited.[28] Henry of Essex became royal standard bearer, but during a skirmish in Wales in 1157, when there was a rumour that the king had been killed, Henry threw away the standard and fled.[29] Henry II took no action against him, and he went with the king on the Toulouse campaign. It was only a private accusation in 1163 by Robert de Montfort, who gained a small part of his lands, which led to a judicial duel. Henry lost the duel and was left for dead on the field. His lands and his castle of Rayleigh were declared forfeit. The monks of Reading Abbey saved his life, and he retired into the abbey as a monk. Henry of Essex ended as a loser, but not for supporting Stephen, or through any action of Henry II.

Aubrey de Vere II was another baron with lands in Essex who had died in 1141. His son Aubrey III had become an earl through defecting to Matilda in 1141, but had returned to Stephen's court and had never been very active in the civil war. He paid Henry to take up his father's office, and seems to have continued in virtually the same position.

Although Henry was prepared to let all and sundry keep their family lands, he was less generous with former demesne lands. It was a sign of favour that Richard de Lucy and Richard de Camville were permitted to keep such lands. Whenever opportunity offered, Henry regained demesne, for example from William of Blois and William of Ypres. This was not an anti-royalist policy, since supporters such as Earl Patrick of Salisbury or Roger of Hereford were subject to the same demands. It was a policy of recovering demesne rather than of punishing former enemies.

At first Henry 'made shift with such sheriffs as were already in place'.[30] There was a purge of sheriffs in 1155, but those newly introduced were often men with experience from the previous reign. The replacement

---

[28] Amt, *The Accession of Henry II*, pp. 64–81.
[29] Gervase of Canterbury, p. 163.
[30] Amt, *The Accession of Henry II*, p. 113.

sheriff in Essex, even in 1157, was still Maurice de Tilty who had been a sheriff under Stephen. Ralph Picot, who had been Stephen's sheriff for Kent, took over for Henry in 1154, and also in Sussex in 1157. Very few of the early sheriffs for Henry II were new men. Richard de Camville had been a Stephen supporter, but was used as sheriff of Berkshire in 1156 and 1157. He kept his own holdings, kept his castle of Middleton Stoney which passed on to his son, and received exemptions from danegeld and taxation.

In administration, Henry introduced some of his own servants, and some of Stephen's men were dropped, including William Martel as chief steward and Baldric de Sigillo as keeper of the seal, though William continued till 1155 as sheriff of Surrey.[31] Only one of Stephen's scribes has been identified as continuing under Henry, but by the end of Stephen's reign there were few operating anyway. Henry made heavy use of men with experience of administration under Stephen, including most notably Richard de Lucy.

Conversely not all the pro-Angevins of the war period gained from its outcome. Many had died before the new reign, including Robert, earl of Gloucester in 1147, Miles, earl of Hereford in 1143, Brian fitz Count in 1151, and Roger, earl of Warwick in 1153. Baldwin de Redvers (1155) and Gilbert de Gant (1156) died early in the new reign.[32] Ranulf of Chester saved Henry much anxiety by dying in December of 1153, allowing him to think again about the over-generous grants made to keep his support.

Waleran of Meulan is difficult to categorise: he had been enthusiastically pro-Stephen, but later deserted his new friends the Angevins for the king of France. As a result he was a loser in Normandy and England, his earldom of Worcester retained by the crown, but not for supporting Stephen. Thanks to the timely desertion to Henry of his twin brother, Robert of Leicester, and his sister-in-law the countess of Warwick, the family fortunes did not suffer alarmingly. Waleran was pardoned in 1162 and lived quietly until his death in 1166, becoming a monk at Préaux. His brother had been a supporter of Stephen's government, but became a figure of importance in the new reign. It showed that Henry was more generous to recruits than Stephen had been. Robert was to act as justiciar for the new king until his death in 1168, before which he became an Augustinian.

Richard de Lucy was another supporter of Stephen who deserted in the last year of the reign. He became useful to Henry, and was trusted to hold the Tower and Windsor and guarantee their passing to Henry on the accession. He was made co-justiciar in the new regime with Leicester. He

---

[31] G. White, 'Continuity in Government', in *The Anarchy of King Stephen's Reign*, ed. King, p. 136.

[32] Amt, *The Accession of Henry II*, p. 24.

also became sheriff of Essex and Hertfordshire and farmed several royal manors.

Robert of Gloucester had been the prime supporter of Matilda, 'the chief of the king's enemies'.[33] His son Philip deserted to Stephen in 1145, making a pact of peace and concord with the king, but Robert's heir William, though 'more devoted to bedchambers than to war', remained with the Angevins, and received the earldom of Gloucester.[34] Henry granted favours to William and his son Robert in 1153 and 1154. Amt and Crouch have suggested that Henry had reservations about Earl William, delaying pardons over tax and danegeld, but he retained the earldom.[35] The doubt may have arisen from the rebellion of William's brother Richard in Normandy in 1154.

David, king of Scots, was another prominent Angevin supporter. Like Ranulf he had been generously rewarded by Henry before the accession. Like Ranulf, he died before the promises had to be fulfilled. David's son Henry had died in 1152, and the grandson who succeeded as Malcolm IV was only eleven. Henry had little compunction in reneging on these promises too. The earldom of Huntingdon was divided, though Malcolm did retain the title.

Miles of Gloucester had become earl of Hereford, and his son Roger inherited the earldom. Roger was largely pro-Angevin, but less devoted to the cause than his father. In 1152 he made approaches to Stephen for 'a pact of inviolable peace and friendship', but he became Henry's main supporter in 1153–54.[36] He rebelled when Henry ignored his earlier promises and demanded Gloucester and Hereford castles. Roger was persuaded to submit by Gilbert Foliot, and was reconciled, but at his death the earldom was not continued. The reduction of earldoms, like the recovery of royal castles, was not an anti-Blesevin policy; it was pursued where opportunity allowed against friend and foe alike. When Roger died in 1155, Henry also took the opportunity of recovering his acquisitions.[37]

Ranulf of Chester had spent more time in the later years of the reign as an opponent of Stephen. His arrest and the seizure of his castles had forced him back into the Angevin camp, as 'the enduring enemy of the king'.[38] He swallowed his pride over Carlisle, and yielded his rights to the Scots,

---

[33] *Gesta Stephani*, pp. 210–11.

[34] W. L. Warren, *Henry II* (London, 1973), p. 35; *Gesta Stephani*, pp. 210–11.

[35] Amt, *The Accession of Henry II*, p. 36; Crouch, 'Earl William of Gloucester', p. 71.

[36] *Gesta Stephani*, pp. 226–7.

[37] D. Crouch, 'The March and the Welsh Kings', in *The Anarchy of King Stephen's Reign*, ed. King, p. 286.

[38] William of Newburgh, eds Walsh and Kennedy, pp. 74–5.

receiving the honour of Lancaster in exchange. After 1146, the Angevins can have placed little trust in Ranulf, but he was useful during 1153. When he died at the end of that year, his son Hugh inherited, but only territories reduced to those held by his father in 1135.

Geoffrey de Mandeville II had hardly been a fervent Angevin either. Stephen had allowed him to recover the family's fortunes and improve upon them. He had gone over to Matilda only during the period when it was prudent to do so after Lincoln. He had been brought down by Stephen for reasons other than those which divided England, and had never really fought for the Angevin cause. His family recovered under Henry II. His son Ernulf was illegitimate, and therefore not disinherited as once thought, while the legitimate sons Geoffrey III and William II in turn succeeded as earls of Essex, the latter becoming a royal justiciar.[39]

Hugh Bigod, earl of Norfolk, had been a constant trouble to Stephen, and was not an easy ally for Henry. Matilda had given him his earldom, which included Suffolk. He provided welcome relief for the Angevins by troublemaking in East Anglia. Stephen's last military success was to wrest Ipswich from Bigod. In 1155 Henry issued a charter confirming his earldom and his possessions, but William of Blois kept Norwich. Henry demanded castles from him, and Bigod remained a discontented and difficult magnate to his death at the ripe age of 83 in 1177. Like many other pro-Angevins, he had not gained much by the change.

Some Angevin supporters were to be disillusioned. Not all would get what they hoped. In Essex, a largely royalist county, William de Helion's family had lost out in order to support Matilda, going with her to Normandy, and accompanying Henry from 1151, but William gained nothing in England.[40]

Other Angevin supporters did profit, however. One example was the family of Eustace fitz John, who had gone over to Matilda in 1138. He had made considerable territorial gains after 1141. His son did homage to Henry, and the gains were confirmed. Henry insisted on the need to confirm all gains made during the previous reign, but he did not reverse many of them. Amt's study of three regions shows that changes were few, whether the area be royalist or Angevin. She concluded that below the level of the magnates, holdings remained stable: 'the *tempus werre* had left the tenurial geography essentially unchanged'.[41]

Let us come to our own conclusion. R. H. C. Davis wrote: 'one of the most puzzling features of Stephen's reign is the way in which it came to an

[39] Holt, '1153: The Treaty of Winchester', p. 298 and n. 24.
[40] Amt, *The Accession of Henry II*, p. 72.
[41] Amt, *The Accession of Henry II*, p. 60.

end'.[42] Can it be made a little less puzzling? Why did Stephen give up so much in the 1153 settlement? The answer is not because he had been militarily defeated. He had won the war against Matilda, or come out stronger than she had. He was not defeated by Henry, and in terms of military force and land in England, was always the stronger. What then is the explanation of his acceptance of defeat in the peace?

Why did he agree to his descendants losing the English throne? Possibly he hoped they would not. No one knew in 1153 how long Stephen would live or how events might modify the agreement. Henry I thought he had arranged for Matilda to get the throne. Everyone knew that Duke Henry had problems on the continent: hostility from France, difficulty with his brother Geoffrey, problems in Aquitaine, problems in Normandy. But accepting that Stephen was prepared to see the agreement enforced, is there an explanation? There are several. There were many pressures upon the king. Stephen had suffered personal tragedy. He was ageing, 59 in 1153: his wife, Queen Matilda, died on 3 May 1152, his eldest son Eustace in 1153, when Stephen 'grieved beyond measure'; he himself was ill and his son, William, suffered a serious accident when riding his horse too fast 'as young people do', and had broken his thigh, which had 'shocked' his father.[43] Such events may have pushed Stephen towards resignation or despair.

He had faced a barrage of criticism for perjury in gaining the throne, now repeated. Henry's propaganda claim to be the lawful heir, improbable at first sight, had perhaps gained by constant repetition. What was thought to be a legal heir to the throne in England must be debatable. No new king since the conquest had been the clear heir by rules of descent: William by conquest in 1066, Rufus rather than Curthose in 1087, Henry I rather than Curthose in 1100, Stephen rather than Matilda in 1135. The Church had become quite awkward with Stephen over recent years: there had been disputes about English elections, including a drawn out problem over York. Ecclesiastics refused to countenance the association of Eustace as the heir. The early death of the more amenable Lucius II (1144–5), was followed by the election of the Cistercian Eugenius III, and a hardening of attitude towards Stephen. Chroniclers, and no doubt others, saw such deaths as that of Eustace as judgements of God, and there were a lot of judgements in 1153–54. Stephen had clearly wanted his son's succession, and briefly in fury imprisoned all the bishops concerned in the refusal of 1152, seizing their possessions. But he could not reverse their decision.

One point which has been neglected is the attitude of Stephen's brother, Henry of Blois, who has been seen as tougher and shrewder than

---

[42] R. H. C. Davis, *King Stephen*, 3rd edn (Harlow, 1990), p. 108.
[43] William of Newburgh, eds. Walsh and Kennedy, pp. 126–7.

his brother. Davis believed he had the qualities his brother lacked.[44] The bishop's actions during the war speak more of self interest than loyalty. Now in 1153, with Theobald of Canterbury, he supervised the peace negotiations, and has received credit for the agreement. But he was Stephen's brother, and so he too was accepting the loss of the English crown to his family. Henry of Huntingdon says the bishop suggested the terms, and the *Gesta Stephani* that Stephen 'yielded to the advice of the bishop of Winchester'.[45] The position of the house of Blois in France should be relevant, but sheds little light. Blois and Champagne had divided on the death of Stephen's brother, Theobald IV, in 1152; but the family was now well in with Louis VII, who married Stephen's sister Adela. The new rulers of Blois and Champagne married the two daughters of Louis VII and Eleanor. But none of this explains why the house of Blois should lose interest in holding England. The best one can say is that compromise was on the cards, not war. It does suggest that Stephen's private state of mind was not the only cause and that the Blesevin position was seen as hopeless without a peace. The bishop of Winchester gained little by his part in the peacemaking. He went into exile, to his old abbey of Cluny, without the king's permission, leaving Henry to demolish some of his castles. Reconciliation was eventually made. One can simply suggest that both Henry of Blois and Stephen were ground down to accepting the loss of England.

Yet for all the personal reasons and all the pressures, Stephen had shown signs of resistance: he had made Eustace count of Boulogne in 1147, had attempted to get him associated in kingship in 1152, and clearly therefore wanted his son to succeed him. He had attacked and taken Ipswich even after the peace negotiations at Wallingford. Even after Winchester, he could annoy Henry by treating the recent castles in a partisan fashion. During his last year he exercised authority with energy, dealing promptly with trouble at Drax. So why the sudden collapse?

One of the most notable developments was in the position of Henry. Within three years, Henry had moved from being a young man with no wealth and little more than expectations, to become a figure of wealth and power. He had been associated in the government of Normandy from 1150; in 1151 he had taken over the duchy and his father's other possessions in greater Anjou. When Eleanor had been divorced by Louis VII in 1152, she had married Henry, and he laid claim to Aquitaine.

---

44 R. H. C. Davis, *King Stephen*, p. 123.
45 Henry of Huntingdon, ed. Forester, p. 294; Henry of Huntingdon, ed. Arnold, p. 289; *Gesta Stephani*, pp. 240–1: 'emollitus consilio Wintoniensis episcopi qui se ad pacem confirmandam medium inter ducem et regem obiciebat'.

Virtually all of western France had dropped into his hands. Nor had this happened by accident. Henry had been forced to struggle and fight for his rights. He had shown himself to have courage and good sense. Men now knew that he was a person of weight, and he was ambitious. Among those who watched these developments were the barons of England. What were their thoughts? Suppose now they fought against Henry? They knew he might become king of England. They would be risking their futures. They stood to lose much by war.

Much interest has been shown recently in the agreements made between magnates in England during the later years of Stephen's reign, the concords, the private treaties. These show that the magnates of England were ready to make peace, to keep stability in their own territories. William of Newburgh says the struggle subsided as they 'wearied of lengthy conflict and their efforts slackened'.[46] Opponents in the war were learning to live with each other. The chronicles suggest that it was not so much the two commanders as their troops who insisted on peace rather than battle. These agreements became almost commonplace, both between allies and between enemies. An early example was that between Robert of Gloucester and Miles of Hereford, perhaps in 1142; they agreed not to do separate deals with their enemies. Their sons, William of Gloucester and Roger of Hereford, made a similar agreement in about 1149.[47]

Such an agreement was made between Ranulf and Robert of Leicester, as a 'final peace and concord', promising not to use more than twenty knights against each other if forced into hostilities through their respective liege lords, and not to erect castles in sensitive areas between them.[48] There were treaties between the earls of Derby and Chester, Chester and Leicester, Leicester and Northampton, Leicester and Hereford, and others: making what Davis called the 'Magnates' Peace'.[49] They make clear the baronial desire for security.

Also the 1150s saw economic malaise: famine, drought, crop failures, hard winters. In France the failure of the grape harvest forced the French to drink beer. There was no feel-good factor. There was a strong desire to see a return to stability and to prosperity.

Not many great men went over to Henry in the key period from 1153 to 1154, but those who did were influential, including Robert of Leicester

---

[46] William of Newburgh, ed. Walsh and Kennedy, pp. 98–9.

[47] *Earldom of Gloucester Charters, the Charters and Scribes of the Earls and Countesses of Gloucester to A.D.1217*, ed. R. B. Patterson (Oxford, 1973), p. 95, no. 95; p. 97, no. 96.

[48] F. M. Stenton, *The First Century of English Feudalism, 1066–1166* (2nd edn, Oxford, 1961), pp. 250–3, 285–8.

[49] Davis, *King Stephen*, p. 108.

and Richard de Lucy. It must have undermined support for Stephen, persuaded men of the direction in which things were going. One significant factor was the knowledge that unless one went over to Henry, family lands in Normandy would be lost.

For a year, though, Henry was in a dubious position. At Dunstable in 1154, he had complained about Stephen's failure to implement the agreement on castles 'by the indulgence or policy of the king', dropping it for fear that 'the light of the concord should be seen to go out'.[50] Already the count of Flanders was involved in a conspiracy with Stephen against Henry.[51] Meanwhile Stephen was taking advantage of the peace; and 'had taken the whole kingdom into his hand'.[52] In March 1154 Henry returned to Normandy, but could hardly have been easy in his mind about the future in England, where he left Earl Reginald to protect his position.[53] It was all much more touch and go than it can seem with hindsight.

On 25 October 1154 Stephen died. It was fortunate for Henry that the death came so soon after the agreement of 1153. The actions of the king since the agreement do not suggest that he was tired of ruling. He 'enjoyed very powerful royal authority'.[54] There was a general desire to keep the peace, and, says William of Newburgh, 'the people hoped for better things from the new monarch'.[55] Henry did not come to England for some time, largely because the weather prevented him sailing. He arrived on 7 December, and was crowned at Westminster on 19 December. He was received by crowds shouting 'Long live the king'.[56]

Stephen had not wished to lose the throne or to disinherit his sons. He had been gradually forced into giving away more than he wanted by the pressure of growing support for Henry, and the hostility to war of the English barons. Personal tragedy, the death of Eustace, the attitude of the church, and the approach of death increasingly inclined him to yield. Henry had sought the throne, had failed to win it by force, but was able to play on the hopes and fears of church and barons. He may not have won a war, but he had survived one. The prospect was of the Matildine war all over again,

---

[50] Henry of Huntingdon, ed. Forester, p. 295; Henry of Huntingdon, ed. Arnold, p. 290; G. White, 'The End of Stephen's Reign', p. 13.

[51] White, 'The End of Stephen's Reign', p. 13; Gervase of Canterbury, p. 159.

[52] *Gesta Stephani*, pp. 240–1.

[53] Richardson and Sayles, *The Governance of Medieval England*, p. 256.

[54] Henry of Huntingdon, ed. Forester, p. 296; Henry of Huntingdon, ed. Arnold, p. 290; White, 'The End of Stephen's Reign', p. 17.

[55] William of Newburgh, in *EHD*, II, p. 323; William of Newburgh, ed. Howlett, p. 101.

[56] William of Newburgh, ed. Stevenson, p. 444; William of Newburgh, ed. Howlett, p. 101.

unless settlement could be reached. By backing down from war, Henry won gratitude from the barons and the church. In the end it was enough to bring him the throne; it was a gamble which paid off.

The reason the pressure against battle was so great soon became clear. It is now a commonplace to point out that medieval commanders normally tried to avoid battle. Medieval subordinates had much the same fears. The barons who had pressured Henry and Stephen into avoiding battle reaped the rewards of their policy. Negotiations were about terms of peace between the leaders, but they were also about deals for the boys. There were very few losers, by arrangement. Most of the great men of Stephen's reign who survived into the new reign kept their lands and their position. Where families did lose, it was through natural wastage, or the result of new opposition to the crown, not vindictive royal policy. Few men could have regretted that Henry's accession came about through agreement rather than battle. The warfare of Stephen's reign had in the end been indecisive, even the peace settlement need not have had the outcome it did, but it was an agreement for mutual benefit of practically all, not a punishment for losers. The surprising realisation that there were no losers in the civil war of Stephen's reign explains the puzzle of the settlement. Men knew what they stood to win or lose, and forced the settlement on their leaders so that they should not lose.

William FitzOsbern, Earl of Hereford: Personality and Power on the Welsh Frontier, 1066–1071

TOBY PURSER

In February, 1071, William fitzOsbern took ten men from Normandy and rode to Flanders. He went, wrote Orderic Vitalis, as 'gaily as if he were going to a tournament'.[1] On Sunday morning, 20 February, Robert the Frisian fell upon fitzOsbern, Philip of France and his own nephew Arnulf, and in the ensuing battle at Cassel, killed fitzOsbern and the young Arnulf. The body of William fitzOsbern was carried back to Normandy and buried with great mourning at Cormeilles. 'The bravest of the Normans, renowned for his generosity, ready wit, and outstanding integrity, he was universally mourned' lamented Orderic. 'Truly the glory of this world falls and withers like the flower of grass, even as smoke it fades and passes.'[2]

What was William fitzOsbern doing in Flanders? Late in 1070, or early in 1071, William the Conqueror dispatched him to Normandy to act as regent of the duchy with the Queen Matilda. Flanders was in a state of disruption at the time. The Conqueror's brother-in-law, Baldwin VI, had died in July 1070 and his two young sons, Arnulf and Baldwin, received Flanders and Hainault, but were to be governed by their mother, Richildis. When Robert the Frisian, son of Baldwin V, opposed her rule, she called upon Philip I of France and fitzOsbern for aid. According to the *Anglo-Saxon Chronicle*, Earl William was to be Arnulf's protector and he intervened – and died – in his capacity as the duke of Normandy's representative. However, it may have been that William fitzOsbern's death at Cassel was the result of a more personal quest. David Douglas believed

---

[1]   M. Chibnall, *The Ecclesiastical History of Orderic Vitalis*, 6 vols (Oxford, 1969–80), II, p. 281. It was not necessarily February when fitzOsbern set out from Normandy.

I would like to thank Chris Lewis for all his friendship, help and advice given unstintingly over the last couple of years and for reading a draft of the paper, Matthew Strickland for offering me the chance to present it at Harlaxton, and my parents for funding the research.

[2]   Orderic, II, pp. 282, 318. This is Orderic's date. Flemish sources say Cassel was fought on Monday, 21 February; see *The Gesta Normannorum Ducum of William of Jumièges, Orderic Vitalis and Robert of Torigini* ed. and trans. E. M. C. Van Houts, 2 vols (Oxford, 1992–95), II, p. 146, n. 5.

Richildis offered herself in marriage to fitzOsbern and placed her son Arnulf in his wardship for that reason.[3] FitzOsbern's wife, Adeliza, had died in 1066 and in 1071 he was on a mission to further his own ambitions. In Freeman's confident words, he perished in a 'mad enterprise after a crown and a wife in Flanders..[4]

William fitzOsbern's death opens up two broad themes central to the entire nature of the Norman Conquest. Firstly, his death was, it seems, a result of both personal ambition and sacrifice in the name of public duty, and it is this duality of motive that is reflected throughout the reign of William of Normandy. Freeman's words could just as well be applied to the ambitious duke on the eve of the Conquest – still more so had William perished at Hastings – and more generally to other great men of William's reign.[5] Odo of Bayeux, Roger II of Montgomery, Robert of Mortain and many others gambled for high stakes. Secondly, fitzOsbern's premature death – and it was premature at a time when all his great contemporaries lived on for another fifteen to twenty years[6] – had a great impact on the nature of the conquest of England, in that his absence created a power vacuum that led ultimately to a revolt and a change in royal policy.

Personal ambition and public service went hand in hand in the young Duke William's duchy. William fitzOsbern was with him from the beginning. And before that his father, Osbern Herfastsson, had died in the duke's service as his steward; his son and heir probably grew up in the ducal household.[7] Osbern, a major support in the reign of Robert the Magnificent, sometimes attested Duke Robert's *acta* as 'Osbern son of Herfast', while his mother was the daughter of Duke Richard I's half-brother, Count Rodulf, lord of Ivry. Though Osbern was only the son-in-law of Rodulf, he inherited the estates and these were passed on

---

3 D. C. Douglas, *William the Conqueror* (London, 1964), pp. 224–5. Douglas followed William of Malmesbury, the only author with this interpretation. Would it be, then, a moralistic tale of the punishment of lust? William of Malmesbury, *De Gestis Regum Anglorum*, ed. W. Stubbs, 2 vols (Rolls Series, London, 1887–9), II, pp. 314–15.

4 E. A. Freeman, *The History of the Norman Conquest of England*, 6 vols (1st edn, Oxford, 1867–79), I, p. 198. In the light of fitzOsbern's staunch loyalty to the duke-king William, this conclusion would seem unlikely. However, the difference of opinion here is used as an example leading to the greater differences over the interpretation of the nature of the power fitzOsbern wielded.

5 Though William, of course, was only seeking a crown; he was already married in 1066.

6 FitzOsbern's brother, Osbern, for instance, lived until 1103.

7 Orderic, IV, p. 83.

intact to his son, William.[8] Furthermore, William's brother Osbern had gone to England with the Conqueror and eventually became bishop of Exeter in 1073, leaving any claim to the Norman lands solely to William.[9]

The *Deeds of Duke William* by William of Poitiers tells how Duke William 'loved fitzOsbern above the other members of his household since they had been boys together'[10] and how he rode into action with Roger de Montgomery before Domfront, in the skirmishes against Geoffrey of Anjou. Roger was to become earl of Shrewsbury in 1069 with enormous powers along the border and was from an early age with the duke, possibly also in his household as a child.[11] FitzOsbern was one of the great men listed at Hastings, present with Roger de Montgomery on the ship-list of the Conqueror, where he was titled 'steward' (*dapifer*), and both were among the top tenants-in-chief in Domesday Book.[12] Together, William the duke, William son of Osbern and Roger de Montgomery grew rich, powerful and successful by mutual aid, marriage-alliances and kinship along with anyone else who stayed loyal. Those not with them were against them, and were either physically rejected or deprived of social connection.[13] The ultimate prize after the consolidation of the duchy and the subjugation of Maine was England, and together they took it and held it. William fitzOsbern was then rewarded richly with the earldom of Hereford, an old and established institution, and given joint authority with Odo over England. The remarkable achievement of these men and their chivalric deeds were celebrated by William of Poitiers, William of Jumièges and the Bayeux Tapestry and continued to fascinate writers of the following century, most notably Orderic Vitalis.

What sort of man was William fitzOsbern? Is it ever possible to see behind the portrait painted by William of Poitiers, who was writing an unashamed panegyric, or that of the Bayeux Tapestry, brilliantly artistic but

---

8   See C. W. Hollister, 'The Greater Domesday Tenants-in-Chief' in *Domesday Studies*, ed. J. C. Holt (Woodbridge, 1986), p. 231, and D. Bates, *Normandy before 1066* (London, 1982), p. 119.

9   S. Keynes, 'Regenbald the Chancellor', *Anglo-Norman Studies*, 10 (1987), pp. 185–222. Bates, *Normandy before 1066*, p. 119, shows that the brother briefly shared the inheritance, probably in the very early 1040s.

10 Guillaume de Poitiers, *L'Histoire de Guillaume le Conquérant*, ed. and trans. R. Foreville (Paris, 1952), p. 264 (henceforth *Gesta Guillelmi*).

11 E. Searle, *Predatory Kinship and the Creation of Norman Power, 840–1066* (Berkeley, 1988), pp. 155–6.

12 See E. van Houts, 'The Ship-List of William the Conqueror', *Anglo-Norman Studies*, 9 (1987), p. 176, who has demonstrated that this is a contemporary source rather than a later, twelfth-century document.

13 For example, Guy of Brionne, the duke's cousin (*Gesta Guillelmi*, p. 18) and Archbishop Mauger, the duke's uncle (*Gesta Guillelmi*, p. 129).

essentially two-dimensional? It may indeed be possible, and I suggest the key to this is through the death of the earl and the revolt of his son in 1075. Orderic Vitalis saw him not only as the bravest of the Normans but as the first and greatest oppressor of the English, hastily supporting the Conquest which claimed thousands of lives. He slew many by the sword and perished by the sword. Orderic's apparent change of heart,[14] motivated perhaps by monastic scruples, reflects the difficulty we have in understanding the man. Writing considerably later, the *Chronicle of Battle Abbey* was more reserved: fitzOsbern was 'a man of admirable probity and very clever', an illustration perhaps of a cool, calculating statesman.[15] William of Poitiers was unequivocal: fitzOsbern was outstanding in valour and counsel in domestic and military affairs and very pious; a conventional view one would expect from the panegyrist, but Poitiers then adds, out of form, a 'very great terror to the English'.[16] The writer of the *Anglo-Saxon Chronicle* would no doubt have agreed with this, for fitzOsbern was clearly one of those in mind when the *Chronicle* describes the oppression caused by the castle-building activities in the Conqueror's absence very early on in the reign.[17]

It would be too simplistic, then, to portray fitzOsbern solely as a 'bold, bad baron' perishing in a mad dash to Flanders in search of further wealth and power. Some letters of Archbishop Lanfranc on the eve of the rebellion of 1075 reveal a very different man, and provide a more immediate image than the distant chronicle sources. 'Never forget your father's distinguished career; the faithful service he gave his lord, his zeal in winning great possessions,' he urged Roger of Breteuil in his first letter voicing concern over Roger's growing dissent. As the news of revolt worsened, so Lanfranc's despair increased: incredible that a son of Earl William, 'a man whose sagacity and integrity and loyalty to his lord and all his friends is renowned in many lands', could bring such shame upon the family and their king. Finally, Lanfranc disowned and excommunicated Roger, and the rebel was exiled to Normandy by the king.[18] Waltheof, the English earl of Northumbria, was not so lucky, and faced execution in 1076.

Further objective evidence of William fitzOsbern's high standing comes from Domesday Book. Although it was compiled fifteen years after his death at Cassel, he is mentioned 34 times in Herefordshire alone, whereas his rebellious son, earl for four years (1071–5), only one year less

---

[14]   Orderic, II, pp. 318–21.
[15]   *The Chronicle of Battle Abbey*, ed. and trans. E. Searle (Oxford, 1980), p. 34.
[16]   *Gesta Guillelmi*, p. 241.
[17]   *The Anglo-Saxon Chronicle* (hereafter *ASC*), trans. G. N. Garmonsway (London, 1953), 'D', 1067.
[18]   *The Letters of Lanfranc, Archbishop of Canterbury*, ed. H. Clover and M. Gibson (Oxford, 1979), nos 30–2.

than his father, receives only one reference.[19] This is a measure of the extent to which the lords and men in the shire remembered him when presenting the returns to the Domesday commissioners, and the impact he had on the shire in such a short period.

It is in Herefordshire that the true measure of William fitzOsbern's power and personality can be seen. The king granted him the earldom and extensive lands in Gloucestershire, Worcestershire, Oxfordshire, Dorset, Berkshire, Hampshire and Somerset, including the Isle of Wight.[20] It is possible that he was titled earl of Herefordshire early in 1067, before the king returned in triumph to Normandy and besides that, he was made vice-regent along with the king's half-brother, Odo of Bayeux, the new earl of Kent.[21] The significance of Herefordshire lay not only in the frontier position it occupied, but also in the long tradition the earldom had as an institution. After the reorganisation of the earldoms of England by Cnut in 1017, Swegn Godwinsson emerged as earl of Herefordshire in the mid 1040s. Swegn was Godwin's first son, and governed Gloucestershire, Oxfordshire, Berkshire and Somerset, roughly the same bloc of land fitzOsbern held.[22] Swegn left England after his father's rebellion in 1051 and never returned, but his place as earl and lord over these shires was taken by Ralph of Mantes, Edward the Confessor's nephew, a descendant of both Charlemagne through his father and Alfred the Great through his mother, Goda, Edward's sister.[23] Following Ralph's failure to defend the shire against the Welsh invaders in 1055, Harold Godwinsson took over the governance of Herefordshire; Domesday Book bears witness to the rich manors he had in demesne. Harold was all but the king's deputy in the 1060s and defeated the Welsh king Gruffudd ap Llwelyn in 1063 in a brilliant campaign with his brother Tostig, earl of Northumbria.[24] William fitzOsbern was thus inheriting a noble title and a well established institution when he took command in 1067.

---

[19]   Earl William; DB; Herefordshire folios 179c, 179d, 180c, 180d, 181a, 181b, 181c, 183b, 184a, 184c, 184d, 185a, 186a, 187a, 187b, 187c (Worcestershire folios for Herefordshire) 163c, 172b; Earl Roger, Herefordshire fol. 180d.

[20]   *Gesta Guillelmi*, p. 239; *ASC*, D, 1066; *Florentii Wigorniensis monachi chronicon ex chronicis* (hereafter Florence), ed. B. Thorpe, 2 vols (London, 1848–9), II, p. 1.

[21]   *Regesta Regum Anglo-Normannorum*, I, ed. H. W. C. Davis (Oxford, 1913), no. 7, 'Willelm eorl'; also nos 8, 22, 24, 26, 28; C. P. Lewis, 'The Early Earls of Norman England', *Anglo-Norman Studies*, 13 (1990), pp. 207–23.

[22]   Florence, I, p. 205.

[23]   A. Williams, 'The King's Nephew: The Family and Career of Ralph, Earl of Hereford', *Studies in Medieval History Presented to R. A. Brown*, ed. C. Harper-Bill, C. Holdsworth and J. Nelson (Woodbridge, 1989), pp. 327–40.

[24]   *ASC*, D, 1063.

He began a strategic castle-building plan immediately, a skill acquired in his rise to power in Normandy. FitzOsbern's marriage to Adeliza, daughter of Roger de Tosny, brought him a considerable dowry and he made Breteuil, 9 miles south-west of Conches his *caput*. This fortress was built and fortified in the 1050s but was not used to his own ends; he held Breteuil as the duke's and guarded it against all ducal enemies.[25] So when castles were built in England to consolidate the new reign, fitzOsbern was placed in command, along with Odo.[26] And in Herefordshire, fitzOsbern organised the building of the great stone castle of Chepstow, one of the earliest stone keeps in the country, possibly begun as early as 1067, dominating the Wye and the Severn estuary. There are five castles named in the Domesday folios for Herefordshire: Richard's Castle and Wigmore to the north, near the Shropshire border, Clifford on the Wye controlling the northern point of the Golden Valley into Wales, Ewyas at the southern point of the Golden Valley, and Monmouth; Chepstow, or *Striguil*, is listed in the Gloucester folios.[27] They lay in a line from north to south along the Welsh border, forming a protective ring around the shire. Clifford was held in Domesday by Ralph de Tosny, fitzOsbern's brother-in-law, and survives today in stone as does Wigmore, if they were not indeed originally stone-built like Chepstow. The strategic importance of these castles is revealed in a letter of Lanfranc when he was pleading for fitzOsbern's son to see reason in 1075: 'Our lord the king of the English greets you and all of us as his faithful subjects in whom he places great trust, commanding us to do all in our power to prevent his castles from being handed over to his enemies: may God avert such a disaster'.[28]

The reality of conquest on the Welsh border and in England as a whole was war. FitzOsbern, Duke William and Roger de Montgomery had been schooled in it from birth; pedigree, marriage and loyalty counted for much but to achieve what these three did demanded military skill, cunning and brutality. Orderic's comment on the new earl's appointment is a reminder of this, for the king set him up 'to fight the bellicose Welsh' and to build strong castles in 'suitable places'.[29] We read in the *Deeds of Duke William* how in 1054 when fitzOsbern and Roger de Montgomery met Geoffrey of Anjou at Domfront, he boasted to them that he would be at Domfront to awake the guards with his trumpet at dawn and described what he would

---

[25] Searle, *Predatory Kinship*, p. 187.
[26] Orderic specifically names fitzOsbern as castellan of York castle, built in 1069; (Orderic, II, p. 223).
[27] DB, Herefordshire folios: Richard's Castle, 186d; Wigmore, 183c; Clifford, 183b; Ewyas, 186a; Monmouth, 180d; Chepstow, 162a (Gloucestershire).
[28] *Letters of Lanfranc*, no. 31, p. 119.
[29] Orderic, II, p. 260; Florence, II, p. 1.

wear, and the horse he would be on, to which fitzOsbern and Montgomery replied that the duke would be there and described his arms and armour.[30] However, the dispute over Domfront and Alençon between the duke and the count of Anjou was resolved not by personal combat but by the brutal mutilation of some citizens of Alençon, an event recorded by William of Jumièges, though passed over by William of Poitiers. The duke apparently ordered the hands and feet of some townspeople to be cut off, in possible imitation of his great uncle Count Rodulf, and the rebellion came to an end.[31] Irrespective of the veracity of this incident, the brutality committed by the Conqueror in the north of England in the winter of 1069, through a devastation that left even Orderic Vitalis shocked over fifty years later, was unequivocal.[32] We assume that William fitzOsbern was present with the duke, advising and carrying out orders, as he had done since childhood. He was the 'terror of the English' and the right-hand man to the king who loved stags more than his subjects and went into Wales with men who, in Orderic's words, 'would dare anything'.[33]

Set-piece battles, however, were rare – the Conqueror only fought three in his lifetime – and castle-building was the order of the day. War was conducted around raids, skirmishes and a scorched earth policy, directed from the motte and bailey castles which acted as shelter and staging posts for the lines of communication into Wales. Duke William's rise to power in Normandy was a story of the subjugation of unfriendly castles, such as the fortress of Brionne, held by his cousin Guy, which took three years to take. Only when William captured or destroyed all these forts could he be secure as duke. Then, in the words of William of Poitiers, he was received with 'huge honour' and men of all ranks bowed down to his dignity.[34]

The emerging picture of fitzOsbern, drawn from narrative sources, charters and Domesday Book, is one of the foremost men of the time; a skilled warrior, harsh, oppressive and brutal; an able ruler in the absence of the king, and cousin and life-long friend to William, a man praised and revered by chroniclers and by the venerable Lanfranc, and a man remembered in Domesday Book fifteen years after his death. He was a benefactor, too. This last role is to be seen in his foundation, with his wife Adeliza, of Lyre c.1046 in the diocese of Evreux and Cormeilles c.1060 in Lisieux.[35] Lyre received English benefactions after 1066; it had the highest

---

[30] *Gesta Guillelmi*, pp. 18–19; and see below, pp. 310–11.
[31] *Gesta Normannorum Ducum*, pp. 124–5; Searle, *Predatory Kinship*, p. 208 and n.
[32] Orderic, II, pp. 232–3; and see below, J. J. N. Palmer, 'War and Domesday Waste'.
[33] *ASC*, 'E', 1087; Orderic, II, p. 260.
[34] *Gesta Guillelmi*, p. 90.
[35] Hollister, 'The Greater Domesday Tenants-in-chief', appendix C, p. 24.

number of churches recorded in Domesday Book and was the greatest recipient of ecclesiastical tithes.[36] These foundations were not exceptional to Normandy before the Conquest; there was a popular trend amongst the ducal aristocracy for the establishment of religious endowments.

Beyond the contemporary and near contemporary sources, however, there are historical constructs which can create misleading portrayals of the real nature of the power William fitzOsbern wielded. The available evidence can be marshalled in various ways which can fail to do justice to Anglo-Norman society and the way it worked. One such construct comes in the form of categorising fitzOsbern and his like. In 1926, W. J. Corbett classified the barons of the Conqueror by placing them into classes A – E by order of their landed wealth, and thereby imposing a rigid hierarchy onto what was in reality, in Holt's words, a 'very fluid society'.[37] Baronial position in society indeed depended upon land but it was only retained through loyalty to the king. Many leading families fell or nearly fell from grace in the forty years after 1066; the earldom of Hereford itself did not exist after 1075 and even the great Odo of Bayeux was brought down in 1082. The earldoms of Hereford, East Anglia and Northumbria fell in 1075; Hugh de Montgomery, Robert of Northumbria and Roger de Lacy were banished in 1095, Robert of Bellême in 1102 and William of Cornwall in 1104. The Clares and Warennes had close calls in 1095 and 1101–03, respectively.[38] Although a family might gain an entrenched position and hand this on to the following generation, it was kinship and allegiance to Duke, then King, William, that counted above all, and the establishment of cordial relationships with his heirs. Of Corbett's Class 'A' list of eleven magnates, seven were the Conqueror's kinsmen.

Another construct, particularly in the case of William fitzOsbern, is the use of the anachronistic term 'palatine earldom'. Both Allen Brown and John le Patourel chose not to employ this term and J. W. Alexander exposed it as the anachronism it truly is.[39] In the case of William fitzOsbern and his earldom, Stenton, amongst others, believed Herefordshire to be

[36] S. F. Hockey, 'William fitzOsbern and the Endowment of his Abbey of Lyre', *Anglo-Norman Studies*, 3 (1980), p. 96.

[37] W. J. Corbett, 'The Development of the Duchy of Normandy and the Norman Conquest of England' in *Cambridge Medieval History*, V (Cambridge, 1926, repr. 1968), pp. 505–13; J. C. Holt, 'Feudal Society and the Family in Early Medieval England I: The Revolution of 1066', *TRHS*, 5th Series (1982), p. 208.

[38] C. Warren Hollister, 'The Greater Domesday Tenants-in-Chief', pp. 219–49.

[39] J. le Patourel, *The Norman Empire* (Oxford, 1976), p. 63; R. A. Brown, *The Normans and the Norman Conquest* (Swansea, 1977), p. 31; J. W. Alexander, 'The Alleged Palatinates of Norman England', *Speculum* (1981), pp. 17–21; and reaffirmed by Lewis, 'The Early Earls', pp. 207–23.

withdrawn from the ordinary administrative system, along with Shropshire and Cheshire; Galbraith and Wightman were both certain that the earl wielded palatinal powers in a palatinal earldom, Wightman even arguing that Worcestershire was a palatinate.[40] But a 'palatine' was a concept unknown to eleventh-century lords and so was the idea of a 'prototype justiciarship'; these are later medieval terms and do not do justice to the nature of William fitzOsbern's power.[41]

Given that William fitzOsbern inherited an old land-bloc which pre-dated Edward the Confessor (in notable contrast to the new creations of Shropshire and Cheshire), and given his kinship with the duke-king and his allegiances and power-building in pre-Conquest Normandy, is it not reasonable to accept that in post-Conquest England, William fitzOsbern was an extremely powerful man? He does not have to be called 'justiciar' or to govern a 'palatine'; in the context of Norman politics and family connections, William fitzOsbern simply *was*. He was remembered in Domesday Book as just 'Earl William', as he was in the charters he attested. The use of the Anglo-Saxon *eorl* in the charters, rather than the Norman *comes*, is indicative of the traditional type of power he had. Similar conditions apply to Roger de Montgomery, made earl of Shrewsbury and Hugh of Avranches, earl of Chester; they were known in the charters and in Domesday Book simply as 'Earl Roger' and 'Earl Hugh'. Everybody knew who they were, for they were the sons of well-known Normans who had themselves supported the duke either in the duchy or at Hastings. As well as the words *eorl* and *comes*, which Crouch believes entirely interchangeable

---

[40] F. M. Stenton, *The First Century of English Feudalism, 1066–1166* (2nd edn, Oxford, 1960), pp. 228–9; V. H. Galbraith, 'An Episcopal Land Grant of 1085', *EHR*, 175 (1929), pp. 353–72; W. E. Wightman, 'The Palatine Earldom of William fitzOsbern in Gloucestershire and Worcestershire, 1066–1071', *EHR*, 77 (1962), pp. 7–8; and *idem, The Lacy Family in England and Normandy, 1066–1194* (Oxford, 1966).

[41] The distinction between concept and terminology seems to remain a matter of debate, for the palatine construct is alive and well according to S. Harvey, 'The People and the Land', *The Agrarian History of England*, II, ed. H. E. Hallam (Cambridge, 1988), pp. 79–121, and F. Suppe, *Military Institutions on the Welsh Marches, 1066–1194* (Woodbridge, 1994), p. 89, n.5, who follows Nelson's thinking that the king created palatine counties; cf. L. Nelson, *The Normans in South Wales, 1070–1171* (Austin, 1966), p. 34. The major revisionist work on terms and concepts is S. Reynolds, *Fiefs and Vassals: the Medieval Evidence Reinterpreted* (Oxford, 1994), which has challenged so much of the traditional understanding of the middle ages, in particular feudalism. See also D. Bates, 'The Origins of the Justiciarship', *Anglo-Norman Studies*, 4 (1981), pp. 1–12.

between England and Normandy at this period,[42] contemporaries used *milites* and *barones* to describe the members of the ruling class. This poses further problems, for if we understand a *miles* to be a humble soldier no better off than a wealthy peasant,[43] then what are we to make of the Domesday references to Robert, count of Eu, William of Braose and Hugh de Montfort as *milites*?[44] These were undoubtedly great men; Robert and Hugh are on the ship-list of the Conqueror and would elsewhere be known as *barones* (as opposed to *homines*) or, in William of Poitiers' words, *potentates* and *summates*.[45] And once the classical and the vernacular titles become interchangeable it might then be possible that William fitzOsbern, earl of Hereford and *vicarus* of England, was also *miles*.[46]

It is clear that at the time of the Norman Conquest, a variety of titles and terms were employed which would not necessarily render the status of such men inherently indefinable to us today, but conversely this should not lead us to impose our own limitations on their position. It merely means that an understanding of the nature of the power fitzOsbern and his colleagues wielded is difficult, probably impossible, to understand fully, but such a realisation would be better than accepting a comfortable fallacy.

It might equally be a mistake to place William fitzOsbern in the category of a 'hero'. This would be to take some of the narrative sources at face-value. Here we confront not the constructs of later historians but those of contemporary writers, already seeking to place the protagonists of their age into a recognisable formula, usually in the form of the classical hero and thereby introducing yet another mode of thought. Chief amongst these is William of Poitiers' *Deeds of Duke William*, which may have influenced the Bayeux Tapestry and certainly did influence Orderic Vitalis. Poitiers was writing a panegyric of the duke, justifying the invasion of England and glorifying the victories of the Conqueror.[47] He was a classical scholar and stylist and there are comparisons between Duke William and Julius Caesar's invasion of Britain throughout. The Trojan War, Caesar's *Gallic Wars* and *Civil Wars* Sallust's *Conspiracy of Catiline* and Virgil's *Aeneid* are all stock sources used. So when the Conqueror's fleet was becalmed at

---

[42] D. Crouch, *The Image of Aristocracy in Britain, 1000–1300* (London, 1992), p. 55, after Lewis, 'The Early Earls', pp. 207–8, 211–12.

[43] S. Harvey, 'The Knight and the Knight's Fee', *Past and Present*, 49 (1970), pp. 3–43.

[44] DB folios 4b, 4c, 65c.

[45] *Gesta Guillelmi*, pp. 26, 44; at one point (p. 16) he describes Nigel vicomte of the Cotentin as *praeses* of the *pagus* of Coutances and these were terms employed by Cicero and Tacitus to mean 'province' and 'guardian'.

[46] Orderic, II, p. 202, calls him *vicarus*.

[47] R. H. C. Davis, *From Alfred the Great to Stephen* (London, 1991), pp. 101–31.

St. Valéry, there is comparison with that of Agamemnon at Aulis; and where the Conqueror refused to return Harold's body to his mother so there is Achilles's treatment of the body of Hector in the *Iliad*. The Bayeux Tapestry's story of Harold Godwinsson rescuing two men from the quicksands of Mont St. Michel looks like a piece of Herculean folklore.[48] Other events might be related more to contemporary jokes or bad omens, such as Conan's escape down a rope from the castle of Dol and the duke putting his hauberk on back to front before the battle of Hastings.[49] These anecdotes owed more to vernacular than to classical literature, but William of Poitiers took them all on board in the writing of his panegyric. The major difficulty when attempting to assess the division between truth and literature is whether men such as William fitzOsbern acted as they did because they modelled their own lives on the legends which they had learnt in infancy, or whether an author asserted that they had behaved in a particular fashion because that was what his literary models demanded.

Although there are passages in *The Deeds of Duke William* that are clearly fabulous, there are some events that appear to be more credible.[50] One event is the time when, after landing at Pevensey, the duke took only twenty-five men on a patrol along the coast, including William fitzOsbern; on the return they had to dismount due to the difficulty of the path, and the duke carried the hauberk of his friend fitzOsbern, who was renowned for his bodily strength. This may indeed be apocryphal, but given the audacious risks taken during the entire campaign, which was itself a huge risk, it does seem to have a ring of truth to it. It shows, without boastful exaggeration how, beneath the trappings of wealth, power, and kinship, the astonishing events described are reduced in a single moment to the duke and his friends laughing and joking as they led their horses along a coastal path.[51]

William fitzOsbern was, of course, present on this occasion, as on all the others. He was quite possibly the chief exponent of the invasion strategy, the 'prime agent in the Conquest of England' as Freeman saw him.[52] It was fitzOsbern who persuaded the dubious Norman barons to follow the duke on the enterprise; and in later legend, when the duke fell on his face leaping onto the shore of England, cutting his nose, it was fitzOsbern who seized the moment, shouting: 'Do not take this as unlucky ... he has claimed England, taking possession of it with both hands and he

---

[48] *The Bayeux Tapestry: A Comprehensive Survey*, ed. F. M. Stenton and others (London, revised edn, 1965), pl. 22.

[49] Bayeux Tapestry, pl. 23; *Gesta Guillelmi*, p. 180.

[50] For example, when Duke William defeated 300 Angevin cavalry and 400 foot with only 50 knights (*Gesta Guillelmi*, p. 34).

[51] *Gesta Guillelmi*, p. 168.

[52] Freeman, *History of the Norman Conquest*, I, p. 198.

has consecrated it as the inheritance of his own lineage by marking it with his own blood.'[53] The Battle Abbey chronicler may have invented this tale, but his choice of William fitzOsbern is telling. FitzOsbern survived only four years of the reign of the duke-king, but clearly made an enormous impact on the historiography of the Conquest; if he did not utter these words, later writers believed he ought to have.

If the contemporary and near-contemporary sources paint a vivid but often elusive portrait of William fitzOsbern and if later historians have added their own particular gloss, then the events after his death go some way to providing a more definite picture of his powers when alive. In 1075, his son revolted. Three men, Roger de Breteuil, Ralph de Gael and Waltheof, son of Siward of Northumbria, plotted a rebellion to overthrow the king and set themselves up as a triumvirate.[54] The plan was dreamed up at the wedding of Ralph de Gael, to Emma, William fitzOsbern's daughter, in Norwich. Ralph de Gael was the son of Ralph the Staller, earl of East Anglia, and had inherited an old established earldom like Roger; Waltheof was a Saxon and had a title that also hailed from the reign of Cnut.[55] All three men had great positions of trust and therefore the betrayal of that trust was so much greater. It was fitting that such a revolt should be planned at a wedding, for marriages were the hub of a society so heavily centred upon kinship alliance. The rebellion failed; the Herefordshire barons remained loyal to the memory of William fitzOsbern and stopped Roger at the Severn. The king threw 'his kinsman' in jail, and Ralph de Gael fled the country, leaving his wife to defend Norwich castle. The Anglo-Saxon chronicler wrote a sanctimonious little couplet to pronounce judgement on the failed revolt:

There was that bride-ale
That was many men's bale[56]

These events were a result of the power vacuum left by fitzOsbern's death. It should be noted that the men of this first Norman revolt of the Norman governance of Britain were of the second generation. The death of William fitzOsbern clearly left such a void that his son, and some other sons of the great men who came over with the Conqueror in 1066, could not cope with the enormity of their fathers' achievements. Little is known of the dispute of 1075, but it seems that part of the problem was over the control of sheriffs. Some sheriffs in the decade after the Conquest were under baronial rather than royal control.[57] Both Roger de Montgomery and

---

53 *The Chronicle of Battle Abbey*, p. 34.
54 The *ASC*, D and E, 1075; Florence, II, pp. 10–11; Orderic, II, pp. 310–18.
55 Lewis, 'The Early Earls', pp. 208–9.
56 *ASC*, D, 1075.
57 J. A. Green, 'The Sheriffs of William the Conqueror', *Anglo-Norman Studies*, 5

William fitzOsbern are known to have been examples of this and Roger wanted to continue his father's powers. This is referred to by Lanfranc in the first of his letters to Roger, where he writes that the king has ordered 'his sheriffs not to hold any courts within your [i.e., Roger's] lands' until he returns.[58] If this was the main bone of contention between Roger and the king it demonstrates clearly that fitzOsbern's son was not given the same powers as his father.

If the hegemony William fitzOsbern had created by his own personal pre-eminence was indeed the result of a combination of kinship, tradition and character, then it would be a unique one, and the king clearly seized the opportunity to break it up after his death with the excuse of the 1075 rebellion. It was replaced by new, smaller power-bases as seen in Shropshire and Cheshire, which, although held by men of old Norman families, were essentially new creations, based around towns rather than shires, in the Norman way.[59] The Conqueror was happy to leave Herefordshire alone, and dismantle the vestiges of the Edwardian earldoms. The execution of Waltheof in 1076 was part of this process.

The power William fitzOsbern wielded was meant for one man only: William himself. His death must have been a tremendous shock to the king, and also occurred at a crucial point of the reign. The deposition of Archbishop Stigand, the possible imposition of knightly quotas[60] and the increasing trouble with the king's son, Robert Curthose, all came in the early 1070s. Had fitzOsbern lived longer, as most of his contemporaries did, there might well have been no rebellion in 1075 and the earldom of Hereford as an Anglo-Saxon institution, and its associate shires of Worcestershire, Gloucestershire and Oxfordshire, might have survived intact. The Norman settlement of England, in particular Herefordshire and southern Wales, might then have taken a different course.

William fitzOsbern embodies the chivalric nature of the Conquest. In an age of heroic battles and extraordinary deeds of derring-do he stands out, but remains a mystery in so many ways. He was never actually titled

---

(1982), pp. 136–7 and J. F. A. Mason, 'Barons and their Officials in the Later Eleventh Century', *Anglo-Norman Studies*, 19 (1990), pp. 243–62. Three sheriffs under fitzOsbern had links with the earl's household: Roger de Pitres, first sheriff of Gloucestershire, Ralph de Bernai and Gilbert the Sheriff in Herefordshire.

58 *Letters of Lanfranc*, no. 31.
59 Lewis, 'The Early Earls', p. 222; J. F. A. Mason, 'Roger de Montgomery and his Sons, 1066–1102', *TRHS*, 5th series (1963), p. 8.
60 If we are to believe Round's thesis, *Feudal England* (London, 1895) or not, according to J. Gillingham, 'The Introduction of Knight Service to England', *Anglo-Norman Studies*, 4 (1981), pp. 53–64.

'earl of Hereford' in his lifetime, but the returns of 1086 show how local people felt otherwise; much written about him was written later, but the different sources are eager to attribute actions and words to him in particular. Even the manner of his death, with which I began, is a bone of contention. However, instead of understanding him and his like as 'palatinal', 'institutional' or even 'feudal', it might be suggested that the solution lies in chivalry. Indeed, the Norman Conquest and the age of the Normans was the first truly chivalric age. Not the complex and ritualistic chivalry of a later age, but rather a way of life simply as seen from the back of a horse – *chevalrie* – with no limit to what one might achieve, and to risk all on the swing of a sword. That was why William fitzOsbern went to Flanders in 1071 with only ten fellow knights. Ambition, imagination and controlled violence rode under the mantle of public service. He was, after all, the 'bravest of the Normans'.[61]

---

[61]   Orderic, II, p. 282.

Valois Powers over Fortresses
on the Eve of the Hundred Years War

CHARLES COULSON

At the outset of his magisterial work, Philippe Contamine renounced the *matériel* of war along with the blood-and-guts of 'les derniers tenants de l'histoire-batailles'[1]. While disdaining 'les amateurs de coups d'épée' his sociological sieve still lets through a great deal of the insidious modernism inherent in 'military history', its monarchism in particular. Castellology knows it well. Though properly far from narrowly architectural, fortress-studies have suffered long from those of the battering-rams and boiling-oil tendency[2] and from those who insist castles are 'rational applications of strategic planning'.[3] The notion that the only good castles were royal ones, so that razing and confiscating 'private castles', or forbidding (as it is thought) their construction, was both right and necessary, sprang from largely-modern castro-phobic royalism.[4] These extremes in Contamine are muted, but military logic alone, not precedent, for him make *châteaux*, *moustier-forts*, *villes-fermées* and fortresses of all kinds hardly more than *matériel de guerre*, compulsorily repaired and manned, requisitioned, *désemparés* or entirely demolished, by force of powers naturally exercised by the king as supreme commander, or by delegation.[5] In

---

1 Ph. Contamine, *Guerre, état et société à la fin du moyen âge: études sur les armées des rois de France 1337–1494* (Paris, 1972), p. vi. For fuller discussion of some issues raised here see my 'Community and Fortress-Politics in France in the Lull before the Hundred Years War', *Nottingham Medieval Studies*, 40 (1996) pp. 80–108.

2 C. Coulson, 'Cultural Realities and Reappraisals in English Castle-Study', *Journal of Medieval History* (1996), including bibliography, pp. 171–207.

3 C. Coulson, 'Hierarchism in Conventual Crenellation: An Essay in the Sociology and Metaphysics of Medieval Fortification', *Medieval Archaeology*, 26 (1982), p. 69.

4 E.g. R. Allen Brown, 'A List of Castles 1154–1216', *EHR*, 74 (1959), pp. 249–60; compare C. Coulson, 'Fortress-Policy in Capetian Tradition and Angevin Practice: Aspects of the Conquest of Normandy by Philip II', *Anglo-Norman Studies*, 6 (1984), pp. 13–38; and *idem*, 'The Castles of the Anarchy', in *The Anarchy of King Stephen's Reign*, ed. E. King (Oxford, 1994), ch. 2.

5 Contamine, *Guerre, état et société*, pp. 8–9, 62, 75, 77, 129, 230–3; compare C.

Contamine's later *La guerre au moyen âge* (1980) a single allusion to 'rendability and jurability', in the twelfth century only, acknowledged the vital customary foundation of these drastic rights, vested not in military command, nor even in *force majeure*, but lawfully in the direct *seigneur*.[6] The Fawtier vision of Capetian infallibility, echoed by Contamine's *monarchie*, even under Charles le Bien Aimé impersonally embodying French nationhood, may be allowable[7] – but not the neglect of the long tradition of fortress-control handed down to Philippe de Valois. To reassert it is to reinstate the seignorial and social dimension, to place central initiative in a truer light, and to suggest that the aims of the war were as much chivalric as national.

What came to be done, stimulated by Poitiers and by restive Estates, with fair accuracy marks the high-tide of governmental intervention in the first half of the war. A decade of disaster since Crécy (1346) had disclosed danger worse than any since Philippe Auguste.[8] Acting for his captive father, after deliberation by the three Estates of Languedoïl, the Regent Charles's Compiègne ordinances of May 1358 added to measures for regional cooperation in defence and for financing some most explicit arrangements for fortresses.[9] Although both consensual and theoretical in wording, calamity speaks in the fifth of twenty-eight heads: 'for that several *chastiaux, fors-maisons et autres forteresces* have been very damagingly lost for default of guard, and others are *en doubte de perdicion*', the captain of the district shall take with him knowledgeable representatives of the clergy, nobility and townships to see if any are not *garniz ou en estat de deffense*, and to compel those whose they are to have it done *senz grant grief de ceuls à qui ils*

Coulson, 'Seignorial Fortresses in France in Relation to Public Policy *c.*864 to *c.*1483', (unpublished Ph.D. thesis, University of London, 1972), ch. 4, i, c; ii, a.

[6] M. C. E. Jones (trans.) *War in the Middle Ages* (Oxford, 1984), p. 109. Note 108 referred originally only to R. Boutruche, *Seigneurie et féodalité* (Paris, 1968–70), ii, p. 38; the translator added C. Coulson, 'Rendability and Castellation in Medieval France', *Château-Gaillard*, 6 (1973), pp. 59–67.

[7] R. Fawtier, *The Capetian Kings of France, Monarchy and Nation (987–1328)*, trans. L. Butler and R. J. Adams (London, 1962). Some of the tone may be due to Fawtier's basic study being of Philip IV.

[8] Contamine, *Guerre, état et société*, pp. 77–8; on the 1356–9 crisis, pp. 44–5, 50, 53–4, 73–4, 77, 85, 87–8, 97–8, 108–9. Coulson, 'Fortress-Policy'; also *idem*, 'The Impact of Bouvines upon the Fortress-Policy of Philip Augustus', *Studies in Medieval History Presented to R. Allen Brown* (Woodbridge, 1989), pp. 71–80.

[9] *Ordonnances des rois de France* (hereafter, *Ordonnances*), iii (Paris, 1732) pp. 219–32. Compare Duke John's largely exhortatory measures in 1349 to defend Normandy against Henry of Lancaster; *Actes Normands de la Chambre des Comptes sous Philippe de Valois*, ed. L. Delisle (Rouen, 1871) pp. 409–13.

seront, euls de ce sommez avant toute euvre. If recalcitrant, so that harm to the *pays* might ensue, the captain shall *emparer*, put in a state of defence and keep them at their owner's cost: 'this all our captains, and each of them, and their deputies shall do'. Moreover, 'should owners be unable or unwilling to guard their fortresses, if prompt distraint cannot be made on their property, then each captain shall *les abatent ou facent abbatre et araser si que dommage n'en viegne'*, negligence or favouritism being punishable, 'any previous ordinance of ours notwithstanding'.[10]

That lords lay and ecclesiastical, and communes, should even hypothetically acquiesce shows that the great among them expected to be executants not victims. Fear of armed bands lodging, levying *appatis* and *rançons* locally from the quasi-legitimate base of a minor fortress,[11] over-rode suffering loss of control, potentially to an upstart captain and alien soldiery. 'Slighting' fortifications demeaned and humiliated. Seizure of goods and revenues supplanted lordship and impugned jurisdiction, nowhere more zealously proclaimed and jealously defended than at the castle, strong-house, fortified precinct and urban *banlieue* ditch.[12] The threat, no doubt, usually sufficed to coerce lesser lords; and the stipulated prior consultation implies negotiation.[13] Appeasing peasant resentment at their disproportionate suffering also weighed; but all allowances made, the responsibilities laid upon the whole nobility might seem to advertise and implement pure martial emergency; were it not that the measures exemplified by the Compiègne ordinance only universalised long-established (but now ill-recognised) fortress-custom.[14]

The force of feudal obligation provided Philippe de Valois and Jean le Bon initially with fortress-facilities as well as with the troop and cavalry services required to oppose Edward III. Since 1341 the gravity of the crisis had become clearer. A good part of the response was to affirm the Valois

---

[10] Similarly in P.-C. Timbal *et al.*, *La Guerre de Cent Ans vue à travers les Registres du Parlement (1337–1369)* (Paris, 1961), p. 107 (1358, 1360); pp. 190–200 (1358, 1372).

[11] E.g. K. Fowler, *The Age of Plantagenet and Valois* (London, 1967), pp. 165–76.

[12] Supersession of communal control of urban defences in war had long been conventional, e.g. *bastides* of Solomiac and Val-Roi-en-Chalosse (1328), and the major monastic town of Corbie, in 1310; *Ordonnances*, xii (Paris, 1777) pp. 500–2, 522–5; *Registres du Trésor des Chartes*, i, ed. R. Fawtier (Paris, 1958), no. 1241.

[13] Magnates' consent significantly was needed to obtain military service from their dependants; they easily gained knighthood and command (Contamine, *Guerre, état et société*, pp. 43–4, 50, 87, 130, 141, 159, 163–5, 168–9, 172, 174–83, 194, 213).

[14] E.g. S. Reynolds, *Fiefs and Vassals* (Oxford, 1994), though thorough, has a single oblique reference only to rendability, in Germany (pp. 469–70).

kingship by flexing the recognitory muscles of military service all the way down the pyramid of tenure. Ritualised social deference by suit of court, once by *albergamentum*, and by the whole unarmed majority of feudal obligations, had much to do with hierarchy but little or nothing with *raison d'état*.[15] In this light, the evolutionary proximity between fortress-customs prior to 1336 and subsequent development becomes much more obvious. Rendability especially had been crucial in consolidating and implementing loyalties during Philip II's great contest with the Angevins (1196–1223). The 1214–34 war of succession in Champagne[16] again showed the dual face of lordly takeover of fortresses (rendability) and of securing guarantees ranging from active benevolence to mere neutrality (jurability). If less vital in time of peace, fortress-customs were certainly not dormant. For this we need look back no further than to the *Coutumes de Beauvaisis*, compiled and commented upon by the royal *bailli* of Vermandois, Philippe de Beaumanoir, around 1283.[17] From the seignorial theory we will then proceed to the sometimes tendentious royal practice in a few salient documents of the crucial reigns of Philippe le Bel (1285–1314) and of *les rois maudits* (1314–28). Fortresses by ancient law were inherently public in character, however seemingly 'private' they were as objects of lordly pride.[18]

The count-bishop of Beauvais, together (be it noted) with his barons, exercised the rights over their vassals' castles still claimed (but already unrealistically) to be a royal monopoly back in 1119 by Louis le Gros.[19] The Valois eventually almost fulfilled it. Thus Beaumanoir: 'the count, and all who hold of him in barony, have this full right over their men *par reson de souverain* that if they have need (*mestier*) of their man's fortress for their war, or to put in their prisoners or munition (*garnisons*), or to protect themselves (*pour aus garder*), or for the common advantage of the *pays*, then they may take them'. Lodging prisoners was not generalised, nor was it usual in charters of recognisance to spell out the lord's reasons; nor, as Beaumanoir also does, the possible illegal abuses of these powers for harassment or oppression. Takeover and lordly entry in need were the fundamentals. In

---

[15] Contamine, *Guerre, état et société*, harps on the centrality of war (e.g. pp. 115–18, 119–25) but not of aristocratic ethos (e.g. pp. 163, 176–8, 190–2, 227, 253–5).

[16] C. Coulson, 'Castellation in the County of Champagne in the Thirteenth Century', *Château-Gaillard*, 9 & 10 (Caen, 1982), pp. 358–61.

[17] *Coutumes de Beauvaisis*, ed. Am. Salmon (Paris, 1899–1900), arts. 1662–6 (pp. 351–3).

[18] Origins examined in C. Coulson, 'The French Matrix of the Castle-Provisions of the Chester-Leicester *Conventio*', *Anglo-Norman Studies*, 17 (1995), pp. 65–86.

[19] *Recueil des chartes de l'abbaye de Cluny*, A. Bernard, A. Bruel (eds) (Paris, 1894), pp. 295–8.

Languedoc they were explicitly arbitrary, due to the *seigneur* be he 'angered or peaceable' (*irato seu pacato*) and in Languedoïl 'in force or without' (*ad magnam vim seu ad parvam*).[20] Beaumanoir softens this by admitting appeals to the king's court but only for misconduct by the lord, ruling out any recourse against his right *pour son besoing cler et aparant*. As normal, costs of takeover must be borne by the lord. He must indemnify the castellan for any resultant damage to the fortress, not asking to be reimbursed for any improvements; and the vassal may stay there in his donjon (*tour*) if necessary for his safety *car ce que nous avons dit que li seigneur pueent prendre les forteresces de leur hommes pour leur besoign, c'est à entendre que leur homme soient gardé du damage et du peril.*[21]

Beaumanoir expected the lodging of prisoners, at least, to be brief. Quite short retrospection gives an atavistic look to his proviso that the mutuality of obligations did not mean the vassal might repossess his lord's fortress, 'as though they were equal', *laquele chose ne doit pas estre*. It is an eloquent nicety. He declares as well another principle: that the lord might compulsorily purchase at fair value any possession of his man 'which seriously harmed his house or his fortress, or the common interest'. Philip IV so acted in 1309 to demolish a *maison forte* too near the gate of the castle of Bourdeilles.[22] Licensing fortification was too seignorially diffused and too honorific a prerogative to serve.[23] Forced acquisition had more potential. Contamine notes it as going beyond 'le pouvoir d'exiger la mise en état' of non-royal fortresses,[24] citing only the justificatory preamble to a charter of 1407 by Charles VI, recording his acquisition by exchange of the castle and *châtellenie* of Taillebourg (Saintonge) from John Harpenden.[25] To Contamine this was one of the war-powers wielded *au départ* by Philip VI, others being interdicting competing *guerres privées*, jousting, trade in war

[20] See notes 4, 5, 6, 8, 16, 18 above.

[21] Charles du Cange (*c*.1668) recognised the importance of this text in his treatise 'Des fiefs [*sic*] jurables et rendables', reprinted M. Petitot (ed.), *Collection complète des mémoires...dissertations sur Joinville*, iii (Paris, 1819) pp. 490–527 (pp. 498 *et seq.*).

[22] *Les Olim, ou registres des arrêts...*, ed. E. Beugnot (Paris, 1839), iii, pp. 338–9; calendared *Actes du Parlement de Paris*, ed. E. Boutaric, ii (Paris, 1867), p. 57.

[23] Coulson, 'Seignorial Fortresses'; for England see my 'Freedom to Crenellate by Licence: An Historiographical Revision', *Nottingham Medieval Studies*, 38 (1994), pp. 86–137; *idem*, 'Community and Fortress-Politics', notes 83, 104–5.

[24] Contamine, *Guerre, état et société*, pp. 230–1, n. 122, referring to *Ordonnances*, viii (Paris, 1750), p. 258: an instance of 1398 in Beaucaire seneschalcy.

[25] Contamine, *Guerre, état et société*, pp. 230–1, n. 123, referring to *Recueil général des anciennes lois françaises*, ed. Isambert *et al.* (Paris, 1822–33), vii, pp. 144–6, whose note that compulsory purchase had not previously been exercised may have misled.

material and prise, together with 'le contrôle de tous les points forts du royaume'. Taking all these as novel components of some implicit War Powers Act is disquieting.[26] Compulsory purchase had long been applied not just to the *fortalicia* or the *corpus castri*, like rendability, but to whole castle-lordships. Obtaining long-term military use of fortresses was incidental and, under the common procedure of *paréage* or coparceny, was shared not exclusive.[27] It particularly suited the expansion of the royal demesne in the Midi. Thus, in 1292, Philippe le Bel concluded at Vincennes a partnership with the abbey of Saint-André of Avignon in the *castrum monasterii*. This was the walled town of Villeneuve-lès-Avignon, which 'castle ...the king understands ...' *necessarium et utile nobis esset et habere in manu nostra*. The monks having apparently refused an outright exchange, the seneschal of Beaucaire negotiated a complex joint-tenure of the town (e.g. the keys were to be in joint custody), allowing the king to build two castles within the *castrum* or new town.[28] One was to be the bridge-tower, the other the great Fort Saint-André, built by Jean le Bon on the hill above Villeneuve from 1363.[29] By ceding a *paréage* in a nearby royal town, but excluding its castle, the crown gained a preponderant control over this major frontier zone, facing imperial Provence and papal Avignon across the Rhône; seemingly an entirely 'strategic' move.

But royal 'necessity' and 'public utility' operated regardless of 'frontiers', vaguely as that term was used, or of 'war' which was more precise. Prosaically, the rationale was that familiar in far-sighted, large-scale noble estate-planning, designed to develop, consolidate and enrich. Temptation to abuse the right expanded with scale. In 1308, Philip's court of the Parlement heard from Amauri of Narbonne that his father had 'some time previously' been deprived of his 'castles' of Talairan and Villar-Fourques by the seneschal of Carcassonne on no better ground than that it was 'on the king's behalf and for his *commodum*'. Compensation had been agreed but never fully paid.[30] Having verified this, the judges ruled that 'by the custom of the *patria* the castles were *licite* ... *retenta*, justly to be kept for ever, once the balance of their valuation was paid over in coined money'. It sounds regular enough – but not so: the crown had already sold

---

[26]   Contamine, *Guerre, état et société*, p. 129.

[27]   One of numerous previous cases is Concressaut castellany, *dép*. Cher, in 1182/3, *Recueil des actes de Philippe Auguste*, i, ed. H.-F. Delaborde (Paris, 1916), pp. 93–4.

[28]   *Ordonnances*, vii (Paris, 1745), pp. 610–16; combining pacts of 1290, 1292; confirmed 1362 by Jean le Bon, and 1394 by Charles VI; see also *Ordonnances*, xv (Paris, 1811), pp. 222–7 of 1293, 1363, 1369, 1434, 1461.

[29]   E.g. F. Enaud, *Les châteaux-forts en France* (Paris, 1958), pp. 131, 180–1.

[30]   *Les Olim*, iii, pp. 312–13; *Actes du Parlement*, ii, no. 3552 (calendar).

both supposedly 'necessary' walled towns and castellanies to one Bertrand Bouchard, revealingly leaving him to make good his title. Amauri next year bought both back, apparently paying twice the value, the court still self-righteously maintaining that they had been lawfully appropriated 'on the king's behalf, as feudal lord'.[31]

No link with the Gascon dispossession of 1294–1303[32] was advanced or would be plausible. The claim of 1407 was neither new nor at all ingenuous that (in Contamine's abbreviation) the king was 'en droit de confisquer et "appliquer à son domaine", moyennant indemnité, les "terres, chasteaux, pors de mer et autres lieux" situés en "frontière" des ennemis, dès lors qu'il l'estime nécessaire à la "garde générale, tuition et defense" de ses sujets et à la "seureté universelle" de son royaume'.[33] This was a bargaining stance. In the 1307 *paréage* in the five castellanies and lands of Saint-Yrieux by Limoges, initiative probably came from the dean and chapter who 'had with difficulty defended them against powerful neighbours in the past'. Since the crown was to assume the fortresses' maintenance, lip-service to 'defence' probably covered up civil pressure and impoverishment.[34] Widows readily succumbed to suasion. Anglesia de Montégut (1309) gave up her portion in the wide Pyrenean lands of Thibaud de Lévis, her late husband, which comprised six 'castles, fortresses and places', for rent assigned in the seneschalcy of Toulouse.[35] She prudently kept her revenues until this was accomplished. Powerful seneschals and *baillis* had opportunities exceeded only by those of magnatial and appointive captains and *lieutenants du roi* in nominal or actual *pays de guerre* in time to come. The fortresses, particularly the walled towns,[36] were unquestionably a major contingent[37] of 'les forces du royaume',[38] but few

---

31 *Registres du Trésor*, i no. 598. Aimeri lost over 2,500 *livres tournois*, plus his revenues while dispossessed.

32 E.g. *Actes du Parlement*, ii, no. 3363: complaint (1306) of damage to Mornac castle (Saintonge) by royal garrisoning in the war. On Gascony *c*.1293–1339, see Coulson 'Community and Fortress-Politics', at length; also the fundamental work by Malcolm Vale, *The Angevin Legacy and the Hundred Years War* (Oxford, 1990), *passim*.

33 Note 25 above.

34 *Registres du Trésor*, i, no. 961.

35 *Registres du Trésor*, i, no. 673.

36 Coulson, 'Seignorial Fortresses', ch. IV, II (a) 2 for detail.

37 E.g. Noyon, in the vital north-east, shows steadily increasing royal intervention at the expense of the bishop: *Actes du Parlement*, i, no. 870 (1294); series II, i (Paris, 1920), nos 3027, 3063 (1340); ii, no. 7439 (1346): compare both *Recueil Philippe Auguste*, i, no. 43 (1181–2); and *Mandements et actes divers de Charles V...*, ed. L. Delisle (Paris, 1874), nos 601, 641, 716, 988, 1329 (1369–76).

towns lacked territory and no fortress was without its appurtenances. Unless, as under time-honoured rendability, the castellan or fortress-holder was deprived only of his capital fortifications (with or without the residential kernel) 'military' protestations are suspect. Pierre-Raimond de Saint-Paul, donzel, heir to a share in the *castrum* of Saint-Paul-Cap de Joux (dép. Tarn), harassed by litigation and the new royal *bastide* of Viterbe, aspired (1308) to make an exchange for a fortress and lands in full jurisdiction within the seneschalcy of Carcassonne.[39] To lose either *château*, or *haute justice* habitually associated with the rank of castellan, meant derogation. He died before implementation and Guillaume Saisset, 'his son and heir', in 1309 accepted instead land only in Toulouse seneschalcy and a promise of compensation for damage done by Viterbe. Valuations were not complete until 1313, Guillaume being short-changed with a miscellaneous parcel of revenues. His father had shared the town of Saint-Paul with the king so his position was weak. The assignment was aborted all the same. It seems the donzel Isarn de Lautrec, styled 'heir by will of Pierre-Raimond', bought out Guillaume's moiety (Louis le Hutin consenting in 1316), inserting himself as *co-seigneur* of Saint-Paul. Philippe le Long, in June 1319, extracted 2,000 *livres tournois* from Isarn for his confirmation and for the concession that the townspeople's consulate (mayoralty) would not be restored without Isarn's consent. These venal manoeuvres by Philip IV, two of his sons and their local viceroys, did not end there. In August 1319, having squeezed Isarn out and gained sole lordship, Philip V took 5000 *petits tournois* from the commune to ratify their pact with his provincial *enquêteurs*, granting both consulate and inalienability from his demesne or from the countship of Toulouse.[40]

The expropriation of the two closely-related joint-lords of the *château* of Leucate (dép. Aude) in the decade after 1302 was in the same vein. Compensation, with an increment for the fine location and 'nobility' of the place, was promised, plus negotiation expenses. The king had nine months to proceed with his option but Aimeri of Narbonne did not agree to sell his mesne rights until April 1309, when he ceded also a *paréage* in his own city, *burgus* and suburb of Narbonne, in return for benefits expected from a new royal Mediterranean port on the Etang de Leucate. His vicecomital rights over Narbonne's fortifications (*forteresse*), eight *châteaux* and the *château ou le monastère* of Levettes, he reserved. In June the coparceners of Leucate received the *châtellenies* of Olonzac, near Béziers, and Villegly (dép. Aude) more or less intact, the fineness of Leucate and the good condition of its

38 Contamine, *Guerre, état et société*, p. 129.
39 Collating *Registres du Trésor*, i, nos 583, 1018–19, 2188; ii, nos 2744, 2942 (1308–19).
40 Entirely typical; see Coulson, 'Seignorial Fortresses', ch. 4, I(c).

buildings allowed for, as promised.[41] Details were still outstanding in October 1310, complicated by the claims of the archbishop (and 'duke') of Narbonne, of the men of Lalme, and of the king of Majorca. The crown gained nothing in fortresses, although it did so in the case of Pontailler-sur-Saône, by Dijon; but as tardily. It took ten years from initial agreement, in 1303, to treasury-assignment to the owner made by Enguerrand de Marigny. Here no 'military' justification of any kind was proffered.[42]

Another forced acquisition, again of castle and territory, does appeal to the king's military role, but perfunctorily. Ribemont, by Saint-Quentin, was laxly allowed to pass hereditarily to the life-tenant's daughter, then to Marguerite de Chambly by purchase.[43] Philip IV's officials did not intervene until 1309, four years after the original alienation, recalling that it was not only the seat of a royal *prévôté* but – *le dit chastel est forteresce ancienne et aussi conme une clef et garde de l'entrée de nostre royaume es parties de là, et que miex est seant en nostre main que en autre*. So it is notable that Marguerite not only kept it, until she could be provided with *un autre manoir suffisant*, but Philip agreed to have it put in better repair for her.[44] She moved house in 1314, about fifty miles south-west to the royal manor of Crouy-en-Thelle, near Beauvais, with high justice thrown in to console her for the delay. Philip V queried the whole transaction in 1319, but only because Crouy had greater revenues than the lady's 'mansion in the castle or house of Ribemont'. He eventually let it stand because Ribemont would cost too much to repair suitably for her. That the castle was 'sited on the frontier between the kingdom and the empire and serves as a refuge for the whole *pays*' was purely incidental. It was the king's personal decision.[45] Given the state of this march, with the severe defeat at Courtrai (1302) not avenged until Cassel (1328), and the already-likely resumption of English pressure *via*

---

[41] *Registres du Trésor*, i, nos 547, 591, 1508. See also above, note 31, for Viscount Aimeri.

[42] *Registres du Trésor*, i, no. 1925.

[43] *Registres du Trésor*, i, nos 572, 2063, 2129, 2283; ii, no. 1319. Compare Baudemont, the fortress initially excluded from a grant of the lands and revenues, then included but under hereditary rendability making it nearly as good as (but less expensive to keep than) the royal castle it formerly was (*Registres du Trésor*, ii, no. 1715); probably Baudemont, dép. Eure, near Château-Gaillard: F. M. Powicke, *The Loss of Normandy* (Manchester, 1961), p. 124 note 176 (ignoring rendability).

[44] Similar provision for exchange of dower castles appear in the 1216 and 1217 reissues of Magna Carta, *Stubbs' Select Charters* (Oxford, 1960), pp. 337, 341 (7). Such care is exceptional in England as in France.

[45] The subscription *de par le Roy* is routine, but not the addition *qui l'a veue et veut qu'elle soit seellée en ceste manière*.

Flanders (as during the Gascon 'confiscation') the case is instructive.[46] Very 'strategic'-sounding hyperbole of this sort was also in common propagandist use in England.[47] Such militaristic phraseology does not translate into ours for all the superficial affinity; nor, at all readily, does medieval 'military' practice.

The pursuit of long-term dispositions of power by buying up castle-lordships is in some contrast to the longer traditions of rendability which provided instantly but temporarily available fortresses, maintained in peace without cost to the superior lord. Fortress-customs differed too in guaranteeing the castellan's right in all respects. Pressure here was monarchical some time before it became truly military. Particularly illuminating are the arrangements made in 1310 with Count Jean of Forez in the Lyonnais, annexed in 1312 from the eastern imperial march.[48] John had obtained the mesne lordship from Philip IV of the *châtellenie* of Thiers in Auvergne and then, in royal style, had exchanged land in the Mâconnais to secure actual possession. At once his right was challenged and the royal sergeant, Berengar Cap-de-Porc, took over and kept the fortress. Under leverage, John agreed that the Marshal should rule whether it was lawfully his but liable to be exchanged for as useful to the defence of the realm, having consulted both the aggressive Charles de Valois and the unscrupulous chamberlain Marigny. If not so declared, Thiers was to be held in liege fief, and consequently jurable and rendable to the kings of France. Alleged 'necessity' ensured that allodial Cervières and the countess's other 'castles and fortresses' were made or confirmed rendable.[49] The verdict nominally in John's favour was suspiciously swift, but etiquette survived. Thiers was duly restored to him with its stores as inventoried under seal of the court of Riom when taken over.

---

[46] Contamine, *War in the Middle Ages*, pp. 87, 258, 300; C. Allmand, *The Hundred Years War, c.1300–c.1450* (Cambridge, 1988) pp. 9–13. *Registres du Trésor*, i, no. 2157 (1314), refers to royal troops put into numerous towns in 1294–1303. For royal captains' powers against the Flemish 'rebels', see *Registres du Trésor*, ii, p. 505, June 1319.

[47] C. Coulson, 'Battlements and the Bourgeoisie: Municipal Status and the Apparatus of Urban Defence in Later Medieval England', *Medieval Knighthood*, 5 (1995), *passim*; also W. M. Ormrod, 'The Domestic Response to the Hundred Years War'; and M. Hughes, 'The Fourteenth-Century French Raids on Hampshire and the Isle of Wight', *Arms, Armies and Fortifications in the Hundred Years War*, A. Curry, M. Hughes (eds) (Woodbridge, 1994), chs 5, 7.

[48] *Registres du Trésor*, i, nos 1147–8, 1253.

[49] In 1334, the count, as royal councillor, intervened to protect his interest in the castles of Rochetaillée and *Caoyl*, rendable and jurable to him as lord (*suzerain*): *Actes du Parlement*, ser. ii, i, no. 942.

In 1338, unsurprisingly anticipating a new wave of expropriations made under colour of defence,[50] new safeguards were negotiated by the Estates into the war-ordinance for Languedoc. Organisational measures for raising and paying the various grades of troops are interspersed with a variety of assurances of continued enjoyment of noble rights including jurisdiction, return of writs and levying distraints.[51] Philippe de Valois then conceded (section 33): 'since supplication has been made on behalf of counts, barons and other nobles that we should refrain (*abstineremus*) from making *paréages* and from acquiring towns, places and castles, whether by way of purchase, exchange or otherwise, be it in direct or in sub-fiefs wherein nobles are known to possess high justice or lordship (*merum imperium*) We ... grant for ourselves and our successors that only when strictly for the kingdom's need will we by any such title further (*ulterius*) acquire fortresses (*fortalitia*) as necessary or useful for the security and protection of our kingdom ... and for any acquired we will make due recompense'. The promise was renewed in 1408 in more general terms,[52] but will also not have outlasted the need to be conciliatory.

Compulsory purchase was limited effectively only by cost, however minimised, but requisitioning under rendability had few constraints, even if honourably observed, and was well-nigh universal.[53] That it was still essentially seignorial is shown by the particularly illuminating clash between Philip IV and the Auvergnat magnate Béraud de Mercoeur, after 1308. Trouble between him and Dreu de Mello had caused both to be summoned to Paris for November, then prorogued to February 1309. Béraud broke his house-arrest at his *hôtel* but attended court under safe-conduct to plead denial of justice and to disown his men's refusal to deliver his castles in the seneschalcies of Auvergne, Beaucaire, Berri, Mâcon and Rouergue.[54] This

---

[50]   E.g. in 1315, Edward II's council resisted as 'highly injurious' Louis X's attempt to buy out the tenant of the vital castellany of Blaye; *Rôles Gascons*, iv, ed. Y. Renouard (Paris, 1962), no. 1486, pp. 576, 580, 582–3.

[51]   *Ordonnances*, ii (Paris, 1729), pp. 120–8; compare *Recueil Général*, iv, pp. 380–2 (1339), confirming (in anticipation) noble privileges in Aquitaine, including *guerra*, as under the English dukes, and tenure undisturbed of *castra, fortalitia aut loca alia*, during obedience; also, *Ordonnances*, vii (Paris, 1745) pp. 193–7, 1388 text including recital of powers to put in garrisons vested in the lieutenant in Languedoc (1340, 1341, 1342).

[52]   *Ordonnances*, ix (Paris, 1755), pp. 360–8.

[53]   Rare examples of the Gascon practice (Coulson, 'Seignorial Fortresses', Appendix B, 3) in French royal licences to fortify of attaching the condition of rendability are *Registres du Trésor*, i, nos 1512, 1512 bis.

[54]   *Registres du Trésor*, i, nos 768, 794–8, 876, all from the exceptionally full MS JJ42A including executive writs; Introduction p. xvi (cp. Chancery Rolls). The Mercoeur castles in 1247, all rendable in chief, are enumerated in the record

coercive use of rendability accords with the new overbearing style of kingship. Béraud warily submitted but stipulated he should not be imprisoned. Later, he denied liability to render castles not held in chief.[55] Hostilities continued, which the Constable, supported by forces of the higher nobility of Auvergne and others, was sent in late May 1309 to suppress. Béraud evaded arrest, being summoned to court again, at all his numerous residences, for July. In June widespread attacks on Dreu de Mello and his ally the lord of Saint-Verain were forbidden. Béraud successfully made his peace and, as constable of Champagne, was in charge in January 1311 of the royal garrisons put into Lyons city and nine of the archbishop's castles, as captain in the Lyonnais. In April 1312 he was formally pardoned.[56]

Measures to assert royal control in an uncertain march, as with the Lyonnais, or to repress disorder, as in the troubles of 1317 when Philippe le Long put troops into numerous towns, partook more of policing than of warfare. Because the defence of the peace and of established authority might employ the same forcible means as the defence of frontiers or the resistance of foreign invasion, war (as we conceive it) can seem to have been more prevalent than it was.[57] In addition, the basic institutions of land-tenure, and realty grants of every kind, expressed their less-than-freehold character so persistently (though far from exclusively) in military terms, that we are easily led to think of a modern state violence as permeating medieval society. Certainly, there were few (not even the clergy, as a class) who could be termed 'civilians', but the social role of martial forms and occasions has few, if any, modern parallels. Buildings, here, are most vital collateral and primary evidence. Just as the architectural features of fortification distinguished the noble's house,[58] and knightly accoutrements and attendants his person, so martial elements proclaimed

---

of homage to Alphonse de Poitiers, in *Layettes du Trésor des Chartes*, iii, ed. Laborde (Paris, 1875), no. 3602.

[55] The king enjoyed no over-riding rendability; sub-rendability was very rare, Coulson, 'Seignorial Fortresses', ii, Index. A full study of rendability etc. is in preparation.

[56] *Registres du Trésor*, i, no. 1498, noting that he had been 'emprisoné' (was this the house-arrest?). Lyons shows increasing royal military intrusion, city and castles: *Registres du Trésor*, ii, nos 1461–3 (1317); no. 1907 (1318); nos 2705, 3101 (1320); Coulson, 'Community and Fortress-Politics', notes 62, 63. 'Garrisoning' of towns was general in the disturbances of 1317 (e.g. Reims, *Registres du Trésor*, ii, no. 1464).

[57] English manipulation of invasion-scares is examined in Coulson, 'Battlements and the Bourgeoisie', especially 1338–90.

[58] C. Coulson, 'Structural Symbolism in Medieval Castle-Architecture', *Journal of the British Archaeological Association*, 132 (1979), pp. 73–90.

and affirmed the identity of the territorial and urban ruling-class, and defined their hierarchy. War has always justified power, if only in the form of taxation. It was not harped on out of paranoia. Philip V was surely not moved by fear that Paris was imminently or remotely likely to be besieged when giving permission to Jean le Mire, his usher at arms and clerk of the crossbowmen, to open through the city wall by his house a doorway suitable for a horseman or pedestrian, subject to the condition that it could be blocked up in case of need or of war (1317).[59] In 1320, when this grant was enlarged by hereditary possession of the Montmartre Gate and of the city wall extending from it to the Porte au Coquillier alongside Jean's *hôtel*, the stipulation that all should be handed back 'in time of war' was standard form, constantly used in such cases. It was also a normal genuflection to military piety to pretend that no deterioration of the defences would be caused. Similarly, a mural tower granted to the royal councillor the abbot of Lagny and his successors (1320) to be 'roofed and used' was to be repossessable 'in case of necessity'.[60] Very typically, and with no less indifference to physical defence, the king intervened (1320) at Reims to stop the burgesses (supported initially by the archbishop) from suing for removal of the close and buildings of Saint-Nicaise which encumbered their *fortalicia* or city wall. Jealous urban lordship, essentially, was appeased by providing that the monks should pay compensation and open their precinct gates whenever access to repair or defend that part of the walls was necessary. Military command denoted public authority at every level.[61]

Much, indeed, was exemplary, symbolic and hierarchical in the 'military' inheritance of the Valois monarchs, and surely remained so.[62] Even the foreboding elevation of the personalised state above the petty *orgueil* of the lesser *seigneur* had, in some sort, been anticipated by and since the time of Saint Louis. Treating as *lèse majesté* refusal of entry to fortresses to royal officials serving writs announced a doctrine of authority remote from Beaumanoir. Philippe le Hardi had punished personally the count of La Marche's sergeant who violently shut out the *prévôt* of Bellegarde from

---

[59]   *Registres du Trésor*, ii, nos 1438, 3109.

[60]   *Registres du Trésor*, ii, no. 3099.

[61]   *Registres du Trésor*, ii, no. 3057. Numerous English examples are discussed in Coulson, 'Battlements and the Bourgeoisie'.

[62]   E.g. M. H. Keen, *The Laws of War in the Late Middle Ages* (London, 1965) has little to do with 'martial law', as it would later be understood, but much on heraldry and the stately *pavane* of honourable courtesies. Even the professional code of the century after Clausewitz was more proximate than the cataclysmic bestialities of the twentieth century: Cyril Falls, *A Hundred Years of War* (London, 1962), p. 394. His whole final chapter on *horrida bella* affords perspective.

Aubusson castle;[63] but also, like his father, he frequently visited his wrath on innocent but eloquent fortifications as the instruments of contempt.[64] So, characteristically, did the lawyers of Philip IV.[65] In 1321, the joint-lords and townsmen of the *château* of Capdenac resisted transference from the seneschalcy of Rouergue to nearby Figeac. Because the viguier of Figeac and his officers had had the wicket gate shut in their faces and had met with violence on two other occasions, the Parlement ruled that 'la principale porte du Château et le portail seraient détruits pour toujours'. The leaves, moreover, of the other gates were to be ceremonially burned in the *place publique,* equally regardless of defence. The lords were stripped of their rights of justice and confined within the walls until they had paid a heavy fine. They continued their resistance to Philip V more circumspectly by litigation.[66] These documents, and those assembled by P.-C. Timbal for the period 1337–69 (but not his commentary), show a fully sociological range of motives far transcending the military.[67] In the interplay of factors after 1338 the role of aristocratic ethos and of royal opportunism was scarcely less than before, even though it may be less conspicuous in military history.

Of the trio *guerre, état* and *société* the greatest was, beyond all doubt, *société* and all that it comprehends.[68]

---

[63]   *Actes du Parlement,* ii, no. 3031. CP Eardisley Castle (Herefs.), 1276: (H.M.S.O., 1901), pp. 162–3. *Calendar of Patent Rolls, 1272–81.*

[64]   *Les Olim,* i, pp. 394–5 (1271); pp. 654 (1266). Fortresses were treated the same as houses: *Les Olim,* ii, p. 231 (1283).

[65]   *Les Olim,* ii, p. 269 (1287, 1291); pp. 346–7 (1292); iii, pp. 86–7 (1302); pp. 175, 182–3 (1306), pp. 822–3 (1313). See also Coulson, 'Community and Fortress-Politics', pp. 82–5, 87–8, and further references.

[66]   *Actes du Parlement,* ii, nos 6291, 6421, 6486, 6727.

[67]   Note 10 above.

[68]   C. Coulson, *Castles and Society: A Social Documentation of Fortresses and Fortifying in France, England and Ireland in the Central Middle Ages* (in preparation).

The Defence of Northumberland: a Preliminary Survey

ANTHONY GOODMAN

The maintenance by the English crown of strongholds and garrisons in both the English and Scottish borders in the later middle ages was a key element in military equations in those regions, and it was one of the crown's biggest continuous military commitments. The aim of this paper is to make a preliminary enquiry into what aims this commitment was intended to fulfil, especially as regards Northumberland, and how successfully it did so. For some of these royal strong points had a dual role. Besides contributing to the defence of the English borders, they were intended to maintain in semblance the claims over Scotland which remained, however fitfully pursued, part of the agenda of English kingship. A question which arises is how this duality of aims affected English frontier defence and border society.

The daunting problems involved in defending England's northern frontiers – problems of terrain, lack of manpower, and inaccessibility – need no rehearsal. In the sixteenth century, a solution was sought, as so often then with strategic conundrums, in classical precedents. According to the author of an *Epystle to the Queens Majestie* (1584), what was needed was a comprehensive and schematic defence system, linked to colonisation, and modelled on Hadrian's Wall. The writer proposed the digging of a trench from the Irish Sea to the North Sea, with strong points built every ten miles, to each of which a plantation of 1,000 acres would be assigned by the crown. The plantations would support communities sufficiently prosperous to pay the wages of the ten gunners manning each strong point. With implausible sleight of hand, this memorialist produced an elegant solution to problems with which generations of royal councillors had struggled; how to defend a geographically open frontier, and to do so with effective regional support.[1]

Traditional government thinking, stretching back to the Scottish Wars of Independence, placed heavy emphasis both on the crown's need to maintain a few key bases in the borders, and on the need to rely on local

---

[1]   H. M. Colvin *et al* (ed.), *The History of the King's Works*, III and IV, 1485–1660 (London, 1975–82), III, p. 613. It is there surmised that the author was Christopher Dacre.

arraying and private garrisoning. The alleged benefits of the maintenance of Berwick were summed up in a parliamentary decision of 1487, a few years after its recovery from the Scots. The estate of the House of York was to be used to subsidise the garrison there:

> The sure keeping of the town and castle ... is a great defence against the Scots and a great weal, surety and ease unto all his [Henry VII's] realm and especial to the northern parties.[2]

A century or so beforehand, the crown's commitment to a similar policy had been reflected in augmentations of its garrisons during truce as well as war. These were responses to the erosion of its control in the Scottish borders in the 1370s and early 1380s. The town garrison of Berwick, nominally less than 100 during times of truce from the late 1360s into the early 1380s, was mustered in time of war (November 1385) at 460.[3] In 1404 the castle and town garrisons were projected for the next seven years as a combined total of 600 in war and 300 during truce.[4] The garrison strength of Roxburgh Castle was increased (27 in 1377, 137 in 1381). In 1400, it was projected at 120 during truce.[5] There was some reduction in garrison strengths in time of truce in the fifteenth century, though not a return to the levels of Edward III's peaceable period, since Scottish royal strategy now focused more directly on the recapture of the remaining castles in Scotland, rather than on large-scale penetration into England.[6]

However, it is questionable whether the crown's Scottish garrisons were best placed for English border defence. They were not strategically and logistically as well placed for it as the garrison of the royal castle at Carlisle was for the defence of the West March. The crown's other castles in the English marches had a highly localised importance. The function of both Bamburgh and Dunstanburgh (the latter annexed to the crown as part

[2] *Rotuli Scotiae in Turri Londinensi et in Domo Capitulari Westmoreasteriensi Asservati* (hereafter *Rot. Scot.*), ed. D. M acpherson and others, 2 vols (London, 1814–19), II, p. 483.

[3] J. Bain (ed.), *Calendar of Documents Relating to Scotland*, 5 vols (Edinburgh, 1881–8), IV, pp. 36 (1369), 46 (1373), 61 (1379), 67 (1381), *Rot. Scot.*, II, p. 76.

[4] *Cal. Documents Scotland*, IV, p. 140.

[5] In 1382 Sir Matthew Redman, as captain of Roxburgh, mustered 30 men-at-arms, 50 mounted archers and 57 sergeants (*ibid.*, pp. 67–8). In 1400 Sir Richard Grey and Sir Stephen Scrope contracted to hold the castle during truce with 40 men-at-arms and 80 archers (*ibid.*, pp. 118–19). In 1377 Sir Thomas Percy had held it with a fee of only £300 p.a., to be contrasted with that of 2,000 marks in 1400 (*ibid.*, pp. 55–6).

[6] In 1421 Lord Greystoke contracted to hold Roxburgh Castle with a fee of £1,000 in peace (*ibid.*, p. 182 – to be doubled in war), a reduction on the contract for 2,000 marks in 1400.

of the Lancastrian inheritance in 1399) was to protect the inhabitants and stock of their adjacent lordship from raids by land or sea – a function strikingly exemplified by the exceptional size of the outer bailey at Dunstanburgh. The chief royal eastern castle, at Newcastle, was too far from the frontier to fulfil a function like Carlisle's castle. Newcastle's defence – rarely tested – depended on the large and impressive circuit of its walls, which provided ample stock protection, and on the wealth and warlike spirit of its burgesses and townsmen, who confidently played communal and individual roles in the defence of Northumberland too.[7]

No royal interest was manifested in the permanent acquisition or the construction of castles in the English borders until the later fifteenth century. The formidable stronghold of Wark-on-Tweed, an excellent frontline defence of a vulnerable sector, was in 1397 sold to Sir Thomas Grey of Heton by Richard II's favourite John Montague, earl of Salisbury.[8] The safekeeping of its companion fortress on the Tweed, Norham Castle, remained the burdensome responsibility of the bishops of Durham. The crown continued to rely heavily on the ability of lords to maintain and defend their own fortifications. It was disinclined to help with costs, though during emergencies the royal council was occasionally prepared to augment private garrisons with troops raised under royal authority. At the start of open warfare in 1384, the warden of the East March, the earl of Northumberland, was ordered to place sufficient forces in Wark and Norham castles. Aid was grudgingly given: the defence of the keeps was left to the lord or his constable.[9] The next year Lord Clifford, leading a retinue on Richard II's invasion of Scotland, was granted ninety soldiers for twenty-nine days to augment his garrison at Brougham Castle (Westmorland).[10] In like manner Henry IV, about to invade Scotland in 1400, ordered the captain of Norham, Sir Thomas Grey, to be sent 150 extra soldiers, and the captain of Harbottle Castle, Sir Robert Umfraville, sixty.[11]

In response to the resumption of large-scale hostilities under James IV (1488–1513), and to the growing problem of reiving by Scottish 'surnames',

---

[7] In 1388 women in Newcastle were outraged by the bishop of Durham's failure to help husbands who fell at Otterburn (L. C. Hector and B. F. Harvey (eds), *The Westminster Chronicle 1381–1394* (Oxford, 1982), p. 349). Roger Thornton (d. 1430), prominent Newcastle merchant, built a tower at Whitton after he purchased it (C. J. Bates, *The Border Holds of Northumberland* (Newcastle, 1891), p. 16 and n. 97).

[8] *Cal. Patent Rolls, 1396–99*, pp. 73, 410. Wark Castle was captured by the Scots in 1399, 1406 and 1420.

[9] *Rot. Scot.*, II, pp. 61–2.

[10] *Cal. Documents Scotland*, IV, p. 77.

[11] N. H. Nicolas (ed.), *Proceedings and Ordinances of the Privy Council of England*, I (London, 1834), p. 124.

often in collusion with English ones, there was some piecemeal acquisition of fortifications by the crown. In 1478 Richard, duke of Gloucester, as lieutenant of the marches, garrisoned the remote fort at Bewcastle, near the Cumberland border, essentially as a forward post on a back route through Bewcastle Waste, intended to facilitate the detection of reivers infiltrating through pasturelands in the Dacre barony of Gilsland and its environs. The post was maintained under the Tudors.[12] In 1507 the crown at last acquired the castle of Wark-on-Tweed; Harbottle was often in the king's lands under Henry VII and Henry VIII, and was permanently acquired by the crown in 1546.[13]

Occasionally, the crown had exploited opportunities to gain more Scottish castles. As a consequence of the defection to the English allegiance of George Dunbar, earl of March in 1400, Henry IV was able to garrison his strong point, Fastcastle, on the Berwickshire coast.[14] In 1483 James III's brother, the duke of Albany, intent on fleeing to England, handed over Dunbar Castle to the English, which they garrisoned until 1485–6.[15] Possession of these coastal castles was potentially useful in assisting the naval supply of English armies, and in hindering attacks on Berwick. In 1491 Henry VII, negotiating secretly with Archibald Douglas, earl of Angus, discussed terms for acquiring Hermitage, his fortress in Liddesdale, possession of which would have helped in curbing the raids of 'surnames' clustered in and around the lordship, though its maintenance would have posed formidable supply problems.[16] The experience of defending Berwick and Roxburgh was a deterrent to such adventures. Both had weaknesses in their defences. At neither site did castle and town defences form an integrated system, nor were their burgesses and their inhabitants likely to have been sufficiently numerous and wealthy to complement the garrisons substantially. Berwick Castle was captured twice in Richard II's reign; on each occasion the town garrison under its separate captain held out.[17]

The consequence of these weaknesses was that the defence of Berwick and Roxburgh, symbols of English domination in Scotland, absorbed resources which might have been concentrated on defences in England.

---

12 Colvin, *King's Works*, III, pp. 233–4.

13 *Ibid.*, pp. 252–4.

14 S. B. Chrimes, 'Some Letters of John of Lancaster as Warden of the East Marches towards Scotland', *Speculum* 14 (1939), p. 18.

15 N. Macdougall, *James III. A Political Study* (Edinburgh, 1982), pp. 188–9, 217.

16 J. Gairdner (ed.), *Letters and Papers Illustrative of the Reigns of Richard III and Henry VII*, I (Rolls Series, London, 1861), pp. 385–7; N. Macdougall, *James IV* (Edinburgh, 1989), pp. 87–9.

17 V. H. Galbraith (ed.), *The Anonimalle Chronicle 1333 to 1381* (Manchester, 1927), pp. 125–6, 192; *Westminster Chronicle*, pp. 104–5.

Once the crown's control over their Scottish hinterlands began to be eroded, in the 1370s, victualling problems were accentuated. John of Lancaster, in a report to the royal council (1411–12), declared that the failure of lieges in the march to cultivate and provide foodstuffs was endangering the security of garrisons. The dearness of victuals in Berwick was causing hardships and loss of morale; no soldier or burgess wanted to stay on.[18] Even in more favourable circumstances, it is likely that a prime concern of captains was to protect corn and pasturage in their bounds, the areas immediately adjacent to their walls. The victualling problems of more isolated Roxburgh Castle were especially acute. In 1400 its captain, Richard Lord Grey, needing to feed an augmented garrison, led raids southwards in search of supplies, into the vicinity of Jedburgh, an area supposedly under English control.[19] Formidably constructed Jedburgh Castle, owned by the Percies, safeguarded a supply route from Newcastle to Roxburgh.[20] The Percy forfeitures early in Henry IV's reign gave the crown an opportunity to strengthen 'the king's dominion in Scotland'. In 1408 John of Lancaster and his heirs were granted the castle, lordship and forest of Jedburgh on similar terms to the Percy grant.[21] However, financial constraints prevented the crown from giving sufficient support. The castle finally fell in 1409, and Fastcastle (also in John's keeping) the following year.[22]

The Scottish threats of the 1380s had induced moves to integrate the defence of 'the king's lordship in Scotland' and the English marches. In 1386 the keepers of Berwick town undertook to ride with the warden of the East March, John Lord Neville, against the Scots. They were to recruit 300 mounted troops, and 190 foot soldiers to guard the town.[23] From the 1380s onwards wardens' commissions normally gave them specific jurisdiction over 'the king's dominions in Scotland'.[24] Captaincies of the crown's border strongholds were frequently granted to the appropriate warden. In 1389

18   Chrimes, 'Some Letters of John of Lancaster', pp. 25–7.
19   *Cal. Documents Scotland*, IV, p. 119.
20   Walter Bower said that Jedburgh Castle's mortar was 'exceedingly strong and hard' (D. E. R. Watt (ed.), *Scotichronicon*, 9 vols (Aberdeen, 1987–), VIII pp. 72–3). The castle must have been quite extensive, as Edward Ilderton's garrison there in 1400 was to be reinforced by the crown with 30 men-at-arms and 40 archers (*Proceedings and Ordinances of the Privy Council*, I, p. 124).
21   *Cal. Documents Scotland*, IV, p. 153.
22   *Scotichronicon*, VIII, pp. 72–5. In 1394 the keeper of Jedburgh Castle, Sir Thomas Strother, had briefly lost it to the Scots, during truce, because most of the garrison were in billets in the burgh (H. T. Riley (ed.), *Johannis de Trokelowe ... Chronica et Annales*, (Rolls Series, London, 1861), pp. 166–7).
23   *Cal. Documents Scotland*, IV, pp. 80–1.
24   *Rot. Scot.*, II, pp. 89–90.

Thomas Mowbray, earl of Nottingham, was appointed both warden of the East March and captain of Berwick. His indenture stipulated that £2,000 of the £3,000 p.a. he was to receive during periods of truce was for the safeguard of the town. This would have left him with a notional force of ninety to employ on other duties, riding or manning private defences.[25]

Did this integration of responsibilities materially assist the defence of the frontier? Southern English chroniclers sometimes picked up news of the involvement of garrison forces in open warfare; for instance, under December 1388 the Westminster Chronicler reported that the captain of Berwick had raided with impunity and profit along the Firth of Forth.[26] Such raids weakened the Scots, but captains' degree of dependence on Scottish supplies in time of truce probably induced selectivity in targeting.[27] Moreover, exhibitions of garrisons' aggressive power were inducements for Scottish raiders to make detours in search of softer pickings in England. The devastation inflicted by raiders on Durham Priory's vills to the south of Berwick is well attested in fifteenth-century estate accounts.[28] Where was the garrison during emergencies? Presumably the mounted troops were patrolling the bounds, rather than exposing them by being caught out past the Northumberland end of the Tweed bridge.

In war, the dilemma of wardens as to how best to safeguard royal castles and marches might become acute, particularly as the loss of a royal castle risked a charge of treason.[29] The Scots exploited the strategic problem in 1388 whilst they ravaged north and south of the Tyne estuary; the warden of the East March, and captain of Berwick, Sir Henry Percy, with unaccustomed passivity waited in Newcastle for the arrival of the bishop of Durham's levies.[30] One reason for his inaction was that he had had to split his waged forces, leaving some to safeguard Berwick. In personal terms this paid off. Whereas his father, the earl of Northumberland, had been lucky to escape a charge of treason for his lieutenant's loss of Berwick Castle in 1384, Percy's reputation was

---

[25] *Cal. Documents Scotland*, IV, p. 88.

[26] *Westminster Chronicle*, p. 375. Bower testified to the severity of the raids carried out by the English captain of Fastcastle, Thomas Holden, who surrendered the castle in 1410 (*Scotichronicon*, VIII, pp. 74–5).

[27] An English protection was issued to Melrose Abbey and lordship in 1405, on condition of supplying the garrison of Roxburgh Castle at a fair price (*Cal. Documents Scotland*, IV, p. 143).

[28] R. B. Dobson, *Durham Priory 1400–1450* (Cambridge, 1973), pp. 274–5.

[29] The issue of the loss of castles (in this case, by surrender) had come to the fore in the Good Parliament of 1376 (G. Holmes, *The Good Parliament* (Oxford, 1975), pp. 131–2).

[30] Percy's need for the bishopric's levies is deduced from *Westminster Chronicle*, pp. 347–9.

nationally enhanced after he was defeated and captured at Otterburn.[31] The Scots thus successfully exploited their opponents' strategic dilemmas. They did so again in their 1389 invasion. The earl of Nottingham, Percy's successor as Warden and captain of Berwick, was taking no chances. He concentrated his main force there, and left Northumberland to its fate.[32] It is notable that the garrisons at Roxburgh and Jedburgh apparently had no deterrent effect in these campaigns. In 1402 the Scots were again undeterred from invading Northumberland, giving Berwick a wide berth. Their defeat at Humbledon Hill was due above all to good English intelligence work, and the superior tactics of the English army.

Royal officials were well aware that some of the king's castles gave little protection to his subjects and that private fortifications were crucial to defence. As we have seen, the crown sometimes provided additional troops to help in manning key private defences. At other times wardens inspected them. In 1379 the wardens of the East March were commissioned to ensure that all laymen with £20 worth of land in Northumberland and the bishopric of Durham resided constantly there, and that all castles and fortalices within twelve miles of the frontier, were adequately supplied and garrisoned.[33] In 1380 John of Gaunt, lieutenant of the marches, was empowered to remove and replace constables of private castles.[34] The importance of defending *fortalicia* was evident during the major invasion of 1388, when resistance in the towers of Ponteland and Otterburn to the Scots, retreating from Newcastle, was a factor enabling Percy to catch up with them.[35]

There were fears among royal officials that the attractions of service (despite John of Lancaster's remarks about its miseries) in the sometimes marginalised royal garrisons might weaken the core of local defences. Indentures with garrison commanders sometimes stipulated that their soldiers were not to be recruited from border shires and adjacent parts. In 1385 wardens and other border retinue leaders agreed that two-thirds of the additional companies which they were to muster for the royal expedition to

31   A Goodman, 'Introduction', *War and Border Societies in the Middle Ages*, ed. A. Goodman and A. Tuck (London, 1992), p. 23.
32   *Ibid.*, pp. 19–20.
33   *Cal. Documents Scotland*, IV, p. 62. The wardens of the West March received similar commissions.
34   *Rot. Scot.*, II, p. 29.
35   K. de Lettenhove (ed.), *Oeuvres de Froissart. Chroniques*, XIII, *1386–1389* (Brussels, 1871), pp. 211–13. The value placed on Otterburn Tower by Sir Henry Percy is reflected by the report in 1404 that he had paid 88 marks p.a. to Piers Stokhalgh to defend it. In 1404 the tower was said to have been 'in great part destroyed' by the Scots (*Cal. Documents Scotland*, IV, p. 652).

Scotland should be strangers to the march.[36] The crown's appointments of 'outsiders' on occasion as wardens and garrison commanders, men who had fields of recruitment elsewhere in the realm, are likely to have been made with this problem in mind. The contrary tendency, to appoint border magnates, may have occurred not only because of their local following, but because their landholding in other parts of the realm, and the contacts they made in the French wars, enabled them to draw in soldiers from outside the borders. Garrison forces were often of both local and 'strange' composition, some outsiders having specialist skills.[37] The existence of such mixed garrisons should induce caution in seeing border defences as inclined to be riven by mutual enmity between borderers and non-borderers. Let us take the situation in Berwick in 1386. The garrison was then reinforced by the retinues of Sir William Drayton and Sir Hugh Despenser, originally intended to reinforce the defence of Ghent.[38] The existing garrison forces and the townsmen are likely to have been united in exasperation at the effect on billets and prices of the influx of newcomers. There is, indeed, little evidence that border defence was hampered by tensions between soldiers of local and 'foreign' origin. In times of intense conflict, they are likely to have been equally consumed by fear and hatred of the Scots.[39] The borderers, well aware that they were a shrunken population, appreciated that in emergencies they needed all the help they could get.

---

[36] Some of these troops were intended to augment the garrisons of Carlisle and Brougham Castles (*Cal. Documents Scotland*, IV, p. 77). There may also have been fears that border garrison troops might desert to defend their own properties.

[37] Among those who received protection from legal process in 1387–88 whilst serving in Ralph lord Lumley's retinue as captain of Berwick town were, besides men from the bishopric of Durham (where his principal estates lay), a draper, a Newcastle merchant, and, from York, a mercer and a taverner/vintner; also, Richard Brynand of Knaresborough (G. G. Simpson and J. D. Galbraith (eds), *Cal. Documents Scotland*, V (London, 1985), pp. 539–41). Brynand had been a leading Lancastrian administrator in Yorkshire (A. Goodman, *John of Gaunt* (London, 1992), pp. 79, 336). For the captain of a remote frontier garrison, it was probably important to retain merchants and estate officials who could help to procure victuals, clothing and other stores from afar.

[38] *Westminster Chronicle*, pp. 147–9, 149 n., 154.

[39] For arguments against cross-border acculturation in the later fourteenth century, A. J. Macdonald, 'Crossing the Border: A Study of Scottish Military Offensives against England, *c*.1369–*c*.1403', unpublished Ph.D. thesis (University of Aberdeen, 1995), p. 241.

Many borderers saw service in the royal garrisons, and raided with them. In his chronicle, John Hardyng, a Northumberland man notable for his hostility to the Scots, recalled with pride Sir Robert Umfraville's exploits as captain of Roxburgh and Berwick. In 1402, he said, Umfraville had sallied out with 140 spears and 300 bows and defeated the Scots, pursuing them for twelve miles into Scotland before returning to Roxburgh.[40] Scions of local noble families, enrolling in royal garrisons, might there refine chivalrous behaviour and military skills, gain the patronage of important strangers, make business connections, and bond with their border fellows. Berwick was their chief nursery of arms, and their theatre of chivalry for a wider world.

Thus the royal fortresses played an important indirect role in border defence, in that they helped to train local gentlefolk in the defence of their 'country', and emphasised the need for co-operation in this among themselves and with 'strangers'. Skills honed and ties made on the actual frontier lines were useful for the defence in depth of Northumberland, where the vulnerability of settlement was emphasised by the way in which it had crumbled, especially at the vulnerable margins. The widespread maintenance of private fortifications in the shire is most strikingly evident in a list compiled c.1415, divided into *Castra* and *Fortalicia* in the shire and its adjoining liberties, with a note of the owners.[41] Thirty-six castles are listed, and seventy-eight *Fortalicia*, all but two of the latter are described as a *turris*. The parts of the shire south of the river Coquet appear as hardly less densely fortified than those north of it. Fortifications were particularly concentrated in three areas – in the north-east, extending down the coast and along the tributaries of the Tweed; along the Aln and Coquet valleys; and north of the Tyne estuary. There were few strongholds in the more barren, less populated inward parts, where the terrain grew rugged and the inhabitants had a reputation for lawlessness – the liberties of Redesdale and Tynedale. Hexhamshire, relative to the coastal plains, was lightly fortified. However, throughout the settled parts of Northumberland, the maintenance of and residence in fortified dwellings was a common feature of 'gentle living'.

The family listed as possessing most fortifications in the shire was the knightly one of Ogle. They had two castles and four towers. Nearly all the castles not held by crown or magnates were, or had been, in the possession of knights or prominent squires. Six out of the fourteen knights named and two of the esquires possessed two or more fortifications. Sir John Heron,

---

[40]   H. F. Ellis (ed.), *The Chronicle of John Hardyng* (London, 1812), p. 373. In 1417 Umfraville sallied from Berwick to attack the rearguard of Albany's army, when it had broken off the siege (*ibid.*, p. 381).

[41]   The document is printed in Bates, *Border Holds*, pp. 13–19.

for instance, held Twizel Castle near the Tweed border; Crawley Tower, north-west of Alnwick, and Eshot Castle, south-west of Warkworth. The majority of the towers were the sole fortification owned by a non-knightly landowner. In Northumberland the maintenance of a castle or tower defined status as well as providing defence.

Northumberland gentlefolk, most of whom were generally resident in the shire, needed household officers, stewards and receivers who were skilled besides in the local kinds of warfare, especially when they had scattered estates to be guarded as well as administered. Reliable kinsfolk and neighbours were vital as office-holders.[42] The great absentee lords – the crown in Tynedale, the archbishops of York in Hexhamshire, the bishops of Durham in Norhamshire, and (in the fifteenth century) the Tailboys family in Redesdale – relied mainly on local knightly families to uphold and defend their rule.[43] In 1438 Walter Tailboys appointed Roger, younger son of Sir John Widdrington of Haughton Castle in Tynedale, as his constable at Harbottle Castle and his lieutenant in Redesdale, in peace and war. According to the indenture, Widdrington was to be 'abiding and dwelling in his proper person with his meinie and household within the dungeon [i.e. keep] of the said castle'.[44]

---

[42]   In Sir Ralph Harbottle's lease in 1499 of Preston Tower to his kinsman John Harbottle, gentleman, there was the stipulation that John and his heirs were to roof the tower (A. M. Oliver (ed.), *Northumberland and Durham Deeds from the Dodsworth MSS in Bodley's Library, Oxford* (Newcastle, 1929), pp. 59–60).

[43]   Sir Thomas Swinburne had been Edward, duke of York's bailiff in Tynedale before Feb. 1390 (Northumberland County Record Office, Swinburne of Capheaton Deeds, 1/81); in 1398 Sir William Swinburne was accused of having ousted John Clavering, appointed by Archbishop Neville as bailiff of Hexhamshire (*ibid.*, 1/96). For the bishops of Durham's grants of the keeping of Norham Castle and shire to leading local lords and knights in the 15th century, see J. Raine, *The History and Antiquities of North Durham* (London, 1825), pp. 7–12. Resident vicars, chaplains, knights, esquires and Newcastle burgesses profited from the special need of distant property owners to have their sources of revenue guarded as well as administered. In 1353, 1364 and 1373 bishops of Durham licensed the Master and Scholars of Balliol to lease the tithes of Long Benton (Balliol College Deeds E1/33, 39, 44). For eleven such leases between 1377 and 1497, E1/43–9, 51–6, 58. The 1383 (46) and 1391 (47) leases had clauses in case of destructions by the Scots, the 1489 and 1497 leases (56, 58) in case of destruction by 'enemies' (English reivers?) or Scots. For Balliol leases of Stamfordham property, E.4. In 1392–3 St George's College, Windsor leased the profits of Simonburn Church for 26 marks p.a. to Sir William Swinburne (Swinburne of Capheaton Deeds, 1/86, 88–90). High profit was anticipated from a large parish especially vulnerable to raiding.

[44]   *Northumberland and Durham Deeds*, p. 222.

For local knightly families such as the Strothers, Ildertons, Greys, Ogles and Middletons, success in defending their own properties and gaining such patronage was often closely allied with success in giving military service to defend the royal castles. Military experience and repute were also necessary for the local careerist and aspirant to gentility, such as Robert Harbottle (died *c*.1419).[45] He may have served as a soldier in a royal garrison.[46] He contracted to be constable of Dunstanburgh castle for life in 1401, and he was sheriff of Northumberland in 1407–8.[47] Over the years 1401–15 Harbottle purchased tenancies in and around Preston, not far from Dunstanburgh.[48] In 1407 the abbot of Alnwick granted him a yearly rent from lands in Preston and elsewhere, in return for past and future good counsel and service, and in 1415 the abbot and convent leased to him for ten years all their lands in Preston, provided that he be of their counsel. They undertook to provide sufficient timber for him to have a substantial new house built there.[49]

In 1418 William de Orde sold Harbottle his watermills at Ellingham, 'now ruinous and wasted by many invasions of the Scots', and other properties there. The first witness was the lord of Ellingham, Sir Robert Ogle.[50] In 1424 Harbottle's son and heir Robert was contracted to marry Ogle's daughter Margery. With her came a plot in Ellingham, whose dimensions were specified in order to facilitate Harbottle's intention to build a fulling-mill, and to divert the Waldenburn, to link it up with the watercourse of another mill which he owned.[51]

The Harbottles could not have been successful entrepreneurs in such an insecure environment without specialised military skills. The perpetuation of such skills among the gentry enabled them to organise their societies for defence, in default of much aid from the crown. This ability helps to explain why, under the Yorkists and early Tudors, despite the occasional renewal of large-scale warfare with the Scottish crown, and the

---

[45] R. Somerville, *History of the Duchy of Lancaster* (London, 1953), p. 357.

[46] In 1394–5 Harbottle was a servant of Sir Matthew Redman (*Cal. Patent Rolls, 1396–99*, pp. 404, 688). Redman's many involvements in border defence had included the captaincy of Roxburgh Castle and Carlisle.

[47] Somerville, *Duchy of Lancaster*, p. 537.

[48] *Northumberland and Durham Deeds*, pp. 155–7.

[49] *Ibid.*, pp. 156–8. Harbottle was holding Preston Tower *c*.1415 (Bates, *Border Holds*, p. 16). In 1413 he was leased the Duchy of Lancaster barony of Embleton, adjacent to Dunstanburgh Castle (Somerville, *Duchy of Lancaster*, p. 537).

[50] Northumberland County Record Office, Blackgate Deeds, ZAN B4/1/2/16–17; *Northumberland and Durham Deeds*, pp. 151–2.

[51] ZAN, B4/1/2/15 (marriage contract); B4/1/2/14 (Ogle's grant concerning new fulling mill). Cf. *Northumberland and Durham Deeds*, pp. 152–4.

growing problem of the 'reiving' surnames, the crown responded only in a piecemeal fashion to arguments for a thorough reorganisation of frontier defences and a fuller commitment to them. Indeed, under these dynasties some features of the royal defence institutions as they had evolved in the later fourteenth century were dismantled. Pay rates for lieutenants in charge of march defences were slashed, and wardenships were decoupled from captaincies.[52] Sir Thomas Darcy's 1503 commission to defend Berwick – in the aftermath of the Anglo-Scottish peace – treats him with a stringency unthinkable in the fourteenth-century era of war and truce.[53] Greater confidence was being placed in border society's ability to defend itself, and reliance on its levies to come to the rescue of Berwick. These changes of perception stemmed from the altered character of Scottish royal strategy and perhaps, towards the end of the fifteenth century, modest growth in population and prosperity.[54]

One border project which the early Tudors were sometimes prepared to pay out for was the updating of the fortifications of Berwick. In part, this reflected continuity with the medieval crown's aims in the borders – the two aims of defending England, and flying St George's flag on Scottish soil as an earnest of ancient claims. In some respects, as we have seen, these aims were not always easily reconcilable. The defence of 'the king's dominions in Scotland' might in some circumstances weaken that of England. However, the continuing royal commitment in Scotland shaped English defences and the character of society in the far north. Service in the royal garrisons provided borderers with opportunities to acquire wages, military skills and chivalrous accomplishments. There they might learn skills and forge bonds which helped them to make local careers and defend properties. The emphasis on the military aspects of kinship and patronage did, indeed, support the practice of feud. However, the frontier life-style proved apt to maintain, generally, patterns of settlement, the exercise of lordship, and allegiance to the crown. Its policy of maintaining garrisons in Scotland helped to create and sustain a society organised for war in Northumberland.

---

[52] S. G. Ellis, *Tudor Frontiers and Noble Power* (Oxford, 1995), pp. 48–9.

[53] *Cal. Documents Scotland*, IV, pp. 333–4, 335. In return for royal favours received, Darcy undertook to augment the garrison with 400 men at his own costs in emergencies, under surety. He and six others had to enter into large bonds for his safekeeping of the town and castle.

[54] In 1417 the duke of Albany besieged Berwick, and the earl of Douglas, Roxburgh. James I and James II both besieged Roxburgh. In 1436 James I abandoned the siege on the approach of northern English levies (M. Brown, *James I* (Edinburgh, 1994), p. 164).

Edward III and the English Aristocracy at the Beginning of the Hundred Years War[1]

ANDREW AYTON

At Ipswich on 17 June 1340, a week before the battle of Sluys, an English knight, William Tallemache, attached his seal to an indenture recording his receipt of an Essex manor in return for life service in peace and war with William de Bohun, earl of Northampton.[2] Tallemache was a seasoned warrior, a veteran of the War of St Sardos, Scotland and Edward III's first expedition to Flanders.[3] He had already served, as an esquire, in Northampton's *comitiva* on several occasions, but in the spring of 1339 after months of inactivity in Flanders he seems to have become restless.[4] In May we find him transferring to the service of Sir John Molyns under whose banner he fought and received the accolade of knighthood during the brief autumn campaign in the Cambrésis.[5] Perhaps it was this dalliance with the ambitious and unscrupulous Molyns that spurred Northampton into offering Tallemache a secure place in his affinity.[6] Whatever the earl's reasons, within days of the indenture being drawn-up and sealed, Northampton and his new retainer were in the thick of it at Sluys, risking,

[1] Unless otherwise stated all manuscript records cited in the footnotes are to be found at the Public Record Office, London. I am grateful to Mr Richard Gorski for reading and commenting on an earlier draft of this article.

[2] DL25/32; printed in M. Jones and S. Walker (eds), 'Private Indentures for Life Service in Peace and War, 1278–1476', *Camden Miscellany XXXIII*, Camden Society, Fifth Series, III (London, 1994), no. 38, pp. 71–2, where the date is given as 20 June, but the *Handbook of Dates* suggests otherwise. Cf. G. A. Holmes, *The Estates of the Higher Nobility in Fourteenth-Century England* (Cambridge, 1957), p. 69.

[3] E101/17/2, m. 4; C71/13, m. 20; *Calendar of Patent Rolls* [hereafter, *CPR*], *1338–40*, p. 386.

[4] Esquire under Northampton: C81/1734, m. 40; C81/1735, m. 15; C81/1750, m. 12; *CPR, 1334–8, p. 530; Treaty Rolls, 1337–9, nos 291, 385, 653.*

[5] Letter of protection dated 8 May 1339; C76/14, m. 13. Four of Molyns's men were knighted during October 1339: M. Lyon, B. Lyon, H. S. Lucas and J. de Sturler (eds), *The Wardrobe Book of William de Norwell, 12 July 1338 to 27 May 1340* (Brussels, 1983) [hereafter, *Norwell*], p. 332.

[6] See Holmes, *Estates*, pp. 69–70 for a discussion of the scanty evidence concerning Northampton's retaining.

as one of that earl's letters put it, *vie et membre* in the king's war.[7]

Alongside them in that fight on St John's day, among Northampton's 135 men-at-arms recorded on the pay roll, was Robert Marny, a knight in his mid-twenties, who had been with the earl in Scotland and at Buironfosse. He was later to combine a life of genteel crime in Essex with continuing regular participation in the king's war.[8] That Essexmen, like Marny, were well represented in Northampton's retinue is easily explained, for their county was one of the Bohun family's landholding strongholds,[9] and traditional ties based on lordship and shared locality counted for a great deal in recruitment.[10] The same explanation probably lies behind the service of William de Pembridge, a Herefordshire esquire in his late thirties, who accompanied Northampton to war on several occasions.[11] But there were others fighting with this earl at Sluys who were from regions far removed from Bohun influence: men like Sir Gerard de Wyderyngton, who, though from the far north of England, responded as often as Marny, Pembridge and Tallemache to the earl's call to arms.[12] Of course, not all of

---

[7] Tallemache's protection, dated 21 June 1340 (C76/15, m 20); Northampton's letter, requesting protections (C81/1734, no 60). Thereafter, Tallemache served loyally under Northampton's banner: e.g. in Brittany in 1342–3 (C76/17, m. 36) and 1345 (T. Rymer (ed.), *Foedera, conventiones, litterae etc.*, revised edn, 4 vols in 7 parts (London, 1816–69) [hereafter, *Foedera*], III, i, pp. 38–9), and on the Reims campaign in 1359–60 (C76/38, m. 17; C76/40, m. 10).

[8] For Marny's military career, see (i) his Court of Chivalry depositions, both dating from 1386; C47/6/1, no. 27; N. H. Nicolas (ed.), *The Scrope and Grosvenor Controversy*, 2 vols (London, 1832), I, pp. 170–1; and (ii) his letters of protection: *Treaty Rolls, 1337–9*, nos 291, 733 (Low Countries, 1338–9); C76/15, m. 20 (1340); C76/17, m. 36 (1342–3); C76/34, mm. 5, 6, 18 (1356); C76/37, m. 3 and C76/38, m. 16 (1359–60). Marny was associated with John, Lord Fitzwalter's Essex gang: J. C. Ward, *The Essex Gentry and the County Community in the Fourteenth Century*, Essex Record Office, 1991, p. 23; J. S. Roskell, L. Clark and C. Rawcliffe (eds), *The History of Parliament: The House of Commons, 1386–1421*, 4 vols (Stroud, 1992), III, pp. 690–3.

[9] On the Bohun estates, see Holmes, *Estates*, pp. 19–25; *Calendar of Inquisitions Post Mortem* [hereafter, *CIPM*], X, no. 639.

[10] See, for example, P. Morgan, *War and Society in Medieval Cheshire, 1277–1403* (Manchester, 1987), ch. 2.

[11] C47/6/1, no. 7. He was still serving under Northampton in 1359–60: C76/38, m. 17; other service is suggested by C81/1734, m. 40; C81/1735, m. 21; C81/1750, m. 12.

[12] Wyderyngton: E101/19/36, m. 5; C71/16, m. 10 (Scotland, 1336); *Treaty Rolls, 1337–9*, nos 291, 317, 693 (Low Countries, 1338–9); C81/1734, m. 24, C76/15, m. 5 (1340); C76/17, m. 36 (1342–3); *Foedera*, III, i, pp. 38–9 (1345); G. Wrottesley (ed.), *Crecy and Calais* (London, 1898), p. 89 (1346); C76/38, m.

Northampton's affinity were actually involved in the battle of Sluys. None of the witnesses named in Tallemache's indenture, for example, can be shown to have been at the battle. Two of them – Sir John Engayne of Dillington and Sir Simon de Drayton – had been soldiers in their younger days;[13] but now they served the earl as attorneys rather than sword-bearing retainers.[14] Indeed, Engayne's career followed what might be termed the classical model for a middle-aged, former fighting knight with a substantial personal estate.[15] Having become the earl's counsellor, Engayne served regularly on commissions and in the 1350s was summoned to Parliament, whilst his sons, John and Thomas, continued the family's martial tradition.[16]

Military service had occupied an important place in these men's lives. They had all personally borne arms, prompted in part at least by an awareness that war was the proper public function for men of gentle birth. For some – those whom we might term 'professionals' – the military life was indeed their *raison d'être*. For others, perhaps the majority, it formed only part of what had, by the second quarter of the fourteenth century, become a more complex genteel lifestyle: a lifestyle in which military and civilian responsibilities, family interests and private passions competed for precedence whilst becoming interwoven. However brightly the warrior *mentalité* burned within him, the extent of a gentleman's experience of war was, therefore, likely to be shaped by his immediate personal circumstances: his commitments, his connections, his 'country'. This can be easily enough seen in the varied careers and backgrounds of the men who served in the earl of Northampton's *comitiva* in 1340. But just how typical of the genteel element in the military community at the start of the Hundred Years War were these men,[17] and how typical of the nobility and gentry at large? Might

---

17 (1359–60).

13   Engayne had served with Bohun in Scotland in 1336: E101/19/36, m. 5. Drayton had been a member of the bishop of Ely's retinue in 1327: E101/18/6.

14   *Treaty Rolls, 1337–9*, nos 288, 373, 707; C76/15, m. 19; C81/1735, m. 14; Holmes, *Estates*, pp. 123–4.

15   G. E. Cokayne (ed.), *The Complete Peerage*, revised edn, 12 vols in 13 parts (London, 1910–57) [hereafter, *GEC*], V, pp. 75–7; *CIPM*, X, no. 433 (died 16 February 1358, aged 55).

16   *Report from the Lords' Committees ... for all Matters Touching the Dignity of a Peer*, 5 vols (London, 1820–29) [hereafter, *RDP*], IV, pp. 605, 608, 612, 615, 618. Sir John Engayne *le fitz* is included in a fiat warrant, possibly for the Sluys campaign: C81/1734, m. 24. Sir Thomas Engayne served with Northampton in France in 1359–60: C76/38, m. 17. See also *GEC*, V, pp. 77–8.

17   'Military community' may be defined as 'those [in local society] with military experience': Morgan, *War and Society*, p. 1. Whilst this is a socially diverse group, embracing both the greatest magnates and the poorest of arrayed

not the pressing military requirements of one of Edward III's foremost captains have stimulated the recruitment of a decidedly atypical group? In terms of their geographical origins, this does not have the appearance of a randomly selected group of Englishmen. Knights and esquires from the Bohun power-bases in Essex and the Welsh marches rub shoulders with a sprinkling of seasoned fighters from the traditionally militarised communities of the northernmost counties of England.

Beyond an investigation of those knights and esquires who actually fought lies a larger question. To what extent were the English aristocracy as a whole, the nobility and gentry, attracted by the prospect of martial service in the fourth decade of the fourteenth century? Was there, as has been suggested by some historians, a significant change in outlook and behaviour taking place, a process of 'demilitarisation'? Or is it simply a matter of diversification of function, a response to the expanding opportunities offered by, amongst other things, administrative service in the shires, combined with changes in the social composition of the secular landholding community? For the historian wrestling with this problem, part of the difficulty lies in the interpretation of apparently contradictory signals in the evidence. On the one hand, the Edwardian period witnessed what Peter Coss has characterised as the 'triumph of chivalric knighthood', involving, for example, a proliferation of heraldic display and knightly effigies in churches.[18] The early fourteenth-century knight's sense of identity, of his social status and his family's honour, had overt martial overtones: 'one consequence of the triumph of chivalry', Coss observes, 'was to reinforce the martial implications of knighthood'.[19] Yet, on the other hand, the aristocracy had a long-established reputation for dragging its feet where overseas military service was concerned. They 'did not give a bean for all of France', it was said, as was amply shown by Edward I's Flemish expedition of 1297, when only 200 men-at-arms were provided from outside the king's household and circle of intimates.[20]

Some historians have argued that by 1337 there had been a shift in attitude, that there was 'among the nobility, actual relish at the prospect of fighting'. The 'bonds of comradeship' which Edward had forged with the aristocracy by his enthusiastic pursuit of chivalric values and by his personal leadership in the Scottish campaigns, and the growing self-esteem

---

infantrymen, this paper focuses on the 'aristocracy', a term which I take to embrace both the nobility and gentry.

[18] P. Coss, *The Knight in Medieval England, 1000–1400* (Stroud, 1993), chs 4 and 5.

[19] *Ibid.*, p. 100.

[20] N. B. Lewis, 'The English Forces in Flanders, August–November 1297', *Studies in Medieval History Presented to F. M. Powicke*, ed. R. W. Hunt, W. A. Pantin and R. W. Southern (Oxford, 1948), pp. 314–16.

of the genteel military community, had moved them to support Edward's 'aggressive designs against France'.[21] The parliament which met in March 1337 certainly endorsed the king's ambitious continental strategy and welcomed the creation of six new earls.[22] But was there really wholehearted backing for the war from the military class? As Edward III contemplated the expedition to Flanders at the start of his continental adventure, how confident can he have been that the aristocracy would indeed back him with their swords? That there was at least some anxiety over this is suggested by the government's willingness to pay *double* the usual rates of pay to all categories of men-at-arms accompanying the king to Flanders in 1338.[23]

Assessment of the extent of the king's success in securing the active support of the nobility and gentry for his French war rests upon a substantial, if incomplete, corpus of records. *Vadia guerre* accounts (pay rolls) have survived for each of the three major royal expeditions up to the truce of Malestroit in January 1343: that is, for the army which landed in Antwerp in July 1338 and eventually fought in the Cambrésis over a year later; the army which in 1340 won the battle of Sluys and then besieged, unsuccessfully, the town of Tournai; and the series of expeditionary forces which served in Brittany in 1342–43. Two of the pay rolls – those for the first Flanders expedition and the campaign in Brittany – are to be found in Wardrobe Books and are well-known to historians.[24] Altogether less familiar is the *vadia guerre* account documenting the English army at Sluys and the siege of Tournai. Indeed, apart from a brief discussion by T. F.

---

[21] J. Sumption, *The Hundred Years War: Trial by Battle* (London, 1990), pp. 180–3. For a very different view, see W. M. Ormrod, *The Reign of Edward III* (New Haven and London, 1990), pp. 12–13, 100.

[22] E. B. Fryde, 'Parliament and the French War, 1336–40', *Essays in Medieval History Presented to Bertie Wilkinson*, ed. T. A. Sandquist and M. R. Powicke (Toronto, 1969), pp. 250–69; G. L. Harriss, *King, Parliament and Public Finance in Medieval England to 1369* (Oxford, 1975), pp. 233–4.

[23] A. Ayton, *Knights and Warhorses: Military Service and the English Aristocracy under Edward III* (Woodbridge, 1994), p. 109.

[24] E36/203, published *in extenso* as *The Wardrobe Book of William de Norwell*; see pp. 325–62 for the pay roll (cf. E101/21/21 and E101/21/31: pay rolls for county-based companies of archers for the period prior to their arrival in the Low Countries). E36/204, the account book of William de Edington's period as Keeper of the Wardrobe, 1341–4; the pay roll for the Breton expeditions occupies fols 105v–110v. For summary analysis, see A. Prince, 'The Strength of English Armies in the Reign of Edward III', *EHR*, 46 (1931), pp. 360–3; and, for the armies taken to Brittany in 1342–3, see Ayton, *Knights and Warhorses*, appendix 2.

Tout and a passing reference by Kenneth Fowler, this important pay roll, buried in the middle of an incomplete royal household 'journal' roll, but filling more than five densely packed membranes, appears to have gone unnoticed.[25]

These three pay rolls enable us to establish with a reasonable degree of accuracy the size and structure of the major royal armies with which Edward III began his French enterprise. They also allow us to determine, at least in outline, the extent of the aristocracy's role. At the start of the French war English royal armies were composed, on the one hand, of retinues recruited by aristocratic captains and, on the other, of shire levies, arrayed – and in some cases led to war – by members of the local gentry.[26] The pay rolls reveal the identities of the captains, from great magnates to relatively humble knights, together with details of their retinues (numbers of men-at-arms and archers, periods of service); and they reveal, if not all the arrayers' names, then at least the men who led the companies of archers to the ports of embarkation and beyond.[27] Also to be found in the *vadia guerre* records are the names of the many minor characters, particularly household servants, who accompanied the king to war.[28] Admittedly, as with most *vadia guerre* records, these three rolls are not free of interpretative problems.[29] Fluctuations in manpower numbers are heavily summarised and periods of service are not always precisely given;[30] and none of the pay

---

25   E101/389/8; the pay roll occupies mm. 11–16. See T. F. Tout, *Chapters in the Administrative History of Medieval England*, 6 vols (Manchester, 1920–33), IV, pp. 106–7; K. Fowler, *The King's Lieutenant: Henry of Grosmont, First Duke of Lancaster, 1310–61* (London, 1969), p. 34, n. 17 (p. 258). Albert Prince's omission of this pay roll from his pioneering 1931 article in the *English Historical Review* appears to have strongly influenced subsequent researchers: e.g. Sumption, *Hundred Years War*, pp. 338–9.

26   For the principal developments in the recruitment and organisation of English armies during this period, see A. Ayton, 'English Armies in the Fourteenth Century', *Arms, Armies and Fortifications in the Hundred Years War*, ed. A. Curry and M. Hughes (Woodbridge, 1994), pp. 21–38. A. Prince, 'The Army and Navy', *The English Government at Work, 1327–1336*, ed. J. F. Willard and W. A. Morris (Cambridge, Mass., 1940), I, pp. 332–93 remains valuable for the period immediately prior to the Hundred Years War.

27   The commissions of array, together with full lists of arrayers arranged by counties, are to be found on the Chancery rolls. Few muster rolls for shire levies have survived, but for this period see E101/21/29 (Shropshire, 1338 and 1339); E101/23/8 (Lincolnshire, 1342).

28   For example, 255 individuals are listed on the pay roll for the Breton campaign: Ayton, *Knights and Warhorses*, pp. 182–3.

29   On this subject, see Ayton, *Knights and Warhorses*, pp. 144–55.

30   Norwell's account does, however, record the creation of new knights, many of them dubbed on 23 October at Buironfosse.

rolls offers complete coverage. In consequence, precise calculation of the numbers of paid troops in these armies is not possible, but the following figures are probably not too wide of the mark.

Edward III landed in Antwerp in the summer of 1338 with approaching 1,400 men-at-arms,[31] about 2,500 archers and various companies of Welsh infantry whose numbers and precise periods of service are difficult to establish.[32] The pay roll suggests some movement of personnel during the following months. Allowing for arrivals and departures, by late September 1339, when the army finally saw action, the numbers of English men-at-arms may have swollen by about a hundred, whilst most of the Welsh infantry had gone.[33] Not included in these totals are the troops provided by Edward's continental allies. Only a few hundred are included on the pay roll, but on paper the network of alliances was intended to yield nearly 7,000 men-at-arms.[34]

The surviving *vadia guerre* records for the Sluys-Tournai campaign appear to be incomplete with regard to 'English' retinues. According to the pay roll, the king fought at Sluys on 24 June 1340 with about 1,300 men-at-arms and probably over 1,000 archers, the majority of whom were serving in aristocratic retinues.[35] About 150 men-at-arms arrived after the battle (though balanced by departures from the army),[36] whilst over 2,000

[31] The pay roll does not give precise manpower numbers for Sir Geoffrey le Scrope's retinue, which served *per convencionem indentatam secum factam per regem et consilium suum. Norwell*, p. 331. However, two witnesses in the Court of Chivalry armorial case between Richard, Lord Scrope and Sir Robert Grosvenor mentioned Sir Geoffrey le Scrope's retinue in 1338–9. One stated that he had served with 40 men-at-arms, the other that he had 10 knights in his company: *Scrope and Grosvenor Controversy*, I, pp. 105, 152.

[32] 445 of the archers, forming a 'free company' of volunteers from various parts of England, actually arrived in mid-August (*Norwell*, p. 360). The Welsh are impossible to document precisely; there were over one thousand of them at various times: cf. Prince, 'Strength of English Armies', p. 361.

[33] E.g., Sir William de la Pole, with 35 men-at-arms, was paid from 16 August; he had 200 archers from 1 March 1339: *Norwell*, pp. 335, 358. Sir Hugh le Despenser appears to have arrived too late to be included in the pay records: *Calendar of Close Rolls* [hereafter, *CCR*], *1339–41*, p. 290.

[34] Sumption, *Hundred Years War*, p. 199.

[35] The pay roll shows that 900 archers were certainly at Sluys. For a further 750 the precise period of service is uncertain, though it is likely that a proportion of these men were at the battle.

[36] The late arrivals included the earl of Oxford's men, who, having been stationed on the Hainault march, joined the earl of Northampton's retinue on 10 July: *Norwell*, pp. 326–7; E101/389/8, m. 11. Oxford was due to leave England with the earl of Warwick towards the end of March (*CCR*, *1339–41*, p. 370; C76/15, mm. 25–6), but Warwick appears to have been at the battle

179

archers, the great majority of the latter serving on foot in archer companies, joined the army later in the summer. However, there are several retinues, probably substantial ones, missing from the pay records. It is likely that Henry de Burghersh, bishop of Lincoln, was accompanied by as grand a company as had served with him during the first Flanders expedition, and yet details of his *comitiva* do not appear on the pay roll.[37] Also absent from the rolls are the earls of Arundel and Huntingdon. There can be no doubt that they actually fought at Sluys. In addition to the evidence of enrolled letters of protection,[38] Arundel appeared in Parliament in mid-July to present an eye-witness report on the recent military operations,[39] whilst the English chronicles attest to Huntingdon's presence (though not Arundel's) at Sluys, serving as an admiral.[40] Also omitted from the list of captains in the Sluys-Tournai pay roll is Robert of Artois, who led the unsuccessful attempt to take Saint-Omer in late July.[41] We can be sure that he arrived *with a retinue* after Sluys, for there are enrolled protections for 49 men

---

of Sluys: the *vadia guerre* record for his retinue makes no mention of service on the Hainault march and begins a new pay period on 24 June, the day of Sluys. William de Sutton, a deponent in the Lovel vs. Morley armorial dispute before the Court of Chivalry in 1386–7, testified that he had been at Sluys with Warwick: C47/6/1, no. 5. The pay roll suggests that Sir Geoffrey le Scrope's retinue joined the army on 31 July (E101/389/8, m. 11), although only three days earlier an order had been issued for six ships to carry him and his retinue from Orwell (C76/15, m. 9). Many retinues show evidence of withdrawals; by far the largest, the departure of 67 men-at-arms on 22 July, affected the earl of Derby's company (E101/389/8, m. 11).

[37] Burghersh's retinue in 1338–9 at its peak fielded over one hundred knights and esquires: *Norwell*, pp. 325–6. Sixty-five men have enrolled protections or attorneys, mostly dated 6 June, for service with the bishop in 1340: C76/15, mm. 21–3, 25. Having had a lucky escape during the siege of Tournai, the bishop died in Ghent on 2 December 1340: Sumption, *Hundred Years War*, pp. 352, 362.

[38] Enrolled protections for Arundel and 21 of his men, and Huntingdon with 9 of his: C76/15, mm. 18–20, 22–4.

[39] *RP*, II, p. 118. For Arundel's service at Sluys, see also *CCR, 1339–41*, pp. 493–4. According to Geoffrey le Baker, Arundel, Huntingdon and Gloucester returned to England after Sluys: E. M. Thompson (ed.), *Chronicon Galfridi le Baker de Swynebroke (1303–56)* (Oxford, 1889), p. 70. Gloucester's pay roll entry shows that he was absent from the siege of Tournai from 16 July until 25 August: E101/389/8, m. 11. Huntingdon had been appointed to the regency council a month before Sluys: *CPR, 1338–40*, p. 528.

[40] E.g. E. M. Thompson (ed.), *Adam Murimuth, Continuatio Chronicarum* (Rolls Series, London, 1889), pp. 106–7. Both earls had been appointed admirals on 20 February 1340: C76/15, m. 32.

[41] Sumption, *Hundred Years War*, pp. 339–43.

intending to serve with him and in early July shipping was being ordered for his passage.[42] Allowing for other omissions from the pay roll, both those we know about and those that we strongly suspect,[43] we should perhaps increase the number of men-at-arms at Sluys to 1,500. There may well have been more in the siege camp outside Tournai: many years later Sir Ralph Ferrars recalled that, at that siege, *chescun liege et gentils avoient ascuns de lour sanc ou affinite.*[44]

The English expeditions to Brittany in 1342–3 involved a series of three expeditions.[45] Sir Walter Mauny served in the duchy in the spring and early summer with no more than 350 men, including about 130 men-at-arms, the rest being mounted archers. The earl of Northampton brought a more substantial force in August. Its size cannot be established precisely, since Robert of Artois and William de Kildesby, who were granted assignments of wool for their retinues, are not included in the *vadia guerre* account.[46] However, at the time of the battle of Morlaix on 30 September 1342, Northampton probably had about 1,100 troops from England at his disposal (with roughly equal numbers of men-at-arms and mounted archers), plus an indeterminate number of Bretons. A third expedition, led by the king, arrived in Brittany in late October. Allowing for the early departure of some magnate retinues and the non-arrival, or very short stay, of most of the arrayed archers and infantry, it would seem that by Christmas 1342 Edward may have had with him about 3,600 to 3,700 men with men-at-arms and mounted archers in just about equal proportions. The pay roll suggests that, overall, about 1,900 men-at-arms served in Brittany during this campaign. Allowing for a certain amount of double counting in that total and the omission of perhaps 150 men-at-arms from the pay roll, we may conclude that as many as 2,000 English

---

[42] Protections and attorneys: C76/15, mm. 20, 22, 24. Passage: C76/15, m. 17; cf. m. 7; E. Déprez, *Les préliminaires de la guerre de cent ans* (Paris, 1902), p. 323, n. 8. One of Artois' lieutenants, the Yorkshireman Sir Thomas Ughtred, brought a company (protections, dated 21 June: C76/15, m. 19) and took part in the battle of Saint-Omer on 26 July; yet Ughtred's only appearance on the pay roll is as the unpaid leader of a small company of archers who were receiving the king's pay from 10 July (E101/389/8, m. 14).

[43] 24 men-at-arms and 24 archers, serving from 24 June until 3 August, are enumerated in a separate pay account for Sir John de Molyns's retinue: E101/22/35. Sir Hugh le Despenser secured protections for himself and 25 men, yet he is missing from the pay roll; and similar evidence exists for Sir Robert Morley: C76/15, mm. 8, 18, 20–4.

[44] *Scrope and Grosvenor Controversy*, I, p. 156.

[45] For details and documentary references, see Ayton, *Knights and Warhorses*, pp. 181–5 and appendix 2.

[46] *Ibid.*, pp. 260–1.

men-at-arms served, most in all likelihood being drawn from the ranks of the gentry.

If the sources which document the size and structure of these armies are far from flawless, the records that reveal the names of men serving in them are perhaps still less satisfactory. Most of these records focus predominantly on the men-at-arms, the genteel combatants, but even within this constituency of personnel the coverage is not comprehensive. There is nothing for Edward III's early French campaigns to compare with the surviving horse inventories from the Scottish expeditions of the later 1330s.[47] The best documentation of this kind that we have are two fairly substantial *restauro equorum* accounts from the first Flemish and Breton campaigns: the first lists over 500 horses (and their owners), of which about 330 were appraised mounts associated with English men-at-arms; the second includes 228 appraised warhorses belonging to 226 individuals.[48] The only surviving muster roll from these early French campaigns lists the 24 men-at-arms serving in Sir John Molyns's retinue from 24 June to 3 August 1340.[49]

Fortunately, the names of larger numbers of knights and other men-at-arms can be recovered from the lists of enrolled letters of protection on the Chancery rolls.[50] 'Protections' are, admittedly, records of intent, rather than firm evidence of service actually performed, and one or two cases of fraud or last minute changes of mind can be discerned in the lists for these campaigns.[51] They also include a sprinkling of

[47] E.g. the force of 500 men-at-arms serving in Scotland under Henry of Lancaster from May 1336: E101/19/36; Ayton, *Knights and Warhorses*, pp. 170–7 and appendix 1.

[48] *Norwell*, pp. 309–25; E36/204, fols 86v–88r; Ayton, *Knights and Warhorses*, pp. 180–4 and appendix 2. The list of horses lost during the Sluys-Tournai campaign is short and composed mainly of unappraised 40s. horses. E101/389/8, mm. 8–9.

[49] E101/22/35; the 24 archers in Molyns's retinue are not named.

[50] On letters of protection and related records as sources for genteel military service, see Ayton, *Knights and Warhorses*, pp. 157–63.

[51] Robert, Lord Lisle was at the centre of what appears to be a case of fraud. In the spring of 1339, in spite of his 51 years (and having been deemed unfit for military service in December 1336), Lisle obtained protections for himself and a number of men who were to serve with him in the king's army. Following the death of his wife, Lisle was excused from joining the army and, shortly after, entered the Franciscan order. However, the king subsequently learned that Lisle's protection had been obtained in order to avoid a court case with the earl of Lancaster. C76/14, m. 14; *CPR, 1334–8*, p. 339; *CCR, 1339–41*, p. 360; *GEC*, VIII, pp. 71–3. John Maddicott has argued that in the late 1330s protections might be used to avoid the attentions of purveyors: *The*

non-combatants, not all of whom are easy to distinguish. Nevertheless, these lists of protection recipients are essential to the study of genteel military service in the early campaigns of the Hundred Years War. A total of 778 enrolled protections are dated to the weeks leading up to the king's departure on 16 July 1338. About 650 separate individuals secured legal protection for the 1340 campaign and 722 for the Breton expeditions two years later.[52] It seems, then, that protections were secured by between a third and a half of all serving men-at-arms. Far fewer genteel combatants are to be found among the men who received charters of pardon in return for spells of military service.[53] For example, there are about 900 service pardons on the Patent Rolls, dating from the period February 1339 to March 1340;[54] but since the great majority of these men are clearly from the sub-genteel strata of the military community, the archers and infantry, these records are of only marginal interest for the present study.

A scatter of further nominal data can, of course, be found in all sorts of places. For example, we learn in the fifteenth-century autobiography of John Carrington that his grandfather, Sir William Carrington, had been scalded in the face at the battle of Sluys.[55] Another unhappy man after that battle was Sir Thomas Latimer. He had been taken prisoner, but at least received a modest royal contribution towards his ransom.[56] Nearly fifty years later no fewer than twenty-one men recalled their involvement in the battle of Sluys in their testimony before the Court of Chivalry.[57] Fascinating though such reminiscences are, they provide no more than icing for the cake. The bulk of our knowledge comes from the pay records and the lists of men who received protections before a campaign or lost a warhorse during it. Taken together, the sources *may* yield the names of as many as half of the men-at-arms serving in a particular army; but such a nominal

---

English Peasantry and the Demands of the Crown, 1294–1341, Past and Present Supplement, no. 1, 1975, pp. 21–2.

[52] 1338: *Treaty Rolls, 1337–9*. 1340: C76/15. 1342–3: C76/17; C76/18; C61/54. Note also the suspension of assizes of novel disseisin; for Sluys-Tournai, see *CCR, 1339–41*, pp. 486–7.

[53] One such is Sir Hugh de Wrottesley: *CPR, 1338–40*, p. 194. On service pardons, see Ayton, *Knights and Warhorses*, pp. 163–6, which provides full documentary references.

[54] There are five large blocks of entries: *CPR, 1338–40*, pp. 217–36, 337–44, 419–23, 436–40, 454–7.

[55] Morgan, *War and Society*, p. 154.

[56] E101/389/8, m. 2. Several chronicles state that Latimer was killed in the battle.

[57] Fourteen in the Lovel vs. Morley case (C47/6/1, nos 2, 3, 5, 6, 7, 10, 13, 17, 19, 20, 27, 59, 92, 106); sevem in the Scrope vs. Grosvenor case (*Scrope and Grosvenor Controversy*, I, pp. 77, 125, 142–6, 198, 240–2).

roll will not be a random sample, since few of the records contributing to it are wholly without bias towards a particular group within the military community. Analysis based upon such a reconstructed army roll should make allowance for this in-built bias in the sources.

What do these sources reveal about the extent of the aristocracy's commitment to the king's war in the late 1330s? Mark Ormrod has argued that Edward III's armies in the Low Countries rested upon a comparatively narrow recruitment base. Attempting 'to do without the massed ranks of the English barons', the king relied upon his personal friends, a group of whom had recently been raised to comital rank, and the military resources of his household.[58] There is *some* truth in this. No fewer than 60% of the men-at-arms who embarked for Antwerp in July 1338 were connected to the royal household – a massive 'household division' by any standards.[59] Looked at a different way, all except one of the king's 62 current household bannerets and knights served in Flanders for all or part of Edward III's protracted first expedition.[60] Even Sir Thomas Lucy, a man with pressing responsibilities on the northern border, remained with the king overseas from July 1338 until February 1340.[61] Using the incomplete pay roll for the battle of Sluys, the household division appears to have contributed a little over 60% (800) of the men-at-arms in the English army;[62] but allowing for the omission of several large, non-household retinues from the pay records,

---

[58] Ormrod, *Reign of Edward III*, p. 100; and, more generally, pp. 12–13, 107–8.

[59] About 850 men-at-arms, including Geoffrey le Scrope's retinue and miscellaneous individuals attached to the household. If we limit our attention to the retinues led by bannerets and knights (including clerks carrying those ranks), we have about 600 men in the household division, which represented 57% of the retinue strength of the army, there being about 450 men-at-arms serving in retinues headed by captains of knightly rank or above who were not attached to the household. Fees and robes: *Norwell*, pp. 301–9.

[60] 17 bannerets and 45 knights; one of the latter, Sir John de Sapy, was absent from the army. During the campaign, 5 of the king's household men were elevated to the rank of banneret, whilst 18 became knights. On 11 October 1339 Sir Thomas de Poynings, a household banneret, died of wounds sustained in the attack on Honnecourt. His son, Michael, having been knighted, took over command of his father's retinue on the following day: *Norwell*, p. 330; H. Maxwell (ed.), *Scalacronica* (Glasgow, 1907), p. 107; *CPR, 1338–40*, p. 39.

[61] *Norwell*, pp. 301, 339–40. On Lucy, see *GEC*, VIII, p. 252; for his family's defence responsibilities, see C. M. Fraser (ed.) *Northern Petitions*, Surtees Society, CXCIV (1981), no. 111; E159/122, m. 56. He was on paid service in Scotland and the Marches during the winter of 1341–2 and the following summer–autumn (E36/204, fols 102r, 103v, 104v, 105r).

[62] Fees and robes: E101/389/8, mm. 9–10, 26–7.

a more likely figure would be in the region of 50% to 55%. For the Breton campaign of 1342–3 it is still lower, 40%, though here we see a household division of stable numbers (800) set within a larger army.[63]

Such heavy dependence on household manpower was not without military advantages. Since the majority of Edward III's household bannerets and knights were veterans from the Scottish wars, he set out on his adventure in France with a well-established team of middle-ranking and junior captains: men who had direct experience of the campaigns which had witnessed a major overhaul of the English fighting machine. This was a heterogeneous group, embracing such colourful figures as the Hainaulter Sir Walter Mauny; men of solid baronial stock, like Henry de Ferrars; and professional soldiers of obscure origins, like Sir John Stryvelyn. Stryvelyn's career is particularly instructive. He was a new recruit to the royal household at the start of the French war, an example of the king's determination to strengthen the household division with reliable, resourceful captains – as Stryvelyn had certainly shown himself to be in Scotland.[64] After the first Low Countries expedition, he was back on the Scottish border for the summer of 1340, but accompanied the king to Brittany in 1342.[65] Stryvelyn was clearly an energetic man and utterly dependable, qualities which characterise the household knights as a whole. Nowhere is this better shown than in the rapid mobilisation of a strike force to relieve Stirling castle in 1341. Eleven royal household bannerets and knights brought with them over 300 men-at-arms; and they performed the task for a little over £1,000, which can only have been regarded as very good value for money.[66]

That the king's household knights played a prominent role in Edward III's Low Countries campaigns should occasion no surprise, for they had traditionally formed the backbone of royal armies.[67] Indeed, the

---

[63]   This takes the three expeditions to constitute a single army and makes allowance for some omissions from the pay roll; but focusing on the army brought by the king in late October, the household division contributed 45% of the army's men-at-arms: E36/204, fols 89r–92r.

[64]   Stryvelyn was keeper of Edinburgh castle in 1335–8; B.L. Cotton MS, Nero C.VIII, fol. 249; E101/388/5, m. 17. See also *GEC*, XII, part 1, 407–8.

[65]   *Norwell*, p. 339; E101/389/8, m. 13; E36/204, fols 102 (Scotland, winter 1341–2); 106v (Brittany, 1342–3).

[66]   E101/389/8, m. 26: 330 men-at-arms, plus a small, unspecified number with Sir John Darcy *junior*. The captains, who included Sir John de Stryvelyn, undertook the task for a fixed sum, calculated at the rate of £30 per 10 men-at-arms. Cf. E. A. Bond (ed.), *Chronicon monasterii de Melsa*, 3 vols, Rolls Series (London, 1866–68), III, p. 49; *CPR, 1340–43*, p. 382.

[67]   J. O. Prestwich, 'The Military Household of the Norman Kings', *EHR* 96 (1981), pp. 1–35; S. D. Church, 'The Knights of the Household of King John:

proportional strength of the military household or 'household division' in Edward III's armies at the start of the Hundred Years War bears comparison with that which has been noted for the armies raised during the reign of Edward I.[68] In Edward III's early French campaigns the dominance of household troops was closely related to the comparative weakness of the comital class and, in particular, to the absence of a militarily-active royal family. In 1359, the massive retinues of the Prince of Wales and the duke of Lancaster, and the presence of a strong group of earls, largely explain why the household division contributed only a sixth of all men-at-arms in Edward III's army.[69]

'Household division' is actually a slightly misleading term. The leader of a retinue might receive fees and robes from the king, but the men whom he recruited would be drawn from the military community at large. A household knight, like Sir Nicholas de Langeford, might bring two esquires,[70] but the king's bannerets' retinues were usually much more substantial. At Sluys they ranged in size from 10 to 79 men-at-arms, often with attached contingents of archers. Some of these men were drawn from specialised regional military communities. There can be little doubt that the men-at-arms whom Sir John de Stryvelyn recruited for his retinues in 1338 and 1342 included a good many tough border professionals, men like himself. It is hardly surprising to find that only one of them required a letter of protection.[71] But, as we have seen, some of the men who took the king's fees and robes at the start of the French war were scions of *baronial* families. As a consequence, the recruitment base of the household division overlapped with the regional lordship networks of magnates. In this way the king's banneret Sir Maurice de Berkeley could rely to some extent upon his family's influence in Gloucestershire and neighbouring counties, an 'intricate and far-reaching ... web of baronial power' as Nigel Saul has

---

a Question of Numbers', *Thirteenth-Century England IV*, ed. P. R. Coss and S. D. Lloyd (Woodbridge, 1992), pp. 151–65.

[68] M. Prestwich, *War, Politics and Finance under Edward I* (London, 1972), pp. 50–7; *idem*, 'English Armies in the Early Stages of the Hundred Years War: a Scheme of 1341', *BIHR*, 56 (1983), p. 109.

[69] Ayton, 'English Armies', p. 25. After 1360 the 'long-established system of household knights' broke down, to be replaced by a smaller number of higher status, more versatile chamber knights: C. Given-Wilson, 'The King and the Gentry in Fourteenth-Century England', *TRHS*, Fifth Series, 37 (1987), pp. 90–2.

[70] *Norwell*, p. 341; E101/389/8, m. 12.

[71] Water de Heslerton, an East Riding man (C76/17, m. 27); see Ayton, *Knights and Warhorses*, p. 192 and n. 286. In 1338 Stryvelyn obtained protection for himself only.

described it.[72] It is, for example, not altogether surprising to find a member of the Mautravers family in Sir Maurice's retinue in 1342.[73] Meanwhile, Berkeley's friend and companion in arms, Sir Thomas de Bradeston, very much a rising star of Edward III's court in the 1330s, built up *his* affinity in the same region from scratch, sometimes drawing on the services of men who also campaigned with the Berkeleys.[74] When we examine the detail of genteel military service, then, the courtier-baron dichotomy becomes blurred.

Edward I's army in Flanders in 1297 can with justification be described as 'essentially the household in arms',[75] but the hosts shipped to the same region by his grandson just over 40 years later were of more complex composition. In July 1338 about 25% (340) of the men-at-arms were serving in retinues headed by an earl.[76] The corresponding percentage figure for June 1340 was probably rather higher: 30%.[77] With the king in 1338 were the earls of Derby, Northampton, Salisbury and Suffolk.[78] Arundel, Derby, Gloucester, Huntingdon, Northampton and Warwick were at Sluys;[79] Salisbury and Suffolk had been taken prisoner the previous April in a skirmish near Lille, whilst Oxford joined the army outside Tournai, having earlier been employed in the defence of the Hainault march.

These men can certainly be described as the 'king's friends': most of them had been raised to comital status by Edward III and they had all fought with him in Scotland. That Edward relied so heavily on this group at the start of the French war was hardly surprising; indeed, he really had no choice. On the eve of the March 1337 parliament the 'community of

---

[72] N. Saul, *Knights and Esquires: the Gloucestershire Gentry in the Fourteenth Century* (Oxford, 1981), pp. 69–75.

[73] Sir John Mautravers *junior*: C76/17, m. 26.

[74] Saul, *Knights and Esquires*, pp. 76–7. Bradeston was also in receipt of Lady Elizabeth de Burgh's livery: E101/92/23.

[75] Lewis, 'The English Forces in Flanders', p. 314, n. 3.

[76] This increases to 30% if we include in the comital total the 75 men-at-arms who accompanied Henry de Burghersh, bishop of Lincoln.

[77] The pay records show 373 men-at-arms in the retinues of earls, but the incompleteness of the pay roll data necessitates a calculation based in part on estimates of retinue sizes.

[78] Laurence de Hastings, who was with the king's army and under twenty years of age, became earl of Pembroke on 13 October 1339: *GEC*, X, 388–91.

[79] The pay roll suggests that Derby, Gloucester, Northampton and Warwick were at Sluys; Arundel and Huntingdon, together with the bishop of Lincoln, were also there. Sumption's assertion that Northampton was involved in the defence of Valenciennes in late May (*Hundred Years War*, p. 314) would seem to be incorrect, for he was in England during the weeks leading up to Sluys (E101/389/8, m. 7; DL25/32).

earls' was in a much depleted state. Edward III's warlike younger brother, John of Eltham, earl of Cornwall, had died a few months earlier, as had John de Bohun earl of Hereford and Essex. John de Warenne, earl of Surrey, had been a vigorous campaigner, but now in his early fifties he was a bit old for *chevauchées*. Between them, Cornwall, Hereford and Warenne had provided over 500 men-at-arms for the large-scale Scottish campaign of 1335.[80] The new earl of Hereford and Essex, Humphrey, appears to have been an invalid,[81] whilst the recently restored earl of Devon was now in his sixties.[82] The earl of Lancaster was a little younger, but blind, whilst his cousin, the king's uncle, Thomas of Brotherton, earl of Norfolk, had taken no part in the Scottish wars after Halidon Hill. He was to die in 1338.[83] The earls of Angus and Buchan were, as their titles suggest, preoccupied with Scotland. This left only the earls of Arundel, Oxford and Warwick, vigorous men in their twenties, who had taken an active part in Edward III's Scottish war,[84] but hardly a weighty enough team of senior lieutenants for an ambitious continental war. Accordingly, in the spring of 1337, they were joined by six new earls, men whom they knew and presumably respected as comrades in arms from the Scottish campaigns.[85]

The honours bestowed in March 1337 had a dual purpose. They were intended, on the one hand, as reward for talented men, who had played leading roles in the coup of 1330 and had fought loyally in Scotland;[86] and, on the other, as practical preparation for the coming war. In expanding the community of earls, Edward III acquired a larger group of reliable captains;

---

[80] R. Nicholson, *Edward III and the Scots, 1327–1335* (Oxford, 1965), p. 248.

[81] Holmes, *Estates*, pp. 20–1. In 1336 the earl sent men-at-arms, including members of his household, to join the king's army in Scotland: *Calendar of Documents Relating to Scotland* [hereafter, *CDRS*], ed. G. G. Simpson and J. D. Galbraith (Edinburgh, 1986), V, no. 763.

[82] *GEC*, III, pp. 466–7. His son, Hugh, received his first summons to parliament in April 1337 and succeeded his father as earl of Devon at the very end of 1340.

[83] Norfolk had apparently intended to serve in Scotland during the autumn of 1337, since there are protections on the Scottish roll (C71/17, mm. 11, 14), but he does not figure as a captain on the pay rolls.

[84] Nicholson, *Edward III and the Scots*, p. 128 and appendices 3–4; Ayton, *Knights and Warhorses*, appendix 1; N. B. Lewis, 'The Recruitment and Organisation of a Contract Army, May to November 1337', *BIHR*, 37 (1964), 1–19; *CDRS*, V, no. 767.

[85] On the neaw earls, see C. Given-Wilson, *The English Nobility in the Late Middle Ages* (London, 1987), pp. 35–40.

[86] Salisbury, Huntingdon, Suffolk and Northampton had been involved in the Nottingham castle coup. For the military experience of the new earls, see n. 84 and Fowler, *The King's Lieutenant*, pp. 30–3.

but it seems that he was also seeking, through the social weight and wealth of these men, to broaden the recruitment base of his armies. Grants of 1,000 marks *per annum* in land, combined with further royal favours, enabled the new earls of Salisbury, Suffolk and Huntingdon to expand their affinities to levels commensurate with their comital status.[87] Hugh de Audley's elevation to the earldom of Gloucester was not accompanied by such a grant: it was an acknowledgement of existing status and wealth. It was also, doubtless, a gesture intended to encourage a seasoned campaigner of relatively advanced years to continue placing well-established recruiting networks, resting in part on the Clare inheritance, at the king's disposal.[88] Given their ages, much more could realistically be expected of the new earls of Derby and Northampton; and by elevating these men, Edward might hope to reactivate and expand Lancaster and Bohun lordship networks for military purposes. Henry of Grosmont, son and heir of the blind earl of Lancaster, already had sufficient resources to support a major campaigning retinue, but comital rank and an annuity of 1,000 marks *per annum*, to last until his father's death, gave him the status and means to build his own distinctive Lancastrian affinity and to play a leading role in the continental war.[89] With the earl of Hereford and Essex also militarily inactive, the elevation of his younger brother, William de Bohun, backed up by £1,000 a year, would enable a vigorous, young captain to revitalise a military affinity based on Bohun lordship.[90] The 'serious decline in names, honours and ranks of dignity', to which the creation patents of 1337 refer,[91] had threatened to restrict the crown's access to the military potential of the gentry by closing natural avenues of recruitment. The expansion of the

---

[87] Salisbury and Huntingdon were in their mid-thirties in 1337; Suffolk was a few years older. On Salisbury, see *GEC*, XI, pp. 385–8; Holmes, *Estates*, pp. 26–8. He became Earl Marshal in September 1338, following the death of the earl of Norfolk (*CPR, 1338–40*, p. 190). On Suffolk, see *GEC*, XII, part 1, pp. 429–32; and Huntingdon, *GEC*, VI, pp. 648–50.

[88] For Gloucester's career, see *GEC*, V, pp. 715–19. The oldest of the new earls of 1337 (he was probably in his forties), Hugh de Audley was the second husband of Margaret, the second of three sisters, co-heiresses of Gilbert de Clare, earl of Gloucester (d.1314). For their portion of the inheritance, see Holmes, *Estates*, pp. 36–7. Although Gloucester died in 1347, his lands passed, through his daughter's marriage, into the hands of Ralph de Stafford, an energetic captain who was raised to an earldom in 1351.

[89] Derby was about 27 in 1337. On Derby's affinity, note that there was 'little continuity from his father's lifetime' and rather more from his grandfather's: Fowler, *The King's Lieutenant*, pp. 185–6.

[90] Northampton was about 25 in 1337. For his career, see *GEC*, IX, pp. 664–7; Holmes, *Estates*, pp. 22–3. Note also Given-Wilson, *English Nobility*, p. 38.

[91] *RDP*, V, pp. 27–32.

community of earls made the genteel military community more accessible to an ambitious king.

The newly created earls would be expected to serve in France with augmented retinues, exploiting in particular the wealth of military experience accumulated during the Scottish wars. In part, this was achieved by the acquisition of permanent retainers, such as we see in the agreement between the earl of Northampton and Sir William Tallemache on the eve of the battle of Sluys.[92] However, only the core of a magnate's campaigning *comitiva* would be recruited by this means and the great majority of genteel combatants were not members of bastard feudal affinities.[93] There was a greater dependence on other sources of manpower: firstly, on those traditional avenues of recruitment that involved less formal ties of lordship and locality; and secondly, on the *ad hoc* employment of freelance 'professionals', many of whom were drawn from families on the margins of the gentry.

A third source of manpower consisted of men who were seeking new allegiances, whether permanent or informal, following the death or retirement of their previous captain. The 85 men-at-arms who served in Scotland under the earl of Cornwall's banner during the late summer of 1336 represent a good example of such a pool of potential recruits. The earl died on 13 September.[94] Thereafter, several of his knights offered their services as independent captains. The most notable of these was Sir Hugh le Despenser. In the spring of 1337 he was restored to some of his father's lands and, as was fitting for the heir to a portion of the Clare inheritance, later served with a retinue that would not have been inappropriate for an earl.[95] However, the majority of the men-at-arms who had been in Cornwall's *comitiva* in 1336 looked to new captains for their future military employment. The principal beneficiaries were the bishop of Lincoln and Sir

---

[92] Cf. the earl of Gloucester's agreement with Sir Robert Bourchier, by which the latter acquired an annual rent of £100; he abandoned it when he became Chancellor in 1340: Holmes, *Estates*, p. 79; *CPR, 1340–43*, p. 75. Bourchier served with the earl in Scotland in 1337–8: E101/35/3; m. 1.

[93] For recent comment, see G. Harriss, 'Political Society and the Growth of Government in Late Medieval England', *Past and Present*, no. 138 (February 1993), pp. 53–5; and M. Hicks, *Bastard Feudalism* (London, 1995), pp. 70–6.

[94] B.L., Cotton MS, Nero C.VIII, fol. 240 (*vadia guerre* account): E101/19/36, m. 1 (incomplete horse inventory); C71/16 (protections). John of Eltham, earl of Cornwall, had served with 100 men-at-arms during the Roxburgh campaign (winter 1334–5) and 135 during the summer campaign of 1335: Nicholson, *Edward III and the Scots*, pp. 246, 248.

[95] *CPR, 1334–8*, pp. 461–2. A few months later Sir Hugh acquired further land following his mother's death: *CIPM*, VIII, no. 132. He served with 72 men-at-arms and 26 archers in 1342–3: E36/204, fols 106r, 108v.

John Molyns, the former faced with the task of recruiting a retinue from scratch at the start of the French war, the latter seeking merely to expand his *comitiva* to a size appropriate to his new-found status.[96] No more than a handful of the earl of Cornwall's men served in the Low Countries with the recently created earls. As far as we can tell, Derby and Salisbury each picked up only one man from this source.[97] Admittedly, neither of these magnates marked the beginning of the French war with an immediately significant expansion in their campaigning retinues. Indeed, Salisbury served in the Low Countries with fewer men-at-arms than he had had in his *comitiva* during the previous winter in Scotland;[98] and it was only with the Breton campaign of 1342–3 that Derby's contingent of knights and esquires showed a sharp increase on the numbers that had served under him in Scotland.[99] Yet we should not assume from this stability of numbers that these retinues were already stable in composition. That only 24 of the hundred men-at-arms on Henry of Lancaster's muster roll in 1336 can be shown to have served with him (now as earl of Derby) in 1338–9 may in part be a result of the incompleteness of our nominal data for the latter expedition; but that nearly two-thirds of the identifiable men-at-arms with him in 1338–9 do not appear on the 1336 muster roll is surely significant.[100] There was, it seems, at the start of the French war an ample supply of knights and esquires who were not constrained by formal or informal ties of allegiance. Derby recruited more widely still in 1345. Having been appointed king's lieutenant in Aquitaine, he contracted to serve with a personal retinue truly befitting his status, consisting of 250 men-at-arms and 250 archers.[101] Yet of the 95 bannerets and knights in the earl's retinue,

---

[96]   At least 10 of Cornwall's men served in the bishop of Lincoln's retinue in 1338–9 (*Norwell*, p. 309; *Treaty Rolls, 1337–9*; C76/14); cf. the bishop's retinue for the diplomatic mission to the Low Countries, winter 1337–8: E101/311/31. The bishop had probably benefited from the fact that his brother, Sir Bartholomew de Burghersh, had served with John of Eltham in 1336 (B.L., Cotton MS, Nero C.VIII, fol. 240). Four of Cornwall's esquires served under Molyns in 1338–9: *Norwell*, pp. 314–15, 332, 357; *Treaty Rolls, 1337–9*; C76/14; see also Ayton, *Knights and Warhorses*, pp. 237–9.

[97]   Philip le Despenser and Mathew Bomsted: *Norwell*, pp. 311–12.

[98]   Salisbury had about 140 men-at-arms in his retinue from December 1337 until mid-June 1338 (E101/20/25, m. 3), but only 121 at Buironfosse in October 1339 (*Norwell*, p. 328).

[99]   Scotland, 1336: 100 men-at-arms. Low Countries, 1338–9: 93. Sluys: 115. Brittany: 182. Fowler, *The King's Lieutenant*, p. 229; E101/389/8, m. 11.

[100] E101/25/12; *Treaty Rolls, 1337–9*; C76/14; *Norwell*, pp. 312–13.

[101] E101/25/9; Fowler, *The King's Lieutenant*, appendix 1. The size of Derby's *comitiva* continued to grow after his inheritance of the earldom of Lancaster in 1345, by which he became perhaps the richest man in the kingdom after the

191

only fifteen had a permanent connection with the earl that involved a grant of land or annuities.[102]

In contrast to Salisbury and Derby, the earl of Northampton's campaigning retinue grew substantially immediately after his elevation to an earldom. From having 56 men-at-arms under his banner in 1336, he served with 89 in 1338–9 and 135 at Sluys in 1340; and having been appointed to an important independent command, in Brittany during the summer of 1342, Northampton accounted for a retinue that included no fewer than 200 men-at-arms.[103] As had doubtless been intended, Northampton was well placed to draw on existing Bohun recruiting networks. As we have seen, Essex offered a promising military community from which to draw recruits, with a proportion of the gentry of this county having established connections with the Bohuns.[104] For example, among the families associated with both Humphrey de Bohun, earl of Hereford (d.1322) and his son William were the Mandevilles of Black Notley. Sir Thomas de Mandeville was with Northampton at Sluys and elsewhere,[105] whilst his son, Thomas, continued the tradition of service with the Bohuns.[106] Data relating to the campaigning retinues of William's elder brother, John de Bohun, earl of Hereford and Essex (d.1336), are sparse.[107] Nevertheless it can be seen that, of the families who are known to have supplied men-at-arms for service with that earl, only three contributed to William de Bohun's *comitiva* in 1336; but following his elevation to comital status (and, a few months later, to the office of Constable of England)[108] at least nine others were represented in Northampton's retinues during the early campaigns of the continental war.[109]

The expanded comital community served Edward III well from the very beginning of the French war. All of the able-bodied English earls

---

king.

[102] Fowler, *The King's Lieutenant*, p. 183.

[103] B.L., Cotton MS, Nero C.VIII, fol. 241; *Norwell*, p. 327; E101/389/8, m. 11; E36/204, fol. 106. The same process of expansion can be seen with the earl of Pembroke: three men-at-arms in 1338–9; 64 in 1342–3; 80 in Aquitaine in 1345 (*Norwell*, pp. 331–2; E36/204, fol. 106; E101/68/3, no. 60).

[104] For the Essex gentry with Northampton during the Crécy–Calais campaign, see Ward, *Essex Gentry*, p. 18.

[105] Holmes, *Estates*, p. 73; C47/6/1, no. 2; C76/15, m. 19; *Foedera*, III, i, pp. 38–9 (1345); Ward, *Essex Gentry*, pp. 19, 22–3.

[106] C47/6/1, no. 47; Holmes, *Estates*, pp. 56, 70 n. 9, 75, 80.

[107] Letters of protection for retinues serving in 1327 and 1335: C71/11, m. 5; C71/15, m. 32.

[108] *CPR, 1338–40*, p. 95.

[109] In 1336: Barinton, Botiller, Bourchier; after 1337: Favelore, Fitz Simon, Fitz Walter, Gernoun, Lancaster, Legh, Mounteneye, Sutton, Wauton.

fought in France on at least one occasion during the early campaigns. With the expeditions to Brittany in 1342–3 the military participation of the earls reached a peak: nine, including Pembroke and the new earl of Devon, played a part in this campaign. Their retinues contributed nearly 900 men-at-arms, a little under half of all of the genteel combatants enumerated on the pay rolls.[110] Edward's injection of new blood into the community of earls had enabled the top stratum of the military community to contribute more manpower to his armies and the heavy dependence on the household division was reduced proportionately.

If some of the earls, notably Arundel and Huntingdon, were directly involved in only one of the early French campaigns (in their case, the battle of Sluys), it cannot be doubted that they supported the king's war in a variety of other ways. Arundel had been co-commander, with Salisbury, of the English army besieging Dunbar during the winter and spring of 1338; and when, in mid-June, Salisbury hastened south to join the king, Arundel was left to supervise the defence of the Scottish border.[111] Similar commitments in the north from July to November 1342 prevented Arundel and Huntingdon from joining the expedition to Brittany, although they would have brought reinforcements to the king had not a truce been concluded in January 1343.[112] It is possible that Huntingdon (and indeed the king) considered that *his* talents lay more in the fields of administration and diplomacy than in war. But it should be recalled that he would have led an expedition to Gascony had it not been cancelled in June 1338, that he served as admiral in 1340 and 1341, and that throughout this period he occupied offices with military functions in England.[113]

With both the northern marches and the south coast under threat of attack at the start of the French war, it made good sense to leave a strong group of militarily-experienced magnates in England. So, along with Arundel and Huntingdon, who on 13 July 1338 were appointed to the regency council,[114] Gloucester, Oxford and Warwick remained in England when the king embarked for Flanders. Their military and managerial talents

---

[110] 893 out of approximately 2,000 men-at-arms (45%): see Ayton, *Knights and Warhorses*, appendix 2, table A, pp. 263–4. A major royal expedition planned for 1341, but not realised, had envisaged a total of 2,590 men-at-arms, of whom no fewer than 1,130 were to be supplied by ten earls (44%): Prestwich, 'English Armies', pp. 109, 111–12.

[111] Prince, 'Strength of English Armies', pp. 358–60; D. Macpherson *et al.* (ed.), *Rotuli Scotiae*, 2 vols (London, 1814), I, pp. 524–5; *CDRS*, III, no. 1267.

[112] E36/204, fols 104v–105r; Sumption, *Hundred Years War*, p. 406.

[113] *GEC*, VI, pp. 648–50. Gascony: Sumption, *Hundred Years War*, pp. 234–7. Admiral: E. B. Fryde *et al.*, *Handbook of British Chronology*, 3rd edn (London, 1986), pp. 137–8.

[114] *CPR, 1338–40*, p. 112.

were not neglected. Warwick, for example, was appointed keeper of Southampton in July 1339, in the aftermath of the devastating raid of the previous October, with a garrison which was intended to number 220 men.[115] Moreover, even the elderly and infirm earls were to be involved in the defence of the realm: they are to be found among the magnates appointed in August 1338 to oversee the array of troops and the keeping of the peace in the various regions of the kingdom.[116] One of these was the earl of Devon, keeper of the maritime land, who, in spite of his 63 years, led the local levies in resisting a French raid on Plymouth in May 1339.[117] Another was the earl of Surrey, who (along with Arundel, Huntingdon and Oxford) was given responsibility for a region's defence during the spring 1339 invasion scare.[118]

If the community of earls undoubtedly pulled their weight in the early years of the French war, what of the role of the untitled nobility, 'the massed ranks of the English barons'? Broadly speaking, the peerage's pattern of service was similar to that of the earls. Of the 60 untitled peers who were summoned to the parliaments of the late 1330s (1337–39), half had either died before the first campaign, were of advanced years or were northern barons with responsibilities on the Scottish border.[119] Of the remainder, a majority served in the French war in 1338–40.[120] Some non-combatant peers were represented in France by relatives.[121] Also to be seen fighting during these years were the leading members of several baronial families which were not currently receiving a parliamentary

---

[115] C. Platt, *Medieval Southampton* (London, 1973), p. 115; Déprez, *Préliminaries*, p. 250 n. 8. During his few weeks in this post, Warwick reported critically on the state of Southampton's defences: SC1/41, no. 171. Bean le Bel has the earl serving with Edward III in the autumn of 1339 (J. Viard and E. Déprez (eds), *Chronique de Jean le Bel*, 2 vols (Paris, 1904–5), I, pp. 154–5), but this finds no support in the pay records. He was summoned to all parliaments and great councils during this period and certainly attended the Michaelmas 1339 parliament (RP, II, p. 103).

[116] *CPR, 1338–40*, pp. 141–2.

[117] Murimuth, *Continuatio Chronicarum*, pp. 89–90. The earl had been one of two keepers of the maritime land of Devon since June 1337: C61/49, m. 26; C61/50, m. 11.

[118] Sumption, *Hundred Years War*, p. 262.

[119] *RDP*, IV; *GEC*.

[120] Lords Bardolf, Beauchamp of Somerset, Burghersh, Cantilupe, Despenser, Deyncourt, Faucomberge, Ferrars, Grey of Codnore, Kerdeston, Monthermer, Morley, Neville of Essex, Poynings, Ros of Watton, Segrave, Stafford, Tibetot, Wylughby.

[121] Lords Berkeley, Charleton, Lucy, Ros of Hamlake and Zouche of Harringworth.

summons.[122] Some of the 'strenuous' peers were royal household bannerets – men like Henry de Ferrars and Thomas de Poynings; but they were a minority. Sir John de Segrave and Sir John de Tibetot brought their own retinues in 1338, whilst others, like Sir Nicholas de Cantilupe, served under greater magnates.[123] Sir Robert de Morley and Sir John Bardolf were admirals during the early years of the war;[124] indeed, Morley distinguished himself leading the English fleet into action at Sluys.

There were some apparently able-bodied peers who, whilst not being closely involved in the defence of the north, did not accompany the king to Flanders in 1338–40, but few of them avoided positions of military responsibility in England. Indeed, the baronial community had already shouldered the burden of co-ordinating coastal defence before the king embarked for the continent. Fifteen of the peers who did not join one of the Flemish expeditions (including some old men) had been appointed keepers of the maritime land in June 1337 and March 1338.[125] In the north during these years the Berwick garrison was headed by a series of men of baronial rank: Sir Anthony de Lucy, Sir Richard Talbot, Sir John de Mowbray and Sir James Audley. Audley's term of duty at Berwick, in command of a hundred men, whom he brought north personally from his castle at Heleigh, ran concurrently with the king's expedition to Brittany.[126] Audley may well have felt that he had contributed sufficiently to the king's wars. But he had missed the Low Countries campaigns and in December 1342 he was ordered to send 20 men-at-arms and 20 archers to Portsmouth for despatch to Brittany. Twenty-two others, including the earls of Surrey and Hereford and sixteen peers, received similar orders.[127] If Edward had indeed been prepared to campaign in France 'without the massed ranks of English barons', it was partly because a substantial proportion of them were unfit for overseas service (a problem which was to some extent reduced by

---

[122]   Roger le Strange of Knokyn; Thomas de Swynnerton; Alan la Zouche of Mortimer (*GEC*, XII, part I, pp. 352–4, 585–8; XII, part 2, pp. 960–1).

[123]   *Norwell*, pp. 312, 331, 333–4, 357; *Treaty Rolls, 1337–9*, no. 346. Cantilupe had served under Henry of Grosmont in 1336: E101/15/12.

[124]   C76/14, mm. 3d, 18.

[125]   Lords Basset of Drayton, Berkeley, Charleton, Chaundos, Columbars, Deyncourt, Fitz Hugh, Fitz Payn, Grandison, Haryngton, Husee, Lisle, Sutton, Welles and Wylyngton: C61/49, mm. 11, 26. See also A. Verduyn, 'The Selection and Appointment of Justices of the Peace in 1338', *Historical Research*, 68 (1995), pp. 8–9.

[126]   E101/23/24.

[127]   *Foedera*, II, ii, p. 1216. In all, 506 men-at-arms and 606 archers were to be mustered at Portsmouth on 1 March 1343. Audley and 11 others received similar orders in late January 1343: C76/18, m. 16.

the promotion of soldier-bannerets to the peerage in the 1340s);[128] but he certainly ensured that many of those who remained in England had a part to play in the war effort.

It remains only to consider whether the gentry were as heavily involved in the French war as the nobility. Each of the three royal expeditions considered in this article fielded at least 1,500 men-at-arms, with about a quarter of these men being knights. As we have seen, the surviving records permit the identification of only a proportion of these men. On occasion, the utilisation of all available sources reveals the names of about half of the men-at-arms drawing the king's pay.[129] Apart from handicapping investigation of the patterns of service within the gentry, the incompleteness of the nominal records prevents us from establishing the numbers of sub-genteel 'professionals' that were serving as men-at-arms. However, the available evidence suggests that, at this stage of the French war, most men-at-arms were recruited from families of gentle rank. If we accept that the gentry of fourteenth-century England consisted of about 9,000 to 10,000 families, with perhaps a 1:3 ratio between 'county' and 'parish' gentry,[130] it would seem that the early campaigns of the French war drew from the lay landholding community a level of military participation which, if not exhaustive, was certainly far in excess of that contributed by the population at large.

---

[128] J. E. Powell and K. Wallis, *The House of Lords in the Middle Ages* (London, 1968), pp. 349–51, 355–6.

[129] See, for example, Ayton, *Knights and Warhorses*, pp. 181–5.

[130] Chris Given-Wilson's estimate (*English Nobility*, pp. 69–83), based on extrapolation from county-level studies of the gentry and the 1436 income tax records, should be regarded as a maximum figure since his 'parish' gentry group is composed of all those within the £5 to £20 *per annum* income range, including 'the poorer esquires, the gentlemen, the lawyers and merchants who had invested in land and acquired "country seats", and some of the richer yeomen'. It is also questionable whether, without the support of a noble patron, a family with an income at the bottom end of the 'parish' gentry income range could easily have provided a fully equipped man-at-arms. It may be significant that the government's schedules of military assessment consistently assumed a higher level of income. For example, the statute of Winchester, as revised during the 1330s, regarded a £20 landholder as a potential man-at-arms, with a £15 income capable of supporting a hobelar: *Foedera*, II, ii, pp. 900–1; M. Powicke, *Military Obligation in Medieval England* (Oxford, 1962), pp. 191–2. In the mid 1340s it was felt that an income of £10 should support a hobelar, whilst a man-at-arms was to be provided by a £25 *per annum* landholder: *CPR, 1343–45*, p. 495.

Moreover, in considering the gentry's contribution to the king's war, we should remember that this was a conflict with many facets. The armies led by the king in person represented the largest, but by no means the only, overseas military commitment facing the crown, whilst whole regional subsets of the kingdom's military community – particularly the manpower of the northernmost shires and the maritime land of southern coastal counties – were tied down by defence responsibilities in the early years of the French war. To consider this point further, let us take as an example the summer of 1339, as the king prepared, after a seemingly interminable delay, to take the field in the Cambrésis. The numbers of English knights and esquires in Gascony, under the overall command of the seneschal, Sir Oliver de Ingham, were admittedly small, probably only a few dozen men.[131] The same applies to Jersey, the only part of the Channel Islands not to have been taken by the French in 1338. It was the responsibility of Walter de Weston, the English sub-warden, but garrisoned at this time mainly by local men.[132] However, larger numbers of English troops were serving in Scotland and the borders. Although Cupar and Perth had fallen to the Scots during the summer of 1339,[133] garrisons were successfully, if expensively, maintained at Berwick, Edinburgh, Roxburgh and Stirling. All told, these fortresses accounted for over 500 men, half of whom were men-at-arms.[134] Field armies might be more substantial, but periods of service were usually brief. The force which failed to relieve the beleaguered English garrison at Perth consisted of about 1,300 men, mostly hobelars; they remained in the king's pay for only three weeks.[135] The manning of these garrisons and the mobile rapid reaction forces watching the Marches

---

[131] On the precarious military situation in Gascony in 1339, see Sumption, *Hundred Years War*, pp. 255–60, 272–3, 275.

[132] The garrison, nominally commanded by Sir Thomas de Ferrars, had a peak strength of 272 during 1339: M. H. Marett Godfray (ed.), 'Documents relatifs aux attaques sur leîles de la Manche, 1338–1345', *La société Jersiaise pour l'étude de l'histoire, Bulletin*, 3 (1877), pp. 22–39; J. H. Le Patourel, *The Medieval Administration of the Channel Islands* (London, 1937), pp. 62–3, 71–4, 127.

[133] Sumption, *Hundred Years War*, p. 276.

[134] Sir Richard Talbot's garrison at Berwick consisted of 138 fighting men, including 65 men-at-arms: E101/22/9 (cf. *CCR, 1339–41*, p. 201). Sir Thomas de Rokeby had 138 men at Edinburgh castle and 113 at Stirling castle, half of whom were men-at-arms: E101/22/20. The size of the Roxburgh castle garrison in 1339 cannot be ascertained, but in June 1340 Sir William Felton had 128 men there, including 78 men-at-arms: E101/22/40. There were also garrisons on the English side of the border: e.g. Carlisle (*CCR, 1339–41*, p. 29); Cockermouth castle, during the summer of 1338, had 12 men-at-arms and 10 hobelars (E101/20/41).

[135] *CCR, 1339–41*, p. 208; SC1/42, nos 94 and 94A.

was the responsibility of the military community of the northern shires. As a consequence, the section of the English gentry within which the fire of the martial instinct burnt most fiercely was prevented from taking an active part in the king's new war in France. The shires north of the Trent did not provide arrayed troops for the French war, and during these years at least we find comparatively few northern knights and esquires in the armies in France.[136] After the siege of Dunbar was abandoned in June 1338 and Salisbury, with the household division, rushed south to embark for the continent, the northern captains – Percy, Neville, Lucy, Mowbray, Clifford, Umfraville and Wake – stayed put, and so, by and large, did the men who had served with them. Men like Gerard de Wyderyngton, a Northumberland knight whom we glimpsed earlier serving at Sluys with the earl of Northampton, were rare exceptions to this general rule; and when *he* wished to accompany the earl of Northampton to Brittany in 1342, having already in May contracted with the crown to serve in the north with ten men-at-arms, he was obliged to employ his brother, Roger, as a stand-in.[137]

Shifting our focus to the military community of the southern coastal counties in the summer of 1339, here too considerations of defence and security were prime concerns of the local gentry. As in the north, a backbone to the defence arrangements was provided by garrisons paid for by the crown. The most heavily garrisoned area was the Isle of Wight, with a force peaking at over 300 men, including nearly a hundred men-at-arms.[138] On the mainland there were perhaps 100 men in the garrison at Southampton, 100 at Dover, and smaller numbers at

---

[136] Ayton, *Knights and Warhorses*, pp. 246–7 and references there. At the southern edge of the northern military community, Yorkshire contributed knightly personnel to campaigns in both Scotland and France: men from the Percy family's oldest landholding heartlands were regular fighters with their lord in the north, whilst others found themselves pulled in two directions. One such was Sir Thomas Ughtred: a veteran of Dupplin Moor and, probably, Halidon Hill, he was keeper of Perth until its fall in August 1339 and leader of the English troops involved in Robert of Artois's unsuccessful Saint-Omer campaign during the summer of 1340 (*GEC*, XII, part 2, pp. 158–61). Judging from the names of those of his men who secured protections in 1340, he was accompanied by a crowd of East Yorkshiremen (C76/15, m. 19). Ughtred was back in Scotland during the winter of 1341–2 (E36/204, fol. 104).

[137] Indenture: *CDRS*, III, no. 1389. In a letter dated 13 October [1342], the earl of Arundel informed the Chancellor that Roger, with 10 men-at-arms, was serving *en le noun le dit Mons. Gerard bien et covenablement arraie* (SC1/39, no. 153). The pay roll shows that during the late summer and autumn of 1342, Roger was serving *literally* in his brother's name: E36/204, fol. 104v.

[138] E101/21/32.

Portchester, Corfe and elsewhere.[139] There were 20 men-at-arms and 50 archers at the Tower and 10 men-at-arms and 20 archers at Windsor castle.[140] Such garrisons certainly drew on the manpower resources of the gentry,[141] but for a county knight or esquire, participation in the defence of the realm usually meant involvement in the defence of the maritime land. About 150 keepers and arrayers of the maritime land were appointed in June 1337 and subsequently renewed, whilst the justices of the peace selected in July 1338, on the eve of the king's departure for France, had similar responsibilities.[142] Over and above this supervisory role were the personal defence obligations of the gentry, particularly their contribution as occupiers of the highest income categories in the revised statute of Winchester, promulgated by Edward III on 30 December 1334 and on several further occasions thereafter. Landholders with £40 *per annum* of lands or rents were instructed to equip themselves and one other man as mounted men-at-arms; those with £20 had only to equip themselves in this fashion. For lesser landholders the established equipment requirements of the statute of Winchester continued to apply.[143] An array list for Norfolk from October 1336[144] and a sprinkling of entries on the Chancery rolls demonstrate that these defence obligations were indeed taken seriously by the Crown. Understandably, the maritime land attracted most government attention. Those, like John de Mowbray, who had withdrawn from their estates near the coast (in his case, Bramber, Sussex), were reminded of their responsibilities.[145] Particularly stinging was the reprimand issued to Bartholomew de Lisle in February 1340 after he had left the Isle of Wight: 'it is not becoming for belted knights to eloign themselves from places where deeds of war may take place, but rather to go to those places and stay there for their honour's sake'.[146]

---

[139] Southampton: Platt, *Medieval Southampton*, pp. 114–15. Dover: E101/22/15 and 16. Corfe and Portchester castles: *CCR, 1339–41*, pp. 56, 65, 411. Pevensey and Hastings castles: *CPR, 1338–40*, pp. 236–7, 271. Winchester and Old Sarum: *CCR, 1339–41*, pp. 7, 64.

[140] Tower (Sir Nicholas de la Beche): *CCR, 1337–9*, p. 446; *CCR, 1339–41*, p. 313. Windsor castle (Thomas de Foxle): E101/21/22; *CCR, 1339–41*, p. 143.

[141] E.g., John Lovel, a Norfolk man, serving at Dover castle in 1339: *CCR, 1339–41*, p. 219.

[142] C61/49, m. 26; C61/50, m. 11; *CPR, 1338–40*, pp. 134–42; Verduyn, 'The Selection and Appointment of Justices of the Peace in 1338'.

[143] *Foedera*, II, ii, p. 900; *CPR, 1334–8*, pp. 137–9; *CCR, 1333–7*, pp. 469–70, 516, 647–8. See also Powicke, *Military Obligation*, pp. 190–1.

[144] E101/19/37.

[145] *CCR, 1337–9*, p. 540.

[146] *CCR, 1339–41*, p. 444.

Given the range of military commitments facing the traditional warrior class in England at the start of the Hundred Years War, commitments involving the defence of the realm as well as the king's expeditions to France, should we not conclude that war was the prime 'public' activity of the gentry at this time? Perhaps we should be wary of insisting on too sharp a distinction between military and 'civilian' service. There were, after all, many men who undertook public service in both military and civilian spheres during their adult lives: it is commonplace to find knights switching, apparently effortlessly, from the shire court to the battlefield.[147] Of those two, three or four gentlemen appointed in each county to commissions of array, many would have had prior experience of judging the calibre of fighting men in the field.[148] Moreover, sheriffs and keepers of the peace, particularly in northern England and in the southern coastal counties, had responsibilities closely connected to the king's war. Military service and administrative work in the shires were not, then, wholly separate activities; and yet surely we should draw a distinction between them. Even if we exclude from consideration all those engaged in the defence of the realm and, further, limit our attention to those who embarked with the king for France in July 1338, then it is clear that there were, at that time, more men of gentle blood taking up arms than there were engaged in shire administration and related activities. This is a particularly striking conclusion since at the time of Edward III's passage to Antwerp in 1338 there *was* a great deal of activity in the shires. Justices of the peace were appointed on 6 July with defence as well as peace-keeping responsibilities. Each commission was composed of four or five members of the local gentry. Above them were seven (later ten) regional commissions of overseers drawn, in the main, from the nobility.[149] At this time, also, elected representatives were preparing to leave for a session of the great council called for the end of July, while continuing in the background was the routine work of sheriffs and escheators.[150] But, all told,

---

[147]   E.g. Saul, *Knights and Esquires*, pp. 55–6.

[148]   Commissions of array for English shires could involve the appointment of a hundred or more individuals; see, for example, *Treaty Rolls, 1337–9*, nos 123–4 (February 1338); 494–6 (April 1338); C76/17, mm. 10d–11d (December 1342).

[149]   *CPR, 1338–40*, pp. 134–42; Verduyn, 'The Selection and Appointment of Justices of the Peace in 1338'.

[150]   *Return of the Name of Every Member of the Lower House of the Parliaments of England, Scotland and Ireland, 1213–1874*, 3 vols (London, 1878), I, pp. 121–3; *List of Sheriffs for England and Wales, to 1831*, PRO, Lists and Indexes, IX (London, 1898); *List of Escheators for England and Wales*, List and Index Society, LXXII (London, 1972).

there were only a little over 300 men engaged in these tasks in July 1338.[151] Adding those who were responsible for arraying archers in the shires during the spring and early summer of 1338 does not greatly inflate the total, since there were in England scarcely a hundred men engaged in this activity (and about a fifth of them have already been included in the total).[152] Even to take account of lesser officials – coroners and chief taxers – does not increase the overall total substantially. To set against this number of office-holders, there were, as we have seen, well in excess of a thousand genteel warriors embarking for France.

Such a level of recruitment, though by no means exceptional, represented a substantial siphoning-off of manpower; but did it result in a shortage of candidates for local administration? It is not difficult to find examples of conflicting responsibilities. In late July 1338 Sir John de Chevereston was unable to serve on a commission of oyer and terminer because he had recently left England in the king's army. A few weeks later, Sir Ralph de Middelneye, who was involved in the same expedition, was given licence to discharge his duties as escheator by a substitute. On 25 October 1342, Sir William Fraunk, who had joined the army bound for Brittany, was replaced by John de Hundon as sheriff and escheator of Lincolnshire.[153] Yet, in truth, the demands of war caused no more than minor disruption: men were replaced without difficulty or were allowed to appoint lieutenants.[154] Thus, recruitment for the army which left England with the king in mid-July 1338 appears to have had very little effect on the appointment of justices of the peace which took place on the eve of the king's departure.[155] The pool of available genteel manpower was large

---

[151] 311 in all. Some men occupied more than one office: 24 men combined the duties of peace commissioners and knights of the shire; John Golafre was simultaneously under-sheriff, justice and parliamentary representative for Worcestershire. I gratefully acknowledge the assistance of Mr Richard Gorski in gathering these data.

[152] *Treaty Rolls, 1337–9*, nos 494–509.

[153] *CPR, 1338–40*, pp. 129, 147; *CPR, 1340–3*, p. 556; *Calendar of Fine Rolls* [hereafter, *CFR*], *1337–47*, pp. 303–4.

[154] See also Saul, *Knights and Esquires*, pp. 52–9; cf. p. 158.

[155] Comparison of a list of those who secured protections, thereby registering their intention to serve with the king, with the list of men nominated to be keepers of the peace by the knights summoned to meetings in April 1338, but not appointed to be justices in early July, reveals that only a handful of the nominees would have been prevented from becoming justices because of their intended military service. Whatever the reason for the crown's disregard of 60% of the nominees, it does not seem to have been because they were planning to go overseas. The protections are listed on the Treaty Roll; for lists of nominees and appointees, and illuminating analysis, see Verduyn, 'The

enough to sustain this level of military participation without interfering with the functioning of local administration. Indeed, it was large enough to include a good many knights and esquires who sought, through lack of ambition, idleness or an overriding concern for their domestic interests, to avoid all forms of public service.[156] Perhaps it was most usual for older men, particularly from 'county gentry' families, to concentrate on shire administration once they had hung up their swords, whilst their sons continued the tradition of military service.[157] Thus, whilst Sir Thomas de Goushill was appointed to a peace commission in July 1338, his son, Nicholas, was preparing to leave England with the king's army.[158] Two years later, he was at the siege of Tournai.[159] However, war was far from being an exclusively young man's pursuit. It is not unusual to find father and son serving together; and a good many of the younger sons of genteel families became career soldiers, with campaigning lives which ultimately stretched over several decades.[160] There were certainly more career soldiers than career administrators in the mid-fourteenth-century gentry; and when we look beyond the careerists, there can be no doubt that, of the forms of public service open to men of gentle blood, that which was performed by the largest number, if only occasionally, was campaigning in the king's armies.

For Edward III at the outset of his continental adventure, much would depend upon the extent to which he could persuade the nobility and gentry to support his war with their swords. Here was a large pool of potential military manpower, men born into a warrior caste, imbued with the chivalric *mentalité* and trained in arms and horsemanship from boyhood. If the majority of knights and esquires were, at most, occasional soldiers, they certainly should not be regarded as amateurs: this was a military reserve from which contract armies could draw a proportion of their personnel for large-scale expeditions of relatively short duration. But how was the king actually to manage the practical business of recruitment? Under Edward III, royal policy took various forms. As we have seen, in the spring of 1337, faced with a shrunken comital class, Edward began the process of

---

Selection and Appointment of Justices of the Peace in 1338'.

[156] Saul, *Knights and Esquires*, pp. 44–5.

[157] *Ibid.*, pp. 56–8.

[158] *CPR, 1338–40*, p. 135; *Norwell*, p. 311.

[159] C47/6/1, no. 29. For Nicholas's career, see Ayton, *Knights and Warhorses*, p. 236.

[160] For examples, see A. Ayton, 'Knights, Esquires and Military Service: the Evidence of the Armorial Cases before the Court of Chivalry', *The Medieval Military Revolution*, ed. A. Ayton and J. L. Price (London, 1995), pp. 81–104.

rebuilding the community of earls, partly with a view to gaining fuller access to the military potential of the gentry. This policy was already bearing fruit by 1342–3, with 900 men-at-arms, nearly half of those in the king's army, serving in the retinues of earls. Other measures, including the restoration of Hugh le Despenser to his father's estates and the creation of a new generation of fighting bannerets, where necessary their new status supported by annuities (and, in some cases, later reinforced by a personal summons to parliament), appear to be directed towards the same goal.[161]

The 'indirect' approach to mobilising the gentry for the king's war, by bolstering the recruiting capacity of captains, was combined with more direct contact with knights and esquires in the shires. This involved both carrots and sticks, enhancements to the terms of service as well as pressure. The provision of pay at double the usual rates for men-at-arms serving in the king's army in both 1338–39 and 1340 was, as suggested earlier, probably a consequence of the crown's anxiety about the aristocracy's attitude to the French war. That anxiety cannot have greatly diminished by 1341, given the protracted nature of the first expedition to Flanders and the anticlimactic, uncomfortable end to the second in the siege camp outside Tournai. But in view of the Crown's dire financial predicament by 1340, such generosity with the rates of pay could hardly be sustained, and it was not to be repeated. Until the introduction in 1345 of *regard*, a bonus payment for men-at-arms campaigning overseas, the terms of service were decidedly less favourable. Indeed, the distraints to knighthood of 1341 and 1344 may indicate a change to a different approach to the problem of how to encourage more of the gentry to fight.[162] However, that the stick had temporarily replaced the carrot in royal recruitment policy in the mid 1340s can best be seen in the short-lived military assessment of landholders on the basis of their landed income.[163] Unpopular as this experiment undoubtedly was, there can be no doubt that it helped to stimulate the massive turn-out of genteel manpower that can be seen from 1345 to 1347,

---

[161] Five household knights raised their banners during the first major expedition to France: Maurice de Berkeley, Thomas de Bradeston, Robert de Ferrars, John de Montgomery, Robert de Ufford junior. Bradeston was granted an annuity of 500 marks (*CPR, 1338–40*, p. 395) and summoned to parliament. See Powell and Wallis, *House of Lords*, pp. 349–51, 355–6.

[162] The distraints may well have been as much aimed at bolstering the community of knights for shire administration (cf. Saul, *Knights and Esquires*, pp. 37–47); but greater recruiting demands on the native population of England would have been one consequence of the collapse of Edward III's strategy of continental alliances.

[163] For details, see A. Ayton, 'The English Army and the Normandy Campaign of 1346', *England and Normandy in the Middle Ages*, ed. D. Bates and A. Curry (London, 1995), pp. 254–8 and references there.

culminating in perhaps 4,000 English men-at-arms at the height of the siege of Calais. Such a level of military participation suggests that there had indeed been under-exploited military capacity in the gentry at the beginning of the French war.

In the late 1330s Edward III's efforts to draw on untapped pools of genteel manpower were less systematic. Perhaps characteristic is the order of 7 November 1338, addressed to 44 individuals, requiring them to appear at Ipswich on 21 December, well equipped and ready for overseas service, on pain of severe consequences for their persons and property.[164] The list of men summoned reads like a roll-call of colourful gentry criminals; all of the famous names of the 1320s and 30s are there, including four members of the Folville family, two Coterels and three Gresleys.[165] It is clear that, as far as the government was concerned, these were men who owed some legitimate service with the sword. Their nefarious skills could no doubt be put to good use in the king's army,[166] where, indeed, they would find many other men quite as fierce and wily as themselves. For every romantic adventurer or virgin soldier in the ranks, there was a battle-scarred veteran from the Scottish wars; and few of the apparently respectable gentlemen whom we have seen in the service of the earl of Northampton and other captains, whether retained or temporarily contracted, were entirely without blemish. It seems likely, for example, that the William Tallemache with whom this paper began and a man of that name who was pardoned for homicide in 1339 were one and the same.[167] Sir Robert Marny, another of Northampton's companions at Sluys whom we glimpsed earlier, later to represent Essex in parliament and one of the venerable deponents in the Court of Chivalry cases of the 1380s, appears to have embarked upon a more systematic criminal career in his home county only after some years of campaigning experience.

It is tempting to explain such behaviour in terms of the corrupting influence of war. What is clear is that, for men of action, honourable service in war and heavy-handed law-breaking in England were not

---

[164] *Treaty Rolls, 1337–9*, nos 890–1. For brief comment on this document, see E. L. G. Stones, 'The Folvilles of Ashby-Folville, Leicestershire and their Associates in Crime, 1326–1347', *TRHS*, Fifth Series, 7 (1957), p. 129.

[165] On the gentry gangs, see J. Bellamy, *Crime and Public Order in the Later Middle Ages* (London, 1973), ch. 3; on the Gresleys of Staffordshire, see M. Prestwich, *The Three Edwards. War and State in England, 1272–1377* (London, 1980), pp. 231–2.

[166] Another member of the Gresley family, Ralph, was probably already with the army (*Treaty Rolls, 1337–9*, no. 365); he served in the Scottish Marches during the summer of 1340 (E101/612/12).

[167] *CPR, 1338–40*, p. 386; *CPR, 1340–3*, p. 188.

incompatible activities. On occasion, military service and crime might be *indirectly* related. Sir John de Norwich's career serves as an example of this. Norwich is perhaps most notable for the fabrication of a family pedigree extending back to the Conquest, but he was also an energetic captain with a career which began during Edward II's Scottish wars.[168] After distinguished service in Gascony early in the French war, he was accused in February 1340 of unlawful seizure of a Ghent merchant's ship near Great Yarmouth.[169] He may well have been driven to this act of piracy by financial desperation, or merely by exasperation with the government. For months he had been seeking payment for his lengthy spell of service in Gascony.[170] His fall from grace was short-lived, however, for he was probably at Sluys and was certainly among those summoned to the great council of April 1342.[171]

Men of daring and enterprise, who, like Sir John de Norwich, had been schooled in the practice of war in the demanding training ground of Scotland and the borders, were of great value to Edward III at the beginning of his continental adventure. Indeed, that Norwich had selected carefully from the pool of available veterans when recruiting his retinue for service in Gascony in 1337 is suggested by the inclusion of such men as William de Thweyt, a young esquire drawn from the minor gentry of Norfolk, who had fought at Halidon Hill and on several subsequent occasions in Scotland. Thweyt's career is unusually well documented, illuminated as it is by his testimony before the Court of Chivalry in 1386.[172] The patchy sources for rank and file military service in the 1320s and 1330s, combined with the difficulties of nominal record linkage, leave us

---

[168] K. B. McFarlane, *The Nobility of Later Medieval England* (Oxford, 1973), pp. 165–6; for Norwich's career, see *GEC*, IX, pp. 763–5.

[169] *CCR, 1339–41*, pp. 367, 382.

[170] Norwich's accounting period began on 19 July 1337 and lasted for 558 days, but payment was very slow in coming: E101/166/11, m. 19; *CCR, 1337–9*, pp. 318, 323. He was owed over £1,500 in early April 1339 and orders were still being issued to pay him in the autumn: *CCR, 1339–41*, pp. 40, 198, 321. In June 1339 Norwich was preparing to leave England with a retinue (ships: *CCR, 1339–41*, pp. 141, 156 and SC1/39, no. 103; protections: C76/14, mm. 3, 7) and may well have joined the king in the Low Countries. On 11 November of the same year he was granted, for good service, an annuity of 50 marks (*CPR, 1338–40*, pp. 397, 452).

[171] In the Lovel vs. Morley Court of Chivalry case in 1386–7, William de Thweyt stated that he had fought at Sluys with Sir John de Norwich: C47/6/1, no. 92. On the council of 1342, see Powell and Wallis, *House of Lords*, pp. 348–9.

[172] C47/6/1, no. 92; A. Ayton, 'William de Thweyt, Esquire: Deputy Constable of Corfe Castle in the 1340s', *Notes and Queries for Somerset and Dorset*, 32 (1989), pp. 731–8.

with no more than glimpses of the military experience of most of Norwich's men,[173] but what evidence we have is certainly suggestive. Several of Norwich's knights had participated in the War of St Sardos, while as many as a dozen of his men can be identified as veterans of the Scottish wars. The actual total must have been higher than this. If, as we have seen, the late 1330s and early 1340s witnessed various initiatives by the government to unlock the latent military potential of the gentry, then Edward III must also have been aware at the very outset of the French war that he already had a pool of seasoned campaigners at his disposal. This was an ambitious, resourceful and, in many cases, unscrupulous community of warriors, into whose midst new recruits, whether younger sons looking for a martial career or their more domestically committed elders seeking no more than an honourable taste of campaigning, would be quickly assimilated. These, then, were the men who in the autumn of 1339 were responsible for breaking the 'thread of silk' which, according to the cardinals, surrounded France.[174]

---

[173] Ten knights and 19 esquires have enrolled protections for service with Norwich in 1337: C61/49, m. 17. The schedule of names which Norwich submitted to Chancery for the issue of protections includes 2 knights and 10 esquires who do not figure among those with enrolled protections (C81/1750, no. 33).

[174] *Chronicon Galfridi le Baker de Swynebroke*, pp. 64–5.

The Organisation of Field Armies in Lancastrian Normandy

ANNE CURRY

The subject of this essay might be seen as embracing the entire military history of the English occupation of France in the first half of the fifteenth century. Indeed, by manipulating the extensive financial documentation which survives from this period, it is possible to reconstruct campaigns, thereby providing details of dates and numbers which, one assumes, are more accurate and complete than those found in contemporary chronicles. I have begun this arduous task of 'reconstitution', and Michael Jones has recently shown how valuable the exercise can be by his study of the relief of Avranches in 1439.[1] But there is obviously neither time nor space to go into detail here on every action of the thirty-five year period between Henry V's first invasion in 1415 and the loss of Cherbourg in 1450. I shall thus be concentrating on some salient general themes relating to the organisational sphere which have emerged from my researches so far. I would like to reiterate, however, that the sources do offer much potential. Even though their study will not go so far as to force a rewriting of the history of the Hundred Years War, it will add an important extra dimension to the subject.

Although extensive, the sources are not without their problems. Only when account books exist can we gain something approaching a comprehensive picture of the military position in English-held territories. Such books are thin on the ground, but we are fortunate that those which survive for the 1420s happen to be for years when there were key campaigns: the account book of the receiver-general of Normandy for 1423–5 thus includes the campaign for the relief of Ivry which led to the battle of Verneuil, and that of 1428–9 the siege of Orleans and its aftermath.[2] As Newhall observed, 'any expedition which lasted more than a

---

[1] M. K. Jones, 'The Relief of Avranches (1439): an English Feat of Arms at the End of the Hundred Years War', *England in the Fifteenth Century. Proceedings of the 1992 Harlaxton Symposium*, ed. N. Rogers (Stamford, 1992), pp. 42–55.

[2] Paris, Bibliothèque Nationale MS français 4485 and 4488 respectively. Of the latter, pages 345 to 476 are printed in L. Jarry, *Le compte de l'armée anglaise au siège d'Orléans 1428–1429* (Orleans, 1892), pp. 87–204. The 1420s are also well served by full or partial account books of the financial officials outside Normandy (see, for instance, B.N. MS fr.32, 510, fragments of the account of

207

month' was allocated its own section in the account where details of payments and musters were given, although the service of individual garrisons was also dealt with in the garrison section.[3] For much of the period, however, we are reliant on the random survival of documents subsidiary to account books which are themselves no longer extant.[4] These consist of orders to pay or to muster, the muster lists, and *quittances* (receipts for pay), for the various garrisons and retinues detailed to field service.[5] On many occasions the survival is not comprehensive enough to reveal the entire composition of an army in the field, nor exactly how long it was kept in being. Thus we can know its total number and intended structure in terms of men-at-arms and archers, but we may not be able to discover which garrisons or retinues were drawn upon to form it.

At no point in the English occupation was there a standing army for the field. Campaigns were conducted by a variety of troops brought together temporarily for the specific action in question. There were essentially five principal sources from which men could be drawn.[6] The first four categories can be studied through the financial documentation of the English occupation of Normandy and northern France as outlined above. First, detachments were drawn from the garrisons within the duchy of Normandy and from other lands under English rule. (Most attention will be given to this particular source of troops.) Secondly, use was also made

Benoit Colenot, *tresorier des guerres*, 1425–6, and B.N. MS fr.4484, the full book of his successor, Andry Esparnon, for 1426–8).

[3] R. A. Newhall, *Muster and Review. A Problem of English Military Administration 1420–1440* (Cambridge, Mass., 1940), p. 123.

[4] The surviving folios of the account of the duchy's receiver-general for 1448–9 (B.L. Additional MS 11, 509) are only marginally useful for current purposes as they deal with a period of truce. The surviving account books of William Allington, treasurer-general from 1419 to 1422 (PRO E101/187/14 and 188/7), are also less helpful; during Henry V's conquests, field campaigns were largely administered through the treasurer of the royal household in his role as treasurer for war, and the details of the latter's expenditure are yet to be elucidated fully. For a discussion of such materials see A. Curry, 'L'administration financière de la Normandie anglaise: continuité ou changement?' in *La France des principautés. Les chambres des comptes xive et xve siècles* (Comité pour l'histoire économique et financière de la France (CHEFF), Paris, 1996), pp. 88–97, and R. A. Newhall, *The English Conquest of Normandy 1416–24. A Study in Fifteenth-Century Warfare* (New Haven, 1924), chapter 4.

[5] For a discussion of the history of the archive see A. Curry, 'English Armies in the Fifteenth Century', in *Arms, Armies and Fortifications in the Hundred Years War*, ed. A. Curry and M. Hughes (Woodbridge, 1994), p. 49.

[6] For an overview of military organisation see Curry, 'English Armies', and C. T. Allmand, *Lancastrian Normandy: The History of a Medieval Occupation 1417–1450* (Oxford, 1983), chapter 7.

of retinues not based in garrisons: these must be taken to include the personal companies of the leading commanders, the retinues held by the *baillis* and by other officials of the civilian administration, as well as the company of the master of the ordnance which might be expanded in the field by the recruitment of extra military craftsmen or of escort troops.[7] Thirdly, at various junctures men without regular garrison or retinue employment, usually termed *vivans sur le pais*, were recruited for temporary field service.[8] Fourthly, the English exploited and developed feudal obligations, calling upon service from native and English landholders in Normandy.[9] Finally, there were the expeditionary armies sent from England in almost every year save those of truce in the 1440s, and usually indented to serve for six months. These armies are well documented in the records of the English exchequer in terms of their organisation within and despatch from England, but it is not always easy to trace their exact use within France. They rarely feature in the financial documentation produced by the Norman and French administrations unless they continued in service beyond their initial period of indenture and thus came to be paid out of local revenues.[10]

Organisation for the field – commonly indicated by the term *la présente armée mise sur les champs* – was usually based upon a combination of the categories of troops noted above, with the intention that they should operate in close co-ordination, even though for purposes of pay they remained in their separate original units. The relative contribution of each element or category is significant, especially for what it reveals about the planning of campaigns. There is an organisational as well as a strategic difference between, for instance, an army assembled quickly in response to an emergency, by drawing on local garrison detachments and easily accessible permanent and semi-permanent companies, and one which was

---

[7]   C. T. Allmand, 'L'artillerie de l'armée anglaise et son organisation à l'époque de Jeanne d'Arc', in *Jeanne d'Arc: une époque, un rayonnement* (Centre nationale de la recherche scientifique, Paris, 1982), pp. 73–83.

[8]   A. Curry, 'Les "gens vivans sur le pais" pendant l'occupation anglaise de la Normandie (1417–1450)', in *La guerre, la violence et les gens au moyen âge. I. Guerre et violence* (Comité des travaux historiques et scientifiques, Paris, 1996), pp. 209–21.

[9]   A. Curry, 'Le service féodal en Normandie pendant l'occupation anglaise (1417–1450)', in *La "France anglaise" au moyen âge* (CTHS, Paris, 1988), pp. 233–57. Note must also be made of Burgundian collaboration on some occasions, although discussion of this falls outside the scope of this essay.

[10]   The use of the expeditionary armies will not be discussed in detail in this essay, but see A. Curry, 'Military Organization in Lancastrian Normandy 1422–1450', unpublished Ph.D. Teesside Polytechnic/Council for National Academic Awards, 1985, pp. 142–71.

planned over several months and intended as a composite, co-ordinated effort involving all or part of a specially raised expeditionary army, a coherent call-out of garrison detachments and companies, as well as use of the feudal summons. In this respect, therefore, a reconstruction of the composition and activity of armies for the field can reveal much about English strategy and planning as well as about the way the war was actually fought. Some campaigns were planned well ahead of the actual action, some were undertaken quickly in response to an emergency, others fell somewhere between these two extremes.[11] When Henry V was in command, planning initiatives lay with the king. After his demise, the royal councils in both England and France each played a role in both planned and emergency situations, although their exact interplay must be postponed for fuller discussion elsewhere. Most expeditionary armies were intended to co-ordinate with other troops raised in France. On some occasions it is made explicit that once in France the expeditionary army would fall under the purview of the council therein. The captains of the expedition despatched in July 1439 were thus under instructions to inform the chancellor and council in France of their arrival and to abide by the latter's directions.[12] Before embarkation, the English council had sent letters to its counterpart in France requesting it to send the troops to places where it would be to the best advantage and honour of the king and his possessions.[13] Accordingly, on 29 July a messenger was sent from the council of Normandy based at Rouen *en certains pors de mer en la basse Normandie pour soy enquerir et savoir de l'armee nouvellement venue d'Angleterre et de quelle part elle descendroit a fin dicelle haster pour estre au secours des ville et marche de Meaux.*[14] We can then trace the movement of troops to Meaux, and their later use in the defence of Pontoise.[15] Emergency situations, however, could interfere with this co-ordination. In May 1436, for instance, it was anticipated in France that Edmund Beaufort's troops would land at Honfleur from whence they would be sent to the southern borders of Normandy, but the English council decided to reroute the army to Calais.[16]

---

[11]   Newhall, *Muster and Review*, p. 123, speaks of first-class campaigns, but does not define the term precisely.

[12]   PRO E10171/4/902, C47/26/28.

[13]   PRO E28/61.

[14]   Rouen, Archives Départementales de la Seine Maritime, Fonds Danquin 11/147.

[15]   B.N. pièces originales 3050 Wydeville 22; Paris, Archives Nationales, K65/1/31, 65/1/3 bis.

[16]   M. K. Jones, 'The Beaufort Family and the War in France', unpublished Ph.D. thesis, University of Bristol, 1982, p. 90.

Within Normandy a further element needs to be borne in mind, the role of the Estates. Given that the financing of military activity depended to a considerable degree upon taxation levied within the duchy, it is not surprising to discover that the levels of grants requested by the English rulers were based upon anticipated military needs, and that the argument put before the Estates might recite these needs and thus provide us with a firm indication of military plans at that stage. The assembly convened at Rouen in October 1431, for instance, was told that there was a need to continue the number currently held in garrison, which was given as 900 men-at-arms and 2,700 archers, and also to have *autre grant nombre pour tenire les champs et pour le recouvrement des places et forteresses de Bonsmoulins* and elsewhere in the area of Lower Normandy. The *grand conseil* had estimated that an extra 300 men-at-arms and 900 archers would be required for this purpose, anticipating that such troops would serve for three months alongside 100 men-at-arms and 300 archers drawn from the garrisons. But in fact the campaign, which was conducted under the command of Robert, Lord Willoughby, lasted two months longer than anticipated, so that in May 1432 the Estates had to be asked for further tax grants to cover the higher costs which had been incurred.[17] Financial accountability was taken seriously. Thus for the siege of Mont-Saint-Michel in 1424 troops from the garrison detachments were paid out of moneys granted for the siege, but the retinue of the commander, Nicholas Burdet, was ordered to be paid from general funds.[18] But changes of plan did occur, the most obvious being the fact that the moneys which the Estates had voted in 1428 to fund a further campaign into Anjou and Maine were diverted instead to the financing of the earl of Salisbury's advance on Orleans. Whilst the English did try to plan ahead, deciding upon campaigns and trying to calculate both military and financial need, unanticipated emergencies might arise during the year. This was increasingly the case as the French closed in on the duchy after 1435, and the English, so to speak, lost control of the timetable of war. Armies might be raised in response to rumoured threats. On other occasions they were put into the field after a disaster had already occurred with a view to damage limitation, such as the armies assembled from November 1440 to May 1441 against the French who were based at Louviers and Conches.[19] Both planning and response were based upon the extensive use of spies. To cite but one example of many: spies were sent to find out the *estat* of the enemy army based at Conflans in August 1441 and to report back to Lord Talbot *a fin quil peust mieulx employer larmee estant soubz*

---

[17] B.N. nouvelles acquisitions françaises 7627/365.
[18] B.N. MS fr. 26047/309.
[19] Various documents relating to these campaigns are to be found in B.N. MS fr. 26067 and 26068, with muster rolls also in B.N. MS fr. 25775 and 25776.

lui en ceste dit ville pour ladvitaillement dudit lieu de Pontoise et Mantes et faire plusieurs autres explois de guerre.[20]

A further consideration related to planning and timing needs to be discussed here – whether there was a notion of a campaigning season. Newhall considered that there was; 'ordinarily garrison duty was a year-round business, while field service, even for a first-class campaign, was likely to be a matter of the summer months only'.[21] His conclusion seems to be supported by the fact that between 1422 and 1450 most expeditionary armies left England between March and July, with the prospect of, in most cases, six months' service ahead of them.[22] As Appendix 1 indicates, the campaigns of the 1420s, both sieges and general clearing-up operations, tended to be concentrated in the period from March to September. Notably, however, the first major siege of Mont-Saint-Michel extended over the winter months, September 1424 – June 1425, by both land and sea, as did the siege of Orleans of 1428–9. The siege of Louviers, however, seems to have been lifted during the winter months of 1430–1, and the land based siege of Mont-Saint-Michel in 1425 was laid only from June to December. There were undoubted (and anticipated) difficulties in maintaining actions over the winter months, especially in terms of victualling and providing forage for horses. The earl of Salisbury was given extra money for troops in the spring of 1427 given *la chierte de vivres* in the Champagne theatre.[23] Extra provisions had to be brought to the siege of Orleans in February 1429, leading to the famous victory of 'Les Harengs' accorded to Sir John Fastolf. Actions after 1435 show more divergence from the campaigning season because, increasingly, they were responsive measures to French moves, such as campaigns aimed at revictualling and protecting outposts of

[20]   B.N. n.a.fr. 7268/487.
[21]   Newhall, *Muster and Review*, p. 123. Recent comments on this issue relating to other periods of warfare are instructive. S. Morillo, *Warfare Under the Anglo-Norman Kings 1066–1135* (Woodbridge, 1994), p. 110, notes a 'tendency for campaigning to cease for the winter, though this was by no means always true ... warfare waged between mid-December and early March was rarer than at other times of the year'. He suggests that this was because winter 'restricted army mobility' because of the impassability of roads and the difficulties of victualling, although he also found evidence of problems with the food supply at other times too. Michael Prestwich's conclusion (*Armies and Warfare in the Middle Ages: the English Experience* (Yale, 1996), p. 7), based on a review of the reigns of John, Edward I and Edward III, is that 'many expeditions took place at much less pleasant times of the year than July and August ... winter did not always mean an end to fighting'. Obviously this is an issue which needs further exploration for the period currently under review.
[22]   A. Curry, 'Military Organization in Lancastrian Normandy', vol. 2, appendix I.
[23]   B.N. MS fr. 4484, fol. 40.

English control. Even so, the siege of Dieppe, otherwise laid over the winter of 1442–3, was lifted for much of January. It is also worth noting that companies might not be kept at a siege for the whole of its duration, but might serve for a certain period before being sent back to base and replaced by other troops drawn from elsewhere. Thus at the siege of Le Crotoy in 1423 it seems that four garrison detachments were present only in May, whereas the contingent from Cherbourg served from July to September and that of Rouen apparently in July alone, during which month ships are known to have operated a blockade.[24]

Most campaigns were begun with some notion of how long they were intended to last. As we have already noted, the expeditionary armies were usually contracted for six months' service although there are cases of longer or shorter periods. Financial considerations played a role here, as did conventions which had developed within the indenture system: a six-month contract had predominated from the 1370s onwards. Identifying the period for which armies raised within France were intended to serve is more difficult, although we saw how the Estates were told in October 1431 that a three-month stint was needed for the recovery of certain places in Lower Normandy. The earl of Salisbury's invasion of Maine, however, was on a much longer time-plan: after an initial period of nine months from December 1424 to September 1425, it was ordered to be continued, although with a lower number of men, for a further twelve months to September 1426. Generally, financial records indicate that garrison detachments and companies tended to serve in blocks of a month or of 15 days (i.e. a half month in accounting terms). Continuations after the initial period of service were also generally for 15 days.[25] The average period for which armies were kept together seems to be about two months, although, as troops were detailed from one place to another during action according to new needs which had arisen, it is sometimes difficult to say where one army or campaign ends and another begins. There were several longer campaigns, butm as noted earlier, companies might not serve for the entire period. Expeditionary armies might be continued in service after the term of their indentures had come to an end. At least 738 of the 2,694 men who had crossed with the earl of Salisbury in 1428 stayed in service in this way.[26] When a campaign was brought to an end, there was what was termed

---

[24] For Cherbourg, see B.N. MS fr. 26046/139; for Rouen, B.L. Add. Ch. 6818 and Rouen, Bibliothèque Municipale, Martainville 198/11 (15); for the naval blockade, B.N. MS fr. 25767/15.

[25] An army under Lord Fauconberg, for instance, served from 24 March to 1 May 1442 and was then ordered to be kept in being initially for a further 15 days (A.N. K67/12/26).

[26] B.N. MS fr. 26051/1002, 1019.

a *cassement* as the army was disbanded.[27]

We must now turn to the vexed question of how the size and composition of an army in the field was decided. Presumably the anticipated strength of the enemy played a part in this decision – hence too the use and significance of spies. Combined with this might be the intended function and leadership of the campaign, which is in turn linked to factors which might be termed 'political' as much as 'military'. Thus in May 1429 Bedford learned that the Dauphin was in the field with a powerful and well equipped army intending to besiege places in English obedience. As a result the duke, we are told, was disposed to put himself in the field with a great puissance in order to approach the enemy and to rebuff him *par bataille si mestier est*. The explanation of why Bedford needed a large army is made explicit: *pour ce que la chose est grande, et desirons que notre dit oncle soit accompagnez ainsi que a son etat appartient ... attendu la puissance de notre dit adversaire*.[28] Not surprisingly, therefore, there was an extensive and varied call-out over the next months, employing various kinds of troops and, perhaps most notably, including an extensive use of companies raised through feudal summons. The link to status is also noted in the organisation of an escort for Queen Margaret as she passed through Normandy en route to England in 1445. The duke of York as lieutenant-general ordered Richard Harrington, *bailli* of Caen, to come to Mantes by 12 March *garny du plus grant nombre de gens de vos charges et retenues que bonnement faire ce pourra ... pour ce quil est expedient que soyons noblement accompagnie pour faire et exhibier honneur et service a ma dicte dame comme il appartient*.[29] For similar reasons the army which accompanied Henry VI in 1430–1 was the largest raised since his father had been active in person in France and it was also indented to serve for the longest period of any army since 1417.

The nature of the intended action was an obvious influence. If battle was anticipated larger numbers were raised. As we saw, this was the case in May 1429, although no battle did arise, in contrast to the situation in 1424. In that year almost every garrison in Normandy was required to send troops for the *journée* of Ivry (fixed for 14 August 1424) and thus participated in the battle of Verneuil on 17 August.[30] This was a major enterprise, therefore, with the garrisons sending almost 1,800 men and a further 700 or so coming from the companies of peers and civilian officials,

---

27 As noted in the section of Esparnon's account relating to the army of John de Luxembourg operating in north-east France in the early months of 1428 (B.N. MS fr. 4484, fol. 74).

28 B.N. n.a.fr. 7627/166.

29 A.N. K66/1.

30 B.N. MS fr. 4485, pp. 274–303. A. Curry, 'Military Organization in Lancastrian Normandy', vol. 2, appendix X.

to join with 2,000 men from England. Admittedly there is less evidence for the *journée* of Le Crotoy in the previous March, but we can be fairly certain that there was no call-out of garrison troops for this event, although garrison detachments had maintained the siege in the previous year. A company of 500 or so had been gathered by the duke of Bedford at Abbeville, probably based on his own household and the companies of leading knights and esquires. It may have been intended that they should join with a small expeditionary force, but as the French offered no resistance, Bedford was able to send Sir Ralph Butler *acompaigne souffisament* to take delivery of the place whilst the duke himself returned to Paris ordering the rest of his company to disband *chascuns en leurs lieux*.[31]

On some occasions the call-outs were not aimed at achieving a specific number but at raising as many troops as possible. On at least three occasions (October 1419, August 1421 and August 1422), Henry V ordered captains and *baillis* to send him all men not needed for local defence, reminding us that the call-out of such detachments was already a means of gathering a field army.[32] In later emergencies a similarly imprecise instruction might be deemed appropriate. Thus early in 1438 a poursuivant of Lord Talbot came from Conches with letters for Sir Thomas Hoo, Sir William Chamberlain, Sir Thomas Kyriell and Foulkes Eyton *ou qui trouve les pourra*, requesting them to join Talbot and Fauconberg's army with *le plus grant nombre de gens quilz pourront en toute haste*.[33] On most occasions, however, it seems that a total was decided upon from the outset and call-outs arranged in order to fulfil this. This gives a clearer indication, therefore, that the English rulers had an idea of how many troops could be raised, and indeed should be raised, aspects which take us back to the question of planning, for the number must have been determined by the perceived requirements of both the field action and of other military commitments, most notably the defence of the garrisoned places. To this end there needed to be a clear idea of how many men were in garrison – hence the various lists of the garrison establishment which are found amongst the archives. For the siege of Tancarville in 1437, for instance, garrison detachments were intended to provide 1,200 men, and Lord Talbot was instructed to find another 800 presumably from retinues of individuals and from the ex-soldiers *vivans sur le pais*.[34] When a number was decided on it was

---

31 B.N. MS fr. 25767/16; Jean de Waurin, *Recueil des Croniques*, ed. W. and E. Hardy (Rolls Series, London, 1868–84), v, pp. 90–1.
32 *Annual Report of the Deputy Keeper of the Public Records*, 42 (1881), pp. 328, 431, 452.
33 B.N. MS fr. 26063/3387.
34 A. J. Pollard, *John Talbot and the War in France 1427–1453* (London, 1983), pp. 72–3.

common for every effort to be made to meet it. Replacements and additions were engineered at the siege of Harfleur, for example, *pour aider a parfournir le nombre ordonne pour la dite siege*.[35] Flexibility was also possible. In 1436, for instance, Thomas Kyriell was ordered to hold 100 men-at-arms and 300 archers in the Pays de Caux *ou autre nombre au dessoubs quil pourra finer*.[36] As noted earlier, the size and composition of the army might be changed during the campaign, according to military needs, both offensive and defensive, and in response to deaths and other such factors.

Most field armies raised within France were intended to have what was regarded by the English in this period as the optimum ratio of one man-at-arms to three archers, although some flexibility was permitted in the face of emergency. So in 1442 Fauconberg was ordered to raise 200 men-at-arms and 600 archers *ou pour et en lieu d'hommes darmes archiers*.[37] Not surprisingly, mounted troops were most commonly required. Thus Griffith Don, captain of Lisieux, faced a dilemma in July 1442 when he was asked to send 10 mounted men-at-arms as well as 30 archers. Although he was supposed to hold 13 mounted men-at-arms in his garrison, he claimed that he had been permitted to have five of them serving as foot. As he noted in the reply to the summons for his detachment, he did not dare send all eight of his mounted men-at-arms because of the needs of local defence, so he only sent five. He was not penalised because it was deemed that there was no cause to do so, *a petit occasion, veu les services par lui fais il ne fust a ceste cause dommaige*.[38]

This incident is known from an order to effect payment. In relatively few cases do we have the actual order sent to a garrison to provide a detachment for field service. A fascinating example survives in the form of a letter from the duke of Bedford to the lieutenant at Falaise, Thomas Gower, asking for troops for the army being raised against enemy threats to Paris in September 1429.[39] Gower is asked to come 'with al the felawship that ye may raise or gete in any wise, on horseback and in fote'. A postscript adds that he should send 'of the best marchers and the best horsed men that ye can or may gete in al the cuntree', and, interestingly, specifically asks for the service of a named individual ('we pray you hertilye that ye sende unto us Henrye Montone with al the retinue and felaship that

---

[35] B.N. Clairambault 201/75, September 1440.

[36] B.N. MS fr. 26060/2799.

[37] A.N. K67/12/26.

[38] A.N. K67/12/1.

[39] B.N. MS fr. 23189, fol. 24, no. 39, printed in J. Stevenson, *Letters and Papers Illustrative of the Wars of the English in France During the Reign of Henry the Sixth, King of England* (Rolls Series, London, 1861–4), II, i, pp. 118–9. The captain of Falaise at this point was John, Lord Talbot.

ye hade loast or moo yf ye may mo gete'), whilst instructing Gower himself
to stay at Falaise for its defence ('an we wol that your self abide stille upon
the sauvegarde of Faloize and that ye take good heed thereunto, boothe day
and nighte and that ye bee wel wer of traisons'). In the account of the
Norman receiver-general for 1428–9, we find payments to Henry Monton
esquire, who mustered with 16 men-at-arms and 32 archers at Rouen on 11
September 1429 along with other detachments.[40] The postscript brings two
matters to our attention: first, that detachments for the field may have been
selected because of their particular skills or equipment, and secondly that
the needs of garrison defence also had to be taken into account.

Linked to the last point made, a study of which garrisons sent troops to
the various field actions is most revealing. The major campaigns, such as
Ivry/Verneuil, required a widespread call-out: indeed their significance is
revealed by the geographical extent of the summons. On other occasions,
various factors can be seen to exert an influence over the choice of
detachments. There was a tendency to summon detachments from the
places nearest to the action. Thus for the siege of Mont-Saint-Michel in
1424–5, for instance, only garrisons in the Cotentin were required to send
contingents. (Further study is needed to see whether some garrisons were
called out more frequently than others or, for instance, whether those on
the frontiers were deemed to be too vulnerable to lose troops even for a
short while.) Another factor seems to have been the command structure.
The garrisons captained by the commander of a siege or campaign were
often called upon to provide troops. This is not surprising in the light of
the powers given to lieutenants for the field to recruit troops, for the most
easily summonable would have been those already in his charge. Thus we
find letters sent in 1445 to the captains of garrisons in York's own lordship
(Bernay, Orbec, Pont-l'Evêque and Lisieux) requesting them to provide an
escort for the duke as he went to meet Queen Margaret.[41] In this context it
is also worth noting that if a garrison captain or field commander was at a
siege or action with a garrison detachment he often had with him an
additional personal company: William Minors was thus present at the siege

---

[40] B.N. MS fr. 4488, p. 574. I have found no further references in the muster
rolls to Henry Monton, unless he was the same person as the Henry Morton
who served in Rouen castle under York in 1437 (B.L. Add. Ch. 191), in Lord
Fauconberg's personal retinue in 1436 and 1438 (B.L. Add. Ch. 11932, B.N.
Clairambault 185/24), and in the field under Talbot in December 1440,
having been recruited by Foulkes Eyton from the *gens vivans sur le pays* (A.N.
K661/61). The fact that Monton's company is in the ratio of 1:2 rather than
the customary 1:3 may indicate that his service was as a result of feudal
obligation (see Curry, 'Service féodal', p. 240).

[41] B.N. MS fr. 26073/5178.

of Guise between May and September 1424 with 12 men-at-arms and 36 archers from his garrison of Harfleur in addition to a personal company of four mounted men-at-arms, 24 foot and 84 archers.[42] Similarly, Sir Thomas Gargrave led a group of three mounted men-at-arms, 30 foot and 83 archers of the retinue of the earl of Warwick, to whom he was lieutenant at Rouen *oultre le nombre des lances et archiers de la dite garnison envoiz au siege.*[43] Regional commanders commonly held a company which doubled as a personal retinue and a troop for field action. The earl of Salisbury as governor of Alençon in 1424 held 100 men-at-arms and 300 archers *pour chevauchee et conduite de sa personne* in addition to his various garrisons.[44]

Let us look further at the mechanics by which troops were called out. As we have seen from the Falaise example, letters from the council, central or regional commanders were sent to those in charge of the garrison. In addition to specifying a number to be sent, or else asking for as many troops as possible, details were provided of the date and place of intended assembly. Orders concerning the garrison contingents were often sent out simultaneously with those for the *semonce des nobles*, or for the raising of *gens vivans sur le pays*. In August 1439, for instance, the earl of Somerset ordered the *bailli* of Caen *quil assemblast toutes* [sic] *gens de guerre tant de sa retenue que dautres aveques les nobles de son bailliage* in order that they should join the earl to serve in the rescue of Meaux.[45] The *baillis* played an important role in the gathering and initial leading of troops, particularly of the *vivans sur le pais* and those raised by feudal summons, and use was made of the traditional means of communicating instructions and orders through the *bailli's* subordinate officials in the localities, the *vicomtes*. An initial alert might be made in general terms, urging that troops be held in readiness or be brought to an initial assembly point, followed by the issue of more specific instructions on precisely where and when to move on for the final muster.[46] In 1442, for instance, garrison detachments and *gens vivans sur le pais* were ordered to assemble at Pontaudemer and Les Andeleys from 17 June, and to move by 15 August to Pont-de-l'Arche or Léry to make musters and to

---

42 B.N. MS fr. 4485, pp. 213–15.
43 B.N. MS fr. 4485, pp. 218–20.
44 B.N. Clairambault 180/86.
45 B.N. MS fr. 26066/3832.
46 See the example cited in Newhall, *Muster and Review*, p. 144 concerning the siege of Tancarville in 1437. Talbot was to raise a company of 200 + 600 and the duke of York was to call out from the garrisons 300 + 900. Preliminary orders went out in July 'for the captains to hold themselves in readiness to send men from their garrisons, the time and place to be designated later'. On 2 August the *baillis* were ordered to proclaim that captains were to bring their men to muster at Jumièges by 7 August.

be paid for service under Talbot and Fauconberg.[47]

Timing could present problems. Bedford's letter to Gower was written at Vernon-sur-Seine on 1 September 1429 and received at Falaise on 7 September. Gower was instructed to have his men with the duke by 9 September, passing via Caen to collect wages from the *bailli* for a month's service, for, as it was noted, Bedford intended to give battle on either 8 or 9 September against the enemy who were assembled at Saint-Denis. The fact that the letter had taken six days to reach Falaise meant that the dates of assembly were unrealistic. As noted earlier, at least part of the company sent as a result of this request did not muster at Rouen until 11 September. A similar example can be cited for the siege of Pontorson in 1427. The siege commander, the earl of Warwick, wrote from his host before Pontorson before mid-day on Wednesday 19 March to Sir John Salvain, *bailli* of Rouen, with news that *devons estre combatus samedi prochain venant ou dimanche ou plus tost par les ennemis.* He asked Salvain to proclaim that English men-at-arms and archers within his *bailliage* should arrive at the siege as early as possible on the following Saturday or Sunday morning. The need for speed was stressed: the letter was said to have been written in haste, the messenger was told to travel by day and night, and the troops were instructed to make their way to the siege *tant de jour que de nuit.*[48] Although we do not know the outcome of this message, in the following April (1428) Salvain showed hesitation over whether to obey Talbot's commands as *governeur du pays du Maine* to go to his aid with *le plus grant nobre de gens darmes et de trait que pourrions recouvrer.* The *bailli* did not wish to go *sans premierement savoir se cestoit la voulente de mondit seigneur le Regent que nous allisons en icellui voyage pour ce que autre fois il nous avoit mande demourer en la dite ville de Roune pour la sauvegarde dicelle place.* As a result he wrote to Bedford in Paris for specific instructions, thus causing an eight-day delay as messages were conveyed between the two capitals.[49]

This reminds us that the fulfilment of orders was not simply a matter of how quickly messengers or troops could move. Another example concerning the garrison of Avranches illustrates other predicaments which might arise. The duke of York had written to various captains ordering them to send troops to Jumièges where they were to muster on 7 August 1437 for service under John, Lord Talbot. On 6 August the *bailli* of the Cotentin, based at Coutances, had the instruction forwarded to John Lampet, lieutenant of the earl of Suffolk at Avranches, requiring the latter to provide eight men-at-arms and 24 archers, but the *vicomte* only managed to get the message to Avranches on 8 August. Lampet set out with the right

---

[47] B.N. MS fr. 2606/4577.
[48] B.N. MS fr. 23189, fol. 40, no. 75.
[49] B.N. MS fr. 26050/870.

number of men but arrived too late. Ordered to return to base, he passed through Pontaudemer where he met a poursuivant with letters from York commanding him to be at Bernay on 2 September with 20 men-at-arms and 60 archers to serve within the army to be commanded by Lord Scales. He thus made for Bernay but, of course he had in his company only the 32 men of the initial call-out. Not surprisingly he subsequently experienced great difficulties when it came to calculating the pay due for the quarter. The situation was not assisted by the fact that in order to ensure the adequate defence of Avranches in his absence he had seen fit to recruit seven *almans* and 47 French, thus exceeding the regulations instituted in October 1434 that only an eighth of the total garrison (Avranches at this stage probably housed 180 men) should be from nations other than England or its subject territories.[50] Co-ordinating the assembly of troops could be problematic given that they were coming from a variety of different locations and sources. The situation could be exacerbated further if expeditionary troops were intended to be part of the campaign, for vagaries of wind, inadequacies of shipping and a series of other difficulties could delay their arrival. Thus in April 1431, 1,200 troops had to be raised under Lords Beaumont and Willoughby *pour certain temps jusqu'a la venue de certaine notre armee qui prouchain soit venuz et descenduz de notre royaume dAngleterre,* in order that they might serve in the field *pour le reboutement des enemis, brigands et autres malfaiteurs estans sur nos dits pays de Normandie et occupans plusieurs petites places et entendre au recouvrement et demolicions dicelles.*[51]

Returning to the mechanisms of troop call-outs within France, we must consider the obligations under which captains of retinues and garrisons had to provide men. On some occasions indentures were issued to cover periods of service in the field. Commanders such as the *lieutenants general pour la guerre* or those charged with the conduct of particular actions usually had the power to issue indentures on behalf of the crown. Warwick exercised this power at the siege of Pontorson, and was further accorded 3,000 *livres tournois* in order to make prests to those captains with whom he indented. The resulting indentures specified service at the siege as well as *partout ailleurs ou il sera ordonne par monsieur le roy, nous* (i.e. the duke of Bedford as Regent) *ou notre lieutenant,* in case the siege should come to a premature end and troops be redirected elsewhere.[52] Garrison detachments did not usually have special indentures to cover their service in the field, although there is a perplexing reference in an order concerning a detachment from Cherbourg for its first month's service at the siege of Ivry

[50] B.L. Add. Ch. 6907. My account adds further details to the mention of this case in Newhall, *Muster and Review,* p. 145.
[51] B.N. MS fr. 26054/1548.
[52] For instance, B.N. MS fr. 26049/692.

(1424) where pay is issued despite the lack of indentures.[53]

Those who held lands were obviously liable to serve under the feudal summons, but in fact the *semonce des nobles* which was exploited by the English also included those 'accustomed to follow the wars'. As expressed in the order of Warwick to Salvain for the siege of Pontorson in 1427, this included *tous anglais et autres demourans en votre bailliage tant hommes darmes comme gens de trait*. It thus gave the power to call to arms those not currently in garrisons and retinues. Summoned to join Warwick *les mieulx habilles que pourront*, they were liable to be reckoned *rebelles et desobeissans au roy* if they did not.[54] Garrison detachments which failed to turn up or were late might suffer the loss of wages. For the siege of Tancarville in August 1437, the *baillis* were ordered to proclaim that *les cappitaines des garnisons nommes en une cedulle attaches soubz le grant seel de la chancellerie de France asdiz lettres narroient envoie le nombre des gens de guerre desclaires en ladicte cedulle pour estre au vii jour dudit mois dAoust receus a mosntres a Jumieges et illec souldier pour servir le Roy au siege ordonne estre mis devant Tanquerville sur paine de perdre ung quartier de leurs gaiges du temps passe et inhabilles destre receus aux gaiges pour ung autre quartier apres et prouchain ensuivant au regard des deffault*. The garrison detachments were subsequently given a week's leeway after this last summons to muster at Jumièges, following which Talbot was given permission to recruit men in place of the *defaillans*, substituting if necessary three archers for one man-at-arms. As we sawm the detachment from Avranches arrived too late and was sent home, having the penalty for default applied. The lieutenant later petitioned saying that he had only received the letter on 6 August and so could not possibly have been at Jumièges the next day.[55] The captains of Caen, Vire and Falaise were also later named as having failed to send the right number of men for the siege of Tancarville and were sentenced to lose *ung quartier de leurs gages du temps passe et inhabilles destre recus aux gaiges pour ung autre quartier apres et prochain ensuite au regard des defaillans*.[56]

This was the stick but the carrot was not lacking. When an army was being assembled in September 1424 under Sir John Fastolf, Sir John Montgomery and Thomas, Lord Scales for the advance into Maine the call up included *et generalement de tous autres quelconques qui y vouldront venir et nous accompaigner*.[57] Bedford's letter to Thomas Gower in September 1429 combines both carrot and stick. First the incentive, 'weteth wel for certain that hit lay never in oure power sith we had the regency of France so wele as it doth now bothe of lordes, landes and other to rewarde men. The

---

[53]   B.N. MS fr. 26047/295.
[54]   B.N. MS fr. 23189, fol. 40, no. 75.
[55]   Cited in Newhall, *Muster and Review*, p. 144.
[56]   B.N. n.a.fr. 21289/136.
[57]   B.N. Clairambault 161/2.

whiche thing we promette yow faithfully for to do largely unto al tho that come to us at this tyme.' (On this same point, it is worth noting that counter-rolls of the garrisons show that gains could be made whilst on field action, although sorties and personal 'aventures' could also be profitable.)[58] Then the (veiled) threat, 'and failleth not her of, as ye love the conseervation of this londe and as ye wol answere to my lordes and us therefore in tyme comyng'.

Bedford's letter to Gower had included in its main text, when it was anticipated that Gower himself would lead the field company, the order that the latter should ensure that in his absence his place was 'surely ordeined fore and kept'. The postscript changed the order, instructing Gower to stay in Falaise for the sake of its safekeeping: 'an we wol that your self abide stille upon the sauvegarde of Faloize and that ye take good heed thereunto, boothe day and nighte and that ye bee wel wer of traisons'. Call-outs of detachments could not be made without some thought for local defence. This is what was on Salvain's mind when he hesitated over fulfilling Talbot's order in 1428, given that the Regent had otherwise ordered him to stay put in Rouen for the safeguard of the place. Cases such as this may have prompted, with effect from October 1429, the introduction of a clause into garrison captains' indentures whereby they were obliged to take their troops anywhere as the king, his regent or their nominees ordered *pour tenir les champs, estre a journees chevauchees ou sieges* under threat of loss of wages.[59] Later indentures specified more closely and emphatically the rates of deductions from pay. The new clause of 1429 also reflects the military situation of the time, for the relative peace of the duchy had been shattered by the successes of Joan of Arc and the need for field service was correspondingly greater. Moreover, *creus* and mobile retinues had been installed in some of the Norman garrisons over the previous months: these were intended to assist in the defence of vulnerable areas and also to serve in the field as necessary.[60] Another important point in the formalisation of the conditions concerning the use of garrison detachments comes in October 1434.[61] In at least 20 garrisons a permanent *creu* was

---

[58] P. Contamine, 'Rançons et butins dans la Normandie anglaise (1424–1444)', *Actes du 101e congrès national des sociétés savantes* (Paris, 1978).

[59] Newhall, *Muster and Review*, p. 128. See, for instance, the indenture for Carentan, B.N. MS fr. 26052/1158.

[60] Curry, 'Military Organization', pp. 235–40, and Map V; Newhall, *Muster and Review*, pp. 124–6.

[61] Curry, 'Military Organization', pp. 263–72, Table VIII, Maps VIII and IX; Newhall, *Muster and Review*, p. 128. See also London, College of Arms Arundel MS XLVIII fols 274r–276v for a declaration of all the garrisons and their companies for the field dated 20 October 1434.

established. This comprised a company of mounted men-at-arms and archers, ranging from 12 at Pont-de-l'Arche to 200 at Verneuil, which was ordered to have its *retrait et logeis* in the garrison and so contribute to its defence, whilst, as its principal function, standing ready at all times for service in the field. Their presence prevented a captain refusing to obey an order for call-out, as a simultaneous revision of the relevant clause in his indenture obliged him to maintain and despatch such troops for service either under himself, his lieutenant or a *chef de montre*. Some of these companies were certainly used in Maine in the spring and summer of 1435,[62] but that at Dreux, forty-strong, probably never left the garrison over the winter months *pour le temps qui est mutible comme chacun scet il* (the captain, William Broullart) *ne les estoit laisse aller dehors pour la securite de la dite place.*[63]

This formalisation went some way towards mitigating the problem of the lack of a standing army for the field, but Bedford's plans were overtaken by the disasters of 1435. Very few of the companies had been placed in the garrisons of the Caux, yet that was where the crisis erupted. The English made some effort to reinforce places in the area, but only when losses had already occurred. After Dieppe had fallen, for instance, a company of one man-at-arms and 20 archers (the ratio and the order for monthly rather than quarterly pay reflecting the emergency nature of their deployment) were put into Caudebec *toute selon la forme et maniere et soubz les conditions et provisions contenues et endentures faites pour les autres gens de guerre ordonnez pour les champs.*[64] As many of the Caux garrisons fell to the French (although not, incidentally, Caudebec) and the English felt vulnerable throughout the duchy, it was necessary to send over more men from England in late 1435 and 1436 because garrison troops had to concentrate largely on defensive duties, and because the *semonce des nobles* was declining in significance as a way of raising troops.[65] *Creus* for the field are found in garrisons after 1436 but there seems to have been no consistent policy concerning their location, at least nothing comparable with Bedford's 'master-plan' of October 1434. In the 1440s, and most notably in the years of truce, they were used as a means of mopping up surplus soldiery as well as improving local defence.[66] Whilst garrison detachments were still called out for field service, it is significant to note that armies deployed for the revictualling of Pontoise in 1441 and for the siege of Dieppe in 1442–3 were dependent on expeditionary troops for about 80% of their strength. This contrasts, for instance, with the situation in the 1420s: the

[62]   B.N. MS fr. 26059/2529, B.N. pièces originales 2135 Ogard 9.
[63]   B.N. n.a.fr. 8637/47.
[64]   B.N. MS fr. 26060/2685.
[65]   Curry, 'Service féodal', pp. 249–50.
[66]   Curry, 'Military Organization', pp. 315–29.

contribution of the expeditionary armies to the sieges of Guise (1424), Pontorson (1427) and Orleans (1428–9), for instance, were 50%, 15–30% and 60% respectively.[67] As the English position was placed under threat it seems that troops could not so easily be withdrawn from garrisons.

Taking the period as a whole, we can see that garrison detachments serving in field armies were sometimes, but not always, led by their captains. The account book of the Norman receiver-general for 1423–5 shows that most of the garrison contingents at the siege of Ivry and battle of Verneuil were led by their captains in person, testimony to the importance of this campaign. But as we saw earlier, Bedford decided that it would be better for Gower (technically lieutenant but in charge because the garrison captain, Lord Talbot, had been captured at Patay) to stay in Falaise than to lead the company to the field for the rescue of Paris in September 1429. In an example drawn from 1437 it seems that the choice of whether to go or stay lay at least to some degree with the garrison commander himself. Nicholas Burdet, captain and *bailli* of Evreux, had been ordered to lead a contingent to serve in the field under Lord Scales, being instructed that the lieutenant of the garrison should also be in this contingent. But Burdet chose instead to remain at Evreux for the *seuretee* of the place. When explaining his reasons for disobeying orders, he claimed that the absence of both captain and lieutenant would have been detrimental to the defence of the town: as he put it, *autrement ne fust demouree homme a qui les autres soldoiers eussent obey*.[68] Lieutenants sometimes led companies in the stead of the captain, but most commonly the company was placed under the control of a senior man-at-arms. Sometimes the latter already held office within the garrison as marshal, the leading of field companies apparently being within his responsibilities. Often, however, the command was temporary, for the duration of the activity alone, and was denoted by the use of the term *chef de montre*, or, less frequently, *conduiseur*. Such men were therefore responsible for the discipline of the troops on campaign and for the receipt and distribution of pay, on which more will be said later. We have already seen some indication of how men were chosen for field activity. The letter to Gower asked for the best marchers and the best horsed. The formalised structures of 1429 and 1434 led to the obvious service of the companies specifically designated for the field, although detachments from the regular garrisons (termed *garnison ordinaire*) are not unknown. The format of a document from November 1440 – where a list of names has had an *incipit* entered later noting the date of muster in the field – suggests that the captain, in this case of Neufchâtel, nominated the men for field service and had their names listed. The list was then sent to the commanders, on this

---

[67] *Ibid.*, Table IV.
[68] Bodleian Library MS Ch. For. 352.

occasion Lords Talbot, Fauconberg and Scales who were assembling an army of 2,400 against the enemy at Louviers and Conches. The list names eight men-at-arms and 20 archers but only four of the men-at-arms are pointed, suggesting that the rest were *defaillans*.[69] What we cannot know is whether they had deserted en route or whether they had never left the garrison in the first place. A study of musters of detachments used in the field suggests that it was often the same men who were chosen for such service, implying that experience, competence and equipment (including horses) may have affected the decision on who should be sent. Two examples may suffice here, one of a man who spent his active career in one garrison, the other who served in several different locations. The first, Osbert Mundeford, appears as a mounted man-at-arms in the garrison of Fresnay-le-Vicomte from 1427. In November 1432, as *chef de montre*, he led a detachment of the garrison for field service under Lord Willoughby. By the following year he was marshal of the garrison and led a detachment from the garrison, as well as his own company of one other man-at-arms and eight archers, in the army of the earl of Arundel which mustered at Bonsmoulins in September 1433. In March 1436, he was ordered to lead a garrison detachment to Rouen and thence to join with Lord Scales in the actions against La Hire. In November 1437 he again led the Fresnay contingent at the siege of Le Crotoy.[70] That he gained valuable experience of command and was seen as a reliable officer is revealed by the fact of his later appointments as *bailli* of Le Mans, treasurer-general of Normandy and captain of Fresnay and Pont-l'Evêque. The career of the second example, John Nelson, is given in Appendix 2. Here we have the impression of a mounted man-at-arms who roved more widely in his service and who had substantial experience of field activity. By May 1441 he had no regular posting, but was one of the *gens vivans sur le pais* who provided a useful source of field troops on several occasions. With many thousands of men involved, we can scarcely say that Mundeford and Nelson are typical, but their careers do give some idea of what experience of field service might have been like for English soldiers in France.

We can also elucidate much about the mechanics of payment, a topic on which Newhall has already commented.[71] It should already be clear from earlier examples that field armies were mustered. Lieutenants for the field, or those designated to the command of specific sieges or campaigns, had the authority to take musters but often delegated it to their leading

---

[69] B.N. MS fr. 25775/1471, muster taken on 29 November at Pontaudemer.
[70] B.N. MS fr. 25770/734 (November 1432), MS fr. 25771/796 (September 1433), MS fr. 25772/1043 (March 1436), MS fr. 25774/1269 (November 1437).
[71] Newhall, *Muster and Review*, pp. 85–6.

officers.[72] Musters were taken at outset and then periodically, often every fifteen, or occasionally eight, days. At the siege of Lagny in 1432, however, Bedford would not allow mustering to be carried out, as the enemy were too close.[73] Furthermore, mustering could be erratic as troops arrived on different days, but to make accounting simpler (for pay was dependent on muster), it often tended to be organised from the beginning of a month or half way through it. Payment was made following first muster. Thus William Breton, *bailli* of Caen, initially did not receive payment for service of his troop at the siege of Le Crotoy as his company arrived late and made no muster during service.[74] The leaders of companies were paid wages in advance for fifteen days or for a month dating from the muster. This was a contrast with garrison service where pay was always quarterly in arrears, but the difference was occasioned by the need for troops to have money in hand to cover victuals and perhaps also the cost of billeting.[75] The payment of wages at the outset of service was also used as an incentive: the postscript of Bedford's letter to Gower adds to various other incentives the following prospect: 'and at Caen we have ordenned your saide retinue to have a *holle monneth* wages in hand'. When the first period of service had expired, further musters were taken and payments made for the next eight days, fifteen days or month. In keeping with the arrangements for the expeditionary armies and the garrisons, the leaders of the companies received pay on their men's behalf, signing a *quittance* to that effect, and were responsible for distributing the money. Transporting cash to the armies in the field was no easy matter, for the officials of the treasury often needed substantial military escorts. When money was late in arriving, commanders had to use their own resources. At the siege of Etrépagny in 1429, for example, Lord Willoughby and Edmund Beaufort, earl of Mortain, had to pay 600 *livres tournois* out of their own pockets to continue the siege which otherwise would have been in danger of *desemparement*.[76] As Newhall has shown, problems could also arise when the regular, quarterly garrison pay was being calculated. As the detachments had already received wages in the field, measures had to be taken to ensure that this was

---

[72] For instance, in the army ordered to advance into Maine under Lord Scales, Sir John Fastolf and Sir John Montgomery in September 1424, Fastolf delegated to Sir William Oldhall the power to take a muster at Argentan and to report names and equipment to the receiver-general of Normandy (B.N. Clairambault 161/2).

[73] B.N. MS fr. 26056/1863.

[74] B.N. MS fr. 26046/151.

[75] See Newhall, *Muster and Review*, p. 123, although he argues for a monthly pay arrangement.

[76] B.N. PO 65 Angleterre 4, 22 Oct 1429, where reimbursement is ordered.

deducted from the pay a captain should receive for his garrison at the end of the quarter. If this was not done, there was a risk that the captain might acquire money for men who had not actually been present in garrison for all or part of the quarter. The various musters and *quittances* had to be checked carefully by the financial administration. The verificatory process was much assisted by the ubiquitous use of garrison controllers from 1429. These agents of the central administration, who served within the garrisons as foot men-at-arms, kept quarterly counter-rolls on which all absences and gains of war were recorded.

Victualling armies in the field was undoubtedly problematic. Sieges presented particular difficulties for besiegers as well as the besieged. As demand intensified with the influx and concentration of troops, and food supplies diminished, their price increased. As we have seen, the earl of Salisbury was given extra funds in 1427 because of *la chierte de vivres* in his expedition into Champagne, and the members of the expeditionary army serving around Montargis in that year were given extra pay to help cover their higher food costs.[77] At the siege of Louviers in June 1431 captains reported that due to shortage of forage they had been forced to send horses away from the siege, along with archers and servants who were responsible for their protection and care. As a result some archers had not been present at the musters for the second month of the siege and there was a danger that pay would thus not be received for them.[78] The provisioning of the besiegers of Dieppe was particularly problematic because the vicinity was relatively wasted (a similar problem had been experienced at the siege of Harfleur). In May 1443 the duke of York ordered the local *vicomte* to assemble food supplies and despatch them to the siege, further instructing that he could send more cider in place of live animals if he wished – an instruction which may place a new interpretation on why the English never succeeded in retaking Dieppe! It was also noted that recurrent demands for supplies in the vicinity were threatening to alienate the local inhabitants, so York suggested that, in order to avoid too much public outcry, the *vicomte* should try to arrange a deal with a couple of Lisieux merchants.[79] Transporting victuals and military equipment was expensive and on occasion dangerous. Thus, a substantial armed escort was needed to convey provisions in November 1442 from Rouen to the *bastide* established before Dieppe.[80]

---

[77] B.N. MS fr. 4484, fols 40 and 69 respectively.
[78] Evreux, Archives Départementales de l'Eure II F 4068, printed in Newhall, *Muster and Review*, pp. 142–3, where he also notes muster rolls made during the siege with some men marked as being with the horses.
[79] B.N. MS fr. 25777/1632.
[80] B.L. Add. Ch. 12158.

Further difficulties arose from the soldiers themselves. Having large numbers of troops moving around the countryside was always potentially risky in terms of maintaining good relations with the native population. The anticipation of problems is revealed in an order concerning the assembly of troops to act as escort for Queen Margaret in 1445, noting that they should be led across country *en bonne regle, en passant le pais le plus doulcement et au moins de grief et foule de peuple que faire se pourra. Et tiengnent leur chemin par les lieux qui declairez vous seront par notre bien ame maistre Michel Pyot secretaire de mondit seigneur le roy lequel pour la cause envoyans par de la.*[81] Extra care, perhaps, had to be taken in the new conditions of truce. Earlier damage may have been occasioned by the demands of war: an inquiry into the low value of the farm of Elbeuf in February 1443 ascribed the loss partly to the fact that the enemy had lodged in the area with 5–6,000 men in November 1440, when local inhabitants had been forced to flee, but it mentioned also the fact that Talbot, Fauconberg and Scales had come into the area with 3–4,000 men, lodging at Elbeuf for nine to ten days *et y firent les gens de guerre moult de maux et de destructions.*[82] Efforts were made to control behaviour on the march and in the camp. At the siege of Orleans something can be known of the activities of the marshal of the host who, along with the provost, was charged with giving justice, reprimanding violence between soldiers and receiving complaints of merchants.[83] The military ordinances of Henry V and of the earl of Salisbury for the campaign into Maine included much on the good regulation of troops in the field.[84] *Ad hoc* orders are also found, many concerning the behaviour of the *gens vivans sur le pays*. In February 1440, for instance, whilst raising an army which included such men, John Beaufort, earl of Somerset, found it necessary to order that the latter should not take horses from the native population when they journeyed to the mustering point at Bernay.[85] The problems which could follow the demobilisation of a field army had also to be mitigated. In January 1433, for instance, we find a certificate issued by Sir John Fastolf, captain of Fresnay, and lieutenant of Caen and Alençon, confirming that he

---

[81] A.N. K66/1.

[82] A.N., Collection Lenoir (Mi. 104) 9, fol. 224.

[83] P. Contamine, 'Les armées française et anglaise à l'époque de Jeanne d'Arc', *Revue des sociétés savants de Haute-Normandie; letters et sciences humaines*, 57 (1970), p. 15.

[84] See, for instance, *The Black Book of the Admiralty*, ed. T. Twiss (Rolls Series, London, 1871), I, pp. 459–72, for the ordinances of Henry V in 1419, and B.L. Cotton Julius CIV for the ordinances of the earl of Salisbury. Of considerable value here is M. Keen, 'Richard II's Ordinances of War of 1385', in *Rulers and Ruled in Late Medieval England. Essays presented to Gerald Harriss*, ed. R. E. Archer and S. Walker (London, 1995).

[85] B.N. MS fr. 26068/3936, 3938.

had been accompanied by men from these garrisons in November and December last in various activities including service in the company of Lord Willoughby, and that he had returned to Fresnay after celebrating Christmas with his wife at Falaise and replacing his men in his garrisons *chacun en sa place sans les souffrir plus vivre sur le pays.*[86]

Troops most certainly deserted from the field armies; this seems to have been a recurrent problem in the case of the expeditionary element.[87] It may be that soldiers serving in the field were required to take oaths that they would provide service: two such examples survive, from the siege of Orleans, and from the rescue of Pontoise in 1441, but it is not clear whether this was common practice.[88] We can be more certain that men were permitted to leave armies, being accorded *congés* to do so,[89] and there was also 'natural wastage' caused by death, injury and capture. In 1449 Sir François Surienne encountered another difficulty following his capture of Fougères when he discovered that the troops of his assault force, drawn from various companies, were now being required by their captains to return to their places.[90] As we saw previously, field commanders were frequently faced with the problem of *defaillans*. Garrisons quite often defaulted on the numbers they were to send, sometimes for good reasons. The captain of Dreux gave several excuses for not sending his contingent to the siege of Tancarville: he claimed that his place was under threat, that its walls were about to collapse and that there was a major dispute amongst the men in his garrison concerning prisoners. Moreover, he had had to detail some of the men intended for the siege to the guard of Chevreuse which had recently been captured.[91] Desertion and reluctance to serve also

---

[86]   B.N. MS fr. 26056/1990.

[87]   For examples from 1424 and 1428, see respectively, B.N. MS fr. 26047/306, printed in S. Luce, *Chronique du Mont-Saint-Michel* (Société des anciens textes français) (Paris, 1879–83), i, pp. 144–6, and B.N. MS fr. 4488 p. 687.

[88]   B.N. MS fr. 26051/996 (December 1428, concerning the *serment* to be taken by men defending the Loire garrisons and the *bastide* at Orleans); A.N. K67/1/38 (29 August 1441, a *quittance* in presence of the *tabellion* of the *vicomte* of Pont-de-l'Arche by Makyn Hilton, marshal of that garrison, for the wages of his troops for 15 days service in the army of Talbot for the rescue of Pontoise, *les susdits promettent de faire le dit service et sy engagent par lobligation des tous leurs biens meubles et heritages presents et avenire*).

[89]   For an example concerning the men of Sir Nicholas Burdet in Elbeuf in July 1441, see B.N. MS fr. 26068/4319. See also the reference in Waurin, *Recueil des Croniques*, V, p. 121, after the victory at Verneuil that the duke of Bedford *donne congie a aucuns de ses captaines pour eulx retourner es garnisons des villes chasteaulx et forteresses quils avoit.*

[90]   Stevenson, *Letters and Papers*, I, p. 291.

[91]   B.L. Add. Ch. 11,992.

took its toll. In 1432 Lord Willoughby noted that of 400 men due to be sent by the garrisons, 160 had not turned up, despite several letters sent by the king and council and by himself; this shortfall he considered a great disadvantage, for without the right number he could not *faire entreprises, chevauchees et mettre sieges*.[92] Sensibly, he, like other field commanders, regularly had powers to recruit substitutes. These were usually raised temporarily from men described as *vivans sur le pais*. Such men constituted up to 40% of the armies for particular field actions, and on occasion were raised in their own right, not simply to substitute for shortfalls in the garrison detachments. In 1443, for instance, a hundred of them were detailed to Neufchâtel and Arques *pour faire diligence de savoir de larmee de Dauphin qui sest mis sus en armes venant es parties de la ville de Dieppe lui faire guerre avec aultres et se mestier est eulx bouter et entrer en la bastide qui de present est de par le roy devant Dieppe*.[93] The earl of Warwick looked even further afield, to the Channel Islands, whence in March 1427 he recruited 300 archers to replace those of the expeditionary army who had deserted.[94]

What conclusions can we come to on the organisation of field armies in this period? Newhall considered that the use of the same forces for garrison and field service was 'one of the complicating features of military-financial administration',[95] and indeed, a study of the immensely complex archive arising from it confirms this interpretation. In a nutshell, it was an administrative nightmare. But did it have military shortcomings? There was a danger that troops withdrawn for field service might render the garrison vulnerable, but save for the example which Newhall cites of Avranches in 1423, it does not seem that it was a cause of English losses. Captains were well aware of their defensive needs, and were prepared to disobey orders to send troops if they felt their place to be under threat. Thus in 1440, although Lord Scales was ordered to send part of his personal retinue to the siege of Harfleur; he kept some men back for the defence of Gavray *pour obvier a plusieurs inconvenimens qui par la deffaut de bonne garde dicellui lieu se feussent peu ensuit*. The treasurer-general sought a reduction in wages as a penalty for ignoring orders, but Scales was pardoned as he had always used his troop in royal service.[96] This scenario is found on many other occasions. But it reveals a difficulty facing the military planners, for they could never be too sure of whether troops summoned would turn up

---

[92] B.N. pièces originales 3051 Willeby 17, which concerns the recruitment of 17 substitutes.

[93] B.N. MS fr. 25777/1647. For further details of the *gens vivans sur le pais* see the article cited in note 8 above.

[94] B.N. pièces originales 238, Beauchamp en Angleterre 12.

[95] Newhall, *Muster and Review*, p. 123.

[96] B.N. n.a.fr. 7628/420.

or not. Even in the 1420s, it had proved impossible to predict what the military needs of the year would be, and as the English moved onto the defensive in later decades, responding to crises became all the more problematic. Yet responses were made, and the English were reasonably successful in regaining the losses they had incurred in 1435–6 because they continued to exploit all of the military resources at their disposal. Only in 1449–50 did the system of field army formation collapse. To a considerable degree, this was due to the effects of the truce which prevailed between 1444 and 1449. Not only did this lead to a major reduction in the size of the garrison establishment, but it also encouraged the systems of garrison and retinue call-out to fall into disuse. The crisis of 1449–50 was also exacerbated by the fact that expeditionary armies were, when they were now most needed, slow in coming as well as inadequate in size and effectiveness of command. It was not so much, therefore, the failure of a system as the lack of political will that drove the English out of their conquests.

Appendix 1: Examples of seasonality of campaigning 1423–1443

1423 April–Sept.	siege of Le Crotoy
1424 May–July	siege of Gaillon
1424 March–Sept.	siege of Ivry, leading to battle of Verneuil
1426 Feb.–July	army under Warwick in Champagne
1426 Sept.–Oct.	siege of Vertus etc.
1427 Feb.–May	siege of Pontorson
1428–9 Oct.–May	siege of Orleans
1430 Apr.–May	Suffolk in Lower Normandy
1430 Mar.–May	siege of Gaillard
1430 Sept.–Oct.	siege of Louviers
1431 Apr.–Sept.	siege of Louviers
1432 Mar.–June	siege of Lagny
1432 Sept. Nov.–Dec.	Willoughby appointed in Lower Normandy, one year from 15 Sept., troops in field in Nov, Dec.
1433	under Arundel for Bonsmoulins, Aug.– Sept.: army in field
1435 July–Sept.	siege of Saint-Denis
1437 Sept.–Nov.	siege of Tancarville
1437 Sept.	Scales in Champagne and Brie
1438 Jan.	revictualling of Montargis
1440 Feb.	Somerset's raid into Picardy
1440 Aug.–Oct.	siege of Harfleur, plus activities in field June–Aug.
1440 Nov.	v. enemy at Louviers and Conches, continued into Jan.–Feb. 1441
1442 July–Sept.	Talbot and York in field
1442 Oct.–Dec.	siege of Dieppe
1443 Feb.–May	siege of Dieppe

Appendix 2: The service pattern of John Nelson*

Date	Commander	Place of Service
Feb. 1429	Sir John Fastolf	field, mustered at Corbeuil
Oct. 1431	John Stanlawe	Verneuil *creu*
Dec. 1431	John, duke of Bedford	Rouen, company for field
May 1432	Robert, Lord Willoughby	ordinary retinue of Willoughby recruited in place of garrison *defaillans*, siege of Saint-Célérin
March 1434	John Marchant (John, earl of Arundel)	muster at Seéz, for sieges of Montfort, Houdan etc.
June 1435	Sir Robert Harling	Verneuil, company for field
Sept. 1435	John Stanlawe	Verneuil detachment at siege of Saint-Denis (where Harling was killed)
Nov.–Dec. 1436	William, Lord Fauconberg	Verneuil garrison
Nov. 1438	William, Lord Fauconberg	personal retinue
Nov. 1440	Edmund Beaufort earl of Dorset	Alençon garrison
Feb. 1441	Edmund Beaufort earl of Dorset	Alençon garrison, but marked 'vacat'
May 1441	Hugh Stanlawe (John, Lord Talbot)	men of no garrison, army mustered at Pont-de-l'Arche v. enemy at Louviers and Conches

*References are, respectively, B.N. n.a.fr. 8602/13; B.N. MS fr. 25770/638; A.D.S.M. Fonds Danquin 3/3/13; B.N. Clairambault 207/111–120; B.N. MS fr. 25771/1825; B.N. MS fr. 25772/948; B.N. MS fr. 25772/989; A.D.E. IIF 4069; B.N. Clairambault 185/24; A.N. K66/1/57; B.N. MS fr. 25775/1502; A.N. K67/1/17.

The Military Organisation of the Reign of Henry VII

KAY E. LACEY

Since 1788 when Francis Grose published his last volume on the history of the English army, an epic study which spanned the period from the Norman conquest to the eighteenth century, numerous scholars have offered contributions on the subject of military history which have included cursory studies of the Tudor period.[1] Few authors have, however, touched upon the reign of Henry VII. At the end of the nineteenth century there was a revival of interest in medieval and Tudor military history, which continued until the end of the nineteen-fifties. There have been sporadic scholarly contributions since, and several recent publications on medieval military history indicate that this subject is once again becoming popular. Yet much of what has been written on the history of the army, the ordnance and the king's small personal bodyguard, who were known as the Yeomen of the Guard, has not been published.[2] It was Sir John Fortescue,

---

[1] F. Grose, *Military Antiquities Respecting a History of the English Army from the Conquest to the Present Time*, 2 vols (London, 1786–8). Sir Charles Oman, *A History of the Art of War in the Sixteenth Century* (London, 1957), included Tudor military history, but was mainly concerned with continental armies. Several historians writing on the reign of Henry VII have briefly mentioned military affairs during the reign; see, for example, J. Mackie, *The Early Tudors, 1485–1558* (Oxford, 1959); R. Lockyer, *Henry VII* (London, 1968, new edn revised by A. Thrush, 1997); A. Grant, *Henry VII* (London, 1985); S. J. Gunn, *Early Tudor Government, 1485–1558* (London, 1995); S. B. Chrimes, *Henry VII* (London, 1972); R. L. Storey, *The Reign of Henry VII* (London, 1968); C. Rogers, *Henry VII* (London, 1991). A good account of the reign and its primary sources is W. Busch, *England under the Tudors*, I, *King Henry VII*, trans. A. H. Johnson and A. M. Todd (London, 1895). In this paper I have not considered the navy of Henry VII, which deserves special consideration in its own right, and forms the basis of my paper 'Sails, Flags, Pennants and Rigging of the Later Middle Ages, with Special Reference to the Navy of Henry VII', given at the National Maritime Museum on 27 April 1996 for a Medieval Dress and Textile Society conference on maritime textiles held in conjunction with the Museum. See also D. Loades, *The Tudor Navy: An Administrative, Political and Military History* (Aldershot, 1992).

[2] A thesis currently in progress by Anita Hewerdine, a student of Dr David Starkey in the Department of International History, London School of

in his *History of the British Army* published in 1899, who drew attention to the formation of the Yeomen of the Guard in 1485, an event which marked a significant development in the history of medieval English military affairs. Subsequently, James Hooker suggested that this body of royal yeomanry may have been patterned on the royal guard of Louis XI, which he speculates Henry may have seen whilst in exile,[3] while John Mackie had already referred to the suggestion made by the late eighteenth-century historian Samuel Pegge that the Yeomen of the Guard, which was a body of archers, was modelled on the French *Petit Garde*.[4] In 1475 Louis XI of France had created a distinct core of gentlemen, the *Grande Garde*, and a lesser guard of 200 archers 'of his body'.[5] There is no record of Henry VII's bodyguard having participated in actual warfare during the reign, although Empson used them in an act of force against Sir Robert Plumpton in 1501.[6] Henry's small personal bodyguard was intended to protect him on public occasions as when, for example, the Guard attended on Henry when he entered London after Bosworth, and at his coronation. The attendance of Henry's small guard at his coronation was in marked contrast to the actions of his predecessor Richard III, who had ordered an unprecedented military presence of 4 – 5,000 northern men to wait outside London during his coronation. It was said, however, that these men were dressed in rusty armour and poorly arrayed and their presence and appearance brought dishonour to the king.[7] Polydore Vergil nevertheless states that when Henry VII acted quickly against the rebellious Francis, Lord Lovell in Yorkshire and Humphrey Stafford in Gloucestershire to deny them the opportunity of assembling more followers, he despatched his whole retinue against them, including his bodyguard, to the total of 3,000 men, even though they were ill equipped, 'for the greater part had made armour for themselves from

---

Economics and Political Science, is on the Tudor Yeomen of the Guard. A study of the military organisation of Henry VII is currently being undertaken by Dr Steve Gunn of the University of Oxford for a book on the subject.

[3] J. Hooker, 'Notes on the Organisation and Supply of the Tudor Military under Henry VII', *Huntington Library Quarterly*, 23 (1959), pp. 19–31.

[4] Mackie, *The Early Tudors*, p. 208, citing S. Pegge, *Curalia* (London, 1791), I, Part iii, p. 4. The source for this belief would appear to be Polydore Vergil and the chronicler Hall.

[5] Pegge, *Curalia*, p. 4.

[6] Mackie, *The Early Tudors*, p. 208.

[7] Mackie, *The Early Tudors*, p. 208. It has been suggested, without any authority whatsoever, that the scarlet of the uniforms of Henry's guard symbolised the dragon of Cadwalader. The red dragon of Cadwalader was borne by Jasper Tudor as his armorial banner, and it was this that Henry Tudor employed as a symbol of his descent from Cadwalader at the battle of Bosworth. The red dragon on a field vert was the royal achievement of Wales.

leather'.[8] By 1509 the Yeomen of the Guard had become a small professional force which numbered about 500 men.[9]

Retaining, the recruiting by lords of gentry followers, could provide stability; a large retinue provided a lord with prestige, and magnate retinues could provide the army with its servants. But they might also be active in rebellion, in local disputes, and in perverting juries. Henry issued prohibitions and condemnations against retaining in 1485, 1487, 1495, 1497 and 1504, which largely repeated Edward IV's act of 1468. The act of 1504 did not apply to servants, officials and lawyers, and allowed those who had the king's authority by licences to recruit men to serve the king in war or otherwise. Henry did not prohibit retaining; retaining which he considered *lawful* was allowable, and a lord was often bound by recognisance to ensure that his retinue would not disturb the peace. Henry's policy effectively limited retaining in his reign, although some nobles circumvented the legislation by increasing the numbers of their estate officers instead.[10] No indentures for private retaining, such as existed before 1485, are known to exist from Henry's reign. Henry was aware of the uses of private retainers; in 1486 he owed his escape from ambush to the retinue of the 4th earl of Northumberland, and in 1487 and 1489 Henry relied upon the resources of Bedford, Oxford and Derby, his household men and the north midlands gentry.[11] The use of licences enabled him to rely more on the support of other gentry, townsmen and royal officers acting under his closest men. By 1507 a foreign observer noted that Henry could call upon 40,000 men of war and an Italian reported that the king did not depend on the military strength of his nobles because he had appointed men in receipt of his fees to perform military services, men who could be

---

[8] *The Anglia Historia of Polydore Vergil, A.D. 1485–1537*, ed. and trans. D. Hay, Camden Series, 72 (London, 1950), p. 11.

[9] A. Cameron, 'The Giving of Livery and Retaining in Henry VII's Reign', *Renaissance and Modern Studies*, 18 (1974), pp. 17–35, at p. 18, n. 4. He states that the Guard 'so far as is known took no part in any engagement during the reign'.

[10] *Year Book I Henry VII*, Mich. pl. 3; J. Strachney, J. Pridden and E. Upham (eds), *Rotuli Parliamentorum; ut et petitiones et placita in Parliamento* [1278–1503] (London, 1832), VI, pp. 287–8; A. Luders, T. E. Tomlins, J. Raithby *et al.* (eds), *Statutes of the Realm*, Record Commission (London, 1810–28), 3 H VII c.15; 10 H VII c.6 and 10; 11 H VII c.18; 19 H VII c.14. See Grant, *Henry VII*, p. 24, and Cameron 'The Giving of Livery', p. 18. Livery (retainers given a uniform or badge), maintenance (protecting a retainer's interests e.g. perverting judicial proceedings on a retainer's behalf).

[11] J. Gairdner (ed.), *The Paston Letters* (Edinburgh, 1910), III, pp. 353, 358–62; Gunn, *Early Tudor Government*, p. 40.

trusted.[12] As Steve Gunn points out, the crown 'was largely dependent for armed force on the recruitment by the nobility and gentry of their own tenants and servants', and Henry attempted to control the existing systems of recruitment by harnessing them. Like Richard III, he secured undertakings from trusted supporters to provide a specific number of men ready to serve when required, allowed his trusted men to have a specified number of licensed retainers (whose names were submitted to his secretary) and he ordered regular musters.[13]

Like his predecessors, Henry maintained control in the provinces through granting overlordship to members of the nobility. He restored the wardenship of the north to the earl of Northumberland a few weeks after releasing him from captivity in 1485, and on his death in 1489, granted the office to the earl of Surrey, who had been released from the Tower for the purpose of quelling the Yorkshire rebels who had killed Northumberland.[14] Henry further rewarded Surrey's loyalty by restoring some of his lands after he had suppressed the Yorkshire rebellion (with the earl of Oxford's retinue) and had achieved military success against the Scots in 1497. Yet Northumberland's powers had been restricted, and Surrey did not hold lands in the north. In 1502 Surrey was replaced by a council under the direction of the archbishop of York. Henry's new policy avoided appointing local potentates and attempted to limit magnate power in the provinces. It is significant that after Prince Arthur's death in 1502, the western marcher lords were required to make indentures with the crown.[15] Henry was tightening his control of retinues. After 1504 Henry was able to exert more control over the number of retinues in the country, and henceforth all men who were royal tenants or holders of lands, fees or

---

[12] L. P. Gachard (ed.) *Collection des Voyages des Souverains des Pays-Bas*, 4 vols (Brussels, 1876–82), I, p. 477; C. A. Sneyd (ed.), *A Relation, or Rather a True Account, of the Island of England*, Camden Society, Old Series, 37 (London, 1847), pp. 45–60.

[13] Gunn, *Early Tudor Government*, pp. 38, 40. A detailed discussion of retaining in the reign may be found in W. H. Dunham, Jnr., *Lord Hastings' Indentured Retainers, 1461–1483* (Yale, 1955), pp. 90–116.

[14] Busch, *England under the Tudors*, I, p. 47.

[15] One indenture survives for William Herbert, earl of Huntingdon (Cardiff Central Library, MS 5.7, f. 78–9, from the MSS collection of Sir Thomas Phillips). On military indentures see A. Compton Reeves, 'Some of Humphrey Stafford's Military Indentures', *Nottingham Medieval Studies*, 16 (1972). Royal indentures for purposes other than retaining survive: T. B. Pugh, '"The Indentures for the Marches" between Henry VII and Edward Stafford (1477–1521) Duke of Buckingham', *EHR*, 71 (1956), pp. 436–41. Cameron, 'The Giving of Livery', p. 20, notes that 'to date no example of private retaining by indenture has come to light'.

offices from the crown were to be retained by the king alone, and all retinue leaders were to be licensed to possess a retinue.[16] Cameron points out that 'there is a very close connection' between the growth of the three retinues of the duke of Buckingham, lord Burgavenny and the earl of Northumberland, and the restrictive statute of 1504.[17]

Dominic Luckett has recently claimed that Henry VII was burdened by debt when he ascended the throne in 1485, without a regular income and living on credit. It was this, and political weakness, that prompted Henry to provide early rewards to his supporters, though his youth and inexperience caused him to distribute 'his *largesse* in an extremely *ad hoc* way'. In the early years of the reign, therefore, Henry's patronage was deficient.[18] This view may be questioned.[19] Luckett also thinks that men once rewarded would be likely to ask for more. There is little evidence of this happening in practice, for although men might ask to exchange their offices with others, they rarely petitioned for further offices. Henry was deliberately parsimonious with his rewards; many men who fought for Henry at Bosworth claimed that they had never been rewarded or even repaid for the expenditure they had laid out, and even by the middle of the reign others stated that they had never received salaries for offices which had been granted to them. Positions might sometimes be awarded by Henry on the basis of recommendation by other crown officers; he personally oversaw the granting of all offices, rewards and fees, and therefore could be expected to

---

[16]   *Ibid.*, p. 22 and n. 2, citing *H.M.C.* 6th Report, p. 444, Lancashire Record Office, D.D.F. 1233. In 1505 Henry reinforced the retaining statutes by a signet letter sent to the steward of Penwortham, Lancashire, forbidding the retaining of royal tenants by anyone other than the king.

[17]   Cameron, 'The Giving of Livery', p. 25.

[18]   D. Luckett, 'Patronage, Violence and Revolt in the Reign of Henry VII', in R. E. Archer (ed.), *Crown, Government and People in the Fifteenth Century* (Stroud, 1995), pp. 145–60, at pp. 145–6. See *idem*, 'Crown, Patronage and Local Administration in Berkshire, Dorset, Hampshire, Oxfordshire, Somerset and Wiltshire, 1485–1509' (Oxford D.Phil. thesis, 1992).

[19]   To ensure that the crown had sufficient personal financial resources Henry followed the example of his predecessor Richard III and claimed the customs revenues from exports and imports as his own. He also acquired revenue from forfeitures, and of course had income from the crown lands. He also retained the income from lands granted to his sons Arthur and Henry. Henry appears to have had more financial problems paying his debts in the 1490s than at the beginning of the reign. Debts incurred whilst in France and Brittany, and 'on his last journey', were not paid until several years after Bosworth. On finance see F. C. Dietz, *English Government Finance, 1485–1558* (University of Illinois, Studies in the Social Sciences, ix, 1920); and N. S. B. Gras, *The Early English Customs System* (Harvard Economic Studies, 1918).

be usually well informed about those subjects whom he employed.[20] Furthermore, it is likely that Henry deliberately excluded certain families from rewards of local offices to prevent them gaining too powerful a position in their localities. The abuses of such power were most marked in Henry's reign in the frequency of complaints against corrupt juries. An attempt to limit the development of powerful families may also be seen in Henry's failure to create new peerages; there were only eight new creations in his reign. This action might be regarded as a shrewd move by Henry, and, coupled with his acts against retaining and liveries, effectively limited opposition to him by overmighty subjects.[21]

Henry, however, needed to maintain a fine balance between providing minimally adequate rewards and maintaining support. It was also necessary for him to ensure that he had military backing when required. Henry's statute of 1487 acknowledged that his security lay in those receiving grants, and in return he required that grantees should provide continued service and must come to the king's aid in time of trouble or war on pain of losing their office.[22] A further statute of 1495 stated that it was a general duty to serve the king, but those who had received offices, fees, or annuities from the crown were bound to defend the king under penalty of deprivation of their grants.[23] Henry thus ensured that the crown received support and military service in times of need. After 1497, Henry resorted more to coercion than favour.[24] In the absence of a standing army, it was necessary for the crown to have the co-operation of the most powerful men in the kingdom; kings depended on their nobilities. The attitude of the crown to the nobility appears to have changed significantly in his reign. Patronage had to be earned through service, not granted in advance, and this had important implications for national security.[25]

---

[20] Evidence for this may be seen in the writs and warrants for issues, Public Record Office C82. The King's Remembrancer of the Exchequer Rolls and the Liberate Rolls were where grants of offices were recorded, while there are also petitions in other Exchequer classes.

[21] On this subject see Cameron, 'The Giving of Livery', pp. 17–35.

[22] 3 H VII (1487), c. 15. *Statutes of the Realm*, II, pp. 522–3.

[23] 11 H VII (1495), c. 18. *Statutes of the Realm*, II, p. 582.

[24] Luckett, 'Patronage, Violence and Revolt', p. 160.

[25] A play written in the 1490s by a lawyer in Cardinal Morton's household provides the message that heredity has no meaning unless accompanied by virtuous actions and that nobility is a matter of behaviour, not birth. This reflects contemporary beliefs about chivalry – high status and respect cannot be inherited but must be earned. See P. Meredith (ed.), *Fulgens and Lucres, by Master Henry Medwall* (University of Leeds, School of English, 1981). On patronage see M. M. Condon, 'Ruling Elites in the Reign of Henry VII', in C. Ross (ed.), *Patronage, Pedigree and Power* (Gloucester, 1979), pp. 109–42. The

According to Luckett, shires which were unproblematic at the beginning of the reign were, by the end of the 1490s, becoming untrustworthy, whereas areas initially volatile were peaceful.[26] He attributes this shift to Henry's distribution of patronage; it was difficult for him to reward everyone with local offices in areas which were predominantly loyal, and he placed allies in areas less sympathetic or hostile, rewarding those not previously supporters. In the south and west Henry rewarded only his closest friends.[27] According to Vergil, some men considered themselves 'ill-rewarded'.[28] Resentment and Henry's demands for war to maintain his position fuelled support amongst the gentry for the rising of 1497. Henry's narrow spread of patronage in the area of the revolt meant few would defend him there, while his own concept of the relationship between the crown and its clients was much to blame.[29] The Croyland continuator comments on Henry's moderation, compared to Edward IV and Richard III, in dealing with his adversaries in the years after Bosworth.[30] Henry attempted to avoid hostility to his rule. Lancastrian shires did not oppose him, and resistance came through the personal influence of Richard's supporters, rather than from county gentry.[31] This was true of Lovell and Stafford's rebellion in 1486.[32] Opposition in the north came from Ricardians with Lovell connections. The north had been Richard III's heartland and there was a north–south divide in 1485.[33] Due to the consequences of the 1483 revolt against Richard, Henry was acquainted with the gentry of Wiltshire, Dorset, Somerset and Hampshire, but knew few from the neighbouring counties of Oxfordshire and Berkshire. It was

---

main study of crown–noble relations is J. R. Lander, 'Bonds, Coercion and Fear: Henry VII and the Peerage', in his *Crown and Nobility, 1450–1509* (London, 1976), pp. 267–308.

[26] Luckett, 'Patronage, Violence and Revolt', pp. 152–3.

[27] *Ibid.*, p. 154.

[28] Vergil, p. 33.

[29] Luckett, 'Patronage, Violence and Revolt', pp. 152–3.

[30] H. T. Riley (trans.), *Ingulph's Chronicle of the Abbey of Croyland* (London, 1854), p. 511.

[31] Luckett, 'Patronage, Violence and Revolt', pp. 150–1.

[32] C. H. Williams, 'The Rebellion of Humphrey Stafford in 1486', *EHR*, 43 (1928), pp. 181–9, at pp. 186–7. This is an extremely important article, frequently overlooked. In 1496 (11 H VII), Henry corrected the original attainder of 1488 (3 H VII), which had omitted Lovell, 'to the most perilous ensample of other being of such traitorous myndys' (PRO E159/272, *Recorda*, Mich. 11 H VII, rot. 18).

[33] Luckett, 'Patronage, Violence and Revolt', p. 152; S. O'Connor, 'Francis Lovell and the Rebels of Furness Fells', *The Ricardian*, 7, no. 96 (March, 1987), pp. 366–7.

this that influenced Henry's patronage in these shires, and thus how effective he was in establishing his rule in them.[34] The opinion of the contemporary lawyer Fortescue was that bastard feudalism had been the cause of the troubles of the previous reigns. Henry's military needs, in the absence of a full-time professional army, made the elimination of this institution impractical, and he needed to maintain the private retinues of great lords for his service: they were his army.[35]

Henry VII had modelled his military organisation upon that of Edward III, raising his armies by commissions of array to the counties, and by indenture. During the planning of the invasion of 1497, Henry had specifically requested that his exchequer officers make a search of the precedents of wars in Scotland from the records of the reign of Edward III to Edward IV.[36] In Henry's reign, soldiers were still recruited largely through feudal obligation, especially for service overseas, and magnates brought with them retinues which varied greatly in size and composition. This meant that specialisation and suitability for various tasks within the army were not regulated by a master plan, and balanced units in the field were not possible. Henry did, however, make annual contracts with certain individuals to supply soldiers who were to serve overseas, and who were to be able bodied, properly equipped and fit for war. Henry's internal security problem was countered by raising the militia, which was the traditional constitutional procedure, and this body was supplemented by retinues of lords and gentlemen. At various times he used armed retainers for garrison duty; a move motivated by the need for their loyalty, especially in the north of England, which had provided core support for Richard III, who was considered to be a Yorkshireman. This explains the appointment of Lord Darcy as governor of Berwick, who was instructed by Henry to put 1,000 of his retainers in the garrison, he and his men being specially exempted by royal licence from the laws against retainers. The ordering of the militia could be clumsy and inefficient, and it was more expedient to use local magnates to raise a force.[37]

On 23 December 1488, Henry issued commissions for musters in every shire to the sheriff to call up archers and soldiers under a loyal captain. The terms of the commission of musters suggests that agreements had been made previously with retinue leaders to provide forces.[38] These

---

[34]   Luckett, 'Patronage, Violence and Revolt', pp. 146–7.
[35]   Sir John Fortescue, *The Governance of England: Otherwise Called The Difference Between an Absolute and Limited Monarchy*, ed. C. Plummer (Oxford, 1926), c.9.
[36]   PRO E404/82/2 (53, or alt. no. 134).
[37]   J. Goring, 'The Military Obligations of the English People, 1511–1558' (Ph.D, London, 1955), pp. 6–8, 13.
[38]   Mackie, *The Early Tudors*, p. 209. T. Rymer (ed.), *Foedera, Conventiones, Literae*

shire-levies were supplemented with indentures to provide troops with gentlemen and noblemen, at fixed rates of pay. A lance with his 'custrell' (an armour bearer or attendant) and page were paid 18*d.* a day, a mounted spear with his 'custrell' received 12*d.*; a master gunner wearing half armour 12*d.* and a demi-lance 9*d.* A mounted archer or bill was paid 8*d.*; an archer, gunner, drummer or bill on foot 6*d.* and a trumpeter 10*d.*[39] Conduct money was also paid at the rate of 6*d.* for every 20 miles, and exact arrangements agreed for the payment of wages. A Treasurer of War was appointed to supervise the whole. Henry appointed his trusted friend and servant Lord Willoughby de Broke as marshal to oversee discipline within the army. In Ireland, Henry's army was supplemented by the hiring of local kerns and gallowglasses. There is evidence from the reign of Henry VII that his troops were not always to be trusted, and in 1491 Thomas Troyes esquire, sheriff of Southampton, was paid at the order of Sir Reynold Bray, knight, for employing men to watch the retinue of Sir James Parker, and Sir Sampson Norton, the night before it departed to Brittany, 'to thentent ther shulde noan of the said army dep[ar]te awey'.[40]

The new method of paying the army was instituted by statute in 1492, for the impending invasion of France. Henry ordained that the nobility should have contracts that stated that they should receive conduct money for their retinues at the same rate as that decreed in 1488, with a month's wages in advance, which was to be paid in ready money after embarkation. This system continued in use throughout his successor's reign as it was efficient and ensured that soldiers were able to obtain their own provisions, which were charged upon their pay. As their magnate was also their paymaster, the troops could have confidence that their money would not be embezzled. The captains of the army were under obligation to guarantee the good behaviour of their men, a duty enshrined in the contracts given to them in 1492. They were obliged to ensure that any of their retinue who caused any offence was to be tried before the marshal's court. The captains received copies of the Statutes and Ordinances for War to make certain they understood their duty.[41]

Early in his reign, Henry VII had provided statutory legislation to ensure that captains did not defraud their troops of pay and instituted penalties against soldiers deserting. This procedure lessened the chance of disorder. Henry VIII had problems of discipline in his military hosts, with

---

etc., 20 vols (London, 1704–35), XII, p. 355; Cameron, 'The Giving of Livery', pp. 272–82.

[39] Mackie, *The Early Tudors*, p. 209.

[40] PRO E36/124 f. 47r.

[41] PRO E163/22/3/3, 3/15, 3/23. The army of 1492 was an army of retinues. See Cameron, 'The Giving of Livery', p. 23.

an ever present threat of mutiny, engendered by the fact that his armies were raised by shire levies under officers with whom they were not familiar. The prohibition of livery and maintenance destroyed the loyalty and ties of retainers; thereafter armies were maintained by coercion rather than feudal obedience. Prior to Henry VIII's reign, Oman states that mutinies in the English army were almost unknown.[42]

Henry relied on the crown's right of purveyance, the royal prerogative to take provisions, horses, carts, and other necessary items at his own price, to provision the army sent against the north of England in 1487.[43] Henry used the royal proclamation to order victuallers to provide bread and ale, and food for horses at a reasonable price, to ensure that his army was supplied on its progress. By 1492, when Henry led his troops into France, he changed his method of provisioning the army, and used private individuals who had contracted to supply victuals under a commercial agreement, which contained severe penalties for non-performance. Henry VIII's provisioning contracts were similar to those introduced by his father,

---

[42]   C. W. C. Oman, 'War: The Art of War', in *Medieval England*, ed. H. W.C. Davis (Oxford, 1902, repr. 1928), pp. 110–49, at p. 144.

[43]   C. Cruikshank, *Henry VIII and the Invasion of France* (Stroud, 1990), p. 55. The best account of the history of purveyance is W. R. Jones, 'Purveyance for War and the Community of the Realm in Late Medieval England', *Albion*, 7, (1975), pp. 300–16. How Henry VII provisioned one of his expeditions may be seen in the preparations to invade France in 1492. He issued commissions early in 1492 for the collection and manufacture of military supplies. The writ of 20 January to James Hede ordered him to take houses, land, vessels, wood, fuel, artificers, labourers and workmen for the making of saltpetre and ordnance. In February commissions were issued only to groups of three individuals in midland and southern counties, to obtain 'chariots', horses, sumpter and draught horses, and labourers to transport the king's ordnance. Another February commission to Thomas Woodrow 'clerk of the king's ordnance', and Richard Bright 'purveyor of the king's avenary', sent them to Southampton to buy litter, hay, carts, barrels, nets, slings, brushes, scythes, sickles etc. It was intended that the army would depart on 20 May from Southampton, and Edward Newchurch, a London pewterer was contracted to supply wheat flour, beer, and beef in February for the army leaving three months later (PRO E405/786G, 39N, 40, 41; C.P.R. 1485–95, I, pp. 394–5; PRO E101/72/3, no. 10, 5). Finally the 88 indentures with the nobility for troop musters to be taken were issued between March and June. Muster sites were at Southampton, Winchester and Portsmouth (PRO E101/73/3, 4, 5, 6). It was at this time that the dry dock at Portsmouth was built for £241 13s. 4d. and also the beerhouse, tower and blockhouse, for £2,099 16s. 4d (PRO E36/285, f.73, 79). Three breweries were also built. Timber was bought and carpenters hired on 9 May, when Henry announced his intention to increase the size of his invasion army (Mackie, *The Early Tudors*, pp. 107, 209–10).

but by the end of the Tudor period the demands on supply meant that the state took over much of the responsibility for foodstuff provision. Henry VIII relied more on purveyance than either Henry VII or Elizabeth I. It has been suggested by Charles Cruickshank that this change was due to the growth of the king's household, which numbered some 2,000 court officials and servants, and his desire to see them adequately fed whilst engaged in the French expedition in 1513.[44]

From February 1492 Henry VII prepared to invade France and in May he announced his intention to increase the size of his invasion fleet. The keeper of the Privy Purse had paid £12 5s. 6d. for 'sphere, spherehedes and vamplates' for the king's guard, and Gilwyn ap Rice received £47 6s. 8d. for horses.[45] Henry also bought a new sword case for himself. For the Sluys campaign in July, the treasurer of Calais, Sir John Turbervyle, was provided with £141 6s. 8d. for 1,885 'jaquettes' for the troops. Sluys fell in October. On the 28th the king had reached Greenwich, and the next day he received his new 'hede peces' decorated with 'golde, perle and stone', from John Shawe, the king's goldsmith and alderman of London, who was paid £1,970 7s. 9d.[46] This sum purchased six 'salettes, horse harneys, and plate' which he had made, and other items obtained by him for the king.[47] When Henry finally crossed the channel in a ship called The Swan, with his minstrels and Dego the Spanish fool, arriving in Calais at 11 p.m. on 2 October, it has been claimed that he had caused the largest army ever to have left England to be sent to France. Apart from the king's own ships, 335 Dutch and 300 English ships transported over 14,000 English troops. Charles VIII had not expected Henry to invade, and he employed diplomacy to make a peaceful settlement, which was concluded on 27 October, after Henry had laid siege to Boulogne. The reputation of English soldiers since the Hundred Years War remained untarnished. 'In the 1490s the French were said to quake at the thought of English troops entering their country against them.'[48] According to Froissart the English were

---

[44] Cruickshank, Henry VIII and the Invasion of France, p. 55. An alternative view may, however, be taken. Contracts with individuals rely upon the ability of the crown to pay for its purchases within a short and regulated period, purveyance does not. Henry VIII's increasing debt may have influenced this volte-face in the system of provisioning.

[45] At Shene on 7 and 8 May.

[46] PRO E36/285 f. 74. On 12 August John Warne, butterer of Calais, was sent a letter of supply from Westminster for beer, oats, cheese and beer – and a new harp case for James Hides.

[47] PRO E404/81 (190 or alt. no. 79). Westminster 29 Oct. 7 H VII.

[48] Cameron, The Early Tudors, p. 23, who gives a figure of 12,680 men going to France with the army. This figure is based upon The King's Retinue into France Whereof the Fourth Part to be on Horseback, and the Other to be on Foot at his Wage

feared because of their cut and burn policies, which caused irreparable harm to the French countryside.[49] Henry, however, was more inclined to peace than war and the treaty of Étaples of 1492 marked the end of hostilities with France.

During the Scottish campaign, which began in July 1497, the Scottish king also refused to engage the English troops but in true chivalric tradition challenged the English commander, Surrey, to single combat, *puissance against puissance* or hand to hand for the gage of Berwick. Surrey declined, as Berwick, he said, belonged to his master.[50] Finally diplomacy achieved a seven-year truce in September. Chivalry and diplomacy went hand in hand. Henry's diplomatic policies, culminating in the truce of 1502, were designed to promote lasting Anglo-Scottish peace. Henry never initiated warfare against Scotland; the campaign of 1496–7 was started by James IV, who supported Perkin Warbeck in the hope of recovering Berwick, which had been retaken by Edward IV in 1482.

It was normal practice for armies to be raised as and when needed. Wars were often planned in advance, and this procedure was usually adequate, though Henry VII was unprepared for Lovell's rebellion in 1486 and was forced to employ his own retinue and the Yeomen of the Guard to suppress it.[51] It is surprising that Henry VII did not thereafter institute a standing army, as on the continent during his reign military affairs were being transformed by the development of standing armies, and the use of the arquebus in preference to the crossbow. Henry VII valued and preferred English archers to other foot soldiers. He regulated the price of yew wood, a large proportion of which was imported by Italians, but did not all originate in Italy as claimed by Mackie.[52] Unshaped yew originating from the Baltic was imported by both the Italians and the Hanse in accordance with legislation that provided for a certain number of bows to be brought with every ton of merchandise. Henry was determined to ensure the continuance of England's superiority in the use of the longbow,

---

(Sir William Le Neve's extracts of Burton Abbey Register, f. 43. B.M. Stowe 440 fol. 79–81); I. Arthurson, *The Perkin Warbeck Conspiracy, 1491–1499* (Gloucester, 1994), p. 5, n. 7; A. Goodman, *The Wars of the Roses* (London, 1981), p. 108.

[49] R. W. Kaeuper, *War, Justice, and Public Order: England and France in the Later Middle Ages* (Oxford, 1988).

[50] Mackie, *The Early Tudors*, p. 147. Hall, p. 481.

[51] Cruickshank, *Henry VIII and the Invasion of France*, p. 165, n. 16. Vergil, *Anglia Historia*, p. 11.

[52] Mackie, *The Early Tudors*, p. 209; M. E. Bratchel, 'Alien Merchant Communities, 1500–1550' (Ph.D. thesis, Cambridge, 1975), p. 140. For bow staves, PRO E404/79/110 (alt. no. 293) 1 Henry VII; E404/80/360; 6 Henry VII; E404/81/96, 97, 7 Henry VII.

although he and his nobles preferred to use crossbows for sport and pleasure. An act of Henry VII had restricted the use of crossbows to nobles and to the wealthy.[53]

Henry's policies remained cautious. There were only two military bodies in England which received continuous finance from the crown, and which might be compared to a standing army. These were the garrison of the east march against Scotland and the Calais garrison.[54] At various times special troops were sent over to Calais; these were known as 'the crew', the split between garrison and crew occurring sometime in the reign of Edward IV.[55] The Calais garrison numbered about 600 men, although the Venetian ambassador in 1500 gives a figure of 800. In the most recent analysis of Calais, David Grummitt gives a total of 700 men in peacetime, and 1,000 in times of crisis.[56] From the reign of Edward IV the men of the Calais garrison included members of gentry and mercantile families, who were paid their fee of 6d. a day like ordinary archers. Control of Calais was vital in the struggle between Lancaster and York. Late in 1484 after the duke of Buckingham's revolt, and the defection of the lieutenant of Hammes to Henry Tudor, Richard III abandoned continuity from the previous reign in the appointment of Calais officers and replaced all these men, except those of Lord Dinham, by knights of the body; in the march the office of the Captain of Calais was revived and given to Richard's bastard son John.[57] Sir

[53] Mackie, *The Early Tudors*, p. 209; *Statutes of the Realm*, ii, 649, 19 H VII c.2, ii. 521, 3 H VII c.13.

[54] The wages of the captain and soldiers of Calais were financed from 1473 (in the reign of Edward IV), by the payment of about £10,000 a year from the wool Staple of Calais, which had been granted the customs duties on wool for this purpose. The king provided an armed convoy for the wool fleets sailing to Calais. *Rotuli Parliamentorum*, Record Commission (London, 1777), VI, pp. 55–61. In the reign of Henry VII the cost of the garrison at Calais was £10,022 4s 8d. The Calais garrison included 24 or more gunners. See PRO E404/79/188 (7 July, 1487), 80/642 (16 July, 1490), 80/364 (6 July, 1492), E405/78 m.40 (July, 1492). A book of Ordinances for Calais survives (PRO E101/198/13). I am grateful to David Grummitt for these references. A permanent military garrison was maintained at Berwick from 1482; M. Hicks, *Bastard Feudalism* (London, 1995), p. 185.

[55] PRO E159/255 Hill 18 E.IV.m.20 ff. In 1477, the wages of a crew sent to Calais amounted to £3,599 p.a. and included men-at-arms at 18d. a day, mounted men at 8d., footmen at 6d., mounted men with lances, and footmen with lances; G. L. Harriss, 'The Struggle for Calais: An Aspect of the Rivalry between Lancaster and York (1450–60)', *EHR*, 75 (1960), pp. 30–53.

[56] D. Grummitt, 'Bastard Feudalism and the Defence of Calais, 1455–1547' (unpublished paper given at the Institute of Historical Research, 29 Feb. 1996).

[57] *Ibid.*

James Blount took the garrison of Hammes with him to support Henry Tudor. Prior to the battle of Bosworth, over two hundred of the Calais garrison, who had expected George, duke of Clarence's son to inherit, fled to Flanders and became mercenaries, fighting for Maximilian, archduke of Austria, at Thérouanne in 1486.[58] They then fought for Margaret of Burgundy, under John, earl of Lincoln and Lord Lovell at the battle of East Stoke, where they were annihilated.[59] It is thus apparent that captains could maintain a personal following, and that military resources in Calais could threaten the security of the crown.

In relation to Calais, Henry was not an innovator but a manipulator. After Bosworth he extended his authority based on bastard feudalism in both the town and marches of Calais. Those who had served him in exile became office holders. Henry challenged bastard feudal relations within the pale; Lord Daubeney was appointed as captain, but the king himself retained the members of the Calais garrison independently of Daubeney and his captains. Henry also extended retaining in the town and marches with life annuities, which according to Grummitt were more stable than short term indentures for war. As Henry achieved more domestic stability and peace, he relaxed bastard feudalism in Calais and changed organisation in the provinces; Calais appointments relied on patronage at court rather than military need. With the resolution of the Perkin Warbeck crisis, Calais no longer faced the threat of warfare; foreign invasion was not a reality. Henry VII's organisation and administration of the Calais garrison differed little from his predecessors, but with the defection of several Calais officers to Perkin Warbeck, it was necessary to take complete stock of the king's Calais possessions and servants with a view to re-organisation.[60] In the muster roll of 1502 all the men retained by Henry retained a small number of men themselves. Henry VII made himself the sole beneficiary of bastard feudalism in Calais.

On the continent before the reign of Henry VII, men-at-arms had begun once more to make extensive use of cavalry rather than dismounting for battle as had been prevalent in the later stages of the Hundred Years War. The difference between Henry VIII's military organisation and that of

---

[58] Arthurson, *The Perkin Warbeck Conspiracy*, p. 6, n. 9; C. S. L. Davis, 'John Morton, the Holy See and the Accession of Henry VII', *EHR*, 102 (1987), pp. 1–30, at p. 27 and n. 3.
[59] Arthurson, *The Perkin Warbeck Conspiracy*, p. 6, n. 11; O'Connor, 'Francis Lovel and the Rebels of Furness Fells', pp. 366–70; M. Bennett, *Lambert Simnel and the Battle of Stoke* (Gloucester, 1987), p. 91.
[60] Henry VII reorganised the financial procedures relating to Calais. Accounts for war, for example, were to be rendered to the royal chamber rather than to the exchequer as previously (PRO E101/414/6, f. 22).

his father's was that his knights fought on horseback in formation. He also took an interest in firepower, causing bronze rather than iron cannons to be produced in his foundry, and the Germans Peter of Köln and Peter Baude made exploding shells for him which were described in 1543 as containing fireworks. In the second half of his reign he hired Germans and other mercenaries armed with *calivers* and arquebuses, yet the bow was still of primary importance. Henry VII rarely hired mercenaries, although in 1492 he paid a Dutch captain £10 for 155 'men of werre of Holland'.[61]

Henry VIII instituted his own armourer's workshop, manned by men trained on the continent, who in documents are often called Germans. Henry VIII's Greenwich workmen were his own servants, wearing his livery and being paid from the Privy Purse.[62] The innovations of Henry VIII with regard to his ordnance were merely a continuation of the policies his father had instituted under the office of the Master of the Ordnance in the Tower of London from the first year of his reign. A Master of the Ordnance had been created by Henry VI in 1456, who appointed John Judde, merchant of London. Fortescue considered that the creation of what he calls 'Master General of Ordnance' in 1483 was of primary importance in the history of the army. Oman also followed Fortescue in suggesting that the office of Master General of the Ordnance was instituted in 1483, and the Tower of London used as an arsenal. Hooker claims that Fortescue's opinion is misguided, as ordnance had little practical consequence in Henry's wars because 'technique was faulty and transport difficult'. If this statement is correct it is hard to understand Henry VII's considerable investment in ordnance, and whilst artillery was of limited importance in Henry's field campaigns, it was used by his navy, in his castles, and in towns such as Winchelsea. The distribution and often manufacture of the ordnance, was co-ordinated from the Tower of London, under the authority of the Master of the Ordnance.[63]

Henry VII's need for shot and ironware for his war against the Scots may have been the main reason for the building of the ironworks in Ashdown Forest. The new method of casting iron was, according to Lower,

[61] Hooker, 'Organisation and Supply of the Tudor Military', p. 23; Oman, 'War: The Art of War', pp. 110–49; PRO E404/81/1.

[62] K. Watts, 'Henry VII and the Founding of the Greenwich Armouries', in D. Starkey (ed.), *Henry VIII: A European Court in England* (London, 1991), pp. 42–6.

[63] S. Bentley (ed.), *Excerpta Historica* (London, 1833), pp. 10–11. O. F. G. Hogg, 'The Passing of a Great Office', *Journal of the Royal Artillery*, LXXIII, n. 2 (1946), pp. 255–60; Oman, 'War: The Art of War', pp. 110–49; Fortescue, *A History of the British Army*, I, pp. 208–10; Hooker, 'Organisation and Supply of the Tudor Military', pp. 19–20.

imported from France, and recent research by Brian Awty has confirmed that ironworkers came from the Netherlands. In particular significant numbers of French ironworkers from the Pays de Bray, south of Dieppe, settled in the Sussex Weald from the 1490s.[64] The use of iron gunstones, in addition to the traditional stone gunstones also made in Sussex, was a significant military development in Henry's reign. Iron gunstones were difficult to manufacture and they had a reputation of shattering. The immigration into England after the Hundred Years War of continental iron-workers was of great importance for the history of English gunfounding and the manufacture of projectiles. Henry was also a pioneer in the English manufacture of bronze guns of varying sizes, and he imported Breton gunfounders to work for him in manufacturing in the Tower of London. Rather than relying totally on imported gunpowder of dubious quality, Henry also appointed manufacturers of gunpowder to serve in his Ordnance. Although large quantities of ingredients for explosives were imported, he was able to ensure that the mixtures would be suitable for his guns. Purity was very important. Gunpowder was corned, using vinegar, for example, which coated the particles with oxygen allowing even combustion. Saltpetre was usually mixed with the other ingredients immediately prior to use. Cannon balls made of cast iron were used in medium sized or small guns, but lead was the preferred metal, as cast iron was often of poor quality. These projectiles could be made at the battlefield; smiths and forges travelled with the artillery train, but they were usually made at an arsenal and transported to their place of use.[65]

Vincent Tuetuler had been king's armourer to Edward IV, Edward V, and Richard III; Henry VII re-appointed him on 20 February 1486 at an annual fee of £20.[66] In 1489 he was paid £8 to provide a 'complete herneys' which was delivered to Earl Boghan, by the king's commission, and the following year received £22 for more 'harneys'.[67] In 1493 his wife

[64] M. A. Lower, 'Historical and Archaeological Notices of the Iron Wares in the County of Sussex', *Sussex Archaeological Collections*, II, 1849, pp. 169–229; B. Awty, 'The Continental Origins of Wealden Ironworkers', *Economic History Review*, 2nd ser. 34 (1981), pp. 524–59.

[65] On gunpowder, see P. Contamine, *War in the Middle Ages*, trans. M. Jones (Oxford, 1984).

[66] PRO E36/125 f.75. Richard III acquired armour for the armoury at the Tower of London, and in the first year of his reign caused his servant Robert Lilborne to buy in Sandwich, from Lewes de Grymaldes, merchant of Genoa, and Gillam de Britayne, merchant of Brittany, 168 harness complete for 5 marks a harness, that is £560 in total. This armour was then delivered into the Tower by the king's servant John Stokes. (PRO E404/78/2 (33); writ payment of £340 6 Feb. I R III).

[67] PRO E404/79 (102), 6 May, 3 H VII; E404/80 (141), 4 Dec., 4 H VII.

Antonia signed for the salary owing to him; when he died in 1504 the king's servant, John De Pounde, known as Crochet, was given the office at the same fee.[68] In 1503 Crochet the armourer had been provided with 20*s* for his house rent.[69] John Van Howden, another man described as an armourer, was appointed in 1501,[70] but in 1502 he was described as a *bombardorum* (sic), otherwise *vibreltor*, that is a gunner, and was granted the place in service held by Clays van Harlam.[71] Another man, William Rabarough, is described in 1486 as *armario* of the king, at a fee of 6*d*. a day. It appears that the position of an armourer could describe more than an artisan involved in the manufacture of harness. Another king's servant making defensive armour was the king's *brigandynmaker*.[72] Raufe de Pontieu, of the king's retinue, was rewarded with this post at £10 per annum, from June 1486.[73] He was still in office in 1508.[74] Peter Wrayton was custodian of the beds and harness, or armoury, in the Tower of London in 1492, and Hugh Aynsley, yeoman, held the same position in the castle of Windsor, from at least 1490.[75]

Sir Charles Oman believed it was Henry VIII who was the first English sovereign to prescribe a fixed uniform for his army. According to his ordinance of 1543 troops were to wear blue coats trimmed with red, with the red cross, and parti-coloured breeches, red and blue, without any livery badges. This uniform was finished with a plain breast and back piece, possibly a leather jack and a steel cap. In previous reigns, Oman claimed, the wearing of the red cross of St George was considered sufficient. But in 1490, the keeper of the king's great wardrobe was paid £25 for 1,000 jackets of white cloth with red crosses, costing 14*d*. each, for the king's army going to Brittany.[76] In his campaigns against France and Scotland, Henry VII provided his army with protective body armour in the traditional

[68]   PRO E404/84/3 (8), 5 Feb., 19 H VII.
[69]   PRO E36/123, 1 Oct.–1 Jan., 18 H VII.
[70]   PRO E404/82 (137), 11 July, 16 H VII [1501]; writ 28 May, 18 H VII.
[71]   PRO E404/84/1 (72), 11 July, 16 H VII [1501]; writ 24 April, 17 H VII [1502].
[72]   PRO E404/79 (7); 23 April, 3 H VII.
[73]   PRO E36/124, f.71; E405/75, f. 15, 20 June, 1 H VII [1486].
[74]   PRO E404/86/2 (4 or alt. no. 126).
[75]   PRO E36/125 f.54, Easter, 7 H VII; E36/124 f.43r, Easter, 5 H VII.
[76]   Oman, 'War: The Art of War', p. 145; PRO E36/124, Easter, 5 H VII. Defensive padded jackets, or jacks, usually lined with iron plates, were commonly worn by English soldiers. These were considered the minimum suitable array for the army, and offered protection from arrows and hand weapons. In 1490 the army sent to Brittany was provided with a total of 2,406 white jackets with a red cross upon them made by several London tailors. (PRO E404/80/383, 4 May 5 H VII).

livery of England. Towards the end of his reign he also provided his marine archers who served on his two most important ships, the *Regent* and the *Sovereign*, with his personal livery of green and white. The delivery at Easter 1495 by Henry Guissenham, from the Keeper of the Wardrobe, of 700 white and green woollen jackets costing £57 16s. 4d., which were provided for the use of Stephen Bull and his company at sea the following August, marks a development in the extension of the wearing of royal livery. Ordinary soldiers usually wore white coats, but Henry's special soldiers were dressed in his livery of white and green.[77] The men who rowed his royal barge along the Thames were also dressed in these colours. When an ambassadorial party of several hundred Danes suffered the loss of their ship, goods and clothes at the hands of English subjects who attacked them off the eastern coast of England and forcibly brought the nobles and gentlemen ashore, Henry, as a matter of honour, personally recompensed them and provided clothes for the most important men in his own livery of green and white. The use of this livery may also have served for protection and as a safe-conduct during their enforced six-week stay in England.[78] Only those men who were closest to the king could wear his colours. Henry VIII inherited this livery from his father, but chose not to extend its use to his army.

To Oman, the military importance of Henry VII's reign consisted rather in what he undid than in what he accomplished. His great feat was the abolition of 'Livery and Maintenance'; the 'household men and badged retainers, who made rebellion so easy, were an abomination to him. He made the giving of liveries and making of private treaties and agreements penal.' A prominent case was that of the earl of Oxford who was heavily fined for having too many retainers wearing the De Vere silver mullet badge. Oman's opinion was that from the tactical point of view Henry's reign was a continuation on a small scale of the Wars of the Roses and more recent historians have reiterated this view, notably Anthony Goodman and Ian Arthurson.[79] Oman further claimed that in the forms of

---

[77] Mackie, *The Early Tudors*, p. 208.

[78] In August 1490, a Danish knight was captured at sea by William Vampage with 224 of his retinued men and 82 others. As this was against a peace treaty, Henry VII decided generosity was necessary, and he transported them from Sandwich to London, where they waited five weeks, whilst he provided them with arms and habiliments of war, 'togas', hose, shoes, doublets, smocks, and frieze cloth for their frocks, and financial restitution. His largesse cost £757 14s. 11½d. Significantly, the most important of these men were dressed in Henry's own livery of white and green (PRO E405/78 f.21, Mich. 6 H VII; E404/80/644–5, Sept. 1490).

[79] Oman, 'War: The Art of War', p. 141; Goodman, *The Wars of the Roses*; Arthurson, *The Perkin Warbeck Conspiracy*, p. 238.

battle, the use of arms and armour, and the arraying of troops, there was little change in Henry's reign; men-at-arms still dismounted to fight, and the archers were positioned at the wings in battle. At the battle of Stoke, bow and bill prevailed over the pikes and hand-guns of the earl of Lincoln's German mercenaries and the Irish javelin-men of Fitzgerald, while at Blackheath, it was the lack of artillery on the part of Lord Audley and the Cornishmen that caused their defeat.. It was the 'thundering discharges of the royal train of cannon', unchallenged by the rebels, which 'settled the day'.[80] On Lord Morley's expedition to Flanders in 1491, the archers performed well against the French, and the English captured the French camp near Dixmude. Cannon did not play any significant part in Henry's English warfare, or in Lord Morley's campaign at Dixmude, but artillery was present at the siege of Boulogne and in Ireland.[81]

Henry was a king who preferred the old ways; 'he merely built upon the foundations provided by the Yorkists and adapted their policies to suit his circumstances'.[82] Ross has demonstrated that Edward IV and Henry VII were very different men, whose methods of and successes in government were not necessarily similar, while to Chrimes, Henry was not 'a creator, but rather a stabiliser' and for this stands 'pre-eminent among British monarchs'.[83] Henry is no longer to be seen as Mackie's 'new monarch', but as a great administrator whose achievement was the enforcement of the law, reinforced by remedial legislation where necessary.[84]

Henry's triumph at Bosworth marks a major turning-point in English history. His personal direction of government created institutions capable of providing ministers whose control over the state provided the Tudor dynasty with the ability to maintain that peace, stability and security initiated by Henry VII. Henry won the battle of Stoke in 1487 without any loss of life of noble or gentleman, using a vanguard comprising an elite force of household men led by experienced commanders such as John de Vere, earl of Oxford. Henry's successes in battle have been attributed to his wise choice of commanders. Grant maintains that 'Henry won and kept his throne, partly at least because he was successful, and probably good at

---

[80] Oman, 'War: The Art of War'.

[81] Mackie, *The Early Tudors*, p. 208–9.

[82] R. L. Storey, *The Reign of Henry VII* (London, 1968), pp. 66–91; Cameron, 'The Giving of Livery', p. 17 and n.3.

[83] C. D. Ross, 'The Reign of Edward IV', in S. B. Chrimes, C. D. Ross and R. A. Griffiths (eds), *Fifteenth Century England, 1399–1509* (Manchester, 1972), pp. 49–66; S. B. Chrimes, *Lancastrians, Yorkists and Henry VII* (London, 1966), p. 322.

[84] Cameron, 'The Giving of Livery', p. 28.

military affairs'.[85] Secondly, Henry maintained internal security through thwarting conspiracies by the use of informers. Unlike his predecessors from the reign of Henry VI onwards, Henry, perhaps learning from their example, did not employ the use of pre-emptive execution immediately after Bosworth, and this explains, Grant argues, why Henry's dynasty survived.[86]

Henry VII himself appears as a conservative and cautious king who used traditional heraldic images, conventional English Arthurian prophecy (which had been utilised by Edward IV to promote his royal standing within continental politics), and traditional crown financial procedures and legal processes to found his Tudor dynasty.[87] Yet Henry's subtle changes in government procedure and financial institutions, coupled with his military innovations, belie the image he presented to his subjects. His reign can be regarded as revolutionary in many ways.

It is apparent that Henry attempted to be a chivalric and pious king. Throughout the reign, the undercurrents of chivalry and diplomacy were of primary importance.[88] Yet Henry's diplomatic achievements have failed to attain the reputation they deserve, and his reign has been marked by criticism of his parsimony and cruelty. Neither has Henry been seen as a great military leader, keen to engage in battle. Rather he has been viewed as

---

[85]   Grant, *Henry VII*, p. 5; on Stoke, see Bennett, *Lambert Simnel and the Battle of Stoke*.

[86]   Grant, *Henry VII*, p. 8.

[87]   Wolffe has confirmed that so far as financial policy is concerned, this assessment of Henry is accurate: B. P. Wolffe, 'Henry VII's Land Revenues and Chamber Finance', *EHR*, 79 (1964), pp. 225–54; *idem, The Crown Lands, 1461–1536* (London, 1970). In the area of feudalism J. G. Bellamy, *Bastard Feudalism and the Law* (London, 1989), has shown this assessment to be valid, but a recent criticism of Bellamy may be found in M. Hicks, *Bastard Feudalism* (London, 1995), pp. 216–17. On the subject of royal propaganda see A. Allan, 'Yorkist Propaganda: Pedigree, Prophecy and the British History in the Reign of Edward IV', in C. Ross (ed.), *Patronage, Pedigree and Power in Later Medieval England* (Gloucester, 1979), pp. 171–92; *idem*, 'Royal Propaganda and the Proclamations of Edward IV', *BIHR*, 59 (1986), pp. 145–54; A. Gransden, 'Propaganda in English Medieval Historiography', *JMH*, 1 (1975), pp. 363–82.

[88]   On chivalry in the reign of Henry VII, see S. J. Gunn, 'Chivalry and the Politics of the Early Tudor Court', in *Chivalry in the Renaissance*, ed. S. Anglo (Woodbridge, 1990), pp. 107–28; R. A. Griffiths, 'Henry Tudor: The Training of a King', *Huntington Library Quarterly*, 49 (1986), pp. 197–218; M. H. Keen, 'Chivalry, Heralds, and History', in R. H. C. Davis and J. M. Wallace-Hadrill (eds), *The Writing of History in the Middle Ages: Essays Presented to Richard William Southern* (Oxford, 1981), pp. 393–414. See also S. Anglo, *Spectacle, Pageantry and Early Tudor Policy* (Oxford, 1969), pp. 52–97; and *idem, Images of Tudor Kingship* (London, 1972), and bibliography there cited.

unwilling to prosecute war, and his Scottish and French campaigns as being insincere, a sham. This view does not accord, however, with the fact that Henry maintained the largest ever English medieval army, and with his enormous financial investment in the English navy.[89] Only in the foundation of the Royal Bodyguard did Henry successfully introduce a French royal model into England, although there are numerous indications in the accounts of chroniclers and diplomatic reports that he intended to follow the example of the French court wherever possible. His attempts to introduce changes into English royal government were, according to his biographers, unsuccessful due to resistance from both his councillors and parliament. His changes in military organisation and structure were, however, uncontested and accepted.

Henry VII introduced numerous innovations concerning military organisation into England. These included the manufacture of iron gunstones and bronze cannons within England.[90] He increased royal employment of foreigners skilled in the use of hand-guns as his guard, as gunners to maintain and fire his artillery, and as manufacturers of gunpowder and body armour. Henry also introduced innovations in the use of gunners in warfare. Gunners accompanied the king at Kenilworth, whilst he awaited attack from the adherents of Perkin Warbeck. Henry introduced changes in the provisioning of the army and navy. For example he kept an artillery store at Greenwich from which guns, bows and arrows supplied the navy.[91] Henry replaced the system of purveyance for both the army and navy, and contracted directly with victuallers to supply goods and foodstuffs.

---

[89] The largest army previously sent to France was in July 1475 by Edward IV, which comprised 11,000 troops. Henry's army sent to France was at least 12,000 strong. See C. Ross, *Edward IV* (London, 1974), pp. 226–39, 295.

[90] For Henry's ordnance see H. L. Blackmore, *The Armouries of the Tower of London*, I, *Ordnance* (H.M.S.O., London, 1976). Bronze was the superior metal for constructing cannons, manufactured by casting at a foundry, but because of the expense, these weapons were usually made smaller. These were stronger, more reliable, lighter and more easily transported than iron artillery. Forged iron cannons, bound by rings, were the most common form of gunpowder weapons, but this method of production was not suitable for making hand-held guns, which were usually of cast iron or bronze.

[91] Mackie, *The Early Tudors*, p. 211; M. Oppenheim, *Accounts and Inventories of Henry VII* (Navy Records Society, 1896), p. 19, n. 2. The Elizabethan serpentine weighed about 400 *lbs* and fired a 5⅓ *oz* ball with about 5½ *lbs* powder. The largest naval guns, serpentines, were used on board Henry's ships and were mostly made of iron, though some were of brass. These breach-loaders weighed about 300 *lbs*, firing shot of about a quarter of a pound with a similar weight of powder.

254

In conclusion, Henry VII's military innovations were precursors of the developments in the organisation of, and technical improvements in, Henry VIII's military affairs. Henry VII should be regarded as laying the foundations for his heir's restructuring of the English army.

War and Domesday Waste

JOHN PALMER

According to Marc Bloch, 'one of the fundamental factors of European civilisation' was its immunity from wholesale and repeated destruction of the countryside after the tenth century. During the preceding centuries, the ravaging of the land over large areas of Europe had been the material condition for the emergence of feudalism, 'born in the midst of an infinitely troubled epoch, and in some measure ... the child of those troubles themselves'. Repeatedly ravaged by 'hordes from without', 'the cultivated land suffered disastrously, often being reduced to desert'. This was 'undoubtedly the most widespread and enduring effect' of the barbarian invasions, leaving 'a reduced population ... confronted by vast stretches of land, formerly cultivated, but now once more reduced to scrub'.[1]

Bloch's thesis has not commanded general assent. Although it is now widely accepted that the principal strategy of medieval commanders was to lay waste the countryside,[2] and although the early medieval economy was overwhelmingly agrarian, largely unprotected by fortifications, and often undefended by armies, some historians have remained sceptical of the ability of medieval armies to cause destruction on anything like the scale that Bloch envisaged, even where the will to destroy was strong and cultural restraints minimal. As one distinguished historian complained, some of his contemporaries portrayed the Vikings – one of the principal 'hordes from without' – as 'little more than groups of long-haired tourists who occasionally roughed up the natives', or even as A Good Thing for native societies and their economies.[3]

Was Bloch's view of the destructive capability of medieval warfare nearer the truth? The debate has been inconclusive, all the evidence which has been brought to bear being insufficient, ambiguous or untrustworthy.

---

[1]   M. Bloch, *Feudal Europe*, 2nd edn (London, 1962), pp. 3, 56, 39, 40.

[2]   This has now achieved the status of a truism. See, among much else, M. J. Strickland, *War and Chivalry. The Conduct and Perception of War in England and Normandy, 1066–1217* (Cambridge, 1996), pp. 258–90; *Anglo-Norman Warfare*, ed. M. J. Strickland (Woodbridge, 1992), pp. 150–5, 199–201, 214–17, 232–4; and S. Morillo, *Warfare under the Anglo-Norman Kings 1066–1135* (Woodbridge, 1994), pp. 98–102.

[3]   J. M. Wallace-Hadrill, *Early Medieval History* (Oxford, 1975), p. 220.

256

But there is one source which has not been pressed into service which offers a real prospect of providing answers. Domesday Book records over 2,000 wasted manors, encompassing more than half a million acres or 1,000 square miles of devastated countryside.[4] Information about these 2,000 manors, moreover, is recorded for two, sometimes three dates, spanning two decades, thereby permitting estimates of the scale of the damage inflicted and of the extent of any subsequent recovery. In addition, Domesday England itself is well-suited to illuminate the impact of early medieval warfare, being – like the continent in the first feudal age – a predominantly agrarian country, largely unfortified, often undefended by local forces, and extensively ravaged by invading armies, savagely so on occasions if we are to believe the native chroniclers.

There are, however, two problems with the data, and both are fundamental: is the waste recorded in Domesday Book real, physical waste; and, if so, is it the result of war? Although many historians have assumed the waste to mean physical devastation and the usual cause to be warfare, Domesday Book itself is rarely explicit on either matter. Both conclusions are therefore open to question, and both have been forcefully challenged, notably in relation to the Yorkshire folios, where the bulk of the waste is recorded. Most of this essay will therefore be devoted to the 'harrying of the north'; but before this is examined in detail, a few preliminary observations on Domesday waste in general are necessary.

The first problem with Domesday waste is that it is rarely explained in the text, which usually contents itself with a terse *wasta, wasta fuit*, or *wasta est*. There are, however, a substantial number of entries which implicitly define waste by noting exceptions to it. Among the ten dependencies of Easingwold, for instance, there were 'only 2 villagers and 4 smallholders with 1½ ploughs' on land for 20 ploughs; 'the rest of the land is waste'. Similarly, the 18 dependencies of Pickering had 'only 10 villagers with 2 ploughs' on land for 27 ploughs; 'the rest waste'. The 14 dependencies of Bridlington could muster 'only 3 villagers and 1 freeman with 1½ ploughs' on land for 30 ploughs, the rest being waste. Northallerton and its dependencies had once had 116 freemen and 66 villagers sharing 80 ploughs; but in 1086 it was waste and was entirely without population or ploughs. South Loftus and its 13 dependencies, worth £48 before 1066 but 'now nothing', could muster only a single villager with one plough on land for 34 ploughs.[5] And so on.[6] Overwhelmingly, the implication of such

---

4   H. C. Darby, *Domesday England* (Cambridge, 1977), pp. 232–59, provides a useful overview of the data and some of the problems it poses.

5   DB: *Yorks.*, 1Y1; 1Y4; 1Y11; 1Y2; 4N2.

6   *Domesday Book seu hiber Consualis Wilhelmi Primi Regis Angliae*, ed. A. Earley, 2 vols (1783); vols III, IV, ed. H. Ellis (1816) (hereafter DB). There are three

entries is that waste meant that there were no men, no plough teams, and no other resources of any consequence.

The reservation – 'of any consequence' – needs emphasis. Too much has been made of the fact that waste manors occasionally had residual values.[7] But the significant feature of those manors described as waste but which actually had some resources is how meagre these were. There were more than 500 manors in Yorkshire described as waste without qualification. Their combined carucage was over 2,600, greater than that of all but half-a-dozen counties. Yet their total resources amounted to two teams, five men, and some minor appurtenances, valued at less than £7. An area the size of a large county populated by just 5 families and 16 oxen scarcely supports the idea that waste does not mean what it appears to mean.[8]

If the normal meaning of waste is uninhabited and uncultivated land, then in the circumstances of the Norman Conquest the most common cause is likely to have been physical destruction, the result of war. The broad national pattern to the distribution of waste strongly supports this conclusion.

Domesday Book records over 2,000 waste holdings distributed among 30 counties, totalling 5,338 hides.[9] Most of these counties, however, had modest amounts of waste, 23 of them accounting for less than 5% of the total. The cause of such isolated or insignificant occurrences of wasted manors cannot be determined. Lincolnshire offers a good illustration of this. The bare statistics of waste in the county – 72 occurrences in 57 vills – might suggest extensive damage and the passage of armies, and Darby's map certainly conveys that impression. But the impression may well be misleading. The wasted holdings are dispersed and they are tiny, averaging

---

dozen such entries in the Yorkshire text, and more in those for Herefordshire and Shropshire.

[7] W. E. Wightman, 'The Significance of "Waste" in the Yorkshire Domesday', *Northern History*, 10 (1975), pp. 55–71, esp. pp. 57–8; D. M. Palliser, 'Domesday Book and the "Harrying of the North"', *Northern History*, 29 (1993), pp. 1–23, esp. p. 11; *idem*, 'An Introduction to the Yorkshire Domesday', *The Yorkshire Domesday*, ed. A. Williams (London, Alecto, 1992), pp. 1–38, esp. pp. 35–6.

[8] Both teams and four of the five men, may in fact not have been intended to be included among the waste: the entry is ambiguous (DB: *Yorks*, 5W34: Cundall). The 1086 value is a mere 1% of the TRE figure, itself almost certainly seriously understated. See note 10 for a discussion of the methodology used for assessing waste.

[9] 2,074 holdings to be precise, if synonyms for waste (e.g. nothing) are included.

a mere third of a hide.[10] Whilst it is possible that much of this waste represents the residual effects of the Conqueror's march from York to Cambridge via Lincoln in 1068, or of military activity in north Lincolnshire in 1069–70, it would be foolhardy to argue the case from such fragile evidence.[11]

It is, therefore, to the counties with significant concentrations of waste that we must look for the evidence of military activity. Among these, seven counties stand out, with Yorkshire well to the front. The losses in Yorkshire were truly staggering, representing more than two-thirds of the total. A long way behind come Shropshire, Herefordshire, and Cheshire, and some distance behind these, Staffordshire, Sussex, and Derbyshire. This list is immediately identifiable as a list of the counties which had borne the brunt of military activity in previous decades: the border counties raided by the Welsh; Yorkshire, Cheshire, Shropshire, Derbyshire, and Staffordshire, harried in the winter of 1069–70;[12] and Sussex, which suffered the first impact of the Norman armies, the battle of Hastings, and its immediate aftermath.

The strength of the correlation between areas of known military activity and the distribution of waste is even more apparent if the data is broken down chronologically. All recorded waste for 1066, for instance, is along the Welsh border. The figures in Table 1[13] refer to waste which is unambiguously stated as having occurred before 1066. They therefore understate the amount of waste in 1066 because many waste entries simply

---

10   The county total – 25 hides – is exceeded by many single waste manors in Yorkshire. The largest waste manor was Wrangle (2 hides), where the waste was due to the sea. See H. C. Darby, *The Domesday Geography of Eastern England* (3rd edn, Cambridge, 1971), pp. 70–3, for a discussion and distribution map. As the example of Lincolnshire shows, Darby's methodology in dealing with waste, which is to count the holdings and vills and plot them as either wholly or partially wasted vills, does not give due weight to the huge disproportion in the size of manors and vills. For this reason I have used hidage/carucage as the least misleading method of portraying the distribution of waste. The hidage is, of course, the only statistic normally provided for waste manors. In the handful of cases where no hidage is available but other statistics are, I have used the teamlands or, failing these, teams as an indication of size.
11   R. W. Finn, *The Norman Conquest and its Effects on the Economy, 1066–1086* (London, 1971), pp. 211–20, attempts to make such a case.
12   This is the list provided by the most contemporary and best informed chronicler: *Chronicon Abbatie de Evesham*, ed. W. D. Macray (Rolls Series, 1863), pp. 90–1; see also R. R. Darlington, 'Æthelwig, Abbot of Evesham', *EHR*, 48 (1933), pp. 1–22, 177–98.
13   My figures differ in some instances from those in Darby's *Domesday Geographies*, which use modern counties in their calculations.

record that the estate *wasta fuit*, leaving it an open question as to whether the date referred to is 1066, *c.*1070, or both. But even if all the *wasta fuit* entries which cannot be confidently attributed to the intermediate date were assigned to 1066, the overwhelming preponderance of waste was still to be found along the Welsh border (96%). It is, in fact, likely that much of the *wasta fuit* in Herefordshire at least is to be attributed to 1066.[14] Herefordshire had been particularly affected by Welsh raids before 1066, with the town itself burnt and much of the surrounding district devastated. In one of its more revealing entries, Domesday Book records that the entire district of Archenfield had been laid waste before 1066 by King Gruffydd and Bleddyn and 'therefore what it was like at that time is not known'.[15]

Table 1: Waste in 1066

Name of County	Total hides	Total waste	% of county waste	% of total waste
Cheshire	550.00	75.42	13.71	26.82
Hereford	1,233.00	131.50	10.67	46.77
Shropshire	1,430.00	70.75	4.95	25.16
Worcester	1,432.00	3.50	0.24	1.24
Totals:	4,645.00	281.17	6.05	100.00

By *c.*1070 the amount of waste had increased by about 240% since 1066, which might be thought to be modest in view of the tumultuous events of the intervening years. In part, this may be attributed to the vagaries of the commissioners, since many of the counties which could be expected to have a substantial amount of waste have no data for an intermediate date.[16] However, another point deserves emphasis. We do have excellent data at all three dates for circuits 1 and 3, which bore the brunt of the initial impact of the Conquest. Yet only in Sussex is any significant concentration of waste recorded, though valuations had fallen drastically in many areas within the ten counties concerned.[17] To the commissioners in these circuits, at least,

---

14 Only 4 Herefordshire entries indicate an intermediate date, a far smaller number than in Cheshire and Shropshire (200 and 87 respectively).
15 DB: *Hereford*, 1, 49.
16 Notably in circuit 6. Circuits 2 and 4 also have data for only two dates – though in circuit 2 it is the 1066 data which is not recorded – but in both cases the amount of recorded waste is modest at each date.
17 J. J. N. Palmer, 'The Conqueror's Footprints in Domesday Book', *The Medieval Military Revolution: State, Society and Military Change in Medieval and Early Modern*

waste clearly implied something more serious than declining values,
however steep.

Table 2: Waste *c*.1070

Name of County	Total hides	Total waste	% of county waste	% of total waste
Buckingham	2,210.00	5.00	0.23	0.74
Cheshire	550.00	265.84	48.33	39.14
Devon	1,142.00	1.13	0.10	0.17
Hereford	1,233.00	58.75	4.76	8.65
Leicester	2,233.00	9.50	0.43	1.40
Northampton	1,280.00	7.75	0.61	1.14
Shropshire	1,430.00	261.07	18.26	38.44
Somerset	2,933.00	2.75	0.09	0.40
Sussex	3,204.00	64.63	2.02	9.52
Worcester	1,432.00	2.75	0.19	0.40
Totals:	17,647.00	679.17	3.85	100.00

The distribution of waste *c*.1070 was broadly similar to that in 1066, but
with a few significant variations (Table 2).[18] Although the Welsh border
counties were still overwhelmingly the worst affected, accounting for
86.6% of the total, they were no longer the only sufferers. Indeed, even
along the Welsh border, the Welsh were no longer responsible for all the
damage. Many – perhaps the majority – of the estates which were not waste
in 1066 but which had been wasted since were clearly the victims of the
Normans rather than the Welsh, particularly in Shropshire and Cheshire,
where the patterns of distribution are sufficiently distinctive to suggest that
much of the recent damage had been inflicted by forces from the north and
the east rather than the west.[19]

Europe, ed. A. C. Ayton and J. L. Price (London, 1995), pp. 26–8.

[18] The distribution of waste *c*.1070 is also affected by the ambiguity inherent in
the formula *wasta fuit*, but once again this only affects the total amount, not
the broad pattern of distribution. The figures in the table are for holdings
which are explicitly stated to refer to an intermediate date or for those *wasta
fuit* entries where the associated valuations imply an intermediate date for the
waste.

[19] H. C. Darby and I. B. Terrett (eds), *The Domesday Geography of Midland England*
(2nd edn, Cambridge, 1971), pp. 94–8, 144–7, 446–9; H. C. Darby and I. S.
Maxwell (eds), *The Domesday Geography of Northern England* (Cambridge, 1977),
pp. 365–76; H. C. Darby, 'The Marches of Wales in 1086', *Transactions of the*

Elsewhere, there is no reason to doubt that the Conquest was responsible, either directly or indirectly, for concentrations of waste. The Exeter Domesday informs us that a small group of ravaged estates in Devon had been laid waste by Irishmen, perhaps during the invasions led by Harold's sons.[20] But the most significant new area of waste c.1070 was, of course, in Sussex. Although the text does not explicitly connect this waste with military activity, the pattern of distribution is so distinctive that there can be no doubt that this was the work of the Norman army in 1066. The wasted holdings, totalling 65 hides, form a tight group in the rape of Hastings, in the area between Hastings itself and where the English and Norman armies clashed in battle. The values of the unwasted manors within this area also plunged dramatically after 1066.[21]

By 1086 the volume of waste had increased almost 16-fold since the Conquest, and its distribution had changed dramatically. Though even worse affected than in 1066, the Welsh border counties now accounted for only 12% of the total. The counties which shared virtually all of the remainder were those that had endured the infamous harrying of 1069–70 (Table 3). The distribution of waste in 1086 therefore strongly suggests that that event was substantially responsible for the overwhelming majority of recorded waste in 1086. Yorkshire, in particular, with a massive 81% of this waste, lies at the heart of the matter, particularly since there are grounds for believing that waste in the county is significantly under-recorded and that Yorkshire's share of all Domesday waste in 1086 may have approached 90%.[22] It is time to look at the criticisms which have been made of the Yorkshire data for waste.

Four major objections have been raised to the customary interpretation of the waste entries in the Yorkshire folios as meaning physical devastation, normally caused by warfare.

The first, which underpins the others, is perhaps best characterised as the common sense view of the effects of military activity. 'Could a comparatively small number of men really have done sufficient damage in the short time available for the land still to have been devastated seventeen years later?' Is it credible 'that large parts of Yorkshire ... could really have been left without a single inhabitant for 20 years?'[23]

---

20   Cheshire, II, pp. 336–7. Darby's maps make the point very clearly.
      DB: Devon, 17, 33–41 and notes; H. C. Darby and R. W. Finn (eds), The Domesday Geography of South-West England (Cambridge, 1979), pp. 273–5.
21   Palmer, 'Footprints', pp. 23–44.
22   In all, about 1,750 carucates in Yorkshire not explicitly stated to be wasted appear to be without resources, making the county total about 5,300 carucates, over 86% of all waste. See below for further discussion.
23   Wightman, 'Waste', p. 55; Palliser, 'Harrying', pp. 4, 20. Anticipated or echoed

Table 3: Waste in 1086

Name of County	Total hides	Total waste	% of county waste	% of total waste
Cheshire	550.00	78.96	14.36	1.80
Derby	699.00	76.56	10.95	1.74
Hereford	1,233.00	232.67	18.87	5.29
Leicester	2,233.00	29.14	1.30	0.66
Nottingham	563.00	37.70	6.70	0.86
Shropshire	1,430.00	189.13	13.23	4.30
Stafford	507.00	82.29	16.23	1.87
Worcester	1,432.00	25.75	1.80	0.59
Yorkshire	10,609.00	3,548.13	33.44	80.71
21 other counties	46,212.00	95.98	0.21	2.18
Totals	65,468.00	4,396.31	6.72	100.00

There is little reason, however, to question the ability of the Norman army to empty the countryside if the Conqueror were intent upon doing so. In the winter of 1069/70 Yorkshire was undefended: there were few towns, no castles, no army, and no leaders. In such circumstances, the Conqueror could divide his army into small contingents to maximise the area he could ravage. This would have been normal military practice, and this is precisely what Ordericus Vitalis tells us the Conqueror actually did, spreading his camps 'over an area of a hundred miles'.[24] Ordericus also tells us that the

---

by F. W. Brooks, *Domesday Book and the East Riding* (East Riding Local History Series 21, 1966), pp. 43–6; A. Raistrick, *The Pennine Dales* (London, 1968), p. 83; *idem*, *The West Riding of Yorkshire* (London, 1970), pp. 40–1; J. le Patourel, 'The Norman Conquest of Yorkshire', *Northern History*, 6 (1971), pp. 7–9; D. Hey, *Yorkshire from AD 1000* (London, 1986), p. 28; P. Dalton, *Conquest, Anarchy and Lordship: Yorkshire 1066–1154* (Cambridge, 1994), pp. 23–5. In a paper given to the Yorkshire Archaeological Society, Professor David Crouch expressed this common sense view in a particularly forthright manner, arguing that it was not physically possible to inflict the sort of damage claimed by the chroniclers; that the medieval economy was resilient enough to recover from any damage within a few years, 'five at most', and that the harrying was 'no more than a routine military operation'.

[24] *The Ecclesiastical History of Ordericus Vitalis*, ed. M. Chibnall, 6 vols (Oxford, 1969–80), II, pp. 230–7. This section of the chronicle made use of a lost portion of the chronicle of William of Poitiers, which would have been both well-informed about military matters and contemporary with the events recorded.

Conqueror made a determined effort to root out the population from the most inaccessible places, combing 'forests and remote mountainous places, stopping at nothing to hunt out the enemy hidden there'. The more prosaic, but contemporary, Evesham chronicle gives substantially the same account, and all other contemporary or near-contemporary chronicles record that the ravaging was of quite exceptional severity.[25]

Another reason for accepting that the Norman army had the capacity to inflict almost unlimited damage in the circumstances of 1069–70 is the unanimous view of contemporary or near contemporary chroniclers that it actually did so. By the same token, recovery could be a protracted affair. The testimony of William of Malmesbury is particularly striking here. He believed – whether correctly or not is almost immaterial – that more than 60 square miles of Yorkshire was still deserted in his own day as a result of the harrying carried out over half a century previously. Symeon of Durham, a native of the area, also believed that the countryside between York and Durham was uncultivated for almost a decade after 1070. For such thoughts to be thinkable, they must represent an approach to reality.[26] 'Common sense' is not a safe guide here. Maitland's dictum that 'agrarian history becomes more catastrophic as we trace it backwards'[27] is a more plausible working hypothesis.

A second, related objection to the interpretation of Yorkshire waste as the result of military activity is that its distribution does not look at all like a military pattern: there are no footprints, no obvious concentrations along major routes. But this objection is based upon a misunderstanding of the nature of the campaign of 1069–70. It was not a campaign with well-defined strategic objectives, in the shape of towns or castles to be defended or captured. The countryside itself was the objective, and many small companies of soldiers were the means to subdue or empty it. These tactics were not of the sort to produce concentrations of waste along major routes. But even had they done so, the Conqueror's footprints would have been muddied, often beyond recognition, by the developments of the next 16 years. One does not need to accept Bishop's elaborate hypothesis of enforced migration from the barren uplands to the more productive lowland manors under the control of the tenants-in-chief to accept the force of his starting premise: that the distribution of waste in 1086 is at best a partial reflection of the situation in 1070, mediated by sixteen years of

---

[25] *Evesham*, pp. 90–1; Palliser, 'Harrying', pp. 2–5 reviews the other chronicle sources.

[26] *Willelmi Malmesbiriensis De Gestis Regum*, ed. William Stubbs, 2 vols (Rolls Series, 1887–89), II, pp. 308–9; *SD*, II, p. 188.

[27] F. W. Maitland, *Domesday Book and Beyond* (Cambridge, 1897), p. 365.

recovery, or at least of change.[28] It is beyond belief that either peasants or lords would have invested scarce resources in redeveloping the poor or marginal land of the uplands if fertile lowland areas were under-populated or even uninhabited. Migration, internal or external, forced or unfettered, is certain to have been involved in the process of redevelopment. It would therefore be unrealistic to expect the waste recorded in 1086 to plot the routes taken by armies almost two decades previously. The absence of such a pattern tells us nothing about the original cause of the waste recorded in the Yorkshire folios. And whether that waste is a direct consequence of the activities of the Conqueror's army, or the displaced, residual effect of those activities, scarcely matters. The fundamental problem remains whether waste in Yorkshire can be taken to be the result of military activity, directly or indirectly. The pattern provides no compelling reason to think that it was not.

One further objection to the traditional view that the harrying of 1069/70 was responsible for the bulk of the recorded waste in Yorkshire has been made on the grounds of military logic. The royal estates were among the most severely wasted in the county. Is it conceivable that the Conqueror would have targeted his own possessions so ruthlessly or, that having done so, he would not have made every effort to restore their prosperity in the following 16 years? The extortionate exploitation of the royal manors is, after all, one of the more obvious characteristics of most counties. Yet in Yorkshire the huge royal estate of some 2,400 hides – greater in extent than many entire counties – was cultivated by less than 100 plough teams and worth less than £150, a fraction of its pre-Conquest value. But though these facts may seem to speak for themselves, the conclusion which has been drawn from them is unwarranted. Far from undermining the traditional view, they actually reinforce it. For the royal estates of 1086 had not, for the most part, been royal in 1066. Almost all the major holdings had, in fact, belonged to the principal rebel leaders of 1069. Targeting *their* estates made excellent military sense. And the fact that recovery had barely begun in 1086 after 16 years of royal control merely serves to underline just how complete the destruction of 1069/70 must have been.[29]

---

28 T. A. M. Bishop, 'The Norman Settlement of Yorkshire', *Studies in Medieval History presented to Frederick Maurice Powicke*, ed. R. W. Hunt, W. A. Pantin and R. W. Southern (Oxford, 1948), pp. 1–14.

29 The estates in the hands of the Siwardsons – about 2,200 hides – had lost almost 90% of their value by 1086, declining from £1,171 to £155. These figures take no account of the additional losses hidden by Domesday's failure to provide a 1066 valuation.

Military considerations, therefore, give no solid grounds for denying the physical reality of Domesday waste. But two arguments of a different kind have been proposed for continued scepticism. The first of these is what may be termed the Wightman thesis. In an influential paper published in 1975, Wightman argued that the term waste in the Yorkshire folios was often used as an administrative device to describe manors 'that had ceased to exist as a result of post-1066 tenurial reorganisation', with no implication of physical damage.[30] His evidence for this view was that some vills with holdings described as waste also contained holdings which were overstocked or had risen in value. In such cases, he argued, the so-called waste manor had, in fact, been absorbed by its thriving neighbour, which was allocated their combined resources for book-keeping purposes; physical waste was not implied.

This was an extraordinary deduction. There is no reason whatsoever why waste and cultivated manors should not have existed side by side; and indeed it is difficult to see how redevelopment could have got under way on any other basis. Moreover, both overstocking and increases in value are commonplace in Domesday Book.[31] A methodology which uses them to diagnose administrative reorganisation is simply not a credible methodology. Yet Wightman argued that this methodology could be applied even when the manors involved lay in different vills, or were owned by different tenants-in-chief, or both.[32] Neither proposition is credible. Since it is the normal practice of the Yorkshire Domesday to name the vills in which a manor lay, the first flies in the face of the testimony of the text. As for the second, it defies belief that a tenant-in-chief would

[30] Wightman, 'Waste', p. 58; W. E. Wightman, *The Lacy Family in England and Normandy, 1066–1194* (Oxford, 1966), pp. 43–54. The scepticism expressed by W. E. Kapelle (*The Norman Conquest of the North: the Region and its Transformation 1000–1135* (London, 1979), p. 277) has not been the predominant reaction, which is better represented by Hey, *Yorkshire*, p. 28; Palliser, 'Harrying', pp. 2, 12–13, and Dalton, *Conquest*, pp. 23–6, 29, 51, 52, 61.

[31] Kapelle, *Conquest of the North*, pp. 160–75, has an interesting discussion of overstocking, though his thesis about its implications for the wasting of the county is unconvincing.

[32] He also suggested that waste may have been an administrative 'accounting device in cases of doubtful or undecided ownership'. But the one instance he cites (p. 62) is a straightforward case of the duplicated entry, Domesday's normal method of dealing with disputed ownership (DB: *Yorks.*, 1W23, 9W71). He also suggests that afforestation may account for some waste, but afforestation is not explicitly recorded in Yorkshire, and forests were sometimes created precisely because the land was already wasted (Darby, 'Marches of Wales', pp. 260–2, 267, 271–2).

266

allow his land – even his waste land – to be absorbed in this way without at least a word of protest, and no such protests are recorded.

Yet it has recently been claimed that the thesis is supported by 'an impressive body of data'.[33] But the paradox is illusory, for appearances here are entirely deceptive. Wightman's anecdotal approach has obscured the fragility of his data. Of some 3,000 entries in the Yorkshire folios, just *eight* are waste holdings which lie in a vill containing a prospering manor held by the same tenant-in-chief. The data as a whole reveals an *extremely* strong negative correlation between waste and improving manors.

The Wightman thesis is therefore unsupported and implausible. There are, moreover, three positive arguments against it. In the first place, there is no contemporary, or indeed later, warrant for waste meaning administrative reorganisation. Secondly, the Domesday scribe had a standard procedure for dealing with administrative reorganisation, which was simply to note the number of manors that had been merged to produce the manor of 1086, to which he assigned their combined resources. The use of the term waste for exactly the same purpose is evidently improbable. The third and most persuasive reason for rejecting the thesis is that its basic premise can be shown to be unfounded. According to Wightman, waste manors lost their separate identity, being absorbed by prospering neighbours. They should, therefore, disappear from the historical record. Yet Domesday Book itself records 434 holdings which had been waste in the past but were no longer so in 1086. In every single case the holding had retained its separate identity. This single fact would appear to destroy the thesis. It is perhaps time it was abandoned.

The final reason which has been advanced for not accepting Domesday waste at its face value appears to be the most substantial. There are a very large number of extremely terse entries in the Yorkshire folios which record no men, no plough teams, and no current valuation. Although some historians have been content to take all or most of these entries as evidence of waste,[34] whether explicitly declared to be so or not, others have voiced suspicions that they reveal nothing more substantial than the ignorance of the Domesday commissioners. William Farrar doubted that the commissioners ever visited north Lancashire, and similar doubts were expressed by Raistrick and Finn about Craven, by Holt about the fief of Roger of Poitou, and by Kapelle about much of the Pennine uplands.[35]

---

[33] Palliser, 'Harrying', p. 12. See Appendix.

[34] Bishop, 'Norman Settlement', pp. 1–14; Darby and Maxwell, *Domesday Geography of Northern England*, pp. 61, 139–42, 212.

[35] W. Farrar, *VCH: Lancs.*, i, 273; Raistrick, *Pennine Dales*, p. 83; idem, *West Riding*, pp. 40–1; R. W. Finn, *The Making and Limitations of the Yorkshire Domesday* (Borthwick paper no. 41, 1972), pp. 29–31; Kapelle, *Conquest of the North*, pp.

More recently, it has been suggested that late additions to the text, which account for a significant proportion of these abbreviated entries, represent 'untenanted' land for which data could not be collected due to the haste with which the text was compiled.[36] Since almost 1,500 entries, affecting over 1,100 vills, are involved, the extent of the damage suffered by the county would be vastly reduced if these interpretations were accepted. Are they tenable?

Before addressing this question, two preliminary difficulties must be resolved: first, are the late additions to the text – the so-called postscriptal entries – *in themselves* presumptive evidence of ignorance; and, secondly, is the omission of the word waste from entries which have no recorded resources significant?

The suggestion that many late additions to the text represent 'untenanted' holdings for which data could not be collected is implausible. Not all postscriptal entries are abbreviated, and only a small proportion of abbreviated entries are postscriptal.[37] Postscriptal status is not a defining characteristic of anything except postscriptal status.

It certainly does not define untenanted holdings, for a minority of these are postscriptal, and many postscriptal holdings are tenanted.[38] But there is a more fundamental problem with these so-called untenanted holdings, postscriptal or otherwise: the very concept is anomalous. Land without tenants, after all, reverted to the tenant-in-chief, who would enjoy the

---

132, 165, esp. note on pp. 268–9; J. C. Holt, '1086', *Domesday Studies*, ed. J. C. Holt (Woodbridge, 1987), p. 61. For Roger's fief, see the discussion of Amounderness below.

[36] D. Roffe, 'Domesday Book : a Re-Interpretation', *EHR*, 105 (1990), 284–309, esp. pp. 323–5; Palliser, 'Harrying', pp. 13–18; *idem*, 'Yorkshire Domesday', pp. 33–8. One of the minor problems with this thesis is that many of the places concerned occur in fuller entries *for the same tenant-in-chief.* E.g. waste holdings among the dependencies of many royal manors are matched by holdings in the same vills on these allegedly untenanted estates. Another problem is that although the argument that Yorkshire was the first county to be inscribed *within its circuit* is convincing, the suggestion that circuit 6 was the first circuit summarised by the scribe is not as persuasive (Roffe, 'Domesday Book', pp. 320–3).

[37] For instance, nine of the eleven blocks of postscriptal entries listed by David Roffe, 'Domesday Book', p. 317, contain no abbreviated entries at all and the remaining two include some full manorial descriptions. Abbreviated entries which are not postscriptal are too numerous to list in full: representative examples may be found on fos. 303a–b, 305d, 306b, 307a, 313a, 314b–c, 320d, 330a–b, 332a–b.

[38] No tenants are named for about 1,200 abbreviated entries, far in excess of the number of postscriptal entries.

resources and make the appropriate return to the inquest. Only if an estate escheated during the inquest would the tenant-in-chief be prevented from doing so in normal circumstances. But circumstances clearly were not normal in Yorkshire in 1086: the sheer number of untenanted estates demonstrates beyond reasonable doubt that they were not recent escheats but estates which had been unexploited and without tenants for years. In that case, the argument that there was no time to gather information has little to commend it.[39] It is more probable that the estates were unexploited and untenanted because they were without resources – that is, because they were waste.

In themselves, therefore, neither postscriptal entries nor untenanted land can be taken as presumptive evidence of the ignorance of the commissioners. Nor, in all probability, can those abbreviated entries which omit the word waste. Where no plough teams, men, or current value were assigned to an estate, the addition of the word waste must at times have appeared redundant, and many of the cases where it was omitted do in fact occur in the lengthier lists of abbreviated entries where the word waste is wearisomely repeated. Two other considerations support this conclusion. In the first place, there are a number of duplicates in which the word waste appears in one entry but not the other.[40] Domesday scholars, however, have learnt to be wary of occasional and possibly eccentric individual examples. A more certain guide is the distribution of the word waste among holdings without resources within the same vill. There are scores of vills containing several holdings without resources, one or more which are described as waste, the other or others not. The sheer number of such cases (Table 4) demonstrates as clearly as possible that the omission of the word waste where an estate has no significant resources is not in itself significant.[41] Such estates should be considered to be in the same category as others with like resources – or lack of them – which are described as waste. The crucial consideration is the amount of information preserved by Domesday Book.

[39] The explanation offered for haste in Yorkshire – that it was the first county in Domesday Book to be inscribed (Roffe, 'Domesday Book', pp. 321–5) – evidently does not apply to Staffordshire, for instance, where a similar list of untenanted royal manors is recorded.

[40] E.g. Bolton, Darton, Penistone, and Rawcliffe.

[41] In the following paragraphs, the word waste is used as a convenient shorthand to describe estates without resources, whether the word waste is used explicitly or not. As with all Domesday statistics, there are problems, the most serious being the difficulty of deciding what information about dependencies is implicitly included in the entry for the manorial centre. The form of the Yorkshire entries for complex manors varies so much that consistent rules cannot easily be applied. However, the orders of magnitude suggested by these figures will not be affected.

With these preliminaries dealt with, we can return to the main question: do the abbreviated entries signify uninhabited land which had gone out of cultivation or merely bureaucratic ignorance? Do they illuminate the dire state of the Yorkshire countryside or only the poor state of the Yorkshire text?

Table 4: Distribution of waste
all holdings in vills containing waste manors

Category of waste	Number of manors in the vill						Total of holdings
	1	2	3	4	5	7	
partial	0	16	7	4	1	0	28
implied	0	67	52	14	13	3	149
none	0	54	55	16	15	1	141
waste	358	237	120	22	16	3	756
Totals:	358	374	234	56	45	7	1074

To answer these questions it is essential to distinguish two types of abbreviated entry: (1) those for which only the hidage of the estate is recorded; and (2) those for which the teamlands, and sometimes the 1066 valuations as well, are also given.[42] In the latter case, a survey had clearly been conducted since this data was the product of the Domesday survey: no historian has ever been rash enough to suggest that it existed prior to 1086. The 1,000 holdings in this group – distributed among 750 vills – can therefore reasonably be presumed to have contained no population and no teams and to have been without any value. A third of the county is thereby accounted as waste.

The estates for which only a tax assessment is provided – about 500 – are more problematic. The tax data may conceivably have been obtained from pre-existing tax lists and its inclusion does not necessarily imply that an inquest had been held. But even if no survey were undertaken, it does not follow that nothing more substantial than the ignorance of the commissioners can be deduced. An entry for the extensive manor of Preston in Lancashire suggests a more plausible interpretation. Here, it is

---

[42] About a third of the valuations are undated, but there is no reason to doubt that they refer to 1066 since they have no resources; they occur alongside holdings with only 1066 valuations (Branton Green, Great Broughton, Burythorpe, Grafton, Kilham, Langtoft, Newham Hall, Penistone, Scampston); and duplicates confirm that several of them do refer to 1066 (Darton and Penistone: DB: *Yorks.*, 1W24; 9W73; 1W23; 9W71).

recorded that of 60 vills belonging to the manor of Preston, '16 are inhabited by a few people, but how many ... is not known. The rest are waste.' If the comparatively fertile area around Preston contained only a few people, the remainder of Amounderness is unlikely to have sheltered that many more. The absence of a detailed survey is therefore not the result of ignorance but of an informed decision by the commissioners that such a survey was neither viable nor useful, given the parlous state of the region. The sparseness of the record of Amounderness therefore points to a significant, though not literal, truth about the condition of the area.[43]

The same may well be true of Craven, for which not even a few people are recorded. This is unlikely to be literally true but may nevertheless reflect a largely desolate landscape, judged to be unable to support a survey and not worth the trouble of surveying.[44] There is no way in which this can be directly tested, but some support for the conclusion is provided by the distribution of waste, which does not – as has been claimed[45] – stop at the boundaries of Craven but which shades away, slowly at first, into areas with at least some values and population to the south and east. There is no sharp line between Craven and surrounding areas which would occur if the absence of information about Craven was an artificial reflection of the organisation of the survey rather than of the reality on the ground.

All of this suggests that the bulk of the abbreviated entries contain little information for the simple reason that there was little to record. This was certainly the case on the fief of the one English landowner to survive as a significant tenant-in-chief. In 1086 Gospatric still held the bulk of the estates he had held before the Conquest, concentrated in the wapentakes bordering Craven. Information about these estates was therefore readily available to Gospatric himself and there are no grounds for suspecting that it was not provided to the commissioners. Yet the proportion of abbreviated entries recorded on Gospatric's fief is typical of the area where most of his estates were located. The same is true of the estates held by other landowners who had held their estates at both dates.[46] This is the

---

43 In view of Holt's point about the fief of Roger of Poitou ('1086', p. 61; cf. note 35), it is worth observing that a return was made for his lands between the Ribble and Mersey even though he had been relieved of these as well as his land in Amounderness.

44 There is, however, no reason to suppose (*Yorkshire Archaeological Journal*, 44 (1995), p. 201) that substantial numbers of Craven manors were omitted from Domesday, which names 40% more places for that area than are recorded near the peak of medieval settlement: R. E. Glasscock, *The Lay Subsidy of 1334* (Records of Social and Economic History, new series, II, 1975).

45 Raistrick, *Pennine Dales*, p. 83; *idem, West Riding*, pp. 40–1.

46 56% of Gospatric's entries in this area are abbreviated, as compared to 59% of all entries; 53% of the entries of other Anglo-Saxon thegns still holding in

clearest possible indication that the abbreviated entries do signify an empty landscape. Their distribution,[47] and some duplicates,[48] further confirm this conclusion, which should occasion no real surprise. For even if we ignore every waste entry in the Yorkshire folios, what remains is dismal. On some 600 manors which are given values for both 1066 and 1086, the decline averages over 60%.[49] In the face of statistics like these, doubts concerning the meaning of waste, and scepticism about the reality of physical devastation, appear to be ill-judged.

In conclusion, what does all this tell us about the effects of warfare? This could well be the subject of another paper, so my observations will be brief. Perhaps the first point to notice is the almost complete absence of waste in the ten counties of circuits 1 and 3. These counties bore all the weight of the Conqueror's two-month long campaign in 1066, which was accompanied by extensive harrying along the length of the 350-mile line of march according to native sources.[50] Yet however serious, the damage had largely been made good within a year or two.[51] Even within the rape of Hastings, where 16 manors were lying waste for some years after 1066, recovery was complete by 1086.[52] The medieval countryside could evidently prove resilient in the face of large armies intent upon inflicting punitive damage, in certain circumstances.

Some indication of what those circumstances might be is perhaps conveyed by the very different experiences of the northern and western counties, where all the indications are that greater damage was inflicted in

---

1086 are abbreviated.

[47] Abbreviated entries occur in substantial numbers in all 3 ridings, in 36 of the 39 wapentakes, and on the lands of 42 tenants-in-chief.

[48] E.g. the entries for Cawthorn, Darton, *Heuuorde*, Houghton, Kirby Hill, Penistone, *Popletone*, Rawcliffe, *Stemanesbi*, and Stockton on the Forest among others.

[49] 60.2%. This figure includes a small number of manors which have values but which are described as either waste or partially waste. If these are omitted, the average falls to 59%.

[50] *Anglo-Saxon Chronicle*, ed. D. Whitelock, D. C. Douglas and S. I. Tucker (London, 1961), p. 144; *The Chronicle of John of Worcester*, ed. R. R. Darlington and P. McGurk (Oxford, 1995), II, pp. 606–7. For a detailed analysis of this campaign, see Palmer, 'Footprints', pp. 23–44.

[51] It is believed that the intermediate valuations are of an early date throughout much of this area, perhaps as early as 1067 in many cases.

[52] These manors, in fact, were in a healthier state than much of the rest of the county, with the valuations virtually back to 1066 levels, a full complement of plough teams, and a markedly higher proportion of men to teams than the county average.

the first place and where recovery was impeded by slighter resources and sparser populations. In Cheshire, for instance, only two of the 53 manors waste in 1066 had recovered at all by *c*.1070. Even twenty years later, two of them were still waste; though by this date the remainder had recovered their prosperity, at least when judged by the low standards of the county.[53] As for the hundred or so manors which became waste after the Conquest, although nine out of ten were no longer waste in 1086, they were seriously under-stocked and their values were 45% lower than in 1066.[54] In Cheshire, therefore, many years had been required for even partial recovery, and complete recovery was a matter of decades.[55]

Even decades were not enough in Yorkshire. Taken at face value, the Domesday statistics show that the devastation of Yorkshire in the winter of 1069–70 had been appalling. Over 80% of all the waste recorded in Domesday Book for 1086 was in the Yorkshire folios, and this understates the real situation. Whole swathes of the county were entirely without plough teams, population, or value. 60% of all holdings were waste or without human or animal resources, and two-thirds of all vills contained wasted manors. Even the prosperous areas of the county in 1086 had lost 60% of their value as compared to 1066.[56] The county had a deficit of roughly 75% of the plough teams and population it might be expected to possess in normal times, including almost all of its free peasantry.[57] At a conservative estimate, more than 80,000 oxen and 150,000 people were needed to make good that deficit.[58] And this was the situation after the

---

[53] The ratios of hidage to teams, population and values (1:0.83, 1:2.7, 1:0.37 respectively) compared favourably with those for the county as a whole. See Darby and Maxwell, *Northern England*, pp. 365–76, for the complexities of the Cheshire record of waste. My figures differ from Darby's in part because he deals with the modern county rather than the Domesday one.

[54] 109 manors were waste *c*.1070 but not, apparently, in 1066. Of these, the 98 which were no longer waste in 1086 had 204 teams on 392 teamlands, their value having fallen from £152 in 1066 to £84 in 1086.

[55] Darby, *Domesday England*, p. 259, has some interesting observations on the extent of recovery by 1086 along the Welsh border.

[56] I.e., the holdings for which we have valuations for both dates.

[57] About 20% of the county was sokeland, which suggests a 1066 population of over 8,500 free peasant families. The ratio of carucage to free peasants on the two sokes where their numbers (224) are recorded for 1066 (DB: *Yorks.*, 1Y2–3) suggests a figure nearer 25%, over 10,000 families (see next note). Both figures take account only of sokeland and so are underestimates. It is not unlikely that numbers were comparable to those of Lincolnshire, which would almost double that number. The number actually recorded for Yorkshire in 1086 was 452.

[58] These figures are based upon the ratio of hides (or carucates) to teams and

county had had 16 years in which to recover. Yorkshire could well have been a desert in 1070.

Yorkshire Domesday therefore reveals something of the damage which could be inflicted by armies prepared to show no mercy to local society, and of the limited capacity of societies to recover from such savagery. If wholesale and repeated destruction of this kind were inflicted on Europe by the 'hordes from without' during the early medieval centuries, then it would be difficult indeed to disagree with Bloch's claim that the devastation they created was one of the fundamental forces which shaped early medieval society.

APPENDIX

The record of prospering manors provides no statistical support for the Wightman thesis.

Of almost 600 cases for which we have comparable values in Yorkshire, only 76 showed an increase in value between 1066 and 1086, just nine of these lying in vills which contained waste manors, *only one* – the figure deserves emphasis – belonging to a tenant-in-chief with a waste holding in the same vill.[59] The tally of waste in neighbouring vills is not much more impressive. Of the 26 undivided vills worth £1 or more which increased in value, only four were adjacent to wasted manors held by the same tenant-in-chief, and only four more to waste manors held by other tenants-in-chief.[60] Since one manor in two contained waste, these figures demonstrate an *emphatic* negative correlation between waste manors and those which had increased in value. It is perhaps worth adding that the manors which showed the largest increases – Conisborough, Coxwold, South Elmsall – were either remote from wasted manors or owed their

population elsewhere in Domesday which suggest a ratio of 1:1.3 for hidage to teams, and 1:4 for hidage to recorded population. To put these vast numbers into perspective, see Darby's comments on comparable figures for the Welsh border counties (*Domesday England*, p. 259).

[59] The vills were Acaster Selby, East Ayton, Buckton Holms, Cawton, *Hindrelage*, Hornington, Hunsingore, Newsham and Skelton. Only three of the manors were valued at more than £1. Neither of the examples that Wightman cites ('Waste', p. 59) are of manors lying in the same vill.

[60] The eight vills were Constable Burton, Leeds, Seamer and Tadcaster (with the same tenants-in-chief), plus Cottingham, Gunby, Topcliffe, and Little Weighton. Settrington was excluded because its wasted neighbour, Buckton Holmes, has been accounted for in analysing the divided vills. Four of these eight manors were of modest size and showed modest increases in value.

increase in value to quite other factors than manorial reorganisation.[61]

Overstocked manors (230) were more common than those that had increased in value. Of 85 divided vills with an excess of teams, only 23 contained waste manors, and just seven of these belonged to the tenants-in-chief of an overstocked holding in those vills. Of the 45 undivided vills which had an excess of two or more teams, just eight had as neighbours vills containing waste. Not one of the 24 manors with an excess of five or more teams lay in a vill with a waste manor, and only two were adjacent to one with waste.[62] The correlation of waste and overstocking is therefore strongly negative.

Thus, even if true, the Wightman thesis would be irrelevant to the problem of war and waste since the number of waste manors with prospering neighbours was so tiny.

---

[61] The increase at South Elmsall was explicitly stated to be due to receipts from the sheriffdom (DB: *Yorks.*, 9W34).

[62] There were 133 overstocked single-manor vills, too large a sample to examine in detail. Of the 45 with two or more excess teams, 10 have been accounted for in analysing the increased valuations. The remaining 35 had 67 neighbouring manors, representing 25 vills with no waste at all, eight containing waste manors held by the same tenants-in-chief as those holding overstocked manors nearby, and two held by other tenants-in-chief.

Military Logistics: the Case of 1322

MICHAEL PRESTWICH

In the summer of 1322 Edward II led a large army into Scotland. This was to be one of the least successful of all English expeditions there. It was not as obviously disastrous as that of 1314, for the Scots did not even attempt to give battle, and there was no defeat to parallel Bannockburn. The Scottish strategy was a safer one than that of 1314, and proved highly effective. Robert Bruce's men simply emptied the land in advance of the English, depriving them of any means of support. The story told later by Barbour in his *Bruce* was that the English found nothing on their march save a single lame cow. Earl Warenne joked pointedly, 'This is the dearest beast I have ever yet seen; it must have surely cost £1,000 or more.'[1] The expedition reached Edinburgh and Leith, from where Edward was forced to retreat. After his return to England, total disaster was narrowly averted at Byland in Yorkshire, when the Scots surprised the English forces, capturing the earl of Richmond, John de Sully and others, but not the king himself. In 1326 Hugh Despenser the Younger was charged with responsibility for these events. He and his father had provided the wrong advice, and not made the proper arrangements for the campaign.[2]

There were many reasons for the English failure in 1322, not least among them the inadequate leadership provided by Edward II himself. Above all, it was the lack of adequate food supplies which proved disastrous. This is one of many campaigns which bring out the importance of victualling to medieval armies. A letter written by one of those present in Henry III's army in Wales in 1245 at Degannwy made the point vividly. Bread cost ten times the normal price. An Irish ship with a cargo of foodstuffs was stranded by the tide, where it was fought over by the English and Welsh. Wine supplies were down to the last tun.[3] The chronicler Jean le Bel witnessed the Weardale campaign of 1327 at first hand, and described the misery of the English cavalry, forced to eat bread

---

[1] *The Bruce*, ed. W. W. Skeat (Early English Text Soc., extra series, 55, 1874, 1877), p. 452.

[2] *Chronicles of the Reigns of Edward I and Edward II*, ed. W. Stubbs (Rolls Series, London, 1882–3), II, p. 88.

[3] *Matthaei Parisiensis, Chronica Majora*, ed. H. R. Luard (Rolls Series, London, 1877), IV, pp. 481–4.

soaked in their horses' sweat. Profiteering Newcastle merchants sold the starving men poor quality supplies at exorbitant prices.[4] There are no such vivid descriptions of the suffering of the men on the 1322 expedition, but there is no doubt that it was lack of supplies which compelled them to retreat having achieved nothing. Yet the ample surviving documentation shows that the government had made elaborate efforts to ensure that the army was properly supplied. The campaign therefore provides a good case-study of the logistics of an early fourteenth-century army.

There is no indication that either Edward or his advisers had learnt much from recent experience of warfare against the Scots. The defeat at Bannockburn should have made clear the dangers of marching a large army north into Scotland, but the campaign in 1322 took the form of a traditional large scale invasion similar to those mounted by Edward I. Such a force required victuals on a massive scale. Whether or not Edward II's officials estimated the needs of the 1322 army on the basis of any set formula, they were certainly well aware that they would be considerable. The evidence of late-medieval diet suggests that provision of food was normally made on a lavish scale. Barbara Harvey's study of the monks of Westminster suggests that they may have each consumed a staggering 6,207 calories on average, outside Advent and Lent. Staggering is perhaps an appropriate word, since nineteen per cent of the energy value of the diet came in the form of alcohol. The proportion of protein was high, amounting to some twenty per cent of the diet. This diet was roughly twice what a modern man consumes. These monks were not exceptional in their greed, for their allowance of food was paralleled by the levels of consumption in secular upper-class households of the later medieval period.[5] Estimates of the victualling needs of castle garrisons suggest that their members may have had a similar profile to Dr Harvey's stout monks. At Neath in 1262, three quarters of wheat, with two quarters of malted wheat and four quarters of malted oats, was allocated each week to a force of fifty-two men. Just over five and a half quarters of provender was allocated for their thirteen horses.[6] Similar calculations exist for English garrisons in Scottish castles during Edward I's attempted conquest, one suggesting that twenty men would need one quarter of wheat a week, and

4 *Chronique de Jean le Bel*, ed. J. Viard and E. Déprez, 2 vols (Paris, 1904–5), I, pp. 59–60.

5 B. Harvey, *Living and Dying in England, 1100–1540. The Monastic Experience* (Oxford, 1993), pp. 62–71.

6 SC6/1212/1 (all documents are in the Public Record Office, unless specified otherwise). Grain was measured by volume, not by weight. There were two gallons to a peck, four pecks to a bushel, and eight bushels to a quarter. A tun would hold about four quarters.

two of malt, along with substantial quantities of meat and fish. Horses required a peck of oats every night. The calorific value was, as at Westminster Abbey, over 5,000 a man.[7]

Recruitment plans in 1322 were ambitious, and the army was a substantial one. Cavalry numbers cannot be calculated with any precision, but it would not be unreasonable to estimate them at 2,000. There were probably at least 12,000 infantry in the normal county levies, and an additional 6,800 provided by a unique demand made on the towns. In addition there were 2,000 men raised separately in Cumberland and Westmorland, making an overall total of at least some 20,000. Further, the earl of Louth brought seventy-three men-at-arms, 304 hobelars (lightly armed cavalry) and ninety-three footsoldiers from Ireland.[8] This was not quite so large an army as that of 1298, but it was larger than many of those which Edward I had marched north into Scotland. The requirements for foodstuffs would have been very considerable indeed.

Planning for provision of sufficient victuals had to begin very early, but there was much less time available in 1322 than there was for most campaigns, since the decision to take the war to the Scots was made only after the defeat of Thomas of Lancaster at Boroughbridge on 16 March. Provisioning arrangements needed to be made as soon as possible, and it was on 24 March, the day before the writs summoning infantry troops were issued, that requests were sent to the sheriffs to collect the quantities needed.[9] This was a familiar technique, which had been extensively developed under Edward I. The traditional royal right of prise, or compulsory purchase for the royal household, had been extended to provide for the massive needs of royal armies. Opposition to the practice had been bitter in Edward's later years. In 1301 prises had even taken the form of 'loans' of supplies, negotiated with the counties, but the crown subsequently reverted to the previous practice of imposing demands.[10] The issue of prise had been an important element in the crisis of Edward II's early years, which led to the publication of the Ordinances of 1311, but hostility to the system had not led to its abandonment. The government in 1322 was well aware of the unpopularity of prise, and at the very time that the king was ordering the collection of victuals for the Scottish expedition,

---

[7] M. C. Prestwich, 'Victualling Estimates for English Garrisons in Scotland during the Early Fourteenth Century', *EHR*, 82 (1967), pp. 346–53.

[8] BL MS Stowe 553 provides details of pay both to cavalry and infantry. See also E2101/16/16. N. Fryde, *The Tyranny and Fall of Edward II* (Cambridge, 1979), p. 128, puts the figure at a minimum of 21,700.

[9] *Calendar of Patent Rolls (CPR), Edward II, vol. V, 1321–4* (London, 1904), p. 93.

[10] M. C. Prestwich, *War, Politics and Finance under Edward I* (London, 1972), pp. 131–2.

republished on 4 April the clause from the *Articuli super Cartas* of 1300 which forbade the seizure of goods without warrant, and without the consent of the owner. Further, Edward reaffirmed this in parliament at York in early May. If properly enforced, this would have prevented the levying of prises on a national scale.[11]

The quantities of foodstuffs to be taken in 1322 were arbitrarily set; there was no discussion or negotiation with local communities. The totals requested from English counties came to 6,700 quarters of wheat, 8,500 of oats, 2,600 of barley malt, 1,500 of beans and peas, and 2,100 bacons. The burden was not equally spread; Yorkshire, Lincolnshire, Nottinghamshire, Derbyshire, Norfolk, Suffolk, Cambridgeshire, Huntingdonshire, Essex, Kent, Hampshire, Surrey, Sussex and Lancashire were listed, as was Cornwall.[12] Ease of transport meant that those counties with easy access to east coast ports suffered greater demands than midland regions. Substantial supplies were also requested from Ireland, totalling 6,000 quarters of wheat, 4,000 of oats, 2,000 of beans, 1,000 of barley malt, 500 bacons, 500 tuns of wine and 500 quarters of salt. On 1 April Gascony was added to the list, with a demand for 2,000 quarters of wheat, and 1,000 tuns of wine. The English royal right of prise did not extend to Gascony, and the royal officials there were told either to take the wheat as a negotiated subsidy, or to pay for it out of tax. If no grant could be obtained, they should pay for the supplies out of the issues of the duchy.[13] The overall scale of all these requests were similar to those that Edward I had made. In 1300, for example, he had asked for 10,000 quarters of wheat, 4,300 of barley malt, 10,300 of oats, 1,000 of beans, and 300 tuns of wine for his Scottish campaign.[14]

It was one thing to issue orders, and quite another to obtain the quantities of supplies demanded. Royal clerks were appointed on 3 April to assist the sheriffs in the task of purveyance, presumably as a result of worries that the requisite supplies might otherwise not be forthcoming.[15] On 15 May orders were issued that all the victuals were to be sent to

[11]   *Calendar of Close Rolls (CCR), Edward II, vol. III, 1318–23* (London, 1895), pp. 532, 557. Curiously, the York statute referred to a decision of Edward I made in the eighth year of his reign (1280) at a Westminster parliament held in Lent. This makes little sense; reference must have been intended to the twenty-eighth year of the reign.

[12]   *CPR, 1321–4*, pp. 93–4. This list does not include Nottinghamshire and Derbyshire; BL Stowe MS 553, f. 40, shows that 300 quarters of wheat, 500 quarters of oats, 1,000 quarters of beans and peas, and 300 bacons were requested from these counties.

[13]   *CPR, 1321–4*, p. 94.

[14]   *CPR, 1292–1301*, pp. 487–8.

[15]   *CCR, 1318–23*, p. 431.

Newcastle upon Tyne by the date originally set for the army to muster, 13 June, despite the fact that this had been postponed until 24 July.[16] The accounts reveal that the sheriffs had considerable difficulties in some cases. For example, Essex was to provide 500 quarters of wheat, and 1,000 quarters of oats. Nottinghamshire and Derbyshire were to produce 300 quarters of wheat, 500 quarters of oats, 1,000 quarters of beans and peas, and 300 bacons. In fact, the sheriffs of these counties came nowhere near to meeting these requests. All that was collected by the sheriff and his officials in Essex, which in the event was combined with Hertfordshire, was 167 quarters of wheat, and 53½ quarters of oats. The sheriff of Nottinghamshire and Derbyshire provided 46 quarters of wheat, 50 quarters of beans and peas, and 10 bacons. This was a year of bad harvest due to drought, but the exceptionally high prices paid in these counties by the sheriffs and their officials, up to eighteen shillings a quarter for wheat, and sixteen shillings a quarter for beans and peas, suggest dishonest accounting. Administrative costs were also high. The cost of the foodstuffs in Essex and Hertfordshire was £150 5s., and the expenses of collection, milling, storage and freightage came to £28 12s.

In some cases, far more grain was collected than had been initially ordered. Norfolk and Suffolk were to provide 600 quarters of wheat, 500 quarters of oats, and 500 quarters of barley. In the event, 1,328 quarters of wheat, 1,084 quarters of barley, 200 quarters of oats and 300 quarters of beans and peas was brought together. Specially appointed purveyors in Suffolk were highly successful, obtaining 513 quarters of wheat and 484 quarters of barley. Notable service was provided by the burgesses of King's Lynn, who provided 600 quarters of wheat, 200 of barley, 300 of beans and peas and 200 of oats. Their prices were much keener than those of Nottinghamshire and Derbyshire; the wheat was acquired at 12s. 6d. a quarter, and the beans and peas at 10s. 6d. a quarter. Tax collectors were also used for purveyance in this year. In Kent, the collectors of the tenth and sixth obtained 500 quarters of wheat, 486 quarters of barley, 32 quarters of beans and peas and 214 quarters of oats. The prices they obtained were lower still. They paid 10s. a quarter for wheat, and 8s. for the beans and peas.[17] It is not surprising that prices varied from region to region, but the scale of the differences suggests that some officials may have been far less than honest, and that some sheriffs were not as reliable as others.

Purveyance was not the only method used to collect the massive amount of stores needed by a medieval army. Another important source of supplies was the merchant community. Merchants could be employed

---

16   *Ibid.*, p. 555.
17   BL Stowe MS 553, ff. 40–41.

directly by the crown, or encouraged to follow the army, offering their goods for sale.

One merchant engaged by the crown was highly successful. The initial proposal was that the Italian Manentius Francisci should go abroad to buy victuals, but in the event he left York, base for the royal administration, went to Louth in Lincolnshire where he stayed six days, then on to Boston for eight days, then six days were spent at King's Lynn. Then he went to Canterbury, spent twelve days in Kent and Essex, before reaching London, and returning directly from there to York. His party consisted of himself, a companion, three horses and four servants. He bought 2,472 quarters of wheat, 1,127 quarters of barley, 1,430 quarters of malt, 140 quarters of mixtillum, or mixed grain, 790 quarters of beans, and 620 of oats. Much of the grain he handed over to the sheriffs of Lincolnshire, London, Kent and Essex, presumably for them to send north. He had some difficulty in persuading them to accept it, since they were anxious to receive no more grain than they could reasonably send for milling. Henry of Shireoaks, royal victualler at Newcastle, acknowledged receipt of 1,198 quarters, or almost half of the wheat in his custody, from Manentius, according to the latter's account. Shireoaks's own account gives a different figure, of 1,258 quarters, received from the Italian: measurement was not always accurate.[18]

In all, Shireoaks had impressive quantities of foodstuffs available. He had 3,788 quarters of wheat in his custody, and 806 tuns of flour. There were 3,822 quarters of barley, 3,137 quarters of oats and 1,202 quarters of beans. The account lists a wide range of commodities besides the great quantities of grain. Bacon was the chief meat, though there were also twenty-one beef carcasses, and herring, cod and salmon all featured. Ginger, mace, cubeb (a spice similar to pepper), and vinegar reveal something of the efforts that were made to add flavour to a fairly unpalatable diet. Much work had to be done in Newcastle on the buildings (such as the great granary belonging to John Scot) and cellars rented as storehouses, and miscellaneous expenditure included the purchase of locks so that the goods could be kept securely. Shireoaks had some difficulty in maintaining his stocks of wine; out of 296 tuns received from Bordeaux and La Réole in Gascony, he recorded losses in ullage amounting to over thirty-one tuns, while a further six tuns went bad. Such losses were not serious, however, when set against an overall wine store totalling a remarkable 1,558 tuns.[19]

Nor was Shireoaks the only royal victualler. John de Louther was in charge at Carlisle, receiving foodstuffs from the western counties and Ireland. There had been worries that the Irish supplies were late, and on 26

---

[18]   *CPR, 1321–4*, p. 90; E101/16/18.
[19]   E101/16/19; BL Stowe MS 553, f. 52.

July the king had written angrily to the earl of Louth, complaining at his own delay in sailing, and at his failure to send supplies.[20] Yet the quantities assembled at Carlisle were considerable. Louther had charge of 1,463 quarters of wheat, 201 tuns of flour, 1,079 quarters of beans and peas, 420 quarters of barley and 1,496 quarters of oats, as well as 208 tuns of wine. The total amount of foodstuffs available to the crown was not quite as great as it had been in 1300, but was nevertheless impressive.[21]

The crown could not provide all the supplies needed by an army, and steps were taken to encourage traders to take advantage of the opportunity to sell goods to the army. During the Welsh wars, Edward I had forbidden the holding of markets in the marches, in order to force merchants to take their goods to the troops. Edward II's administration did not go so far, but considerable efforts were made to provide the appropriate writs of protection and safe-conduct for those who assisted the war-effort. On 6 April Selo Susse, described as a king's merchant, received protection to go overseas with three ships to purvey oats for the coming campaign.[22] Protections for merchants bringing victuals to Newcastle began to be issued on 20 April. On 7 May a considerable number was issued to merchants who were going south to buy victuals, which would be sent to York and Newcastle.[23]

In addition to the efforts made by the crown, it was normal for magnates to make some arrangements themselves for provisioning. There is rarely much surviving evidence for this, and the campaign of 1322 is no exception. It is, however, known that Andrew Harclay sent some of his men abroad in April to buy food supplies, and other leaders of substantial contingents must also have organised some of their own provisioning.[24]

The victuals collected together at Newcastle and elsewhere should have been sufficient for the campaign, provided it did not last too long. The major problem on the 1322 campaign was that few of the victuals reached the army, which set out on 10 August. In particular, it was no use collecting large quantities of victuals if there were not enough ships to carry them north. Orders to prepare ships had been issued on 1 March, 'to set out in the king's service against the Scotch rebels and certain rebellious magnates of this realm'.[25] This, of course, was before Lancaster's defeat at Boroughbridge on 16 March. It was on 25 March that the Cinque Ports were asked for their service for the expedition against the Scots. On the

---

20   E101/16/16.
21   *Ibid.,* ff. 47v.
22   *CPR, 1321–4,* p. 90.
23   *Ibid.,* pp. 109–10, 115–18.
24   *Ibid.,* p. 90.
25   *CCR, 1318–23,* p. 524.

same day protections were given to some forty-five merchants and shipmasters who were being sent south from Yorkshire to buy victuals which were to be brought to Newcastle and York. On the next day a credence was issued for Alexander le Convers to seek ships from ports in the south and west.[26] The bishop of Norwich and Walter de Norwich, an exchequer official, were appointed to negotiate an aid of ships from the seaports.[27] By 17 April the king was able to write to Ipswich, Dunwich, Orford and other East Anglian ports thanking them for the grant of ships, which were to serve for two months. The Yarmouth grant was for a forty day period.[28] On April 20 the king asked for ships from Yarmouth and the other ports of Norfolk and Suffolk, so as to deal with the threat of the Flemings, who, it was suspected, were assisting the Scots by preying on English shipping taking supplies north. In late April and early May further writs of protection were issued in favour of shipowners who were going south so as to collect victuals to be brought to York and Newcastle.[29]

By early May all was clearly not going smoothly. Information came to the king that the ships of the Cinque Ports were trading in distant parts. Instructions went out on 10 May ordering them to return to their home ports without delay, though it is not clear how such orders could have been sent to the shipmasters. On 11 May orders were issued to assist the men of Blakeney in Norfolk to obtain the assistance of the nearby ports in the preparation of the ship they were to send to Scotland.[30] On 25 June the king, as a result of news that there was a naval threat to the country, asked for additional vessels. The original number from East Anglia was fourteen; now there were to be twenty more, all to serve for eight weeks.[31] These were to be substantial ships, with double crews, intended more for escort work than for the actual carriage of the vital foodstuffs. This was very late to act. A further fleet was to be assembled from the ports south of the mouth of the Thames.[32]

One frequent problem in obtaining naval assistance was the conflicts which often broke out between the men of the Cinque Ports and those of other seaports. In 1297 the difficulty had been virtual war between the Yarmouth men and those of the Ports; this time there was trouble between the Ports and sailors from Southampton, Weymouth and other southern seaports. Orders were issued to try to prevent the 'homicides, depredations

---

[26] *Ibid.*, pp. 533–4; *CPR, 1321–4*, pp. 86–7.

[27] *CCR, 1318–23*, p. 462.

[28] *Ibid.*, pp. 546–7.

[29] *Ibid.*, p. 540; *CPR, 1321–4*, pp. 109–10.

[30] *CCR, 1318–23*, pp. 549–50.

[31] *Ibid.*, pp. 462–3.

[32] *Ibid.*, pp. 465–6.

and burnings of ships' on 18 August.[33]

There was considerable alarm at the possible effects of Flemish piracy on the victualling operations. On 20 April the men of the Cinque Ports were ordered to be ready to go against the Flemings, who were said to be infesting the coast, and preventing victuals from being brought north.[34] On 6 May Edward II complained to the count of Flanders that a proclamation had been issued in Flanders, ordering all Englishmen to leave the land. Those who had not done so had been detained. The next day saw further orders on the same lines as those of 20 April issued to the Cinque Ports.[35] The accounts for the campaign reveal that one ship, the *Notre Dame de Guistres*, with a cargo of 126 tuns of flour, was captured and robbed on the voyage north to Newcastle, between Blackminster and Hull.[36]

The plan had been to bring the supplies north by sea, to the port of Leith, which was reached by the army on 20 August, but far too few ships were available. The Wardrobe account book lists a mere twenty-one vessels, which was much too small a fleet, taking victuals from Newcastle to Leith.[37] Holy Island was used by the English as a staging post, for John Abel was sent there by night from Wooler, to bring back news to the king of the arrival of the victuals there. The *Charity* of Colchester was one ship which did reach Leith, but she was wrecked on arrival there, her master receiving £5 for unloading the cargo. This had consisted of fifteen tuns of flour, twenty ox carcasses, sixty bacons, and twenty pounds of bread.[38]

The failure of the attempt to bring the victuals brought military failure. The army was not plagued by desertion on the scale of some previous English campaigns in Scotland, but without adequate supplies it could achieve little. Edward and his advisers had no option other than to retreat south. When the army returned to the border on 2 September, the majority of the troops were dismissed. The king wrote letters sealed with the privy seal on 17 September from Newcastle to the archbishop of Canterbury and the bishop of Winchester. He did his best to put a good face on events. The campaign was, of course, described as a success, for there had been no resistance. In the letter to the bishop of Winchester, however, Edward explained that he and his army, which was greater than any in his day or previously, had reached Edinburgh, and had gone on to the Firth of Forth. There was no resistance, but no victuals had reached the army. Flemish ships had attacked and captured the victualling ships, and the army had

---

[33] *Ibid.*, pp. 490–1.
[34] *CPR, 1231–4*, p. 102.
[35] *CCR, 1318–23*, p. 549; *CPR, 1321–4*, p. 111.
[36] BL MS Stowe 553, f. 54.
[37] *Ibid.*, ff. 77–77v.
[38] *Ibid.*, ff. 67v, 77.

been compelled to return to the Borders, destroying territory as it went.[39]

There was one bonus for the crown as a result of the failure of the campaign. Shireoaks's account reveals that his sales of victuals yielded some £6,000. Some were sent to the garrisons in the north-east, such as Barnard Castle, Dunstanburgh, Bamburgh and Norham, but much was simply sold for profit after the failure of the royal campaign. At Newcastle, most of the goods were sold by Shireoaks's successor, John de Polhou, on 28 October.[40] Overall, sale of victuals raised an astonishing £13,808 2s. 8d., rather more than the annual farms from the sheriffs, and equivalent to the clear receipt from Gascony at this period. Even so, the crown did not make a profit in this way from its victualling arrangements, for the overall cost of the operations had come to £15,467.[41] It would be quite wrong to see purveyance as either a form of, or as a tempting alternative to, taxation. It never provided the crown with a means of raising substantial sums of money.

The campaign of 1322 provides an example of the failure of the English government to ensure that troops were provided with adequate supplies. Other campaigns showed the victualling system in a better light.[42] Under Edward I the story had been one of improvement and growing sophistication in the organisation of military supply. By making use of the network of local officials under the control of the sheriffs, and by using established distribution networks, above all water transport, very substantial quantities were collected to meet the orders issued by the central government. In 1297 over 11,000 quarters of wheat and almost 14,000 quarters of oats were shipped to Gascony and Flanders. In the Scottish wars supply bases were established at Berwick and Skinburness, near Carlisle. The victualling officers there, Richard de Bromsgrove and James de Dalilegh, had charge of very substantial quantities of supplies, and it proved largely possible to meet the demands both of the English garrisons in Scotland, and of the great armies that marched north with such regularity. There were certainly some problems. Food was short before the battle of Falkirk in 1298. Shortage of fodder for the horses meant that many died in the winter of 1301–2. At Aberdeen in 1303 the king had neither money nor food, and had to rely on 'loans from merchants, who had brought goods there to sell to provide sustenance for the men of our

---

[39] E163/4/11, nos 8, 73, 81. Nos 8 and 81 make no mention of the role of the Flemings.
[40] BL Stowe MS 553, f. 123.
[41] Ibid., ff. 18, 55v.
[42] For a broader discussion of the problems of victualling armies, see M. Prestwich, *Armies and Warfare in the Middle Ages: The English Experience* (Yale, 1996), pp. 245–62.

army. So we ask all those who love our profit and our honour to ensure that the merchants from whom goods have been taken for our use in this way are speedily paid..[43] In general, however, the royal officials involved in victualling achieved all that could have been asked of them. The very regularity of Edward I's campaigns eased their task in some respect, for it meant that victualling bases were permanent, and the routines of food collection were well-established. The situation in 1322 was very different. It was three years after the last major campaign, the attempted recapture of Berwick in 1319, and the crown no longer had an established supply headquarters on the Scottish border.

In his Scottish wars, Edward III used similar methods to those attempted in 1322. His officials may, indeed, have drawn some lessons from the failures of that campaign. In 1333 great emphasis was placed on the role of Manentius Francisci, though when it became clear that he could not deliver all that was needed, there was an appeal to merchants to bring goods north for the campaign, and orders for purveyance went out to sixteen counties in the midlands and the south. Less than a fifth of what was requested was received. In 1335 very considerable efforts were put into collecting an adequate naval force to protect the supply routes so vital to the English operating in Scotland.[44] The account of Robert Tong, royal victualling officer at Newcastle, for 1336–8, shows the scale of the operation winding down. He bought 1,000 quarters of wheat from the bishop of Durham, bringing the overall total in his charge to 1,284 quarters. He also bought 1,094 quarters of oats from the bishop, and had 176 tuns of flour, twenty-two quarters of beans, and 254 fish in store.[45]

When it came to the French war, however, the needs of the English armies began to change. France offered far greater potential to live off the land than had been the case in Scotland, and it was no longer necessary to make arrangements for victualling on such a scale as in the past. Another factor was that armies were smaller. There were some substantial estimates made, but these were for naval expeditions. One was drawn up for an expedition in the 1340s, and put needs at 4,000 quarters of wheat, 6,000 of oats and 1,000 of oats. Another, for a naval force with 4,000 men who were to serve for four months, put their needs at 5,400 quarters of wheat, 8,250 of barley, and 2,400 of beans and peas, with substantial quantities of bacon, dried fish and cheese in addition.[46]

Armies, however, needed less than naval expeditions, for they could be expected to live off the land. The account of William of Dunstable, royal

[43]   Prestwich, *War, Politics and Finance*, p. 136; E101/371/21, no. 96.
[44]   R. A. Nicholson, *Edward III and the Scots* (Oxford, 1965), 113–15, pp. 206–9.
[45]   E101/19/6.
[46]   C47/2/29; C47/2/31.

purveyor in seventeen counties in 1338–9, shows that even in the early stages of the war, when the king was in Flanders, demands for food did not approach the levels of Edward I's reign. Dunstable assembled 1,961 quarters of wheat, 2,394 quarters of malt, 226 quarters of beans and peas, a mere seven quarters of oats, 127 cattle of varying ages, 651 sheep together with some beef and bacon carcasses and 136 cheeses.[47] In contrast, Richard atte Magdalayne, keeper of the royal victuals at Southampton in 1339, did not account for any foodstuffs 'because he did not receive any victuals in the said town to keep for the king, as he declares under oath'.[48]

The fact that smaller quantities were collected than had been the case forty years previously did not reduce the unpopularity of the system of purveyance. A constant accompaniment of the activities of purveyors was the complaints of those whose foodstuffs had been taken. This was a part of the background to the crisis of 1297, and by 1311 the Ordainers feared that popular rebellion was possible as a result of purveyance. The complaints about purveyance were many and serious, and less than a decade after the 1322 campaign the *De Speculo Regis* would condemn the practice in bitter terms, warning Edward III that the people might well rise up against him as result of such exactions.[49] In Lincolnshire in 1341 out of 767 presentments against officials, 227 charged them with illegally taking goods, while 96 complained that goods taken had not been paid for. In Huntingdonshire William de Wallingford, royal victualler, was accused of receiving £7 13s. 6d. to leave the lands of Ramsey Abbey alone. Many offences were hardly serious in themselves. In Nottinghamshire, John of Oxford, deputy for William de Dunstable, was accused of taking fifty-four eggs from Richard de Wannesey at Newark.[50] Taken as a whole, however, the volume of grievances demonstrates that there was a serious problem.

Changing patterns of warfare, with smaller armies conducting *chevauchées*, raids whose purpose was to ravage French territory with forces that could live off the land, transformed the situation. The last major national demand for victuals came in 1351, and aroused a storm of protest. The old methods were largely abandoned in favour of the use of contract

---

[47] E101/21/4.

[48] E101/21/35. See also the account of William de Wallingford of victuals received in Brabant and Antwerp for the royal household, in *The Wardrobe Book of William de Norwell, 12 July 1338 to 27 May 1340*, ed. M. Lyon, B. D. Lyon and H. S. Lucas (Brussels, 1983), pp. 57–8.

[49] J. R. Maddicott, 'The English Peasantry and the Demands of the Crown 1294–1341', *Past and Present Supplement* I (1975), p. 24. This article provides a most important discussion of the impact of purveyance.

[50] *The 1341 Inquest in Lincolnshire*, ed. B. W. McLane (Lincoln Record Soc., 78, 1977), p. xxvii; E101/21/38.

merchants. Purveyance was increasingly reduced to its traditional role of providing for the daily needs of the royal household. This was unpopular enough, but the scale of the problem was far less than it had been in the late thirteenth and early fourteenth centuries, though it must be doubted whether many were convinced by the replacement in 1362 of 'the hateful name of purveyor' by that of 'buyer'.[51] Indeed, purveyance for the household continued to be a grievance. In terms that could have been written in the fourteenth century, a late sixteenth-century author condemned purveyors as men of 'perverse and crooked nature, hurtful to many, odious to all'. The practice of household purveyance was finally abandoned by Charles II.[52]

The 1322 campaign shows that the apparently robust system developed under Edward I could fail in its purpose. The high prices recorded by some sheriffs suggest possible corruption, or at best incompetence; the success of Manentius Francisci suggests that the use of merchants might be an effective alternative to the traditional forms of purveyance. It was, however, the failure to provide adequate shipping in the face of Flemish hostility that was the prime reason for the decision to order the army to retreat. There were alternatives to be tried. The Hundred Years War was to see the crown move increasingly away from the traditional methods of purveyance, towards the use of contract merchants and, where possible, to armies living like locusts off the land through which they marched. The change eased the domestic political problems that resulted from the imposition of purveyance, but it did not necessarily bring improvement for the troops. Henry V's army in 1415 would run out of food supplies after no more than eight days' march.[53] The battle of Agincourt may have demonstrated that victory did not necessarily depend upon full stomachs, but that was hardly a secure principle upon which to fight a war.

---

[51] C. J. Given-Wilson, *The Royal Household and the King's Affinity: Service, Politics and Finance in England 1360–1413* (1986), pp. 41–8, 111.

[52] A. Woodworth, 'Purveyance for the Household in the Reign of Queen Elizabeth', *Transactions of the American Philosophical Society*, n.s. 35 (1945), pp. 37, 76 and *passim*.

[53] *Gesta Henrici Quinti*, ed. F. Taylor and J. S. Roskell (Oxford, 1975), p. 66.

The Forgotten Battle of Bevershoutsveld, 3 May 1382: Technological Innovation and Military Significance

KELLY DeVRIES

As all historians can testify, sometimes significant events in history can be overshadowed by other events which, in their time, seem larger or more earth-shaking. Such often happens in military history, when a later victory won on the battlefield or at siege removes the gravity of an accomplishment by the defeated party at an earlier engagement. (Undoubtedly, Edward I would find it rather odd that a foe which he defeated with relative ease at the battle of Falkirk in 1298 would, nearly seven hundred years later inspire an Academy Award winning film.) Such also is the case with the battle of Bevershoutsveld, fought on 3 May 1382 outside of the town of Bruges between the forces of that town and their rivals from the neighbouring town of Ghent. The Ghentenaars won, but this battle was greatly overshadowed by the succeeding conflict fought at Rosebeke between the Ghentenaars and the young French king, Charles VI. By that time and because the French were the victors at Rosebeke, how the Ghentenaars defeated their Brugeois counterparts at Bevershoutsveld had been forgotten. However, it may have been at Bevershoutsveld where gunpowder weapons first decided the outcome of a battle.

During the years between 1347 and 1379, the county of Flanders had been able to remain relatively neutral in the political and military conflicts which occurred in the more southern portions of France. This neutrality allowed the region to support France politically while being economically dependent on England without interference from either kingdom.

But in 1379 the Hundred Years War would again shift to the southern Low Countries, and it would ultimately involve not only England, France, and the southern Low Countries, but the duchy of Burgundy as well. In fact, this would mark the first political and military entrance of the duke of Burgundy into the region that would later be dominated by him and his descendants.[1]

The conflict began merely as a revolt by the town of Ghent against the Flemish count, Louis of Male. Louis' reign had not been an easy one. He

---

[1]   R. Vaughan, *Philip the Bold: The Formation of the Burgundian State* (London, 1962), pp. 16–38.

had ascended to the comital throne as a relatively young man on the death of his father, Louis of Nevers, who had been killed at the battle of Crécy. And for the first few years of his reign he was forced to work under the strict economic, if not political, aegis of King Edward III, the man who was responsible for his father's death. In addition to this insult, Louis of Male had barely escaped being tied to the English king by marriage.[2] Even after the English political concern for his county had abated, Louis found himself constantly at war ideologically with his subjects, who still favoured the English, especially as their cloth-making industry demanded English wool, while he was by tradition and obligation tied to the kings of France. Still, although the threat of English economic desertion was always present, Louis succeeded in guiding his county along the line of neutrality between the two warring kingdoms.[3]

Louis' domestic politics were not so tranquil. Often Louis would favour one town over another regardless of its size or legal traditions. At one time or another all three of the major towns of Flanders rose against Louis of Male. Ypres revolted in 1359–61, 1367, 1370, 1371, and 1377; Bruges revolted in 1351, 1367, and 1369; and Ghent revolted in 1359–60 and 1379–85.[4] What ultimately prompted the rebellion of 1379 were two comital acts prejudicial to Ghent: firstly, Louis infringed the town's privileges of *bourgeoisie* by arresting one of its burgesses, and secondly, he permitted the town of Bruges to construct a canal from Bruges to the Lys river, which, had it been completed, would have destroyed Ghent's monopoly of the river and its traffic.[5]

In response, the Ghentenaars rose up against the count, and on 5 September, they murdered his bailiff to the town, Rogier van Outrive.[6] A popular government was immediately installed in the town, and legates were sent to the other regions of the county announcing the rebellion of

2   See Jean le Bel, *Chronique de Jean le Bel*, ed. J. Viard and E. Deprez (Paris, 1905), II, pp. 135–9 and Jean Froissart, *Chroniques*, in *Oeuvres de Froissart*, ed. Kervyn de Lettenhove (Brussels, 1868), V, pp. 149–62.

3   H. Pirenne, *Histoire de Belgique*, II: *Du commencement du XIVe siècle à la mort de Charles le Téméraire* (Brussels, 1903), pp. 172–8.

4   See Vaughan, *Philip the Bold*, pp. 19–20.

5   For a discussion of the Ghentenaar complaints against Louis of Male see Pirenne, *Histoire de Belgique*, II, p. 188; Vaughan, *Philip the Bold*, p. 20; J. J. N. Palmer, *England, France and Christendom, 1377–99* (Chapel Hill, 1972), p. 20; and L. Mirot, *Les insurrections urbaines au début du regne de Charles VI (1380–1383)* (Paris, 1905), p. 68.

6   M. Vandermaesen and M. Ryckaert, 'De Gentse opstand (1379–1385)' in *De Witte Kaproenen: De Gentse opstand (1379–1385) en de geschiedenis van de Brugse Leie*, ed. M. Vandermaesen, M. Ryckaert, and M. Coornaert (Ghent, 1979), pp. 12–14 and D. Nicholas, *Medieval Flanders* (London, 1992), p. 228.

Ghent and asking others to join the independence movement. Bruges and Ypres submitted without bloodshed and the remaining parts of the county quickly joined in the rebellion. Only the towns of Oudenaarde and Dendermonde remained faithful to the count, and they became the rebels' first target. Oudenaarde was besieged on 7 October, and Dendermonde, the town to which Louis of Male had fled, was assaulted by rebel forces on 10 November.[7] Both withstood many attacks and artillery bombardments, both from gunpowder and non-gunpowder siege weapons, until Louis, using his father-in-law Philip the Bold as principal agent, sued for peace. The peace of Pont-à-Rosne, as this was called, which was signed on 30 November, issued a pardon to the rebels, set up town commissions which would inspect Flanders and the count, banished Louis' chief councillor and deprived him of his office, and restored all town privileges.[8]

However, by May 1380, Louis was unwilling to continue to abide by this peace treaty. This time it was the Flemish count who took the military initiative, and it at first brought him success. By the end of May he had captured Bruges, by August Ypres, and by September Courtrai. During this time he had also laid siege to Ghent. Yet, by November, Louis' supplies were running out, and he was forced to raise his siege of the rebellious stronghold and press for peace. Peace was restored to the county on 11 November. This time Louis was able to consolidate his authority over Ypres and Bruges, and he received monetary reparations from other, smaller rebellious towns.[9]

Yet again, in March 1381, Louis broke the peace and besieged Ghent. However, despite his being supported by money and forces from Burgundy, and despite his being able to apply a blockade on Ghent which included help from the duchy of Brabant and the counties of Holland and Hainault, Ghent would not succumb to the count's siege which lasted throughout the rest of the year and into 1382.[10] By April 1382, another

---

[7] On these sieges see Vandermaesen and Ryckaert, 'De Gentse opstand', pp. 14–15; Vaughan, *Philip the Bold*, pp. 20–1; D. Nicholas, *The Van Arteveldes of Ghent: The Varieties of Vendetta and the Hero in History* (Ithaca, 1988), p. 141; and *idem, Town and Countryside: Social, Economic and Political Tensions in Fourteenth Century Flanders* (Bruges, 1971), p. 333.

[8] See Vandermaesen and Ryckaert, 'De Gentse opstand', p. 15; Pirenne, *Historie de Belgique*, II, pp. 191–2; Nicholas, *Medieval Flanders*, p. 228; *idem, Town and Countryside*, p. 333; and E. Perroy, *The Hundred Years War*, trans. W. B. Wells (London, 1951), pp. 188–9.

[9] Vandermaesen and Ryckaert, 'De Gentse opstand', p. 15; Pirenne, *Histoire de Belgique*, II, pp. 192–3; Vaughan, *Philip the Bold*, pp. 22–3; and F. Lot, *L'art militaire et les armées au moyen âge en Europe et dans le proche orient* (Paris, 1946), I, p. 451.

[10] On the siege of Ghent see Vandermaesen and Ryckaert, 'De Gentse opstand',

peace conference was held, this one at Tournai. But the Ghentenaars, newly confident in their ability to withstand Louis' siege attempts, and led by Philip van Artevelde, the son of the great rebel leader of the 1340s, Jacob van Artevelde, refused to agree to a truce.[11] On 3 May they attacked the town of Bruges, fighting a battle outside the walls of the town at Bevershoutsveld. Bruges was taken, and Louis of Male, who was in Bruges at the time, was forced to flee to the safety of Lille during the night.[12]

Victory was to be short-lived, however. Although almost all of Flanders joined the rebellion, with Dendermonde and Oudenaarde again as the only hold-outs,[13] independence was not to last long. Louis, making his escape, quickly travelled to Paris where he petitioned his father-in-law, Philip the Bold, and Philip's nephew, the young French king, Charles VI, for aid against the rebellion. The French king could hardly refuse such a petition, especially after Philip convinced his nephew that to allow the Flemings to rebel would fuel the already hot fires of independence in other French towns. The king was further convinced when he received word that the Flemish rebels had violated French territory by attacking several small towns around Tournai.[14]

---

p. 16; Vaughan, *Philip the Bold*, p. 23; Nicholas, *Medieval Flanders*, pp. 228–9; and M. Haegeman, *De anglofilie in het graafschap Vlaanderen* (Courtrai, 1988), pp. 63–6.

[11] Vaughan, *Philip the Bold*, p. 23; Nicholas, *Van Arteveldes*, p. 169; and Haegeman, *De anglofilie*, pp. 66–8. On Philip van Artevelde's early life and his governance of Ghent from 1379 to 1382 see Nicholas, *Van Arteveldes*, pp. 99–159.

[12] On the battle of Bevershoutsveld and Louis of Male's flight see Vandermaesen and Ryckaert, 'De Gentse opstand', p. 16; Nicholas, *Van Arteveldes*, pp. 172–5; Nicholas, *Medieval Flanders*, p. 230; Haegeman, *De anglofilie*, p. 82; Pirenne, *Histoire de Belgique*, II, pp. 193–5, 198; Vaughan, *Philip the Bold*, pp. 23–4; Mirot, *Les insurrections urbaines*, pp. 84, 144–5; Palmer, *England, France and Christendom*, p. 20; Lot, *L'art militaire*, I, p. 451; and F. Lehoux, *Jean de France, duc de Berri: Sa vie, son action politique (1340–1416)* (Paris, 1966), II, p. 68.

[13] Nicholas, *Van Arteveldes*, pp. 175–8; Pirenne, *Histoire de Belgique*, II, p. 195; Mirot, *Les insurrections urbaines*, pp. 145, 148; Lot, *L'art militaire*, I, p. 451; H. Delbrück, *Geschichte der Kriegskunst im Rahmen des Politischen Geschichte*, III: *Mittelalter* (2nd edn, Berlin, 1923), p. 442; and F. Autrand, *Charles VI* (1986), p. 131.

[14] On the petitions of Louis to Philip the Bold and Charles VI see Nicholas, *Van Arteveldes*, pp. 181–3; Pirenne, *Histoire de Belgique*, II, p. 197; Vaughan, *Philip the Bold*, p. 16; Perroy, *The Hundred Years War*, p. 189; Autrand, *Charles VI*, p. 124; Mirot, *Les insurrections urbaines*, pp. 145, 159; Palmer, *England, France and Christendom*, p. 20; Lot, *L'art militaire*, II, p. 451; Lehoux, *Jean de France*, II, p. 68; and J. Favier, *La guerre de cent ans* (Paris, 1980), p. 384.

The king gathered his forces and proceeded to Arras, reaching there on 3 November. In the following days, a council of war was held at Seclin in which it was decided that the French would cross the Lys river at Commines. From there they would proceed to Ypres and then to Bruges, and ultimately they would besiege Ghent. At the same time, the council sent peace envoys to the rebels bidding them to accept a truce; it was refused.[15]

The council's plan was followed without much deviation in its first two phases. The Lys river was crossed at Commines with only a little resistance from the Flemings,[16] and Ypres surrendered on 21 November without a battle.[17] But before the French army could move to Bruges, scouts reported that the Flemish force had massed between Ypres and Bruges near West Rosebeke. Philip van Artevelde, knowing that his force was superior in numbers, and perhaps mindful of the great Flemish victories over the French in the past, at Courtrai and Arques, for example, as well as his own recent victory at Bevershoutsveld, believed that it was to his advantage to meet the French in open battle. He selected an advantageous terrain, ordering his troops on the side of Goudberg, a small hill, and he awaited the advent of the French force.[18]

The battle of Rosebeke was fought on 26 November 1382.[19] It was a resounding defeat for the Flemish rebels, and among their dead lay Philip van Artevelde. The remains of the rebellious army fled to the safety of

[15]   On Charles' council of war see Delbrück, *Geschichte der Kriegskunst*, III, p. 443. On the peace offered to the Flemish rebels see Autrand, *Charles VI*, p. 124; Mirot, *Les insurrections urbaines*, p. 161; and Lehoux, *Jean de France*, II, p. 69.

[16]   On the conflict at the bridge of Commines see Nicholas, *Van Arteveldes*, p. 184; Autrand, *Charles VI*, pp. 126–8; and Delbrück, *Geschichte der Kriegskunst*, III, p. 443.

[17]   On the surrender of Ypres see Nicholas, *Van Arteveldes*, p. 184; Autrand, *Charles VI*, pp. 129–30; and Delbrück, *Geschichte der Kriegskunst*, III, p. 443.

[18]   On the Flemish army and numbers see Autrand, *Charles VI*, p. 131; Delbrück, *Geschichte der Kriegskunst*, III, pp. 443–4; and Lot, *L'Art militaire*, I, p. 452. On the French numbers see P. Contamine, *Guerre, état, et société à la fin du moyen âge: Études sur les armées des rois de France, 1337–1494* (Paris, 1972), p. 198.

[19]   On the battle of Rosebeke see Nicholas, *Van Arteveldes*, pp. 184–7; Nicholas, *Medieval Flanders*, p. 82; Pirenne, *Histoire de Belgique*, II, p. 198; Haegeman, *De anglofilie*, p. 82; Favier, *La guerre de cent ans*, p. 385; Autrand, *Charles VI*, pp. 131–3; Delbrück, *Geschichte der Kriegskunst*, III, pp. 442–6; Lot, *L'Art militaire*, I, pp. 451–2; F. Mohr, *Die Schlacht bei Rosebeke* (Berlin, 1906); M. de Maere d'Aertrycke, *Recherches concernant quelques questions controversées à propos des batailles de Courtrai et Rosebeque* (Annales internationales d'histoire, Congrés de Paris, 1900), Ie section, pp. 150–60; C. Oman, *A History of the Art of War in the Middle Ages* (London, 1905), II, p. 376; and P. Contamine, *War in the Middle Ages*, trans. M. Jones (London, 1984), p. 230n.

Ghent and other nearby towns. The siege of Oudenaarde was raised, and the French army moved to Courtrai. Bruges surrendered to Charles there, promising to submit to the governance of Louis of Male, to accept Clement VII as pope, and to pay a reparation of 120,000 *livres parises*.[20] The French were unable to proceed further against Ghent, however, and the town would not surrender for two more years.[21]

While the commentary of modern historians on the battle of Bevershoutsveld pales in comparison to that on the later battle of Rosebeke,[22] there are several contemporary sources which discuss what occurred there: from the northern Low Countries, Jan Beka's *Chronographia*; from England, the *Westminster Chronicle* and Thomas Walsingham's *Historia Anglicana*; from France, the *Chronique des quatre premiers Valois*, the *Chronique du religieux de Saint-Denis*, and Jean Juvenal des Ursins' *Histoire de Charles VI*; from Flanders, the *Chronicon comitum Flandriae*, the *Chronique de Flandre*, the *Rijmkroniek van Vlaenderen*, the *Chronique des Pays-Bas, de France, d'Angleterre et de Tournai*, the *Kronyk van Vlaenderen van 580 tot 1467*, Oliver van Dixmude's *Merkwaerdige gebeurtenissen vooral in Vlaenderen en Brabant van 1377 tot 1443*, Theodore Pauwel's *Alia narratio de ducibus Burgundiae*, Adrien de Budt's *Chronicon Flandriae*, and, especially, from Hainault, Jean Froissart's *Chroniques*.[23] It is from them that we get the following tale.

---

20   See Autrand, *Charles VI*, pp. 134–5.
21   See Pirenne, *Histoire de Belgique*, II, pp. 199–200, and Nicholas, *Medieval Flanders*, p. 230.
22   See notes 12 and 19 above for a comparison of modern works which discuss these two battles.
23   Jean Beka, *Chronographia de Jan de Beka*, ed. H. Bruch ('s Gravenhage, 1973), p. 345; *The Westminster Chronicle, 1381–94*, ed. and trans. L. C. Hector and B. F. Harvey (Oxford, 1982), pp. 27–31; Thomas Walsingham, *Historia Anglicana*, ed. H. T. Riley (Rolls Series, London, 1864), II, pp. 61–2; *Chronique des quatre premiers Valois (1327–1393)*, ed. S. Luce (Paris, 1862), pp. 302–3; *Chronique du religieux de Saint-Denis*, ed. L. Bellaguet (Paris, 1839), I, p. 351; Jean Juvenal des Ursins, *Histoire de Charles VI*, ed. Michaud and Poujoulat, in *Nouvelle collection des mémoires pour servir à l'histoire de France depuis le xiiie siècle jusqu' à la fin du xiiie siècle*, II (Lyons, 1851), p. 351; *Chronicon comitum Flandriae*, in *Corpus chronicorum Flandriae*, I, ed. J. J. de Smet (Brussels, 1837), pp. 240–8; *Chronique de Flandre*, in *Istore et croniques de Flandres*, ed. Kervyn de Lettenhove (Brussels, 1880), II, pp. 246–7; *Rijmkroniek van Vlaenderen*, in *Corpus chronicorum Flandriae*, IV, ed. J. J. de Smet (Brussels, 1865), pp. 869–71; *Chronique des Pays-Bas, de France, d'Angleterre et de Tournai*, in *Corpus chronicorum Flandriae*, III, ed. J. J. de Smet (Brussels, 1856), p. 275; *Kronyk van Vlaenderen van 580 tot 1467*, ed. P. Bloomaert and C. P. Serriere (Ghent, 1839), I, pp. 242–4; Oliver van Dixmude, *Merkwaerdige gebeurtenissen vooral in Vlaenderen en Brabant van 1377 tot 1443*, ed. J. J. Lambin (Ypres, 1835), pp. 10–11; Theodore Pauwels, *Alia narratio de ducibus Burgundiae*, in *Chroniques relatives à l'histoire de la Belgique sous la*

Ghent, the contemporary chroniclers record, was suffering from severe hunger at the beginning of 1382.[24] The Flemish harvests had been destroyed from the constant warfare of the preceding three years, and what little good was available in 1382 had gone to Bruges which had been supported by Count Louis of Male since March of the previous year. As well, only a modicum of supplies had been provided from the allies of Ghent, among them Liège, and this was quickly disposed of by the citizens of the rebellious town.[25] Therefore, it was expedient that the Ghentenaars attack and defeat Louis of Male and Bruges to try and free their town from its hunger. At least that is the rationale given by the southern Low Countries' chroniclers. The anonymous author of the *Rijmkroniek van Vlaenderen* writes:

> There was no time to spare. / They must fight or die / of hunger; and to rid them of their need, / they decided in their council / to go against Bruges.[26]

Other sources, notably the French chroniclers and the *Westminster Chronicle*, see this act as something quite different, an act of treason. Here the Ghentenaars rebelled not only against their comital lord but also against their king.[27]

For some reason, Louis of Male did not expect an attack to come from Ghent against Bruges. Although he knew of Ghent's situation – indeed, he counted on his blockade of Ghent and the ensuing hunger to incite the town to submission – he reckoned that this submission would come long before there would be any military action. Jean Froissart recounts:

> Of all their needs and affairs was the count of Flanders, who resided at Bruges, informed, and how those of Ghent were so constrained and so taken by hunger that they could not survive much longer. So you can

---

domination des ducs de Bourgogne (textes latins), I, ed. J. J. de Smet (Brussels, 1837), p. 340; and Jean Froissart, *Chroniques*, in *Oeuvres de Froissart*, ed. Kervyn de Lettenhove (Brussels, 1870), X, pp. 1–38.

[24] See Jean Froissart, X, pp. 1–3; *Chronicon comitum Flandriae*, p. 240; *Rijmkroniek van Vlaenderen*, p. 869; Oliver van Dixmude, p. 10; and Adrien de Budt, p. 340.

[25] Jean Froissart, X, pp. 5–8.

[26] *Rijmkroniek van Vlaenderen*, pp. 869–70:
Doe ne was daer gheen langer sparen,
Si moesten vechten, of bliven doot
Van honghere; ende te scuwene de noot,
So vonden si in haren raet
Voer Brugghe te treckene ...

[27] *Chronique des quatre premiers Valois*, p. 302; *Chronique du religieux de Saint-Denis*, I, p. 351; Jean Juvenal des Ursins, p. 351; and *Westminster Chronicle*, p. 27. The *Westminster Chronicle*, not supporting the kingship of Charles VI, naturally leaves out the last issue.

believe and know that he was not much concerned about their poverty, nor also were those men of his council who wished to see the destruction of this town.[28]

He may also have felt that the town of Ghent, filled not with soldiers, but with clothmakers, merchants, bankers, and tradesmen, would not have the desire or skill to fight against anyone else, even others of similar non-military occupations. In this he failed not only in his judgement, but also in his reading of recent Flemish urban history.[29]

The Ghentenaar force was not large; contemporary chroniclers estimate that their numbers were only between four and eight thousand men.[30] However, they did have a large number of gunpowder artillery pieces accompanying the force, with Jean Froissart recording the presence of two hundred carts full of this type of weaponry.[31] These guns seem to have been brought by the Ghentenaars in anticipation of a siege of Bruges. Facing them was a comital army of between twenty and forty thousand soldiers, a force which the *Chronique de Flandre* calls 'une moult puissant compangnie de gens de guerre'.[32]

But, despite their overwhelming numerical advantage over the Ghentenaars and despite also seeing the approach of their opponents from a long distance away, the Brugeois and their army were not prepared for battle. Why this was so can only be guessed at. However, there is some indication that the Brugeois, together with whatever soldiers were there to protect the count and the town, were celebrating the Holy Blood Processions, a most important and still practised local holiday. Indeed, the

---

[28] Jean Froissart, X, p. 9: 'De toutes ches besognes et affaires fu li contes de Flandres qui se tenoit à Bruges, enfourmés et comment chil de Gand estoient si astraint et si menet que il ne pooient longhement durer. Sy poés croire et savoir que de leur provreté il n'estoit mies courouchiés, ne ossi n'estoient cil de son conseil, qui la destruction de la ville de Gand veissent volentiers'.

[29] For an excellent survey of the economic history of fourteenth-century Ghent and the townspeoples' occupations see D. Nicholas, *The Metamorphosis of a Medieval City: Ghent in the Age of the Arteveldes, 1302–1390* (Lincoln, 1987). On the numerous conflicts of Flanders in the fourteenth century see K. DeVries, *Perceptions of Victory and Defeat in the Southern Low Countries during the Fourteenth Century: A Historiographical Comparison* (Ph.D. Dissertation, University of Toronto, 1987).

[30] For estimations of the Ghentenaar numbers at Bevershoutsveld, see Jean Froissart, X, p. 22; *Chronique de Flandre*, II, p. 246; Oliver van Dixmude, p. 10; and *Kronyk van Vlaenderen*, I, p. 242.

[31] Jean Froissart, X, p. 22.

[32] The *Chronique de Flandre* (II, p. 246) estimates the number of Brugeois at more than 20,000 while Jean Froissart (X, p. 30) numbers these troops at more than 40,000.

Chronicon comitum Flandriae claims that the captain of Bruges, Hallard de Poucke, refused to attack the Ghentenaars because of this holiday.[33] Those who did go to fight, almost all of the chroniclers declare, were drunken, because, in the words of Oliver van Dixmude, 'they had been drinking all day'.[34] The *Chronicon comitum Flandriae* agrees: 'Many of the Brugeois were drinking, and drunk, and full of food.'[35]

Another excuse for the lack of preparation by the Brugeois was simply their surprise at encountering a force from Ghent attacking their town. For although they could see their approach, the Brugeois seemed to be amazed that such an onslaught was being attempted against them. The *Rijmkroniek van Vlaenderen* reports that the attacking army so surprised the Brugeois that they were forced to order themselves 'hastily'.[36]

On the other side, the Ghentenaars were in high spirits and were well organised. Jean Froissart claims that on the morning of the battle the Ghentenaars celebrated seven masses. After each mass, the monks accompanying the army preached to the rebel soldiers likening their situation to that of the people of Israel who were held in bondage by the Pharaoh of Egypt until freed by Moses. Froissart recounts the preacher's sermon:

> And so, good people, you are held in servitude by your lord, the count, and by your neighbours of Bruges, whom you have come to attack, and with whom you will without a doubt fight.[37]

The preacher then concluded his oration by promising the Ghentenaars that they would be victorious:

> because God, who can do all things, is everywhere and knows all things, will have mercy on you ... And in this quarrel, you have justice and a very reasonable cause. So you ought to be very bold and much comforted.[38]

---

33 *Chronicon comitum Flandriae*, p. 248.

34 Oliver van Dixmude, p. 11: '... want zy al den dach ghedronken hadden'.

35 *Chronicon comitum Flandriae*, p. 240: 'Insuper plures Brugensium erant potati et ebrii et epula gravati ...' See also *Chronique de Flandre*, II, p. 247 and *Kronyk van Vlaenderen*, I, p. 243.

36 *Rijmkroniek van Vlaenderen*, p. 870.

37 Jean Froissart, X, p. 26: 'Enssi, bonnes gens, dissoient chil Frère-Prêceur en leurs sermons, estes-vous tenu en servitude par vostre signeur le conte et vos voisins de Bruges, devant laquelle ville vous estes venu et arresté, et serés combatu, il n'est mie doubte.'

38 Jean Froissart, X, pp. 26–7: 'Car Dieux qui tout peut, tout set et tout congnoist, ara merchy de vous ... et en ceste querelle vous avés bon droit et juste cause par trop de raisons. Sy en devés estre plus hardy et mieux conforté.'

After these masses, Philip van Artevelde harangued his army, reiterating the justice of Ghent's fight and claiming that the town's citizens had frequently sought peace, independence, and self-governance from the count, but that they had never received these. He told them that nothing could be gained from retreating to the town without attacking Louis of Male's army, and that they should think of Ghent and their women and children who were there. The army then breakfasted on the last of the town's foodstuffs.[39]

In this way the two armies prepared for battle. The Ghentenaars were high spirited, organised, and prepared to fight and die for their town. The Brugeois were disorganised and lacked both leadership and morale. They were also undoubtedly inebriated and fatigued by the celebrations of the day. Still, they went out of the town to fight with the Ghentenaars in what Theodore Pauwels describes as a 'long battle of great malice'.[40] In the end the Brugeois were defeated. The *Rijmkroniek van Vlaenderen* recounts the action:

> Many pious men fled out of Bruges / in order to fight the Ghentenaars. / The armies, as you know, / met together on both sides. / There men saw terrible fighting / which cost many men their lives. / But those of Bruges were driven back / and they were forced to yield the field.[41]

But why did the Brugeois lose the battle of Bevershoutsveld? Even though they lacked the preparation and morale of their Flemish counterparts, they still had overwhelming numerical superiority, and this superiority it seems drove the soldiers of Bruges to flee the protective walls of their town. This in itself invites an interesting query: why did the Brugeois have to fight a battle at all when it is likely that the Ghentenaars, extremely low on supplies, could not have won a lengthy siege against their town, especially as such a siege would certainly have brought a relief force from the French king in support of his faithful lord? Indeed, Thomas Walsingham is so surprised by the Brugeois wish to fight a battle that he surmises, erroneously, that the town was not protected by walls, but by

---

[39] Jean Froissart, X, pp. 27–8.
[40] Theodore Pauwels, p. 235. See also the *Chronique des quatre premiers Valois*, p. 302.
[41] *Rijmkroniek van Vlaenderen*, p. 870:
    menich vroom man huut Brugghe,
    Om te strydene up die van Ghent.
    Die battaeljen, sy hu bekent,
    Ghinghen toe an beede zyden:
    Daer sach men vreeselike striden,
    Dat meneghen man coste zyn leven.
    Maer die van brugghe worden verdreven,
    Ende moesten wyken van den velde.

deep ditches which were easily crossed.[42] Of course, the Ghentenaars had brought their gunpowder weapons with them in order to shorten the length of any siege which they might have to fight. Yet at this point in time, so early in the history of gunpowder weaponry use, only a few fortified locations had fallen to this new military technology.[43] However, without question this is the reason for the presence of gunpowder weapons among the Ghentenaar force. Philip van Artevelde believed in using these weapons for sieges, and he would employ his guns against Oudenaarde following his victory at Bevershoutsveld.[44] But van Artevelde was not forced to use his guns against the walls of Bruges. For the Brugeois had left them to do battle on the plain outside of the town. Instead, he would use them in another, much less conventional way.

As the Brugeois exited from their town, they faced a Ghentenaar army arrayed in well ordered lines. Seeing this array may have caused some of the Brugeois to lose face and retreat, although it was definitely not the whole of the army, as Adrien de Budt claims;[45] the majority of troops seem to have remained to fight. This group, still larger than the Ghentenaar army, moved forward. It is here that Philip van Artevelde decided to use tactics different from those common in these types of conflicts. Instead of waiting to receive the Brugeois attack, he fired his guns into their oncoming force. Then, he wheeled his troops on an axis, to where the sun shone in their opponents' eyes, and attacked the approaching Brugeois troops. Jean Froissart describes this action:

> The Ghentenaars placed themselves on a hill and they gathered themselves all together. Then they fired more than three hundred cannons all at the same time. And then they turned around on a hub and ordered themselves, placing the Brugeois with the sun in their eyes which distressed them greatly. Then they attacked them crying 'Ghent!' At the moment that the Brugeois heard the voices of the Ghentenaars and the firing of the cannons and saw that they were about to be brutally attacked, they, like cowards and villains, opened their lines and allowed

---

[42] Thomas Walsingham, II, p. 61.

[43] I know of only two such victories that preceded the battle of Bevershoutsveld. The first of these came in 1374 when the French used them to bring down the town walls of Saint-Saveur-le-Vicomte. This was followed in 1377, at the siege of Odruik, when Philip the Bold, duke of Burgundy, used cannons which fired 200 lb balls to bring down the walls of the castle. See K. DeVries, 'The Impact of Gunpowder Weaponry on Siege Warfare in the Hundred Years War', in *The Medieval City Under Siege*, ed. I. A. Corfis and M. Wolfe (Woodbridge, 1995), p. 229.

[44] Jean Froissart, X, pp. 57–62. See also DeVries, 'The Impact of Gunpowder Weaponry', p. 229.

[45] See Adrien de Budt, p. 340.

the Ghentenaars to enter among them without putting up any defence. And they flung down their weapons and fled.[46]

The *Chronique de Flandre* confirms what Froissart writes:

The Ghentenaars moved themselves and their artillery forward. Which artillery fired a blast with such a furor that it seemed to bring the [Brugeois] line directly to a halt.[47]

The Brugeois fled in a hurried rout, rushing for the safety of their town. The Ghentenaars pursued them, showing little mercy. Jean Froissart writes:

The Ghentenaars followed the Brugeois harshly and boldly, and wherever they encountered anyone they attacked him and killed him ... So I must say to you that in this chase there were many killed, wounded, and cast down, for they made no defence, nor were there any more wicked people than those of Bruges, nor any more recreant, nor any who held themselves more cowardly according to their great arrogance which was shown when they came onto the battlefield.[48]

There were large numbers killed on both sides, with some contemporary chroniclers citing a tally of 10,000 Brugeois and 4,000 Ghentenaars slain.[49] The anonymous author of the *Chronique du religieux de Saint-Denis* writes:

---

[46]   Jean Froissart, X, pp. 31–2: 'Adont ceulx de Gand se missent en ung mont et se recueillirent tous ensemble et fisent tout à une fois desclicquer plus de IIIc canons, et tournèrent autour de ce plasquiet, et misent ceulx de Bruges le souleil en l'ueil, qui mout les greva, et entrèrent dans eulx, en escriant: "Gand!" Sitost que ceulx de Bruges oyrent la voix de ceulx de Gand et les canons desclicquer, et que il les veirent venir de front sur eulx et assailir asprement comme lasches gens et pleins de mauvais convenant, il se ouvrirent tous et laissièrent les Gantois entrer dans eulx sans d'effence nulle et jettèrent leurs bastons jus et tournèrent le dos.' The *Chronique du religieux de Saint-Denis* (I, p. 168), though praising Philip van Artevelde for his tactics, misunderstands what the Ghentenaars did in this battle. See also Jean Juvenal des Ursins, p. 351.

[47]   *Chronique de Flandre*, II, p. 247: 'Ils se reboutèrent tous en leur artillerie que ils firent à coup tirer par telle fureur que ce sembloit ung droit fourdre venant d'en hault.'

[48]   Jean Froissart, X, pp. 31–2: 'Il poursuivirent ceulx de Bruges asprement et hardiment, et là où il les raconsuivoient, il les abatoient et ocisoient ou sus eulx passoient ... Si vous di que en celle chace il y ot mout de mors et de desconfits et d'abatus; car entre eux point de deffence il n'avoient, ne onques si meschans gens que ceulx de Bruges ne furent, ne qui plus recréamment, ne laschement se maintinrent selonc le grant boban que au venir sus les champs fuit il avoient.'

[49]   Jean Juvenal des Ursins, p. 351 and *Chronique du religieux de Saint-Denis*, I, p. 168.

A large number fell. Not long after the attack was the land coloured red, marked with much blood. And on both sides were many killed or fatally wounded.[50]

Furthermore, this intermingling of the two sides presented a problem when the mass of troops reached the town gates. The *Kronyk van Vlaenderen* reports that because both the Ghentenaars and the Brugeois reached the gates at the same time, the keepers of these gates were unable to close them, thus allowing the attackers easy entrance into the town:

> The Ghentenaars saw the Brugeois fleeing quickly, so they followed them strongly in order to enter the town with them ... The keepers of the gates dared not close the gates in order to protect the people who were fleeing into the town. When they saw the Ghentenaars approaching, they tried to close the gates, but as they did so, a Ghentenaar threw a pike between both of the doors of the gates, and by this they were unable to close the gates.[51]

Once inside the town, the slaughter continued. All partisans of Louis de Male were killed, including, the *Chronicon comitum Flandriae* records, many fishermen.[52] On the other hand, Thomas Walsingham takes solace in the fact that no alien merchant was slain that day; Englishmen were especially spared.[53] 'Many good men were killed', notes the *Rijmkroniek van Vlaenderen*,[54] and Adrien de Budt reports that more could have been killed had not nightfall put an end to the slaughter:

> victory fell to the Ghentenaars, having perpetrated a slaughter of citizens; and except for the darkness of night giving aid to the fleeing citizens, a

---

[50] *Chronique du religieux de Saint-Denis*, I, p. 168: ' ... ingentique cede, non diu post adgressum jam rubricaret tellus, multo distincta cruore, et utrinque multi corruerunt moribundi aut letaliter vulnerati'.

[51] *Kronyk van Vlaenderen*, I, pp. 243–4: 'Die van Ghendt siende de Brugghelingen vastelijc vlien, sy volghden starckelijc an van achtere, om met hemlieden in te comene ... De wachters die de poorten wachten, sy dorsten de poorten niet sluten, om haer volc dat vaste in quam ghevloen, mar als sy saghen die van Ghendt ancomen, sy pijnden hem de poorte te slutene, nemar yeer dat sy toe ghinc, een Ghentenare schoet sine pyke tusschen beide de bladeren van de poorten, ende by dien soe ne conste de poorte niet toe.' Other chroniclers also comment on the Ghentenaars' easy access to Bruges: see Jean Froissart, X, pp. 33–4; *Chronique de Flandre*, II, p. 247; *Rijmkroniek van Vlaenderen*, pp. 870–1; *Chronicon comitum Flandriae*, p. 240; *Kronyk van Vlaenderen*, I, p. 243; *Chronique des Pays-Bas*, p. 275; and Adrien de Budt, p. 340.

[52] *Chronicon comitum Flandriae*, p. 240. This keeps with the image of Ghent's problems with river traffic.

[53] Thomas Walsingham, II, p. 62.

[54] *Rijmkroniek van Vlaenderen*, p. 870: 'So bleef menich goet man doot'.

greater massacre would have been done.[55]

However, the chief prize of the rebels, Louis of Male, was not to be found among the dead or captured, for the count had successfully escaped from his enemies. The *Chronique de Flandre* does insist that Louis was nearly slain in the battle outside of the town, but that he was saved after his horse was killed by a Ghentenaar soldier who was then killed himself; but the *Chronique de Flandre* is alone in this assertion.[56] Other sources refer only to certain legends of the count's escape from within the town. Some of these report that Louis was aided in Bruges by a craftsman named Simon van Cokermoes who insisted that Louis flee from the defeat and save himself. The *Chronicon comitum Flandriae* reports the conversation held between the two men:

> The lord prince, Count Louis, wished to enter the town square with his horse, but he was not permitted. One Brugeois craftsman, Master Simon van Cokermoes, hit the horse of the prince, and the prince said, 'O Simon, who have you hit?' He responded, 'Lord Louis, I know what I do. I did not hit you, but your horse. You must make haste to get away from here!'[57]

Simon van Cokermoes then led Louis of Male outside of the town to safety.

A more colourful story of Louis' escape comes to us from Jean Froissart. Froissart begins his account by writing:

> So God was clearly there for the count since he delivered him from this peril and saved him, for no one had ever been in such great peril as before, nor was it over, as I shall relate.[58]

He then reports that after the battle the count remained alone and was chased from street to street in Bruges. About to be captured, Louis came upon the poor house of a young widow. Identifying himself, he asked for aid in return for a handsome reward. Without any reluctance, the woman quickly hid the frightened count in the loft with her sleeping children. A

55 Adrien de Budt, p. 340: 'cessit Gandensibus victoria, maxima civium strage perpetrata; et nisi tenebrositas noctis civibus fugiendi auxilium praetitisset, occisio major fuisset'.

56 *Chronique de Flandre*, II, p. 247.

57 *Chronicon comitum Flandriae*, p. 240: 'Dominus princeps comes Ludovicus volebat intrare forum cum equo suo, non est permissus; sed unus Brugensis faber, dominus Simon Cokermoes percussit equum principis, ac princeps dixit: "Och Symon! quem percutis?" respondit: "Dominus Ludovice! scio quid facio, non vos sed equum vestrum percussi; expediatis vos per hinc."'

58 Jean Froissart, X, p. 36: 'Si fu Dieu propement pour luy quant de ce péril il le délivra et saulva, car oncques en si grant péril en devant n'avoit esté, ne ne fut depuis, sicomme je vous recorderay présentement.'

mob of rebels soon entered her house to search it for the hiding king, whom the widow denied having seen. Unable to find Louis, they left without capturing him. Froissart concludes his story:

> All was heard by the count of Flanders who was hidden in this poor loft. So you are able to imagine that he was greatly afraid for his life. God, what could he have been thinking about? When in the morning he was able to say: 'I am one of the greatest princes of the Christian world,' to find himself that night to be in such humble circumstances. It can easily be said and thought that the fortunes of this world are not very stable. Again it was fortunate for him that he was able to save his life. Always this perilous and cruel adventure ought to be a great remembrance for his entire lifetime.[59]

Without the Flemish count's capture, there was to be no end to the rebellion. The battle of Rosebeke would have to be fought and lost.

The use of gunpowder weapons by the Ghentenaars at the battle of Bevershoutsveld is unique and special. It seems that van Artevelde did not expect to use his guns to fight a battle, anticipating instead that their fire would shorten his siege of the town. And while he did take them to Rosebeke, he could not duplicate his Bevershoutsveld tactics, losing his life in that combat. Still, what had been solely a siege weapon from at least the mid-fourteenth century was used by van Artevelde and the Ghentenaars at Bevershoutsveld to decide the victory of their smaller force over the larger Brugeois army in battle. This was the first such decisive use in the history of western Europe. From this time on, gunpowder weapons would begin to be found more and more on the battlefield, at Aljubarrota in 1385, at Castagnaro in 1387, at Tongres and Othée in 1408, at Agincourt in 1415, at Cravant in 1423, at the battle of the Herrings in 1429, at Bulgneville in 1431, at Formigny in 1450, at Castillon and Gavere in 1453, at Blore Heath and Ludford Bridge in 1459, at St Albans in 1461, at Montlhéry in 1465, at Huy and Brusthem in 1467, at Grandson and Murten in 1476, at Nancy in 1477 and at Bosworth in 1485.[60] The battle of Bevershoutsveld deserves not to be forgotten.

---

[59] Jean Froissart, X, p. 38: 'Toutes ces paroles avoit oyes li contes de Flandres qui estoit couché et cati en ce povre litteron. Sy povés bien ymaginer que il fu adont en grant effroy de sa vie. Quel chose povoit-il là, Dieux, penser, ne ymaginer? quant au matin il povoit bien dire: "Je suis li uns des plus grans princes dou monde des chrestiens," et la nuit ensuivant il se trouvoit en celle petitesse, il povoit bien dire et ymaginer qu les fortunes de ce monde ne sont pas trop estables. Encores grant heur pour luy quant il s'en povoit yssir, saulve sa vie.'

[60] See Kelly DeVries, *Medieval Military Technology* (Peterborough, 1992), pp. 147–8.

The Myth of the Military Supremacy of Knightly Cavalry

MATTHEW BENNETT

'Horsemen armed [with the couched lance] had an advantage over men
fighting on foot as absolute as that which, a millennium later, men armed
with breechloaders had over enemies armed only with spears.' Thus Sir
Michael Howard in *War in European History*, Chapter 1, 'The Wars of the
Knights'.[1]

The title of the paper might seem rather tautological. After all, 'knightly
cavalry' could be rendered as 'horsey horsemen'; but there is a reason for
this apparent clumsiness. What do we call the mounted warriors of that
equally absurdly titled period of history – the middle ages – in order to
explain their role in warfare? They called themselves *equites*, and for
well-known reasons (which I shall not go into now) the generic name for
soldiers, *milites*, also came to convey the idea of an armoured cavalryman.
The various vernaculars provide: *chevalier, caballeros, Ritter*, and (from Old
English) *cniht*.[2] It is unfortunate for English speakers that we are saddled
with the word knight, since it is so value-loaded, although some historians
take evasive action when confronted by it, and with some justice. A recent
study of the background to the First Crusade in southern France is entitled
Knightly Piety, but the author prefers the words 'arms-bearers' throughout
when talking about the military classes' involvement in the novel activity of
armed pilgrimage.[3] Is this too extreme a stance to take, or is there still some
validity in the 'K'-word?

Now the whole issue would be a great deal easier if the term 'knight'
was not used to carry – in popular literature and school textbooks at least –
the weight of representing the whole medieval social order, which used to
be called 'feudalism'.[4] For an academic audience this word has been
deconstructed into oblivion, but such phrases as 'The Age of the Knights'
find their way into more scholarly works, too. Warfare then, in the age of

---

[1]   M. Howard, *War in European History* (Oxford, 1976),p. 2.
[2]   See M. Keen, *Chivalry* (London, 1984), ch. 2, esp. pp. 27–43; P. Contamine,
      War in the Middle Ages, trans. M. Jones (Oxford, 1984), ch. 2, esp. pp. 31,
      36–43, 50–9.
[3]   M. Bull, *Knightly Piety and the Lay Response to the First Crusade: The Limousin and
      Gascony c.970–1130* (Oxford, 1993).
[4]   See S. Reynolds, *Feudalism* (Oxford, 1994).

the knights, is perceived as knightly warfare. And what is knightly warfare? Why, the lance attack à l'outrance, as everyone knows:

> The basic strategic principle was to give immediate battle with a mass charge. After the initial clash in which manoeuvrability was at a minimum, the medieval battle became a melée of individual struggles.[5]

Nor is the knight, as an individual fighter, credited with any tactical skill or flexibility on the battlefield:

> On the whole, a knight was a very brave combatant and an ardent warrior but a mediocre soldier, virtually incapable of carrying out a plan that he could not grasp or a manoeuvre different from one which involved accosting the enemy from the front and throwing himself recklessly as soon as possible into the most intense melee.[6]

Both the works just cited were published almost a decade after Malcolm Vale's *War and Chivalry* completely revised current ideas about its subject; that chivalric warfare was out-of-touch with reality.[7] Rather he shows that it was in the mainstream of technological and tactical developments in the fifteenth century. Now, it might be argued that I have chosen easy targets to set up as Aunt Sallies for my ideas, but de Wailly's book is the most recent study of Crécy (and widely read) while Machiavelli's *Art of War* (it hardly needs saying) is a seminal text. Seminal text, that is, to post-1500 historians, who are often alarmingly ignorant of periods preceding their own (a charge that can also be levied against later medieval historians, on occasion). There is a strong argument to be made that it was not the 'Art of War' that changed in the sixteenth century – there was no 'Military Revolution', rather the advent of printing spread military ideas, as in so many other fields, so as to give an impression of novelty.[8]

The essential problem with both these quotes is that they place that mythical, unitary figure 'the knight' at the centre of medieval warfare. Recently, I tried to redress the balance against the dominance of this myth, by publishing an article in a popular journal of military history; but given the nature of its readership, I had to hold back from some of the closer analysis of campaigns and battles which had been part of my original

---

[5]   *Machiavelli's The Art of War*, ed. N. Wood (Pennsylvania, 1990), introduction.

[6]   H. de Wailly, *Crécy: Anatomy of a Battle* (Poole, 1989), pp. 36–7.

[7]   M. Vale, *War and Chivalry* (Oxford, 1981). Even an historian as percipient as Philippe Contamine can fall into much the same trap, as K. DeVries, *Infantry Warfare in the Early Fourteenth Century* (Woodbridge, 1996), pp. 4–5, points out, citing Contamine, *War in the Middle Ages*, p. 229.

[8]   M. Bennett and N. Hooper, *Cambridge Illustrated Atlas of Warfare: The Middle Ages 768–1487* (Cambridge, 1996), 'A Military Revolution', pp. 152–3, elaborates this argument.

thesis.[9] It is these matters to which I want to turn in the present paper. To a certain extent, this may appear restricted in that I find myself tackling the exponents of what might be termed 'old military history' on their own terms. That is to say, the great man and decisive battle approach to warfare, which has been deserted by most academic historians, but which still dominates popular perceptions of what military history is.[10]

Yet what follows is about battles, distant in place and time and spanning over a millennium. In so doing, I am, I admit, following the approach of those historians, represented by Sir Charles Oman, who first created the idea of the 'thousand-year rule of the knight' and presented warfare as dominated by the charges of heavy cavalry.[11] The timespan is delineated as beginning with the battle of Adrianople (AD 378) and ending with Crécy in 1346 (although Courtrai 1302, Bannockburn 1314, and Mortgarten 1315 also feature in the canon). In between, this interpretation proposes that infantry were swept from the battlefields of Europe and 'the knight' ruled supreme. Now, there is obviously so much wrong with this approach as possibly to render its refutation unnecessary (were it not that the misguided views are still so influential today).

I shall begin, as the traditional military historians do, with the battle of Adrianople. The most recent analysis of the course of events is by T. S. Burns, a historian of the Ostrogoths.[12] He points out that when Valens led his men against the 'Gretungi', they were defending a wagon-laager in the classic steppe manner. His main source, Ammianus Marcellinus, blames poor march discipline for the Romans putting in piecemeal attacks upon the encampment. The right wing arrived first, but suffered a repulse. At this moment the 'Gothic' cavalry arrived and smashed into the retreating troops. The Roman left wing had by now fought its way to the wagons, but it was

---

9   'The Knight Unmasked', *Military History Quarterly: The Quarterly Journal of Military History*, vol. 7, no. 4 (Summer, 1995) (American Historical Publications), pp. 8–19.

10 The British Channel 4 series *Great Commanders* is a good example of this approach. Not only that, but by leaping from Caesar to Nelson and Napoleon it omits eighteen centuries of warfare – including the middle ages! The series was shown on British terrestrial television Winter 1994 and repeated Summer 1996. It has also been shown world-wide on satellite channels.

11 Sir Charles Oman, *History of the Art of War in the Middle Ages*, which began as a brief essay of 134 pages (Oxford, 1885), was expanded to 667 pages for a new edition (London, 1898) and was further revised and expanded to two volumes (London, 1924). An unrevised reprint has recently been produced (London, 1991). All references are to the last edition. For the supposed dominance of cavalry, see I, pp. 356–8.

12 T. S. Burns, *A History of the Ostrogoths* (Bloomington, 1984); *idem*, 'The Battle of Adrianople: a Reconsideration', *Historia*, 22 (1973), pp. 336–45.

deserted by its cavalry. This meant the infantry of the centre were now attacked on both flanks, compressed together and unable to defend themselves properly. Valens took refuge with two of his household regiments, whilst his general Victor rode off to bring up the Batavians who were in reserve. But they had made off also, leaving the emperor to his fate. Now, it is difficult to see how this chapter of accidents could have been made into a decisive victory for 'barbarian' cavalry. But it has. The attack of the Gothic cavalry may even have been the result of a pre-planned ambush such as the Goths attempted at Ad Salices the previous year. The point is that 'barbarian' cavalry did not dare tackle Roman forces on equal terms.[13]

I do recognise that cavalry was becoming more important in western warfare generally in the fourth century. The armies of the later Roman Empire were substantially different from those fielded before the third century crisis. They were what Byzantine armies continued to be, mobile field armies made up of specialist troops often recruited from outside or on the borders of the empire. Warfare on the eastern frontier, especially with Sassanid Persia, had produced a higher cavalry component in these armies, perhaps as much as a third, in contrast to the infantry legions of the High Empire. Such troops increasingly came to resemble the warbands of important leaders, whether with Roman or barbarian names. This happened in the western part of the empire too. The political and military crises of the late fourth and fifth centuries produced the circumstances where the senatorial aristocracy of Gaul became local protectors in a way easily comparable to the invasion period of the ninth and tenth centuries.

Here, for example, is Sidonius Apollinarius describing the deeds of his brother-in-law Ecdicius when repelling a Visigothic attack on the Auvergne in 474, by reputedly scattering a thousand opponents with only eighteen of his own men:

> You came back at leisure to the city (Clermont) ... The courts of your vast house were filled with your retainers. They kissed the very dust of your feet, they handled the heavy bridle, clotted with blood and foam, they lifted the saddles, steeped in sweat, from the horses of your warriors, they unclasped the fastenings of your hollow helmet, they vied with one another in loosing the folds of your greaves, they counted and measured the terrible dints in your coat of mail ... Need I say how, after this, you with your own private resources, collected a public army and

---

[13] For Ad Salices see Ammianus Marcellinus, Bk. XXXI, ch. vii. I owe this reference and idea to Roy Boss. Cf. Oman, *Art of War in the Middle Ages*, I, 13–14: 'the first great victory won by that heavy cavalry which had now shown its ability to supplant heavy infantry of Rome as the ruling power in war'.

chastised the enemy for their incursions.[14]

This description sounds like that of any medieval hero, and with reason, for cavalry played an important role in what was evidently a war of raid and counter-raid. Nor should we be surprised to find cavalry warfare practised in Gaul. After all, Caesar had commented over six hundred years earlier on the value of Gallic cavalry. The question I am addressing is, though, whether cavalry became the dominant force in warfare, sweeping infantry from the battlefield. Of course, as John Gillingham and others have pointed out, the question is actually misframed, since decisive battle-seeking strategy is post-Clausewitzian theory, not terribly relevant to most medieval warfare.[15]

But the argument runs that the Franks developed a cavalry force, which after the mid-eighth century suddenly became much more effective owing to the introduction of the stirrup. Or rather, used to run. Bernard Bachrach has pointed out the flaw in Lynn White Jnr's original thesis, since stirrups do not seem to have been widely used in western Europe until *after* the Carolingian expansion, not before it. Nor should the literary conceit which has Charles Martel's men of the north standing like a wall of ice be taken literally to suggest a dismounted response to a mounted Muslim raid, which was then replaced by 'new' cavalry forces.[16]

There is no description of the mounted element in Charlemagne's armies winning victories by cavalry charges. The mobile troops of horsemen referred to as *scarae* have a strategic, rather than tactical, role, being especially used to garrison fortresses. In a sense, this is the real model to be drawn from Carolingian warfare, which continued to be an accurate representation of 'medieval' warfare. Charles' concern for the equipment of his warriors was also a continuing factor in war-worthiness. His wealthy vassals were expected to serve as armoured cavalry.[17] Karl Leyser has

---

[14] T. Hodgkin, *Italy and Her Enemies*, 6 vols (Oxford, 1888–99), II, pp. 499–500.

[15] See John Gillingham, 'Richard I and the Science of War in the Middle Ages', *War and Government in the Middle Ages: Essays in Honour of J. O. Prestwich*, ed. J. Gillingham and J. C. Holt (Woodbridge, 1984), pp. 78–91 and J. Gillingham 'William the Bastard at War', *Studies in Medieval History Presented to R. Allen Brown*, ed. C. Harper-Bill, C. Holdsworth and J. Nelson (Woodbridge, 1989), pp. 141–58. Both articles are reprinted in an invaluable collection, *Anglo-Norman Warfare*, ed. M. Strickland (Woodbridge, 1992), pp. 194–207, 143–60 respectively.

[16] The much-overrated 'impact of the stirrup' theory was popularised by Lynn T. White Jnr., *Medieval Technology and Social Change* (Oxford, 1962) and criticised by B. S. Bachrach, 'Charles Martel, Mounted Shock Combat, the Stirrup and Feudalism', *Studies in Medieval and Renaissance History*, 7, (1970), pp. 49–75.

308

examined the implications of this in relation to the Ottonian cavalry of the tenth century. In this case there can be no doubt that in order to defeat the Hungarians in the field, at the battle of the Lech, Otto I's *loricati* were instructed to close-up, shelter from the enemy's arrows behind their shields and make contact with lance and sword. In a sense this anticipated another continuing trend, that of the moral and physical superiority which western cavalry seem to have enjoyed over more lightly equipped easterners, as commentators such as the Byzantine princess Anna Comnena continued to remark.[18]

But this did not necessarily mean that armoured cavalry enjoyed such an easy superiority in western Europe. John France's examination of warfare in tenth-century Frankia draws attention to the *regii equitatus* (household cavalry?) described by the chronicler Richer. Apparently they placed an important role in defeating a number of opponents, including Vikings. Louis IV's victory over a Viking force in 943 is depicted as that of horse over foot, but most encounters are described in such a way as to make it impossible to determine the tactical significance of one arm or another.[19]

So we arrive, fairly swiftly, at the eleventh century, when evidence begins to thicken considerably, and come to the exceedingly well-reported battle of Hastings. This used to be read as confirming the superiority of 'knights' over axe-wielding footsoldiers. When it is paralleled by other near-contemporary 'Norman' victories over Swabian swordsmen at Civitate (1053) and the Byzantine Varangian Guard made up of English and Scandinavian axemen at Durazzo (1081), this interpretation would seem to be confirmed. Indeed, I used to believe it. I no longer do so.

Stephen Morillo has observed that Hastings was an unusual battle. This was the comment of contemporary witnesses, too: one side standing tight-knit and still, the other possessing mobility. From Hastings has grown up the idea that the Anglo-Scandinavian tradition of fighting on foot was inflexible in the face of 'new' tactics. But there is the problem that we have practically no other battle accounts with which to compare Hastings. The

---

[17] See Bennett and Hooper, *Atlas*, for a convenient summary and S. Coupland, 'Carolingian Arms and Armour in the Ninth Century', *Viator*, 20 (1989), pp. 29–50.

[18] K. Leyser, 'The Battle of the Lech, 955', *English Historical Review*, 50 (1965), pp. 1–25, reprinted in *Medieval Germany and its Neighbours 900–1250* (London, 1982), pp. 43–67; Anna Comnena, *Alexiad*, trans. E. R. A. Sewter (London, 1969), p. 416, on the supposed invincibility of the Frankish knight and his weakness once dismounted.

[19] J. France, 'La guerre dans la France féodale à la fin du IXe siècle et au XIe siècle', *Revue belge d'histoire militaire*, 20 (1985), pp. 177–98.

Old English poem *The Battle of Maldon* does describe the English as fighting in the same way, with their commander Byrthnoth dismounting to show his intention of not deserting his sworn companions. Now, I am not saying that the English on the eve of the Conquest fought in exactly the same way as their Frankish opponents for whom cavalry was certainly important; but it is possible to see Harold taking up the tactical option of dismounting because the situation warranted it.[20]

It is striking (though perhaps explicable) that most of the dismounted English are shown on the Bayeux Tapestry as equipped in exactly the same way as William's mounted knights.[21] It is also possible to find comparable examples of armoured cavalry dismounting, both in the early twelfth-century Anglo-Norman world (as is well known), and much further afield in 1148, at Damascus, where the German crusaders dismounted to fight 'as is the Teutonic custom in a crisis'.[22] It is also worth mentioning that this is precisely what the barbarian leader did when confronted with Julian's cataphracts at Argentoratum (Strasbourg) in 357, and proved able to throw back the cavalry, despite both men and horses being armoured all over.[23] Perhaps it is possible to suggest that commanders who led armoured men on horseback had a 'menu' of choices as to how they deployed them, depending upon the tactical situation. So instead of seeing 'knightly cavalry' as wedded to their horses, we should be impressed by their versatility and all-round skills – a kind of western Samurai.[24]

But to return to Hastings. One factor to which Stephen Morillo draws attention is the lack of any kind of controlled pursuit of the first retreat on William's left wing. Certainly there is no mention of a mounted reserve to exploit such a situation, although we know how useful this was at Tinchebrai (1106) and Halidon Hill (1333) (to cite two well-known examples as shorthand). But then, we only have the 'Norman' accounts to rely upon, which had no reason to record, or even to be aware of, a reserve. Morillo posits a foot counter-attack led by Harold's brothers Gyrth and Leofwine, which collapsed when they were killed (all guesswork, of

---

[20]   S. Morillo (ed.), *The Battle of Hastings: Sources and Interpretations* (Woodbridge, 1996), esp. ch. 18, 'Hastings: An Unusual Battle', pp. 219–27; 'The Battle of Maldon', *Anglo-Saxon Poetry* trans. S. A. J. Bradley (London, 1982), pp. 518–29.

[21]   For the best modern edition see D. M. Wilson, *The Bayeux Tapestry* (London, 1985). Most of the armoured men (*huscarls?*) carry the kite-shaped shield.

[22]   J. Bradbury, 'Battles in England and Normandy' in Strickland (ed.) *Anglo-Norman Warfare*, pp. 182–93 and other articles *passim*. See also J. Bradbury, *The Medieval Archer* (Woodbridge, 1985), p. 45 (and fn. from where the quote comes).

[23]   Ammianus Marcellinus, Bk. XVI, ch. xii, esp. paras. 34–5.

[24]   I owe this idea and term to my friend Roy Boss.

course).[25] But the fact that the Frankish-style cavalry proved unable to break into the infantry formation is significant.

It took several feigned flights (in which I am prepared to believe) and archery support to thin out and shrink the English line enough to enable the knights to gain level ground and break into the infantry formation. Although far from contemporary, in his *Roman de Rou*, the mid twelfth-century Norman poet Wace understands the decisive moment of the battle to be when William and his companions drove in amongst the foot, splitting them up and bowling them over by the weight and strength of their warhorses. And even if not primary information for Hastings, it certainly tells us what was credible a hundred years later.[26]

The crucial component in William's victory was his use of combined arms: infantry spearmen, archers and cavalry to wear down his enemy. The same is actually true of Durazzo, where the Varangian Guard had charged the 'Norman' cavalry on foot, astonishing the knights and driving them back into the sea. It was only when they rallied and deployed to 'pin' further attacks by the foot that Guiscard brought up his crossbowmen to shoot down the axemen, eventually forcing them to take cover in a church which was promptly fired.[27]

Two clear points emerge from these battles, which I believe hold good for almost any period up to the invention of the plug-bayonet and platoon firing in the late seventeenth century. First, that infantry could not advance against cavalry with any expectation of ultimate success. Second, that cavalry, no matter how well-equipped or motivated, could make no impression upon foot soldiers who kept their formation.

This second point is supported by the account of a skirmish outside Shaizar, in northern Syria, where Tancred, prince of Antioch, attacked the city militia with his household knights:

---

[25]   Morillo, 'Hastings', p. 224.

[26]   Wace, *Le Roman de Rou*, ed. A. J. Holden, 3 vols, Société des anciens textes français (Paris, 1970–3), II, p. 212, ll. 8,765–70. For recent studies of medieval warhorses see: R. H. C. Davis, *The Medieval Warhorse* (London, 1989); A. Hyland, *The Medieval Warhorse* (Stroud, 1994); and my critique of their approaches, M. Bennett, 'The Medieval Warhorse Revisited', *Medieval Knighthood V* (Woodbridge, 1995), pp. 19–40, pointing out that the animals rarely exceeded 15 hands despite exaggerated claims. My argument has received recent archaeological support in J. Clark (ed.), *The Medieval Horse and its Equipment c.1150–c.1450*, Medieval Finds from London 5, esp. pp. 22–32.

[27]   Bennett and Hooper, *Atlas*, pp. 82–3. M. Mathieu (ed.), *Guillaume de Pouille: La Geste de Robert Guiscard*, Istituto Siciliano di Studi Bizantini e Neoellenici (Palermo, 1961), pp. 224–7, and *Alexiad*, pp. 145–8, for a description of the battle of Durazzo.

On a day (in Spring 1111), a number of footsoldiers came out of Shaizar. The Franks charged them, without disturbing their formation. Thereupon Tancred became angry and said, 'You are my knights and each of you receives pay equivalent to the pay of a hundred Muslims. You have these sergeants (by which he meant the infantry) in front of you, and you are not capable of moving them!' They answered, 'Our only fear was for our horses. Otherwise we would have trampled them and pierced them with our lances.' Tancred replied, 'The horses are my property; I shall replace any one's horse that gets killed.' They then made several charges against the men of Shaizar, and lost seventy horses, without being able to get the men out of their position.[28]

There are several things of interest in this account, not least the mention of *restor* in Tancred's duty; but it is noticeable that the author, Usamah, although a Syrian Muslim, was very well aware of the social distinction between horse and foot, and he uses the French loan-word *sarjand* to describe the infantry.

I will mention in passing, as others have, the ability of well-ordered footsoldiers to hold off knightly cavalry in almost any time or place. The close-order of crusader foot served to keep their Muslim opponents at bay, even the Turkish horse-archers who were capable of throwing western knights into disorder by shooting their horses. Bows and especially crossbows (which could knock over these light cavalry both man and horse) were particularly effective, and in combination with shielded spearmen repelled even the most heavily-equipped Muslim cavalryman.[29] Then there is the example of the Italian city militia at Legnano (1176), (although the battle could not have been won without cavalry support) and Bouvines (1214) where Brabançon spearmen defied the French knights, only to be eventually let down by the imperial horse, and eventually overwhelmed by French foot.

So we should not be surprised by the defeat of French chivalry at Courtrai in 1302. What strikes me about the battle is how the French foot and Genoese crossbowmen prepared the ground for the defeat of the Flemings, in the approved 'combined arms' manner, only for the cavalry to flounder, predictably enough in totally unsuitable conditions in which to deliver a mounted charge. And this is what they seem to have done, despite there being a good argument for dismounting the knights before attacking. Contemporaries blamed that proverbial French weakness, pride, and they

---

[28] *The Autobiography of Ousama,* trans. G. R. Potter (London, 1929), p. 89.
[29] See R. C. Smail, *Crusading Warfare 1099–1192* (Cambridge, 1956) pp. 125–30, 156–65 and M. Bennett, 'The Crusaders' "Fighting March" Revisited' (forthcoming).

were probably right to do so.[30]

Weakness of command and control (usually portrayed in chronicles as the result of a rash commander), is a problem for all arms, but especially cavalry, which obviously moves much faster and is carried away by its own excitement. The same problem was exemplified at Crécy half a century later. The duke of Wellington complained in the Peninsula that his cavalry always seemed to get 'out-of-hand', so as to be practically useless, so ill-disciplined cavalry were not restricted to the medieval period. This is not to deny the feeling of utter disdain for mere footsoldiers expressed by Philip VI at Crécy, when, according to Froissart, he encouraged his knights to ride over their auxiliary Genoese crossbowmen because they were a rabble which was getting in the way.[31] But it should not be forgotten that almost two decades earlier he (or his commanders) had proved competent enough to deploy the French knights in order to overwhelm the Flemish foot at Cassel (1328). It must be said, however, that the Flemings had not improved their chances by attacking the French camp, so rendering themselves as vulnerable to counter-attack as the English at Hastings.[32]

Just how the cavalry-infantry balance worked is exemplified, I feel, by the Franco-Flemish encounter at Mons-en-Pévèle, near Lille in 1304. It was the only large-scale battle of that year, with heavy casualties on both sides. Most historians ascribe victory to the French. The *Annals of Ghent* (which may not give the whole picture, admittedly) assert a Flemish victory. Whatever the case, the *Annals* certainly provide a flavour of the tension of the situation, of the cat-and-mouse game of infantry confronted by well-equipped and well-mounted knights.[33] The Flemings advanced strategically (though not tactically) against the French and took up a position 'in a long and deep line', protecting their rear with baggage wagons. Troops were specially detailed for the purpose of 'making a sort of fortification' with them and removing a wheel from each vehicle in order

---

[30] The most recent study of Courtrai has been made by DeVries, *Infantry Warfare*, pp. 9–22.

[31] Jean Froissart, *Chroniques*, in *Oeuvres de Froissart*, ed. Kervyn de Lettenhove, 29 vols (Brussels, 1869–77), V, p. 49.

[32] DeVries, *Infantry Warfare*, pp. 100–11, also deals with Cassel, blaming the Flemish infantry for their rash advance, exposing themselves to a mounted counter-attack; and Crécy where the reverse was true, the cavalry attacking rashly (pp. 155–75).

[33] *Annales Gandenses*, ed. and trans. H. Johnstone (London, 1951), pp. 65–76, is used for the description of the battle which follows. DeVries, *Infantry Warfare*, pp. 32–48, gives a more detailed account based on a wider range of sources, the majority of which claim a French victory. The incautious Flemish assault late in the day did result in the death of several of their leaders, but many of the Flemings seem to have escaped.

313

that the French could not get round behind and easily drag them away. Whilst this was happening there was an exchange of shooting between the crossbowmen of both sides. Then the French crossbowmen made way for their cavalry, who made a 'feint charge' at the opposing infantry, causing the Flemish crossbowmen (who were presumably skirmishing in front of their main battle line) to cut the cords of their crossbows and hurl them at the French horses' legs. The Flemings expected to fight at an advantage in this position (remembering Courtrai), but the French knights reined in their horse and stood with only their spearpoints touching those of the Flemish foot. Even allowing for some poetic expression, the protagonists in this remarkable impasse could have been only a few feet apart.

Apparently, some Flemish crossbowmen had retained the use of their bows, for they proved able to drive back the French horse, just out of range (about 200 yards away?), where they then waited. Then small groups of Flemish foot went out to attack the French line, and in return troops of French cavalry also engaged the infantry. The French knights were greatly helped by *bidauts* (lightly armed javelineers) who skirmished amongst them ('under the bellies of their warhorses') throwing darts, sticks and stones. Then the French brought up a stonethrowing engine, which hurled stones as big as a man's fist into the unit formed by the men of Ypres. This was presumably a *balista* of somewhat limited range, as the Yprois were able to stage a raid and break it up. Justifiably, the *Annals* refer to the fighting as more like skirmishing (*preludia belli*) than real combat, and negotiations began.

During the lull, the French took the opportunity to send bodies of horse and foot around both flanks of the Flemish line, seeking to attack it from the rear. Fighting resumed and was particularly heavy on the Flemish left where the men of Ghent were stationed. The French sent in groups of horsemen in successive charges, but the Ghenters dared not pursue them in small groups, for fear of being cut off by the 'powerful French horses'. Nor could they leave their position en masse, as this would enable the French cavalry to sweep in between them and the wagons which protected their rear. Something to this effect happened on the right flank, where a troop of French horse sought to separate the Flemish from the wagons, but they were repelled. So they made a wider sweep to the rear and the footsoldiers who accompanied them tried to drag away some of the wagons, to let the knights in. This manoeuvre was also prevented when the Flemish mounted the wagons in their defence (shades of Adrianople!).

Such inconclusive fighting went on for much of a long, hot day, during which more men fell by heat-exhaustion than arms. Many French tired of the action and went off to plunder the Flemings' camp. As sunset neared, the Flemings launched a mass assault on the by now thinned French line, and drove them back into their camp. In a dramatic encounter, the king had to be rescued and the Oriflamme was lost along with its bearer. This was a humiliation for Philip, but the Flemings also suffered heavily from a mounted counter-attack after their ranks had been disrupted by fighting in the camp. They retreated after dark, in good order according to the *Annals*, leaving many dead, including some prominent leaders, and with barely half of them unwounded.

This dramatic account illustrates the strengths and weaknesses of knightly cavalry very well. Like the Normans at Hastings they could only make headway against a broken infantry line. With better missile support the French cavalry might have been able to exploit gaps in the Flemish formation as the English knights had been able to do at Falkirk a few years earlier (1298). But when English bows were turned against the French from the mid-fourteenth century onwards, they were to cause knightly cavalry severe difficulties. Its horses were always vulnerable to arrows. I have suggested elsewhere that the tactical expedients devised by French commanders indicate how alert they were to the problem they faced in massed archery. The recently-rediscovered French battle plan for the Agincourt campaign devised by Marshal Boucicault shows how well he understood the value of 'combined arms'. Missilemen, dismounted men-at-arms and a cavalry force were all intended to play a role in countering the English tactical system.[34]

Malcolm Vale has explained, in much greater detail, the implications of technological and tactical developments in the fifteenth century, and how the man-at-arms fitted into them. He points out that the crude interpretation stressing cavalry dominance up to the early fourteenth century replaced by infantry dominance in the 'Age of the Swiss and the Longbow' completely misrepresents the real balance between horse and foot. He sees the *gendarmerie* of heavy cavalry as *more* important in the fifteenth century and 'the only permanent element of the French royal army for most of the sixteenth century'.[35]

It should not be surprising that the crude 'thousand-year rule' stereotype of cavalry dominance can be overturned by a closer study of individual campaigns and periods of warfare. One basic rule, which I am happy to define, is the perennial problem an infantry force faced when attacked by a mobile, knightly cavalry. Both Anglo-Scandinavian-style infantry in the eleventh century and Flemish foot in the fourteenth century – arguably the best-motivated footsoldiers of their respective ages –

---

[34] M. Bennett, 'The Development of Battle Tactics in the Hundred Years War', *Arms, Armies and Fortifications in the Hundred Years War* (Woodbridge, 1994), pp. 1–20; idem, *Agincourt, 1415* (London, 1991), pp. 62–6.

[35] Vale, *War and Chivalry, passim*, the quote is from p. 128.

suffered defeat if they advanced to the attack. This is why I am unhappy with the supposed 'Infantry Revolution' of the fourteenth century. Only a combined-arms force with a substantial missile component could even attempt this, and even then it was still better to wait on the defensive, in a prepared position, if victory was to be assured. On the other hand, even the best equipped mounted men of any period could not hope to overthrow a determined infantry line, without missilemen to break it up, enabling the horsemen to force their way into the breaches. So knightly cavalry were generally as impotent before well-trained foot as the French cavalry against British infantry squares at Waterloo. There were moments when, under a good commander, with a well-balanced all-arms force, men-at-arms could achieve their tactical potential. It is actually more interesting to try and analyse when and how this came about than to set against the out-dated stereotype of knightly dominance supposed 'revolutions' of infantry or other arms.

Provoking or Avoiding Battle? Challenge, Duel and Single Combat in Warfare of the High Middle Ages

MATTHEW STRICKLAND

Immediately prior to the battle of Hastings, William of Poitiers has Duke William offer to submit his claim to the English throne to judgement by either Norman or English law. If Harold refuses, however, then William is prepared to engage him in single combat for the kingdom to avoid 'the double slaughter of two armies':

> If he [Harold] refuses these conditions, I do not think it right that either my men or his should perish in conflict over a quarrel that is not of their making. I am ready therefore to risk my life against his in single combat to decide whether the kingdom of England should by right be his or mine.[1]

Harold naturally refuses such a challenge, leaving William and his encomiast firmly in command of the moral high ground; Poitiers is able to laud the duke for his supposed willingness to risk his own life to avoid general bloodshed, and to vilify Harold for his fear of submitting to the divine will. Whether or not Duke William ever issued such a challenge, the proffer of judicial combat was for William of Poitiers an important preliminary in his sustained depiction of Hastings as trial by battle, the *judicium Dei,* in which the duke triumphs over a perjured usurper.[2]

The theme of battle as a judicial duel on a grand scale, a collective ordeal in which God bestowed victory upon the side whose cause was most just, is well known.[3] So too are the related concepts of prayer, fasting and

---

[1] *Guillaume de Poitiers: Histoire de Guillaume le Conquérant* (William of Poitiers), ed. R. Forville (Paris, 1952), pp. 176–81; *English Historical Documents (EHD), II, 1042–1189,* ed. D. C. Douglas and G. Greenaway (2nd edn, London, 1981), p. 224. I would like to thank Dr Graeme Small for his helpful comments on this paper. Errors and omissions are, of course, mine alone.

[2] This theme permeates Poitiers' account of the pre-battle negotiations, while the Normans begin the fight 'even as in a trial for theft it is the prosecuting counsel who speaks first' (William of Poitiers, pp. 171–81, 188–9; *EHD,* II, p. 240).

[3] See K. G. Cram, *Iudicium Belli: Zum Rechtscharakter des Krieges im deutschen Mittelalter* (Münster, 1955); P. Contamine, *War in the Middle Ages* (London, 1984), pp. 260–1; and M. J. Strickland, *War and Chivalry: The Conduct and*

confession before combat, the use of relics and the invocation of saints, the promulgation of penitential edicts (such as those following the battles of Fontenoy, 841, of Soissons, 923, and of Hastings, 1066), and the founding of votive abbeys such as Battle and La Victoire.[4] Here, however, I wish to examine the closely related but less familiar theme of the role of the judicial duel as a *substitute* for full-scale battle, and to set it within the wider context of the formal challenge to battle and the single combat of champions before assembled armies.[5] These not only offer valuable insights into pre-battle ritual but also show how mechanisms ostensibly designed to initiate full-scale combat could equally be used to delay or circumvent the clash of armies.

In the *conventio* between the earls of Leicester and Chester, drawn up sometime between 1148 and 1153, it was stipulated that neither earl was to lay ambush or snares for the other unless he had defied him at least fifteen days in advance.[6] The clear implication was that once war had formally been declared, the use of guile, ruse and ambush was considered perfectly legitimate and far from unchivalrous, provided an existing truce, respite or safe conduct was not violated. Nevertheless, though the pages of Anglo-Norman chroniclers abound with examples of surprise attack and low cunning,[7] one of the most striking features of contemporary warfare was the custom of sending a formal challenge to an enemy, stating time and place for combat.[8] Gilbert Crispin, the biographer of Herluin of Bec, believed that during the reign of Duke Robert the Magnificent (1027–35), Herluin's powerful lord, Gilbert of Brionne, 'advised his enemies by messenger of what he proposed to do and when, not just beforehand, but several days in advance', in order to 'advertise his strength'.[9] Though

Perception of War in England and Normandy, 1066–1217 (Cambridge, 1996), pp. 59–60.

[4] Contamine, *War in the Middle Ages*, pp. 265–70, 296–302; Strickland, *War and Chivalry*, pp. 60–8.

[5] For this theme in the later middle ages, see P. Contamine, 'L'idée de guerre à la fin du Moyen Age: aspects juridiques et éthiques', *Académie des Inscriptions et Belles-Lettres. Comptes rendus des séances* (Paris, 1974), pp. 70–86.

[6] F. M. Stenton, *The First Century of English Feudalism* (2nd edn, Oxford, 1961), pp. 251–2, 287.

[7] Strickland, *War and Chivalry*, pp. 124–31.

[8] For formal declarations of war itself, at least from a canonical standpoint, see F. H. Russell, *The Just War in the Middle Ages* (Cambridge, 1975, repr. 1979), pp. 6, 49, 54, 89, 101, 140, 194, 203; and K. DeVries, 'Medieval Declarations of War: An Example from 1212', *Scintilla*, 4 (1987), pp. 20–37. I am grateful to Kelly DeVries for drawing this paper to my attention.

[9] *Vita domni Herluini abbatis Beccensis*, in J. A. Robinson, *Gilbert Crispin, Abbot of Westminster: A Study of the Abbey under Norman Rule* (Cambridge, 1911), p. 88.

Crispin himself was writing after 1093, and thus at a considerable distance from these events, it was precisely this form of challenge that the Norman *Consuetudines et justicie* of 1091 sought to prohibit as an integral element of private warfare, when it forbade anyone to carry a banner, wear a hauberk, sound a horn or send a challenge (*cembellum*) when seeking out an enemy or exercising distraint.[10]

The formal challenge was a public assertion of a lord's power and aggressive intent, intended to swell his martial reputation and to intimidate the enemy. The reciprocal display of bravado, threat and insult between two opposing war leaders is clearly shown in William of Poitiers' account of how, in an attempt to raise Duke William's siege of Domfront (c.1049 x 51), Geoffrey Martel, count of Anjou, informed the Norman envoys

> that he would be at Domfront the next morning to arouse William's watch with his trumpets. He gave notice of the horse he would ride into battle, his shield and his armour. To this they replied that he had no need to wear himself out by advancing further, for he whom he sought would straightway appear before him, and in their turn they described the horse, the arms and the armour of their lord.[11]

---

[10] C. H. Haskins, *Norman Institutions* (Harvard, 1918), p. 283. The term *cimbellum/cembellum* itself appears but rarely. J. F. Niermeyer, *Mediae latinitatis lexicon minus* (Leiden, 1976), p. 179.cites only one other source in which it occurs with the meaning of a challenge, namely the *Chronica Boemorum* of Cosmas of Prague (c.1045–1125) This relates how in 1087 twenty Saxon knights appeared before the forces of King Wratizlaus, *ut eos provocarent cimbello*, while during the civil war of 1107 *filius patrem cimbello et pater filium provocat duello* (*Die Chronik der Böhmen des Cosmas von Prag*, ed. B. Bretholz, *Scriptores Rerum Germanicarum in usum scholarum ex Monumentis Germanicae Historicis separatim editi*, n.s. II (Berlin, 1923), Bk II, c. xxxix, p. 143; Bk III, c. xxxi, p. 202).

[11] William of Poitiers, pp. 38–40; translation from R. A. Brown, *The Norman Conquest* (London, 1984), p. 21. The difficulty of recognition afforded by armour when worn (as before the mid-twelfth century) without an armorial surcoat is vividly demonstrated by the *Gesta Stephani*'s account of how, at the siege of Exeter in 1136, a relief force led by Alured, son of Judhael of Totnes, mixed with the royal army besieging the castle and effected a sudden entry, 'for among so many clad in mail, it was impossible for one to distinguish one from another' (*Gesta Stephani*, ed. and trans. K. R. Potter (Oxford, 1973), pp. 36–9). As at Domfront, knights might be recognised simply by distinctive equipment and harness. Thus Orderic noted how in the war between Robert of Bellême and Hugh of Grandmesnil, 'Theobald, son of Walter of Breteuil, and Guy "the Red (*Rubicundus*)" were killed there: the first was called "the white knight (*candidus eques*)" because his horse and all his trappings were white; the second "the red (*rubeus*)" because he was covered in rubies' (*The Ecclesiastical History of Orderic Vitalis* (Orderic), ed. and trans. M. Chibnall, 6

In this instance, which appears to blend a challenge to single combat with a general proffer of battle, William of Poitiers uses the device to highlight both the duke's personal courage and the arrogant pride of his Angevin opponent. Yet, as a former knight, he must have been very familiar with such conventions,[12] and in this description we vividly glimpse the practical concerns with personal recognition in the period before hereditary arms and the 'science' of blazon.[13] But, as Poitiers was no doubt well aware, the significance of the challenge went far beyond this. For in Duby's words, such rituals belonged:

> to the standard libretto of that grand opera being performed – splendid vociferations, splendid gestures – on the stage of feudal warfare, where what mattered, as much as any exchange of blows, was to intimidate, to frighten, to convince the adversary by words and dumb-show.[14]

Equally, the challenge fulfilled a variety of other important functions. In a judicial sense, the challenge was a form of summons closely analogous to that for the wager of ordeal by battle. It was for this reason, as Leyser has noted, that Nithard was careful to stress that before the battle of Fontenoy in 841, Louis the German and Charles the Bald informed their

---

vols (Oxford, 1969–80), IV, pp. 232–3). Nevertheless, many knights seem to have worn marks of distinction, though their exact nature (possibly 'proto-heraldic' shields) is uncertain. In the rout following the battle of Brémule, 1119, Peter of Maule and some of the other French fugitives 'threw away their cognizances (*cognitiones suas*)' to avoid recognition. At the siege of Breteuil the same year, the commander of Henry I's garrison, Ralph de Gael, fiercely engaged the besiegers on the arrival of an Anglo-Norman relief army, hurrying 'from gate to gate, frequently changing his arms (*arma*)' to avoid recognition (Orderic, VI, pp. 242–3, 246–7).

[12] As Orderic Vitalis (Orderic, II, pp. 258–9) noted in this regard, William of Poitiers 'had been a brave soldier before entering the church, and had fought with warlike weapons for his earthly prince, so that he was all the better able to describe the battles he had seen through having himself some experience of the dire perils of war'.

[13] For the important development of heraldic devices see P. Gras, 'Aux origines de l'héraldique', *Bibliothèque de l'École des Chartes*, 109 (1951), pp. 198–208; A. Ailes, 'Heraldry in Twelfth-Century England', *England in the Twelfth Century. Proceedings of the 1988 Harlaxton Symposium*, ed. D. Williams (Woodbridge, 1990), pp. 1–16; idem, 'The Knight, Heraldry and Armour. The Role of Recognition and the Origins of Heraldry', *Medieval Knighthood IV. Papers From the Fifth Strawberry Hill Conference*, ed. C. Harper-Bill and R. Harvey (Woodbridge, 1992), pp. 1–21; and D. Crouch, *The Beaumont Twins: The Roots and Branches of Power in the Twelfth Century* (Cambridge, 1986), pp. 211–12.

[14] G. Duby, *Guillaume le Maréchal ou le meilleur chevalier du monde* (Paris, 1984), trans. R. Howard as *William Marshal: The Flower of Chivalry* (London, 1985), p. 64.

brother Lothar not simply of the day but the very hour at which they would march to battle.[15] Similarly, the ritual of keeping the field of battle for one or more whole days marked a form of seisin of victory, analogous to the early Germanic method of possessing real estate.[16] In 992, Fulk Nerra had challenged Conan, count of Rennes, to battle at Conquereuil, and it was similar considerations that underlay the famous letter supposedly sent by Frederick Barbarossa, prior to his departure on the Third Crusade in 1188, formally defying Saladin and offering him pitched battle in November, 1189, 'in the field of Zoan'.[17]

In tactical and strategic terms, a challenger might hope to bring his enemy out to battle at a fixed time and place chosen to his advantage, and so avoid the uncertainties of surprise attack. Such a safeguard was not always successful. Following the rout of Winchester in 1141, Patrick, earl of Salisbury, and other supporters of King Stephen sent word to John fitzGilbert that if he would await them they would attack him the next day. John replied that he would on no account wait, and the royalists unwisely took this as a statement that he intended to retire from his castle at Ludgershall before their advance. Instead, John laid an ambush and fell upon the unsuspecting royalists miles from his castle, killing many as they had not yet donned their hauberks or helmets.[18]

---

[15]   Nithard, *Historiarum Libri IV*, ed. P. Lauer as *Nithard, Histoire des fils de Louis le Pieux* (Paris, 1926), II, pp. 75, 78; J. Nelson, *Charles the Bald* (London, 1992), pp. 117–18; K. Leyser, 'Warfare in the Western European Middle Ages: The Moral Debate', in K. Leyser, *Communications and Power in Medieval Europe. The Gregorian Revolution and Beyond*, ed. T. Reuter (London and Rio Grande, 1994), p. 192.

[16]   Contamine, *War in the Middle Ages*, p. 261.

[17]   *La Chronique de Nantes*, ed. R. Merlet (Paris, 1896), ch. 44; B. Bachrach, *Fulk Nerra, the Neo-Roman Consul, 987–1040* (Berkeley, 1993), pp. 41–2 and n. 96, who notes the particular significance of the chosen site, as this was where Fulk's father Geoffrey Greymantle had defeated Conan ten years previously. For Frederick's challenge, see *Itinerarium peregrinorum et gesta regis Ricardi*, ed. W. Stubbs (Rolls Series, London, 1864), pp. 34–6. The authenticity of this letter, and of Saladin's reply, have been contested; see H. E. Mayer, 'Der Brief Kaiser Friedrichs I, an Saladin vom Jahre 1188', *Deustches Archiv*, 14 (1958), pp. 488–94.; A. Waas, *Geschichte der Kreuzzüge* (Freiburg, 1956), I, p. 190, n. 114; and P. Muntz, *Frederick Barbarossa* (London, 1969), p. 390, n. 1.

[18]   *L'Histoire de Guillaume le Maréchal* (HGM) ed. P. Meyer, 3 vols (Société de l'histoire de France, Paris, 1891–1901), II, 283–354, and particularly ll. 287–9 for Patrick's challenge. I have followed S. Painter, *William Marshal, Knight-Errant, Baron and Regent of England* (Johns Hopkins, 1933), pp. 8–9, in ascribing the challenge to Patrick of Salisbury, as the *Histoire* erroneously places Stephen as the leader of the royalist forces in this incident (cf. *HGM*, III, p. 7, n. 2 and p. 3, n. 1). The use of such ambiguity recalls Henry of

Challenges might be used as a diversion for attack or withdrawal. In 1119, for instance, Henry I ordered Robert Goel, castellan of Ivry, to challenge Amaury de Montfort and his knights to combat on the banks of the river Eure, while he himself attacked and burnt Amaury's comital city of Evreux.[19] In 1194, when being pursued by Richard near Vendôme, Philip Augustus sent a message telling Richard to expect a hostile attack that same day. Richard replied that he was prepared, and that if the attack did not come, he would come against Philip the next day. Philip then attempted to slip away while Richard's men made ready. The ruse failed, however, for the following day, Richard overtook Philip's rearguard near Fréteval and inflicted considerable losses on the French, coming within an ace of capturing Philip himself.[20]

Indeed, rather than the prelude to inevitable conflict, challenges might as frequently serve as a deliberate means of avoiding battle. As at Fréteval, many challenges were designed merely to call the enemy's tactical bluff. Thus despite his high words at Domfront, Geoffrey Martel in fact judged the moment unpropitious for an attack on William and withdrew.[21] Others were issued in the confident assumption that an opponent would be very unlikely to accept the proffer of battle. Thus in August 1173, rather than attacking Louis VII's army as it lay besieging Verneuil, Henry II deliberately halted at nearby Breteuil. He drew his forces into battle array then sent a challenge to Louis to the effect that unless he withdrew from Normandy – which he might do unmolested – Henry would come against

Blois's reply 'I will get ready' to a summons by Matilda in 1141 when he feared for his safety. She believed him to mean he was preparing to come to her court, whereas he instead summoned all the royalist forces he could muster to Winchester (William of Malmesbury, *Historia Novella*, ed. K. R. Potter (London, 1955), p. 58).

[19]   Orderic, VI, pp. 230–1.

[20]   *Chronica Rogeri de Hovedene* (Howden), ed. W. Stubbs, 4 vols (Rolls Series, London, 1868–71), III, pp. 255–6; *Radulphi de Diceto decani Lundoniensis opera historica* (Diceto), ed. W. Stubbs, 2 vols (Rolls Series, London, 1876), II, p. 117; William of Newburgh, *Historia Rerum Anglicarum* (Newburgh), in *Chronicles and Memorials of the Reigns of Stephen, Henry II and Richard*, ed. R. Howlett, 4 vols (Rolls Series, London, 1884–90), IV, p. 419; *Oeuvres de Rigord et de Guillaume le Breton, historiens de Philippe Auguste*, ed. H.-F. Delaborde, 2 vols (Paris, 1882–5), I, p. 129; II, *Philippidos*, Bk. IV, ll. 530–68.

[21]   William of Poitiers, p. 40. For the tactical and strategic background to this incident see J. Gillingham, 'William the Bastard at War', *Studies in Medieval History Presented to R. Allen Brown*, ed. C. Harper-Bill, C. J. Holdsworth and J. L. Nelson (Woodbridge, 1989), pp. 141–58, reprinted in M. J. Strickland (ed.), *Anglo-Norman Warfare* (Woodbridge, 1992), pp. 143–60, at pp. 149–51.

him in force that same day.[22] Henry, who knew his man, guessed that the French king would retire rather than face him in the field. Henry's surmise was correct, though Louis used the subsequent peace negotiations as a decoy whilst he burnt part of Verneuil, before withdrawing in haste to France.[23]

Such instances of pre-emptive challenges only serve to reinforce the now orthodox view that most commanders shunned battle wherever possible.[24] Should armies stand their ground and confront one another, however, then another form of challenge might occur, namely the challenge to combat between champions. This might take one of two forms; a duel simply as a prelude to group combat, in which a champion sought to boost both his own martial reputation and the morale of his army; or a judicial duel in which the outcome of combat between champions was to decide matters of contention and thus avoid a general engagement. 'War', wrote Powicke:

> was a great lawsuit. The truce was very like an essoin, a treaty was drawn up on the lines of a final concord, the hostage was a surety, service in the field was the counterpart of suit of court. The closeness of the analogy between the field of battle and the law court is seen in the judicial combat. Trial by battle was a possible incident in all negotiations.[25]

Thus it was that the challenge to combat between champions before assembled hosts might assume the form of a judicial duel. Such challenges are recorded from at least the fifth century,[26] and closely reflected the prevalence of the ordeal by battle within Germanic society.[27] The wager by

---

[22] Diceto, I, p. 375; Newburgh, pp. 174–5.

[23] *Gesta regis Henrici secundi Benedicti Abbatis (Gesta Henrici)*, ed. W. Stubbs, 2 vols (Rolls Series, London, 1867), I, pp. 54–5; Diceto, I, p. 375; Newburgh, p. 175.

[24] See, for example, J. Gillingham, 'Richard I and the Science of War', *War and Government in the Middle Ages. Essays in Honour of J. O. Prestwich*, ed. J. Gillingham and J. C. Holt (Woodbridge, 1984), pp. 78–91, reprinted in Strickland (ed.), *Anglo-Norman Warfare*, pp. 194–207 at pp. 197–9; *idem*, 'William the Bastard at War', pp. 145–8.

[25] F. M. Powicke, *The Loss of Normandy* (Oxford, 2nd edn, 1961), p. 242.

[26] Gregory of Tours, for example, believed that in 496, the Alamanni and Vandals decided to settle a territorial dispute by champions rather than pitched battle, and when the Vandal champion was defeated, their king, Trasamund, swore to carry out his promise to withdraw. Whether he did so, however, is not recorded (Gregory of Tours, *Histoire des Francs*, ed. R. Latouche, 2 vols (Paris, 1963–5), I, p. 77; *The History of the Franks*, trans. L. Thorpe (Harmondsworth, 1974), pp. 107–12).

[27] For an extended discussion of trial by battle, see G. Neilson, *Trial by Combat* (Glasgow, 1890); and R. Bartlett, *Trial by Fire and Water* (Oxford, 1986), pp. 103–26, and especially pp. 113–15, where the important distinction is noted

battle is found in the majority of barbarian law codes, though not those of the Goths, and was seemingly absent (unlike the ordeals of fire and water) from Anglo-Saxon England.[28] While the eleventh century witnessed its prohibition in Iceland and Norway,[29] wager of battle was introduced into England by the Normans: Domesday Book reveals offers made to settle pleas *per iudicium vel per bellum*, while the *Leis Willelmi* allows an Englishman charged with a capital crime by a Frenchman to choose between wager of battle or the ordeal of the hot iron.[30]

It is unsurprising, therefore, to find the theme of judicial combat very much to the fore in William of Poitiers' description of the battle of Hastings. As we have seen, Poitiers uses the challenge to a judicial duel as a potent motif to hammer home the justice of the Norman cause and William's supposed reluctance to avoid bloodshed. Yet even if William did in fact offer Harold single combat, neither Duke William nor his biographer can have been in the least surprised that Harold did not take up the challenge. No leader would stake the fate of a kingdom or of an important territory on a single duel, particularly if they could command forces as powerful as – if not more so than – those of the challenger. Rather, the challenge to a judicial duel was often the last gambit of a numerically or strategically disadvantaged opponent, hoping to offset the military superiority of the enemy by the personal prowess of individual knights. Thus Fulcher of Chartres records how in 1098, before the great battle outside Antioch, the crusaders offered the Turks combat 'between five, or ten, or twenty or even a hundred knights chosen from each side, lest in the case of all fighting at once a great number should die'.[31] The

---

between regulated private combat and trial by combat as an ordeal. For early examples of the judicial duel in Europe, see M. W. Bloomfield, 'Beowulf, Byrhtnoth and the Judgment of God: Trial by Combat in Anglo-Saxon England', *Speculum*, 44 (1969), pp. 545–59, at pp. 549–51.

[28] Bartlett, *Trial by Fire and Water*, pp. 104–5; cf. Bloomfield, 'Beowulf', pp. 545–6, 557–9.

[29] For the duel in Scandinavia see G. Jones, 'Some Aspects of the Icelandic "Holmganga"', *Journal of English and Germanic Philology*, 32 (1933), pp. 203–24; M. Ciklamini, 'The Old Icelandic Duel', *Scandinavian Studies*, 35 (1963), pp. 175–94; Bartlett, *Trial by Fire and Water*, pp. 105, 114–15.

[30] *Domesday Book*, ed. A. Farley, 2 vols (London, 1783), II, 146b, 176, 213; Neilson, *Trial by Combat*, p. 32 and n. 2; F. Liebermann, *Die Gesetze der Angelsachsen*, 3 vols (Halle, 1903–16), I, p. 486; *EHD*, II, p. 421, c. 6.

[31] *Fulcheri Cartonensis Historia Hierosolymitana*, ed. H. Hagenmayer (Heidelberg, 1913), Bk I, c. xxi, pp. 247–8; trans. F. R. Ryan as *Fulcher of Chartres: A History of the Expedition to Jerusalem, 1095–1127* (University of Tennessee, 1976 edn), p. 103. This offer of battle by a limited number of champions is also noted by Albert of Aachen (*Alberti Aquensis Historia Hierosolymitana, Receuil des historiens*

Turks, fully aware of the dire straits in which the crusaders found themselves, rejected the challenge outright.[32]

Such expedients, however, were consistently resorted to by the weaker opponents of the Anglo-Norman and Angevin kings. Thus according to Suger, in 1109 Louis VI proposed to determine possession of Gisors and Bray *lege duelli*, at first offering combat between a few select nobles then himself challenging Henry I in person.[33] Later in his reign, Henry faced a second challenge for far higher stakes: in 1127 William Clito challenged Henry to a duel at Gisors for possession of the whole duchy of Normandy.[34] Likewise, Jordan Fantosme believed that in 1173 William the Lion proposed to decide his claim to Northumberland against Henry II by single combat.[35] But in every instance, the more powerful opponent not surprisingly refused.

Clearly, in the majority of cases the challenger cannot have expected an opponent to submit to the arbitration of champions, and the proffer of a judicial duel seems rarely to have been taken at face value by either side. Rather, the discussions it raised might serve on a pragmatic level as a mechanism to postpone imminent bloodshed by offering an honourable pretext for parley and renewed dialogue. But as – if not more – important, it could be employed as a valuable weapon of propaganda to seize the moral high ground. A readiness to submit claims to the judgement of God proclaimed the justice of one's cause, while if an opponent refused, he could be labelled as one who, fearing the legitimacy of his position, preferred all-out bloodshed to the acceptance of divine arbitration.

For this very reason, rather than simply refusing the challenge outright, the recipient might in turn attempt to gain a diplomatic and psychological advantage by returning the challenge couched in terms he

des croisades, Historiens occidentaux, 5 vols (1841–95), IV, c. 45, pp. 420–1). This detail is not recorded by the two authors present at Antioch, but both mention the challenge to combat by the Christian army (*Gesta Francorum et aliorum Hierosolimitanorum*, ed. R. Hill (London, 1962), pp. 66–7; Raymond d'Aguiliers, *Historia francorum qui ceperunt Iherusalem*, ed. J. H. Hill (Philadelphia, 1968), p. 79).

[32] As Fulcher records, 'This was the demand, but it was not conceded by the Turks. They trusted in their great numbers and strength and thought that they would conquer and destroy us' (Bk I, c. xxi, pp. 248–9; trans. Ryan, p. 103).

[33] Suger, *Vie de Louis VI Le Gros*, ed. H. Waquet (Paris, 1929), pp. 106–10; *Suger, the Deeds of Louis the Fat*, trans. R. C. Cusimano and J. Moorhead (Washington, 1992), pp. 72–4.

[34] A. Luchaire, *Louis VI le Gros, annales de sa vie et de son règne, 1081–1137* (Paris, 1890), nos 4 and 5: Orderic, IV, pp. 472–4.

[35] *Jordan Fantosme's Chronicle*, ed. and trans. R. C. Johnston (Oxford, 1981), ll. 334–5.

knew to be equally unacceptable. These considerations are highlighted by two incidents occurring in the Angevin-Capetian conflicts of the 1180s and 1190s. In August, 1188, the forces of Philip and Henry II confronted each other outside Gisors. Philip suggested that their dispute should be settled by the combat of four champions, but his mockery was readily apparent by his stipulation that the Angevin team should be composed of William fitz Ralph, the seneschal of Normandy who was too old for battle, and three other knights well known to be incapable warriors. According to the *Histoire de Guillaume le Maréchal,* William advised Henry to turn the tables on Philip by proposing that the combat should be held before the emperor or the king of Navarre, a neutral court where Henry could choose his own champions. These were to consist of the Marshal, and three other experienced knights, Earl William de Mandeville, John de Fresnai and Osbert de Rouvrai. Philip naturally refused. If we are to believe the *Histoire,* his insulting jest had been countered by a more serious proposal, which the Angevins knew full well Philip would not accept, but whose refusal would now rebound unfavourably on him.[36]

In spite of this, it is intriguing to find that in 1194, following recurrent breaches of a newly established truce between Philip and Richard,[37] Ralph of Diceto noted that the Capetian again proposed that their differences should be settled by judicial combat between five champions on each side 'so that the issue should make manifest to the people of both realms what was the mind of the Eternal King as to the rights of the two earthly sovereigns'.[38] Diceto's scanty account does not reveal the diplomatic intentions underlying the French king's proffer. Possibly he was using the challenge to prove the legality of his conquests during Richard's captivity, or merely as a method of postponing the renewal of an imminent war which only waited on Richard's amassing of forces and money. He may even have hoped that Richard, who would insist on being one of the champions, would be slain in the ensuing duels. Certainly when Richard had protested bitterly against his exclusion from the list of four champions proposed by the Marshal in 1188, William had replied that it would be folly to risk the life of the heir apparent in such a fray.[39]

Whatever his motives, however, Philip was seemingly again hoist with his own petard. The offer 'pleased the king of England greatly, provided that each of the kings should be one of the five combatants on his own side and that they should fight each other on equal terms, armed and

---

[36]   *HGM,* ll. 7429–781.
[37]   Howden, III, p. 276.
[38]   Diceto, II, p. 121.
[39]   *HGM,* ll. 7619–39.

equipped alike'.[40] Philip may have been a sound general, but he was no match for Richard in hand to hand combat, and was left with little option but to drop his challenge.

Here in the context of war we have a practice analogous with, indeed possibly influenced by, a strategy of litigation common in later eleventh-century France, whereby the ordeal was proposed only to be subsequently avoided. In his perceptive discussion of this process, Stephen White argues that:

> proposing the ordeal, accepting it as proof, and, finally cancelling it were all tricky and dangerous but potentially effective bargaining ploys that different participants in a court hearing could use as instruments of self-empowerment to move an unusually protracted and embittered lawsuit toward a favourable and workable settlement. Sometimes ... they were executed from positions of great strength; at other times, they were acts of desperation. Sometimes they worked, and sometimes they backfired.[41]

Yet whatever its intellectual failings, the judicial duel in the law courts was a workable legal process while conducted within a lord's discrete and unquestioned jurisdiction. Once transferred to a situation of war between two princes, however, the process became untenable because of 'the obvious impossibility of securing guarantees that the issue would be regarded as a verdict'.[42] Neutral courts might be sought, as in 1177 when Henry II had arbitrated between the kings of Navarre and Castile; champions accompanied the delegations in case of trial by battle, but the matter was eventually settled by diplomacy.[43] It was inherently unlikely, however, that the protagonists would abide by the outcome of any duel even if held before a disinterested third party. And in the case of Angevin against Capetian, impartiality was clearly impossible if proceedings were held in the court of the French suzerain. Thus, ironically, the very efficacy of the challenge of champions as a diplomatic or tactical manoeuvre as seen in 1188 and 1194 rested on the tacit recognition of its *de facto* impossibility. Nevertheless, the pretence might be carried a long way. The Norman exchequer roll for 1198 refers to payment for 'the champions of the king, who were taken to the isle of Andely against the king of France'.[44]

---

40 Diceto, II, p. 121.
41 S. D. White, 'Proposing the Ordeal and Avoiding It: Strategy and Power in Western French Litigation, 1050–1110', *Cultures of Power. Lordship, Status and Process in Twelfth-Century Europe*, ed. T. N. Bisson (Philadelphia, 1995), pp. 89–123, at p. 92.
42 Powicke, *Loss of Normandy*, p. 242.
43 *Gesta Henrici*, I, pp. 139–43, 151–4.
44 *Magni rotuli scaccarii Normaniae sub regibus Angliae (Rot. Scacc. Norm.)* ed. T.

If the actual fighting of judicial duels was impractical in situations of real war, the motif was nonetheless popular in twelfth-century literature. Thus the single combat between Tristan and Morholt, fought on the island of St Sampson over the tribute of young men and girls owed from Cornwall to Ireland, forms a central part of the *Tristan* legend.[45] Likewise, in Geoffrey of Monmouth's *History of the Kings of Britain*, King Arthur is challenged to a duel on an island in the Seine by the giant Frollo in order to avoid pitched battle between the British and Roman armies; the winner is to inherit the kingdom of the other.[46] Likewise the genesis and literary evolution of the legendary judicial duel fought for the rulership of England between Edmund Ironside and Cnut can be traced from the *Anglo-Saxon Chronicle*'s account of their meeting in 1016 at Olney by Deerhurst, where there is no mention of a duel, through William of Malmesbury and Gaimar where the theme of a challenge is introduced but actual combat avoided,[47] to Henry of Huntingdon and Walter Map, where a fierce fight ensues in which Edmund triumphs.[48] Clearly a popular tale in the twelfth and thirteenth centuries, Matthew Paris incorporates it into his *Chronica Majora* complete with a fine illustration (Pl. 46).[49] Yet even in romance, there were

---

Stapleton, 2 vols (Society of Antiquaries of London, 1840–4), II, p. 481.

[45] J. Bédier, *Le Roman de Tristan par Thomas*, 2 vols (Paris, 1902–5), I, 84–8; *The Romance of Tristan by Beroul*, trans. A. S. Fredrick (Harmondsworth, 1970), pp. 40–1.

[46] *The Historia regum Britanniae of Geoffrey of Monmouth*, ed. A. Griscom (London, 1929), pp. 448–50; trans. L. Thorpe, *The History of the Kings of Britain* (Harmondsworth, 1966), pp. 224–5; Cf. J. Gillingham, 'The Context and Purposes of Geoffrey of Monmouth's *History of the Kings of Britain*', *Anglo-Norman Studies*, 13 (1991), pp. 99–118.

[47] Though Symeon of Durham notes that Olney was an island, the theme of judicial combat significantly is first introduced by William of Malmesbury, who has Edmund challenge Cnut only for the latter to decline (*Symeonis monachi opera omnia*, ed. T. Arnold, 2 vols (Rolls Series, London, 1885), II, p. 153; William of Malmesbury, *De gestis regum Anglorum*, ed. W. Stubbs, 2 vols (Rolls Series, London, 1887–9), I, p. 217). Gaimar picturesquely has the two kings meet fully armed in a ship moored in the Severn, with their armies ranged on opposite banks, but a compromise is effected without combat (Geoffrey Gaimar, *L'Estoire des Engles*, ed. and trans. T. D. Harris and C. T. Martin, 2 vols (Rolls Series, London, 1888), ll. 4267ff).

[48] Henry of Huntingdon, *Historia Anglorum*, ed. D. Greenaway (Oxford, 1996), pp. 360–1; Walter Map, *De Nugis Curialium*, ed. and trans. M. R. James, revised by C. N. L. Brook and R. A. B. Mynors (Oxford, 1983), pp. 424–7; C. E. Wright, *The Cultivation of Saga in Anglo-Saxon England* (Edinburgh and London, 1939), pp. 184–98.

[49] *Matthaei Parisiensis, monachi sancti Albani, Chronica majora*, ed. H. R. Luard, 7 vols (Rolls Series, London, 1872–3), I, pp. 498–9.

echoes of reality; the island setting of such literary combats reflects the traditional location of duels on islands not just in Scandinavia – from whence the duel was termed the *Holmganga* or 'island-going' – but also in much of Europe, including post-Conquest England and Scotland.[50] That the tradition was still very much alive in the late twelfth century is indicated by the sending of the Angevin and Capetian champions in 1198 to the isle of Andely.

The majority of single combats, however, whether in literature or reality, were not waged in the formal context of a judicial duel but rather simply as the pitting of martial skill and strength between champions. As Pope Nicholas I pointed out to Charles the Bald in 867 when criticising the judicial duel as a sinful temptation of God, the combat between David and Goliath was a contest between champions and not a judicial duel; it was therefore not a valid precedent for ordeal by combat, although it had often been wrongly cited as such.[51] The common preserve of many warrior aristocracies, the single combat before assembled hosts has a long ancestry, visible *inter alia* in biblical, classical, Celtic and Germanic tradition.[52] Among the barbarian peoples, we find the duel of champions among the Ostrogoths, Lombards, Bavarians and Franks throughout the early middle ages. Thus, for example, if Procopius may be believed, the battles of Faenza in 542 and Busta Gallorum in 552 opened with single combat between Ostrogothic and Byzantine champions, while continuity of tradition is suggested by Liudprand of Cremona's account of a duel between a Lombard and a Bavarian champion at Pavia in 889 before the hosts of Wido and Centebald, son of King Arnulf.[53]

The sources, though meagre and predominantly literary, suggest equal familiarity of the convention of single combat among the Anglo-Saxons, despite the apparent absence from pre-Conquest England of ordeal by battle. Beowulf's principal opponents are the monstrous race of Cain and the hoard-guarding dragon, but the hero is said to have slain the Frankish champion Daegrafen with his bare hands.[54] In *The Battle of Maldon*, the Vikings' access to the mainland from Northey island is barred by three

---

[50]   Jones, 'Some Characteristics of the Icelandic *Holmganga*', pp. 203–24; Neilson, *Trial by Combat*, pp. 61–76.

[51]   *Patrologia cursus completus, series latina*, ed. J. P. Migne *et al.*, 221 vols in 222 with supplements (Paris, 1878–1974), cxix, cols 1142–6.

[52]   See V. G. Kiernan, *The Duel in European History* (Oxford, 1988), ch. 2 'Ancient and Primitive Analogies', pp. 19–30, for the anthropology of the duel.

[53]   T. Hodgkin, *Italy and Her Invaders*, 6 vols (Oxford, 1892–9), IV, pp. 444–5; *Antapodosis*, I, xx–xxi, in *The Works of Liudprand of Cremona*, trans. F. A. Wright (London, 1930), pp. 48–50.

[54]   *Beowulf*, ed. and trans. M. Swanton (Manchester, 1978), ll. 2497–508.

Anglo-Saxon champions, Wulfstan, Aelfhere and Maccus, who hold the causeway until their lord, the ealdorman Byrhtnoth, makes the fatal decision to give 'ground all too much to the hateful folk' and allow them across to fight.[55] The theme of a hero holding a narrow place against the odds is a common one in epic literature, visible, for example, in the *Waltharius*,[56] a German tenth-century Latin epic, and in the tale known to Henry of Huntingdon, William of Malmesbury and the late-twelfth-century interpolator of the 'C' version of the *Anglo-Saxon Chronicle*, of how a lone Norse axeman held Stamford Bridge against Harold's army in 1066 until attacked by boat from below and slain by a spear thrust up under his byrnie.[57]

The story, moreover, of the single combat between an unnamed Anglo-Saxon champion and the Norman *jongleur* or *histrio* Taillefer before Hastings quickly became an important (and increasingly elaborated) feature of the Norman tradition concerning the battle.[58] Though unmentioned by William of Poitiers, the *Carmen de Hastingae Proelio*, possibly the earliest source, regarded Taillefer's victory as an omen of divine favour, presaging a general triumph of the duke's forces in the collective ordeal of battle itself. After juggling with his sword and cheering on William's army by reminding them of the heroes of the chansons, Taillefer slays the Saxon champion and cuts off his head:

> Turning his eyes on his comrades, he displayed this trophy and showed that the beginning of the battle favoured them. All rejoiced, and at the same time called upon the Lord. They exulted that the first blow was theirs, both a tremor and a thrill ran through brave hearts and at once the men hastened to close shields.[59]

---

[55] *The Battle of Maldon*, ed. D. Scragg (Manchester, 1981), ll. 74–83, 89–95.

[56] J. Knight Bostock, *A Handbook of Old High German Literature* (2nd edn, revised by K. C. King and D. R. McKlintock, Oxford, 1976), pp. 259–70.

[57] Henry of Huntingdon, pp. 386–9 and p. 388, n. 160; William of Malmesbury, *Gesta Regum*, II, p. 228; *Anglo-Saxon Chronicle*, 'C', *s.a.* 1066 (*EHD*, II, p. 149); Wright, *Cultivation of Saga*, p. 240 and Appendix 59, and pp. 239–40 and 298. Huntingdon repeats a similar tale, *s.a.* 1010, of how a single Anglo-Saxon defended the church tower of Balsham, Cambs., against a Danish army (Henry of Huntingdon, pp. 348–9); cf. the same motif employed by Jordan Fantosme, who has a lone knight in the keep at Brough in 1174 defy the entire Scots army (*Jordan Fantosme's Chronicle*, ed. and trans. R. C. Johnston (Oxford, 1981), ll. 1493–1505).

[58] The references to Taillefer's duel are collected and discussed in *The Carmen de Hastingae Proelio of Guy, Bishop of Amiens (Carmen)*, ed. C. Morton and H. Muntz (Oxford, 1972), Appendix B, pp. 81–3.

[59] *Carmen*, ll. 390–408; cf. *Le Roman de Rou de Wace*, ed. A. J. Holden, 3 vols (Société des anciens textes français, Paris, 1970–3), ll. 8035–60.

Whether in the light of recent rehabilitation of the *Carmen* as a contemporary authority we choose to accept the veracity of Taillefer's duel,[60] the poem nonetheless powerfully conveys the great psychological advantage enjoyed by an army whose champion had drawn first blood. Much later, the poet John Barbour stressed how, prior to the battle of Bannockburn in 1314, Robert Bruce's victory in single combat over Sir Henry de Bohun greatly cheered the Scottish army. Had the king been worsted or slain, however, the effect on Scottish morale might have been disastrous, and Barbour noted that despite his success, Bruce was sharply rebuked by his nobles for putting his own life at risk.[61]

The striking image furnished by the *Carmen* of a *jongleur* before a battle singing chansons about battle in an epic poem on a battle is an important reminder of the complex interaction between literature and reality.[62] The narrative mode of the chansons and romances themselves habitually portrayed combat as a series of successive single encounters, and a considerable body of literary scholarship has focused on the formulaic descriptions of the attack with couched lance then sword in these

---

[60] For a review of the debate surrounding the dating of the *Carmen*, and for powerful arguments for its authenticity, see E. M. C. van Houts, 'Latin Poetry and the Anglo-Norman Court, 1066–1135: The *Carmen de Hastingae Proelio*', *Journal of Medieval History*, 15 (1989), pp. 39–62.

[61] *John Barbour, The Bruce*, ed. and trans. A. A. M. Duncan (Edinburgh, 1997), pp. 448–53; cf. G. W. S. Barrow, *Robert Bruce* (3rd edn, Edinburgh, 1988), p. 218. Though one of the most famous of single combats, this incident was neither a judicial duel nor the result of a formal challenge; seeing Bruce dressing the ranks of his men, Sir Henry merely charged him unannounced, but paid the price for his rashness with his life. Mounted on a lighter and more manoeuvrable palfrey than his opponent's great destrier, Bruce was able to avoid the charge, and, as Bohun passed, cleft his helmet and skull with his battle axe. A more formal combat between champions occurred before the battle of Halidon Hill, 1333, when a knight from Edward III's household, Robert Benhale, slew a giant Scots champion named Turnbull (*Geoffrey le Baker, Chronicon*, ed. E. M. Thompson (Oxford, 1889), p. 51; R. Nicholson, *Edward III and the Scots* (Oxford, 1965), p. 134 and n. 3).

[62] An equally forceful example of the extent to which life could mirror art within the chivalric culture of the later middle ages is the famous incident (*c.*1318) related in Sir Thomas Grey's *Scalachronica* in which Sir William Marmion's lady gave him a gilt crested war helm, 'commanding him to go to the most dangerous place in Britain and [there] cause this helmet to be famous'. Accordingly Marmion chose Norham castle, sallied out single-handedly to attack a group of Scots, and nearly lost his life before being rescued by the castle's constable, Sir Thomas Grey, the chronicler's father (Sir Thomas Grey, *Scalachronica*, trans. H. Maxwell (Glasgow, 1907), pp. 61–3).

engagements.[63] As Martin Jones has recently argued, a serious attempt to describe pitched battle in romance literature has to await the adaptations of Chrétien in the late twelfth and early thirteenth centuries by Wolfram von Eschenbach and Hartmann von Aue.[64]

In turn, such vernacular literature cast a long shadow over descriptions of single combat in historical or quasi-historical writing. We have already noted the prominence of judicial combat as a literary motif, but equally an epic triumph in single combat might be ascribed by chroniclers to favoured benefactors of a religious house[65] or to a patron's dynastic forebears. Thus, for example, in his *Historia Gaufredi ducis,* John of Marmoutier has his hero Geoffrey le Bel slay a giant Saxon champion 'from beyond the sea' following a 'tournament' between Normans and Bretons supposedly *c.*1128.[66] The incident is clearly apocryphal; such deliberate killing did not take place even in the nascent tournament, while the champion's lance 'like a weaver's beam' and his beheading seem drawn directly from the biblical account of Goliath. A widely popular motif in

---

[63] See, *inter alia,* J. Rychner, *La chanson de geste. Essai sur l'art épique des jongleurs* (Geneva and Lille, 1955), pp. 139–46; and M. Jones, 'Chrétien, Hartmann and the Knight as Fighting Man', in *Chrétien de Troyes and the German Middle Ages,* ed. M. H. Jones and R. Wiseby (Woodbridge, 1993), pp. 90–7 and references there cited.

[64] M. H. Jones, 'The Depiction of Battle in Wolfram von Eschenbach's *Willehalm', The Ideals and Practice of Medieval Knighthood,* II, ed. C. Harper-Bill and R. Harvey (Woodbridge, 1988), pp. 46–69.

[65] Hence the annals of Dunmow priory, *s.a.* 1216, have a splendid but wholly fictitious tale of single combat involving the house's benefactor Robert FitzWalter, one of the leading baronial opponents of King John. On one occasion when the armies of the kings of England and France confronted each other, an English knight had challenged any of the French side to joust (*hasti ludere*) 'for the love of his lady'. Immediately, FitzWalter, serving with the king of France, sprang into his saddle without the aid of a squire, unhorsed his opponent and presented the French king with the captured mount. Impressed by such prowess, John remarked that it was truly a fortunate ruler to have such a knight in his *comitiva,* whereupon FitzWalter's friends revealed the knight's identity and professed FitzWalter's loyalty. John thereupon reinstated him, and FitzWalter stood by him henceforth (W. Dugdale, *Monasticon,* ed. J. Caley *et al.,* 6 vols (London, 1817–30), VI, p. 147).

[66] John of Marmoutier, *Historia Gaufredi ducis,* in *Chroniques des comtes d'Anjou et des seigneurs d'Amboise (Chroniques des comtes d'Anjou),* ed. L. Halphen and R. Pourpardin (Paris, 1913), pp. 182–3. For a discussion of John of Marmoutier's work and his portrayal of Geoffrey see J. Bradbury, 'Geoffrey V of Anjou, Count and Knight', *The Ideals and Practice of Medieval Knighthood, III,* ed. C. Harper-Bill and R. Harvey (Woodbridge, 1990), pp. 21–38.

manuscript illumination,[67] the combat of David and Goliath was explicitly acknowledged as an influence by the author of the *Chronica de gestis consulum Andegavorum*, when he has Count Geoffrey Greygown (960–987) slay a Danish champion, Ethelulf, who 'like a new Goliath', had challenged and killed a number of Franks in single combat outside Paris.[68]

Yet in addition to biblical influence, it has been suggested that the author of the *Deeds of the Counts of Anjou* was here drawing on an account by Richer of an actual duel between a German and Frankish champion when Otto II's army was encamped outside Paris in 978.[69] According to Richer, the German champion rode to the fortified bridge over the Seine and, when his repeated offers of single combat went unmet, heaped insults upon the Franks. Stung by the German's repeated taunts, Hugh Capet urged his *milites* to wipe out these slurs, to cover themselves in glory and to gain a reward for their bravery. Of the many who then came forward, one of Hugh's vassals, Ivo, took up the challenge, and slew the German in view of both armies. Then stripping his foe of his arms and equipment, he presented them to the duke, who granted him his reward.[70]

Though the veracity of Richer's own account has been called into question,[71] it has been firmly defended by Ferdinand Lot, who pointed to the existence among the vassals of Hugh Capet of one Ivo, who had received a benefice by 981.[72] Yet irrespective of its ultimate historical validity or the extent of literary embellishment, Richer's tale (as with Taillefer's duel in the *Carmen*) nevertheless reflects familiarity with the convention of single combat and indicates many of its essential features. A bridge as the place of a challenge furnishes an early example of the kind of site favoured for the setting of the later *pas d'armes*,[73] while the defiance and taunting of an opponent reminds us that the insulting and abuse of an enemy, so common in the chansons, were essential counterpoints to praise and honour in a martial society obsessed with pride and reputation.[74]

---

[67] See, for example, *English Romanesque Art*, ed. G. Zarnecki, J. Holt and T. Holland (London, 1984), pp. 57, 110–11; and C. M. Kaufmann, *Romanesque Manuscripts, 1066–1190* (London, 1975), fig. 69.

[68] *Chroniques des comtes d'Anjou*, pp. 38–9; Geoffrey, 'like another David', also beheads the Dane.

[69] *Richer, Histoire de France (888–995)*, ed. R. Latouche, 2 vols (Paris, 1930, 1937), II, pp. 92–5.

[70] *Ibid.*

[71] *Ibid.*, p. 93, n. 3, where Latouche comments, 'le récit de ce "combat singulaire" a une allure légendaire'.

[72] F. Lot, *Les derniers Carolingiens (954–991)* (Paris, 1891), p. 101, n. 1, and p. 402, pièce justificatif no. 4.

[73] Keen, *Chivalry*, p. 203.

[74] Strickland, *War and Chivalry*, pp. 98–131.

Stripping the vanquished opponent of his arms and armour represented not simply the seizure of valuable booty but also the infliction of further shame and degradation,[75] which in some cases might even extend to the mutilation or beheading of the defeated champion's corpse. Conversely, the bestowal of the defeated champion's arms on the victor's lord, an act deeply rooted in Germanic tradition,[76] conferred upon him associative honour and kudos from the triumph of his own champion.

Above all, Richer's account reinforces Maurice Keen's stress on 'the strong streak of individualism' so readily apparent in chivalry,[77] and takes us to the essential *raison d'être* of such duels; the desire of an individual warrior to display skill in arms and, by triumphing against an elite opponent, to gain martial glory. Such valour might well elicit booty and princely largesse, but duels were undertaken predominantly to augment a knight's prowess and honour by proof of his worth as a fighting man. In the romances, as Martin Jones has perceptively noted concerning the series of single combats in Hartmann von Aue's *Erec*, 'the quest for *aventiure*, that is, for martial challenges of the kind that Guivreiz obliges Erec to accept ... is a regular component of the life of knightly excellence', and for the knight 'a means of maintaining his combat fitness as well as his reputation'.[78] Repeated challenges to combat against one or more enemy knights may have been a staple *topos* in the adventures of the itinerant heroes of Chrétien and his redactors, but it was one not wholly divorced from reality. If we may believe Anna Comnena, at a time when the tournament was still nascent in northern France, Frankish knights might seek combat even in time of peace through challenges to all comers, in what were clear antecedents of the later, more highly developed *pas d'armes*. As a Frankish noble reportedly told the Emperor Alexius at Constantinople in 1096:

> ...at a cross-roads in the country where I was born is an ancient shrine: to this anyone who wishes to engage in single combat goes, prepared to fight; there he prays to God for help and there he stays awaiting the man

---

[75] Thus after his victory in single combat at Pavia in 889, the Lombard champion Hubald similarly stripped his dead Bavarian opponent of his armour and left his corpse in the middle of the river Vernavola (*The Works of Liudprand of Cremona*, trans. Wright, p. 50).

[76] In *Beowulf*, for example, the first act of the victorious hero on returning home from the court of Hrothgar is to bestow on his lord Hygelac the arms and equipment that were his reward for slaying Grendel and his mother. As he tells Hygelac, 'By my actions there, prince, I brought honour to your people.' Earlier, he had presented Hrothgar with the 'sea-plunder' of Grendel's head and the hilt of the giant's sword after his undersea duel with Grendel's mother (*Beowulf*, 11. 2145–95, 1634–70).

[77] Keen, *Chivalry*, p. 250.

[78] Jones, 'Chrétien, Hartmann and the Knight as Fighting Man', pp. 107–8.

who will dare to answer his challenge. At that cross-roads, I myself have spent time, waiting and longing for the man who would fight– but there was never one who dared.[79]

Instances of formal duels before battle or during siege such as those described by the *Carmen* and by Richer are comparatively rare outside literary sources. Nevertheless, the predominantly castle-based hostilities of the eleventh and twelfth centuries gave rise to a host of small-scale but sanguinary *melées*, that were in effect a series of concomitant single combats. Orderic, for example, noted how in 1098, Angevin knights sallied out from Le Mans to engage Rufus's army: 'Chivalrous feats (*militaria facinora*) were accomplished on both sides: for renowned champions from both armies strove to prove their valour and to earn the laurels of war from their leaders and comrades.'[80] Similarly at the siege of Bellême in 1113, knights from the garrison rode out against Henry I's forces to engage in single combat (*singulari certamine dimicaturi*),[81] while outside the walls of Breteuil in 1119, the garrison commander, Ralph de Gael, mortally wounded a Flemish champion who had vanquished Ralph the Red and Luke of la Barre.[82] Orderic's often detailed knowledge suggests that feats of arms undertaken even in such relatively minor skirmishes were still vibrant currency in the oral traditions on which he drew.

Though duels between lone champions appear largely absent from the preliminaries of larger pitched battles such as Tinchebrai, 1106, and Brémule, 1119, a series of individual combats might nevertheless precede the clash of the main armies. In Wolfram von Eschenbach's *Willehalm*, which seems to reflect closely the realities of battle, picked knights, referred to as *tjostiure*, highly skilled in the use of the lance, ride ahead of the closely-ordered units (*scharn*) to engage their enemy counterparts, and such jousts (*tjoste*) take place each time fresh battalions enter the fray.[83] Likewise, the *Histoire de Guillaume le Maréchal* describes how in the tournament, individual jousts known as *commençailles* took place immediately prior to the main teams coming together in the *melée*.[84] It seems likely that this practice

---

[79] *The Alexiad of Anna Comnena*, trans. E. R. A. Sewter (Harmondsworth, 1969), X:10, p. 326.
[80] Orderic, V, pp. 242–3.
[81] Orderic, VI, pp. 182–3.
[82] Orderic, VI, pp. 246–7.
[83] M. H. Jones, '*Die tjostiure uz vunf scharn*', in *Studien zu Wolfram von Eschenbach. Festschrift für Werner Schröder zum 75. Geburtstag*, ed. K. Gärtner and J. Heinzle (Tübingen, 1989), pp. 429–41.
[84] *HGM*, ll. 3499ff, 5517ff, 6057; K. T. G. Webster, 'The Twelfth-Century Tourney', *Anniversary Papers Presented to G. L. Kitteridge* (Boston and London, 1913), p. 232; Barker, *The Tournament in England*, p. 141.

mirrored that in actual combat, save that in the tourney these jousts were *à plaisance*. Such outriders may have had a tactical purpose, to engage and vanquish battalion leaders or to exploit gaps in the ranks of an enemy unit that was becoming disorganised. Whatever their purpose, however, their employment shows that in a well-ordered force, individual combat was seen to co-exist with and augment group manoeuvres, which depended on corporate discipline and tight cohesion for success in the *melée*.[85] For when not undertaken in such a controlled context, the urge to engage in single combat could have a highly detrimental effect on a unit's fighting efficiency.[86]

That this practice of engaging in individual hastiludes before larger group combat was prevalent in the earlier twelfth century is revealed by William of Malmesbury, when describing the discomfiture of Stephen's army outside Lincoln in 1141 by the Angevin forces of Robert, earl of Gloucester:

> The royalists first attempted that prelude to the fight which is called jousting (*quod iustam vocant*), for in this they were accomplished, but when they saw the 'earlists', if the expression may be allowed, were fighting not with lances at a distance but with swords at close quarters and, charging with their banners in the van, were breaking through the king's line, then all the earls to a man sought safety in flight.[87]

Although Malmesbury's use of the word *justa* is cited by both Ducange and Niermeyer as the earliest known instance of the term,[88] it is clear that by the 1140s it was in common currency, reflecting considerable familiarity with such hastiludes. Clearly, however, Stephen's supporters had expected neither the form of *tjoste* seen in *Willehalm*, which were fought very much *à outrance* and to the death, or full-scale battle. Rather, they had hoped for a consciously limited form of combat, in which feats of arms might be displayed before the assembled hosts but without much bloodshed, exactly the type of engagement which Henry of Huntingdon saw as characterising the desultory skirmishes between royalist and Angevin forces during the siege of Winchester later that same year:

> Conflicts took place every day, not in pitched battles but in the excursions of knightly manoeuvres. Valiant exploits were not unrecognisably confused as in the darkness of war, but the prowess and glory earned by individuals appeared in the open, so that for all the participants, exalted in the splendours of illustrious deeds, this interlude

---

85 Jones, '*Die tjostiure uz vunf scharn*', pp. 429–41.

86 Below, pp. 342.

87 *Historia Novella*, p. 49.

88 Ducange, *Glossarium mediae et infimae latinitatis*, ed. L. Favre, 10 vols (Niort, 1883–7), III, pp. 947–8; Niermeyer, *Mediae latinitatis lexicon minus*, p. 569.

was a source of gratification.[89]

As Henry of Huntingdon shrewdly observed, the more restrained nature of these combats stemmed from the context of civil war; many of the nobility sought to shun a decisive engagement both because of close ties of kinship among the Anglo-Norman aristocracy and because of the desire to maintain the political *status quo* to their own political advantage.[90] The result, at the siege of Winchester at least, was a form of engagement poised between the bloody melées which had characterised so much of the castle-based warfare within or between the territorial principalities, and the tournament. And it seems no coincidence that the tournament itself, prohibited in England before 1135, first emerges in the kingdom during the troubled reign of Stephen, an emergence closely connected with the weakening of royal authority.[91]

Nevertheless, in the tournament it was not until the second quarter of the thirteenth century that jousting itself gained prominence; the exploits of Ulrich von Lichtenstein epitomise a growing emphasis on spectacle and on audience facilitated by increased geographical circumscription of the lists, on Arthurian pageant and on the desire to highlight individual feats of arms formally lost in the chaos of the *melée*.[92] Even then, however, group combat long held its own as the key component of the tournament, with hastiludes confined to the vigil or 'vespers' of the tournament and regarded, as once in battle itself, essentially as a prelude to the *melée* itself until well into the fourteenth century.[93]

But if in Anglo-Norman England and northern France single combats achieve little prominence outside epic and romance, they abound in crusade sources. For nowhere was the yearning to exhibit individual prowess more prominently displayed than in Outremer, in a theatre of war where religious zeal fuelled the desire for glory through martial deeds. During the protracted siege of Acre, 1189–91, for example, negotiation and

---

[89] Henry of Huntingdon, pp. 740–1.

[90] Thus at Crowmarsh in 1153, although Stephen and Duke Henry mutually desired a pitched battle, the magnates on both sides refused to countenance this and forced an agreement on them both (Henry of Huntingdon, pp. 766–7). At Lincoln in 1141, the resolve of 'the disinherited' and those irrevocably committed to Robert of Gloucester's cause to force the issue by pitched battle clearly took both Stephen and his supporters by surprise. Similarly at the siege of Winchester, it had only been the arrival of Queen Matilda that precipitated a serious engagement. Cf. above, pp. 119–20.

[91] William of Newburgh, p. 422; J. R. V. Barker, *The Tournament in England, 1100–1400* (Woodbridge, 1986), p. 8.

[92] R. Barber and J. Barker, *Tournaments: Jousts, Chivalry and Pageants in the Middle Ages* (Woodbridge, 1989), pp. 49–53.

[93] Barker, *The Tournament in England*, pp. 139–41.

fraternisation were interspersed with duels, while even the children in both camps challenged each other to mock combat.[94] Joinville recounts how at the same city in 1252, a Genoese knight he names as Jean le Grand was escorting back a group of serjeants into Acre when 'one of the enemy started to call out to him in the Saracen tongue that he would tilt with him if he were willing'.[95] Accepting the challenge, Jean then saw a group of about eight Turks whom he charged instead, running one through with his lance and striking two others with his sword before withdrawing in safety. 'These three fine strokes', notes Joinville approvingly, 'were delivered in the sight of the lord of Arsuf, and were also witnessed by the leading citizens in Acre and all the women who had gathered on the walls of the city to watch the fight.'[96] To have performed such a feat of arms against the infidel in full view of many, including ladies and esteemed lords, and in a setting where fine blows would not go unnoticed unlike in the thick of battle, was exactly the kind of scenario for chivalric deeds of which knights must have dreamed.[97] Jean le Grand was still more fortunate in having Joinville to record the incident quite literally blow by blow.

Enemy champions might be well known to each other and challenge opponents by name. Thus the Syrian emir Usamah, whose memoirs are replete with tales of single combats, records how 'one the of most valiant Frankish knights' from the army of Antioch sallied from the Christian camp and called out for the Muslim champion Jum'ah al-Numayri, whom he had long wanted to encounter. Disappointed to find him absent, the knight charged and routed four other Muslim horsemen.[98] In his *Estoire de*

---

[94]   Beha-ad-Din, *The Life of Saladin*, trans. C. L. Conder (Palestine Pilgrims' Texts Society, XII, London, 1897), pp. 161–2. For a (doubtless apocryphal) archery duel between a Turk and a Welshman, see *L'Estoire de la Guerre Sainte par Ambroise* (Ambroise), ed. G. Paris (Paris, 1871); trans. M. J. Hubert and J. L. La Monte as *The Crusade of Richard Lion-Heart by Ambroise* (New York, 1941), ll. 3731–70.

[95]   *Histoire de St Louis par Jean, sire de Joinville* (Joinville), ed. M. N. de Wailly (Société de l'Histoire de France, Paris, 1868), p. 196; trans. M. R. B. Shaw, *Joinville and Villehardouin: Chronicles of the Crusades* (Harmondsworth, 1963), p. 302, where the knight's name is rendered as Giannone.

[96]   Joinville, pp. 196–7; trans. Shaw, pp. 302–3.

[97]   As Geoffrey de Charny was later to stress in his *Livre de Chevalerie*, feats of arms in war against the pagan won far more glory than those performed merely in the tournament; *The Book of Chivalry of Geoffroi de Charny*, ed. and trans. R. W. Kaeuper and E. Kennedy (Pennsylvania, 1996), p. 84 ff; Keen, *Chivalry*, pp. 12–13.

[98]   *An Arab-Syrian Gentleman and Warrior in the Period of the Crusades. Memoirs of Usamah ibn-Munqidh* (Usamah), ed. P. K. Hitti (Columbia, 1929; reprint, Princeton, 1987), pp. 96–7.

la Guerre Sainte, Ambroise singles out certain combats between individual Frankish knights and prominent Turkish warriors within the context of larger engagements,[99] and was able to identify by name certain Turkish champions who were killed.[100]

Knights' urge to break tight formation and engage in individual combat was often overwhelming on a 'fighting march', when they were faced with the incessant harrying tactics of the Turkish horse archers. Usamah describes with admiration how in 1111, as Tancred's host withdrew to Antioch under Turkish attack, a Frankish knight had sallied out and charged into the midst of the Turks. His horse was slain and he was wounded, but he succeeded in cutting his way back on foot to the host. Usamah himself saw the Frankish knight when given safe conduct on pilgrimage, and wondered at his numerous scars earned in this engagement.[101]

But though such feats might display great courage, they could also threaten corporate discipline and endanger an army by disrupting the tight cohesion essential to guard against Turkish tactics.[102] The military orders were well aware of the temptations of brother knights to engage in spontaneous single combat without orders and strictly forbade it.[103] Ambroise records how a Hospitaller, Robert des Bruges, had broken ranks from Richard's army in 1192 to attack and slay 'a certain well armed Turk', 'an illustrious act of valour', as Ambroise noted, 'had it not involved the breaking of the rule of his order'. The Grand Master, Garnier de Naplouse, made the knight dismount in disgrace and read him the rule; and Robert

---

[99] Hence, for example, he records the great difficulty Peter de Préaux had in overcoming a redoubtable Turk, who could not be taken alive and was only slain by Peter and his men after a bitter struggle (Ambroise, ll. 7563–70); and the emir who was run through by Andrew de Chauvigny but not before he had pierced and broken Andrew's arm with his lance (*ibid.*, ll. 7571–82).

[100] Notably Ayas al Tawil, one of Saladin's marmlukes, slain on 1 September 1191, two days before the great battle of Arsuf; 'a man of gallantry and of such strength and mastery that there was no man who could beat him, and none even dared compete with him. He had so huge a lance there were no larger two in France' (Ambroise, ll. 6020–32); *Itinerarium*, p. 13; and Beha-ad-Din, pp. 284–5.

[101] Usamah, pp. 97–8.

[102] Strickland, *War and Chivalry*, pp. 115–17.

[103] *La Règle du Temple*, ed. H. deCurzon (Paris, 1886); trans. J. Upton-Ward, *The Rule of the Templars* (Woodbridge, 1992), cc. 242–3, 611–15. It is testimony to the intense pressure sustained by the Hospitallers in the rearguard at the battle of Arsuf, 1191, that one of the two knights who broke ranks against orders, and thereby precipitated a general and premature charge, was the Marshal of the Hospital (Ambroise, ll. 6421–36).

was only saved from being severely disciplined by the intercession of the nobles in the army who applauded his courage.[104] For all their austere lifestyle, plain arms and quasi-monastic rule, the new knighthood of the military orders was no less prone to seek personal, as well as corporate, glory than the *militia saecularis*.[105]

The prevalence of single combat in crusading texts such as Ambroise or Joinville emphasises the great desire not only to perform but also to record feats of arms against the paynim.[106] The motif of single combat between Frankish champions and their Muslim counterparts became a powerful and ubiquitous symbol in both art and literature of the triumph of Christendom. Thus of the ten famous stained glass roundels depicting the First Crusade that once decorated Suger's St Denis (which date from *c*.1144 but survive only in eighteenth-century engravings), two depict the individual victories of Count Robert of Flanders and of Duke Robert Curthose of Normandy in such duels,[107] scenes which may well have been based on their actual feats of arms during the great battle near Ascalon in August 1099.[108] But even before his death in 1134, Anglo-Norman writers were crediting Curthose with a series of imaginary victories in single combat with pagan leaders, including Kerbogha of Mosul himself, with these feats gaining increasing elaboration in vernacular epics such as the *Chanson d'Antioch*.[109]

Legendary feats accrued with equal rapidity around the figure of Richard Coeur de Lion. His remarkable relief of Jaffa in August, 1192, and its subsequent defence by the king with only a handful of knights and a force of footsoldiers against Saladin's far larger army was already being vaunted in epic terms by Ambroise, a contemporary and probable

---

[104] Ambroise, ll. 9908–46.

[105] Strickland, *War and Chivalry*, p. 117 and n. 98.

[106] Thus even in a brief notice concerning the Second Crusade, a local chronicler such as John of Hexham could proudly note the triumph of Robert de Mowbray over a Saracen emir in single combat (*Historia Johannis, prioris Haugustadensis ecclesiae*, ed. J. Raine, *The Priory of Hexham, ils Chroniclers, Endowments and Annals*, 2 vols (Surtees Society, 44, Durham, 1868), I, p. 154).

[107] C. W. David, *Robert Curthose, Duke of Normandy* (Cambridge, 1920), Appendix G, pp. 249–52, while the glass roundel depicting Robert Curthose's duel is reproduced as a frontispiece; cf. G. Paris, 'Robert Courte-Heuse à la premier croisade', *Comptes Rendus des séances de l'Académie des Inscriptions et Belles-Lettres*, 4th series, xviii (1890), pp. 190–215.

[108] David, *Robert Curthose*, p. 116. Duke Robert slew the standard-bearer of the Egyptian grand vizier, Malik al-Afdhal, and later presented the standard to the Church of the Holy Sepulchre (*Gesta Francorum*, pp. 95, 97).

[109] The growth of these legends is fully discussed by David, *Robert Curthose*, pp. 190–202.

eye-witness, in his *Estoire de la Guerre Sainte*.[110] Richard's exploits at Jaffa gave rise to the thirteenth-century romance the *Pas de Saladin*, in which Richard and twelve peers hold a narrow defile against an entire Saracen host, and the romance itself states that many halls were decorated with paintings of this great feat of arms.[111] *Pace* Walter Scott's *The Talisman*, Richard and Saladin never in reality met, let alone vied with each other in single combat. Yet by 1251, Henry III could commission a painting of 'the duel of King Richard' for his palace of Clarendon, indicating that a legendary tale of Richard unhorsing Saladin in a joust had become well established by the mid-thirteenth century, and was probably current in Anglo-Norman vernacular literature considerably earlier.[112] Lloyd has emphasised the extent to which both Henry III and Edward I were influenced by the crusading prowess of their Norman and Plantagenet forebears, and the murals at Clarendon, as well as other decorative schemes similarly ordered in 1251 for royal chambers in the Tower of London, Winchester Castle and the palace of Westminster, may well have included Robert Curthose's duel with Kerbogha, as a fitting counterpart to Richard's single combat against Saladin.[113] Certainly Coeur de Lion's joust re-occurs as a widespread motif on a number of decorative tiles, such as those dating *c*.1250 from Chertsey abbey, Surrey (Pl. 47).[114] Both tale and image, which were very closely linked,[115] had an enduring appeal. With the Middle

[110] Ambroise, ll. 11,035-652.

[111] G. Paris, 'La légende de Saladin', *Journal des Savants* (1893), pp. 284–99, 354–66, 428–38, 486–98 at pp. 491–6; and R. S. Loomis, 'Richard Coeur de Lion and the Pas Saladin', in Medieval Art, *Proceedings of the Modern Languages Association*, 30m, (1915), pp. 524–5, especially p. 524 n. 22.

[112] For a full discussion of the development of the literary motif of Richard's single combat with Saladin, see Loomis, 'Richard Coeur de Lion and the Pas Saladin, pp. 510–20, at pp. 509–18; and J. Gillingham, 'Some Legends of Richard the Lionheart: Their Development and Their Influence', in *Riccardo Cuor di Leone nella storia e nella leggenda* (Accademia Nazionale dei Lincei, Problemi attuali di scienza e di cultura, 253, Rome, 1981), and reprinted in *Richard Coeur de Lion in Myth and History*, ed. J. Nelson (London, 1992), pp. 51–69.

[113] S. Lloyd, *English Society and the Crusade, 1216–1307* (Oxford, 1988), pp. 198–200; T. Borenius, 'The Cycle of Images in the Palaces and Castles of Henry III', *Journal of the Warburg and Courtauld Institutes*, 6 (1943), p. 45.

[114] Loomis, 'Richard Coeur de Lion and the Pas Saladin', pp. 514–16; *idem*, 'Illustrations of Medieval Romance Tiles from Chertsey Abbey', *University of Illinois Studies in Language and Literature*, 2 (1916), pp. 20–7, 84–5; E. S. Eames, *Catalogue of Medieval Lead-Glazed Earthenware Tiles in the Department of Medieval and Later Antiquities, British Museum*, 2 vols (London, 1980), I, pp. 144–5, 192–4.

[115] Loomis, 'Richard Coeur de Lion and the Pas Saladin', pp. 514–18.

English romance, *Richard Coeur de Lion*, the epic reaches its summation, with Richard fighting Saladin with a great wooden beam placed across his horse's neck, thus cutting swathes through the Saracen ranks,[116] while nowhere does this *pas Saladin* find more dramatic visual expression than in the early fourteenth-century Luttrell Psalter (Pl. 48).

It has been possible here only to touch on the complex interaction between art, literature and chronicle narrative in relation to the powerful and ubiquitous motif of single combat. Equally, its depiction in Anglo-Norman sculpture, mural painting and manuscript illumination must be the preserve of more detailed and specialist studies, such as the important discussion by J. J. G. Alexander of the combat between virtues and vices in the *Psychomachia* of Prudentius and other allegorical texts.[117] Rather, I have tried to suggest that the theme of challenge, duel and single combat offers a valuable microcosm of the chivalric thought-world. The challenge was a flexible instrument, used as much to avoid major engagements as to initiate them, and employed as a psychological weapon to outface an opponent or to buy time for tactical withdrawal or attack. Similarly, the proffer of judicial combat through individuals or groups of champions was a complex mechanism deployed in varying circumstances to defuse situations of imminent bloodshed, to proclaim the justice of a cause and to achieve moral advantage, or as an unrealistic last gambit of a desperate protagonist. Realpolitik ensured such wagers of battle normally remained mere diplomatic manoeuvrings, except in epic and romance where champions fought and pledges were honoured. Beyond the context of judicial duels, the desire of knights to engage in single combat was profound, informed by and reflected in vernacular literature. Single combat was the ultimate test of prowess, a key means of gaining repute (*los*), and all the more so if one's opponent was an enemy of the faith.

Let us conclude with an incident occurring during the Third Crusade. In August, 1192, having saved the citadel of Jaffa at the eleventh hour by a daring sea-borne assault, Richard had then mounted a brilliant tactical defence of a dangerous position when faced by a numerically far superior Muslim force. Yet not content with having driven off repeated Muslim assaults, Richard took the war to the enemy by challenging any of the Turks to single combat.[118] Doubtless Richard's counsellors despaired of such rashness, but its effect is reflected in the fact that we learn of the incident not from Ambroise or other Christian sources, but from Saladin's own scribe and confidant Beha-ad-Din. As Beha-ad-Din is honest enough to

116 Gillingham, 'Some Legends of Richard the Lionheart', pp. 53–4.
117 J. J. G. Alexander, 'Ideological Representation of Combat in Anglo-Norman Art', *Anglo-Norman Studies*, 15 (1992), pp. 1–24.
118 Beha-ad-Din, p. 376.

admit: 'I have been assured by men who were there, that on that day the king of England, lance in hand, rode along the whole length of our army from right to left, and not one of our soldiers left the ranks to attack him.'[119] Beha-ad-Din's remarks sharply reveal the way in which a challenge could intimidate and shame the enemy whilst enormously augmenting the reputation of the successful challenger. Perhaps the Luttrell Psalter was not so wide of the mark after all.

---

[119]   *Ibid.*

Armour and Military Dress in Thirteenth-
and Early Fourteenth-Century England[1]

FRÉDÉRIQUE LACHAUD

Two years ago, a manuscript from the library of the late Alan G. Thomas
was purchased at Sotheby's by the Royal Armouries. It is an indenture
dated 10 July 1282, which records the loan of 18*s.* of silver and several
pieces of armour to William de Chervile of Reydon (East Suffolk) by Hugh
de Reymes (or Reymis), son of Gilbert de Reymes, of Wherstead. The
pieces of armour listed in the indenture are: an aketon, a haubergeon, a
colret, a bascinet, a pair of gloves of whalebone, a pair of poleyns, a pair of
cuisses and a surcoat, the whole equipment being estimated at 6 marks.[2]
Hugh de Reymes was from a landed family, but he and his father had made
their fortune in trade and both were Ipswich burgesses.[3] As for William de
Chervile, he appears to have held a knight's fee in Reydon: his rank is
indicated by the seal attached to the indenture, which represents a knight
on horseback. The loan was probably connected with the writs of military
summons sent to all sheriffs in May 1282, in preparation for a new
campaign in Wales: the writs announced an ordinance in council according
to which every person holding lands to the annual amount of £30 had to
provide himself with a good horse and suitable armour.[4] Obviously,
William de Chervile already owned some kind of military equipment, at
least some offensive weapons, but the acquisition of a complete suit of
armour presented difficulties for him, and he had to pledge two pieces of
land as security for the loan. His was not an isolated case. The difficulties
faced by combatants in the thirteenth century in purchasing the necessary
defensive equipment for the battlefield have often been stressed, and are
usually regarded as being one of the reasons behind the reluctance of many

[1] Unless otherwise specified, all references are to documents kept in the Public
Record Office in London.

[2] Trustees of the Royal Armouries, I. 875. The text is edited in Appendix 1. I
wish to thank Dr Dora Thornton for giving this reference to me.

[3] For the destinies of the family, see P. Dixon, *Aydon Castle, Northumberland*
(London: H.M.S.O., 1988), p. 7ff.

[4] *Parliamentary Writs*, I, p. 226. William de Chervile, however, does not appear in
the muster roll drawn up at Rhuddlan at the beginning of August (*ibid.*, I, pp.
228–43).

potential knights to undertake knighthood, in spite of various incentives and regulations.[5]

Beyond general considerations, however, we know little of the way individual combatants would actually protect themselves on the battlefield in the thirteenth century. Work on armour in this period has traditionally been dominated by the study of visual evidence, such as illuminated manuscripts and funeral effigies, and of a very few extant pieces.[6] In this paper, I would like to suggest that the study of documentary evidence may still yield some information of interest on the attitude of the king and nobles concerning the provision of military equipment to their troops, as well as on the technical evolution of armour and on the composition of military equipment for the individual combatant.[7]

A category of documents rich in relevant information is that of financial accounts for expenditure by the king. There we can find indications about the stock of armour deposited in the Tower of London, the work of armourers employed in royal service,[8] as well as the provision of military equipment for the royal family and for some privileged members of the court, such as the wards of the king. A well-known example is that of John of Brittany, the second son of the duke of Brittany, who was brought up in the household of his uncle: during the 1280s, the king regularly provided him with military equipment for the tournament or for

---

[5] This was already pointed out by J. E. Morris, *The Welsh Wars of Edward I* (Oxford, 1901), p. 49. See also B. C. Keeney, 'Military Service and the Development of Nationalism in England, 1272–1327', *Speculum*, 22 (1947), pp. 534–49; and for an analysis of this position M. Prestwich, '*Miles in Armis Strenuus:* The Knight at War', *TRHS*, 6th series, 5 (1995), pp. 201–20, esp. p. 207. Also N. Saul, *Knights and Esquires: The Gloucestershire Gentry in the Fourteenth Century* (Oxford, 1981), p. 24.

[6] The best study of armour in England is still C. Blair, *European Armour, circa 1066 to circa 1700* (London, 1958). For recent work on iconography and extant pieces, see I. Peirce, 'The Knight, his Arms and Armour c. 1150–1250', *Anglo-Norman Studies,* 15 (1992), pp. 251–74.

[7] I have left aside the corpus of romances, already exploited in various works. For instance P. A. Sigal, 'Les coups et blessures reçus par le combattant à cheval en Occident aux XIIe et XIIIe siècles', *Le combattant au Moyen Age,* Société des Historiens Médiévistes de l'Enseignement Supérieur Public (Paris, 1991), pp. 171–83; and L. M. Paterson, 'The Occitan Squire in the Twelfth and Thirteenth Centuries', *The Ideals and Practice of Medieval Knighthood. Papers from the First and Second Strawberry Hill Conferences,* ed. C. Harper-Bill and R. Harvey (Woodbridge, 1986), pp. 133–51.

[8] For instance C. 47/3/11: expenses of the king's armourers, 1274–80. See T. F. Tout, *Chapters in the Administrative History of Mediaeval England,* 6 vols (Manchester, 1920–33), IV, p. 439 ff., for general considerations on the Tower as armoury.

the battlefield.[9] Several decades later, the Wardrobe accounts contain information concerning the military equipment of Gilbert de Clare. In 1306–7, for instance, he was given a haubergeon, an aketon and a gambeson, a gorger, some head-gear (two bascinets, a helm and a chapel de fer) and extremely elaborate leg-harness (a pair of *jambers*, a pair of sabatons, two pairs of poleyns, a pair of greaves), as well as some equestrian equipment, robes and tents.[10] (Appendix 3) We also find mentions of occasional gifts to men who had escaped from the jails of the king's enemies,[11] or to foreigners come to serve the king.[12] This was particularly the case with a group of Gascon knights who came to England in the 1290s after the loss of their property at the hands of the French: they became part of the royal household and were provided with military equipment suitable to their rank.[13]

More generally, the king showed some concern for the equipment of his men. In March 1254, for instance, Henry III ordered the treasurer to pay 30 marks or the equivalent of this sum in cloth or wine to fourteen men-at-arms of his household, because they had been obliged to pledge

9   M. Prestwich, 'Royal Patronage under Edward I', *Thirteenth Century England, I, Proceedings of the Newcastle upon Tyne Conference 1985*, ed. P. R. Coss and S. D. Lloyd (Woodbridge, 1986), pp. 43–4, for John of Brittany. For his tournament equipment, see *Records of the Wardrobe and Household 1285–1286*, ed. B. F. and C. R. Byerly (London, 1977), nos. 41, 60, 247, 321.

10   Gilbert de Clare, lord of Thormont, was a member of the entourage of Edward of Caernarvon (M. Altschul, *A Baronial Family in Medieval England: The Clares, 1217–1314* (Baltimore, 1965), p. 160), but the importance of the equipment suggests that it may have been destined for his cousin, the grandson of Edward I and future earl of Gloucester, a member of the entourage of Queen Margaret since 1301.

11   B.L. Additional MS 7,965, fol. 53r: 11 marks to a valet of Sir Hugh Bardolf, who had lost all his military equipment when he had been made prisoner by the men of the king of France, in order for him to buy some new *armuras* because he was returning to Gascony to his lord (February 1297). Also *Liber Quotidianus Contrarotulatoris Garderobae 28 Edward I, A.D. 1299–1300*, Society of Antiquaries of London (London, 1787), p. 156, for money given to men who had been imprisoned by the king of France and who were sent by Edward I to the garrison of Berwick-upon-Tweed after their reaching England, in order for them to buy some military equipment (January 1300).

12   E. 101/3/19, m. 1 (1276–7): mention of the payment of military equipment for Reynold Macere, knight of Germany. He was a household knight by 1285–6: *Records of the Wardrobe and Household 1285–1286*, p. xl.

13   B.L. Additional MS 7,965, fol. 53v: mention of military equipment purchased for some knights of Gascony who have escaped from the jails of the king of France (Arnaud de Gavaston, Raymond de Caupenne and Bertrand de Panissau), for themselves, their *commilitones* and their squires.

their military equipment after being left without pay for a lengthy period.[14] Was the king responsible, however, for the provision of military equipment to men fighting for him? Here and there in the financial accounts of the royal government we find mentions of provision of arms and armour to troops, as the following examples will suggest. Between August 1215 and September 1216, the Close Rolls record numerous payments for the equipment of men fighting for the king.[15] In February 1225, several knights leaving for Gascony with Richard of Cornwall received money from the king for their equipment.[16] In the summer of 1244, Henry III organised a demonstration of force in Scotland, and a handful of knights received military equipment for the occasion.[17] An account dated 1276–7 records payments to some members of the royal household for military equipment, probably for service in Wales: a squire of the queen received 50s. for this purpose, a squire of the king 40s., master Bertram, the *ingeniator* of the king, received 75s. Finally a group of knights, including some Gascons, received large sums of money to provide themselves with military equipment, as well as the earl of Bangor and his retinue.[18] In July and August 1297, money was given to Peter Bidau de la Testere, a merchant of Bayonne, and to his *socius*, to Geoffrey de Montravel, to Gilbert son of the earl of Stratheam, to the sons of the earl of Menteith and to Ginellus de Montravel, a valet of the household, to serve in the French war.[19] In the late winter of 1307, when John Botetourt, a banneret in the royal household, headed two *chevauchées* in Scotland to track down Robert Bruce, several knights and mounted serjeants of the household who accompanied him on his raids had their equipment provided for by the king.[20] In some of those cases the king seems to have graciously provided equipment expeditions abroad, while in others the equipment provided was accounted for as a prest on wages. What is common to all those deliveries of equipment is service abroad or exceptional circumstances such as the situation of urgency of the end of John's reign.

Very specific categories benefited more systematically from the provision of military equipment by the king. This was the case with the archers and crossbowmen of the king. Provided with offensive weapons

---

[14] *Close Rolls 1253–1254*, p. 226.
[15] *Rotuli Litterarum Clausarum in Turri Londinensi Asservati, 1204–27 (Rot. Litt. Cl.)*, ed. T. D. Hardy, 2 vols (Record Commission, 1833–44), I, pp. 226b, 229a, 230b, 231a, 233b, 240b, 241a, 266b, 274b, 286a.
[16] *Ibid.*, II, pp. 16b and 18.
[17] *Calendar of Liberate Rolls*, II, pp. 243–6.
[18] E. 101/3/19, m. 1.
[19] B.L. Additional MS 7,965, fol. 56.
[20] E. 101/369/16, fols. 7r. and 28.

from the royal stores, they were also given targes, and sometimes bracers of *cuir-bouilli*.[21] Occasionally they received pieces of clothing, such as in 1276–7, when a crossbowman in the service of the king received a piece of sindon, a silk in general use in military equipment, 'of the suit (*secta*) of the other crossbowmen'.[22] This is quite similar to later military uniform and was in any case distinct from the courtly livery of woollen cloth distributed to the rest of the household. The provision of military equipment to crossbowmen and archers may be explained not only by the fact that they were considered as an important element of military organisation, but also because they formed a kind of bodyguard around the king. The king was also concerned with the armament of his ships, such as in January 1225, when haubergeons appear among the arms necessary for the serjeants and mariners of the king.[23] Finally royal garrisons had to be equipped.[24] Royal accounts frequently mention the provision of crossbows, targes and other military equipment for garrisons.[25] In many cases, however, indentures were contracted with captains coming with their own retinues, and they were responsible for the equipment of their troops.[26] Inventories of castles give

21 This appears frequently among the royal accounts. See for instance *Rôles gascons*, II, no. 67 (Westminster, 5 June 1276). C. 47/22/2/57: purchase of crossbows by James de Molyns, 1300–1, for the war in Scotland. *Close Rolls 1242–1247*, pp. 5, 24, 175 for crossbows and quarrels sent to the king. *Close Rolls 1253–1254*, p. 169 (15 September 1253): letter ordering the mayor of Bordeaux to send 200 targes, together with the same number of crossbows and baldrics, to the king. For a bracer of *cuir-bouilli* of the Tudor period, see *Henry VIII. A European Court in England*, ed. D. Starkey (London, 1991), no. xi. 37.

22 E. 101/3/19, m. 2: order to provide Walter of Kent, a crossbowman in the service of the king, with sindon to make himself some equipment of the suite of the other crossbowmen of the king, for a cost of 20s.

23 *Rot. Litt. Cl.*, II, p. 13. Also *ibid.*, II, p. 51a (July 1225).

24 See general considerations on the place of garrisons in the household system in T. F. Tout, *Chapters in the Administrative History of Medieval England*, II, p. 137.

25 For instance *Close Rolls 1268–1272*, p. 232 (October 1270): targes and other equipment for the castle of Gloucester. For the provision of equipment for the royal garrisons, see E. 101/371/8/141 (*temp.* H. III): purchase of crossbows and of baldrics for crossbows for garrisons.

26 For instance, *Documents Illustrative of the History of Scotland, 1286–1306*, ed. J. Stevenson, 2 vols (Edinburgh, 1870), II, pp. 314–16: indenture dated 21 October 1298 between some royal officials and Sir Robert de Hastang for the guard of the castle of Roxburgh. Also *Calendar of Documents Relating to Scotland Preserved in the Public Record Office*, ed. J. Bain, 4 vols (Edinburgh, 1881–8), II, no. 1002, for a similar agreement concerning Stirling Castle, also *Calendar of Documents Relating to Scotland*, v (*Supplementary*), A.D. 1108–1516, ed. G. G.

us some idea of the difficulties encountered in maintaining the equipment of a garrison in good order. In January 1275, the castle of Exeter was viewed when its keeper left. The castle itself was in a poor state, with most of the building in ruins. From the stock of the garrison next to nothing was left: three hauberks, a haubergeon and a horse cover of mail, all rusty and not worth above 20s., as well as a pair of mail chausses, in slightly better shape.[27] In November 1276, Edward ordered the sheriff of Northumberland to view the castle of Bamburgh. There again the account was quite damning: the castle was in ruins, and from the equipment of the garrison, the officers found only three hauberks and three haubergeons, of no value at all, as well as three gambesons, two helms and eight chapels de fer, all of which were completely decayed.[28]

In short, apart from the garrisons, the king took only a systematic interest in the armament of his ships and in the equipment of his crossbowmen and archers. A similar pattern has been underlined for France by Philippe Contamine, who stresses that the king rarely interfered with the equipment of his army, except for the navy and artillery.[29] There was no general policy to provide armaments for the royal household, and the occasional provision of military equipment was very limited in comparison with the number of combatants. This explains why the absence of

---

Simpson and J. D. Galbraith (Scottish Record Office, 1986), no. 376, an indenture dated 30 July 1304 between Sir John de Botetourte, Sir John de Benestede and Sir Walter de Bedwynd on one part, and Sir Matthew de Redmayne on the other. Matthew will keep the castle of Dumfries with 5 men-at-arms, 10 crossbowmen and 10 archers for the period from 1 August to 20 November 1304 for the sum of £60 paid by the king to him. For a similar agreement with John de Segrave for Berwick Castle (1303–4), *ibid.*, no. 383.

[27] C. 145/33/36. Also view of the castle of Bamburgh (1276–7): mention of crossbows and quarrels (C. 145/34/1).

[28] C. 145/34/1 (13 November 1276). For military equipment kept in royal castles, see *Pipe Roll 5 Henry III*, p. 129 (1221): mention of hauberks, covers of iron, mail chausses and helms in the castle of Richmond (Yorkshire). Also *Pipe Roll 26 Henry III*, p. 282, for targes kept in the castle at Windsor. An interesting document, dated 1278, lists the store of the garrison of Carmarthen castle left by Llywelyn ap Gruffydd: it lists 3 chapels de fer with visors, 4 round chapels de fer, 14 bascinets, 4 pairs of plates, 3 aketons, 3 pairs of gloves of whalebone, 2 gorgers of linen, 1 hauberk, 6 haubergeons, 4 corsets, 1 pair of mail chausses, 92 large quarrels and 256 small ones, 5 lances, 6 whole pieces of whalebone, 67 crossbows of various types and 12 baldrics. Some of the baldrics and crossbows were immediately redistributed to the men of the king (E. 101/3/23).

[29] P. Contamine, *Guerre, Etat et société à la fin du Moyen Age. Etudes sur les armées des rois de France, 1337–1494* (Paris & La Haye, 1972), p. 121.

household members on leave to fetch the equipment they needed is often recorded. We see this particularly well during the Scottish wars, when the members of the royal household occasionally left for England for this purpose.[30] The individual combatant serving in the context of the feudal levy was supposed to equip himself; as for the members of his own retinue, the king assumed that the wages and fees they received were sufficient for the provision of military equipment. While lost or sick horses were replaced, and saddles and clothing provided, arms and armour were normally at the cost of the individual household member.

The same policy was adopted by the nobility, and this is reflected in indentures of retinue, which, to my knowledge, are silent on the question of arms and armour, except when service in the tournament was expected.[31] Horses, saddles and robes were usually part of what a lord would give to his men, but not arms, whether offensive or defensive. The only evidence for the provision of arms that I have been able to find in an indenture of retinue for our period is that between Aymer de Valence, earl of Pembroke, and John Darcy in November 1309: this specified that, in time of war, John, who was entering the household of the earl of Pembroke as a valet, was to receive his mount and his armour from the earl. But the second part of the indenture, which specifies what John Darcy would be entitled to after taking the order of knighthood, does not mention armour any more. In this case, it seems that the lord was ready to help with the equipment of his valets, but this did not extend to the household knights.[32]

Knights and barons serving in the royal army with their retinues, whether for feudal service or for pay, or both, were clearly expected to turn up well equipped, a demand reflected in the wording of the writs of summons, which usually specified that service was due with arms and horses.[33] In 1202, a letter of King John to the knights of Flanders, Hainault and Brabant, offering them money and land for service, specified that they

---

[30] For instance E. 101/370/16, fol. 15r. (31 May 1307): mention of the leave of Nicholas Golston and William de Craye, gone to England to purchase some military equipment for their own use.
[31] Indenture between Sir John Bluet (of Raglan), a knight, and William Martel, a valet, Ellcestre, 10 August 1297. 'Private Indentures for Life Service in Peace and War 1278–1476', ed. M. Jones and S. Walker, *Camden Miscellany*, xxxii, Camden Fifth Series, III (London, 1994), no. 7; e *en tornemens en tens de pees od un graunt cheval de armes, le quel le dist Johan lui trovera et armure bonne et avenaunte saunz nule defaute pur seon cors.*
[32] *Ibid.*, no. 15.
[33] See for instance a writ addressed to Henry de Lacy, earl of Lincoln, and others in *Parliamentary Writs*, I, p. 222 (6 April 1282): *cum equis et armis decenciori et meliori modo quo poteritis parati si necesse fuerit exinde proficisci.*

had to present themselves completely armed.[34] If the king had to intervene to improve the equipment of private retinues, then he usually deducted the amount spent from the pay, if there was pay involved. Such was the case when John of Brittany was assigned to keep Scotland in September 1307, with 120 men in his company:[35] half were to be of his own retinue, taking 10 marks daily for their sustenance, and they had to be properly equipped by the earl himself. The contract specified that if the retinue was not properly equipped, the king would provide another sixty men-at-arms, a deduction being made eventually on what the earl would be paid.[36]

This general policy is reflected in Assizes of Arms, which list the military equipment the king's subjects were to have ready at hand. Writs of summons to military service sometimes quote Assizes of Arms and underline the necessity of coming well armed to the muster.[37] According to the Assize of Arms of 1181, the owner of a knight's fee or the freeman who owned chattels to the value of 16 marks was to have a hauberk, a helm, a shield and a lance. The category below that, of freemen with chattels to the value of 10 marks, was to have a haubergeon, a chapel de fer and a lance. The burgesses and all the community of freemen were to own a protection called a *wambais*, that is to say a padded and quilted garment, a chapel de fer and a lance.[38] In the writ of 1242 for enforcing watch and ward and the Assize of Arms, the body armour of the various categories is designated by the same terms, except that the *wambais* has been replaced by the *pourpoint*. According to this document, those who had £15 of land or chattels worth 60 marks had to have a hauberk, a chapel de fer, a sword, a knife and a horse. Those belonging to the category below that, with £10 of land, or chattels worth 40 marks, were to have a haubergeon, a chapel de fer, a sword and a knife.[39] An Assize of Arms dated 1230 only mentions the

---

34 *Foedera, conventiones, litterae*, ed. T. Rymer, 20 vols (London, 1704–35), I, p. 129 (27 May 1202).

35 See I. Lubimenko, *Jean de Bretagne, comte de Richmond. Sa vie et son activité en Angleterre, en Ecosse et en France (1266–1334)* (Lille, 1908), pp. 58–60.

36 *Calendar of Documents Relating to Scotland*, v (*Supplementary*), no. 515c.

37 *Close Rolls (Supplementary) of the reign of Henry III, 1244–1266*, p. 5: summons for the levy of foot soldiers with bows, arrows, lances and gisarmes in the counties of York, Westmorland, Cumberland and Northumberland (June 1244).

38 Text in W. Stubbs (ed.), *Select Charters and Other Illustrations of English Constitutional History from the Earliest Times to the Reign of Edward I* (9th edn rev. by H. W. C. Davis, Oxford, 1913), pp. 183–4.

39 *Ibid.*, pp. 362–5. See H. M. Cam, *The Hundred and the Hundred Rolls. An Outline of Local Government in Medieval England* (London, 1930, reissued 1963), p. 189, for the correction of the date of this document. There are a few differences between this text and that concerning the keeping of the peace in *Fleta*: the

hauberk and the haubergeons for the first two classes, without any other specification.[40] The following year, the writ for assembling the *jurati ad arma* describes the combatants as the *loricas et hauberionos et purpunctos*.[41] The stress on body armour points out the fact that it was considered paramount in defining one's place on the battlefield. Whether the Assizes of Arms were really effective is another matter. At first sight, rolls of muster such as the one drawn up in the summer of 1277 seem to offer a rather negative answer to this question, because the equipment listed is very motley. In fact, most combatants of knightly rank seem to have come properly equipped to the muster of 1277, since nothing particular is said about their equipment. What was listed in detail in this review was the armour of serjeants, and this was clearly the category which turned up with the less satisfactory equipment: most of them rode uncovered horses, some only had a quilted armour, an aketon or a pourpoint, and a chapel de fer. But many also owned a haubergeon, which after all reflects the regulations of the Assizes of Arms.[42]

Assizes of Arms and occasional gifts of military equipment by the king give us an idea of some of the elements of the military wardrobe. Occasionally, the accounts of the royal wardrobe offer a more precise picture of the complete wardrobe of a combatant. Such was the case in July 1297 when Geoffrey de Creal, a mounted serjeant of the king, received, for the French war, the following equipment for a total cost of £11 10s. 2d: an aketon, a gambeson, a pair of horse trappers, a pair of cuisses, a haubergeon, a bascinet, a chapel de fer, a gorger, a pair of gloves of plate, a crossbow, a saddle and a targe. In the same source, the equipment of Gilbert, the son of the earl of Strathearn, is also described in detail: an aketon, a gambeson, a pair of horse trappers, a pair of cuisses, a hauberk, a bascinet, a chapel de fer, a gorger, a pair of jambers, a lance, a sword, a knife and a gown, for a total of £10 11s.[43] The son of the earl of Strathearn had a hauberk among his equipment, which may be an indication of his

---

equivalences between land and chattels are not the same. For those who have 100s. of land, the gambeson is replaced by the pourpoint in *Fleta. Fleta*, ed. H. G. Richardson and G. O. Sayles, *Selden Society*, 72 (London, 1955), I, c.24, p. 63.

40   *Close Rolls 1227–1231*, p. 398.

41   Text in Stubbs, *Select Charters*, p. 355; *Close Rolls 1227–1231*, p. 595.

42   *Parliamentary Writs*, I, pp. 198–211.

43   B.L. Additional MS. 7,965, fol. 56. Also *ibid.*: gift in July 1297 from the king to Alan and Peter sons of the earl of Menteith of 2 aketons, 2 gambesons, 2 pairs of horse trappers, 1 hauberk, 1 haubergeon, 2 bascinets, 2 chapels de fer, 2 pairs of cuisses, 2 pairs of jambers, 2 gorgers, 2 pairs of gloves of plate, 2 saddles and 2 targes for the war in France, for a total cost of £27 7s. 4d.

knightly rank. But overall his equipment was less costly than the one provided to the mounted serjeant, who clearly fought as heavy cavalry.

The systematic study of wills may also yield information of this kind.[44] But arms were often part of the chattels handed down from father to son without being included in testamentary dispositions.[45] Inventories of personal goods are more promising. In 1290, for instance, Philip de la Garderobe, a member of the royal household,[46] left some of his personal belongings, to be taken care of, at the house of a certain William de Mewy. Philip was in fact fleeing from justice, for having broken into the royal treasury in the castle of Carmarthen. The goods he had left at William de Mewy's house were eventually confiscated and inventoried by royal officers: they found a gambeson, priced 2s., a haubergeon, with a bascinet and a *colret*, the whole priced 3s. 4d., a pair of cuisses priced 2s., as well as three ells of white cloth, a Welsh shirt, a robe, a hood, an old *houce* (probably a horse-trapper), a crossbow with a baldric and some quarrels.[47]

Another source which may offer an insight into the possession of military equipment is constituted by court rolls. Some court cases seem to demonstrate that, while offensive weapons of all kinds were omnipresent in daily life, defensive arms were probably fewer and very prized. A court case in Devon, dated 1201, shows a certain Richard of Launcells accusing the men of Henry fitz William of having broken into his house and stolen his hauberks, helms and mail chausses, as well as all sorts of other objects, and

---

[44] A well-known legacy of this kind is that of Fulk de Pembridge, 1325, leaving his armour to his sons: B.L. Stowe Charter 622, analysed in M. Prestwich, *Armies and Warfare in the Middle Ages. The English Experience* (New Haven & London, 1996), p. 26. Another well-known example is that of the will of Nicholas Longespee, bishop of Salisbury, dated 1295 (legacy of armour for men and horses to his ward, to Johan de Herterigg, William de Braybrok rector of the church of Wittenham, and to William de Barneuil; the rest of the armour is to be distributed among the other men-at-arms of the bishop): A. R. Malden, 'The Will of Nicholas Longespee, Bishop of Salisbury', *EHR*, 15 (1900), pp. 523–8. For another example of a legacy of arms, see the will of Hugh de Nevill, dated 1267 (M. S. Giuseppi, 'On the Testament of Sir Hugh de Nevill, Written at Acre, 1267', *Archaeologia*, 2nd series, 6 (1899), pp. 351–70).

[45] M. M. Sheehan, *The Will in Medieval England. From the Conversion of the Anglo-Saxons to the End of the Thirteenth Century*, Pontifical Institute of Mediaeval Studies, Studies and Texts 6 (Toronto, 1963), pp. 284, 293.

[46] He was perhaps the sumpterman of the arms of the king mentioned in the roll of robes of 1288–9 (*Records of the Wardrobe and Household 1286–1289*, ed. B. F. and C. R. Byerly (London, 1986) no. 2929.)

[47] C. 145/49/40.

finally his horses, to the total value of 100 marks.[48] In a Norfolk case dated 1220, Reginald de Wervelton brought a case against William de Wudecrofte, saying that he had deposited a hauberk, a pair of mail chausses, a chapel de fer, a pourpoint and a lance at William's house, and that the latter was refusing to return this equipment to him.[49] In the summer of 1296, Master Thomas the doctor accused Thomas Brun of having broken into his house at St. John's of Perth and of having stolen some armour there to the value of 26s. 8d.; another case was that of Robert fitz Payn, who accused three men of having broken into his house at Berwick, and of having taken his armour from his chamber, to the value of 100s.[50] A court case of 1214 in Cornwall mentions that a certain Baldwin Tyrel had opposed the entry of the rightful lord in his tenement *armatus lorica et purpuinto et capello ferro in capite, et tenuit unam magnam hachiam in manu sua*. But a witness to the scene stated that although the said Baldwin Tyrel had an axe in his hand, he did not wear a hauberk nor a pourpoint nor a chapel de fer, an indication, it seems, that his action was not premeditated.[51]

Coroners' rolls provide detailed information about offensive weapons, their use, and the type of injury they inflicted. Here and there also, mention of defensive equipment crops up. A case in Bedfordshire, dated June 1271, concerned a certain Hugh Priest, a felon who had broken the king's peace and who was eventually killed. The inquiry revealed that he had a sword and that he was wearing an aketon at the time of his death.[52] The systematic study of this type of source should give us some useful information not only about individual military equipment but also about the way it was used.

The study of written evidence also yields some technical information which may help to complete our knowledge of the evolution of armour from effigies and illuminated manuscripts. An example of this is the indications contained in written sources concerning the variety of mail equipment available in the thirteenth century. First of all, the documentary evidence shows that the iron wire used to make the rings of mail equipment could be of varying thickness, which cannot be inferred from iconography. In an inventory of the castle of Berwick drawn up sometime after 1296, we find three 'hauberks de gros fer'.[53] This variation in the size

---

[48]   *Select Pleas of the Crown, 1200–1225*, ed. F. W. Maitland, *Selden Society*, I (London, 1888), no. 84.

[49]   *Curia Regis Rolls*, VIII, pp. 205 and 306.

[50]   *Calendar of Documents Relating to Scotland*, pp. 191 and 193.

[51]   *Select Pleas of the Crown, 1200–1225*, no. 115.

[52]   *Select Cases from the Coroners' Rolls, A.D. 1265–1413*, ed. C. Gross, *Selden Society*, ix (London, 1896), p. 29.

[53]   E. 101/7/7.

of the metal links led to some pieces being much heavier than others. In August 1215, five light 'covers' and five thick 'covers' were to be handed out from the royal stores to the half-brother of the king, William Longsword.[54] In September 1216, the king ordered his haubergiers to make two light 'covers' of iron and two light hauberks for his nephews.[55] In March 1246, several pieces of armour 'of Chaumbely' appear among the personal arms of the king: four hauberks, one haubergeon, five pairs of mail chausses.[56] 'Chaumbely' was the locality today known as Chambly (Chambly-le-Hauberger in a seventeenth-century map), situated about 25 miles east of Senlis (between Neuilly-en-Théle and Beaumont), north of Paris: it was particularly famous for its hauberks.[57] One wonders what would have made the mail of Chambly specific: perhaps a particular process in the making of the iron wire for the rings, or a particular kind of riveting.

A piece of mail equipment which raises difficulties of interpretation is the 'cover' (Lat. *coopertorium*). This was made of mail, since iron wire was regularly purchased to repair or enlarge 'covers'. It is often mentioned alongside body armour, for instance in 1238–9, when six hauberks, four pairs of mail chausses and four pairs of iron covers (*coopertoria ferrea*) were purchased for Henry III.[58] In 1246, Henry III ordered the sheriff of London to send him six hauberks, six pairs of mail chausses, ten haubergeons and six *coopertoria ferrea* for himself, as well as one hauberk, one pair of mail chausses and one pair of iron covers for a knight entering the order of the Temple.[59] Occasionally the clerks specify that they are referring to a cover for a mount. The inventory of the castle of Exeter drawn up in 1274–5 mentions a horse-cover of iron (*cooperturam ferream unius equi*).[60] It is probable that at other times they just used the term 'cover' on its own. The expression 'pair of covers' would therefore refer to the fact that the horse cover was made of two parts: the tester and the crupper.[61] Such horse-covers were pictured on the wall murals of the Painted Chamber of

---

[54] *Rot. Litt. Cl.*, I, p. 226b.

[55] *Ibid.*, I, p. 286a.

[56] *Calendar of Liberate Rolls*, III, p. 30.

[57] C. Gaier, *L'industrie et le commerce des armes dans les anciennes principautés belges du XIIIe à la fin du XVe siècle* (Paris, 1973), p. 164.

[58] E. 352/32, m. 5.

[59] C. 62/22, m. 20. Also C. 62/22, m. 5, 16 (*quedam coopertoria de Chaumbely*), 21. Also E. 372/79, m. 21d. (1234–5). Also *Rot. Litt. Cl.*, i, pp. 121a (July 1212), 121b (1212), and 143b (1213).

[60] C. 145/33/36.

[61] *Records of the Household and Wardrobe 1285–1286*, no. 214 (21 February 1286). *Rot. Litt. Cl.*, I, p. 121b (1212).

Westminster,[62] and they frequently appear in illuminated manuscripts (Pl. 49).

The introduction of plates of metal, whalebone or *cuir-bouilli* in body armour is one of the main features of the evolution of defensive armament in the thirteenth century. Plates of metal were flat pieces of iron cut and shaped by the armourer, hence the term 'plates'. *Cuir-bouilli* was leather hardened using various processes, and it was a relatively effective protection. Whalebone was widely used for gloves and ailettes. While the representation of plate-armour on effigies or on iconographic documents is usually limited to the poleyn, a protection of the knees, or to the ailette protecting the shoulder (Appendix 3; Pls 50, 51 and 52; cf Pl. 54), documentary evidence suggests that plate was used extensively from the mid-thirteenth century onwards, at least for the equipment of the military elite. For instance, an iron piece was purchased for the equipment of the earl of Ross in 1302–3, at a cost of 100*s.*, and this was probably cut into plates (Appendix 2). Whalebone and leather were much favoured for the armour of children: the equipment provided for Alphonso, the son of Edward I, in 1274, included an aketon, an embroidered gambeson, a sword with an embroidered scabbard, a bascinet and a helm of leather.[63] Whalebone and leather were also used for tournament armour. The well-known example of the Windsor tournament of 1278, where the combatants were provided with swords of whalebone and a whole body armour of hardened leather, hints at the fact that for some types of tournaments at least combatants would wear a specific equipment.[64] The line between tournament and war was, however, a thin one, and many pieces of equipment, such as the ailettes, knee-caps or gloves, would often been made from whalebone or *cuir-bouilli*.

Plate was especially favoured to re-inforce the protection of the legs. Legs were first protected with gamboised and then mail chausses (*chaucon*),[65] maintained by laces just under the knee. Cuisses of mail are often recorded

---

[62] Reproduced in P. Binski, *The Painted Chamber at Westminster*, The Society of Antiquaries of London (London, 1986), pl. xxv.

[63] C. 47/3/11, m. 3 (1277–8): 'Item pro broudura j gambizon' ad opus domini Alfonsi filii regis xxx s. Item pro j aketon' empto ad opus eiusdem x s. Item pro una galea de coreo depicta viij s. Item pro uno bacinetto empto ad opus eiusdem iij s. Item pro j gladio cum j vagina brodata vj s. viij denarii.'

[64] 'Copy of a Roll of Purchases for a Tournament at Windsor Park in the Sixth Year of Edward I', ed. S. Lysons, *Archaeologia*, 1st series, 17 (1814), pp. 297–310 and J. R. V. Barker, *The Tournament in England, 1100–1400* (Woodbridge, 1986), pp. 162–87.

[65] E. 101/3/23 (inventory of arms at Carmarthen castle, 1278): mention of a *paria chaucon*.

in the documentation, and also appear in illuminated manuscripts (Pl. 52).[66] In the course of the thirteenth century, plate was used increasingly to protect the legs. During the stay of the royal household in Gascony in 1286–9, an armourer of Toulouse provided some shin-guards of plate (*gambers*) for the king, priced 3*s*. 9*d*. sterling.[67] Toulouse had been an important centre for the making of armaments ever since the Albigensian crusade and it is therefore not surprising to see the king purchasing some equipment there made according to the latest fashion. Shin-guards or *jambers* would sometimes end with a protection for the upper of the foot, the *wampes*: among the armour provided for the earl of Ross in 1302–3, for instance, we find a '*peyre jamberis ove les wampes*' (Appendix 2). Greaves and *jambers* were probably distinct pieces of equipment, because we see them side by side in the same documents: among the armour provided for Gilbert de Clare in 1306–7 there were a pair of *jambers* and two pairs of greaves (Appendix 3). The loan of armour of 1282 mentions *mustilyers*, and a document of October 1253 *musteleria*.[68] The term came from the Old French *mustel*, meaning calf of the leg; the description given in the document of October 1253, *unas mustelerias ferreas cum perticula ferrea supra pedem*, refers to a piece of armour complete with protection for the upper of the foot. It seems therefore that the *perticula ferrea* mentioned in this document was the same as the *wampes*, vamp in modern English, that is to say the upper of the shoe (Appendix 2), but it is difficult to say whether this was different from the sabaton, the *soullers de guerre* mentioned among the equipment delivered to Gilbert de Clare (Appendix 3). The whole system of leg-defence could be completed by stirrups with toe-caps.[69]

Another type of plate protection already mentioned, the ailettes, protected the shoulders and displayed the heraldic arms of the combatant. Already in the early thirteenth century, documentary evidence also mentions another type of shoulder protection, the *spaundlers*,[70] but whether it had a function similar to that of the ailette, or whether it was worn under the surcoat, is unclear (Pl. 52). As to gloves of plate, they frequently appear in the documentation in the last decades of the thirteenth century, when they probably replaced the mail mittens of the great hauberk (Appendix 3). Whalebone was used to make such gloves: two pairs of gloves found in the

---

66 Such as on B.L. Royal 2.A. xxii, fol. 220, c. 1250. For documentary evidence see C. 62/22, m. 16 (1246).
67 *Records of the Wardrobe and Household 1286–1289*, no. 910.
68 *Close Rolls 1253–1254*, p. 174.
69 C. 62/22, m. 16 (March 1246): mention of *estruvielers ferri cum antipeditibus*.
70 *Rot. Litt. Cl.*, I, p. 229 (24 September 1215).

castle of Carmarthen in 1278 were said to be of *baleyne*,[71] and it is also the case for the pair of gloves borrowed by William de Chervile.

Plate was also used increasingly to protect the chest. This was of relatively small dimensions and always fixed inside a garment of fabric. There are several terms referring to garments reinforced with plate. The inventory of the castle of Carmarthen dated 1278 mentions four corsets. In the same document, some 'pairs of plates' also appear, and this may refer to a kind of padded garment reinforced with two plates on the chest or on the chest and the back. Among the armour for the earl of Ross, we find some *pissanes*, probably similar to the pairs of plates (Appendix 2).

Over the hauberk, the mounted combatant wore a surcoat, a garment in the shape of a large flowing tunic which usually displayed heraldic devices (Pls 49–52). Although the practice of wearing a surcoat probably went back to the mid-twelfth century,[72] numerous manuscript illuminations show combatants still in the mid-thirteenth century wearing mail without a surcoat (Pls 51 and 53).[73] Several decades later, however, it had become an indispensable part of the equipment of the aristocratic combatant: even the knights who were more modestly equipped had at least a surcoat in their equipment, as is shown in the indenture for a loan of armour in 1282 (Appendix 1).

The accounts of the royal wardrobe show that this piece of military equipment was generally cut out of sindon, a light and bright silk which was the main material used in the thirteenth century for the making of surcoats, horse-trappers, pennons and banners, and lined with linen. The expenses for the preparation of the armour of the earl of Ross in 1302–3 included the purchase of 20 ells of red sindon, 6.5 ells of white sindon, 4 ells of plain linen, 8.5 ells of red linen and 9 ells of worsted. Six workers were hired for eight days for the task of tailoring the military equipment (Appendix 2).

Heraldic devices could be large-sized, or in the shape of small devices 'powdering' the background: for instance, an account of the king's armourers for 1275–6 mentions horse-trappers of green cloth 'powdered' with shields with the arms of England, and other horse-trappers 'powdered'

---

[71]   E. 101/3/23.

[72]   See Peirce, 'The Knight, his Arms and Armour', pp. 256–8.

[73]   C. Gaier, 'L'évolution et l'usage de l'armement personnel défensif', *Armes et combats dans l'univers médiéval* (Brussels, 1995), pp. 125–49, esp. pp. 143–4. Claude Gaier has shown that the coat-armour appeared in the Pays de Liège during the last decade of the twelfth century; but its diffusion was not general before the second quarter of the thirteenth century, and some illuminations of the mid thirteenth century still omit the coat-armour.

with the leopards.[74] Various techniques were used to create heraldic devices on surcoats and horse trappers. Patterns were usually cut out of some contrasting material, and sewn to the background fabric according to the *appliqué* or to the *intarsia* technique.[75] Expenses for the military equipment of Edward of Caernarvon in 1301–2 included the making of horse-trappers with leopards of yellow sindon on a red background.[76] An example of *appliqué* work has come down to us in the shape of a seal-bag: dated 1248–60, it shows the arms of William de Fortz, earl of Albermarle, and of his wife Isabel, and it may have been cut out of the decoration of a surcoat.[77] Surcoats were also painted: in 1208, for instance, 3s. was spent on painting the banners and surcoats of the king, and a total of 69s. 10d. for gilding the same pieces.[78] In the last decades of the thirteenth century, while there was a growing fashion for ostentatious excess, embroidery seems to have been resorted to increasingly for the decoration of military equipment.[79] Shields could also be made of parchment: the account of the expenses of John of Brabant, in 1292–3, mentions the purchase of small shields of parchment with his arms.[80] There are also mentions of chapels de fer decorated with painted or enamelled arms.[81]

In the late thirteenth century, another type of garment worn over the hauberk, the tabard, appears among the military wardrobe of the aristocracy as well as of more modest combatants. In the king's treasury in 1299–1300, there was a tabard (*alverum*) with pearl embroidery representing the arms of England, Flanders and Bar.[82] In 1296, as mentioned earlier, a certain Thomas Brun was accused by Master Thomas the doctor of having stolen from his house in St John's town of Perth several pieces of military

---

74 C. 47/3/11, m. 2 (1275–6).
75 In 1306–7, two knights of the king's household, Simon de Montacute and his son William, were given a cloth of green, two pieces of common sindon and one piece of reinforced sindon to cover their armour. The patterns were probably cut out of the half-piece of blue sindon and of the one and a half pieces of yellow sindon they also received (E. 101/370/11/8).
76 E. 101/361/17, m. 2 (1301–2).
77 British Museum MLA 56, 8–19, 1: see F. Pritchard, 'Two Royal Seal Bags from Westminster Abbey', *Textile History*, 20 (1989), pp. 225–34.
78 *Rot. Litt. Cl.*, I, p. 109a.
79 See F. Lachaud, 'Embroidery for the Court of Edward I (1272–1307)', *Nottingham Medieval Studies*, 37 (1993), pp. 33–52.
80 E. 101/353/4/3, roll of expenses of Thomas and Henry sons of Edmund and of John of Brabant (1292–3).
81 C. 47/3/28 (final account of the household of Henry and Thomas of Lancaster, 1296–7), m. 3.
82 *Liber Quotidianus Contrarotulatoris Garderobae*, p. 343.

equipment, including a tabard worth half a mark.[83] The heraldic tabard of the fifteenth century, with its peculiar square cut and its large sleeves, is familiar to us, but it is not at all certain that the tabard of the late thirteenth century was of this shape.

The documentation mentions several types of gamboised garments worn by combatants: pourpoint, aketon and gambeson, which could be worn on their own by combatants of modest fortune, as the Assizes of Arms suggest. But they were also a component of the equipment of the military elite. In 1208, 183 ells of rautine, a kind of woollen cloth, were purchased for a pourpoint for the king.[84] This shows that this garment could be extremely thick and probably a very effective defence against blows. But there were also some light 'pourpoints' recorded among the military equipment of King John in 1215, and these were probably worn with another type of chest armour.[85] In a later example, we see a gambeson transformed into an aketon, but we do not know what made them distinct (Appendix 2). Aketon and gambeson appear alongside each other in the wardrobe of Gilbert de Clare, but it is impossible to know whether they would have been worn together (Appendix 3).

The combatant would wear, over a quilted cap in many cases,[86] various types of head-gear: mail coif, helm (*galea*), chapel de fer (Pls 50, 51 and 52),[87] or bascinet (Appendix 2). The mail coif was often the only head-defence of the combatant (Pls 51, 52, 53 and 54). In the last decades of the thirteenth century, coifs often appear to have been separate from the rest of the hauberk: a '*coyf de mayle*' is for instance mentioned in an inventory of armour dated of the reign of Edward I.[88] Claude Gaier has stressed that the adoption of a separate coif made a specific protection for the neck necessary: this explains the presence of the *coler* or *colret*,[89] and of the gorger in the accounts (Appendices 1 and 3). It is possible that while the *coler* was of mail, the gorger was of linen, probably quilted; but the two terms may have been used interchangeably.[90] Over the mail coif other head-gear could be worn. In the thirteenth century, the helm, of conical shape, enclosed the

---

[83]   *Calendar of Documents Relating to Scotland*, II, p. 191.

[84]   *Rot. Litt. Cl.*, I, p. 109a.

[85]   *Ibid.*, I, p. 229.

[86]   There was sometimes a quilted coif attached to the piece of head-gear: C. 47/3/11, m. 2 (1276–7): *Item pro j cerebro empto ad j galeam regis [viij] d.*

[87]   C. 145/34/1 (view of the castle of Bamburgh, 1276–7): mention of *duas galeas et octo capell' ferreas putrefactas et nullius valoris.*

[88]   E. 101/13/37.

[89]   C. 62/22, m. 16 (1246): mention of a double colret and of a colret of iron.

[90]   E. 101/3/23 (inventory of arms at Carmarthen castle, 1278): mention of 2 gorgers of linen.

whole of the head (Pls 49 and 54). At the end of the century helms were often provided with a visor.[91] This piece of head-gear could be sumptuously decorated: some arms of the king kept at Chester castle in 1246 included two gilded helms with precious or semi-precious stones.[92] Others were decorated with a crown (*capellum*) (Pl. 49):[93] such helms may be seen on the equestrian seals of Henry III and Edward I. Another piece of head-gear was the chapel de fer (Pls 49–52 and 54). Its use was obviously not restricted to the ranks below that of knight since chapels de fer are mentioned among the arms of the king kept in Chester castle in 1246: a chapel de fer 'de Aundeyne' (probably of Andenne, on the Meuse), another with spikes, and another covered with felt.[94] The chapel de fer also appears among the arms of Gilbert de Clare (Appendix 2). Some chapels de fer were ornamented with knobs of metal.[95] The bascinet, finally, was an egg-shaped piece which was directly attached to the mail shirt, and usually provided with a visor. In the inventory of Carmarthen castle drawn up in 1278, there were three iron chapels with a visor, four round iron chapels, as well as fourteen old and 'weak' bascinets.[96] All these pieces were found together in the same wardrobes: the armour purchased for Gilbert de Clare included two bascinets, one heavy and the other light, a helm, and a chapel de fer (Appendix 2).

Finally, the systematic study of documentary evidence should help us to establish a more precise correlation between the place of the combatant on the battlefield and his rank on the one hand, and his military equipment on the other. We may stress this point on the basis of the equation between hauberk and knightly rank. Indeed, the hauberk of mail is usually considered to have been the basic piece of equipment for the combatant of knightly rank in the thirteenth century. This was a mail shirt that covered the chest, the head, the arms and the upper parts of the legs, down to the knees or to the middle of the thighs (Pl. 53). The permanence of the hauberk has often been underlined: effigies and manuscript illuminations of the first half of the fourteenth century still show a hauberk quite similar to the garment worn in the late twelfth century. But documentary evidence underlines the variations in the shape of hauberks in the course of the thirteenth century. Some documents of the reign of John mention 'large' hauberks (*lorica larga*) and 'great' hauberks (*lorica magna*): this was perhaps a reference to the great hauberk which appeared in the later decades of the

---

[91]   E. 101/13/37 (*temp.* Edward I).
[92]   C. 62/22, m. 16. Also *ibid.*, m. 5: purchase of 4 helms with precious stones.
[93]   *Rot. Litt. Cl.*, I, p. 143b (1213): mention of crowns on helms.
[94]   C. 62/22, m. 16.
[95]   C. 47/3/11, m. 2 (1276–7).
[96]   E. 101/3/23.

twelfth century,[97] a variety with long sleeves ending in mittens protecting the hands (Pls 51, 52 and 53).[98] After the reign of King John the expression 'large hauberk' seems to disappear from the documentation, a fact that is difficult to explain. Another difficulty is raised by the expression 'pair of hauberks' that one encounters in the documentation, for instance in a document dated 1246.[99] This might refer either to two hauberks, or else to the hauberk and the chausses, or to the hauberk and the quilted garment worn under it. One also notes the mention of 'small hauberks' (*loriculi*) in a document of 1261: these were perhaps shorter hauberks.[100]

As for the term haubergeon, it appears in documentary evidence in the course of the last decades of the twelfth century. Like the hauberk, the haubergeon was made of mail, and sometimes of mail of Chambly,[101] but it may have covered part of the arms only, and was probably shorter than the hauberk (Pl. 53). It is usually assumed that the haubergeon was the body armour of those who could not afford a complete hauberk,[102] and the documentation goes some way to confirm this. For instance, an order sent to the mayor and good men of York in July 1244 specified that they had to provide the knights and valets of the king with fifteen hauberks and the same number of haubergeons.[103] One presumes that the hauberks were meant to be worn by the knights and the haubergeons by the valets. In Assizes of Arms, hauberks are listed among the armour necessary for the highest class of combatant, while haubergeons are reserved for categories below that. We notice an important shift, however, in the terminology with the Statute of Winchester (1285), which does not mention the hauberk any more, but only the haubergeon.[104] In fact, if the documentation suggests that during the second half of the thirteenth century the hauberk was still considered as an attribute of the military elite, the haubergeon was also part of its equipment. Haubergeons were made or purchased for Edward I.[105] Gilbert de Clare also owned some haubergeons (Appendix 3), while the loan of armour mentioned earlier lists a haubergeon and an aketon, as well

---

[97]   *Rot. Litt. Cl.*, I, p. 229 (23 September 1215).

[98]   C. Gaier, 'L'évolution et l'usage de l'armement personnel défensif', pp. 141–2.

[99]   C. 62/22, m. 20.

[100]   *Calendar of Liberate Rolls*, V, p. 29 (12 April 1261): view of the state of the castle of Sherborne (Kent) by some officers of the king who found there 8 decayed hauberks and 5 small hauberks (*loriculos*) among other equipment.

[101]   C. 62/22, m. 16 (1246): mention of hauberks, cover and mail chausses of Chambly.

[102]   For instance C. Gaier, 'L'évolution et l'usage de l'armement personnel défensif', p. 142.

[103]   *Close Rolls 1242–1247*, p. 216 (28 July 1244).

[104]   Stubbs, *Select Charters*, pp. 464–6.

[105]   Also C. 62/22, m. 20 and 21 for haubergeons purchased for the king (1246).

as a surcoat, but no hauberk. The use of the haubergeon by the military elite may have been already widespread in the twelfth century, since we see some *halberjolis* purchased for the king in 1165.[106] It is probable that the development of the haubergeon was parallel to the development of specific leg-defences, first of mail and then of plates, and that it became popular with the military elite for that reason.

The authors of a recent book have underlined the difficulties raised by the systematic comparison between various sources for the study of costume and armour, in particular between documentary evidence and other sources.[107] The systematic study of documentary evidence, however, should inform the historian about the way military equipment was provided, about its technical evolution and finally about the cost of armour and the consequences this had on the recruitment of armies. Finally, I would like to stress the need to address those questions on the basis of a large study of the various types of evidence.[108] Indeed, however tempting it may be to interpret the indenture registering a loan of armour mentioned at the beginning of this paper as evidence for the difficulties of the knightly class in England, we ought, before attempting to draw any general conclusion, to place this document in the context of the evolution of the knightly class as well as of the manufacture, trade and techniques of military equipment.

---

[106] *Pipe Roll 11 Henry II (1164–1165)*, p. 53.
[107] F. Piponnier and P. Mane, *Se vêtir au Moyen Age* (Paris, 1995), pp. 19–20.
[108] This could be done on the example of the study carried out by Claude Gaier for the southern Low Countries: C. Gaier, *L'industrie et le commerce des armes dans les preincipautés belges du XIIIe à la fin du XVe siècle* (Paris, 1973).

APPENDIX 1
A Loan of Armour, 10 July 1282
(The Trustees of the Royal Armouries, Accession Number I. 875)

Omnibus Christi fidelibus hoc presens scriptum visuris vel audituris, ego Willelmus de Cherebile de Reydone salutem in domino. Noveritis me teneri Hugoni de Reynns de Wersted filio Gilberti de Reynns de Wersted in solucione octodecim solidorum bone et legalis monete. Et ex mutuo recepisse unum aketun et unum haubergoun et unum colret et unum bacin et unum par cirotecarum de baleyne et unum par de mustilyers et unum par de quisouz et unam tunicam armeriam de sidone precii sex marcarum bone et legalis monete. Pro quibus quidem octodecim solidis et pro qua quidem armura prenominata duas pecias terre mee arabiles in villa de Reydone cum viis et semitis et cum libero introytu et exitu et cum omnibus aliis aysiamentis et libertatibus ad predictas duas pecias terre spectantibus eidem inpingnoravi. Quarum una pecia terre que vocatur Scottispiktib jacet inter terram Roberti de Reydone ex una parte et viam que se extendit de aula Roberti de Reydon versus ecclesiam ex alia et alia pecia terre que vocatur Haylond et continet sex acras et habunttat uno capite super Arnoldispirie et alio capite super curiam dicti Willelmi de Cherevile. Reddendo eidem Hugoni de Reynns dictos octodecim solidos argenti in aula de Wersted die sancte Margarete virginis anno regni regis Edwardi filii regis Henrici decimo sine ulteriori dilacione. Preterea solvendo etiam eidem Hugoni de Reynns totam predictam armuram in adeo bono statu quo eam ab eo recepit vel precium armure supra appositum die sancti Michaelis anno regni regis Edwardi filii regis Henrici decimo sine aliqua ulteriori dilacione. Et si contigat me in aliqua solucione predicta ad aliquem predictum diem aliquo modo difficere volo et concedo quod dictus Hugo de Reynns habeat et teneat inperpetuum dictas duas pecias terre cum omnibus supradictis et eorum pertinentiis sibi et heredibus suis vel suis assingnatis sine aliqua condicione mei vel heredum meorum vel assingnatorum faciendo inde per annum unum clavum gariophili ad Pascha. Pro omnibus serviciis sicut continetur in carta feofomenti eidem facta quam cartam Robertus de Reydone penes se habet in equali manu per assentum nostrum. Ita videlicet quod si non solvero dictos octodecim solidos et totam prenominatam armuram in tam bono statu quod eam ab eo recepi vel precium armure supra appositum licite poterit dictus Robertus de Reydone dictam cartam feofomenti dicto Hugoni de Reynns sine aliqua condiccione vel perturbacione tradere. In cuius rei testimonium huic presenti scripto ad modum cirograffi confecto: uterque nostrum alternatim sigillum apposuit. Datum apud Reydone die Veneris proxima post translacionem sancte Thome martiris anno regni regis Edwardi filii regis Henrico decimo.

Translation:

To all the faithful in Christ who will see or hear this writing I, William de Chervile of Reydon, address my salutations in the Lord. Know that I owe Hugh de Reymes of Wherstead, son of Gilbert de Reymes of Wherstead, the sum of eighteen shillings of good and legal money. And as a loan I have received an aketon, a haubergeon, a colret, a bascinet, and a pair of gloves of whalebone, a pair of mustiliers, a pair of cuisses and a coat armour of sindon, the whole being worth six marks of good and legal money. For the said eighteen shillings and for the said armour I have pledged to him two arable pieces of my land in the village of Reydon with the ways and paths and free access to come and go, with all the facilities and liberties touching the said two pieces of land. One of those pieces, called Scottispiktib, is situated between the land of Robert de Reydon and the road which goes from the hall of Robert de Reydon to the church; the other piece of land, called Haylond, which contains six acres, lies between Arnoldispirie and the court of the said William de Chervile. And I am due to pay to the said Hugh de Reymes the said eighteen shillings of silver in the hall of Wherstead on the day of Saint Margaret the Virgin in the tenth year of the reign of King Edward, son of King Henry, without any further postponement. And if it happens that I alter the said payment on the said day in any way, I will and concede that the said Hugh de Reymes will have and will hold in perpetuity the said two pieces of land with all the aforesaid things and everything touching them, his heirs and those assigned by him making afterwards to me or my heirs or those assigned by me the payment of one clove at Easter without any condition, this being for all the services as one contained in the charter of enfeoffment made to him, Robert de Reydon having the said charter with him as a trustee by our consent. That is to say, therefore, if I do not render the said eighteen shillings and all the aforesaid armour, in a state as good as the one I received it in or the price of the armour listed above, the said Robert de Reydon will legally be able to hand the said charter of enfeoffment to the said Hugh de Reymes without any other condition or trouble. As a testimony of this each of us has in his turn his seal to the said writing which is in the form of a chirograph. Given at Reydon the Friday after the translation of Saint Thomas the Martyr, the tenth year of the reign of King Edward, son of King Henry.

APPENDIX 2
Purchase of Armour for the Earl of Ross in 1302–3
(Public Record Office, E. 101/11/5)

Memorandum de dezpenciz fetis per le meyn Gefrei Merre pur lez armures le Cunte de Ros a Dunfermelyn lan xxxj. Adezprimis pur j gambessoun achate dunt fu fet un aketun pur le cunte lx s. pur un autre gambessoun pur le cunte xl s. pur un pissane e un gorger achate xxx s. pur un chapel de fer xxx s. pur un bacinet viij s. pur un peyre jamberis ove les wampes e un peyr poleyns x s. viij d. pur un colret de fer v s. vj d. pur xx aunys de sandal vermayl pris laune xiiij d. xxiij s. iiij d. pur vj aunys e demy de sandal blaunk pris laune xviij.d ix s. ix d. pur viij aunys e demy de tele vermayl pris laune iiij d. ij s. x d. pur ix aunys de worstede pris laune iiij d. iij s. pur saye achate ij s. viij d. pur fil xvj d. pur iiij aunys de aylisham x d. pur chaundelye xix d. ob. pur les gagis de vj valez qui eyderunt sur lez overis per viij jours prenaund le jur chekun de valez vj d. xxiiij s.
Summa xij li. xiij s. vj d. ob.

Item pur un fer pur le corps au conte c s. qui fut achate de Wauter de Rye.

[*deleted:* Pro comite de Ross]
Summa vij li. xiij s. vj d. ch'. Inde recepit xj die Novembris anno xxxj x m. et vj die Decembris anno xxxij c s. Et sic debitur ei vj li. ij d.

Dorse: Arma pro Comite de Ros. Anno xxxj per G. de Merre [In'...]

366

APPENDIX 3
Military Equipment Delivered to Gilbert de Clare
in 1306–7 (Public Record Office, E. 101/369/20)

[m. 1]

Pur Gilbert de Clare un aketon' e un gaumbeison pris de x li.
Un par de trappes pris iiij li.
Item pur la fazoun del aketoun, gaumbeisoun, trappes argent e sey c s.

Item une sale de deaus posts de xiiij pee de haut, e de xl pee de long e une
chaumbre de deus postz ad garderob de xx pee de long e x peez de lee. Une
panetrie e boterlerie od un post qe ad noun potence de xiij pez de haut e de xx
peez de loung. Une estable de treis postz de xiiij peez de haut e l peez de long, e
une autre estable de deus postz de xiiij peez de haut e xl peez de long. Canevace
pur les tentes avauntdites mil aunes pris de xvij li. pris del c xxxiiij s. des queus ccc
e di. de canevace inde e pur tendre les ccc e di. del canevace avaundite iij li. x s.

Item pur la fazoun de treis meisouns od la garderobe vj li.
Item pur la fazoun del estable de treis postz l s.
Item pur la fazoun de la Potence xx s.
Item pur le merin e la charpentine de meisme le merin e la fazoun du fer iiij li. x s.

Item en cordes, en quir e fil pur les tentes avauntdites l s.
Item robe pur soun cors de la Pentecost lx s.
[deleted: Item robes pur sa meigne cest assavoir pur treis valletz un clerk vij
valletz de mester iiij sometors e deus garsouns pris per cacun xij li.]

Summa totalis [deleted: lxxj li.] lix li.

[m. 2]

Pur Gilbert de Clare ij bacinez lun pesaunt e lautre leger pris de j mark.
Item j heaume de guerre e j chapeu de guerre pris de c s.
Item j peire jaumbers j peire soullers de guerre j peir de poleins pris de ij m.
Item ij peire de greves j peire de poleins fourbe pris de xx s.
Item ij peire de gaunz de plate pris de xx s.
Item j hauberioun e j gorger' pris de c s.

Summa xiiij li.

Item ii seeles pur grandz chevaux e ii freiens pris de lx s.
Item ii eskus pris xl s.
Item j seale pur soen cors de la Pentecust x s.

Summa cx s.

Item j vallet qi puisse prendre garde des tentes qaunt il sunt debrisez qi les puisse amender.

[*struck through:*] Pur Gilbert de Clare vi esqueles dargent pris vij li. xiij s. pris de lesquele xxvj s.
Item vj saussers dargent pris de xxxvj s pris du sausser vj s.

Summa ix li. ix s.

Item j pot de arrem de v galouns du peis de xxxviii livres pris de ix s. vj d.
E j autre pot de iiii galouns du peis de xxvj livres pris de ix s.
E le tierz pot de iii galouns du peis de xxii livres pris de v s vj d.
E j potenet de j galoun du peis de x li. pris de ij s vj d.
E j paele de xvj galouns pris de xviii s.
E j autre paele de x galouns pris de xii s.
E j graate pris de xij d.
E j gredil pris de ij s. viij d.
Summa lx s ij d.

Barilz ferrez x pris de la pere vj s. viij d. lxxiij s. iiij d.
[*deleted:* Barilz ferreez xv pris de l s. pris de la peire vj s viij d.]
Item vj peire de petiz barils a chenne pris de xij s. pris de la peire ij s.
Item ij barils pur sausse pris de ij s.

[*deleted:* Summa lxiiij s.
Summa totalis xxxv li. iij s. ij d.]

[   ]n carriage ij carettes cheskune carette de iiij chevaux e despenses pur meisme
[ ] cariage de Loundres iesques au roi.

[   ]xvij s. vj d.

Summa xxvj li. xvij s. [vj] d.

Dorse: [   ] Gilbert de Clare [   ]

[ ] indicates that the document is not legible.

This account for de Clare is of particular value in revealing not only the extensive garniture that one of the greatest magnates of the realm might possess, but also equestrian equipment and the more mundane items needed for campaign such as carts, barrels and kitchen utensils. The provision and use of tents, which might act as important symbols of rank and wealth when in camp, is a comparatively neglected subject which would repay further study. This equipment was certainly prepared for the Scottish campaign of 1307; if one accepts its owner is Gilbert, grandson of Edward I rather than as Gilbert, earl of Thormont, then it may be that he was wearing some of the armour recorded here when he rode to his death at the hands of the Scottish spearmen at Bannockburn in 1314.

1. Caernarfon Castle, the Eagle Tower.
© History of Art Photo Library, University of Warwick (R. K. Morris)

2. Caernarfon Castle, river façade.
© Cadw: Welsh Historic Monuments (Crown Copyright)

3. Caernarfon Castle, the King's Gate.
© Cadw: Welsh Historic Monuments (Crown Copyright)

4. Harlech Castle, general view from the south-west.
© Cadw: Welsh Historic Monuments (Crown Copyright)

5. Conwy Castle, view across the estuary to the inner ward.
© Cadw: Welsh Historic Monuments (Crown Copyright)

6. Dolbadarn Castle, the tower.
© History of Art Photo Library, University of Warwick (R. K. Morris)

7. Herstmonceux Castle, the gatehouse.
© History of Art Photo Library, University of Warwick (A. Watson)

8. Ingham parish church, Norfolk, tomb of Sir Oliver de Ingham (R. K. Morris)

9. Wells, Bishop's Palace, detail of chapel roofline (R. K. Morris)

10. Leeds Castle, general view of the moat (R. K. Morris)

11. Leeds Castle, the *gloriette* (R. K. Morris)

12. Acton Burnell Castle, exterior from the south.
© History of Art Photo Library, University of Warwick (R. K. Morris)

13. Acton Burnell Castle, interior looking west.
© History of Art Photo Library, University of Warwick (R. K. Morris)

14. Wells, Bishop's Palace, general view from the north.
© History of Art Photo Library, University of Warwick (R. K. Morris)

15. Wells, Bishop's Palace, great hall interior.
© History of Art Photo Library, University of Warwick (R. K. Morris)

16. Bristol Cathedral, south choir aisle and Berkeley tombs.
© Conway Library, Courtauld Institute of Art

17. London, Old St Paul's Cathedral, tomb of John of Gaunt
(Dugdale, *History of St Paul's Cathedral*, 2nd edn, 1716).
© History of Art Photo Library, University of Warwick

18. Kenilworth Castle, great hall, view from the keep.
© History of Art Photo Library, University of Warwick (R. K. Morris)

19. La Ferté-Milon, entrance façade.
© History of Art Photo Library, University of Warwick (R. K. Morris)

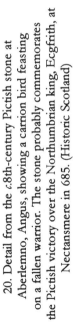

21. A fragment of a sculptured frieze from Winchester (c.11th century) depicting a warrior, possibly departing from the battlefield, and a wolf standing over a prone figure. (Conway Library, Courtauld Institute of Art)

20. Detail from the c.8th-century Pictish stone at Aberlemno, Angus, showing a carrion bird feasting on a fallen warrior. The stone probably commemorates the Pictish victory over the Northumbrian king, Ecgfrith, at Nectansmere in 685. (Historic Scotland)

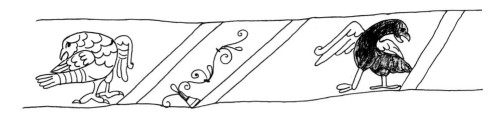

22. The Bayeux Tapestry, birds and beasts in the margin above the final battle scenes (Jennie Hooper)

23. A raven pecks at the eyes of a decapitated head, placed on a pole on the prow of Noah's Ark, detail from an early 11th-century Canterbury MS of Aelfric's *Hexateuch* (BL, Cotton MS Claudius. B. IV, fol. 15r) (Jennie Hooper)

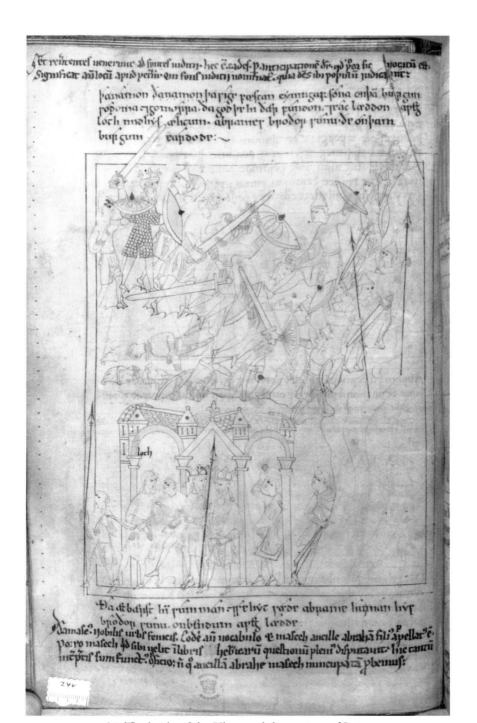

24. The battle of the Kings and the capture of Lot,
from BL Cotton MS Claudius. B. IV, fol. 24v (Aelfric's *Hexateuch*).
(Conway Library, Courtauld Institute of Art)

25. Additional MS. 44985, f. 4v. The use of the grappling hook. Italian, late 14th century.
(British Library)

26. Royal MS 20 B XI, f. 3. Exercises for recruits. French, early 14th century.
(British Library)

27 (left). Royal MS 15 E.I,
f. 209. Cannon and
accoutrements. Flemish,
late 15th century. (British
Library)

28 (below). Cotton MS Nero
C.iv, f. 14. The Massacre of
the Innocents. English c.1150.
(British Library)

29. Add. MS. 23145, f. 37v. St Maurice.
French, late 14th century.
(British Library)

30. Eg. MS 859, f. 27. St Maurice.
German, 15th century.
(British Library)

31. Royal MS 12 F XIII, f. 11v. Mail armour. English, early 13th century. (British Library)

32. Royal MS. 10 E.IV, f. 65v. Single combat.
Italian with English illustrations, early 14th century.
(British Library)

33. Arundel MS 66, f. 45. Constellation of Argo. English c.1490.
(British Library)

34. Yates Thompson MS. 12, f. 40v. The siege of Jerusalem. French *c*.1250–1260.

35. Yates Thompson MS. 33, f. 155v. The battle of Hastings. French, late 15th century.

36. Royal, MS 19 D.I, f. 111. The siege of Saianfu. French, mid 14th century.
(British Library)

37. Stowe MS 17, f. 243v. A siege engine. Maastricht, *c*.1300. (British Library)

38. Royal MS 16 G.VI, f. 388. Two trebuchets in action. French, 1325–1350. (British Library)

39. Cotton MS Nero D.ix, f. 77v. A battle scene. French *c*.1470. (British Library)

42. Royal MS 16 G IX, f. 76v. An army advancing in formation. Flemish, c.1470–1480. (British Library)

43. Harley MS 326, f. 90. An army on the move. English, c.1480. (British Library)

40. Burney MS 169, f. 21v. The destruction of Thebes. Flemish, 1468–1475. (British Library)

41. Cotton MS Nero E.ii, pt. 1, f. 124. Roland fights Feragut. French, early 15th century. (British Library)

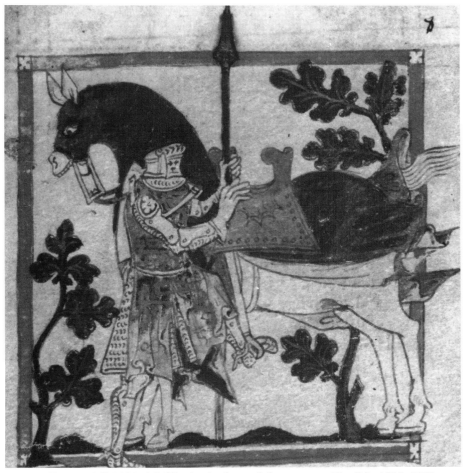

44. Egerton MS 3028, f. 8. The beginnings of plate armour. English, 1325–1350.
(British Library)

45. Add. MS 47680, f. 44v. A primitive cannon, English, 1326–1327. (British Library)

46. Matthew Paris's depiction of the legendary duel between Edmund Ironside and Cnut, from his *Chronica Majora* (c.1240–58). Though the incident occurs *sub anno* 1016, Paris conventionally portrays the kings in armour and equipment of his own day and assigns Cnut a fictive blazon. (Corpus Christi College, Cambridge, MS 26, p. 160. The Conway Library, Courtauld Institute of Art)

47. Two lead-glazed tiles from Chertsey Abbey, Surrey, c1250, showing Richard Coeur de Lion's joust with Saladin. (The British Museum)

48. Richard I unhorsing Saladin, from the Luttrell Psalter, c.1325–35, a dramatic rendition testifying to the continued popularity of the motif of the 'pas Saladin'. (British Library, MS Add 42130, f. 82)

51: Two knights from a
13th-century Apocalypse
(Bodleian Library, MS Auct.
DIV 17, f. 7v). The
left-hand figure wears a
chapel de fer and surcoat,
the other has gamboised
cuisses with poleyns.

52: Over his hauberk, this horseman from the Metz Apocalypse, c.1250–55, wears an
armorial surcoat with reinforced shoulders, and mail chausses reinforced with poleyns.
(Médiathèque de Pontiffroy, Metz, MS 1 184, f. 5)

49: Horses with mail barding, from Thomas of Kent's *Roman de toute chevalerie*, c.1240–50. (Cambridge, Trinity College MS 0.9.34, f. 20)

50: A knight from the Ormseby Psalter c.1310, showing a chapel de fer, ailettes, poleyns and couters. (Bodleian Library, MS Douce 366, f. 55v)

53: King Offa setting out on an expedition from Matthew Paris's *Vie de Saint Auban*, c.1245–52 (Dublin, Trinity College MS 177, f. 55v). The warrior blowing his horn on the far left wears a chapel de fer, while the trumpeter to the right wears a shorter hauberk (haubergeon) than that of the king. Offa's arms appear on both his shield and the rear cantle of his saddle, and the knight to his left bears an armorial surcoat which repeats the arms of his shield.

54: The knights engaged in this late-thirteenth-century battle scene ride barded horses and wear a variety of head protection, including close helms and chapels de fer. Many, however, still wear only coifs of mail. (Bodleian Library, Bodley Rolls, row 3)